PUBLICATIONS

OF THE

STATE DEPARTMENT OF ARCHIVES AND HISTORY

# THE PAPERS OF
# WILLIAM ALEXANDER GRAHAM

# The Papers of
# William Alexander Graham

---

Edited by

J. G. DE ROULHAC HAMILTON

---

VOLUME TWO

1838-1844

Raleigh
State Department of Archives and History
1959

iii

# CONTENTS

# FOREWORD

This is the second in a series of approximately seven volumes containing the papers of William Alexander Graham. The first volume was published in 1957 and other volumes will follow as soon as funds become available.

Dr. J. G. de Roulhac Hamilton, professor emeritus of the Department of History of the University of North Carolina, who has edited three other series for publication by the Department, has edited this volume and looks forward to the time when all the Graham material will be published.

William A. Graham was active in the political life of the State for many years. He was a Whig and served in the General Assembly, as Governor, United States Senator, Secretary of the Navy, and Confederate States Senator. This volume covers the period when he served in the House of Commons as Speaker, and as United States Senator. It also covers the period when he campaigned for Governor. The next volume will begin when he became Governor.

September 1, 1959,
Raleigh.

D. L. Corbitt, Head
Division of Publications.

# LIST OF LETTERS

## Letters Written By William A. Graham Printed in This Volume

| Place | Date | Written to |
|---|---|---|
| Raleigh | Jan. 9, 1838 | Susan Washington Graham |
| Raleigh | Dec. 4, 1838 | Susan Washington Graham |
| Raleigh | Dec. 8, 1838 | Susan Washington Graham |
| Raleigh | Dec. 10, 1838 | Susan Washington Graham |
| Raleigh | Dec. 23, 1838 | Susan Washington Graham |
| Raleigh | Jan. 6, 1839 | Susan Washington Graham |
| Raleigh | Jan. 13, 1839 | Susan Washington Graham |
| Raleigh | Feb. 3, 1839 | Susan Washington Graham |
| Hillsboro | Feb. 23, 1839 | Susan Washington Graham |
| Hillsboro | May 16, 1839 | Susan Washington Graham |
| [Hillsboro] | June 1, 1839 | Susan Washington Graham |
| Hillsboro | June 8, 1839 | Susan Washington Graham |
| Hillsboro | Aug. 31, 1839 | James W. Bryan |
| [Hillsboro] | Oct. 20, 1839 | David L. Swain |
| Hillsboro | Dec. 14, 1839 | James W. Bryan |
| Raleigh | Jan. 8, 1840 | Susan Washington Graham |
| Greensborough | April 18, 1840 | James W. Bryan |
| Hillsboro | Aug. 15, 1840 | James W. Bryan |
| Surry County | Sept. 15, 1840 | Richard C. Puryear and others |
| Williamston | Sept. 15, 1840 | James J. Williams and others |
| Raleigh | Nov. 18, 1840 | James W. Bryan |
| Raleigh | Nov. 21, 1840 | James W. Bryan |
| Raleigh | Nov. 24, 1840 | Susan Washington Graham |
| Petersburg | Dec. 7, 1840 | Susan Washington Graham |
| Washington, D. C. | Dec. 10, 1840 | Susan Washington Graham |
| Washington, D. C. | Dec. 16, 1840 | William Gaston |
| Washington, D. C. | Dec. 20, 1840 | James W. Bryan |
| Washington, D. C. | Dec. 21, 1840 | Susan Washington Graham |
| Washington, D. C. | Jan. 1, 1841 | Susan Washington Graham |
| Washington, D. C. | Jan. 9, 1841 | Susan Washington Graham |
| Washington, D. C. | Jan. 25, 1841 | Susan Washington Graham |
| Washington, D. C. | Feb. 1, 1841 | Susan Washington Graham |
| Washington, D. C. | Feb. 9, 1841 | Susan Washington Graham |
| Washington, D. C. | Feb. 13, 1841 | James W. Bryan |
| Washington, D. C. | Feb. 15, 1841 | Susan Washington Graham |
| Washington, D. C. | Feb. 23, 1841 | Susan Washington Graham |
| Washington, D. C. | March 4, 1841 | Susan Washington Graham |
| Hillsboro | March 29, 1841 | James W. Bryan |
| Washington, D. C. | June 4, 1841 | Susan Washington Graham |
| Washington, D. C. | June 8, 1841 | Susan Washington Graham |
| Washington, D. C. | June 12, 1841 | Susan Washington Graham |
| Washington, D. C. | June 13, 1841 | James W. Bryan |
| Washington, D. C. | June 19, 1841 | Susan Washington Graham |

| | | |
|---|---|---|
| Washington, D. C. | June 26, 1841 | Susan Washington Graham |
| Washington, D. C. | July 2, 1841 | Susan Washington Graham |
| [Washington, D. C.] | July 4, 1841 | Susan Washington Graham |
| Washington, D. C. | July 6, 1841 | Susan Washington Graham |
| Washington, D. C. | July 18, 1841 | Charles Plummer Green |
| Washington, D. C. | July 22, 1841 | Susan Washington Graham |
| Washington, D. C. | July 24, 1841 | Susan Washington Graham |
| Washington, D. C. | July 25, 1841 | Susan Washington Graham |
| Washington, D. C. | July 26, 1841 | David L. Swain |
| Washington, D. C. | July 28, 1841 | Susan Washington Graham |
| Washington, D. C. | July 30, 1841 | James W. Bryan |
| Washington, D. C. | Aug. 1, 1841 | Susan Washington Graham |
| Washington, D. C. | Aug. 6, 1841 | Susan Washington Graham |
| Washington, D. C. | Aug. 8, 1841 | Susan Washington Graham |
| Washington, D. C. | Aug. 13, 1841 | Susan Washington Graham |
| Washington, D. C. | Aug. 16, 1841 | Susan Washington Graham |
| Washington, D. C. | Aug. 17, 1841 | William Gaston |
| Washington, D. C. | Aug. 22, 1841 | Susan Washington Graham |
| Washington, D. C. | Aug. 27, 1841 | Susan Washington Graham |
| Washington, D. C. | Aug. 29, 1841 | Susan Washington Graham |
| Washington, D. C. | Sept. 5, 1841 | Susan Washington Graham |
| Washington, D. C. | Sept. 12, 1841 | Susan Washington Graham |
| Washington, D. C. | Sept. 13, 1841 | James W. Bryan |
| Washington, D. C. | Dec. 5, 1841 | David L. Swain |
| Washington, D. C. | Dec. 22, 1841 | James W. Bryan |
| Washington, D. C. | Jan. 6, 1842 | David L. Swain |
| Washington, D. C. | Feb. 10, 1842 | James W. Bryan |
| Washington, D. C. | Feb. 23, 1842 | John M. Morehead |
| Washington, D. C. | March 8, 1842 | James W. Bryan |
| Washington, D. C. | April 11, 1842 | James W. Bryan |
| Washington, D. C. | May 2, 1842 | Messrs. Gales and Seaton |
| Washington, D. C. | May 10, 1842 | David L. Swain |
| Washington, D. C. | May 14, 1842 | James W. Bryan |
| Washington, D. C. | May 20, 1842 | Paul C. Cameron |
| Washington, D. C. | July 7, 1842 | Samuel F. Patterson |
| Hillsborough | Sept. 24, 1842 | Calvin H. Wiley and others |
| Hillsboro | Sept. 24, 1842 | Charles P. Green |
| Washington, D. C. | Dec. 21, 1842 | James W. Bryan |
| Washington, D. C. | Jan. 14, 1843 | James Webb |
| Washington, D. C. | Feb. 17, 1843 | Charles P. Green |
| Hillsboro | April 30, 1843 | James W. Bryan |
| Raleigh | June 22, 1843 | Willie P. Mangum |
| Hillsborough | July 22, 1843 | Weston R. Gales |
| Hillsboro | Aug. 5, 1843 | Weston R. Gales |
| Hillsboro | Aug. 31, 1843 | J. H. Hedges |
| Hillsboro | Sept. 1, 1843 | James Graham |
| Hillsboro | Nov. 26, 1843 | James Graham |
| Hillsboro | Dec. 18, 1843 | George E. Spruill |
| Hillsboro | Dec. 28, 1843 | James W. Bryan |
| Raleigh | Jan. 26, 1844 | James W. Bryan |

| [Hillsboro] | Feb. 16, 1844 | New Hanover Committee |
|---|---|---|
| New York | Feb. 19, 1844 | Democratic Whigs of New York City |
| Hillsborough | April 11, 1844 | Richard Hines |
| Lexington | June 20, 1844 | Susan Washington Graham |
| Hillsboro | Nov. 25, 1844 | James W. Bryan |
| Hillsboro | Dec. 15, 1844 | James Graham |

## Letters Written To William A. Graham Printed in This Volume

| Place | Date | Written by |
|---|---|---|
| Washington, D. C. | Jan. 6, 1838 | James Graham |
| Washington, D. C. | Jan. 21, 1838 | James Graham |
| Nassau Hall | Jan. 26, 1838 | J. McKay and J. J. Witherspoon |
| Washington, D. C. | Feb. 20, 1838 | James Graham |
| Washington, D. C. | Feb. 25, 1838 | James Graham |
| Washington, D. C. | April 8, 1838 | James Graham |
| Greenesboro | April 18, 1838 | Hugh Waddell |
| Washington, D. C. | June 7, 1835 [1838] | James Graham |
| Raleigh | July 23, 1838 | Edward B. Dudley |
| Boston, Mass. | Aug. 5, 1838 | James Graham |
| Chapel Hill | Aug. 13, 1838 | William R. Walker |
| New York | Aug. 18, 1838 | James Augustus Washington |
| Saratoga Springs, N. Y. | Aug. 22, 1838 | James Graham |
| Brandon, Miss. | Oct. 13, 1838 | James A. King |
| Macon, Miss. | Oct. 24, 1838 | Victor Moreau Murphey |
| Woodville | Nov. 26, 1838 | Josiah T. Granbery |
| Brook-Land [Ala.] | Dec. 2, 1838 | Eliza B. Witherspoon |
| Washington, D. C. | Dec. 14, 1838 | James Graham |
| Newbern | Jan. 3, 1839 | James W. Bryan |
| Washington, D. C. | Jan. 4, 1839 | James Graham |
| Chapel Hill | Feb. 18, 1839 | Clarke Moulton Avery |
| Washington, D. C. | April 1, 1839 | James Graham |
| Davidson College | April 6, 1839 | Literary Societies of Davidson College |
| Brook Land [Ala.] | April 15, 1839 | Eliza Witherspoon Goldthwaite |
| Raleigh | April 16, 1839 | Weston R. Gales |
| Newbern | May 13, 1839 | James W. Bryan |
| Van Buren, Ark. | June 8, 1839 | Jesse Turner |
| Randolph Macon College | Aug. 25, 1839 | Jno. S. Wright, J. L. Smith and Jas. L. Mullen |
| Newbern | Sept. 26, 1839 | James W. Bryan |
| Wilmington | Nov. 30, 1839 | James Graham |
| Washington, D. C. | Dec. 5, 1839 | James Graham |
| Philadelphia | Dec. 10, 1839 | Henry W. Miller |
| Washington, D. C. | Dec. 22, 1839 | James Graham |
| Washington, D. C. | Jan. 31, 1840 | James Graham |
| Washington, D. C. | Feb. 3, 1840 | James Graham |
| Washington, D. C. | March 19, 1840 | James Graham |
| Washington, D. C. | April 5, 1840 | Kenneth Rayner |
| Washington, D. C. | April 8, 1840 | James Graham |

| | | |
|---|---|---|
| Raleigh | April 24, 1840 | William H. Battle |
| Washington, D. C. | May 10, 1840 | James Graham |
| Egypt | May 19, 1840 | James W. Bryan |
| Washington, D. C. | May 20, 1840 | James Graham |
| Charlotte | May 26, 1840 | James W. Osborne |
| Raleigh | May 30, 1840 | Charles Manly |
| Washington, D. C. | May 31, 1840 | James Graham |
| Washington, D. C. | June 16, 1840 | James Graham |
| Washington, D. C. | July 3, 1840 | James Graham |
| New York | July 7, 1840 | James A. Washington |
| Washington, D. C. | July 13, 1840 | James Graham |
| Newbern | Aug. 9, 1840 | James W. Bryan |
| Charlotte | Aug. 26, 1840 | James W. Osborne |
| Saratoga Springs | Aug. 29, 1840 | James W. Bryan |
| Charlottesville | Sept. 4, 1840 | James Graham |
| Newbern | Nov. 12, 1840 | Matthias E. Manly |
| Pittsboro | Nov. 22, 1840 | Maurice Q. Waddell |
| Newbern | Nov. 26, 1840 | Matthias E. Manly |
| Newbern | Dec. 9, 1840 | James W. Bryan |
| Raleigh | Dec. 27, 1840 | William Gaston |
| Raleigh | Jan. 19, 1841 | George E. Badger |
| Hillsboro | Feb. 1, 1841 | Cadwallader Jones |
| Dockery's Store | Feb. 8, 1841 | Isaac Dockery |
| Mobile [Ala.] | Feb. 8, 1841 | Jesse Carter |
| Raleigh | Feb. 9, 1841 | Thomas Ruffin |
| Washington, D. C. | Feb. 9, 1841 | Joel R. Poinsett and N. C. Paulding |
| Raleigh | Feb. 16, 1841 | George E. Badger |
| Charlotte | Feb. 21, 1841 | Daniel Moreau Barringer |
| Raleigh | March 25, 1841 | Charles L. Hinton |
| Chapel Hill | March 25, 1841 | James Phillips |
| Newbern | April 3, 1841 | James W. Bryan |
| Halifax | April 5, 1841 | Bartholomew F. Moore |
| New York | April 7, 1841 | Nicholas Carroll |
| ———— | April 12, 1841 | Daniel Webster |
| Washington, D. C. | April 8, 1841 | Nathaniel P. Tallmadge |
| Washington, D. C. | April 28, 1841 | George E. Badger |
| Chapel Hill | May 31, 1841 | Robert B. Gilliam |
| [Washington] | June 1, 1841 | John Bell |
| Charlotte | June 4, 1841 | Thomas J. Holton |
| Raleigh | June 7, 1841 | Duncan Cameron |
| Hillsboro | June 8, 1841 | Frederick Nash |
| Raleigh | June 9, 1841 | Henry W. Miller |
| Sandy Grove | June 15, 1841 | William R. Albright |
| Brandon [Miss.] | June 24, 1841 | James A. King |
| Newbern | June 30, 1841 | Matthias E. Manly |
| Washington, D. C. | July 2, 1841 | Daniel Webster |
| Hillsboro | July 7, 1841 | Priestley H. Mangum |
| Hillsboro | July 9, 1841 | Edmund Strudwick |
| Wilmington | July 10, 1841 | Edward B. Dudley |

| | | |
|---|---|---|
| Washington, D. C. | July 15, 1841 | James Graham |
| Fayetteville | July 20, 1841 | ———— |
| Raleigh | July 29, 1841 | William Gaston |
| Greensboro [Ala.] | Aug. 6, 1841 | William F. Strudwick |
| ———— | Aug. 15, 1841 | James W. Osborne |
| Raleigh | Aug. 19, 1841 | William Gaston |
| Boston [Mass.] | Aug. 22, 1841 | Henry K. Burgwyn |
| Edenton | Aug. 30, 1841 | Thomas S. Hoskins |
| Charlotte | Oct. 16, 1841 | James W. Osborne |
| Raleigh | Nov. 9, 1841 | B. Baker, H. W. Miller, C. L. Hinton |
| ———— | Nov. 29, 1841 | David L. Swain |
| Raleigh | Jan. 5, 1842 | William Gaston |
| Chapel Hill | Jan. 11, 1842 | David L. Swain |
| Raleigh | Jan. 18, 1842 | William W. Holden |
| Philadelphia | Feb. 14, 1842 | George McClellan |
| Chapel Hill | Feb. 16, 1842 | Elisha Mitchell |
| Hillsborough | Feb. 16, 1842 | James C. Turrentine |
| Moon's Creek | Feb. 17, 1842 | G. Robertson |
| Plymouth | Feb. 20, 1842 | J. A. Norcom |
| Carthage | Feb. 26, 1842 | George C. Mendenhall |
| Hillsboro | March 2, 1842 | Priestley H. Mangum |
| St. Augustine, Flo. | March 10, 1842 | Citizens of Florida |
| Raleigh | March 11, 1842 | David W. Stone |
| Forestville | March 16, 1842 | Daniel S. Crenshaw |
| Newbern | March 19, 1842 | James W. Bryan |
| Greensboro | March 22, 1842 | Ralph Gorrell |
| Washington | March 25, 1842 | Samuel L. Southard |
| Raleigh | April 4, 1842 | Charles L. Hinton |
| Raleigh | April 7, 1842 | John M. Morehead |
| Morganton | April 22, 1842 | Tod R. Caldwell |
| Wentworth | April 22, 1842 | William R. Walker |
| Edenton | May 9, 1842 | Thomas S. Hoskins |
| Hillsboro | May 12, 1842 | Priestley H. Mangum |
| Yale College | May 17, 1842 | Denison Olmsted |
| Newbern | May 24, 1842 | James W. Bryan |
| Panther Creek | May 25, 1842 | Nicholas Lanier Williams |
| Hillsboro | May 30, 1842 | Priestley H. Mangum |
| White Oak | May 30, 1842 | Giles Mebane |
| Scotts Creek | May 31, 1842 | J. Kerner |
| Sandy Grove | June 3, 1842 | W. R. Albright |
| Hillsboro | June 7, 1842 | Henry K. Nash |
| Hillsboro | June 8, 1842 | Hugh Waddell |
| Hillsborough | June 13, 1842 | John W. Norwood |
| Granville | June 15, 1842 | William A. Johnson |
| Van Buren, Ark. | June 15, 1842 | Jesse Turner |
| Greensboro | June 22, 1842 | Jesse H. Lindsay |
| Oxford | June 23, 1842 | James T. Littlejohn |
| Raleigh | July 1, 1842 | Weston R. Gales |
| Germanton | July 1, 1842 | John F. Poindexter |

| | | |
|---|---|---|
| Washington, D. C. | July 7, 1842 | W. Forward |
| ——— | July 7, 1842 | J. H. Long |
| Roxboro | July 8, 1842 | John A. Barnett |
| White Oak | July 10, 1842 | Giles Mebane |
| Raleigh | July 12, 1842 | Charles L. Hinton |
| Pittsboro | July 13, 1842 | Frederick J. Hill |
| Louisburg | July 14, 1842 | Daniel S. Hill |
| Roxboro | July 16, 1842 | Edwin G. Reade |
| Raleigh | July 20, 1842 | Samuel F. Patterson |
| Salisbury | July 24, 1842 | John M. Morehead |
| Chapel Hill | July 25, 1842 | William H. Owen |
| Mobile [Ala.] | **July 26, 1842** | James Martin |
| Pittsboro | July 27, 1842 | Frederick J. Hill |
| Ridgeway | July 30, 1842 | Charles Plummer Green |
| Ridgeway | Aug. 2, 1842 | Charles Plummer Green |
| Huntsville | Aug. 5, 1842 | Richard C. Puryear |
| Raleigh | Aug. 8, 1842 | Samuel F. Patterson |
| Hillsboro | Aug. 12, 1842 | Henry K. Nash |
| Henderson | Sept. 17, 1842 | From Committee |
| Frankfort, Ky. | Sept. 23, 1842 | Frankfort Whig Committee |
| Ridgeway | Oct. 5, 1842 | Charles P. Green |
| Newbern | Oct. 25, 1842 | James W. Bryan |
| Raleigh | Nov. 20, 1842 | Charles L. Hinton |
| ——— | Nov. 28, 1842 | George C. Mendenhall |
| Columbia, S. C. | Dec. 4, 1842 | William C. Preston |
| ——— | Dec. 4, 1842 | George C. Mendenhall |
| Hillsboro | Dec. 5, 1842 | Edmund Strudwick |
| Raleigh | Dec. 7, 1842 | George C. Mendenhall |
| Raleigh | Dec. 8, 1842 | George C. Mendenhall |
| Raleigh | Dec. 9, 1842 | John A. Young |
| Raleigh | Dec. 10, 1842 | George C. Mendenhall |
| Raleigh | Dec. 11, 1842 | George C. Mendenhall |
| Raleigh | Dec. 13, 1842 | George C. Mendenhall |
| Raleigh | Dec. 14, 1842 | George C. Mendenhall |
| Raleigh | Dec. 14, 1842 | George C. Mendenhall |
| Raleigh | Dec. 14, 1842 | Joseph B. Hinton |
| Raleigh | Dec. 16, 1842 | George C. Mendenhall |
| Raleigh | Dec. 18, 1842 | George C. Mendenhall |
| Wilmington | Dec. 18, 1842 | Hamilton C. Jones |
| Cincinnati [Ohio] | Dec. 18, 1842 | S. O. Butler |
| Raleigh | Dec. 18, 1842 | George C. Mendenhall |
| Raleigh | Dec. 19, 1842 | Charles L. Hinton |
| Raleigh | Dec. 19, 1842 | Henry K. Nash |
| Raleigh | Dec. 31, 1842 | Charles L. Hinton |
| Hillsboro | Dec. 31, 1842 | Susan Washington Graham |
| Raleigh | Jan. 12, 1843 | George C. Mendenhall |
| Raleigh | Jan. 12, 1843 | George C. Mendenhall |
| Raleigh | Jan. 13, 1843 | George C. Mendenhall |
| Hillsboro | Jan. 16, 1843 | John Umstead Kirkland |
| Raleigh | Jan. 20, 1843 | Charles L. Hinton |

| | | |
|---|---|---|
| Raleigh | Feb. 1, 1843 | Charles L. Hinton |
| Cottage Home | March 6, 1843 | Robert Hall Morrison |
| Washington, D. C. | March 16, 1843 | E. Dyer |
| Raleigh | March 26, 1843 | James Graham |
| Washington, N. C. | March 30, 1843 | Joshua Tayloe |
| Halifax | April 20, 1943 | Bartholomew F. Moore |
| Halifax | April 20, 1843 | Bartholomew F. Moore |
| Tarboro | May 23, 1843 | Bartholomew F. Moore |
| Rutherfordton | May 25, 1843 | James Graham |
| Rockbridge County, Va. | Aug. 5, 1843 | Charles P. Green |
| Raleigh | Aug. 12, 1843 | George E. Badger |
| Randolph-Macon College, Va. | Sept. 18, 1843 | John Howard |
| Raleigh | Oct. 10, 1843 | Thomas P. Devereux |
| Beaufort | Oct. 13, 1843 | James W. Bryan |
| Newbern | Oct. 19, 1843 | James W. Bryan |
| Rutherfordton | Nov. 5, 1843 | James Graham |
| Conaconara | Nov. 6, 1843 | Thomas P. Devereux |
| Neuse River | Nov. 15, 1843 | Charles L. Hinton |
| Washington, D. C. | Dec. 3, 1843 | Daniel M. Barringer |
| Raleigh | Dec. 11, 1843 | George E. Spruill |
| Washington, D. C. | Dec. 27, 1843 | Daniel M. Barringer |
| Salisbury | Dec. 29, 1843 | John Steele Macnamara |
| Chapel Hill | Jan. 21, 1844 | Reuben Clarke Shorter |
| Charleston | Jan. 22, 1844 | William Blanding |
| V. Furnace | Jan. 30, 1844 | James Graham |
| Oxford | Jan. 31, 1844 | Robert B. Gilliam |
| Oxford | Feb. 2, 1844 | Robert B. Gilliam |
| Wilmington | Feb. 4, 1844 | New Hanover Committee |
| Franklin | Feb. 5, 1844 | John Y. Hicks and others |
| New Orleans | Feb. 6, 1844 | Henry Clay |
| Windsor | Feb. 17, 1844 | Thomas Turner |
| New York | Feb. 19, 1844 | Henry E. Davies and others |
| Hillsborough | March 1, 1844 | Hugh Waddell |
| Pleasant Gardens | March 2, 1844 | S. Bulow Erwin |
| Allamance | March 6, 1844 | Thomas Ruffin |
| Sommerville [Tenn.] | March 16, 1844 | Calvin Jones and others |
| Pittsborough | March 21, 1844 | Hugh Waddell |
| Asheboro | March 29, 1844 | Hugh Waddell |
| Fairntosh | April 6, 1844 | Paul C. Cameron |
| Raleigh | April 8, 1844 | John M. Morehead |
| Newbern | April 13, 1844 | James W. Bryan |
| Raleigh | April 15, 1844 | Henry Clay |
| Raleigh | April 15, 1844 | Thomas P. Devereaux |
| Oxford | April 27, 1844 | Robert B. Gilliam |
| Lincolnton | May 4, 1844 | Haywood W. Guion |
| Oxford | May 7, 1844 | Robert B. Gilliam |
| | | Hugh Waddell |
| Cottage Home | May 7, 1844 | Robert Hall Morrison |
| Raleigh | May 11, 1844 | John M. Morehead |
| Lincolnton | May 13, 1844 | Bayles M. Edney |
| Attaway-hill | May 16, 1844 | Francis Joseph Kron |

| | | |
|---|---|---|
| Rutherfordton | May 30, 1844 | W. E. Mills and others |
| ———— | ———— | W. E. Mills |
| New Orleans | June 4, 1844 | James Graham |
| Rutherfordton | June 17, 1844 | William E. Mills |
| Lincolnton | July 22, 1844 | Charles Cotesworth Henderson |
| Newbern | Aug. 3, 1844 | James W. Bryan |
| Rockingham | Aug. 5, 1844 | John W. Cameron |
| New York | Aug. 27, 1844 | Nicholas Carroll |
| Raleigh | Sept. 21, 1844 | George E. Badger |
| Raleigh | Nov. 9, 1844 | Christopher C. Battle |
| Staunton, Va. | Nov. 18, 1844 | William D. Cooke |
| Raleigh | Dec. 5, 1844 | Hugh Waddell |
| Raleigh | Dec. 15, 1844 | Hugh Waddell |
| Raleigh | Dec. 20, 1844 | John M. Morehead |

## Speeches and Other Writings of William A. Graham Printed in this Volume

Speech upon Election as Speaker....................................................Nov. 19, 1838

Speech at Close of Session...........................................................Jan. 8, 1839

Speech in United States Senate on the Bill to Establish a Permanent
Pre-emption System in Favor of Settlers on the Public Lands ..........Jan. 7, 1841

Speech in the Senate on Roanoke Inlet...........................................Jan. 29, 1841

Speech in the Senate on Roanoke Inlet...........................................Jan. 28, 1842

Speech on Lewis Williams in U. S. Senate ......................................Feb. 24, 1842

Speech on the Loan Bill in U. S. Senate..........................................April 13, 1842

Speech on the Distributing Clause of the Apportionment
Bill in the U. S. Senate .............................................................June 3, 1842

Campaign Speech at Fayetteville...................................................June 1, 1844

## Miscellaneous Letters Printed in this Volume

| By | Place | Date | To |
|---|---|---|---|
| Members of the Whig Party | Raleigh | Jan. 12, 1839 | Lewis Williams Edmund Deberry Aug. H. Shepherd Abraham Rencher James Graham Edward Stanly |
| Walter Gwynn | ———— | June 22, 1840 | Edward B. Dudley |
| Sam F. Bridge | Boston | April 10, 1841 | Daniel Webster |
| William H. Owen | Chapel Hill | July 25, 1842 | "Dear Sir" |
| James Graham | Washington, D. C. | Aug. 24, 1842 | The President of the U. S. |
| James Graham | Washington, D. C. | Aug. 29, 1842 | The President of the U. S. |
| Calvin H. Wiley, et als. | Henderson | Sept. 17, 1842 | ———— |
| James P. Espy | ———— | ———— | Friends of Science |
| Richard Hines | Raleigh | Oct. 18, 1843 | Willie P. Mangum |
| Weston R. Gales | Raleigh | Nov. 2, 1843 | Hugh Waddell |
| Robert Hall Morrison | Cottage Home | Mar. 9, 1844 | Susan W. Graham |
| James Cornick | Norfolk | Nov. 27, 1844 | John M. Morehead |

# Miscellaneous Documents Printed in this Volume

# Symbols Used to Designate Depositories of Graham Papers

| | | |
|---|---|---|
| A | | North Carolina Department of Archives and History |
| U | | The Southern Historical Collection of the University of North Carolina |
| A | Bryan Mss. | North Carolina Department of Archives and History |
| U | Gaston Mss. | The Southern Historical Collection of the University of North Carolina |
| U | Lindsay Patterson Mss. | The Southern Historical Collection of the University of North Carolina |
| U | T. J. Green Mss. | The Southern Historical Collection of the University of North Carolina |
| U | James Webb Mss. | The Southern Historical Collection of the University of North Carolina |
| U | Cameron Mss. | The Southern Historical Collection of the University of North Carolina |

1838

*From James Graham.*                                    U.

Washington, January 6th, 1838.

\*   \*   \*   \*   \*

Congress is now actively employed. Calhoun's position is very unpleasant. The Whigs and he have dissolved all connection, and the leaders of the Van Buren ranks are obviously disposed to throw him over board.

The friends of the administration are tardy in presenting their Sub Treasury scheme; they are trying to compromise with the Conservatives. I think their efforts will be unavailing. The President and his party appear disponding. Some of the Whigs are desirous *now* to nominate a Candidate for the Presidency. I am *utterly opposed* to any nomination now or before next December. Whenever a nomination is made, the Whigs will be weakened and somewhat divided among themselves. Let us fight on therefore for *great measures;* for a good and *uniform Currency,* for *our equal share of the public Lands,* and so on until after the Elections are over next Fall in the large States, and after we have enlightened public opinion on great principles and sound policy then let us select a suitable Candidate *to carry out our principles.* The want of a Candidate on our side will disarm all the little superficial politicians who never can discuss measures, but always trade on a borrowed Capital, and discourse largely upon the supposed merits or demerits of men. In this way next summer we may *kill off a large number of the pickaune politicians in No. Ca.* and the Country, and destroy the man-worship which has pervaded the whole Country and created so much noisy & unprofitable discussion. The first year of Mr. Van Buren's Presidential term has not yet expired. The Van Buren men are desirous and anxious to see the Whigs *now* nominate their man.

I do not credit the reports that the Cabinet is to be reorganized. The President entertains in most splendid and sumptuous style. The City is now very gay and many strangers are still coming in.

*To Susan Washington Graham.*                    A.

Raleigh, Tuesday night,

Jany. 9th, 1838.

My Dear Wife

. . . I then purchased Mr. Spencers (where Mr. Waddell formerly lived) at $1175. and am to get possession the 1st. of Feby. Every one says that I have gotten a great bargain in it. Mr. C. Jones upon hearing of it, offered to exchange for it his house (formerly Maj Davies) and seemed anxious to do so. I have every prospect of being able to sell it again for at least an equal price, should we not like it on trial. There are three acres of ground, on which are all the necessary outhouses, stables, an office with two rooms, a garden, and yard somewhat improved, and near to a good Spring. The dwelling house is not as good as I could wish, but I hope with a little repair it will answer our present purpose, at least until our affairs are more settled. It has no rooms upstairs, but four below, three of which have fire places. I took the dimensions of the rooms, supposing we could make some provision of furniture when we meet.

The Parlour is 19½ by 15½ feet
dining room    20 by 15½   ″
Bed room    15½ by 12½   ″

These have fire places, and I suppose we will want carpets at least for two of them. Of the kinds you will judge. I think you might as well have your beds, etc., boxed before you leave New B. and sent by the first opportunity. Such other furniture as we want immediately we can purchase now, and send for the residue to the North. I believe it will be better for us to go into the house soon after we return, as an agreeable boarding house cannot now be had, and we can now most advantageously lay in supplies for the year, and begin our garden in time to make it to our liking. I hope you may be better pleased with the place than I fear you now are. It is the best however that I can now do. I will write to Lincoln and have our kitchen ware and such other articles as can be procured there, forwarded at once. The servants you wish, from your own negroes, may be perhaps sent by the waggon which may bring your furniture. I am truly glad to learn that you will soon come to me; It seems long since I saw you & my Dear

Son. If Mary does not come with you I hope Mother will send her as soon as we get into our own house. I will meet you at any place and day you may name after the middle of next week. I am very busy here, and write you in great haste.

* * * * *

With ardent desire to see you,
I am, my dearest Wife.

*From James Graham.*                                    U.

Washington, Jany 21st, 1838.

* * * * *

The contested Election from Missippi has engrossed the whole time and attention of the House. The result is quite doubtful. I think Prentiss[1] and Word [2] have some fair prospect of success. Prentiss is a dissipated lame man of fine talents, and made an able and eloquent speech in behalf of his claim. Parties are so nearly divided here that each side is afraid to move out and shew their plans. The Sub Treasury will come up after the contested Election and consume much time. I think it can't pass, tho' great efforts will be made for it.

Washington is quite gay, and I have been out in company more than usual, and my health is better than it ever was. There is a strong disposition manifested among a few Whigs to nominate their favourite candidate for the Presidency. This would be suicidal. The large majority of the Whigs now say they will not fix upon their Candidate for 9 or 10 month yet, and in the mean time they will fight on great principles. I hope our friends in No. Ca. will act discreetly in this matter. The Game is our's if we play it with Judgment. Let us keep down men and push forth prominent measures. It requires some exertion on the Part of our influential friends to keep down candidates for the Presidency, because small men (taking mind for standard) can't get along unless they have some man to applaud and another man to abuse, but this is

---

[1] Sergent Smith Prentiss (1808-1850), a native of Maine, educated at Bowdoin, a lawyer, who moved to Mississippi, and had served as a Whig in the lower house of the legislature. The contest resulted in his favor, and he served in this congress only. He later moved to Louisiana.

[2] Thomas J. Word, a native of Surry County, North Carolina, who, in 1832, before moving to Mississippi, was a member of the commons. He was seated, but served only in this congress.

the way to enlighten the People and kill off demaguges by shewing them that we are going for the Country and not for a Party.
I hope our friends in No. Ca. will bring out *talented and popular
candidates* in all the Counties for the Legislature and spare no
pains to carry the election.

I am making an effort to get a great *Daily line* of Stages from
*Raleigh* by Buncombe to *Nashville* in Ten. When the Rail Road
is finished to Raleigh this line will be a great one and much used.

I saw Badger here (one day only) on his way to Philadelphia.
He appeared dejected. Shocco Jones is here living high and entertaining largely. He is no favorite here in public or private.

Mrs. Jos Gales gives us a splendid Party every friday evening,
and we have 3 and 4 in the week beside.

The Theatre is open every night and some fine starrs on the
boards.

*From J. McKay and J. J. Witherspoon.*        U.

Nassau Hall, Jany 26, 1838.

As the organs of the American Whig Society, it becomes our
agreeable duty to inform you of your election as an Honorary
member of that Society. The objects of which are the promotion
of Friendship, morality, and literature, objects which, we are confident will meet with your warmest approbation. Trusting that
you will permit us to enroll your name in the Catalogue of the
members of the A. W. Society.

We remain with the highest respects,
Your most obedient Servants.
From J. J. Witherspoon.

Dear Uncle[3]

If you can find a leisure moment if would give me great satisfaction in hearing from you. I received a letter from Pa, a few
days since, He mentioned that the Family were all in good health

I expect to graduate next August, if nothing should happen
between this and that period, to marr my expectations. I find my

---

[3] Written on the same page by John James Witherspoon.

College exercises to become a source of pleasure to me every day. I have just reached that period, when my studies become interesting and useful.

I hope you will permit me the pleasure, of enrolling your name in the Catalogue of which my Father, and Brother, are graduates. If you should find it convenient to answer this, I would request you to write on a seperate sheet, As I will have to read it in the Hall.

Give my love to Aunt and to any of my relations with whom you may meet,

Your Nephew

P.S. We have 250 Students in College  I believe it is in a more prosperous condition than it has ever been.


*From James Graham.*　　　　　　　　U.

Washington, Feb. 20th, 1838.

On yesterday Clay spoke on the Sub Treasury. He gave Calhoun the most *dreadful Castigation* I have ever witnessed. I never before saw Clay go into the *Ring* of debate with such bold defiance. He said, to use Calhoun's own words, in letter lately published in So. Ca. He Calhoun had left the Whigs because a victory was about to be won by the opposition but it would not enure to *Calhoun and his party,* and so Calhoun and all his party had gone over to the Administration. Yes all his party—horse, foot, and draggoon, and who are they? Why the Senator marched over to his new ally (T. Benton) Solitary and alone, Clay told him. He went over to his new Allies, *suspecting* and *suspected.* After Clay spoke 3 or 4 Hours he concluded. Calhoun rose and said Clay has *misrepresented* and perverted his argument out and out and he would at his own good time pay off and Settle the accounts between them.

Clay rejoined he would leave to the Senate wheather he had misrepresented or perverted him. He said he was always willing to receive debts due him; that he sought neither Contention or quarrel with any man and he was determined to avoid none with Calhoun.

They were both as mad as they could be. On this day Calhoun will answer him, and the debate will be violent and bitter. I must go to the Senate to see the Giants fight.

*From James Graham.*                                    U.

Washington, Feb 25th, 1838.

On last evening we had *a Duel* 4 miles from here in Maryland. Watson Webb [4] of N. York, editor of Courier & Enquirer, came here and challanged Cilly[5] (a member from Maine) for having said in debate he was *bribed* and *bought* by the United States Bank. Graves[6] of Ky. carried the challange to Cilley who refused to accept, alleging Webb was not a gentleman. Graves then challanged Cilley who accepted and selected Rifles to fight with. They fought at 80 yards distance and the *third fire* Graves shot Cilley through the body and he died instantly. Wise and Menifee[7] were the seconds of Graves, and Jones[8] of Wisconsin and Bynum[9] were the seconds of Cilley.

Watson Webb is desirous it is said here to get a fight out of Bynum or Duncan[10] of Ohio.

The City is much excited and I apprehend we shall have some other fights.

Congress is getting on very slowly, and I think very little will be done this Session. The Sub Treasury scheme is still under discussion in the Senate but I think it cannot pass either branch of Congress.

There are a great number of strangers here, and the City is very gay.

---

[4] James Watson Webb (1802-1884), of New York, journalist and diplomat, obtained a lieutenant's commission in the army, and served from 1819-1827. His usual title of General was purely honorary. He was a noted duelist, and consequently, frequently in trouble. Becoming editor of the *Courier and Inquirer,* he was shortly one of the most important figures in that day of personal journalism. From an ardent follower of Jackson he became a Whig, on the Bank issue. He was strongly anti-Abolition, but a Free-Soiler. Appointed Charge to Austria in 1849, he was not confirmed. Lincoln made him minister to Brazil, where he spent eight years. He is credited with inducing Napoleon III to withdraw French troops from Mexico.

[5] Jonathan Cilley (1802-1838), of Maine, a native of New Hampshire, where he was member and speaker of the lower house, who had entered congress in 1837.

[6] William Jordan Graves (1805-1848), of Kentucky, Whig member of congress, 1835-1841. He later served in the state legislature, and was an elector in 1844.

[7] Richard Hickman Menifee (1809-1893), of Kentucky, graduate of Transylvania, a lawyer who, after brief service in the legislature, was a member of congress, 1837-1839, and an elector in 1840.

[8] George Wallace Jones (1804-1896), of Iowa, a native of Indiana, a graduate of Transylvania, lawyer, soldier in the Black Hawk War, who became territorial judge in Michigan, then delegate to congress, 1835-1837, delegate from Wisconsin, 1837-1838. Moving to Iowa, he was United States senator, 1848-1849, and minister to New Grenada, 1859-1861.

[9] Jesse A. Bynum.

[10] Alexander Duncan (1788-1853), of Ohio, native of New Jersey, who, after brief service in each house of the legislature, was a member of congress, 1837-1841, 1843-1845.

*From James Graham.* U.

Washington, April 8th, 1838.

I received your letter a few days since and regretted to learn you had been sick. I fear you don't take exercise enough now since you have a Lot. A little regular work with an Axe or Hoe every good day would raise your muscles and give you more vigerous robust health. I have lately had a bad cold, but my general health has been good. Judge Cameron was here on yesterday and Dined with me in company of a number of Members. I went with him to see Clay, and he was much pleased with the interview. Wm. B. Shephard is here in very bad health; He is Dispeptic.

I presume if you become a Candidate for Orange you will scarcely go to Tennesee this Spring or Summer.

The Corn I sent you is the *Baden Corn* of Maryland and it is said produces from 4 to 8 ears to the stalk.

The Sub Treasury is not yet taken up in the House. I think it cannot pass but great efforts will be made to carry it. The recent defeats in the elections have discouraged the administration. I fear the Whigs in N. Carolina will not be so active as they ought to be. They ought to have a Central Committee in each County, and one or *two* Committee-men in each Captain's Company who should be furnished with *materials* and *points* to make known to the people and expose the evil deeds of the party.

I think the Whig Candidates ought not to come out on the presidential Candidates at this campaign, But denounce the acts and proposed measures of the administration.

\*  \*  \*  \*  \*

My negroes are doing badly and 3 of them have run off. No money can be made by farming during the derangment of the Currency.

[P.S.] If I can be of any service to my friends in Orange by sending speeches I would do so, If had a list of *names* and *Post offices.*

Mangum ought to go out freely, I presume his acquaintance among the people is nearly worn out.

I think the Expunging Question he should say nothing about to the people. It will be attributed to his former defeat. The *Currency* and *pub Land* are the 2 strong questions with the people. The discount and losses we sustain on our money is very great and the Farmer and Consumer pays it all finally.

---

*From Hugh Waddell.*                                    U.

Greenesboro', April 18th, 1838.

\*   \*   \*   \*   \*

I know not in what language to express my distress at hearing of yr. late indisposition; it took me wholly by surprize. I had fondly hoped to have the pleasure of meeting you on my arrival here and there are many things which I had desired to say to you, in relation to the future, which made me anticipate more than the usual pleasure of meeting you.

Altho' I confidently expect you will be much better before this reaches you, yet one of my present purposes in writing is to beg that you will not suffer a slight or even a *great* apparent amendment to tempt you to come here during this Court.

In the first place, it is so generally understood that you are unwell that few of yr. clients will return and by the time you could get here, *others will be* employed in new business, and moreover I know that a long and fatiguing ride may be very injurious to a convalescent and may prevent your going to Rockingham. And above all, the present is a season of the year at which it behooves you as well as myself to take care how we tamper with cold or other affections of the lungs.

---

*From James Graham.*                                   U.

Washington, June the 7th, 1835. [1838]

I very much regret to learn from your last letter that your health is still delicate. If it is proceed from the consequences of the Fever you had last summer, as you apprehend, it will go off by degrees. After I had the Fever I was much debilitated and Dr. John McLean prescribed some Bay tree Bark; that is, the inner skin or membrane of the Coucumber tree: fill a bottle 2/3 full of the bark and then fill it up with good French brandy and after standing 24 hours take a small wine glass full before breakfast, and also before dinner. It gave my stomach tone and my system strength; you can dilute it with a little water if you like. You ought to take *regular exercise* in the morning and evening as much as you can bear. Use the warm bath once a week when the weather is dry and warm and use the flesh brush every day. Ride on horseback to your Courts and Electioneering and when you tire the least in riding dismount and walk, 2 or 3 hundred yards; this will brace and strengthen you. This sedentary life we lead is very destructive to health and few constitutions will sustain it. Do not permitt the Doctors to give you too much medicine. If you resolve to go to the Springs write me when and where and probably I may meet you there. The White Sulphur and the Red I presume are the best. Congress will probably adjourn in or about the 9th. of July. I will be here until the 15 or 16 and then leave for N York and Boston—a short trip—and then return through here in August by the Springs home.

We had as you have seen a fight in the House between Bell and Turney[11] from Ten. It was soon adjusted and the debate proceeded. Two day since we had another strange scene between Biddle[12] and Downing[13] of Florida. The former in debate applied the word falsehood and the latter supposed he intended it for him. He immediately sprung to his feet, picked up an Inkstand and moved towards Biddle, but was stoped by the intervening members. They are both Whigs and the debate was on the Bill to suppress Indian hostilities. Their mutual friends think they have reconciled the difficulty. This Indian Bill has given rise to a very wide debate, I participated in it on two occasions. I sustained the Treaty of 1835 and the policy of the Genl. Government towards the removal of the Indians; but did not justify the conduct of Georgia. I will write out one speech and publish it. It is rumored here the cabinet is to be much changed the last of this session. I believe it, but do not know who is to succeed. The sub Treasury is to be up next week. I think it will be rejected by *a few votes* only.

I think Strange and Brown are both very uneasy since *they voted against the repeal of the Specie Circular.*

---

[11] Hopkins Lacy Turney (1797-1857), of Tennessee, served in the legislature, 1828-1837, as a member of congress, 1837-1843, and as United States senator, 1845-1851.

[12] Richard Biddle (1796-1847), of Pennsylvania, a lawyer, member of congress, 1837-1840. He was the author of "Life of Sebastian Cabot."

[13] Charles Downing (d. 1845), a native of Virginia, member of the legislative council of the Florida Territory, and delegate to congress, 1837-1840.

The papers in N. C. ought to hold them up to the public indignation for that vote; distinctions and differences without cause are invidious and odious to our people.

The Whigs here, you have seen, have determined to postpone the presidential question until next fall come a year. The object is to fight for principle and give the public mind time to cool. I do not think the Whig candidates in N. C. ought to be drawn into that question *now,* but expose the measures of those in power, and stand up for the Constitution, the union and the people regardless of any President.

*From Edward B. Dudley.*                          A.

Raleigh, July 23, 1838.

In obedience to your message by Mr. P. Cameron, I send you herewith a half dozen reports of the Engineer in charge of draining the swamp lands for the State.

These lands are immensely rich & will be commensurately valuable when drained.

I have no doubt the work will pay the State handsomely & releave the country from a very unhealthy atmosphere & impart comparative health & contentment to the Citizens. What now pays a tax on 6¼ to 12½ *cents* per acre value, will be increased to the value of 40 to 80 *dollars!* per Acre! the price which the improved lands now sell at.

A very small amount of money has as yet been expended on this work. The time has been occupied in tracing titles & surveys, which preliminaries are mostly despatched & the Engineers are now employed in locating two Canals from Alligator & Pungo lakes & seeking contractors to engage in the work.

The Money appropriated for the work has been loaned out by the Literary Board & paying into the Treasury interest every 90 days, which has so far exceeded the expenditures.

Any information which I can furnish you from this office or place, shall be done with great pleasure.

With my sincere good wishes for your success in the election & good health through the *firery* ordeal of convassing.

I am very truly
Yours

*From James Graham.* U.

Boston, August 5th, 1838.

I have been here one week and will stay 2 or 3 days longer when I will leave for Saratoga and perhaps Niagara. Providence never made a poorer Country; and the People never made a Richer country than New England. I ask myself every mile I travel how they live on such a sterile soil? Their Exports are *Rock* and *Ice, Irish Potatoes* and *Onions*. Every Body here (from the garrett to the cellar) works and makes money, and then *takes care of it*. I have been to Lowell and saw all the factories. I found them making steam Machinery for Russia! Printing Calico's, and all sorts of Machines at work. This place is a Mine of great Treasure to Massachusetts. The water power in North Carolina is superior to that of Lowell, but we suffer it to run to waste and buy of them.

I have been to Lynn, the great Shoe town, and to Nahant, the celebrated sea bathing place, where I dined with a party of the Nobility of Boston. I have been *very kindly* received and treated in this City. The most opulent men here are as plain as our North Carolina people. Mr. Abbott Lawrence,[14] the late member of Congress, has shewn me great attention and all the City and environs. Prentiss of Missippi left here on yesterday.

I hope before this day next week the Whigs in N. C. will be triumphant in the Elections and then I hope you will travel to the Virginia Springs—White and Red Sulphur; at all events be sure to take more *regular exercise* than you have done and acquire more robust health.

If you determine to go to the Virginia Springs and write me *to Washington* I will try and meet you there.

I spent one week in Newport, R Island, and bathed in the sea before I came here. I met Senator King of Alabama and much of the fashion of New York, Philadelphia, Baltimore, and Charleston there.

I stoped only one day in the City of N. Y. & Phila.

I hope to get home by the last of August or first of September.

---

[14] Abbott Lawrence (1792-1855), of Massachusetts, merchant and importer, a Whig member of congress, 1835-1837, 1839-1840. Member of the Canada Boundary Commission, 1842, refused a cabinet post under Taylor. He was minister to Great Britain, 1850-1852; founder of Lawrence Scientific School, of Harvard.

*From William R. Walker.*[15]                            A.

Chapel Hill, August 13th, 1838.

I was graduated a few months ago. And have determined to commence the study of law immediately. I did expect to read with Governor Swain. But the number of students here is so great as to occupy not only every comfortable room in college but also in the village. There is one however which I have in contemplation & I shall ascertain in a few days whether or not it can be procured. If not I must seek a situation elsewhere. My object therefore in writing to you is to ascertain whether or not I can read with you and upon what conditions. You will oblige me by writing as early as is convenient. I selected Governor Swain not because I esteemed him a better lawyer than all others, but because he is always at home and can bestow more attention upon a student than those whose practice calls them abroad.

Permit me to congratulate you & the country upon your election. I regret very much that Messrs. Mangum & Waddell have not been equally fortunate. I regret it not only in consequence of their talents & politics, but also in consequence of the low and groveling means restorted to by their successful V. B. Competitors.

Yours, Very respectfully

*From Dr. James Augustus Washington.*                    A.

New York, August 18th, 1838.

\*      \*      \*      \*      \*

. . . I am very glad to see that Van Burenism is prostrate in N. C. and I wish that he were equally so in every county of the State. As Mangum was in favour of the sub-Treasury, it is not to be regretted that he was not elected, although otherwise a Whig, I have heard. It is highly honorable to yourself to have been the only one on your ticket who succeeded. How is it that the ticket otherwise failed? I am very sorry that your friend Waddell was not elected and I presume you must very much regret his failure as it will deprive you of a pleasant companion & valuable friend. Wm. Haywood I understand is not a member of the

---

[15] William Richmond Walker of Caswell County.

next legislature, which is a matter of congratulation considering his subserviency to Van Buren. I wish that it would not too much interfere with your professional business to permit you to oppose successfully Montgomery's re-election to Congress.

My love for N. C. makes me very desirous to see her no longer misrepresented by party collar men. I would however no doubt be far better for you not to go to Congress until you shall go as a Senator, as it seems to be impossible to attend satisfactorily or advantageously to the practice of the law and to the duties of Congress; such I believe is your own opinion.

* * * * *

The Atlantic Steamers will create a revolution on the Sea as great as railroads upon land. They have brought Europe more nearly to us almost than New Orleans. It is astonishing, the regularity of the trips of the Great Western. Fourteen days is the time allowed & she has perhaps not varied more than a day from that time. Her last trip to New York was 14½ & the trip before to Bristol was only 13 days. She sailed yesterday at the hour appointed although the weather was quite unfavourable. It has been well said that old Neptune has been bearded at last. Mr. Biddle[16] was lately in New York and appeared to anticipate, I have understood, most extensive & important results from the influence of Atlantic Steam Navigation upon Europe & America. It was a subject which seemed to afford him the greatest pleasure. His financial operations will no doubt be very materially benefitted by the change, but he is a man of enlarged views & looked to its influence upon a much more extended scale. Emigration to this country will no doubt still further increase & will be composed of still greater numbers of intelligent & wealthy individuals, and fewer loco-focos proportionately it is to be hoped. I am very glad that the rail road will pass within forty miles of you; it will at least I trust enable me to see Susan & yourself here frequently.

My love to all.
Yours sincerely

---

[16] Presumably Nicholas Biddle (1786-1844), of Pennsylvania, the distinguished scholar, financier, and author. A graduate of Princeton, after having been denied graduation at the University of Pennsylvania, because of his youth, he studied law, was secretary to the minister to France, travelled widely, and was apparently entered upon a literary career when he was drawn into public life during the War of 1812. After service in the state senate, he became a director of the United States Bank, and in 1822, its president. His connection with Jackson's attack on the bank is, of course, well known.

*From James Graham.*                          U.

Saratoga Springs, N. Y., August 22d, 1838.

I have been here one week and will stay one more. The water has improved my health. The Crowd is very great of fashionables.

This Country looks very much like the Flat Rock part of Buncombe. Gov. McDuffy [17] is here on his way to England to borrow Two Millions of Dollars for So. Ca. to build up Charleston. I have been very much in his company. He is the plainest man at the Springs, and says but little about politicks. He is rather inclined to the Sub Treasury *by way of Experiment,* but thinks when public opinion will justify it a U. S. Bank is the best mode of regulating the Currency.

Van Buren is down in this State. He can't rise. The Whigs will carry the State in Nov' next.

I have made a large acquaintance here, mostly of the people in the city of N. York. They are a social clever people without any very profound acquirements. The Grahams of that City are here and have expressed great pleasure at meeting me.

On yesterday I visited the Ground where Genl. Burgoyne surrendered to Genl. Gates about 13 miles from here. I will go no further North but return by N. York and Philadelphia home in 2 or 3 weeks, so as to get home by the middle of September.

If I get no letter from you at Washington stating you are out of Hillsboro I will probably return that way.

Do take regular and active Exercise and improve your health.


*From James A. King.*                          A.

Brandon, Miss., Octr. 13th, 1838.

You are doubtless aware that I removed to this State during the last Spring.

I have settled in this place (Brandon) about twelve miles East of Jackson the seat of Government, and am in all respects pleased with the place. I have discontinued my operations as *a farmer* in Ten., & shall resume them in this I think with better prospects in the coming winter.

---

[17] George McDuffie.

I passed thro. Ten. & brought my negroes; now I have them
(a few) hired upon advantageous terms. I have not yet determined
whether I shall remain here, or Settle in Jackson during the
winter. This is a more agreeable place to live in, but not so good
a location for a lawyer as Jackson. The amt. of business done
here is immense, at least so it seems to a N. Ca. Lawyer. In many
of the Courts the returns vary from 1000 to 3000. The collection
business is all that is worth anything here, and all that is requisite
is that a man should know how to draw a declaration; there are
comparatively few litigated cases.

*   *   *   *   *

I congratulate you on the result of the elections in N. Ca. &
in your County so far as your election is concerned. I regret
Waddell's defeat & in this State all Whigs are much disappointed
at Mangum.

In the Space of a few weeks I hope that I shall hear that you
are Speaker of the House of Commons. I am almost sorry that I
did not remain in the State one year more. It would have afforded
me sincere gratification to have been in the Majority *one time,*
but I am content that the Whigs are in the ascendant. My health
I am glad to say, has been entirely restored; indeed it has been
better during the last Summer than at any time within the last
six or eight years. I find no sort of inconvenience in attending to
my business or from any cause whatever, so far as my health is
concerned.

I now expect, in fact, I have determined, to visit N. Ca. next
Summer. I wish to go there for a variety of reasons, and amongst
others I am not exactly sure but that I shall attempt some matri-
monial enterprise, but of this curia vult advisari.

*   *   *   *   *

*From Victor Moreau Murphey.*                    A.

Macon, Miss.,
24th. Octo, 1838.

After the most animated contest that ever occured in this
County I have the pleasure of announcing to you my success over
the *"Brag* Nag" of East Mississippi. Never has such a scene of
suspence, anxiety, and conjecture been witnessed since the days

of the celebrated defeat of "Santa Anna" in Orange. It was nearly
a dead heat. My Majority was only five votes. The Democrats
have claimed a majority of forty in the County & since the result
has been ascertained they are certainly the most haggard looking
set upon earth. The race of Henry & Eclypse would have been
equalled as to betting had I not dissuaded my friends from risking
their money, being satisfied that the majority for either would be
small.

You may now throw open the old "Post office & kick up a
little row to my especial honour. The great probability is that
we shall now be enabled to prevent the reelection of Judge
Trotter [18] —God grant it! He does not represent the wishes of
a large majority of the people of this State—He is a real *"Sub."*

I was compelled carry heavy weights, Henry Clay & a National
Bank, and the vulgar prejudices of fools upon the subject of our
local Banks was made to operate against me.

I was determined to let you know the result, if success attend
me, & after a real jollification with my friends must beg off from
saying anything more.

If I have done any good in my life, it was in adding something
to the Whig strength in this County.


*Speech upon Election as Speaker.* [19]

November 19, 1838

*Gentlemen of the House of Commons:*

I tender you my thanks for this mark of distinction. Without
experience in the duties of the chair, I must needs bespeak in
advance the generous indulgence of the House. If, however,
by a diligent, faithful, and impartial administration of those
rules and forms of proceeding which you shall adopt for your
government, any requital can be made for your kindness, no efforts
on my part shall be spared. What those rules of proceeding shall
be, is yet to be ascertained by your sanction—and to that subject

---

[18] James F. Trotter (1802-1866), a native of Virginia, a Democrat, was, by appointment, United States senator from February to July, 1838, when he resigned. Dr.
Murphey's fears had no grounds, as he did not seek re-election. He had already
seen service in both houses of the legislature, and later he was supreme court
judge, and professor in the state university.

[19] From the *Hillsborough Recorder,* November 22, 1838.

I invite your attention. But all who are conversant with deliberative assemblies will readily admit, that written rules, and the best intended exertions of a presiding officer, are of but little avail, for the preservation of decorum, unless a *spirit* of order pervades the House, — and, after all, greater reliance must be placed upon the mutual respect, the forbearance, and gentlemanly courtesy of members, than upon compulsory enactments.

This is the first time, gentlemen, in the history of our State, when a session of the General Assembly has not been held for a period of two years. If the occasion shall not demand of us double the ordinary quantum of labor, it at least requires redoubled zeal, fidelity, industry, and vigilance over the public interests. Whatsoever of wisdom and knowledge may fall to the lot of each individual member, will be no more than requisite, to the fulfilment of his duties here. "To make us love our country, it ought to be lovely," and a heavy responsibility attaches to those interested with its Government, if they contribute not all that in them lies to impart to it this character. But properly to discharge those high duties, it is necessary that prejudice shall be cast aside, passion subdued, personal collision avoided, and our minds left free to the impulses of patriotism and reason — thus conducting our deliberations we may confidently hope that they will proceed with harmony, and result in benefit to that people to whom our highest loyalty and best service are due.

## *From Josiah T. Granbery.*[20]          U.

### Woodville, Novr 26th, 1838.

Presuming on our early acquaintance & friendship, I have taken the liberty of asking your attention, as also to solicit your influence, in a small matter to the legislature, but of much importance to me.

There has been a petition gotten up in this County praying for the passage of a law to prohibit all persons from fishing within two miles of the mouth of Perquimans River and as Mr. Nixon[21] and myself last Spring established one within that distance, it is

---

[20] Josiah Thomas Granbery (1806-1862), of Perquimans, planter, and fishery operator, member, commons, 1835-1838.

[21] Possibly John Nixon, of Perquimans. There were many of the name in that section of the State.

no more or less than a Prayer to abolish our fishery. The plea set forth is that we prevent the fish from going up the River, one which no man in this community, at all acquainted with fishing believes for one moment, as you will percieve from the counter petition. I will however mention a few facts connected with our fishing, with a view of enabling you to judge Correctly of the merits of their Petition.

We fish on the Albermarle sound about one & a half miles from the mouth of Perquimans River. (Which now is some two miles and a half wide at its mouth) with a Seine *sixteen hundred yards long,* which is laid out entirely in the waters of the Sound at about the *same distance* from the Shore, where the Sound is from Six to eight miles wide We make some four hauls a day, and from the time the seine is laid out until the ends of the net are again at the Shore, it cannot be to exceed one hour and quarter, by which it will seen that the Seine is not in the deep water more than five hours in twenty four. So that the Short time the seine is in the deep water and so small a proportion of it that is utterly impossible that it can afford any obstruction whatever to the passage of the fish. I will farther remark that any restriction such as lay days will be tantamount to prohibition, for it must be obvious to every reflecting man that when the water is some eight miles wide and forty in length, that much time must necessarily be lost by Stress of weather as it is not infrequently the case, that whole days together are lost from high winds.

As to the relative value both private and publick of our fishery, & those on the river, I refer you to the counter petition.

I am well aware, that I am addressing you on a subject that it is not expected you are acquainted with, but I hope, that I have made it inteligeble to your comprehensive mind. I am convinced that at the first glance, you will see the injustice of their petition, and that justice & truth will ever find an advocate in you.

Your attention (in a small degree) to this matter will place me under lasting obligation to you.

With the highest regard.

N. B. When I say four hauls a day I mean the twenty four hours as they take a large portion of the night, for instance we start at 4 Oclock in the morning & stop about 9 at night.

*From Eliza B. Witherspoon.* A.

Brook-Land, Dec. 2d, 1838.

My Dear Uncle

We were much pleased a a short time since to hear from you by Dr. Webb.[22] I was absent from home while he was here, or I should have written by him, & as Ma grows older & her cares increase, her aversion to writing seems to increase with it. We had an afflicted family the past Summer, during the months of August & Sept there was not a day but we had some severe sickness.

\* \* \* \* \*

I see by the papers you have been chosen Speaker of the House, although an honourable, , I should think a tiresome seat. I suppose you have your two little boys with you, to entertain you at night with their prattle.

\* \* \* \* \*

The crops are generally short except in the Cane Brake, the Droubt the last Summer was exceedingly severe. The crop upon our home plantation was almost entirely cut off. We have made a pretty good one in the Cane Brake.

In late letters from my Brother John he seems to be doing very well at Princeton. Graham purposes going in the Spring. The schools around Greensboro are very inferior & it is difficult to get a private teacher to remain longer than six months, so that my Brothers labour under many disadvantages in entering a classical institution.

Pa thinks of visiting Mobile in a day or two & I think it Probable I shall accompany him, he dislikes to travel alone & one of us generally accompanies him. I shall not remain very long. After spending a long Summer at home, it is quite a treat to spend a short time in a City. I made a short visit to Mobile last Spring.

I was at the Marriage of William Webb a few nights since, he has married a clever girl, with a red head, but some of his friends I believe thought he might have done better, if he had waited awhile.

---

[22] Probably Dr. Henry Y. Webb (1808-1878), of Greene County, Alabama, native of Hillsboro, or Dr. Robert Dickens Webb, of Marion, Alabama. Both attended the University of North Carolina.

Your old friends Mrs. Strudwick & Mrs. Young visit us occasionally. . . . Mr. Strudwick's family speak of spending the next Summer in Carolina & if I can get a good opportunity I shall except your kind offer in spending at least a part of the Summer with you. I am anxious to visit my Mother's relations, having been seperated from them the greater part of my life I feel a desire to know more of them than I do at present. . . . I think you would feel quite at home in Ala. their are so many of your old friends here, but your *ties* to Carolina seem to increase so rapidly I almost despair of ever seeing you here, & particularly as our State adhears so minutely to the administration. I doubt if you would be so popular as you are at home. Pa is still a true friend to Henry Clay, & the Bank, & I believe almost prays he may live to see him President, political excitement runs higher hear now than I have ever known it, they are holding public meetings through out the State for the purpose of choosing Candidates for the Next Congress, but unless I cease this tyrade I fear you will think I am fond of *Poly ticks*.

\*    \*    \*    \*    \*

*To Susan Washington Graham.*                          A.

Raleigh,

Tuesday night, Decr. 4th, 1838.

My Dearest

It is a dark gloomy night and I gladly avail myself of my leisure and the absence of Company to commune with my beloved. I am so anxious again to see you & my dear Boys that I had well nigh take the stage to visit you on Saturday. I was fearful however of a change of weather, and of my inability to return in time to open the Session of the House on Monday. This is one of the inconveniences of the station I occupy, but for which I would surely have gone.

My bro. James and Mr. Morrison arrived in the stage on Saturday night, and the latter is still here, staying with Dr. McPheeters.[23] His health is much improved, & promises an entire

---

[23] The Rev. William McPheeters (1779-1842), of Raleigh, native of Virginia, the first minister of the Presbyterian Church in Raleigh. A man of great power and influence, and much beloved, within and outside of his own denomination. He was a trustee of the university, and received the degree of D.D. from it. He was also a trustee of Davidson College, of which he was offered the presidency.

restoration. The object of his visit is to procure an act of Incorporation for the College over which he presides. It is somewhat doubtful whether he will succeed to the extent of his wishes.

Bro. James tells me that the spirit of emigration among the people of the West is more rife than ever; among others Uncle J. Davidson of Mecklenburg, and his whole family, will most probably move to Florida. Malvina Graham has reluctantly abandoned the idea of going with you to New Bern.

The Plantation which I have been cultivating in Lincoln has been rented for the ensuing year, and I am endeavouring to have my negroes removed to Hillsboro' by the 1st. of Jany. to be hired there. I have written by this mail to Mr. Turrentine to hire out Charity (for I regret that you are troubled with her) and to dispose of the servants you leave on your departure as well as to overlook our Lot during our absence. I think you had better leave Alfred to take care of the houses &c with directions to pay strict attention to every thing, feed the cow and calf & keep the gates closed. You will please inform Mr. Turrentine soon of the servants you desire to be disposed of, and how long you will be probably absent. Regulate that by your own wishes. Your Br. insisted that I should go to Kinston as soon after the adjournment as practicable, to attend to the division of lands. He desires if possible to adopt some mode of division, by which land may be received by some of the Heirs in lieu of personal estate by others, and expressed a wish that the Egypt plantation [24] may be assigned to Mrs. Bryan. I fear such a mode may be subject to legal difficulties, but hope we may do all for the best, when we get together. I hope you will allow yourself time to spend several days here, as it appears long since I saw you, and will probably be still longer untill we meet again. Genl. Barringer's family are still here. I have not yet sought lodgings for you but will do so, & let you know before you come. A Bill to divide Orange passed the House of Commons today. Whether it will get through the Senate I can't tell. Resolutions have been introduced censuring the administration of the General Government which will probably pass. There is much speculation here as to the course of our Senators in Congress, if they be adopted.

When you leave home it will probably be best to come to Chapel Hill or Morings the first day, as it would require an early

---

[24] In Craven County.

start to enable you to come through in a day. Let me know before
hand, and I will endeavour to meet you a few miles from town;
should you require more money than you have, apply to Mr.
Kirkland, or let me know and I will send it. Mr. Walker will
probably be willing to go & stay in the office during your absence
if you desire it, that however I leave to you.

*    *    *    *    *

The Govr. is to give a large dance on Thursday evening; unless
I can engage your ladyship for a set, I shall hardly venture to
caper on my broken legs.

Teach my babes to say "Father" and be assured of my unfailing
affection.


*To Susan Washington Graham.*                          A.

Raleigh, Decr. 8th, 1838.

My Dearest

I avail myself of the politeness of Col Jones to write you, and
send a toy with some kisses to Joseph. I fear however that unless
I see him soon that I shall go entirely out of his recollection.

*    *    *    *    *

Col. Preston & Genl. Thompson of S. C. were at the Govrs. being
on their way to Congress. Of course they were quite lionized.
Seawell Jones was master of ceremonies as usual. Some gentlemen
have already arrived as delegates to the Convention on Internal
Improvement, which is to meet here on Monday. I have not
heard of the arrival of Mr. J. W. Bryan. My friend Mr. Clingman
came on yesterday. He staid a night at Judge Ruffin's, & says
that Miss Elizabeth was dangerously ill of pleurisy when he left
— not expected to survive.

We hear this evening from the North that the Legislature of
Pennsylvania has been dispersed by a mob which went from
Philadelphia to Harrisburg in consequence of a contest about
the election at the former place.[25] It is a subject of the deepest

---

[25] Election day had seen rioting and violence in Philadelphia County, and Whigs
and Democrats claimed fraud. When the legislature met to canvass the returns,
a mob drove the speaker of the lower house from the chair, and threatened
bloodshed. Governor Ritner, who had been a candidate for re-election, was refused
troops by President Van Buren, and then called out the state militia. The matter
was finally adjusted, and Porter, the Democratic candidate, declared elected.

concern to all friends of good Government, and may be attended with the most serious consequences. We wait with anxiety further particulars. Bro. James has arrived safely in Washington, as I learn by a document received from him this afternoon. . . .

Kiss the dear little fellow for me, as I am unable to interest him by any thing I can send. How much I would be delighted to see you all this evening!

Mr. Morrison is still here. His act of Incorporation for the College has passed the House of Commons with almost unanimity. The Baptist Church here is again in trouble. Last Saturday night I was applied to for leave to Mr. Jordan [26] to preach in the Commons Hall on Sunday which was given. Mr. Holland, who applied, stated that the adverse faction had locked up the doors of the Church and would not allow them to go in.

\* \* \* \* \*

*To Susan Washington Graham.* A.

Raleigh, Decr. 10th, 1838.

10 o'clock night.

\* \* \* \* \*

Your Bro. John & Mr. J. W. Bryan arrived yesterday evening as delegates to the Internal Improvement Convention. They will remain untill you come & probably untill you may desire to leave here. Mr. Henry Bond [27] is with them. Mr. Thos, Burgwyn [28] & Dr. Chapman [29] from New Bern & many other delegates from other quarters are also here. The Convention organized this evening by appointing Judge Saunders President. What they may do, I do not know, but it seems a respectable body in numbers and character.

The Gov. of Pennsylvania has ordered out the militia to suppress the mob which disturbs the assemblage of the Legislature.

\* \* \* \* \*

---

[26] The Rev. William Hill Jordan (1803-1883), a native of Bertie County, graduate of the university, who, in addition to this pastorate, filled others in Wilmington, Wadesboro, Lilesville, in North Carolina, Clarksville and Petersburg, Virginia, Sumter, South Carolina, and Morristown, Pennsylvania.

[27] Probably Henry Francis Bond (1814-1881) of Kinston.

[28] Thomas Pollock Burgwyn of New Bern.

[29] Samuel Edward Chapman (1807-1862), a graduate of the university, M.D. of the University of New York.

I can't yet form an idea of the time of adjournment of the Legislature, though probably about the 1st. or 2nd. week in Jany.

You can give Abram my cloth vest if you think proper, or the older velvet one. Please have the clothes for Isaac & the other servants attended to.

I shall probably not write you again till I see you.

*From James Graham.*                                               U.

Washington, Decm, 14th, 1838.

I have seen the Resolutions before your Legislature.[30] They are well drawn and will make an impression before the People. There should be little time consumed in the discussion. The Whigs should select *only 3 or 4 speakers* to debate them; and let the best speeches be written out with care and published in pamphlet form for distribution among the Members to scatter among their constituents. The speeches will be commentaries on the propositions contained in the Resolutions, and explain the doctrines and principles of the *Republican Whig party.*

The Whigs in Congress begin to think they must give up Mr. Clay. The Ohio Members say their preference for Clay caused them to loose Ohio in the last election. In Pennsylvania, Indiana, Illinois, and Michigan too, it is said Clay cannot run successfully, but will destroy the Whig ticket, if he is their Presidential candidate.

The Anti Masons will not vote for Clay or any other Mason. In the new States it is said Clay has injured himself very much by denouncing the settlers *in harsh and bitter terms* on the public Land. Clay having been twice run & defeated for the Presidency, and there being *a strong prejudice* in the minds of "the many voters" against him: his prospects are diminishing rapidly. Harrison's [31] friends say they are unwilling to split the party, but that

---

[30] The resolutions, introduced by Kenneth Rayner, condemned as a violation of the Constitution, and an act of party servitude, the action of the Democrats in expunging the resolutions of censure of Jackson, and demanded its repeal. They further condemned the Sub-Treasury plan, the right of preemption of public lands, the power and patronage of the President, and the extravagance of the administration. They demanded the distribution of the proceeds of sale of public lands. Without a direct statement of the fact, they amounted to instructions to the North Carolina senators to vote for such action, but the use of the word was studiously avoided. They passed by practically a party vote.

[31] William Henry Harrison, later President.

Harrison never having engaged in the active and animated party topicks of the Country has no political prejudices against him, and having won many military Laurels in the Late war, he is the only man who can defeat Van Buren. There is a strong disposition here to bring into the field another and new candidate, and I am among that number. In a great contest like the approaching one for the Presidency, it is difficult to satisfy all parts of the Country, and we must all make reasonable sacrifices to sustain such men as will advocate correct principles. I can't *now* say that any one, or if any one who, will be brought out, but the Whigs all admit that every thing depends upon a *popular Candidate*. It is in vain for the Politicians to coerce the people into the support of any Candidate. They must take the most available candidate of their own views and principles. I am very desirous to start some candidate upon whom No. Ca., Virginia, Georgia, and Tennessee could unite upon Republican Whig principles. The Whigs in N. C. can maintain their ascendency in the State, if they do not attempt to carry and *force* upon the people some candidate whom they do not desire, and as N. C. *has always been* overlooked and neglected *by all Presidents,* I see no reason or policy which should induce us to sacrifice our principles and prominent men at home to render Homage to any candidate not of our own views. Heads they win, tails we loose. I am and shall remain uncommitted until I am better satisfied about the presidential candidate. Clay's friends in N. Carolina I know will be slow to surrender him. The New Jersey Delegation in Congress say they were very near loosing all their Elections by attempting to carry Clay in the last contest. John Sergeant says in Pennsylvania the strength of the Whigs, or rather whatever strength the Whigs have there is owing to the popularity of Gen. Harrison. I mention these opinions to shew you the present aspect of popular sentiment so far as developed here from different States. I think now (what I wrote you last Spring), the Whigs in N. C. should not pledge themselves prematurely to any one, but go in solid Column against Mr. Van Buren and the Sub Treasury. Our Editors in N. C. are the greatest fools I ever met with; they asked my opinion last Spring as to the time and manner of coming out for the next President, I advised them *not then to stir* that Question; and forthwith they began to hoist the Clay Flag, and I have no doubt lost 15 or 20 Whig members to the Legislature by so doing. Gales led the way being flattered and wheedled into it by some sap headed South Carolinians, who used N. Carolina as a feeler to sound public opinion to the South. Van Buren has no hold upon the people of N. C., and can't get the vote of the State, unless some unpopular Candidate be taken up by the Whigs and then his rash enemies may give him the vote of the State. The prominent Whigs in N. C, should consult together with deference and respect for the opinions of each other on this question. I see no reason for hasty & rash action but wait until a candidate of *sound principles* and *fair prospects* shall be announced as brought out not only to run but to beat. Then if we can go for him we will do it, and if not we will still maintain our principles.

I do not believe from present or past indications Clay can get the vote of N. C., or a majority of the Whig States. Members who last Spring said he could, now give it up. I think he will be withdrawn from the contest before next March. Some of his friends from Kentucky have intimated as much to me.

I have *apprised* you of the movements and signs here that our friends in N. C. may act with prudence & discretion and not be disappointed or distracted in going for a candidate for the next presidency. My present impressions are not favourable to Harrison, but still I will wait untill I learn his history and character, his principles and policy. I am told he will come out as strong as *aqua fortis* against Abolition & the Sub Treasury.

I do not desire *to be prominent* or *public* on Presidential matters, but I have droped you these suggestions because public opinion is unfolding new lights and in search of men whose popularity will forward (not retard) good and successful results in the future.

I wish the Legislature would direct a recognisance survey and Estimate by an able civil Engineer from Beaufort Harbor to Ashville in Buncombe to ascertain if a Rail Road cannot be constructed through the heart and centre of our State. I would examine the ground from Beaufort to some point on the Cape-Fear a little below the Junction of Haw & Deep Rivers and then continue on the Ridge South of all the Waters of Deep River and Cross the Yadkin either at Stoke's Ferry, or a little lower down at the mouth of the Uwharre and then, (either up to the Island Ford on Catawba River and Morganton,) or on to the Ridge north of Long Creek in Mecklenburg to the Catawba River 3 Miles above Tuckesege ford and the south fork north of Long creek in Lincoln and up to Robert Winters or Jacob Fulenweders:

near that join the Charleston Rail Road. If the Rail Road from Raleigh were extended so as to join this line below the junction of Haw and Deep Rivers then would a direct and great High way for Travellers *from New York to New Orleans* be through North Carolina and Tennessee. One Central western Rail Road we ought to have in N. C. and I would make a Road to Beaufort, which is a healthy place and a much better Harbour than Charleston.

The Defaulcation of Sub Treasury officers is alarming to the Party. The public money is *going going going,* and I fear will soon be all gone to Europe.

No wonder the Government is insolvent when the Treasury is constantly robbed by our Agents and officers as fast as they can get their britches Pockets full.

The Van Buren Party here look drooping and dejected, they are obviously waiting and hoping for a division in the Whig Ranks. They are drilled Regulars; we are Raw and undisciplined militia.

I hope you take regular active exercise every good day. farewell

*To Susan Washington Graham.* A.

Raleigh, Decr. 23rd, 1838.

My Dear Susan

I send you this as a Christmas gift, a poor one, it is true, but still valued, I doubt not, as a testimonial of the fidelity & affection of your *chere ami.* It is now Sunday night, and I have the pleasing hope, that my letter will reach you on Christmas day, & remind you, that you are not forgotten though absent. I promise myself no extraordinary pleasure during the holidays. Several members of the Legislature are visiting their homes, and those here are not much disposed to business. I can't yet say how long the Session will continue but think it will be at least two and probably three weeks. The resolutions of Mr. Rayner[32] passed the house of Com-

[32] Kenneth Rayner (1808-1884), of Bertie, member of the commons, 1835-1836, 1846-1850; state senator, 1854; delegate to convention of 1835, member of congress, 1839-1845; member of commission on "Alabama" claims, solicitor of the treasury, 1877-1884. An ardent Whig, he became a leading member of the American (Know Nothing) party, and wrote one of its secret degrees. After the war, he supported President Johnson, and wrote anonymously a campaign life of him. He then became a supporter of Grant, and a Republican.

mons last Friday by a majority of 7 Votes, No regular speech having been made after that of Mr. Hoke,[33] which was in progress while you were here. They are confidently expected to pass the Senate. What course our Senators in Congress will take, we have as yet no means of knowing. The more general impression is, that they will resign. Gov. Swain has tendered his resignation to the board of Trustees, to take effect next June.[34] He is uncertain as to his future destination. Genl. Barringer's family have appointed the day after Christmas for their departure. Three members of the Legislature have been bound by Mr. Justice Badger to appear at the next term of the Court of this County for cruelly beating a free negro, on a charge of having stolen a watch from one of them. Of which it is since ascertained that he was altogether innocent.

\*    \*    \*    \*    \*

I am exceedingly glad that you have had clear days since you left & hope, that you journied without accident. With Sister Eliza's kind aid I doubt not but you were as much relieved of the trouble of the children as circumstances would allow. If you do not wish any of the servants from below, and you can ascertain that they have been well treated the past year, please ask your Bro. John to hire them for us again. If he thinks they will not be abused on the Rail road I would not object to their going there. although I would prefer to hire them to planters; those in Lincoln I will have bro't to Hillsboro & hired there.

How are my dear Boys? [35] Would that I could see them, & yourself, tonight.

I heard today a good sermon from Mr. Lacy[36] who was assisted in the services by Mr. Merideth.
Kinston.

---

[33] Michael Hoke.

[34] Swain evidently withdrew his resignation. I have found no public notice of the resignation, and the minutes of the Board of Trustees contain no mention of it.

[35] Graham's second son, John Washington, was born July 22nd., 1838. In later life he was a graduate of the university and a tutor there, a lawyer, Confederate major, delegate to the convention of 1868, and state senator, 1870-1872, 1877-1879, and 1907-1909.

[36] Presumably the Rev. Drury Lacy (1802-1884), native of Virginia, who attended Washington College (now Washington and Lee University), and was graduated from Hampden-Sydney. After teaching for a time, he attended the Union Theological Seminary there. He held pastorates at New Bern and Raleigh, was president of Davidson College, 1855-1861, Confederate chaplain, and then taught in Raleigh from 1865 until shortly before his death.

1839

U.

## A PARTY

*Will be given Complimental to the* GOVERNOR *and* MRS.
DUDLEY, *at the Eagle Hotel, on* FRIDAY EVENING *next,
to which the Managers request the pleasure of your
Company, at 7 o'clock.*

| | |
|---|---|
| L. D. WILSON,[1] | W. W. CHERRY,[6] |
| R. K. SPEED,[2] | J. T. MOREHEAD, |
| M. A. WILCOX,[3] | KENNETH RAYNER, |
| H. L. ROBARDS,[4] | WM. P. WILLIAMS,[7] |
| T. G. SCOTT, | E. H. WINGATE, |
| S. W. WHITING,[5] | C. C. BATTLE,[8] |

Managers.

*January 1st.* 1839.

*From James W. Bryan.*          U.

Newbern, Jany. 3d, 1839.

I hope the Whigs will by no means repudiate the idea of sending Delegates to Harrisburg; if we are to cut ourselves loose from

---

[1] Louis Dickson Wilson (1789-1847) of Edgecombe County. He was a member of
the commons, 1815-1819, state senator, 1820, 1824-1832, 1838-1846, (speaker, 1842);
delegate to the convention of 1835, and several times a presidential elector. He
rose from captain to colonel in the Mexican War.
[2] Rufus King Speed (b. 1810), of Chowan and Pasquotank counties. A native of
Virginia, with Indian blood, a physician who was active in politics. He represented Chowan in the state senate, 1838-1840, 1870; and Pasquotank in the convention of 1861, and in the senate, 1866.
[3] Major A. Wilcox, member of the commons, from Halifax.
[4] Horace Lawrence Robards (1814-1867), of Granville, graduate of the university,
a miner and hotel proprietor, member of the commons, 1838.
[5] Seymour Webster Whiting, of Raleigh, treasurer of the Raleigh and Gaston
Railroad.
[6] William W. Cherry (1805-1845), of Bertie, teacher, merchant, and lawyer, and
state senator. He served in the commons in 1844.
[7] William P. Williams, of Franklin, a member of the commons. He was a senator,
1830-1832, 1842.
[8] Christopher Columbus Battle (1814-1859), of Edgecombe, Governor Dudley's
private secretary. He was a soldier in the Mexican War, and later moved to
Tennessee.

the Whig party of the North let us hear it from some one who can speak by authority, for as to the prevalent opinion that the dictu of isolated persons, as it were, are to constitute our rule of action, I myself cannot come into it. Our strength and success consist in Union & as this Harrisburg Conv. was proposed as a sort of middle ground upon which to reconcile the distracted opinions and preferences of the Whigs, let the South meet them there and I guarantee that the Meeting will be productive of most beneficial results. We Croak too much and are disposed to condemn without a hearing.

I argue with you upon the subject of nominating Mr. Clay; he is my first and I may almost say my only choice, for however highly we may think of the other gentlemen, you know they cannot run at the South. Leave the question of nomination therefore at present to the Convention & if we fail there, it will not then be too late to nominate him here; we will run a ticket for him at all events in this State.

Whilst personally I am pleased with the nomination of Mr. Morehead for Govr., I must express to you the opinion that Judge Settle would have obtained in our part of the State one third more votes, but we will leave nothing undone for Morehead here.

If you do not shove the Beaufort road along *pari passu* with the rest we will Kick up *a tremendous dust here!* I expect the whole scheme will fail & the failure here would be more acceptable than the partial success in another part of the State as they seem determined that these projects shall go hand in hand.

*From James Graham.*                                        U.

Washington, Jany 4th, 1839.

Our Senators received their Resolutions from Raleigh on or before last Tuesday (New Year's day). Brown told me he had received them at that time. He also asked me if I had any news from Raleigh? I told him none, except the Legislature would adjourn on Monday next the 7th. I gave that information to him that he might have no excuse to say "he did not know When the Legislature would adjourn". I have said nothing to our Senators myself, but Stanley[9] talks every day to them about their resigning

---

[9] Edward Stanly.

and I understand *they are much confused* & consulting their friends as to the proper course to take. I still think *they will not resign.*

They are higgling and harping about the word *Instruct* not being inserted, but that is all prevarication. The Legislature have told them modestly and decently to "Go out of my House" but they seem to think the Legislature should have said "you Damned Rascals I instruct you to go right straight out of my House." I think nothing short of one of Paddy's hints will remove them. To resign would be a bitter Pill to them. It would be like drawing their eye tooth. It is much better for the Whig cause they should not resign. And our Editors should open their batteries forthwith *upon them* and *their party* for violating their own doctrines— they preach one text and practice another, they give medicine to others which they will not take themselves. They keep the word of promise to the ear, while they break it to the sense, they con sider Instructions and Resolutions a very good Ladder to climb into power on, but altogether inconvenient to go out of power upon that very same Ladder. This is the forked-tongue-doctrine of the Spoils Party who have the people constantly in their mouths and never in their hearts.

The two legged Sub Treasury advocates must have two ways to deceive the people:

> one to cheat them out of their *votes:*
> the other to defraud them out of their *money.* Our Senators are both very *Aristocratic Democrats ! !*

*you* had better say but little about them, let time develope what they intend to do. They are in deep distress, and may God increase their pain, untill they repent of their sins and pitiful party devotion.

They may, in time, feel so unworthy and guilty as to *resign;* their pride (not their principle) may at last come to this conclusion.

Charles Shepherd[10] has just published a *Primmer* to his constituents in which "he gives in his political Experience": his matchless discovery of the sinful nature of Banks, that Abolition is for the North, and the Sub Treasury for the South, and therefore he swears allegiance to *Van* and *the Spoils!*

---

[10] Charles Shepard (1807-1843), of New Bern, graduate of the university, a member of the commons, 1831-1832, now completing the first of two terms in congress.

*To Susan Washington Graham.*                    A.

Raleigh, Jany 6th, 1839.

Sunday night.

My Dear Susan

I recd your kind letter of the 30th. ult. at a time when I stood somewhat in need of your comfort. On the day it came to hand, I had a severe boil which confined me to my bed with a high fever, but as I was exceedingly desirous to attend to my duties in the House during the few remaining days of the Session, I have managed to keep my feet every day except that one, though it has been with much pain and fatigue. I am decidedly better however today, and hope that I shall get through the remainder without much difficulty, though I anticipate quite a trial tomorrow. It has been appointed as the day for adjournment, and the meeting will be at sunrise in the morning. From the quantity of business on the table, the Session will probably continue all day, & then a portion will probably be unfinished.

The past week has been quite an important one. A Bill has passed giving the aid requested to the "Raleigh & Gaston Railroad Company,"—enabling them to borrow $500,000 and pledging the credit of the State for its payment. Also a Bill appropriating $750,000 to assist in building a Railroad from Fayetteville to the Yadkin River, And making an appropriation to survey the proposed Inlet at Nagshead. On Friday evening letters were received by the Speakers of the two Houses from Messrs. Brown & Strange, Senators in Congress saying that they had learned from correspondents at Raleigh, that Resolutions had passed the Legislature on some subjects of Federal politics, & desiring to know whether such resolutions were intended to *instruct them.* Resolutions were promptly passed by both Houses declaring that the Resolutions are sufficiently plain & intelligible to be understood by any one desirous of understanding them, and that it would be inconsistent with the self respect of the General Assembly to make any reply to the Communication from the Senators. A most amusing debate took place afterwards on a motion to enter it on the Journals, in which explanations were given of charges against two members of the administration party of eavesdroping at a meeting of the Whigs.

I proposed yesterday in Committee a plan for common schools[11] which was unanimously approved in the House of Commons; it will go to the Senate in the morning. I forget however that you are not a politician and perhaps take but little interest in what I have been writing.

A public Ball was given to the Gov. & lady at Guion's last Thursday & a party at Mr. Iredell's to Miss Mary Jones of Hillsboro on Friday evening. My state of health prevented my from attending either.

I ventured last night to the theatre with Judge Gaston & Mr. Battle to witness the performance of Miss Davenport an English girl of 11 years of age, who is truly a surprising actress.

Mr. Turrentine writes me that he has hired our negroes & laid in 1900 lbs of Pork [for] me. He entered the house with a key of his own, and obtained there the smoke House & cellar keys. Mr. Walker is staying in my office. Mr. Palmer of Hillsboro was here yesterday. There is nothing new there.

I have nearly finished without saying any thing of my Boys. I wish I could see them & my dearest this evening. I have not heard from your Bro. & Mr. B. and am somewhat at a loss whether to go to New Bern as soon as the Assembly rises or wait to argue my cases in the Supreme Court. I would prefer the latter and think I could promise to be in Kinston a fortnight hence with certainty. If they think it indispensable that I shall come earlier however I will do so, say the last of this week, & write me.

Genl. Barringer's family will leave tomorrow for Ten.

* * * * *

New Bern.

*Speech at Close of Session.*[12]

*January 8th., 1839.*

*Gentlemen of the House of Commons:*

I beg leave to detain you a moment, whilst I express my gratitude for the flattering terms in which you have been pleased to approve my conduct as your presiding officer. I wish I were conscious of having deserved such unqualified commendation. I

---

[11] *North Carolina Laws, 1838-1839,* Chap. VIII.
[12] From *Hillsborough Recorder,* January 17th, 1839.

appreciate it, however, as a not unmerited testimonial of the purity of my motives of action, and my unfeigned desire to do right. The scenes through which we have passed have been often of an exciting character, but I have been gratified to observe that there has been no interruption of the kindest personal relation between individual members; and with the utmost pleasure I declare, that I have never been associated with any deliberative assembly in which there was exhibited so little asperity of temper, and so much of kind and cordial feeling, as has been uniformly manifested in the present House of Commons.

Though this occasion has been impatiently expected as the moment which was to relieve us from public cares, and restore us again to the objects of our affection, that heart must be insensible to the best feelings of human nature, which is not in some degree saddened by the malancholy reflection that we part, many of us, no doubt, *forever*. On the great ocean of life our courses lie in different directions. For a brief season we have met here to deliberate on the public weal. We now renew the voyage, and each one resumes the way from which he has been for a time diverted. Whatever fortune may await us, I trust, gentlemen, we shall recollect with pleasure the social intercourse we have enjoyed here—that our acquaintance has been extended, new friendships have been formed, and our knowledge of the moral, and intellectual, as well as the physical resources of our common country, enlarged.

Wishing to you, each and all, health, happiness, success in your various pursuits, and a safe and speedy return to your families and friends, I bid you a respectful and affectionate farewell.

A.

Raleigh,

Jan'y 12th., 1838. [1839] [13]

*To, The Honorable Messrs*

LEWIS WILLIAMS
EDMUND DEBERRY[14]
AUG. H. SHEPPERD          REPRS. FROM
ABRAHAM RENCHER          NORTH CAROLINA.
JAMES GRAHAM
EDWARD STANLY

Gentlemen

                    At a meeting of the members of
the Whig party, held before the adjournment of the recent Session
of the General Assembly of this State, the subject of nominating
a Candidate for the next Presidency of the United States was
considered, and the series of resolutions inclosed herein was
unanimously adopted.

In compliance with the second Resolution, the undersigned
have been appointed a Committee to communicate to you the
opinions of those who were there assembled from all parts of the
States, and have supposed that they could most effectually discharge the duty thus devolved on them by transmitting the
Resolutions in extenso, that you may be informed not only of the
Whig party here upon this important subject, but that you may
be apprized of the plan of operations which is deemed best calculated to insure success. We deem it proper further to add that
in our opinion Mr. Clay is the only Candidate of the Whigs who
has the least prospect of uniting the party throughout the State.
Indeed, several members of the General Assembly declared openly
that he was the only Candidate whom they themselves were
willing to support, and certainly the only one who could expect
to receive the vote of their constituents.

---

[13] Draft in Graham's handwriting. There is no indication as to the other members
of the committee.

[14] Edmund Deberry (1787-1859), a native of Montgomery County, who was state
senator 1806-1811, 1813-1814, 1820-1821. Whig member of congress, 1829-
1831, 1833-1845, 1849-1851.

We have not deemed it expedient to make a public nomination because it was believed to be premature, and that such a mode of presenting a Candidate was not approved by our people. But we deem it due to candour to say, that unless Mr. Clay shall be our Candidate, we believe it will be useless to form an opposition ticket in the electoral Canvass. And the main purpose of this letter is to request you to urge upon our friends in other States the necessity [of] uniting with us upon this question. It will [be] seen that we have thought it expedient to defer a final nomination untill November, but this is merely to await developments in other States, and with no expectation of the adoption of a different Candidate.

We are, Gentlemen, with utmost Respect,

Your Obed't Serv'ts,

[*Enclosure*]

*Resolutions*[15]

1. Resolved—that the members of this meeting do express their decided preference for Henry Clay of Kentucky, as the Candidate of the Whig party for the next Presidency.

2. That a Committee of 13 gentlemen be appointed by the Chair to correspond with the Whig members of Congress from this State, and such Whigs elsewhere, as they may deem judicious, insisting on the nomination of Mr. Clay, and informing that he is the unanimous choice of the Whigs in this Legislature, and that no other Candidate now in nomination has a reasonable prospect of receiving the Electoral vote of North Carolina.

3. That the members of this meeting will recommend to their constituents, (and do pledge themselves to each other zealously to endeavor to procure their approbation of the same) to appoint delegates in primary assemblies to meet in Convention in the City of Raleigh on the 2nd. Monday of November next, to propose Candidates for the offices of President & Vice President of the United States, and also of Governor of North Carolina.

---

[15] These resolutions were adopted just before the adjournment of the legislature by the Whig members of the two houses. The copy is in Graham's handwriting, and presumably, he was the author. They were first published by the *Standard,* and then several Whig papers published them. They can be found, for example, in the *Star and North Carolina Gazette,* Feb. 27, 1839.

4. That the said Convention when assembled, shall allow a representation to each County in proportion to its ratio of representation in the House of Commons—and shall be invested with power to determine on the expediency of sending delegates to the National Convention proposed to be held at Harrisburg in December, 1839, for the purpose of nominating a Candidate for the Presidency, and if they shall deem it proper, to appoint delegates thereto.

4. That Charles Manly, Weston R. Gales, Charles L. Hinton, Thomas J. Lemay, John H. Bryan, & Henry W. Miller, Esqs., be requested to act as a central Committee, and to disseminate such intelligence among the several Counties as they shall deem calculated to advance the Whig cause in this State.[16]

*To Susan Washington Graham.*                                  A.

Raleigh, Jany. 13th, 1839.

My Dear Wife

I hope this letter will be the last that I shall send, before I have the pleasure to see you. I have been hurrying my business in Court, & hope that I can leave here on Wednesday morning, so as to reach New Bern, if you are not at Kinston on Thursday night.

I feel wearied with my long stay here, and am getting exceedingly impatient to share again the society of my own family. My health is much better this week, than it was last, & is still improving.

Our Session closed on Tuesday morning, and all seperated, I believe, with kind personal feelings. My Valedictory in return to a vote of thanks was exceedingly brief, as you will perceive in the papers. We have heard nothing from Washington since the last Resolution in relation to our Senators, except that they are in a great tribulation as to the course they will pursue, and are asking the advice of friends, etc. Mr. Badger will leave here tomorrow for the City of Washington to appear in the Supreme Court of the United States, on behalf of our State in a suit for large bodies of land in our Western Counties. We are of course all anxious

---

[16] On August 29th, 1839, this Committee, as will be seen later, issued a call to the Whig party.

that he shall succeed in the cause, and make a display which shall be creditable to the State.

I have declined going to Hillsboro', before I go down the Country, as Mr. Turrentine has been kind enough to attend to our affairs there. Though it has been so unseasonably warm for four or five days past, that I am somewhat apprehensive about our Pork.

Franklin Grist [17] arrived here last night but there is so much travel in the Hillsborough stage although it goes daily, that he will not be able to get a seat untill day after tomorrow. He is quite well, and desirous to get on. I will write to Mr. Walker to get his Books, etc., for him. As also to attend to your requests about the smoke house.

Your two letters written since you left me have been a long time on the road or in the office here. The last dated 2nd inst. I did not get untill yesterday. I do not see your Bible in the room but will endeavour to have it gotten for you. My time has been so much occupied in endeavouring to make my stay here as short as possible, that I have not been in society, nor heard any thing in the way of news.

Gov. Swain's family left yesterday for Chapel Hill. He has determined to leave that place in June, but has not concluded what to do.

Your Bro. John wrote me a note by the mail of last night, saying that Sister Eliza had been there a few days ago, and had Joseph with her. Tell him that Father will get a little waggon for him when he goes home. I am the more anxious every day to see the dear little fellows & their still dearer Mother. A few more days I hope will restore me to them again.

Miss Mary Jones will leave tomorrow for Hillsboro'. I am told she has made quite a sensation in the *beau monde* of the metropolis.

\* \* \* \* \*

[P.S.] Judge Gaston who is with us, was robbed of his trunk as he came up. He supposes it was cut off the stage near Waynesboro. The season here for four or five days past, has been as mild as the latter part of April.

I hope you have sent the Carriage to the Shop & had such repairs done to it as it needs. You can make any arrangement in

---

[17] Franklin R. Grist (1828-1912), the son of Mrs. Graham's sister, Elizabeth Heritage Washington (Mrs. Richard Grist).

relation to the sale or exchange of negroes with Mother, that you desire.

Gov. Iredell is selling off his servants. He had sold a good cook before I heard of it, or I would have purchased her for you.

\*    \*    \*    \*    \*

*Address of the Republican Whig members of*          U.
*the General Assembly of 1838*
*to the People of*
*North Carolina.*[18]

Fellow Citizens:

Among the acts of the last session of the General Assembly, you find a series of Resolutions, upon subjects of great interest in our National affairs. These were not adopted without violent opposition from the minority, who supported the present administration of the General Government, & who, of course, with few exceptions, uphold that which the resolutions condemn, and reject that which they recommend. This opposition has lost none of its zeal, but appears to have much increased in acrimony, since the adjournment of the Legislature. First, the proceedings of "a party meeting" of members at the Capitol, was put forth, next came the address of a Committee of members of that meeting. Circular letters have been published, public meetings called, and popular harangues delivered, in which the course of the General Assembly has been denounced in terms of bitterest censure. That all this indicates alarm on the part of the minority, lest the doctrines and practices of our Federal rulers, which have been thus rebuked, shall be no longer tolerated, is sufficiently evident, but that the resolutions of the majority afford any ground for alarm to the people, is, we think, incapable of demonstration. On the contrary, there is far more reason to dread that unless the sentiments they express shall be carried out in the practical administration of the Government, the balance of that Government will be overthrown, and the free constitution of our Fathers

---

[18] From a rough, and evidently incomplete, draft, in Graham's handwriting, found in the Graham papers. (See letters of Weston R. Gales to Graham, April 16th, 1839, and Graham to the North Carolina Whig members of congress, Jan. 12th, 1839.) So far as I can discover, the address was never published, or completed. It bears no date.

degenerated into an elective monarchy. The undersigned Committee were appointed by their Whig brethren in the Legislature to address you in vindication of these Resolutions, at such time as they might find convenient. Although it has been longer delayed than they had desired, they now proceed to acquit themselves of that task. For the sake of easy reference, a copy is inserted of the

## Resolutions

### relating to the General Government.

Whereas, we believe that a great crisis has arrived in the political history of our country, on the issue of which, we conceive the safety of our free institutions to depend: And whereas, we consider it our bounden duty, as the representatives of the freemen of North Carolina, to express in calm and dispassionate language, our opinions on the great questions which have been for some time, and some of which are still agitating the public mind:

I. *Resolved therefore,* That this General Assembly do condemn in the most decided manner, that act of the Senate of the United States expunging the records of that body, as a palpable violation of the plain letter of the Constitution, and as an act of party servility, calculated to degrade the character of the Senate.

II. *Resolved,* That resolutions ought to be passed by the Senate of the United States, condemnatory of that act, and rescinding the resolution authorizing it to be done.

III. *Resolved,* That this General Assembly do condemn the Sub Treasury system which this Administration is endeavoring to establish, as another item in that series of fatal experiments of this and the past Administration, which are the main source of that derangement of the currency, and prostration of commercial credit, that have been so severely felt of late in every branch of industry, and which, if suffered to become a law, will, by its tendency to augment Executive power, to unite the purse and the sword in the hands of the Executive, and to destroy the credit system by the exaction of specie in the Government dues, ultimately change the real character of our Government, and place in peril the liberties of our country.

IV. *Resolved,* That we consider the Public Lands of the United States as the common property of all the States, and that we therefore condemn the late Act of Congress allowing settlers on the Public Lands, the right of pre-emption at the minimum price. as an act of gross injustice to the old States, who originally ceded them, or who contributed to a common fund for their purchase.

V. *Resolved,* That we believe that the proper and equitable disposition of the public domain, is to divide the proceeds arising from their sales, among the several States of the Union, according to the ratio of their federal population.

VI. *Resolved,* That we do most solemnly protest against the wasteful extravagance of the present Administration, and their profligate expenditure of the public money, which not only creates a demand for heavy taxation in order to meet the exorbitant appropriations of the General Government, but which tends to the corruption of public morals, and the degradation of the national character.

VII. *Resolved,* That the power and patronage of the Executive Department of the Federal Government have increased to an alarming extent, and ought to be diminished.

VIII. *Resolved,* That our Senators in Congress will represent the wishes of a majority of the people in this State, by voting to carry out the foregoing Resolutions.

IX. *Resolved,* That the Governor of this State be requested to forward a copy of these Resolutions to each of our Senators in Congress, with a request that they lay them before the Senate of the United States; and one to each of the Governors of the several States of the Union, with a request that they lay them before their respective Legislatures.

It will be seen that they relate 1st. to
Expunging the Journals of the Senate.

The Constitution enjoins that "Each house (of Congress) shall keep a Journal of its proceedings, & from time to time publish the same, excepting such parts as may, in their Judgment, require secrecy, and the Yeas and Nays of the members of either house on any question, shall, at the desire of one fifth of those present, be entered on the Journal." This plain declaration of the duty "to keep a Journal," It appears to us impossible to misunderstand. It is one of the most ordinary duties of a deliberative body, required in written Constitutions, that the proceedings of that body may be clearly manifested to its constituents. Its end is not wisdom, but truth. When made out and published, the Journal of the Senate becomes as much the property of the Nation as the Library of Congress, as a vessel in the Navy, or as the Capitol in which Congress holds its deliberations. And with as little propriety might either house of Congress attempt to explode or destroy any of these, as to mutilate, to alter or expunge it. That they may repeal or rescind, any previous resolution of their own body is not denied, but when the Senate, in 1837 did violence to the Journal of 1834, they acted not only without the warrant of the Constitution, but in direct violation of it. It is not, however, as a merely literal violation of the Constitution that we condemn that act. But because it, in effect, sanctioned the monstrous doctrines set up in the Executive protest, that he is the only constitutional keeper of the public Treasure, and that the Senate, a coordinate branch of the Legislature, representing the sovereign States of the Union, had no power to express an opinion of his conduct, unless upon an Impeachment instituted by the other House. It was, moreover, avowedly designed to humble and degrade that body for having dared to do so by resolution, and to be to them in future times a beacon and a warning never to do the like again. Without undertaking to review the question first in dispute between the President and the Senate, (which is no less than the momentous one, whether the Executive or the Legislature has the authority to controul the custody of the public funds) we affirm that the Senate, as one of the attributes of its Legislative power, has a perfect right to form and to declare its opinions, in relation to the official conduct of the President upon any subject. This freedom of thought & of speech, in regard to all the acts of Government, is not only guaranteed to every citizen, but its full and free exercise is one of the highest duties of a Legislature. Their office is not merely to enact new Laws, but to look into the practical execution of the old,—and, if found to be either improperly expounded or administered by any Judicial or Executive officer, from the highest to the lowest, either branch of the Legislature may, and ought to, express its dissent, either by proposing a new Law, or declaring that the old has been misinterpreted.

This is equally true of infractions of the Constitution, although they are not armed with power to enforce their own construction, they are nevertheless authorized & bound to notice any material violation of either the Constitution or Laws, that public attention may be directed to it, and that it may undergo examination, at least in the public mind. This necessary right in a Legislative Assembly of a few people, would never have been questioned to the Senate of the United States but for its being also invested with certain judicial powers. These, we submit, are added to, but do not impair or abridge either its Legislative powers or duties. Senators are not to be less vigilant & faithful in investigating the acts of public officers, nor less bold in avowing their opinions respecting them, than the members of the House. Otherwise the intention of the Constitution is but half fulfilled, and the peculiar rights of the States committed to their charge, may be trampled under foot with impunity. That they may err in the performance of this duty is admitted, but to that, they are liable [as] in all other acts. But whether, in any particular instance, they may be right or wrong, we assert the authority of the Senate whenever, in their belief, the Constitution or Laws have been infringed by the President, or any subordinate officer, to speak out in the language of freemen, as the Commons and even Lords of England, on so many memorable occasions, have been accustomed to speak of the acts of the King and his Ministers, as our ancestors in their consecrated struggles for liberty, did of the sovereign & Colonial Governors, and as every free citizen feels it his birthright to do, of the acts of all public servants. The sedition Law of 1798, subjecting to indictment any person who should publish matter deemed libellous of the President, or other high officers of Government, was justly condemned by popular indignation, though it allowed the truth of such matters as a sufficient defence. But the construction of the Constitution implied in the act of expunction, & maintained by its advocates, will not permit the representatives of the twenty-six States of America, charged in an especial manner, with the care of their interests, to pass any resolve as to the conduct of the President, though however true, just or merited; even, maybe, to reprove usurpation, correct error, or protect their body in the just enjoyment of its rights. In that construction Your General Assembly was invited to concur by a communication from the Legislature of the State of Missouri, approving the mutilation of the record of the Senate, & highly commending the efforts of one of her Senators for his agency in procuring its accomplishment. Being thus called to the consideration of the subject, and unwilling by silence to give an implied assent to an act, which we verily believe has degraded the character of the Senate, & deprived it of much of its usefulness to the Country, and to doctrines which, if generally concurred in, will at no distant day, concentrate in the President all the powers of Government, we deemed it proper to declare our disapprobation in unequivocal terms. That our Senators, whether present or future, may perceive that they are required to be vigilant sentinels, as well as diligent, faithful lawgivers. That the Senate, (so far as it can be aided by us) may be raised from its self abasement, & restored to the confident exercise of its Constitutional powers & duties, and that it may be manifested to our sister States & to the world, if this orb in our political system is to be stricken out, or to remain in the dim eclipse into which [it] has been cast by the devotion of party, to an Executive magistrate, that it will not be with the concurrence, or without the solemn protest of the Sovereign State of North Carolina.

2nd.                    The Subtreasury System.

This is the new plan proposed for collecting & keeping the public monies of the United States, which has been urged upon the Country with so much pertinacity by the Executive & his partisans, although it has been twice rejected by the representatives of the people in Congress, and as is well known, would have shared the same fate again at the last session, had not its advocates prudently declined to call it up for a vote of the House. Its outlines may be briefly stated. It requires, 1st., that all the public revenues shall be paid by the people in Gold & Silver coins, and, 2ndly., that they shall be kept by individuals untill they are wanted for disbursement, and not deposited in Bank as heretofore. However, it may be attempted to vary its features at different times, to make it more comely to the public eye, these are its prominent characteristics, as recommended by the President and Secretary of the Treasury, and without which it has been pronounced by its ablest advocate, Mr. Calhoun, "a solemn farce." And it is argued with most fervid eloquence, that this is not only the wisest plan which has ever been devised, but that it is the only one which is allowed by the Constitution, that all former systems which have been pursued were not merely inferior to this in point of utility, but were not justified by the limited powers conferred on the General Government. Those who accuse Washington & Jefferson and Madison of not understanding the Constitution, or not administering the Government according to its provisions, and who hold that Hamilton & Gallatin & Dallas

& Crawford all failed to perceive and to adopt any scheme of finance equal to this modern discovery, ought [to] be at least expected to be charitable to others, who, perceiving the subject in a different light, see quite as numerous & as fatal objections to their *theory* as *they* do the *practices* of their predecessors. This is more especially to be expected when it is remembered that, with exceedingly rare exceptions, the same persons who are now so strenuous in support of the Independent Treasury were, but little more than two years ago, as vehement & clamorous in favour of the State Bank deposit system. When that experiment commenced in the autumn of 1833, they predicted, with the most undoubting confidence, that those Banks would not only keep the public money safely, and pay it out whenever wanted, but would furnish a currency which should be at par every where in the Union, afford exchanges, & give accommodations to trade upon better terms than had been done at any time before. Through their agency it was said, that the circulation of small notes was to be suppressed, & Gold & silver made sufficiently abundant to supply at least all the demands of Commerce under twenty dollars. Every Farmer was to have his purse full of Gold, and it was to circulate as freely as "the waters flow down the Mississippi." Not only are these promises to be found in the prophetic declaration of party Orators, but were put forth with equal boldness in Executive documents, & echoed in the reports of the Committees of Congress. Look through the Messages of the President, V. B., and the long, blundering reports of the Secretary of the Treasury in 1833, 4, 5, & 6, and you will see, not merely what was hoped and expected, but triumphant boastings that the Golden age, which had been foretold, was now at hand, and that "the experiment had succeeded." Scarcely had the last of these congratulations ceased to vibrate in our ears, untill the explosion took place. The Banks everywhere suspended specie payments, *those which had been so much praised and patronized by the Executive being the first to lead the way.* That that experiment would fail, we were prepared to expect. Although, did the occasion permit, we think it might be shewn that the suddenness of the catastrophe, as well as the extent of its ruin, are fairly attributable to its administration. Its authors, confessing their failure, now insist on a new experiment. If this shall be allowed them, it will hardly be for the skill in finance which was exhibited in administering their late system, or the success which attended it. Their project may therefore be judged of, without encountering *infallible* authority. Does it derive any recommendation from its success elsewhere? What State of the American Union has applied it to its own fiscal affairs? None? In those foreign Countries where it has been tried, have industry & enterprize been encouraged, are the people as prosperous, and are their Agricultural manufactories or commerce as flourishing as in those Nations who have pursued other systems? If so, its advocates are bound to tell us where. It is difficult to foresee the result of great pecuniary experiments, and hence the greater the propriety of relying upon experience, rather than mere speculation, but as far as we are able to anticipate, the practical workings of this plan we see in it nothing to be desired.

1st. As to the exaction of specie in all payments to Government. This, we believe, would produce incalculable mischief. The precious metals are not sufficiently abundant to afford a currency for all the business of the world. In modern times especially large quantities, both of Gold and silver, which might have been coined, have been consumed in the arts, both useful and ornamental, whilst the supplies of these which were formerly derived from Mexico and South America have, in the last thirty years, greatly diminished. In the mean time, the labor of a larger portion of our race than ever was before employed in like manner, (aided by every species of improvement in machinery) has been employed in producing articles for sale, and requiring an additional supply of money to give them circulation. Hence paper currency has been invented as a representative of, & in part, a substitute for, coin, and hence Banking has been allowed as a legitimate branch of business. Banks have been established in all the States of the Union, and their paper constitutes by far the largest portion of our actual currency. That this will continue to be the case in all transactions of business among the people, where large sums change hands, we presume no one will deny, who adverts either to the scarcity of the precious metals, the power of the Legislatures of the States to establish Banks, and the free exercise of that power in every member of the Confederacy. No one State can prevent this, even within her own limits. For, although in ours, the circulation of the Banks of the State does not furnish the entire currency, the residue is not specie, excepting a small amount, but consists of the notes of the Banks of other States. So long as this currency is founded on a sufficient specie basis,

and is convertible into specie on demand, it answers every purpose of Gold & silver, and is more convenient in many respects.
To compel it to be always redeemable in specie & therefore equal
to it, is the first duty of the States granting a Charter, and the
failure so to redeem should be visited with the heaviest penalties.
But we are not now inquiring whether such ought to be the currency of the Country, but stating the fact that [it] is, and our
opinion founded on the necessity of things, and the nature of our
Confederacy, that it will in all probability, continue to be. If,
therefore, we are not to have hard money for the commerce and
business of the people, why is it to be exacted from them in payment of dues to Government? It is sometimes alledged that it is
to prevent fraudulent & dishonest Banking. If this be the design,
why place the honest and knavish on the same footing? Why
reject the Bills of those Banks who adhere to their Charters in
every particular, & always pay specie on demand, and thus depreciate their credit equally with those who make no attempt at
redemption? To reject those which are not redeemed, is not only
just but salutary, but to reject all, because some are spurious, is
to destroy instead of endeavouring to correct. If the injury reached
only the Banks, it might be matter of less moment. But is it not
at once perceived that when so large a money dealer as the Government of the United States will take nothing but specie, that
the best Bank notes depreciate in comparison with it, and whilst
the Government officers & employees are receiving payment in a
superior currency, thus adding directly to their salaries as established by law, that the people whose servants they are, must be
content with an inferior one, and when called on to make payments to Government, must pay a premium in addition to the
revenue.

Suppose that your Legislature, instead of protesting against
this system, had passed a Law applying it to our State affairs, &
requiring all County and State taxes to be paid in Gold & silver.
Would it not have been denounced with universal indignation?
The whole County and State tax may be estimated at $300,000.
annually. The State tax alone at $75,000. The former sum could
not be yearly collected from the people in specie, without great
sacrifice. Imagine, however, that our Sheriffs only collected the
State taxes, 75 or 80 thousand dollars in Gold & silver, and pay it
into the Treasury at Raleigh. This operation would be severely
felt by the people in the progress [of] a few years. Its direct effect

would be to accumulate specie at the seat of Government, but to drain it from the Country, paying the taxes. True, it would go out again, in payment of Gov't expenses but in much larger sums than those in which it came in, and but little of it would ever reach the great body of those by whom it was contributed, except at a premium.

The subtreasury system is only the same thing on a larger scale. The revenues of the General Government are derived from sales of the public lands, and from duties on foreign goods. They amount at present to 30 or 35 millions of dollars per annum. If they should be required to be paid in specie, would not the consequence be, to gather a greater amount of the precious metals at the lands offices on the frontier, and the custom Houses of the great Cities, which would be withdrawn from the general circulation of business.

*To Susan Washington Graham.*                          A.

Raleigh, Feby 3rd, 1839.
My Dear Wife

I arrived here last night in safety in company with Mary and Eliza & Laura Washington from Waynesboro. The latter has come to Raleigh to school & her sister accompanied her to stay a few days.

You have, I presume, learned from Mr. Bryan that I had the misfortune to lose my pocket Book, and to have it robbed of the money it contained. It has perplexed me much, and I almost despair of ever being able to regain it. We had a most uncomfortable ride from New Bern, and I was very much exhausted from fatigue when I reached Waynesboro, at 10 o'clock P.M., and after a little refreshment at the house of our kind friend Mr. R. Washington I retired and slept soundly. In dressing the next morning I discovered that the Book was missing from the pocket of my pantaloons, which were more shallow than I have been accustomed to wear. It no doubt escaped on the ride from Kinston to Waynesboro, during which I several times drew my watch, to observe the time by the light of the moon. After inquiring at the Tavern I took a horse & sulkey, which Mr. W. kindly lent me, & returned to Kinston, stopping and making inquiries & search at the only place at which I had gotten out, Walters. I waited at Kinston untill the return of the stage next day and your acquaintance, Capt. Swift, who was a passenger, had the goodness to hand it to me. It was discovered by him & the other passengers just after they had taken their seats in the stage after breakfast at Maples 12 miles from New Bern on Trent road. You will recollect that it was in the mail stage that it was lost, which travels Trent road, into which I had been forced at Kinston by the stoppage of Guion's line there. Mr. Swift knew it to be mine by the papers it contained, being the bills of sale from your Mother, sundry notes due to me for near $200., and receipts, etc., all of which were left in it & uninjured. On the night I lost it there were passengers with us, a Baptist clergyman Mr. Gardner & Mr. Williams a New York merchant, an acquaintance of Mr. Burgwyn—neither of whom could be suspected—they went on to the Hotel at Waynesboro & took the Wilmington line next morning. If it was not discovered by the bookeeper & servants, it went unmolested at 4 o'clock next morning on return to New Bern. Mr. Cutter and Mr. Carraway were passengers down all the way from Waynesboro, and as neither of them could be capable of the theft, the only persons on whom suspicion can rest are the drivers of Wiswel's line, untill the arrival at New Bern, when possibly servants might again have an opportunity. I have regretted ever since I left Kinston that I did not return to New Bern for the purpose of conferring with Mr. Cutter which I could have done before the return of the stage on Saturday night. But I had kept Guion's stage waiting to carry me to Waynesboro on Friday evening, and the weather was so exceedingly wet, that I returned to the latter place. I wrote to Mr. Cutter from Waynesboro urging him to have such steps taken for the recovery of the money as he may deem best. The book contained 3 Gold pieces of $5. Bechlers coins, of which you have some. These I hope may lead to the detection of the thief, there were 2 silver half dollars, and I think a 20 cent piece, 3 Bills of $100, 3 of $50, as well as I recollect & smaller Bills, all of the Banks of this State amounting in the whole to about $650. I have a distinct recollection of a $4. Bill recd. at Kinston, also of 2 of $20. on Bank of C. Fear. If I were well acquainted along the line I should not despair of recovering it, but at present I have but little hope. I regret the loss the more, as the most of it is a portion of your patrimony, all of which I had hoped to preserve for you & my little ones. If any prospect of discovery is seen write me immediately. I have written to Mr. Bryan & Mr. Cutter, and desired to do so to others but dislike to trouble them, and do not know that it would be of any advantage.

*     *     *     *     *

I shall remain here tomorrow and go to Hillsboro' on Tuesday; the roads are said never to have been worse. Dr. Scott, dentist, came down today from Chapel Hill; the trustees have suppressed the disorders there & suppressed the third society which had recently sprung up. The French teacher there, Mons. Maret, has drawn a draft on the Trustees & received monies from Mr. Hooper in Charleston, and it is believed, has run off with the whole. The example of the Government officers at New York & elsewhere seems to be making rogues of the whole country.

The Supreme Court will sit two weeks yet. If I succeed as well in some other cases as I have done in two already decided I hope to repair some portion of my recent losses.

*     *     *     *     *

The Stockholders of the Raleigh and Gaston Railroad Co. meet here tomorrow to determine whether they will accept the terms of assistance offered them by an act of the last Legislature. New Bern.

*From Clarke Moulton Avery.*[19]          A.

University of N. Ca., Feb. 18th, 1839.

The Dialectic Society over which I have the honor of presiding has instructed me to make you the within communication:

In accordance with a regulation subsisting between the two literary associations at this place, whereby an annual orator is chosen alternately by these two bodies, the members of the Dialectic Society have proceeded to an election and I take great pleasure in announcing to you your appointment by a unanimous vote, to deliver an oration before the two literary societies of the University on Wednesday the day preceding the ensuing Commencement day.

---

[19] Clarke Moulton Avery (1819-1864), a native of Burke County, educated at the university. He was elected a delegate to the state convention that the people rejected in 1861. He rose from captain to colonel in the Confederate army, and was killed in the Wilderness.

Your fellow members express through me, their sincere hope that you will accept of the nomination thus tendered and permit me to add my individual wish that their proposition may meet at your hands a favourable reception.

For I doubt not but you will do honor not only to yourself, to the Society of which we are proud to claim you as a member, but also to your native state.

Under the expectation of being informed of your determination at as early a period as convenient, I remain with great respect, Your humble & obedient servant.


*To Susan Washington Graham.*          A.

Hillsboro', Feby. 23rd, 1839

\*    \*    \*    \*    \*

I also regret that no discovery has yet been made in relation to my loss. Could I have any reasonable proof of the guilt of the persons suspected I would go down and institute a prosecution. It is lamentable to think that the deed would be perpetrated by such persons. It has long since been said that "justice though slow of foot, seldom fails to overtake the guilty."—I shall therefore "bide my time" and possibly it may yet arrive.

I have been exceedingly busy ever since my arrival from New Bern. Have had the greater part of the Garden turned up with the spade, a few seeds planted, fences repaired, Bacon hung up and smoking, Lots ploughed, etc. My hands arrived with the waggon from Lincoln on last Monday while I was absent at Guilford Court, and I wish I had the benefit of your counsel in disposing of them. There are eight children among them, who will interfere very much with the hiring of the others, and yet cannot be kept about the Lot. I have partially bargained for the Lot opposite us, as the family there have become a great nuisance, and think I shall place one of the women & children there for the present. I have been able to procure no suitable farm. I went last Saturday to look at one two miles from town above the race course, which would have suited well as to situation & buildings but had not a sufficiency of wood to fence it, and was exceedingly poor. I have two horses and a waggon which were brought from Lincoln; the waggon is one of the best I have ever seen. I wish to sell the whole, but am apprehensive that I cannot get a sufficient price for them. Bro. John has sent you some more Flower boxes, but as that is not in the culinary department, I shall leave them unfilled untill you return.

I took the stage to Guilford Court, and was gone but three days. On my return it was upset in the night about 8 o'clock, by running on a high bank near the road. I fortunately received no serious injury, though I am somewhat bruised on the side of the head, shoulder and hip. The horses did not run, & we lifted it up again, and came in, about 12 o'clock at night.

I went with Mary to attend the concert of Mons. and Madame Couderbeck last week; there was quite a large audience, but I thought the music was rather refined for our tastes.

\* \* \* \* \*

A young gentleman from Granville named Lassiter is now reading in my office.

\* \* \* \* \*

*From James Graham.*                                    U.

Washington, April 1st, 1839.

\* \* \* \* \*

The City is full of street news about *changes and removals* in the offices here and in the Departments. It is all Conjecture yet; but there is no doubt of many removals in Contemplation, and soon as the Elections in Virginia are over the work of *Decapitation* will commence. One report is that Forsyth is going to England; Poinsett [20] to be Secretary of State, and Stephenson [21] to return and be Secretary of War. And it is said, (which may Heaven grant) old Woodbury is going to Russia, He is a Bear and Russia is his climate. Kendall, it is said, is going into the

---

[20] Joel Roberts Poinsett (1779-1851), of South Carolina, diplomat and statesman. Educated in Europe, he travelled widely. He was diplomatic agent to South America, 1810-1814. Returning to South Carolina, he began to practice law. He was a member of the South Carolina assembly, 1816-1818, chairman board of public works, 1818-1821, member of congress, 1821-1825. He developed an intimate friendship with Jackson, who sent him on a special mission to Mexico in 1822, and then appointed him minister in 1825. He returned in 1830, in time to become a leader in the Anti-Nullification party in South Carolina, acting also as Jackson's confidential agent. He served as secretary of war, 1837-1841. He opposed the Mexican War, and the movement for secession, in 1850-1851.

[21] Andrew Stevenson.

Treasury Department. This is swaping a fool for a Knave, or rather a Bear for a Wolf.

*From Literary Societies of Davidson College.* U.

Davidson College, N. Ca.,

April 6th, 1839.

Sir

The Literary Societies of this Institution, through us their committee, request you to address them publickly, at the close of the present college session, which will be the last of July next, or on the first of August.

This choice has been made heartily by the members, and under the conviction that your compliance will afford much gratification to a large surrounding community.

Anxiously hoping for your consent, we only add the expression of our high regard for your personal character.

Very Respectfully,

WM. H. MOORE,[22]
R. N. DAVIS,[23]
O. D. McNEELY,[24]
R. E. SHERRILL,[25]

Joint Comm.

---

[22] William H. Moore, of Lancaster County, South Carolina, after graduation, attended the Columbia (S. C.) Theological Seminary, became a Presbyterian minister, and died while very young.

[23] Robert Newton Davis (1818-1871), of Hopewell, Presbyterian minister, pastor at Lincolnton, 1850-1870.

[24] Oni Davis McNeely (1811-1881), of Mecklenburg County, later attended the Union Theological Seminary at Hampden-Sydney, Virginia, became a Presbyterian minister, and moved to Alabama.

[25] Richard Ellis Sherrill (1816-1897), of Lincoln, after graduation taught for four years, and then became a Presbyterian minister. The rest of his life was spent in Tennessee, Texas, Mississippi, and Kentucky, where he held various pastorates.

*From Eliza Witherspoon Goldthwaite.*    U.

Brook Land, April the 15th, 1839.

You will doubtless be much surprised, My dear Uncle, at the contents of this communication. When I wrote you last Dec I was upon the eve of a visit to Mobile, intending only to remain a few weeks, but upon my arrival I found so many of my old friends, & schoolmates, that I was induced to remain the entire winter. Whilst there, I renewed an acquaintance of several years standing with Judge Goldthwaite,[26] & became so much pleased with him as to be induced to give him my hand on the 10th. inst. (last Wensday) We were married very privately in the morning, & went to my Brother's in Greensboro, & dined with a few friends. Although the affair had been on hands all winter, I was married very unexpectedly, or I should certainly have written you about it before it took place.

As I am now married it would not be expected for me to give you an impartial description of my "liege Lord," he was 37 years of age on the tenth, is a short, stout man, something Pa's size with light hair & blue eyes, & I have the pleasing satisfaction I believe of saying that my friends were all gratified.

I expect to remain at home until the first of July. We expect then to leave for the North, by way of Nashville, Lexington, by the Lakes, on as far as Canada, & hope to return through the Middle States, & I trust My Dear Uncle I shall be able to spend a week with you in Hillsboro. We will most probably settle in Mobile. We would leave earlier in the season for the North, but the Supreme Court meets the first of June & will necessarily detain us until July.

\* \* \* \* \*

My Father is much engaged at this time planting, he is very much interested in the Morves Multicoulis,[27] has also a number of Silk Worm, & to hear him expatiate upon it, you would fancy

---

[26] Henry Barnes Goldthwaite (1802-1847), a native of New Hampshire, who moved to Alabama, by way of Richmond. A lawyer of distinction, he was also, for a time, editor in Montgomery, and a member of the legislature. He moved to Mobile in 1831, was on the supreme court from 1836-1843, when he resigned to make an unsuccessful race as a Democrat for congress. He returned to the supreme court for the short period before his death. He was the brother-in-law of Justice John A. Campbell.

[27] *Morus multicolorus,* a variety of mulberry, presumably suitable for feeding silkworms.

you could almost see the Money *growing*. I have been at home but a short time, & know very little about the news of the up Country. I spent a gay & pleasant winter, the City was unusually gay a series of Balls & parties, & an unusual number of Stars at the Theatre, & I believe I participated in most of the amusements. I heard of you occasionally through the medium of the News Papers. I flattered myself a part of the winter, that I should have the pleasure of spending a part of the next Summer with you, but so it is, you see young Ladies are uncertain characters, & instead of the giddy girl, I suppose *I shall have to be the stayed Matron in future.*

*From Weston R. Gales.*                          A.

Raleigh, April 16, 1839.

At a meeting of the Whig Central Committee last night I was directed, as Secretary, to drop you a line enquiring when we may expect the Address to the People of the State, which you were selected to prepare, and in anticipation of which provision was made for a large edition. Be good enough to write me immediately on this subject. Enquiries from all quarters of the State have been addressed to us, on the subject, and the necessity of speedy action insisted on. We should have it in our power to publish it immediately on its reception.

I had the pleasure of receiving your recent letter on the subject of our Congressional Candidate, and though I regret exceedingly your determination, I cannot object to your reasons. Similar considerations, but more imperative, in their nature, will interpose a barrier to my becoming a Candidate. We have taken steps, however, to have a District Convention and will endeavour to have some one in the field.

From James W. Bryan.                          U.

Newbern,

May 13, 1839.

The man who was suspected of having your money, etc., has had quite an affair in town today & made an attack upon Mr.

Washington and myself about it. He armed himself with his pistols and dirk and announced that he intended to "do execution" as soon as he could meet with us. We met opposite the Church Corner in the Street and had a "bout" on the spot. He believed that I was the instigator of the matter & that I had made the attempt to have him indicted, etc., he says he intends "to write you on the spot" and demand your author, etc., and I have thought it prudent to advise you of the same; he demanded the name of the persons who gave the information from Mr. Washington, but he, deeming it imprudent to divulge them as the investigation is still going on, refused to gratify him. So you see we are likely to have something of a war about your money at last.

\* \* \* \* \*

The Bishop[28] has been with us, preaching to admiring and delighted audiences. On Sunday night he preached to the negroes, who crowded the Church to suffocation & if he never saw "nodding" in perfection before he must have been gratified that night to his heart's content; his most appropriate and admirable discourse was lost upon one half of his sable congregation.

Newbern is most wofully dull and I often wish that I could enjoy the luxury of inhaling the pure and invigorating air of your mountain country.

I received a letter the other day from the Philanthropic Society, requesting me to deliver the address before the Alumni and graduates at the ensuing Commencement, and I should have consented to do so but for a prior engagement in N. York about that time, and I could then have done myself the pleasure of visiting Hillsboro' once more "but as it is" I do not know when I shall see you all "at home."

\* \* \* \* \*

The contest waxes warm between Mr. Shepard [29] and Col. Biddle[30] and the better opinion seems to be that Col. B. will beat him; it is however in my opinion impossible to arrive at any correct conclusion in the matter, although I believe Col. B's. prospects are improving every day.

---

[28] Bishop Ives.
[29] Charles Shepard, the incumbent, who was successful in retaining the seat.
[30] Samuel Simpson Biddle (1811-1873), a graduate of the university, and a prominent business man of New Bern. He was a member of the state senate at this time.

*To Susan Washington Graham.* A.

Hillsboro', May 16th, 1839.

My Dear Wife

I reached home from Caswell on Saturday afternoon after your departure. Sister Eliza and the children were all well, but the House was quite solitary to me in the absence of my Susan. I remained with them untill the afternoon of Sunday, and then went on horseback to Person whence I have returned today.

\*     \*     \*     \*     \*

Mr. B. also mentions that the Grand Jury of Craven had had quite a laborious and searching investigation relative to the thief who stole my money; they made no presentment, but strongly suspected the individual who is generally believed to have it. He hopes that a little more time may make further disclosures on the subject.

Joseph and John have both had severe colds this week and I learn were quite sick on yesterday. I am happy to say that they are both better today. Jo is running about the office (where I write) quite cheerfully, amusing himself at the people passing who have been to see a show of wild beasts in town today. Col. Jones' carriage has just gone by. He says "It ain't Abe & Tom, Derry." He still clings to his Aunt and does not appear to miss you much, but looks sad when asked, "where has Mother gone?" I will have his carriage put up for him tomorrow. John has been sleeping soundly ever since I came home, which I hope will relieve him entirely from his cold.

We have had plentiful rains, and our Garden vegetables appear to be growing luxuriantly, but running to vine too much.

\*     \*     \*     \*     \*

. . . Nothing has been determined as yet, by the Whigs of this district, relative to the canvass for Congress. I still fear that I shall be embarassed by a nomination, but must persist in my determination.

Mr. Bryan writes me that it will be a warm & close contest between Shepard and Biddle, and that the better opinion is that the latter will succeed.

The New Bern Spectator says that the Report of the duel [31] of Jo. Jones is all a Hoax.

Mr. Pollock [32] has left no will as is now generally believed, and his property will therefore be divided equally between Mrs. Devereux and the Burgwyn family. Mr. Burgwyn has already removed into the "Stanly House," and left Henry in possession of his. I shall go next week to Guilford County Court & close the week after with the Court here. The Convention of the Episcopal Church will sit next week in Raleigh. I believe Mr. M. is quite disappointed in not having to go to New Bern.

\*   \*   \*   \*   \*

New York.

### Newspaper Account of
### Speech declining Congressional Nomination.[33]

### May 31, 1839.

Mr. Graham then addressed the Convention, and said, he had had the honor to be informed by the committee of his nomination; and the position he now occupied was one of greater embarrassment than had fallen to his lot since he had been in any way connected with public affairs. To be deemed worthy of the station by so respectable an assembly, was a distinction which he highly valued, and for which he expressed his profoundest gratitude. He was aware that many of his friends had been pleased to speak of him, among those from whom a candidate would be selected by the Whigs of the district. He had, therefore, reflected on the subject, with every disposition to comply. He trusted that he had not been backward in making personal sacrifices when it was believed that his services might be useful to his countrymen; and nothing now should prevent his acquiescence in the wishes

---

[31] There was, in 1834, considerable publicity with respect to a duel supposedly fought by Jones in Rhode Island. The governor took notice of it, in a public proclamation, offering a reward of five hundred dollars for his arrest. Jones then issued an absurd counter-proclamation, ridiculing Governor Francis, and offering a reward of a barrel, and forty pounds of feathers, for a delivery of the Governor to him at Cape Lookout. See Marshall DeLancey Haywood, in *Biographical History of North Carolina*, VI, pp. 333-334.

[32] Thomas Pollock, of Craven, a very wealthy member of a family long prominent in North Carolina. The bulk of his estate was inherited by Thomas P. and Henry K. Burgwyn, and Thomas P. Devereux.

[33] From the *Hillsborough Recorder*, June 6th, 1839.

of the Convention, but what was, to him, a moral necessity. Circumstances of a merely private and domestic character had imposed on him duties which it would be criminal to neglect, and which absolutely forbade his acceptance of the nomination. These he had stated to the committee, somewhat in detail, and had the satisfaction to believe that they would be deemed sufficient by them, for the course he had adopted. But, sir, said Mr. G., this affords no cause for dispair or discouragement,—"Sparta has many a worthier son than he," who stands before you. The great principles which he, in common with this convention, advocated, depended not for their success upon any individual candidate. He hoped that no one would do him the injustice to suppose that he was actuated in his determination by any apprehension of an unfavorable result in the election. Knowing that it would be out of his power to accept, even if the seat in Congress were tendered to him, he had made no inquiries as to the probability of his success. But humble as were his claims, he would have no hesitation in placing them before the people of the district, in accordance with the desire of the Convention, but for the causes to which he had before alluded. Again thanking his fellow-citizens here present, as well as those whom they represented, for this manifestation of their continued confidence, he begged leave, most respectfully, to decline their nomination.

*To Susan Washington Graham.*      A.

Saturday Evening,

June 1st, 1839.

My Dearest Susan

It is Saturday evening, the Court here has ended, & with it my Circuit for this Spring. I have come home, played with my Boys, and dined, and you only are wanting to make me entirely satisfied. I always experience a feeling of vacancy at the close of a Court, especially at the end of a long circuit unless I can retreat to the bosom of my family.

*   *   *   *   *

The Convention to nominate a Candidate for Congress in this district met here on yesterday, and I have never in my life been more embarrassed than by their solicitations. They had urged the nomination upon me individually before they met, and I thought assented to my refusal. But on my return to the Court House yesterday afternoon I met a numerous committee on their way to my house to announce that I had been selected by the unanimous voice of the Convention & that they would take no refusal. I retired with them to Mr. Waddell's office, and there for an hour it was pressed with renewed zeal. Nothing but the most deliberate determination, which I had formed beforehand, and the promise I had made to you, prevented me from yielding. I am not entirely satisfied that my course is the proper one—I fear it has given offence, as I have no doubt it has disappointment and mortification, to many pure patriots & as disinterested friends as man ever had. And more may depend on it, than might at first be imagined. I thought however of my home and family, the orphans committed to my care and my numerous engagements arising out of these relations. At the request of the Committee I appeared before the Convention and made my apology in person. Mr. G. W. Haywood was then nominated, and a Committee appointed to write him. It is not yet known whether he will accept. The Whigs will generally vote for him here, and with an extensive personal popularity in Wake, he may, I hope, succeed.

Bro. James writes me that he has no opposition. Bro. John will be here with Malvina & Julia Scott in a few weeks. He went with them to the celebration of the 20th. of May at Charlotte, where the girls attended a ball. Dr. Webb has his house now full. His son and son in Law & their families having arrived from Alabama.

The Episcopal convention abandoned all hope of continuing their school at Raleigh, and resolved to sell out the lands about the buildings, and propose to the Diocese of S. C. to join them in establishing a Theological Seminary there.

* * * * *

[P.S.] Mr. Pollock is said to have died much indebted—so much so that many of his negroes will be required to be sold, of whom there is only about 1200 in all.
New York.

*From Jesse Turner.*[34]                          U.

Van Buren, Ark.,

June 8th, 1839.

It is a long time since I saw you, though I have a distinct and vivid recollection of you. Occasionally through the medium of the Newspapers I see accounts of your course as a public man. I am gratified to find you doing battle so manfully in the Whig ranks, and fervently hope should you again be a Candidate for Congress that you may obtain the object of your wishes, a seat in the next Congress. When I left North Carolina I little thought ever to hear of the election of Dr. Wm. Montgomery to Congress but alas! Sir the times are sadly out of joint, the dark and turbid waters of Jacksonism alias loco focoism have swept over the land like a tornado, and oh! my Country how much of merit, of worth, of talent and of high souled patriotism have been lost in that bitter flood, while the *putrid fungi* of democracy have been borne upon the surface of that broad stream to station, wealth, and honor.

My father and many other relatives reside in Orange, and there my own eyes first opened on the light, and I have all that Nationality about me so characteristic of N. Carolinians, and having been wedded to the Whig cause since boyhood, you can probably form some conception of the ardour of my desire for the success of the Whigs in N. C. What position my relations occupy in regard to parties I know not, my father is far advanced in life and I presume takes little interest in politics but he should be a Whig as he had the honor to be a Whig and a soldier of the Revolution. I hope they are with you in your elections. If not, apprize them of my views and wishes on the subject;—perhaps it may have some little influence with them.

I had the honor to be a member of the last Genl. Assembly of Arkansas and flatter myself that I made altogether a favorable impression. But the Potent democracy are in the ascendency here, though we are giving them war to the knife, and the knife to the hilt.

---

[34] Jesse Turner (1805-1894), of Van Buren, Arkansas, a native of Orange County, who studied law at the university and later under Archibald D. Murphey. He moved to Alabama in 1830 and to Arkansas in 1831, where he was a Whig state legislator, able judge, Federal district attorney, and a delegate to the secession convention and the convention of 1874.

I should be pleased to hear from you on matters and things in general.

*To Susan Washington Graham.*                               A.

Hillsboro', June 8th, 1839.

My Dear Susan

This is the anniversary of our wedding day, and I undertake the task of writing you with even more pleasure than usual. Were I a poet, I would forthwith indite for you an epithalamium. As I am not, I must content myself in simple prose with assuring you, from my inmost heart, that my affection yet "goes hand in hand even with the vows I made to you in marriage." Our three years dwindle in my imagination to a few months, and the whole scene is present to my memory as if it were but yesterday. The gathering of friends, the illumined hall, the group of attendants, the maiden blush of my bride, the junction of hands, the plighting of vows, & sealing kiss, are all before me in vivid rememberance. Would that you could be with us today, that we might talk over each trivial event of the occasion, & imprint them more deeply in our memories. May we be apared to witness many happy returns of this day & never be separated on the recurrence of another.

Let me not however consume my letter in expatiating on the recollections inspired by the return of the 8th. of June.

Sister Eliza and the children are well. . . . Sister has had them out several evenings to ride with her. She took Jo a few days ago out shopping with Mary & herself. I found them at Mr. Kirkland's store, & walked with them to Mrs. Vassines; he was quite delighted with the boys & good things there, some of which we bought for him, and soon began to feel quite at home. Begining however to daub his dress with Icecream, his Aunt took the Glass out of his hand; this threw him into a furious rage, and he set up a savage squall, which he kept up through the street untill he reached home, showing more indomitable passion than I had ever before seen in him. His Aunt had then I believe to give him a switch, he all the while threatened to tell Pape. His health is very fine, and he has improved in talking, but will still not do it except when he is in the humour.

I have sold one of the horses, but have not been able to dispose of the extra negroes.

Mr. G. W. Haywood [35] accepts the nomination for Congress.

Mr. Allen, the *cher ami* of Miss Cain, was here last week, and by some sudden whim of the lady was discarded. He went off apparently much mortified. Albert Anderson was married this week in Perquimans to a sister of his former wife, and is expected in a few days at Mrs. Palmer's.

You have probably heard from New Bern of the engagement of Miss Julia Burgwyn to Mr. McRae.

* * * * *

Since I commenced writing my Cask of Madeira which I imported has arrived. If you were here I would broach it that we might take a bumper to the *day we celebrate*.

I shall go to the Supreme Court the latter part of next week, & remain perhaps a fortnight. . . .

We have an abundance of cherries and fair prospects for every kind of crop & vegetable. A waggon has brought your Saddle, clock, & Tea Caddy from New Bern.

* * * * *

[P.S.] A young gentleman by the name of Myers from Anson arrived today, and is to read in my office.

Mr. C. Shepard was at the Convention in Raleigh & I hear from good authority is engaged to Miss Watson. It is near night. I must bid you,

Adieu.

New York.


*Election to Literary Society.* U.

Randolph Macon College, 25th. August, 1839.

Sir

It affords us insurpassable pleasure to inform you of your election to Honorary Membership in the Franklin L. Society of Randolph M. College : And much more would our pleasure be increased, could your reply to this but bring us the gratifying intelligence of your acceptance.

---

[35] George Washington Haywood (1802-1890), a son of "Treasurer" John Haywood. He was a lawyer of Raleigh.

And we, the appointed, feel ourselves highly honored in being the humble organ by means of which you are made acquainted with your election.

| | |
|---|---|
| Jno. S. Wright | Committee |
| J. L. Smith | of |
| Jas. L. Mullen | Correspondence |

*To James W. Bryan.*

U. Bryan Mss.

Hillsboro, Aug. 31st, 1839.

Your letter came to hand as I was setting out for my first Court since my return, and our Court here occurring this week has delayed a reply untill now.

\*     \*     \*     \*     \*

Mrs. Washington left us a week ago for Raleigh, whence she was to go to New York with Mr. R. Washington. . . . She left Charity here, and we supposed though she was hardly willing to admit it, that her only object in coming, was to get her again into Carolina. Many attempts were no doubt made to decoy her off, and she would perhaps eventually have yielded.

\*     \*     \*     \*     \*

I arrived in the County just in time to vote, but it was of no avail. I think however, all things considered that this district & especially this County has shown no decline of Whig strength. We shall keep our forces rallied, and have no idea of a surrender.

You will see by the papers that the Guilford people have appointed delegates to the Raleigh Convention on the 2nd Monday of Novr. to nominate Candidates for the Prest., Vice Prest., & Gov. of the State, & proposing J. M. Morehead for the last. I hope your counties below will send delegates to that Convention & that some of you who are capable regulating affairs will come up. There will probably be a diversity of opinion as to the Vice Presidency, and perhaps as to sending delegates to Harrisburg.

What think you of Seward [36] of N. Y. for V. P? Would he do as well as Talmadge, and be exempt from the sin of expunging? Morehead will come out as strong as *aqua fortis* against Abolition and can get 2000 votes in Guilford to begin the race. I hope my friend Col. C. Jones will not allow the V. B. party to run him. A gentleman from Raleigh says that Brown and Haywood are more spoken of, than any body else on that side.

Our Court this week has appointed Commissions on the subject of schools under the act of Assembly.

The Bishop is preaching here, on his way from Buncombe. Judge Bailey[37] is to begin our Circuit next week at Granville. He has been here some time, looks badly & says he will stay here this winter and may come to reside among us. We have more lowlanders here this season, than have been for some time past. J. B. Skinner[38] and family are among them. He has told us of many marvellous matters, such as dining with a friend in Phila. on a feast which had been prepared *every article* in Paris, and imported in Glass hermetically sealed, etc.

I shall go to Granville next week by request and will probably take it into my Circuit.

We have the most abundant crops of every thing, but money, and are feasting on the finest fruits imaginable.

Our Love to all.

*From James W. Bryan.* U.

Newbern, Sept. 26, 1839.

The late Storm which was a very severe one Came near "making a finish" of your Warehouse. The river runs up a north

[36] William Henry Seward (1801-1872), of New York, graduate of Union College, who had served in the state senate, 1830-1834, had been defeated for governor in 1834, and was now governor. He was elected as a Whig to the United States senate in 1849, and served until 1861, becoming a Republican in 1852, and after being defeated for the Presidential nomination in 1860, served as secretary of state under Presidents Lincoln and Johnson.

[37] John Lancaster Bailey (1795-1877), a native of Pasquotank County, educated at the university, lawyer, member of the commons, 1827-1829, state senator, 1832. delegate to the convention of 1835, a judge of the superior court, 1837-1863.

[38] Joseph Blount Skinner (1780-1851), of Edenton, a brilliant lawyer, effective legislator, successful planter, and pioneer in the fishing industry on Albemarle Sound. After a short stay at Princeton, he read law under Samuel Johnston and after twenty years of practice, retired. He represented the borough of Edenton in the commons in 1807, and 1814-1815. He represented the County in the state senate in 1833, and in the convention of 1835.

course from it about a Mile or more & it is in one of the most
bleak and exposed situations in the town. The wind and the
rain & waves came down upon it with fury & violence with nothing to obstruct them for a mile or more & away went a part of
the Wharf & the underpinning of the House; the windows were
"Stove in" and I expected that it would be a mass of ruins. I
have had it raised to a proper level and underpinned all round
with blocks at a cost of $25.91 which I have charged to you in the
administration a/c preserving the bills & recpts for you. But this
is but a beginning of the repairs. I have had the wharf examined
and an estimate made of the necessary expenses to be incurred in
preserving it and they fall but little short of $100. I have been
unwilling to incur the responsibility of having the repairs made
without consulting you. Wharfing is the most expensive of all
kinds of labour; it is laborious, the materials are costly and difficult to be procured. The repair, however, of the wharf is essential
to preserve the House. The high tides now will wash the Wharf
away as the storm has cut it up very much. It will however afford
me pleasure to do in the premises whatever you may deem best,
etc. I should however be glad to hear from you about it, as I can
now obtain a workman (no easy matter here) & I have promised
to let him hear from me, as soon as I could learn your wishes on
the subject.

We are very much like the English gentlemen who met each
other at the Cheltenham Springs on their return from India after
amassing great fortunes, looking at the gold or copper in each
other's skins, With this difference that they lost their ruddy hue
in amassing wealth & gold, & we ours in sucking miasma & getting
poorer both in body and purse, but never mind as soon as the
white frost comes we will get fat like the Rabbits & forget it all!

The news from the N. Y. money market seems to Create Something of a panic here & our Banks will be compelled it is feared
to Curtail their discounts & consequently to produce both a pressure in the small way & disable our Merchants from buying at
fair prices the coming in Crops. Our Notes are at 5 pr. Cent
discount and from the large quantity of N. C. money Carried on
this season by N. C. Merchants in Consequence of the Banks not
being able to furnish them with Northern funds, I should not be
surprised if they got to 10 pr. ct. discount—a fine shave of them
will be made in N. Y.

We are not doing much in the way of politics. Our friends insist on my going to Harrisburg, but I really do not see how I can do it. I am so much engaged and have so much of one thing or another to attend to that a trip there in cold weather, would seem to be the *ultima thule* of all my jaunts, and besides I need rest and quietude above all things and do not care to have any thing more to do with public life, although I shall "go my death" for Clay. We shall hold a District Meeting & also send Delegates to Raleigh.

We are dragging on slowly with our Courts and have thus far had a poor harvest of it. Settle says that he has seen us on this Circuit for the last time & that he intends to resign etc. Donnell talks of coming to the Bar again & I reckon would like to take his old post, but I suppose Candidates for Judicial appointments will hereafter be as thick as blackberries.

\* \* \* \* \*

*To David L. Swain.*              A. Swain Mss.

### October 20th, 1839.

I have just rec'd your note, & send by the Stage my N. C. Journal, and file of Minerva for 1815, 16, & 17. I purchased them from Dr. Murphey, with a portion of his Father's Library. You will therefore be kind enough to take especial care of them, & have them returned to me as soon as you are satisfied with their perusal.

Can you afford me any aid in reclaiming my Father's manuscripts which were lent to J. S. Jones? If I knew where he made deposit of his effects (if there be any such place) I would cause search to be made there.

My family is now well, though we have lost two little negroes within the last week. We hear from New Bern that Mr. James Bryan has lost his eldest son.

*From James Graham.*                                    U.

Wilmington, N. C.

Nov. 30th, 1839.

I am now on the Steamer Vanderbilt within sight of Wilmington on my way to Washington. I was up set on the Cumberland Mountain in Tennessee and had my Right Arm injured. I found I could not go up the Ohio River, and my injured arm prevented me from travelling by Stage, so I floated down the Missippi River to N. Orleans; by Mobile, Pensacola, Augusta, and Charleston to this place.

I am in company with two Senators, Fulton[39] of Arkansas and Walker of Missippi, and a very fine fellow, Judge Cross,[40] a new member from Arkansaw. My Arm is nearly well. We expect to reach Washington on next Monday morning, after which I will again write you.

*From James Graham.*                                    U.

Washington, Decm. 5th, 1839.

I reached this City on last Monday morning about day light. The Members met on Monday about 12 oclock in the Capitol. The Clerk began to call the Members elected and proceeded until he came to N. Jersey When after calling one Member elected, he stated there was a contest about the remaining Seats and he refered that question to the House to decide. The debate has now on that question been progressing in a most desultory manner, and no one can tell when it will terminate. The debate thus far has been decorous and free from much excitement, but I think it will wax warmer before the close.

Brother Joseph you know left Five children : George, Lydia Ann, Albert, Mary Sophia, and Joseph. I have never seen Five more promising children. I made diligent inquiry to find some

---

[39] William Savin Fulton (1795-1844), a native of Maryland, soldier of the War of 1812, moved to Tennessee, and was military aide to Jackson in Florida in 1818. He moved to Alabama in 1826, was appointed secretary of Arkansas Territory in 1835, and elected United States senator in 1836, serving until his death.

[40] Edward Cross (1798-1887), a native of Tennessee, went to Arkansas Territory in 1826, and was Federal judge. He was a Democratic member of congress, 1839-1845; a judge of the state supreme court, 1845-1855; a railroad president, 1855-1862, and state attorney general, 1874.

suitable person to become their Guardian, and came to the conclusion that Buckly Kimbrough was clearly the best appointment
that could be made in that quarter. He is a plain man of good
moral character and fair business habits. He is said to be out of
Debt and is no speculator. He consented reluctantly to become
their Guardian.

There are 32 negroes belonging to the Estate all named in the
Inventory returned by the Administrator About 2/3 of the
negroes are working the farm and this year will make about 56
Bales of Cotton. The remaining 1/3 are Hired out. They have
had a worthless overseer who is now discharged. I have advised
Sister Sarah if she can find a competent Lady to teach, to employ
and introduce her into her house to teach her children and also
be some company for her. Sister Sarah's health is pretty good and
she is doing quite as well as could be expected in her situation.
But still her task and trials are extremely difficult & embarrassing.

\* \* \* \* \*

## *From Henry W. Miller.*[41]                                    U.

### Philadelphia, Decr. 10th, 1839.

I am here on my way home from the National Convention. I
doubt not but you have heard before this that Genl Harrison was
nominated for the Presidency & John Tyler for the Vice Presidency, by the Convention. I know that our friends in North
Carolina will feel much disappointment at not getting the man
of their choice. But could they have been present during the deliberations of the Convention, they would have been satisfied,
that, though Mr. Clay enlisted the partialities of a large majority
of the *members* who were present, he could not under any circumstances command a majority of the electoral votes of the
States represented. The New York Delegates alleged it was impossible to carry that State for him and they could not be prevailed on to cast their votes for him. The Delegates from North
Carolina were the last to yield. Kentucky, Maryland and Virginia
gave up Mr. Clay as hopeless and pledged their zealous support

[41] Henry Watkins Miller (1816-1864), a native of Virginia, who settled in Raleigh
after graduation from the university. He became a distinguished lawyer, was an
enthusiastic and influential Whig leader, and had a widespread reputation as an
eloquent public speaker.

to the nomination before our Delegation could be induced to surrender their preferences. It was then our duty to offer in behalf of our Whig friends at home a zealous cooperation. You shall have a copy of the proceedings as soon as they are printed and I have but little doubt that Mr. Clay's letter to the Convention thro' the Kentucky Delegates will be satisfactory to all his friends. It is confidently believed that Genl. H. will carry New York, Pennsylvania, Ohio, Indiana. Maryland, Massachusetts, New Jersey, Kentucky, Vermont, Deleware, Rho: Island, & Michigan and Connecticut, Virginia, Tennessee and North Carolina put down as doubtful but the first considered by their Delegates as strong for Harrison as Clay. The nomination was received with great enthusiasm by the Convention. Mr. Tyler was nominated unanimously on the first ballot.

I fear that the disappointment of our friends in N. C. will induce them to denounce the nomination before they give it proper reflection, but I hope they will pause. I know when they hear all that can be said in justification of the course taken by the Convention they will be content. They should remember that the object of the Whig party is to break down the corrupt powers that rule. I have been mistaken in the character of Genl H. He is with us on all the great questions of the day—Against abolition, Voted against the Missouri restriction, is for Mr. Clay's land bill, and opposes the Sub Treasury. Messrs Tyler, Leigh and in fact the whole Southern Delegation declared that the Whigs of the South would be perfectly satisfied with his political principles. It is hoped that the *true* friends of the Whig cause will exert themselves to the utmost to counteract, or forestal, any precipitate opposition to the Nomination. It was the best could be done—*all* that could be done, except to break up the party, & give the Spoilers unmolested possession of the Country. The Delegation join in the request that no exertion may be spared.

My respects to all friends.

*To James W. Bryan.*          U. Bryan Mss.

Hillsboro, Decr. 14th, 1839.

... I have now vacation for a few weeks, after having been absent nearly all the fall. My receipts for the year have been good, but there is a dull prospect for the next. I have been desirous to get a plantation in this vicinity on which to settle my hands or a part of them next year, but have not done so as yet, and the weather has been so unfavourable as not to allow one to go out to examine those offered.

Judge Bailey passed around our riding very pleasantly. We learn from very authentic sources that Judge Saunders is to be the V. B. Candidate for Governor. If so, I presume, that delicacy would compel him to vacate the bench. Morehead is diligently preparing ammunition and expects an actual Campaign through the State, though in this he will probably be governed by the course taken on the other side. Congress, I fear, will go near a dissolution of the Government at this session—if such it may be called; there seems no prospect of organizing the House at present.

I last night recd. a letter from Miller on his return from Harrisburg announcing Harrison and Tyler. We would, of course, have all much preferred Clay, but I hope will unite cordially in support of Harrison. His letter is written at the request of the N. C. delegation and urges that the nomination be at once adopted. Our friends here will be satisfied, & make a strong effort for him. My brother has always told me that Harrison was much stronger in the mountain district than Clay. And I am far from believing the chances in the State desperate. The calculation at Harrisburg elects him without any vote South of Potomac. Mr. Leigh declares that he, H., has no principle adverse to the South. He is in favour of Clay's land policy against abolition and the Subtreasury. I hope you will see our friend Moore and get him to take him up with zeal. Wadsworth of Craven was against him last Session; I presume he will not prefer V. B. to him, and that is now the question.

I recd. with deep sensations of sorrow the intelligence of the loss of your son,[42] and would have early offered the assurance of my sympathy, but that I knew you possessed sources of consolation far more assuaging to grief than any that I could afford.

My family is well & all join in tendering their best wishes.

---

[42] John Washington Bryan, who died at the age of five years.

*From James Graham.*                                      U.

Washington, Dec. 22d, 1839.

I have been very much confused since Congress met as no one could tell one moment what course of proceeding might be adopted the next. We succeeded you perceive in preventing the Van Buren men from electing their Speaker. But they have gained their Clerk by the *unholly Allience* of Nullification and Loco-Focoism.

Genl Harrisons nomination was not unexpected to me, or rather I did not believe Mr Clay would be nominated. The general prejudice which was lodged in the public mind against that distinguished Statesman induced the convention to surrender his name. I mentioned this same idea to you in a letter last winter while you were in the Legislature, and objected the Whigs nominating Mr Clay in advance of the decission of the general Convention, because it presented a false issue to the people and roused old political prejudices which would operate against the Whigs. Harrisons friends are very sanguine. I am not intimately or sufficiently acquainted with his public life to know what impression he will make before the people. My intention is to support any respectable man against whom no serious charge can be sustained in opposition to Mr Van Buren. Abolition is charged upon Harrison, His friends say the charge is false and I have seen nothing yet to satisfy me it is true. His whole History will be reviewed and presented to the people, and we shall soon learn all his views opinions and policy. I believe the people will take him up much sooner than the politicians. He was a soldier in his boyhood and A Major General in his Manhood and never sustained a defeat from the enemy. He was appointed Gov of the N W Territory by Mr Jefferson. He was Representative & Senator in Congress from Ohio. He has for the last nine years been in retirement on his Farm on the Ohio River, where I am informed by one of his Nbrs., *he labours with his own hands a portion of every day.* This gives him a robust constitution and a green old age. He is poor, but comfortable in his circumstances, and that is clear & conclusive evidence of his Honesty. His Ambition has been to serve the people, not to steal their money. When He served the Country, "the spoils did not belong to the victors." The public Treasury did not belong to the Sub Treasury office holders. I am trying every opportunity to learn truly Harrisons whole character and opinions and to act and declare for him if his conduct is free from objection. I am glad to find the Whigs are all united against Van but some will not go for Harrison.

If it be ascertained N Carolina will not go for Harrison we had better let the Presidential go against us *by Default,* and stand by and mentain our Principles. I think the S. Carolina Whigs and Georgia will pursue that course.

Still if Harrisons principles when Developed will justify it, they may go for him. In N. Carolina the great Contest and decisive battle will be fought next August for the State Legislature. And the Candidates should arm themselves from this time to that, by laying by Extracts from N. papers and Documents to use when needed.

I wish I was better pleased with Harrison than I am, but I am apprehensive those who are not well pleased with his nomination, will have to reverse and change the Question, and ask themselves *which is the Worst?* and make up their opinions and decissions on that Question.

I was very much pleased with my visit to New Orleans. It is very far superior to any thing I anticipated. It is a great and delightful City. I spent two days there.

Genl. Henderson of Texas passed here a few days on his return from France. He is a polished gentleman and recently married to a Lady of Philadelphia.

## 1840

*To Susan Washington Graham.*        A.

Raleigh Jany. 8th. 1840.

My Dear Wife

I arrived here safely at 1 o'clock on yesterday, though I travelled in considerable apprehension as the drivers had no lamps & received no light except what was afforded by the snow. Just after daylight, about half a mile from Morings the stage broke down & I was obliged to get out, & walk about 1/4 of a mile. The latter however was done while they were fixing up the stage, which soon overtook me. The stages on that line are old and crazy and it is not surprizing with their customary bad management that accidents should often occur.

I am staying at Rogers', as yet in a great crowd as the V. Buren Convention is in Session here & pretty fully attended. It will probably dissolve tomorrow when I hope to be more comfortably situated. Judge Saunders, it is ascertained, will be their nominee for Gov, Messrs. Haywood [1] & Henry[2] declining. The former is at New Bern, but expected here daily.

\* \* \* \* \*

Mr. Bennehan,[3] who is here tells me that Judge Cameron's family have gone to St. Augustine, & will not return untill May. Miss Ann is no better, but all the rest improved.

\* \* \* \* \*

I hope to finish my business here in the course of next week, but am not sure that I can do so. Raleigh is improving. Mr. Freeman is constructing a handsome house near Judge Camerons. A very large Engine house of brick is being built at the depot below the Hotel.

*From James Graham.*                              U.

### H. of R.,

### Jany 31st, 1840.

I have recd your two letters from Raleigh. I am pleased to hear you have a third son.[4] Surely you have luck for Boys.

I have induced Rayner to write to Anderson on the nomination of a Judge   You see from the Papers Congress will do very little this Session. The disorder and loquacity increases. We have stoped Abolition for this Session *by refusing* to receive their Petitions. This unfortunate subject has generally been used *here* by Demagogues to try and make *political Capital to trade and trafick* upon at home. I am happy to see the Raleigh Register is edited with more spirit than formerly—The paragraphs are *short and pithy.* That takes and *sticks* with the people.

---

[1] William H. Haywood.
[2] Louis D. Henry.
[3] Thomas Davis Bennehan (1781-1847), graduate of the university, planter, and merchant of Orange County. He was the brother-in-law of Judge Duncan Cameron, and was a highly respected and influential citizen.
[4] William Alexander Graham, Jr. (1839-1923), later a student at the university, graduate of Princeton, Confederate major, farmer in Lincoln County, state senator, 1874-1876, 1879-1881, commissioner of agriculture, 1908-1923.

Harrison is rising and gaining ground in all quarters every day. The more he is slandered and libeled, the more his character & conduct are elevated. If each County in N. C. would in due season nominate proper *ardent candidates for the Legislature,* who will well inform themselves as to Harrison's History and present it truly to the People there is no doubt he will carry the State in August which will decide the complexion of the State for 8 or 10 years. The August Election will determine, the presidential Contest in N. C., the next Senator in N. C. and the future policy of the State. Harrison will carry *the Farmers and Boys,* who have no file-leader and winn all the wavering and doubtful. It is fair in war to refer to the gallant deeds and noble sacrifices of Harrison in defence of our Country and those who oppose and abuse him will run great risk of being called *Tories.*

We in N. C. should *begin in time* and inform and *enlist the young men* who are full of enthusiasm and patriotism. Try and secure the officers of the Militia and Civil officers. The Battles of H. will tell after they are recited and understood.

I have made the above suggestions for you to improve on. This contest between Power and Right; or the President against the People requires the friends of freedom to start the Ball Rolling *in time* to effect useful purposes.

*From James Graham.* U.

### H. of R.,

### Feb. 3d, 1840.

I think the Republican Whigs in N. C. should quickly organize in each County in the State. Appoint about 3 Persons, in each County at or near the Court House as a central Committee to collect and distribute information among the People. Then appoint 2 or 3 *popular* and *influential* men in each Captain's Company to inform their neighbours of public measures and public men. *Particularly* of Harrisons life, and long and eminent public services. The Whigs are *very wrong* in keeping up their war and abuse of Jackson. He is an old man out of office, and it *only strengthens* Van. We ought not to go out of our way to grapple with *a Lion* when we are *Fox-Hunting.* The Whigs have the game in their own hands if they will play it well.

If the young and *ardent* men are once informed of "old Tip's" *many brilliant victories* they will break loose from their Fathers and Leaders and go for that man who has served his Country long and faithfully and grown poor to make his countrymen free and independent. Very much can be done now before the canvass commences by giving information to certain influential men and securing them as leaders. Many of our best Citizens say *Party Spirit* has got too high, and they want a *retired Farmer* to come in and go for *the people* a while, as the Party has been served long enough.

The Whig papers in N. C. should look to the Madisonian and quote Extracts from it. It is conducted with spirit and ability.
[P.S.]   If men who once supported Jackson would come out for Harrison they will win over many.

<br>

*From James Graham.*                                    U.

### H. of R.,

#### March 19th, 1840.

I have ordered the Papers you last directed and herein inclose the Rect. I have also sent to each of the persons on your List a brief Life of Harrison, And will forward more when you send me more names. Send a full proportion of the names of *young men* who belong to Van Buren families. You know young men are apt to be struck with Military Glory.

The Van Party will tell the Whigs they did not like a military man when Jackson was President! That you know is a *two edged* sword. And as they once went for Jackson why will they not support Harrison?

Be careful in selecting your Candidates. Two or three of them should be talking men and the others selected for their family connections, sectional interests, and personal popularity. New Candidates have one advantage over old ones, that is they have no charges against them for old scores.

I think the Republican Whigs do themselves great injustice in attempting to justify the conduct of all the Banks. I have never done it. I denounce the Bad Banks and advocate Gold and Silver and good Specie paying Banks and I denounce the Administration for refusing good Bank paper and by its oppressive measures injuring all the Banks by drawing out and hoarding up Specie.

The Hard Times, the *Reduction of Wages* and *prices of produce and property* & stagnation of business will do much to awaken & inform the people. The People should be reminded continually of this. Van Buren has had and now has a Majority in both branches of Congress and must be responsible for the present state things. The Sub Treasury is and has been in *partial operation* and all without any Law or rule but the *President's will*. In 34-5 Levi Woodbury reported to Congress the State Banks were good Agents for the Government and *had lost less* than any agents ever employed. Now in 1840 the said Levi Reports the State Banks have lost *more* than any agents we ever had. He is like an old Jockey's Son, who when about to mount a Horse always asked his "Daddy must I ride him *to sell,* or *to buy."* I will write soon to Morehead. He ought to propose to Saunders to go into the distant parts of the State. Morehead is unknown personally at a distance & Saunders is known all over the State. I disapprove of *indiscriminate* and violent opposition of the Whigs to *all* the acts of the administration. That course strengthens the Tories and injures the Whigs. The people love *fair play*. This constant cry of Wolf won't do. No charges should be made but those that can be *sustained clearly*. I do not know much of Morehead, but I fear he will charge too much *without proof*. Van Buren was *opposed* to the war, and *tried* to elect Clinton[5] over Madison;[6] And He was opposed to the admission of Missouri into the union without *restricting* slavery. While old Tip was for our Country and our Country's Cause against Great Britton, and for the South against Abolition.

The *Sub Treasury* and the *enormous Defaulcations* are the crying sins of *his Majesty*. All power in the hands of *one man* and *no Accountability*. Van Buren asks Congress to issue *5 Millions more of Treasury Notes for 2 years and no longer!* This is the old song and the old tune. Two years and no longer!!!! This is the fourth time his Majesty has thus importuned us with those *seductive* words two years and *no longer*. Treasury Notes are the Nest Eggs for the Treasury Bank over which the President is to

---

[5] George Clinton (1739-1812), of New York, member continental congress, 1775-1777; brigadier general of militia, and later of the continental line; governor of New York, 1777-1795, 1801-1804; president of convention of 1788; vice president, 1805-1812.

[6] James Madison. The reference is to the election of 1808.

set *hatching* more power and whenever opposed in his grasping measure He, like an old Hen, is to *Cluck* and say "two years and *no longer*" until the Treasury Government Bank is hatched and presented in full form

Mr Clay speaks of [page torn] and entering [page torn] from Congress, but has not Resolved to do so yet. He is cordial in his support of Harrison. I board with his Colleague *Crittenden*[7] and *Corwin*[8] of Ohio: and Clay dined with us after his return from Richmond. He appears quite sanguine of Va., but stated perhaps his opportunities were not so good as others to form correct opinions. Very much may be done before Candidates are announced by enlisting certain influential persons. And if the *first* man in the Neighbourhood be against us, try the *Second,* and divide the influence. Much may be done by appealing to the pride of people to *act* for themselves, and not permit any would-be leader to *dictate* to them.

\*    \*    \*    \*    \*

I wish you would write to some person in Person County and tell them to send a written list of influential persons and their post offices to me and I will send them documents.

The Whigs should have a Ticket in every County next August. It will bring out the people to vote for Governor.

*From Kenneth Rayner.*                        U.

Washington City, April 5th, 1840.

I received your letter some time since, touching the executive appointment, of a Judge of the Superior Court of our State; and should have replied to it at the time, but that I could not have done so in a matter satisfactory to yourself, inasmuch as I had been previously requested by several friends, to interpose as far as

[7] John Jordan Crittenden (1787-1863), of Kentucky, student at Washington College (now Washington and Lee University), was graduated from William and Mary; attorney general of Illinois Territory; aide to Governor Shelby in the War of 1812; member lower house of the state legislature, 1811-1817, (speaker), 1825, 1829-1832; United States senator, 1817-1819, 1855-1861; Federal district attorney, 1827-1829; attorney general of the United States, 1841, 1850-1853; U. S. senator, 1842-1848; governor of Kentucky, 1848-1850; member of congress, 1861-1863.

[8] Thomas Corwin (1794-1865), of Ohio, native of Kentucky, lawyer, member of the lower house of the legislature, 1822-1823, 1829; Whig member of congress, 1831-1840; governor, 1840-1842; elector, 1844; United States senator, 1845-1850; secretary of the treasury, 1850-1853; Republican member of congress, 1859-1861; minister to Mexico, 1861-1864.

my humble aid could avail any thing, in favour of Mr. A. H. Shepherd [9] for the same appointment, not knowing at the time, that the name of Mr. Winston[10] would be before the Council. So I concluded to remain silent on the subject, between the two applications, coming as they both did from my friends. This, I hope you will accept as an apology, not only for my failing to comply with the request of your kind letter, but also for my silence at the time.

Congress is still "Dragging its slow length along," doing but little (in fact, nothing) for the benefit of the Country, but sinking itself more and more every day in the estimation of the sober and reflecting portion of the Community. Sir, it is lamentable to see to what a depth of degradation the Congress of the U. S. is sinking, and has already sunk. The Senate has long since, surrendered its high character for independence and character, and has for years been bowing in abject submission at the footstool of power; and the House of Reps is "following in its footsteps," with as much exactness as is Mr. Van Buren in those of his "illustrious predecessor." And I believe the alarming increase of executive power, within the last few years, is mainly owing to the low standard of character and publick morals, which prevail in Congress; for as the latter has lost power, and publick confidence, the former seems to have grasped it. The scenes of violence and disorder that prevail in our house, are much more befitting a bear-garden, than the legislative Council of a great and (self-styled) free nation. I assure you that I never saw disorder, such indecorous conduct, such want of independence, such servile subjection to party leaders in the legislature of No. Ca. even in its most partizan and Van-Buren-devoted days, as I have witnessed in our house, and I believe I might add such dearth of character and talent. And you know that you and I have served together in the Legislature of our State, when party tyranny ruled us with a "rod of iron," and when virtue and independence seemed to constitute a crime in the possession. I was then disposed to undervalue the character of our people, and the intelligence of our State. Since I came here, I have discovered my error, and I am now more devoted to my own State, and have more confidence in the virtue & intelligence of her people, than I ever had; for I find that other States, those too that make great professions in

---

[9] Shepperd.
[10] Patrick Henry Winston of Rockingham County.

regard to character and talent, send men here, of whom the old North State would be ashamed. The violence and disregard for all order peculiar to the present session, seems mainly to have originated in the outrageous course practiced in regard to the N. Jersey election. That conduct was in utter violation of all law, all precedent, all order; habits of disorder were then contracted, which still adhere to us, which clog our progress at every step, and which in fact impart a revolutionary character to all our proceedings. When is this thing to end? When will the people look for succour and protection, when instead of looking upon Congress with veneration, they look upon it with contempt? Had Congress been sitting in a large City, long ere this the members would have driven by a mob from the doors of the Capitol. The V. Buren presses say the Whigs are equally to blame for this, with the other party. I deny the fact, for although some of the Whig party have acted with violence, yet it was *defensive,* in its character. It was for the purpose of *repelling* violence. The course of the present Ho. of Reps. has been revolutionary during the whole Session, and we have been compelled either to defend ourselves with nerve and vigour, or to yield the contest, and retire in disgrace from our seats. I ask when is this to end?—The people must come to the relief of our free institutions, through the peacful medium of the ballot box; or else we have the alternative of revolution on the one hand, or the yoke of bondage on the other. For a more practical despotism never existed in any age or country, than that which represses all the talent and energies in our house, and weighs down the prosperity and commerce of this *once* free people.

But is there no hope that the people will come to their own relief? There is. If there is any thing in the "signs of the times," the eyes of the people are opening, their fears are arousing, their indignation is exciting; and in a few months more, this corrupt dynasty will be hurled from the high place of power, which they have so long desecrated, and *honest men* will occupy their places. The accounts which we receive from all parts of the Union daily, all concur in stating the rapid progress of Harrison and reform. We are in high spirits here, and are cheered not only with the hope, but the absolute belief of an overwhelming victory. "The party" are evidently alarmed, and well they may be, for from all sections from Maine to Florida, we receive the same "glad tidings," that we are not only maintaining our ground, but that we are making heavy inroads upon the enemy. As to N. York, Mr. Tallmadge says it is certain for 20,000 Majority for Harrison. The late rupture between the Radicals & the Moderates of "the party" in Pennsylvania, render that state safe for us by 10,000, as I am correctly informed by men who know.

We are all looking with great anxiety to the Connecticut elections which take place next week; the Whig members from that State assure me, they will carry it by 3,000 majority. Massachusetts and R. Island are considered equally safe; the V. Buren party give up Ohio, Indiana, Illinois, & Michigan, & Kentucky. Virginia, N. Carolina, Maryland, Delaware, & N. Jersey, & Louisiana are debateable ground. In these States however, all the accounts state that the Whigs are fully organized, and prepared for action. So far as No. Ca. is concerned, we *can* carry it, and we *must* carry it. I know we have the power, if we can make it available. The only difficulty will be in getting our friends to the polls, and in order to do this no pains should be spared, "no stone left unturned."

There is one thing I think of the utmost importance. The Whig Electors should by all means, Canvass their districts,—not in July, for the Candidates for the Legislature can do that, except perhaps in Counties where there is no Whig candidate, but in the months of September and October, just previous to the Presidential election. For no matter how high may be the spirit of our friends in August, it will cool off before Nov. unless means are used to keep it up. Recollect the election 4 years ago. With a majority of near 5,000 in August, we were beaten more than 3,000 in Nov. And the V. Buren party will not forget that; they even now speak of our apathy as the grounds of their success. There is also another matter of great moment, The Whigs should run Candidates for the Legislature in every County in the State, whether there is any prospect of success or not. It will be a means of aiding us in the Governor's election, and then it will keep up the district organization of our party in each County preparatory to the great battle in Nov. I know it will be in your power to do much in regard to these suggestions, while riding your Circuits, and by correspondence and conference with the leading men of our party.

Why not the lawyers in your Circuit address the people at each Court, and actually preach a Crusade against the corruptions of the times. The times require it, patriotism requires it, the suffering situation of the Country requires it.

Now I know you are "an older, and abler soldier" than myself, and need not any suggestions from me; you will however pardon my zeal, when you reflect that comes from an old friend, and co-labourer in "the good cause." And do not, I beseech you, suffer the Legislature to go against us. Of all political matters dearest to my heart, after defeating V. Buren, is to turn "neck and heels" out of the Senate of U. S. the "noble pair of brothers" who now *mis*-represent our good old North State in that body. Could you once witness their attempt to "break a lance" with such men as Clay, Webster, Crittenden, etc (and they are both remarkable for it) as a North Carolinian, you would hang your head in shame. May the Lord deliver us from their clutches is my prayer!

From all parts of No. Ca. the news is good, and some of us receive news daily. Fisher's is the only district that gives me any uneasiness, and I hope Morehead will devote much of his time to that section of the State.

The treasury Note bill has passed, after a long and stormy debate. The party attempted to force it through without suffering the Whigs to debate it, as they did in their final action on the N. Jersey case. We however had it in Committee of the whole, and there we were determined to keep it, and there we did keep it, 'till every Whig who wished it, had spoken on the subject. 'Tis true we suffered much from privation and exposure, but then we gained our point, which was discussion. The speeches of Thompson of So. Ca., Biddle[11] of Pen., & Barnard [12] of N. York were of great power, and can not fail to have their influence before the Country.

We remained in Session, at one time for 29 hours, meeting on Tuesday 12 M., and not adjourning 'till Wednesday 5 P.M., and then we forced them to adjourn, without taking the question, although they swore when the house met on Tuesday that they would have the question before they adjourned. As often as they attempted to report the bill to the house, by a party vote, our friends refused to vote, and thus left them without a quorum, and whenever we moved to adjourn, or to report progress, they defeated us by a party vote.

For the better part of the past week, the House has been discussing Bell's favourite measure to prevent the interference of

[11] Richard Biddle.
[12] Daniel Dewey Barnard (1797-1861), native of Massachusetts, who, after graduating at Williams College, practiced law in Rochester. He was a member of congress, 1827-1829. He moved to New York, was a member of the assembly, and from 1839 to 1845 was again in congress. He was minister to Prussia, 1850-1853.

office holders in elections. Bell made a very strong speech on the subject. The bill cannot pass, for while the V. Buren party will oppose it in a body, there are many Whigs who do not like some of its provisions.

The Sub-Treasury will soon be up, and then there will be another warm and protracted debate. It will pass, if the party *wish* to pass it. That however is doubtful, if they could possibly avoid it. The Whigs, however, will not suffer them to evade this issue.

We shall probably be here 'till July, perhaps later, if they succeed in getting up a war panic, which they are evidently attempting to do, for you know it is an old scheme to get up a war-cry, whenever they get hard pressed.

Well really I must be *boring* you with this long letter, you will excuse it. I feel deeply in regard to these matters, and I also feel, that I am writing to one, whose position and character in No. Ca, places it in his power to do much—very much—for the good of the Country at large.

I should be happy to hear from you, and to know your opinion of our prospects in the State whenever you may have leisure to do so.

I am with much respect
Yours sincerely.


*From James Graham.* U.

Washington, April 8th, 1840.

. . . I have sent the Lives of Harrison to all the persons in Orange and Person named in your List. Should you or any one from there send more I will attend to it.

The following objectionable subjects should be urged against Van Buren and his party.

1st. In 1837, He contracted a *new public Debt of 10 Millions* the first year he was in office.

2d. He and his Party during the last Congress *increased* the Regular Standing Army from 7,000, to *12,500* nearly double in time of Peace. The Florida war has been mainly kept up by Militia.

3d. Van & his Party have sent out an Exploring Expedition consisting of 5 or 6 Ships to Circumnavigate South America in search of unknown Lands, & Islands, different *Beasts, Birds* and *Batts*, which will cost 3 or 4 Millions of Dollars. And both these *extravagant schemes* are put in motion while we are obliged to borrow money & make large new Debts.

4th. Frequent and enormously large Defaulcations of public money and although the President *well knew* of those fraudulent Defaulcations and public losses, he did not Remove the *offending swindlers,* but kept them in office.

5th. The Independent Sub Treasury which is a sort of Barrell with an open *Bung* turned down and a small spill at Top. It runs out faster than it runs in. The Treasury is now empty and there is very little coming in. This paper money hating and hard money loving administration has just authorized the issue of Five Millions of paper money—Treasury Bank Notes. This is a fair sample of Mr. Van Burens principles and practises. They are at right Angles with each other very much like + the Cross Keys at the Cross Rhodes. One Text to preach by and another to practise by. This Cross eyed conduct and Indian Rubber Policy I do not admire.

\* \* \* \* \*

Try hard to get energetic and popular men as Republican Whig candidates in Orange. Men of tact. The Issue is narrowed down to this single simple proposition; will the people support General Harrison, or *General Ruin?* That's the question.

Harrison and good prices, or Van Buren and Insolvency? Our friends should hold on and use that word *Republican* it is an expressive and potent word; & we should appropriate it to our own Cause. It is a host before the people.

*To James W. Bryan.*          U. Bryan Mss.

Greensborough,

April 18th, 1840.

I am here attending the Superior Court of Guilford and avail myself of some leisure to write you. Genl. Saunders was here and addressed the people on Thursday last, and I am told, expects to be at New Berne on Thursday next, at the time appointed for Mr. Morehead to be there. Morehead has entered the canvass in good earnest and I have thought it proper to advise him through you, of some of the grounds assumed here by Saunders.

1st. then, he charged that Genl. Harrison had never said anything since he became a Candidate for the Presidency, against abolition. This is contradicted by the Vincennes speech, the Letter to Sherrod Williams, and Letter published in the last Raleigh Register to a Gentleman in New Orleans all in 1836, in the heat of the Canvass. Other declarations are perhaps familiar to you.

2nd. He urges that Harrison's name was stricken from the resolution proposing medal, etc., in 1816, and although it passed at the next session 13 Senators names stand recorded against it. You know that in fact, it passed *unanimously* after the investigation acquitting Harrison of the false charges preferred against him. Hull's Life 286.

3rd. that Harrison resigned before the War ended. See causes—Hull 280 to 285.

4th. He has documents from the Sec. of Treasury for the purpose of showing that more money was lost to the Government under former administrations, Adams for example, than under V. B. and Jackson, setting off the losses by *failures* of Merchants to *pay Custom House Bonds* against the thefts of Swartwout, Price etc. Morehead should by all means have the document of the Ho. Reps. containing the correspondence between Woodbury and his defaulters No. 297, I think, shewing that under the present dinasty, for the first time in the History of the Government, theft and embezzlement have been tolerated and justified on the ground of party service etc.

5th. He has a letter recently obtained from some one at Washington stating that instructions were sent to our Ministers in England and France, directing suits to be brought against Swartwout & Price, but that by the French Law (they both being there) no such suit could be sustained. He didn't read the whole letter, tho' I presume it was from Forsyth. Examine the treaties and Law of nations to see whether they might not be demanded as Fugitives from Justice. It is not pretended that any attempt has been made to bring them back.

6th. He defends Mr. Poinsett's Military project, by saying that Genl. Washington recommended one similar and that Genl. Harrison did also when a member of the Senate. Tell Morehead to see wherein these differ.

7th. He harps on Abolition and boasts that 27 V. B. men voted against receiving Petitions at this Session. Stanly's late speech and appendix contains the answer to that; besides I am told that 38 of the party in the North, voted in favour of receiving them.

8th. He abandons hard money only wants to regulate Banks; the Sub T. will do that. That he didn't justify the suspension, but the resumption by State Bank in which he owns stock.

9th. Whigs are as much blameable for extravagant expenditures as the Party.

A. H. Shepperd was here, and called out by the people replied successfully. He stated that Adams had been the second choice both of Saunders and himself in 1824, and Saunders made no reply. Two V. B. leaders in this County afterwards came to Shepperd with a Whig to know if he had so stated. Shepperd replied yes, and Poindexter, being present said he had heard Saunders say so in 1824 and that 100 men in Stokes would prove it. Saunders has heretofore denied it. I write all this trash not to be used, of course, but to apprize Morehead of the present drift of his opponent.

I left home on Sunday last. My family were quite well. Susan has been promising herself a visit from Mrs. Bryan this Summer. I need not say, that we shall be more than pleased to see you, and will endeavour to accompany you in some jaunts to the neighboring Country; that is to say Susan and the children would accompany you for a week or two to Rockingham Springs, etc., should you incline to go. For my own part, I shall be probably engaged in the summer campaign during July and a part of August. I think a summer at Hillsborough would be quite as beneficial to Mrs. B. and yourself as one in the mountains, and we will endeavour to make it agreeable.

I have undertaken the culture of a farm in the neighborhood of Hillsborough, and am making divers experiments in agriculture with what success, time and the seasons will determine.

Judge Dick is holding our Court and is going slowly on. He has adjourned over to day to go to his Plantation.

Our friends who have heard M. think he is deficient in political information. On that account I have written the foregoing leaf, which you can tear off and give him, to put him on inquiry and prevent his being surprized. He is a fine fellow and I hope you, Manly & others will aid him all you can.

*From  William  H.  Battle.*[13]                       U.

Raleigh, April 24th, 1840.

\* \* \* \* \*

How goes the political world with you? Every thing which we
hear now seems to be cheering our cause. Every mail brings intelligence of some new Whig victory. May the good cause speed
until every nook and corner of our wide spread country is freed
from the devastating influence of Van Burenism, which is but
double distilled Jacksonism, and is the very worst ism with which
any Country pretending to be free, was ever afflicted. I hope the
Whigs will give a good account of themselves in Orange next
summer. In my old county, Franklin, there are strong hopes of
sending a partial if not total delegation to the Legislature of the
right principles. When there, week before last I heard of some important changes in our favour, and found the Whigs in the finest
kind of spirits.

*From  James  Graham.*                                 U.

Washington, May 10th, 1840.

I have just returned from Baltimore where upon invitation I
have been attending the young Men's Convention.[14] The Scene
was imposing and magnificent beyond description. There were
about *Twenty thousand Gentlemen* marching in one line of
Procession with Banners and Badges and Motto's indicating the
States, Districts & principles of those whose divisions marched
under them. There were speeches delivered during two days;
and shouts & Huzza's, to all and every thing. The Crowd was

---

[13] William Horn Battle (1802-1879), who, after graduation from the university,
studied law under Leonard Henderson. He represented Franklin County in the
commons in 1833-1834, became reporter of the supreme court, and a member of
the commission to revise the statutes, and moved to Raleigh in 1839. He was a
judge of the superior court, 1840-1848, when he was appointed to the supreme
court, but not being elected, served on the lower court again to 1852. Elevated
then to the higher court, he served until 1868, when he returned to private practice, and again revised the statutes. Upon the reopening of the university, he
became professor of law.

[14] The Young Men's Convention, referred to, was a large and enthusiastic meeting
of Whig politicians, which, in spite of its name, was composed chiefly of those of
fairly ripe years. Its character set a standard for the enthusiasm characteristic of
the following campaign of the Whig party, which inaugurated the hullabaloo
appeal to the emotions of the unthinking which characterized political campaigns
of all parties for many years thereafter, and is by no means unknown today.
James Graham's comment upon it is interesting.

so large but few could hear, or know any thing that was said. When Bascome, a Methodist preacher came forward on the stand to open the meeting *with prayer;* two thirds of those on the out side of the crowd were *shouting* and *Hizzawing,* supposing he was making a political speech. We had all sorts of speaking from the very best to the very worst. The whole affair reminded me of a big Methodist Camp Meeting; zeal and enthusiasm & acclamation were omnipotent. I believe a great multitude of Men, are like a great multitude of *Buffalo's,* they will run over every thing, and often over each other.

North Carolina was very well represented in numbers & talents, though they were nearly all Boys, or very young Men. The Loco foco's are becoming rabid and desperate. They will *die hard*: and struggle to the last. We have some Whigs in Congress that can *out-Democrat* and *out-Demagogue* them. Such chaps as Duncan[15] and Bynum[16] are distressed at seeing an *opposition Line* to their Demagogical Democracy. I hope in Orange you are smart in enlisting smart and popular young men in every neighbourhood to aid the Whig cause.

In Ohio, Wheat is now selling at *Twenty five cents a Bushel;* and Corn at *sixteen cents a Bushel.* Hard-money-prices make hard times to every body, but the *office holders* and the *rich Capitalists.* Labor and Industry are ground into dust & Ashes.

Your County Republican Whig Candidates ought to keep constantly among the people until the Election. Tell the people you are for Gold & Silver money just as long and as far as it can be had and found. But where is it? There is more in the Earth in North Carolina than any other State; and yet all candid men know we have not enough, not half, nor quarter enough to answer the trade and business of our own State. The Rich men may command gold and silver, but the poor people cannot.

The officers and Tax Collectors ought not to be allowed to sell the last Shillings & Sixpences off the necks of little children in order to get in Hard Money $25,000 every year to pay President Van Buren his annual salary. Genl. Harrison is willing to take just such money as the people take in a trade between two neighbours. He is for equal rights to all free men. He is for Gold & Silver, as long as we can find a Penny weight, or coin a Dollar. But like we Farmers have to do, when we can't get Bacon and

---

[15] Alexander Duncan of Ohio.
[16] Jesse A. Bynum.

Beaf enough to feed every body in our household, we are obliged to use Cabbage and Potatoes along with our Meat to make it go far enough to feed and fill all, and the poor as well as the Rich. And if Squire Van Buren should come to my Farm when Meat was scarce, I don't see why he should be *foundered* on Bacon and Beaf, while the rest of the family could'nt get one morsel of Meat, but must work hard and live on Cabbage and Potatoes *only,* that King Martin might be *surfeited* with meat. Bacon & Cabbage is good eating for her Farmers and good enough for any President. In like manner good Metal and good Paper constitute a good currency. Simple comparisons take with the people.

Call on the Van Buren Men to show & explain Where, and how, and When, they are going to get Gold & Silver enough to answer the purposes of Trade and business.

Denounce *bad Banks* and the abuse and excess of Banking; but shew that the Banks never can be made good or compelled to do their Duty and keep their Notes at *Specie par* until the Government receives their paper when it is good; and then the plain working people are inspired with confidence and will take such Bank notes as the Government (the great Creditor) takes. Our friends loose much by becoming the general & indiscriminate advocate of Banks. That is wrong in principle and wrong in policy.

Whenever the Government ceases its war on Banks and will receive the Notes of good specie paying Banks. I will do all I can to compel them to pay specie for all their Notes. I will not defend the conduct of all the Banks. The course of some of them is and has been *Censurable.* But the conduct of the Administration, has been that of an Arch Seducer, they have persuaded and prevailed on the Banks to impregnate and flood the Country with Bastard paper money; and then to hide their own shame and conceal their own destructive measures they (Seducer-Like) charge the Whole blame on the Banks. The Locofocos are like an ill-natured old woman who Whips her child until it cryes; and then, she Whips it for crying. You should call on the Van Buren men to say if they propose to *destroy* the Banks of N. C. If they say yes; then they propose to destroy a large part of our Revenue and the Taxes destroyed in Bank must be imposed on the people and collected in gold & silver.

I have given you a few hints to simplify and make plain. I think the Whigs may gain Orange but they can only do so by activity & industry.

Strange, Fisher & Connor have all gone to N. C. I presume they are political missionaries sent out by the Magician to buy votes.

Try and get Dr. Smith to take the stump *now* and hold on making speeches. My Respects to Sister Susan. I have sent her a good many seeds, I hope she got them.

*From James W. Bryan.*                    U.

Egypt,

May 19th, 1840.

\*    \*    \*    \*    \*

The lines of party are tightly drawn down here, but we have broken through those of our opponents and are making sad ravages upon their ranks. I am nearly worn out with my Circuit and political speech making, in fact I think this Canvass (unless my health becomes very robust) closes my connexion with public life. I am too feeble, and the excitement incident to the Canvass and the stirring times which it gives rise to are very detrimental to my health; but I have put my hand to the plough in this matter & I am sure I shall not look back.

I addressed the citizens of Greene on Thursday last and was succeeded by Morehead & Saunders who kept it up until 9 or 10 o'clock at night. I left Snow Hill before sundown to go partly on my way home & understand that before they closed a personal matter of a very disagreeable character passed between them, one giving the lie, etc., but that they settled it to their mutual satisfaction before they left. We shall certainly carry Morehead through triumphantly in this part of the State unless the signs of the times are most wofully deceptive. Saunders does not seem "to take" with the people, in fact his manner is repulsive to them, and his having been on the Bench lately makes them reluctant to approach him, & they keep up that distant but deferential respect which is usually evinced for a Judge. Consequently they do not seem to chime in with him or his sentiments, or to evince the "hail fellow well met" cordiality which it is very evident they feel for Morehead.

I am now nearly through my District, & when I shall have given all the Counties a taste of the Glories of Harrison, I shall pull up stakes and wend my way to your more salubrious region & endeavour to take some rest from business and politics. When we reach your town we purpose forming a programme of our future peregrinations, etc.

\* \* \* \* \*

We have had an Association at Fort Barnwell, but it happening during my Circuit, I had not the pleasure of attending. I believe they made no converts & were not much encouraged.

The times are so horribly out of joint that Jno. Washington finds it exceedingly difficult in collecting; he told me that he was trying hard to collect funds enough to settle with you.

I rec'd a letter the other day from our agents in Illinois, who stated that we had lost another quarter section in consequence of the lands not being given in; this is really a pretty tale from men who acknowledge themselves to be our agents, and admit that they are, & have been always in ample funds to pay all dues! In fact if some one of us does not go on there, we will loose all the lands in Illinois & I think we will make more by going and attending to them than by remaining at home & the estate of course ought to pay the expenses incident to the same. I wish you could make it convenient to go, it would be a pleasant trip with the present facilities for travelling.

I have hands at work upon your Wharf and Warehouse in Newbern; the work and materials will cost about $150, the work on the Wharf & timber am't to $100. & I expect it will cost $50 to fill it up. The Warehouse I had repaired some time since at a cost of between $25 & $30.

\* \* \* \* \*

We shall send from Craven I think three Whigs, also a gain of one Whig from Greene & I have strong hopes of a Whig Senator from Onslow, the great Citadel of Locofocoism in this part of the State. We have revived the Spectator at a burdensome expense and I wish it's circulation could be promoted in some way or other.

*From James Graham.* U.

Washington, May 20th, 1840.

Fisher has just returned from Salisbury and says the indications are very good for Van Buren and Saunders through out his district. I do not believe it. He boasts that the Merchants, Lawyers, Doctors and rich people who wear Broad Cloth are all for Harrison, but the Farmers, Mechanicks and working folks who wear *Home spun* are for Van Buren. This is the old *Text* of Demagogues. I have always accomodated my *habits* and *Dress* to the People when electioneering and taken the Text out of the mouth of such low fellows. I have always dressed *chiefly in Home spun* when among the people. I was raised in it and am at home in it. When a gentleman is dressed in fine broad cloth and silk and stops to stay all night with a plain poor working man, He often renders the man and all his family unhappy, because they think they cannot entertain him in the same stile he lives at home. I have actually some times felt my self a *sort of Nuisance* when too well dressed in obscure sections. But if a Candidate be dressed Farmer-like he is well received and kindly remembered by the inmates of the Log Cabin, and there is no sensation among the children or the *chickens.* In Orange I presume you will be a Candidate, and as usual the *low party prejudice* will be urged often against your profession of the Law. To that you have a short reply. That you a supporting a *Farmer* for the Presidency, while the loco foco's are going for a Lawyer in the person of Mr. Van Buren. Try & get Dr. Smith immediately to address the People in all parts of his District. Your Hillsboro Recorder is too grave and long in all its Articles to *catch* and *win* the attention of the people. *Short, pithy articles* only will do for the crowd. Wit, Pleasantry, & Anacdote are the weapons for execution. Arguments like cannon will not do for every day fighting.

I think the Republican Whigs may make a great deal out of the *persecutions* and prejudices & falsehoods propagated against Genl. Harrison. If the People once believe any man is persecuted, or unfairly dealt with there is great sympathy felt for him. Harrison's friends may make much out of the abuse and slander which is heaped on him. He not only was longer in service in the war than any other Genl officer and won more victories; but He was the only Genl officer who always Whiped the British and Indians in the United States, still more, he *actually followed them to Canada* and whipped them again at the Thames *on their own soil.* He whipped them on our Land, and then, on their Land, at home & abroad.

North Carolina will immediately be flooded with Papers and speeches for the Van Buren men. They have $30, or 40 millions of the public money in their keeping and using, and they will spend it freely to buy and bribe the people with the public **money.**

If there should be any complaint about my sending Papers in Orange, The Whigs may answer that at once by asking them If I had sent Van Buren's Messages instead of Harrison Lives would there be any complaint among the faithful?

When I had my Contested Election, the Van Buren Members of Congress sent Bushels of Papers into my District and some of the members lived as *far North as New Hampshire.*

The Plan drawn by Poinsett, and endorsed and *Recommended* by Van Buren to organize the Militia and convert them into a standing Army of 200,000 men, is a strong ground of attack on the administration. N. C. and S. C. and Georgia & Florida are to make *one Division.* They are to meet at some Central Point twice a year to Drill and Muster. Now how would the Militia of Orange like to be marched off to Columbia or Augusta *twice a year,* to be disciplined by some Regular federal officer!!! Leave their Wives and Children, loose their Crops and incur heavy private expenses, all in time of Peace to learn *from a Federal Van Buren officer* how to shoulder a Musket, and **Ramdown** a Cartridge. This wild, mad and expensive proposition emanates from the same administration that so *in*gloriously conducts the Florida war. Genl Van Buren's projects *on Paper* are a good deal like his achievements *in the field.* The Sub Treasury I think will pass. It is and has been in practical operation and has produced much distress and Ruin. If the green tree produces such bitter fruits, what will be the poisonous products of the Dry?

Do not be a Candidate at all; or do all that may become a man to be elected. Mix with the common people. They vote for those whom they like.

*From James W. Osborne.*                                  U.

Charlotte,

May 26th, 1840.

\* \* \* \* \*

In Mecklenburg we have at length a ray of promise on the horizon of politics. There is an obvious depreciation of party enthusiasm with Van Buren men; many have openly renounced the trammels of party obligation while individual ambition and internal furor are destroying unanimity and concert. We may not carry the County. Of my own success as a candidate for the

Senate I am now sanguine. I do hope you will carry Orange. The acquisition of that County with the gain in the senatorial districts of the mountains, and the small counties of Cabarrus and Yancey will give us such a number as will secure the legislature beyond any contingency—

Morehead will have your brother's district I am informed by intelligent observers with a majority not short of four thousand. If the East will do its duty we will obtain such a majority as will place Harrison beyond the reach of his competitor.

When you write me advise me of your own prospects, & the prospects generally in the Eastern region.

*From Charles Manly.*                                    U.

Raleigh, 30 May, 1840.

We have procured for the Dutch Country One Thousand Copies of "Lives of Harrison in the Ginuine dutch, with pictures." If you can spread them in Orange, Lincoln, Stokes & Ashe it will help. I have taken the liberty of sending them in a Box to you marked "C. C. Battle." Mr. Allen Brown's wagon will deliver them to you free of charge.

I shall take about 200 Copies with me to Chapel Hill next week for D. M. Barringer.

I hear from all parts of the State we are going it with an *all fired sluice.*

Hurrah for Tip.

*From James Graham.*                                    U.

Washington,

May 31st, 1840.

Mongomery has published one of his demagogical speeches and made some statements in relation to Rainer[17] which the latter denies. An angry correspondence in the Globe was the consequence. The Drs last letter pronounced Rainers letter & *statement to be false.* Rainer after seeing the Drs last letter met him in the Capitol (but out of the House) near the Post Office and without saying one word walked up to him and Slaped his Jaws; Whereupon M. struck R. with a stick on the shoulder and

---

[17] Kenneth Rayner.

broke it. R. then struck M. divers times with a stout stick until he was pulled away from M. In striking, R. held his stick by the small or lower end, and his sword flew out of the stick, but he made no effort to use the sword. There was no injury done. I did not happen to be present to witness the scene.

The Sub Treasury Bill is under discussion and I have no doubt *it will pass*. The Party are becoming rabid and furious at the thought of defeat. I have no doubt they will use exertions such as were never known to carry N. C. in August. I think the Whigs cannot take higher and better ground than that the election of Genl Harrison would alley and *destroy party spirit*. He is and has been in retirement 10 or 12 years working his farm, and his feelings are not embittered with party strife. He fought for the whole Country, and he would, if elected, be the President of the whole people and not the tool and Head of a mere party. God grant the speedy arrival of such a time. We want a change of men, a change of measures and some *Change* in our pockets to pay taxes with & buy salt and necessaries once more.

When the people are called on for Debt and Taxes these hard times, it is a favourable opportunity to remind them of good money and the duty of Government to assist and Compell the Banks to resume by taking their Notes whenever they pay specie for their paper.

*From James Graham.*                                      U.

### H. of R.,

### June 16th, 1840.

You must fight hard and constant in Orange. Our friends make a great mistake in Defending Harrison *only; our true policy is to Charge Van Buren Strongly* and make his friends defend him, or condemn him. Make them say *before they* people: Do they approve his *bauses* & *usurpations,* and *defaulcations?* And giving away the public Land to buy votes in the new States and all other questions, Tarriff and internal improvements by U S?

A new case has just come. Lieutenant Hoe,[18] a Virginian of the Navy, was tried for some affair before a Court Martial at *Pensacola* and the Court permitted *two negroes to be witnesses* and give evidence against him, and he was *convicted.* He appealed

---

[18] This name, as here spelled, does not appear in the register of Officers of the Navy. The name *Hooe* appears twice. Lt. Emmett R. Hooe died 1847, and is clearly the one mentioned here.

from the Judment of the Court, and took the Case before the highest tribunal, President Van Buren. Van Buren took time to examine the Case and approved it, by endorsing on it, that he thought or saw *no grounds* to reverse the decision of the Court & and confirmed the Judgment.

The Northern man with Southern principles is still showing his feelings for *Cuffy*. He thinks negroes and slaves (for one of the witnesses was the *slave of the prosecutor*) may give evidence against a white man in a slave territory. Well according to Van's opinion, A *Rich slave holder* may prosecute *a poor man* and call as a witness, his own slave and *convict him* on the testimony of *black negroes*.

Van thinks free negroes should vote; but He goes further, and says it is his solemn Judgment that a *black Slave* shall give evidence *against a white man* in Slave States! ! !

By this Rule of the President, *property, Reputation, liberty* and *Life* itself may be taken away from us by the evidence of a Negro Slave.

This decission is a part and parcel of his Missouri Restriction and preventing Slaves from going into Arkansas & Florida.

Van's friends only want to get Harrison to come out strong against Abolition votes. And this Florida negro slave witness case proves that Van is *fishing for Abolitionists* with abolition *Bate*. Tappan[19] and Company will like such damnable deeds.

*From Walter Gwynn,[20] to Edward B. Dudley*     U.

22nd. June, 1840.

\* \* \* \* \*

As to the success of draining the Swamp Lands & more than realizing the expectations of its most sanguine advocates you must

---

[19] Benjamin Tappan (1773-1857), of Ohio, native of Massachusetts, printer and engraver, and later a lawyer; member lower house of the legislature, 1833; soldier, War of 1812; state judge of various grades; Federal district judge, 1833-1839; Democratic United States senator, 1839-1845.

[20] Walter Gwynn (1802-1882), a native of Virginia, graduate of West Point, who resigned from the army in 1832, and became an eminent and widely sought consulting engineer. As this letter indicates, he was in the employ of the state for two important projects. He was president of the Portsmouth and Roanoke Railroad, 1842-1846; president of the James River and Kanawha Canal Company, 1846-1847, and chief engineer, 1847-1853; was head of the commission to locate the proposed University of the South, 1857-1858; and during the Civil War, he served first with a state commission as brigadier general of engineers in North Carolina, but later was commissioned colonel, under General Jeremy F. Gilmer, Confederate, chief of engineers.

be under no apprehensions. I have satisfied myself perfectly on this point & look upon it as the most important work in its results now going on in the Southern Country.

In relation to Nag's head, my conclusions are very satisfactory to *myself*. Genl. McRae[21] is the only person who has seen my report and he expresses an entire concurrence with my views.

I have much to say in relation to the Rail Road which I would rather not write, particularly as I shall have the pleasure of seeing you so soon.

A true Copy of a letter on file in the Executive Office.

M. C. Battle
P. Secty.

June 24th, 1840.


*From James Graham.*        U.

H. of R.,

July 3d, 1840.

The Deed is done, the Sub Treasury passed finally this House on yesterday: 124 in the affirmative, and 107 in the negative, majority 17. The Whigs had a number of members absent by sickness and otherwise. Fisher went off to N. C. and did not vote. If all our men had been present, and the *lawful* members of N. Jersey in their seats and this House had not *elected five men* in their stead, we would have defeated them by *one vote*. I spoke about Two Hours and a half against the Bill just before the vote was taken, and will write out my speech when I get time. We had a *real Row* in the House just after the Bill passed; some of the opposition members denounced the Measure as one which power had dictated. At length Pickins[22] (whom the opposition had tried to draw into the debate) rose and pawed and squalled like a Cat with its Tail in the Door and after foaming and frothing a considerable time, he closed by moving the previous

---

[21] Alexander H. McRae, of New Hanover, soldier in the War of 1812, major general of militia for many years, and author of a manual of military organization and training. He was superintendent during construction, and later, president of the Wilmington and Weldon Railroad.

[22] Francis Wilkinson Pickens (1805-1869), of South Carolina, was educated at the University of Georgia and South Carolina College, and became a lawyer. He served in the state legislature, 1832-1834, and was elected to congress as a nullificationist, and served from 1834 to 1843. He was minister to Russia, 1858-1860, and governor of South Carolina, 1860-1863.

question. The indignation of the opposition broke over all rules
and he was hissed or rather Taunted by crying aloud in con-
temptuous derission, "Well done South Carolina Chivalry," and
similar phrases, but the noise was so great that no one could hear
well and it looked like we should have a general fight. If Pickens
had not retreated under cover of the previous question, he would
have been badly *Tomahawked,* and I think he well knew it. We
are quiet to day.

The bustle of winding up the Session has commenced and will
continue to the end. I presume we shall adjourn about the 21st.
inst. I hope you Candidates are all busy and active you ought
all to be out every day and work hard. I am glad your H Recorder has convicted Montgomery, Hawkins, and Co. of suppressing the truth, *the whole truth* in the *Thumb-Paper* issued
*by Fraud* & signed by *conspiracy* of the party and witnesses.

Carry the Law and shew the Fraud *in Suppressing* the Truth
and *deceiving* the people to injure an Honest & faithful old
Soldier. Caution the people against similar impositions. When
they catch Members of C at such *tricks,* they may look out for all
sorts of slanders.

I cant leave here until a week or Ten days after the Adjournment. I wish to write a short Circular and my speech and they
are both quite vexatious. I think I will go to the Virginia Springs
when I leave and spend a few weeks.

I am in the midst of noise and confusion


*From James A. Washington.*                              U.

New York, July 7th, 1840.

I wish I could be with you, Susan and the others of the family
at the gathering at your house. I sometimes feel a longing desire
to be in the midst of my family or to have some or all of you
here. You have however been purchasing a farm of late near
Hillsboro, and therefore contemplate I presume to remain there
permanently. I wish it were so that we could all be together or
near each other. I am sometimes astonished at my remissness in
writing home, which surely proceeds from any thing else than
a want of affection or interest. I keep constantly busy—if not in
attendance upon private patients, upon those of public institutions, being Physician to the Half Orphan Asylum, to the Lying
In Asylum & to the New York City Dispensary; of the two latter

institutions there are also other physicians however. I had intended, again and again, to write you, but have postponed it till now.

*     *     *     *     *

I have just received from France some anatomical models which I think would interest you exceedingly. One of them is peculiarly interesting. It represents a man about 4 feet high with the skin removed and the muscles, blood-vessels and nerves exposed. Muscle after muscle may be removed until you come down to the bony frame work or skeleton and they may be again replaced in a very short time, and the whole human structure may be thus taken apart and put together like any other piece of curious mechanism, so as to enable you in less time than it would seem possible, to understand the various functions of life. I have also large models of the Eye, of the Ear, of the foetal heart, also of the brain & spinal marrow, etc., which are likewise extremely interesting and instructive. The models are made of a material which is so tenacious that it would hardly injure by being thrown upon the floor. It is when about to be manufactured so soft as to run into moulds and when dry very firm and somewhat elastic. There are models which would interest Susan as a materfamilias, which I need not describe. I presume her curiosity as well as your own will be sufficiently awakened by what I have said to induce you both to come on and visit us as soon as you can conveniently. When public lectures were delivered in Paris winter before the last, I think, by the inventor, with his models, to illustrate his courses, the crowd was so great as to require the interference of the Police. I do not contemplate producing so great a sensation. Had I however, more self possession and a tongue more at my command I should take much pleasure in lecturing upon Popular Anatomy and Physiology with such aids to give interest to my lectures. Had I no other object than to make a fortune it would be effected by traversing the country as an itinerant lecturer. The knowledge which could be communicated and the sound advice upon the preservation of health and the proper culture of the physical, intellectual and moral powers to insure their greatest vigour and best condition, would be a noble field of effort; but my duties are at the bedside of the sick and in every sphere of life duty well performed will render our lives useful to others.

*   *   *   *   *

In closing let me say Success to Tippecanoe—notwithstanding Dr. Montgomery and M. T. Hawkins.

*From James Graham.*                                    U

H. of R.,

July 13th, 1840.

I have sent two of my Circular letters in one envelope to each of the names you sent me from Orange Person and Caswell. I have sent you two by mail and two letters by Wm. H. Thomas[23] of Haywood Co., N. C. who is now on his way home.

My Circulars are all in the Mail and on the Road to N. C. (2,500) I am fearful they will be *delayed* in the post offices until *after* the Election. Still I hope they may get on in time.

Since my Circular was known to be published and read there has been a great demand for it by southern members. If the Whigs in Orange should think it will do any good in exposing that *Dirty Thumb paper* of Montgomery & Hawkins They can have one or two thousand printed for Circulation. I made it *short* and *plain* so that *all men* might read and understand.

M. & H. have come out with a second letter trying to sustain their false charges and *gross impositions* on the people. by trying to trade and trafic and make capital upon the prejudices of the People by exciting the passions of the *poor* against the *Rich*. He who protects the *honest poor man,* his conduct is worthy of imitation and all praise; but the *demagurge* who will *pretend* to be the friend of the poor to deceive the poor, *is a wolf in sheeps clothing.* Such fellows remind me of the *Butcher* who tolls the in-

---

[23] William Holland Thomas (1805-1893), of Haywood County, who began his interesting career as a clerk in a Qualla Town store, and later went into business for himself, with much success. He became deeply interested in the Eastern Band of the Cherokee Indians, and was adopted by them, and finally was elected their chief. He was their agent in Washington, and spent some of the time there from 1836 to 1840, and all the time from 1841 to 1848, working in their behalf, to their great benefit. He was a member of the state senate, from 1848 to 1862. He was a pioneer in western North Carolina in his advocacy of good highways and railroad development. Opposed to secession, he threw himself into the struggle, and raised, equipped, and commanded Thomas's Legion, composed of two companies of Cherokees, and fourteen of white men. He also raised four cavalry companies, one of artillery, and one of engineers.

nocent Lamb along with *salt* until he gets him into the Pen and then he cuts his throat.

Prepare *in time* at each *election precinct* & have 3 or 4 active & popular men stationed to aid you on the day of Election. That is a day *for action,* and not argument by our friends. If suitable men be stationed on the ground when the people light to hitch their horses tickets may be given them and march in plattoons to the Polls, still leaving one or two men to watch for others—and so soon as the votes are given let the parties return and look for more votes. In this way you get on smoothly and operate effectively. Guard the Polls well against fraud.

Let your friends be early on the ground on the morning of the Election and open the polls soon in the day, & move actively until the votes are all **taken.**

Montgomery & Hawkins, & many more followers of Van Buren were in the Legislature of N C in 1827 when they ordered the public money to be deposited in the Banks. Inquire of the People, if they are willing to pay their *Taxes only in Gold & Silver.* Where is the money? There are but 80 Millions of specie in U S, and 15 Millions of people. Well we must pay our debts before we divide. The expence of each year since Van Buren came into power is: in 1827—37 millions; *in 1838—39 millions+*; In 1839— 37 millions. They say they are going to reduce. I would rather *see* than hear tell of Reduction:

But take 35 millions only as the govt Expence. 35 from 80 leaves 45—well 15 (millions of People) into 45 will go *3 times,* that is 3 Silver Dollars or $3 in Specie to each individual. Ask the people if they are willing to vote that each person in this great nation shall have but $3. It wont pay Taxes, buy necessaries, or leave any currency to trade on.

This silver scheme of the President will carry all the gold & silver out of N. C. and heap it up in N York and Charleston where specie only will be recd.

You can improve on these Hints

+about one half of all the Specie in U States. [James Graham's note.]

*Broadside*                                                U.

July, 1840.

### Negro Evidence Against White Men.

The Position of the Administration defined—

Van Buren's cloven foot shown—

Negroes to be Witnesses in
all United States Courts against White Men! ! !

In Lieut. Hooe's case, Negro Witnesses were received against
a white man—an Officer in the Navy—a Southern man—and in
a slave-holding Territory—and he was convicted. The President
of the United States was appealed to by Lieut. Hooe, and earnestly entreated to interfere and save him from the sting of a disgraceful punishment, on a conviction supported by Negro testimony. But Mr. Van Buren refused to hear—he refused to see any
thing wrong in the proceedings, and therefore declined to give
redress—so that a gallant young man who had bravely served
his Country was disgraced—reprimanded and dismissed from the
squadron to which he belonged. Mr. Key, the Van Buren Attorney of the District of Columbia, gave a written opinion, that
under the law of the United States, Negroes were good Witnesses
against white men, and therefore the Court in Lieut. Hooe's
trial had acted rightly.

When this shameful trial was first heard of, many Whigs said,
if this testimony could be received in Courts Martial against the
officers and soldiers of the Army and Navy, so could it be against
ALL OF US, in the Federal Courts. This was at first denied, and
it was attempted to make a difference between the two cases;
but now the whole truth is discovered. The opinion of Mr. Van
Buren, of his Naval Secretary, of his District Attorney, and of
his Newspaper, the *Globe,* became known amongst the faithful—
apology is no longer attempted—what has been done is openly
justified, and it becomes at once an article of the Locofoco creed,
that Negroes may lawfully be admitted as Witnesses against
White men—and the Officers appointed by Mr. Van Buren to
prosecute in the United States Courts, do not hesitate openly to
proclaim, that if the Courts will allow them to do so, they
will offer such black Witnesses against any white man whatever,

and will, upon such testimony, convict him of any crime., whether it concerns his character, his person or his life—so far as they can. Such is the despotism of Party—such the degradation to which Van Buren seeks to reduce the once gallant and high-spirited South.

Read the Certificates which follow. Certificates from men of as much truth as live in the world. Read, men of the South! Read, white citizens of North Carolina! and say if you are willing, that your lives—aye, and the lives of your children, shall depend on Negro testimony? Will you support a man like Van Buren, who professing to have Southern feelings, declares that Negroes ought to be Witnesses against white men.

Are you for equality between Negroes and yourselves—between black women and your wives—black children and your children. If you are, vote for Van Buren, and for Van Buren Candidates. But if not—then go to the polls—and vote against every man who supports Van Buren, and thus show your detestation of the man who has grossly insulted the South by declaring *that Negroes are good Witnesses against White Men!*

---

THE CERTIFICATES ABOVE REFERRED TO:

No. 1.

W. R. GALES TO THE HON. JAMES IREDELL.[24]

Raleigh, July 23, 1840.

*My dear Sir,*—I took occasion yesterday in an Address which I delivered to the People, to allude to certain declarations said to have been made in your presence, as I learn from highly respectable authority, by James B. Shepard,[25] Esq. United States Attorney for the district of North-Carolina,—declarations which, if rightly reported to me, go to assert to the fullest extent, the

[24] James Iredell (1788-1853), of Raleigh, a son of Justice James Iredell (1751-1799), of the Supreme Court of the United States. Educated at Princeton, he became a lawyer, was a soldier in the War of 1812, a member of the commons, 1813, 1816-1818, and speaker, 1817-1818; judge, 1819, governor, 1828, and a democratic member of the United States senate, 1828-1831. He was later reporter of the state supreme court for twelve years.

[25] James Biddle Shepard (1815-1871), native of New Bern, graduate of the university, state senate, 1842, house of commons, 1844, United States district attorney, Democratic candidate for governor, 1846, who had a wide reputation as an orator.

principle recognized and sanctioned by Mr. Van Buren, in Lieut. Hooe's case. Believing that the doctrine in that case, sanctioned by Mr. Van Buren, is fraught with danger to our institutions, particularly when a Southern man is found ready to enforce them, I felt it not only my right, but my duty, to make such comments thereon as appeared to me warranted by the facts of the case. I was however greatly surprised, when I alluded to Mr. Shepard's declarations, to hear Major Rand, one of the Administration Candidates, read from the stump, a Communication from that gentleman, in which he denies having used the objectionable language charged upon him. This places me, Sir, in a delicate situation. If I have wronged Mr. Shepard, pray afford me the means of doing him justice before the people. If I have not wronged him, and he has, in the excitement of party discussion, used language which he now seeks, after cool reflection to justify, I ask at your hands that you will afford me the necessary weapons of self-defence. I have charged, that he, Mr. S. said openly, that as United States Attorney, he would be willing to introduce Negro testimony into the Federal Court, and leave it to the Judge to decide as to admissibility; and that he further declared, that he would rely more upon the evidence of a free negro than he would upon that of many a white man. If this statement is substantially correct, please say so. If not, inform me what Mr. Shepard did say, and oblige

Yours, truly,
Weston R. Gales.

---

## No. 2.

### James Iredell To James Shepard, Esq,

Raleigh, July 23, 1840.

Dear Sir:—I have just understood that at a muster in this County, on yesterday, a letter from you relating to a conversation I had with you a few days ago, at the Post Office, in relation to Negro testimony in the Federal Courts, was produced and read. I have been called on by the Whig Candidates, for a statement of the substance of that conversation, and feel myself not only at liberty, but bound to give it, as the conversation was a public one, in the presence of at least fifteen or twenty persons, and as I apprized you that I was adressing you as the Representative of the General Government in the Federal Courts of North-Carolina, and would use your answer before the people. As the purport of your letter may have been misunderstood by the gentleman who communicated to me its contents, I respectfully ask a copy of it, that I may do you no injustice in the Certificate I intend to give.

My Certificate will be given this afternoon, and the copy of your letter, (if you send it to me) shall be returned this evening.

Your respectfully,

JAS. IREDELL.

---

No. 3.

*(Copy of Mr. Shepard's letter, as furnished to Mr. Iredell by himself.)*

---

*Tuesday morning, July* 24, 1840.

JAMES B. SHEPARD TO N. G. RAND,[26]

DEMPSEY B. MASSEY,[27] AND JAMES M. MANGUM.[28]

GENTLEMEN:—I have understood that in several public Speeches delivered by different individuals, the accusation has been made against me of saying, that as District Attorney of the United States, I would admit free Negro testimony against White Men, whenever a fair opportunity offered. I do not hesitate to pronounce the charge either gross misrepresentation, or an unworthy attempt to pervert the truth.

Very respectfully, your obedient servant,

JAMES B. SHEPARD.

---

No. 4.

JAMES IREDELL TO W. R. GALES.

*Raleigh, July* 23, 1840.

Dear Sir:—At your request, I do not hesitate to repeat to you the substance of a conversation which occurred between Jas. B.

---

[26] Nathaniel G. Rand, of Wake, was a member of the commons, 1825-1826, 1830-1833, 1836-1842, 1854-1856.

[27] Dempsey B. Massey, of Wake, was a member of the commons, 1838-1842.

[28] James M. Mangum, of Wake, was a member of the commons, 1838-1842.

Shepard, Esq. District Attorney of North Carolina, and myself, at the Post Office, in this city, some four or five days ago.

I met Mr. Shepard at the Post-Office soon after the arrival of the Northern mail, and before the door of the office was opened, (some fifteen or twenty persons, I presume, were present,) I commenced the conversation by alluding, rather jocularly, to the question which had been discussed that morning in the Tippecanoe Club. Whether Mr. Van Buren had ever shown, by his acts, any republican principles, and asked Mr. Shepard if he could adduce any? Some conversation ensued, which it is unnecessary to relate, as it does not apply to the subject of your letter. I then mentioned to Mr. Shepard the conduct of Mr. Van Buren in relation to the case of Lieut. Hooe, of Virginia, and his approval of the proceedings of a Court Martial, held in a port in Florida, in which negroes had been introduced as witnesses against Lieut. Hooe, and asked him to say, whether he, as the District Attorney of the United States for the district of North Carolina, and therefore representing the Government in all the Courts of that District, would offer to introduce Negro testimony against white men in any of the said Courts, stating to him that, in my opinion, there was no difference in regard to this matter between the rules of evidence in a Court Martial, sitting in a slave-holding State, and a Federal Court, Circuit or District, sitting in a slave-holding State. To this inquiry, I understood Mr. Shepard to reply distinctly, that he would offer such testimony, that is, Negro testimony, against white persons. I expressed my surprise, and told Mr. Shepard I had asked him, as District Attorney, because the people of the State had a right to know by what rules they were to be tried in the Federal Court, to which, in certain cases, they were equally as amenable as to their own State Courts, and that I should make a public use of his answer. I then repeated my question—Mr. Shepard said, it was an *abstract* question; but on my telling him it was an important practical question, in which the people of this State were deeply interested, he replied, that if he had no doubt that the Negro testimony could be introduced against white men under the laws of the United States, he would introduce it; if he had doubts, he would offer the testimony to the Court, and be governed by their opinion. In the course of the conversation, Mr. Shepard *did* say, that there were Negroes, or many Negroes, that he would believe in preference to some white men, or to many white men—the precise words I do not undertake to repeat—but this was the substance. Indeed, in all I have said in relation to this conversation, I cannot give you the exact words, or the precise order in which the conversation occurred, but I cannot be mistaken in saying, I have given you the substance and the meaning of Mr. Shepard's language.

I may be pardoned for adding, that, condemning as I do most strongly, the course of Mr. Van Buren, in relation to Lieut. Hooe's case, I did hope and expect, that when I asked Mr. Shepard the questions I did, that he, although a Van Buren partizan and District Attorney of the U. States for North Carolina, but still born, education and living in a Southern State, would have joined me most heartily in reprobating the introduction of Negro testimony against white men, particularly in our own, or any other Slave-holding State. My disappointment and chagrin were great, when I saw him even hesitate upon this subject, and still greater when he expressed the sentiments I have mentioned.

I may add too, that I had not then, nor have I now, the slightest personal animosity against Mr. Shepard, nor the most remote desire to injure him personally.

Yours,

JA. IREDELL.

---

## No. 5.

### CERTIFICATE.

We, the undersigned, do certify, that we were present at the conversation above alluded to by Gen. IREDELL, and believe his statement of it to be substantially accurate.

| | |
|---|---|
| JNO. M. MASON, | J. A. CAMPBELL. |
| GEO. W. MORDECAI, | WM. PEACE,[30] |
| WM. BOYLAN, | BERNARD DUPUY, |
| GEO. LITTLE,[29] | JAMES LITCHFORD,[31] |
| | GEO. W. POLK, |

[29] George Little (1810-1876), of Raleigh, who was, prior to the Civil War, active and influential in Whig politics.

[30] William Peace (1773-1865), of Raleigh, educated at the university, a merchant of considerable wealth, director of the Bank of the State, founder of Peace Institute.

[31] James J. Litchford (1825-1894), a merchant of Raleigh.

*From James W. Bryan.*                                    U.

Newbern,

Aug. 9th, 1840.

Your majority in Craven is 100—in Carteret between 80 & 100—in Jones 49—in Pitt we learn about 200—in Beaufort Co. (official) 414—in Washington County 237—in Wayne the vote, we learn, stands Graham 317, Shepard 884.

Street [32] is elected over Chadwick,[33] Whig, to the Senate in this Co. by two votes—this election can easily be set aside in favour of Chadwick if it should become necessary. Street has received a number of illegal votes, and Chadwick is truly and honestly elected.

Washington[34] and Guion[35] are elected (Whigs) to the Commons, by large majorities. Howard [36] is elected in the Senatorial district of Jones and Carteret, and Foy,[37] Whig, from Jones, in the Commons. Piggott,[38] Whig, is elected from Carteret. Wm. Ferrand,[39] Loco, is elected to the Senate in Onslow, & Cox in the Commons. We have gained a member in Lenoir;[40] he has heretofore been an "independent," but will vote with the Whigs now. Speight [41] has beaten Taylor[42] (Whig) in the Senatorial district of Greene and Lenoir—and Edwards[43] has beaten Horn, Whig, in Greene. This is all the election news we have.

We reached home safely and leave for Beaufort the last of this week. I have only time to write you this short note.

---

[32] Nathan H. Street, of New Bern, state senator, 1846, 1860.

[33] Samuel Chadwick, of New Bern, member of the commons, 1854.

[34] William Henry Washington, of Craven, member of congress, 1841-1843, of the commons, 1846, and of the state senate, 1848-1852.

[35] Henry T. Guion, of Craven, member of the commons, 1846.

[36] James W. Howard, of Jones, member of the commons, 1831, 1834-1835, state senator, 1842, 1846.

[37] William Foy, of Jones, member of the commons, 1844-1846.

[38] Jennings Piggott, of Carteret, member of the commons, 1846-1850. In December, 1862, he was elected to the Federal congress in a so-called election, ordered by Edward Stanly as military governor, but was not seated.

[39] William Pugh Ferrand, of Onslow, briefly a student of the university, a physician, member of the commons, 1826. He was not elected nor was Cox.

[40] Jesse Jackson, of Lenoir, member of the commons, 1844-1846.

[41] Edwin G. Speight, of Greene, member of the state senate, 1842-1850.

[42] John W. Taylor, of Greene, member of the commons, 1840-1842.

[43] James G. Edwards, of Greene, member of the commons, 1844-1848.

*To James W. Bryan.*          U. Bryan Mss.

Hillsboro', Aug. 15th, 1840.

Our election in Orange has resulted in a decisive victory over Locofocoism.

Polls—G.[ov.]  Morehead  1664  Saunders  1549  Maj  115.
        S.,[enate]  Mangum  783  Allison  730  Maj  50.
C[ommons]  Graham  1720  Holt[44]  1686  King[45]  1656  J. Grahams[46]  1564  Stockard[47]  1566,  Trolinger[48]  1563,  Jones 1571,  Horner[49]  1480,  Sheriff  Turrentine[50]  W[hig]  1784, Shaw V[an Buren], 1404.

So you will perceive that we have carried the election of Governor, Senator and three out of 4 Commoners, and the fourth was only lost by the folly of our friends, in voting for Jones at this precinct, from merely personal considerations. You see that his majority is but 7 votes over J. Grahams although he was 30 stronger than the vote of party at Hillsborough precinct. The triumph, however, is great though not perfect and has quite crushed the spirits of the Locos.

Our labors were uninterrupted almost untill the election—Besides the electioneering resignations of Messrs. Brown and Strange, Montgomery came home and threw himself into the scale of our competitors, made a speech for them in one of their strongest sections after the campaign had closed. But it was all in vain; the real Whig strength of the County when fully displayed surprized many of our own friends. My vote in this election, is the highest that has been ever given to any individual in a contest for the Legislature.

In Wake all is lost and Saunders majority is 127. In Guilford, Morehead has a majority of about 1800 and in Davidson of 900. On the stage waybill last night is "good news from Stokes" but no details. You have no doubt heard of the triumphs in Halifax

---

[44] Michael William Holt (1811-1858), who began his political career as a member of the commons in 1804. He was state senator in 1820-1821, and again in the commons in 1840, and was the first senator from Alamance after its creation, in 1852.

[45] Nathaniel J. King had served in the preceding session of the legislature.

[46] James Grahams cannot be identified. He lived in the northern part of Orange. This was his sole election to the legislature.

[47] John Stockard served in the commons, 1826-1830, 1833-1836, 1838, 1842, 1848.

[48] Benjamin Trolinger, a Democratic wheel-horse, who had served in the preceding legislature.

[49] William Horner, a Democrat.

[50] James C. Turrentine, the incumbent.

and Northampton. I regard it as now certain that we shall have a majority in the Legislature of at least 15 on joint ballot, and will elect Morehead by 4,000 maj.

Brown is haranguing in the mountains, and Strange on the Cape Fear, but it will "signify nothing." We will endeavour to get Smith into the field immediately, but I fear he has not energy enough for the crisis.

My family are all in good health. Both your children appear improved. I am myself sunburnt almost to the complexion of the redman, but am invigorated by the exercise and excitement of the campaign. Mangum kept the field constantly untill the day of election. Old "Santer Anner" has been terribly bedeviled, and is deeply mortified.

I saw at Carvills last summer a small treatise on the roads of that State, etc. May I trouble you to purchase it and send me as well as any other information on the construction etc. of Turnpike roads? I wish it, with reference to our contemplated road from Raleigh to Greensboro. Be pleased also to purchase for me a neat family Bible with a blank register, etc., and a copy of the New Testament in large type for Susan. She wrote you a few days ago requesting the favor of buying for her a piano and inclosing a check for $260. Please ship the whole to the care of White and Blume, Petersburg, Va., and inform me of the cost of the books, that I may forward it directly.

I believe we have nothing in the way of news except the elections; the affair between Gov. Iredell and Shepard [51] occasioned some fighting among the certifiers, the particulars of which I have not heard. Barnett is beaten in Person 15 votes.

*From James W. Osborne.*                                    U.

Charlotte,

August 26th, 1840.

\*     \*     \*     \*     \*

We have had an ardent struggle and a glorious result. It exceeds the most sanguine expectations of the Whigs and is overwhelming to their adversaries. They were not prepared for such

---

[51] This has reference, probably, to the certificate of Iredell, with reference to James B. Shepard's attitude towards the employment of Negro testimony in the case of Lieutenant Emmett R. Hooe.

a disaster. Mr. Haywood of Raleigh, who is yet the presiding genius of the *faction*, had laid his calculations before their leaders in this region, had minutely detailed the state of affairs in each County—in a manly spirit had conceded that the result of the canvass for the office of Governor was doubtful, but that they should feel defeated if their majority in the Legislature was not as great as ten or twelve. I do trust that among other beneficial results of our victory we may never hear more of him or his calculations.

I was overjoyed at the result of your canvass in Orange. Your election was always too certain in my own estimation to admit of apprehension, but I feared and felt deeply for our friends Mangum, Holt, and King. To friend Holt give my respects and congratulations. It was almost unreasonable to expect anything from a people whose political prejudices are so inviolate as in Mecklenburg. The worst doctrines of the worst era have been long since imbibed and cherished among the people of Mecklenburg. I stemmed a heavy torrent of political prejudice, besides resisting almost single handed base personalities and low scurrility.

If the polls were now purged, among my friends a general impression prevails that I am elected. The effort however—tho' strongly urged to do so—I shall not make. It is possible that I may see your City during the month of October. If so, I shall be most happy to make the acquaintance of your fair cousin.

In this region there is some speculation as to the choice of Senators. Mangum, with several prominent Whigs, I regret to learn, is not acceptable. Gaston, Badger, & yourself are among the persons towards whom conjecture points. I need not assure you how gratifying your election to that distinguished station would be to my own feeling, not only because it would be a theatre on which the highest honors within reach of an American citizen may be won, but because of my feelings as a relation, and the earliest recollections of my boyhood.

Business will place it out of my power to visit Raleigh during the session. At that time I will be in Alabama looking after a cotton plantation, and its various interests.

I think the Whigs should take ways and means to keep the good spirit alive until November. The Locos have no hope but from our supineness.

*From James W. Bryan.* U.

Saratoga Springs,

Aug. 29th, 1840.

We reached here on Tuesday last, & found quite an agreeable company assembled at the Springs. We stopped at the United States Hotel & soon made a very agreeable and fashionable acquaintance. The Court of Errors is in session here, and I have been a constant attendant on their sittings. Many of their most distinguished Lawyers have addressed the Court, and on today a cause of much interest involving the right of Trinity Church to a large portion of their city property was taken up. Mr. B. F. Butler is now addressing the Court in reply to an argument made by a Mr. Warner for the Claimants, (Pltffs) and he will be succeeded by D. B. Ogden on the same side. If you think seriously of ever leaving old N. C. come to N. York and your future will be made at the Bar; their best lawyers with one or two exceptions are very ordinary men, and they are crowded they tell me with more business than they can possibly attend to and that too which commands fees worth receiving. Our people are too poor and their cases to insignificant ever to pay a lawyer in N. C. for his services unless he resorts to a system which they would deem extortion. When I return to N. C. I will shew you how their causes are prepared for argument in the Court of Errors.

We have made many interesting acquaintances & seen many grotesque looking beings here; the present fashionable style is to have the hair to grow from the corners of your mouth and meet in a tuft under the nose, so that you may keep it moving in gentle undulations with the breath of your nostrils. A larger tuft projects from the extremity of the chin like the top of a little pine sapling, and the more you grease the whole concern when eating the more luxuriant and rich it becomes. There are several ourang outang looking fellows here, who would certainly produce a miscarriage upon some of our delicate married females if they were not exceedingly fashionable themselves. I think I could make money by shewing them in N. C. So much for the men; the women are some of them no better. They wear on their rumps little mountains, not quite as high as the hill on which Mr. Norwood lives, which elevate the whole body of their clothes, exposing their beautiful legs and "calves" and give them a bobbing about motion, which adds very much to their grace and gentility. I saw one of them in St. Thomas' Church in N. Y. with a tumor on so large that it was with much difficulty she could squeeze into the pew door with the thing. I am within bounds when I say that it was as large as a dinner pot. What a thing it must be in warm weather!

I have advised with some of the Whigs, and they intend to congratulate our State on their late Signal Success, at their Convention which meets at Syracuse on the 16th. of next month. I should be glad to hear from our State. Who are to be the Senators & who the Judge in place of Judge Toomer? [52]

Col. Ruffin (the Judge's brother) is here, with a large party from Alabama, and we are the sole representatives from the old North State.

*     *     *     *     *

I was exceedingly gratified to perceive that you had obtained so large a vote and that so many of your ticket had succeeded.

Gen'l Scott [53] is here, and it is said would like to know whether it would be agreeable for him to follow in the footsteps of Gen'l Harrison, as it seems to be generally conceded that he will be the next President. We are much pleased with Lt. Gov. Bradish [54] here; he is very courteous and polite and quite a "Lady's man." Ann and Cousin Eliza are delighted with him.

Well—Can you read this? for I have been unable in the whole establishment to get a pen! As I did not intend the characters for heiroglyphics I hope you will make it out.

*     *     *     *     *

[52] John De Rosset Toomer (d. 1856), of Cumberland, briefly a student at the university, an able lawyer, a judge of the superior court, 1818-1819, appointed to the supreme court in 1829, and not elected, again a judge, 1837-1840. In the interim, he was a member of the commons, 1826, state senator, 1831-1832, and a delegate to the convention of 1835.

[53] Winfield Scott (1786-1866), native of Virginia, who had had a brilliant army career, beginning with the War of 1812, and who was, at this time, the ranking officer in the army. Mentioned for President in 1839, he never lost hope until after Lincoln's election. He and Graham were to head the Whig ticket in 1852.

[54] Luther Bradish (1783-1863), of New York, a native of Massachusetts, a graduate of Williams College; lawyer, soldier in the War of 1812; diplomatic commissioner to Turkey, 1820; Whig member assembly, 1827-1830, 1835-1838; (speaker, 1838), lieutenant-governor, 1838-1842; president of the New York Historical Society, 1849-1863.

*From James Graham.*                                    U.

Charlottsville,

Sept. 4th, 1840.

I have been at Washington since Congress adjourned sending off Papers of various sorts to all parts of N. C., and lastly I have sent out 4000 Copies of my speech, and the Congressional Committee have just ordered *Ten Thousand* of them to be published for other States. I have stayed so long I believe I will go by the Virginia Springs and stay a week and then go to Guiandot and take the Ohio River for Memphis, Ten., so as to reach home the last of October. . . .

*    *    *    *    *

I think your prospect to be elected a Senator in place of Brown, whole *full Term* is vacant, may be very good. I think you had better extend some marked civility to the members of Assembly, while of course you would say but little on that subject except to confidential friends. You will of course first run for the Speaker's Chair.

Every *possible effort* should be made to carry the presidential election in Nov. There is great danger from *fancied security.* Four years ago when Dudly was elected, the Whigs reposed upon their laurels while the friends of power gathered strength from defeat and disciplined their forces and won victory.

My contested Election was the result on the part of my friends of supposed Security and they did not go to the Polls. I tried to prevail on them to be active, but they laughed at me when I talked of danger. Let every County and Captains company have its organization and persons appointed in each Company to go round among the people a few days before the election to prevail on them to be sure to go and vote; let no one stay at home. Dr. Smith should be active, and speak often at public places. The young men *are the Boys for this Contest;* they are captivated with military glory. There is more *Huzza* in old Tip, than any body is aware of. Make *no issues* with Jackson, let him alone; give his letters the go-bye. *hold Van up,* on the Sub Treasury the *Militia Army,* the negro testimony, the Expenditures, the Defaulters, the want of Capacity to manage the Florida War, which has now lost 25 millions.

A change of men is necessary to investigate frauds. Power will never condemn itself. Low wages and prices. Every thing depends on efficient and systematic arrangements. Each of our N Papers should keep a *standing column of the Majorities* in Kentucky, 16,000, Indiana, 9,000, Virginia, 3,000, Louisiana, 25,000 and N. Carolina, 8,700. This will encourage friends and discourage enemies. Have *no* festivals or barbecues. Send out *short tracts, Extracts,* Letters or *Speeches,* where the facts can be seen quickly and Clearly. I do believe N. C. *is in great danger.* The *Presidential purse* & *foreign* interference will be actively exorcised. Warn our people of its approach. Our Ancestors in the Revolution *made Gov. Martin take water,* when he was the tool of the King; now let us make President Martin's foreign tools, pimps, and parasites, and slaves of power and the Palace *take water,* or run them up a Gum.

If Van had not the public money (30 or 40 Millions) in his britches pocket, he could not stand-up long enough to be knocked down in this contest. But no matter what a President does or says, at least 7 *excuses* can be offered for him, one for each of the five loaves and two fishes in the Treasury. The *weakest King* in Europe is dangerous with the public money in his pocket. And the most talented man in any Kingdom can't do much harm without the money.

Let the Whigs hold on to the word & name *Republican* on all occasions and put it on their Ticket.

In the Presidential contest *every vote counts,* hence in counties like Caswell they should be active & organize.

If you carry *Orange* in Nov., the Whigs will hold it for years, and if you do not, *the loco's* will be hard to beat. You can do much by enlisting substantial Farmers and Mechanicks, but above all attend *to the young men in this election,* Give them songs & anacdotes, they are often better than reasons and arguments before the People.

I have sent my speeches to all the persons on the lists I had from Orange, Person, & Caswell and five speeches *to each* of the Whig electors in the State.

The members elected in each county to the Legislature can do much if they will be active. Gov Morehead by writing to his friends in different parts of the State can do much to encourage them to action.

\*    \*    \*    \*    \*

My health is good, I have derived great benefit from the constant use of a *Flesh Brush* and *regular Exercise,* if I could work two hours every day, I should have first rate health—I am fearful you do not exercise enough.

*Political Invitation*                    U.

Surry County, Sept. 15, 1840.

SIR:

The Whigs of Surry County, grateful for the success of their cause, as manifested by the result of the late elections in this and in other States of the Union, and believing that their principles, if known and understood, would be more generally, if not universally adopted, have determined to hold a meeting of the friends of Harrison and Reform, at the town of Rockford, in said county, on Tuesday, the 20th. day of October next.

The undersigned, acting in behalf of their Whig brethren, most respectfully invite you to attend on that occasion, to partake of the festivities of the day, and to cheer and animate us by your example. Your known devotion to the cause, gives an assurance, we hope, that we shall not be disappointed in having the pleasure of your company.

Richard C. Puryear, Nathaniel Boyden, Columbus Franklin, Henry P. Poindexter, Francis P. Clingman, Nicholas L. Williams, William D. Somers, Josiah Cowles, Nathan Hunt, T. J. Williams, Benj'n F. Menafee, Isaac Jarratt, Tiry Glenn.

Com. of Invitat'n.

*Invitation to speak at Williamston.*          U.

Williamston,

Sept. 15th., 1840.

A Convention of the people this and other adjoining Counties will be held at Hamilton on the 21st. day of October next, at which place extensive preparations are being made for a festival on that Occasion.

Your zeal and energy in the great Cause of Harrison reform have induced your Committee to express to you their admiration of your efforts and earnestly desire that your convenience will permit you to meet our fellow Citizens on that Occasion.

With Sentiments of great regard,

Your Ob't Serv'ts,

Jos. J. Williams, Jno. B. Griffin, S. W. Bagley, J. H. Burnette, S. M. Smithwick, Wm. J. Ellison, C B. Russell.
Committee.


*From Matthias E. Manly.*                    U.

Newbern, Nov. 12th, 1840.

My dear Graham

Several persons in this part of the State feeling the necessity of a resident judge in the district have pressed me to allow my name to be put before the Legislature for one of the vacancies to be filled by that body this winter.

I have said that with the approbation of some of my friends in the Legislature and elsewhere I would consent.

What think you of it?

I have much confidence in your judgment as well as in your friendly regard and shall feel perfectly safe in your hands.

After consultation with the members of the house of Commons from this County, (who are my friends), with my brother, and any others whom you may think proper to consult, I know you will be able to mark out such a course as will best become all parties.

I am actuated in yielding to the wishes of gentlemen and allowing myself to be put before the Legislature by an impression that my habits of acting, thinking, & speaking are better suited to the bench than the bar: and I doubt not a similar impression has influenced the selection of myself in preference to others who are equally well, if not better qualified in other respects.

The gentlemen of the bar in this part of the State, with the cooperation of the Governor placed me before the Council in the Summer, but I was not the choice of that body. Of this, I dare say, you have had an account.

I mention now to show that I ought not to be considered in the light of an opponent of the executive appointments, but on the contrary as one who has been opposed in an unusual manner and who is seeking to be reinstated in the position where the Council found him.

May I rely upon your accustomed frankness for your exact views in relation to this matter, and upon your friendship for such advice and aid as may be needful in the progress of it?

This is the day of the election for President and Vice President. I hope and believe it has resulted in North Carolina, as elsewhere, in such a manner as to shake and put down all selfish and un-principled politicians for a century to come.

We have heard only from a few precincts in this county

|          | Harrison      | Van Buren |
|----------|---------------|-----------|
| Newbern  | 139 Majority  |           |
| Ives     | 17            | 29        |

These two Whig precincts shew a Whig gain In August New-bern gave a majority of one hundred and ten only for the Whigs, and Ives a majority of twenty one for the loco party

I fear you will be a little bothered to agree upon two fitting persons to fill the vacant seats in the Senate of the U. S. Com-promise must be resorted to and the best selected without ref-erence to their local positions.

I should like to be in Raleigh and throw in my mite of counsel in the premises. If you decide to dispose of the Judgeships earlier [illegible] I may yet be with you.

*To James W. Bryan.*          U. Bryan Mss.

Raleigh, Nov. 18th, 1840.

You will perceive by the Register that the Legislature has been organized, by the appointment of the old Speakers and Clerks in both houses. Many of our friends had desired that Gales should be elected, instead of Stone in the Senate, but a few seemed rather disposed to patronize dullness and Locofocoism, than to hazard the imputation of proscription. The V. B. men desired in the Commons that they should not be obliged to vote in the election of Speaker, and suggested that no vote should be taken. They seem exceedingly amiable, but are confident in the belief that they can controul one of the appointments to the Senate U. S. It seems now to be conceded that Mangum will be elected to Brown's seat, and the long term. There will be some difficulty in relation to the other. L. Williams is here, and came prepared

to make war on Mangum, but perceiving the current of public
sentiment, he is said to be changing his tone and going for the
other seat. He can do nothing for himself, but has a fraction of
the party who may be mischievous. Badger is in a bad humour and
says he thinks we have a bootless triumph. He has anxious friends
but can't get a majority of the party. I believe he will be satisfied, however, as it is designed to recommend him by Legislative
Convention for the office of Atto. Genl.

Swain has a considerable anxiety, and may get a considerable
number of votes. Gov. Owen brings but one vote from his Congressional district, and (although the choice of the people of
Raleigh) cannot succeed except after many trials. W. B. Shepard,
I think, can do nothing. It is said that Williams, on finding that
his own prospects are not the brightest, is for Aug. Shepperd.
I have not moved myself on the subject, though some of my
friends are busy in making inquiries, and say that if Badger &
Swain are disposed of, I shall be certainly chosen. There is to a
grand Caucus tonight to make arrangements, and probably to
determine the election.

I have received a letter from our friend Manly in relation to
the Judicial appointment. Please say to him that I have not yet
been able to satisfy myself on the subject, & that I will write him
by the mail of Friday. Battle, I presume, will be reappointed.
Hall,[55] so far as I can now judge, will not. D. F. Caldwell of
Salisbury is a Candidate and will be formidable, whether to success or not, I cannot say. Indeed every body is so agog, about the
election of Senators that there are few developments about anything else.

I have not seen your brother since my arrival. McQueen[56] is in
the field for Atto. Genl. and Badger proposes Edwd. Stanly.
Guinn, Gaither, and Bynum[57] are Candidates for Sol. in the

[55] Edward Hall (1795-1877), of Warren, son of Judge John Hall, graduate of the
university, who had been appointed by the governor a judge of the superior court.
He failed of election later.

[56] Hugh McQueen, of Chatham and Wake, briefly a student of the university,
lawyer, member of the commons, 1829-1833, state senator, 1834-1835, delegate
convention of 1835, and attorney general, 1840-1842. He was editor of the Columbian
Repository, the Emerald, and the Raleigh Star, all for brief periods, and the
author of a manual of oratory. Little is known of him today, but his reputation
for brains and ability has defied the years.

[57] John Gray Bynum (1813-1857), of Stokes, Lincoln, and Rutherford, a graduate
of the university, state senator, 1840, 1850, member of the commons, 1854. He was
editor of the Carolina Gazette, and author of the Western Address of 1851. He
studied law under Judge Gaston, and became a highly successful practitioner. He
was brilliant, forceful, and aggressive.

mountain riding, and Dodge,[58] Horn,[59] Jones[60] & Genl Cook [61] in the next one to it. The last are a thirsty trio. I neglected say that Judge Gaston has been written to by Clingman, asking his consent to run for the Senate, and the reply was expected last night. But I have not heard what it is. He is said to have written a letter to Chatham[62] putting himself at the command of his friends, etc. He will be strong if brought forward, but cannot get some members of the party at all.

*   *   *   *   *

I will write from here to Judge R.[63] in relation to the Reporters office. I have not seen him since the summer term of the Court.
[P.S.] The Presidential election has been a perfect hurricane. The majority in N. C. will be 12,000.
Judge Barbour[64] adjourned his Court on Monday. He has been occupying Mrs. Taylor's office, & had many visits from Candidates for Clerks, doorkeepers, etc., on my account. He is a pleasant old gentleman & a great talker.

---

[58] James R. Dodge (1795-1880), a native of New York, aide to his father, a general officer in the War of 1812, he came to the state more or less by accident. Wrecked on his way to Charleston in 1817, he landed at Norfolk, drifted to Petersburg, where he studied law under the famous David Robertson, who introduced him to Judge Ruffin, who befriended him, as did a number of prominent lawyers. He settled in Stokes, and married a niece of the famous Williams brothers, was solicitor, clerk in the legislature, and, finally, clerk of the supreme court at its Morganton division, 1847-1858. He became the intimate friend of Ruffin, Badger, Graham, the Manlys, Henderson, Morehead, and Gaston. He was a nephew of Washington Irving.

[59] Probably Nicholas Horn, of Surry, a member of the commons, 1802-1812, 1814. His name was not presented.

[60] Hamilton Chamberlain Jones (1798-1868), a native of Virginia, a graduate of the university, who read law under Judge Gaston, and then settled at Salisbury, where he founded the *Carolina Watchman,* which became an influential Whig paper. He was a member of the commons, 1827, 1829, 1838-1840, 1848; solicitor, 1840-1848; and reporter of the supreme court.

[61] Probably James Cook, of Davie County.

[62] I have been unable to discover to whom Judge Gaston was supposed to have sent it, and it is not likely that such a letter was written. The correespondence in the Gaston Papers has a number of such requests to him, and his reply in every case, was a courteous refusal.

[63] Judge Thomas Ruffin.

[64] Philip Pendleton Barbour (1783-1841), of Virginia, a graduate of William and Mary, member of the delegates, 1812-1814, member of congress, 1814-1825, (speaker, 1821-1823), 1827-1830, judge of the Federal district court, associate justice of the supreme court of the United States, 1836-1841. He refused many other important posts.

*To James W. Bryan.*                    U. Bryan Mss.

Raleigh, Nov. 21st, 1840.

I wrote Mr. Manly by the last mail, advising him to come to Raleigh forthwith. It is now conceded even by Badger, the God-father of Hall, that he has failed to realize the public wish, and that he will not do. Caldwell of Salisbury declines, and there is no certainty as to the other Candidates, who they may be, or what will be their prospects. Swain is now talked of, Roberts[65] of Buncombe, & Winston—the last of whom will probably be a Can-didate for Atto. Genl. however. Your brother refuses to receive it, Moore[66] of Halifax & Iredell are now mentioned in connexion with it. But the wishes of neither is known to me.

There was a party meeting on Wednesday evening at which there was no little wrangling in relation to the election of Sen-ators. Williams or (as he is here called) "Panther Creek," was represented there by the members from his district headed by Boyden[67] & Bynum. They refused to be governed by the wishes of a majority for some time. But after another resolution that the party would support no one who was not a friend of a Bank of U. S. and the distribution of the public lands, they finally assented, and Monday night was appointed for the filling of the appointments. Mangum was then nominated for the long term & called out on the questions already mentioned, he avowing his consent to both. Shepard was then nominated by Speed for the short term—2 years. My name was then added, and Boyden men-tioned Williams, Badger, Gaston, & Swain as probable Candi-

---

[65] Joshua Roberts (1795-1865), a native of Cleveland County, a lawyer, who lived in Macon County, and later in Buncombe, where he established the first newspaper in western North Carolina.

[66] Bartholomew Figures Moore (1801-1878), of Halifax, a graduate of the univer-sity, a Whig lawyer, who served in the commons, 1836-1846, and was deeply interested in internal improvements, and care of the unfortunate. He was attorney general, 1848-1851, and one of the commission to revise the statutes, 1851. He was bitterly opposed to secession, and declined to take an oath to support the Confed-erate constitution. He was an influential member of the convention of 1865, and he wrote the code for the freedman, notable for its moderation, which the legis-lature adopted. He opposed congressional reconstruction.

[67] Nathaniel Boyden (1796-1873), a native of Massachusetts, who, after graduation from Union College, came to Guilford, and then to Stokes, as a teacher. He studied law, was a Whig member of the commons from Stokes, 1838-1840, and, moving to Salisbury in 1842, was state senator in 1844, and a member of congress, 1847-1849. He was a delegate to the convention of 1865, again member of congress, as a Republican, 1868-1869, and a justice of the state supreme court, 1872-1873.

dates. Dr. Hill[68] proposed Gov. Owen. And Dr. Hellen[69] nominated you. Shepard[70] & myself were called on for our opinions as Mangum had been, & he gave his full approval of a Bank, tho' at the last Session he proposed three and made a speech which is said to have condemned the idea of one. He is also anxious to have the Federal Government patronize Nags Head, & rallies the support of his section on that question. Mr. Pettigrew[71] is here doing something for him, and attempts are also making on the members from your district in his behalf. The contest for the short term will be between him and myself, and our friends believe I shall receive the nomination of the party by a large majority. Mangum will be elected, I think, to the long term without difficulty, though I hear today that the war will be renewed upon him at the next meeting, and it may be attempted to be shewn that he has given written pledges against a Bank. Much acerbity may be produced but his election cannot be prevented. I have not spoken of the subject except in the circle of those, who have mentioned the matter to me. I find my nomination acceptable in many quarters that I had formerly doubted. But for the hope which has by some been entertained untill now of electing Gaston or Badger, I believe I would receive the nomination for the six years. I have had no conversation with the members from the New Bern riding. Attempts I know, are made to carry them for Mr. S. and their Eastern feelings are strongly appealed to. Without them, I believe the party nomination can be had, though I presume that some of them, at least, will be with us. I have perceived much jealousy among portions of the Whigs, and fear that the Session will not pass over without some defection from the ranks.

I will write you again after the nominations are determined on, Provided they are made by Wednesday.

I learn from your brother, that you will be here the last of next week. Nothing of consequence has been introduced as yet, and but little will be done untill after the elections.

[68] Frederick Jones Hill (1790-1861), of "Orton," Brunswick County, and of Chatham, physician and planter, state senator, 1835, delegate to the convention of 1835, member of the commons, 1836-1842.

[69] Isaac Hellen, of Carteret, member of the commons, 1818-1820, 1822-1823, state senate, 1840, 1844.

[70] William B. Shepard.

[71] Ebenezer Pettigrew (1783-1848), of Tyrell County, who attended the university in its opening year, was an extensive planter, was state senator, 1809-1810, and a member of congress, 1835-1837.

. . . The Railroad Companies are both beggars for patronage
& in debt.
[P.S.] Mr. J. Hawks is here, a Candidate for Judge but looks
lonesome.

*From Maurice Q. Waddell.*[72]                     U.

Pittsboro, Novr. 22d, 1840.

My Dear Graham

I learn with much pleasure thro an individual travelling thru
our Village that you have been elected by the Legislature to the
Senate of the United States,[73] this at all times and under any circumstances would have been gratifying to your friends, but peculiarly so under existing circumstances. Here was a party in the
Legislature with sufficient majorities in both Houses to accomplish any end they desired with the State before them to choose
their Senators; there were aspirants to office *aged* and *dignified;*
there were others who believed all that was necessary to insure
their election was to let themselves down from their *high estate*
and claim the places they believed the community was ready to
grant them, without having ever once rendered important service
to the cause which gave the Whigs the ability to clothe them
with such authority. Under all these circumstances it is gratifying
to see that the talents and Patriotism of one so young in years as
yourself Should overcome the projudices which I feared might
operate against your claim, in the general belief that *age* rendered an individual more sapient; so I believe Hugh [74] reckoned
Judge Norwood as an advocate of when he insisted that the Judge
would neither listen or place confidence in any one at the Bar
unless he was an *old fool.*

Your friends have cause to be proud of this distinction and as
one of them you must excuse the liberty I take of writing you congratulations upon the subject.

As a member of the Senate of the United States it is possible
after Genl Harrisons inauguration you may have my name before
the Senate for the office of Receiver of the Land office at Natche-
toches, Louisiana. This cannot occur however until the next Session of Congress as there will be no Senate after the 4th March

---

[72] Maurice Quince Waddell (1838-1888), of Chatham, a brother of Hugh Waddell,
studied briefly at the university, served in the commons, 1838, 1846, and was clerk
and master in equity.
[73] The traveller had evidently been only informed of the nomination of Graham
by the Whig caucus, as he was not elected until the 24th. See his letter of that
date to Mrs. Graham, and also the legislative journal.
[74] Hugh Waddell.

next until the next meeting of Congress which will confirm all appointments by the President but in the mean time Genl Harrison will vacate the seat of the present incumbent, I have no doubt, and ought to do so, and I will be greatly obliged to you to represent me favourably at Washington so that when application is made my claims (if any I have) may be strengthened. The Situation is one which will suit me remarkably well in connection with my other business then I can make it a lucrative one.

Any and all interest you will take in this matter for me will be thankfully received by your friend.

*To Susan Washington Graham.*    A.

Raleigh, Nov. 24th, 1840.

My Dear Susan:

I was this day elected to the Senate of the United States, for the residue of the term of Mr. Strange, it being for two years after the fourth of March next. Mr. Mangum was elected to the vacancy of Mr. Brown, and also for the term of six years after the fourth of March.

Though my appointment is grateful to my feelings, as a manifestation of public esteem unusual to one of my age,[75] it is still a

---

[75] Whig editorial comment upon Graham's election was almost universally favorable, and a number of Democratic papers expressed pleasure at his selection, if a Whig had to be chosen. The two editorials which follow, are examples of Whig sentiment:

"It was a remark of Lord Bacon, we think, that men are apt to be envious of those near their own age and condition, who may be raised to exalted station. This may be a reason why a shade of dissatisfaction, to some, accompanied the announcement of Mr. Graham's election, over many *grayer, not sounder,* heads. He is probably the youngest member of the Senate. But the idea will at once strike every one at all acquainted with Mr. Graham, that another member of the Senate cannot be found, combining more of usefulness—more of the decision of business habits with highly accomplished talent. And he will carry into that august body more weight than any man of his age in the State. Besides, he is a Whig—mild, firm, consistent, liberal,—but every inch a Whig. Under all the circumstances, a more satisfactory appointment could hardly have been made from the host of North Carolina patriots."

*Greensboro Patriot,* quoted
in *Hillsborough Recorder,* Dec. 10th,
1840.

"I rejoice that our State is at length represented by men who will do her justice. The calm dignity of Mr. Graham's character, his firm and unflinching integrity, and his cool, accurate, and judicious intellect, will place him high, I think, in the Councils of the Nation.

We do not present him to the United States as a rival for Henry Clay in eloquence, to Daniel Webster in vastness of intellect—or to Prentiss in sparkling wit—but with pride and confidence we present him, as pure in morals, sage in council, prompt in action, and determined in purpose—as a man—every inch of him, a man—and a gentleman."

Letter in *Raleigh Register,* quoted
in *Hillsborough Recorder,* Dec. 17th.
1840.

subject of painful reflection on many accounts. I will resign my seat as Speaker & as a member of the House of Commons from Orange, and will be in Hillsboro on Friday.

Please to defer your leaving home untill I come up, and I will accompany you to this place next week.

*   *   *   *   *

I could write you much in unbosoming my heart, on the event which has just taken place, but I hope to be with you soon, and am compelled to bring my letter to a close.


*From Matthias E. Manly.*                              A.

Newbern,

Nov. 26th, 1840.

You have placed me under the greatest obligation by the kind terms of your letter of the 20th.

It would have been earlier replied to but for my constant engagements during the past week in the services of the Bank over which I preside. From a letter however, written to my brother the contents of which I begged him to communicate you will have learned my present determination not to visit Raleigh; & the reasons therefor.

I think the recent triumph of the cause of the republic should inspire the legislature with pure patriotism even in small matters. Let no prejudices or partialities sway but let the judges be selected from the whole field of choice with a single view to fitness. Subsidiary to this, it seems to me not improper to bestow them in such a way as to distribute throughout the state the benefits as well as the burthens of government. There is not a Circuit Judge east of the city of Raleigh. The Gentlemen of the Edenton riding insisted upon their rights a few years ago & a judge was conceded to them (Judge Baily) He has since removed to the west.

It is surely not now an unreasonable expectation in the east, when there are two vacancies to fill that the selection of one should be made from amongst her citizens; or in this circuit that she should have her regular turn after Edenton in an attempt to furnish to the country a resident eastern judge.

One consideration I have forborne to mention heretofore It is known to you that I had the nomination of the Executive in the last winter & that the council refused to concur  As no reasons have ever been given for this extraordinary course it operates as a kind of stigma. This I am desirous of wiping out & placing myself at least in as sound a condition as I was in anterior to the time when my friends here sent my name to the Governor of the State.

I leave this matter however where it properly belongs to the justice and patriotism of the General Assembly, & my own peculiar interest in it to you and others who will act in my behalf.

I have been rejoiced to hear through various channels that you are likely to receive a nomination and appointment to the Senate of the United States to fill one of the vacancies in the delegation from this State.

I trust this has already been done. Early in the summer when Judge Gaston & myself were discussing the public desire that *he* should be one of the Senators, your name was frequently mentioned & we both concurred in the opinion that the appointment to one place ought to fall upon you beyond doubt. Since that time I have frequently mentioned it in this district & feel persuaded that you will receive a handsome [support?] from our delegation. Nothing I assure you gives me greater pleasure than to hear of the advancement in life of my old school fellows

I am a little surprised that the name of Judge Gaston should still be bandied about as a candidate for a seat in the Senate. He has repeatedly & positively declined it & it is unjust to him to hold him up now as a mere target to be shot at. I suppose those who speak of him in this connexion do so from the most friendly motives but it is nevertheless unfair to him & towards the true candidates. It leads many to believe that the Judge really wants to be nominated *which I know is the farthest possible from the truth.*

We have learned with some surprise down here that our fellow townsman Mr. Bryan was in nomination for the Senate. *This is doubtless without his knowledge & against his decided wishes;* as I have reason to know that he has advocated your appointment with earnestness wherever he has had a fitting opportunity. This is just to Mr. B. for I take it from your relations that he has made known to you his intentions to give you his support & if after this he had procured and sanctioned the bringing forward his own name it would be uncandid

*Hellen* is Bryans friend but acts in this case without consultation.

*To Susan Washington Graham.*                      A.

Petersburg,

Monday night, Decr. 7th, 1840.

My Dear Wife

Having some leisure on my hands here I have concluded to give you some account of our journey. I had expected to reach Washington City yesterday afternoon a 2 o'clock, but we have met with a series of delays from the snow and ice which keeps us now here, and probably will forbid our arrival for two days more.

On Saturday we had a wretched day but travelled quite comfortably in the cars, in which there was a stove & a good fire, arrived about dark at Gaston, & there learned that the train from Petersburg had not come out. The consequence was that we were obliged to lodge there for the night in a badly kept Hotel. The next morning (Sunday) we started after ten, on a thick ice, & after running five miles broke the axel of the tender which carried the boiler of the engine. This occasioned a halt for about 2 hours & after jogging along as we could over the ice, arrived at Belfield, 20 miles from Gaston, just before night. No train having yet come out from Petersburg, & the ice continuing thick, we concluded after a parley, to stop there untill this morning.

Set out about ten (with a bright sun for the first time since our departure) & encountering sleet thicker & thicker as we advanced, arrived here with some difficulty at 4 this afternoon, are now at the Bolingbroke Hotel and expect to go on to Richmond in the morning, but it is doubtful whether farther than that tomorrow.

Messrs. Mangum Stanly & others who left Raleigh on the day before us, did not get here untill Saturday 12 o'clock, A. M. were detained untill this morning & are now probably no farther than Richmond. Genl. Thompson of S. C. who was with them narrowly escaped being killed about 2 miles from here as they came in. He had gotten out of the car and was walking ahead as they came slowly through the snow, being muffled up in his cloak, & not hearing very well, the front car ran on him, knocked him down just along side of the rail, and the whole train passed over him, ripping his cloak & clothes along the back and pressing him down so as to bruise and lacerate his face, but without material injury except a severe stunning. I think that we shall perhaps overtake them at Richmond tomorrow and get on to Washington the next day—that will be three days later than I expected when leaving

Raleigh. Such a storm is altogether unusual so early in the season, & has no doubt delayed a large number of the members of Congress.

Bro. James and Messrs. Conner, Hawkins, Williams, of Ten., and Thompson, of Miss., & his lady are with me. I have suffered but little from cold, & all things considered, esteem myself fortunate in getting along even so well as I have.

\*    \*    \*    \*    \*

*From James W. Bryan.*                                      A.

Newbern, Decr. 9th, 1840.

I regretted exceedingly that I was deprived of the pleasure of seeing you at Raleigh on my recent visit to that place, as I had much to say, which the limits of a letter will not admit of. I am very reluctant to be numbered among that almost Scythian horde denominated office seekers, and do not desire to be placed in that relation to the Executive and shall not consider myself as such in the remarks which I wish to submit to your better judgment and sounder discretion, both of which I wish you to exercise, and advise me of, in this matter. I find that I have entirely failed to attain that strength and health, which I hoped to secure by my late summer excursion. Whilst in N. Y. our mutual friend, Dr. Washington, advised me that a residence in such a climate as Italy would entirely restore me to health as I had no disease of a fixed character & was perfectly sound in my system. I immediately turned my attention to Naples, & though that whatever may be my views in relation to that Mission, the present incumbent (Mr. Throop) [76] ought by all means to be removed in consequence of his connexion etc. with the Swartwout defalcation & that he had not proved a faithful & efficient officer of the Govt. & was so far as the developments made in that case would bear me out, unworthy of his present situation, etc. I believed that I could represent the Govt. there with credit to myself & our Country & that a residence there for some time would restore myself & family to good health. I have conversed with mo one except Dr. W. in relation to this matter & address you now as much to consult you

---

[76] Enos Thompson Throop (1784-1874), of New York, Democratic member of congress, 1815-1816; judge, 1823-1827; governor, 1829-1833; charge to the Two Sicilies, 1838-1842.

upon the propriety & expediency of it, as to induce you to promote my views if it should become expedient for me to seek it.
I claim no merit for my services in the late campaign for feeble
as they were, I consider that I only discharged a duty to the Country in contributing my mite towards its' regeneration. I disdain
also to be considered an office seeker; the emoluments in this
case cannot be an object & will not defray the expenses, etc. No
inducement save the paramount consideration of my health could
induce me to leave the U. S. & as I can regain that & discharge
my duty to the Country at the same time I presume, I shall not be
charged with an undue degree of selfishness.

I presume Mr. Mangum & the N. C. delegation would aid in
this matter, but I trust you will not let me be placed in the position of a seeker, for as I might possibly attain the same object by
going to Florida, I would willingly do it if it were a fit place (at
present) for a white man to carry his family there. Do let me know
your views freely & unreservedly & I assure you they shall be received in the proper spirit & with great kindness of consideration.

The present Collector at Ocracoke, Silvester Brown,[77] is in my
opinion unfit for his office, has left it several times on Electioneering tours & was the author of a hand bill against me because I
was opposed to the administration in my last Election; he is a
brawling partisan in our County Elections & extremely meddle-
some & officious & has in every instance, I believe, brought his
patronage in conflict with the Elections of the County. If possible he ought to be turned out. Joseph S. Fowler of this place
would make an excellent officer & is an applicant for it; if he
should fail Isaac Hellen the present Senator from Carteret would
discharge the duties of the office with much ability & wishes also
to be considered an applicant.

If the matter should come before the Senate or President do
advise me of it, I promised these gentlemen to write to you &
Mr. Mangum & advise you of their intentions—I hope you will
mention the matter to Mr. Mangum.

Your appointment seems to have given very general satisfaction
but I find that Mr. Mangum is the cause of much heartburning
among some of the Whigs. I am sorry for it and trust that they
will calm down & become united on the subject. You having been

---

[77] Sylvester Brown was a highly respected citizen of Beaufort County. He was the
father of George Hubbard Brown (1850-1926), a justice of the state supreme court,
1905-1920. His daughter, Elizabeth, was the wife of James Edward Shepherd (1847-
1910), chief justice of the supreme court of North Carolina.

so recently to Raleigh & being better informed no doubt of their doings than I am, renders it unnecessary to send you my *modicum* of news from that quarter. I was truly pleased at the result in Orange, of the Election to supply yours and Mr. M's places; it is quite a triumph to Waddell.

Do let us hear from you & give us the *on dits* of the great & knowing ones at Washington.

P. S. Mr. Saml. Oliver a Merchant & an old and worthy citizen of this place will be an applicant for the appointment of Post Master of this town & desires me to secure the good offices of yourself & Mr. Mangum. I can safely recommend him to you both, in every point of view.

*To Susan Washington Graham.*                    A.

Washington City,
Thursday evening,
Dec. 10th, 1840.

After writing you from Petersburg, I passed that afternoon to Richmond, having been overtaken by Messrs. Calhoun, Preston, Fisher & many others with whom I journied to this place. On yesterday we came from Richmond arriving here about dark.

Today I appeared in the Senate, took the prescribed oath and selected a seat, have been introduced to a large number of members of both Houses of Congress, among whom the Whigs have all greeted me with much cordiality. Messrs. Clay, Webster, Davis,[78] Crittenden & King of Ala. were particularly kind and complimentary. Mr. Benton also did me the honor to come to my seat & introduce himself with offers of civility.

I have not yet taken quarters for the Session. I am at present at Brown's Hotel where I shall probably continue for several days before I make a permanent location for the Session. I shall most probably however establish myself on Capitol Hill within convenient distance of the Capitol itself.

*     *     *     *     *

The snow here has been very deep (some say 1½ feet) and prevented a quorum from attending the Senate untill yesterday. It

---

[78] John Davis (1787-1854) of Massachusetts, lawyer, a National Republican member of Congress, 1825-1834; resigned to become governor, serving 1834-1835; Whig United States senator, 1835-1840, resigning in December again to become governor, serving 1841-1843. He was again a senator, 1845-1853.

now covers the whole country & there is fine sleighing in the streets. I have been out no where except to the Capitol, & have heard but little news. There is some speculation as to the new Cabinet,—indeed a good deal is begining to be said about it but no one yet speaks with certainty as to who will fill the different departments. But I much fear that N. C. as usual will be over-looked.

\* \* \* \*

There is much gratulation among the Whigs at the great triumph they have achieved, and the amounts of money won by some of them. Mr. Botts[79] the member of the House from Richmond Va. has won $13,000.

Pray write me frequently, take care of our dear children & continue to me your love. . . .

New Bern.

*To William Gaston.* U. Gaston Mss.

Washington City,
Dec. 16th, 1840.

Speculation is busy here respecting the formation of the new Cabinet. The President elect is expected in Washington about the middle of Jan. and designs to go hence to Va. to spend the interim until the 4th of March. Our delegation propose in the most delicate manner possible, to bring to his notice the fact that, in the past history of the Government but few of the citizens of N. C. have been called to any of its higher offices and respectfully to suggest that some appointment of distinction is befitting, if not due to, the State. If he shall be disposed to gratify us and will take our councils in making a selection, we shall unanimously recommend your name, should he tender either the office of Secretary of State or the mission to England or to France. In assuming this liberty, I hope a pardonable one, we would of course apprize him that your wishes on the subject are unknown. Should he offer to the State the office of Attorney General, Mr. Badger would be designated—our consultations, as yet, have extended no further. It is generally be-

---

[79] John Minor Botts (1802-1869), of Virginia, lawyer and farmer; Whig member house of delegates, 1833-1839; member of congress, 1839-1843, 1847-1849, later, a bitter opponent of secession, and of the Confederate administration. He was a delegate to the Southern Loyalist Convention of 1866.

lieved here among the Western friends of General Harrison that Mr. Crittenden of Ky. will be appointed the Attorney General and Mr. Ewing[80] of Ohio, Post Master General; there are many rumors as to the other seats in the Cabinet, but nothing is ascertained. Mr. Clay, of course, will not take office, and it is believed, would prefer that Mr. Webster should not. The latter, however, it is supposed will be offered the State or Treasury department, and is expected to accept. Mr. Bell is mentioned in connection with the War, Mr. Southard [81] with the Navy and Mr. Sergeant with the Treasury departments, but my limited acquaintance does not enable me to say what is the latest or most credible report.

On yesterday Mr. Clay made quite a spirited speech on a resolution introduced by him proposing a repeal of the sub-treasury act and instructing the Committee on Finance to report a Bill accordingly. He was replied to by Messrs. Wright,[82] Calhoun, Anderson[83] of Ten. and Hubbard [84] of New Hampshire. Mr. Calhoun stated among other things, "that he feared a majority of the people of the United States were against the Independent Treasury" but denied that a majority was in favor of any other system of finance—that gentlemen of the opposition could never support the system of deposite banks and that an United States Bank was unconstitutional etc. Today Mr. Webster made a most able speech on the proposition to refer part of the President's message to the Committee on

[80] Thomas Ewing (1789-1871), of Ohio, a native of Virginia. Educated 'at Ohio University, he became a lawyer, served as senator in congress, 1831-1837; secretary of the treasury, 1841; secretary of the interior, 1849-1850; and again senator, 1850-1851. He was a delegate to the peace conference in 1861, supported Johnson's policy of reconstruction, was a delegate to the National Union convention in 1866. Johnson appointed him to replace Edwin M. Stanton as secretary of war, but he was not confirmed.

[81] Samuel Lewis Southard (1787-1842), of New Jersey, graduate of Princeton, served in the legislature, 1815; judge of the state supreme court, 1815-1820; Democratic elector, 1820; senator in congress, 1821-1823; secretary of the navy, 1823-1829; governor, 1832-1833; again senator, as a Whig, 1833-1842, (president *pro tem,* 1841-1842).

[82] Silas Wright, Jr., (1795-1847), of New York, a native of Massachusetts, graduate of Middlebury College, became a lawyer and went to New York. He was a member, state senate, 1824-1827; brigadier general of militia, 1827; Democratic representative, 1827-1829; re-elected but never qualified, senator, 1833-1844; governor, 1844-1846.

[83] Alexander Outlaw Anderson (1794-1869), of Tennessee, soldier War of 1812; government agent to remove Indians from Alabama and Florida; senator in congress, 1840-1841. He moved to California, where he served on the supreme court, 1851-1853, when he returned to Tennessee. He later lived in Mobile.

[84] Henry Hubbard (1784-1857), of New Hampshire; lawyer, member state legislature, 1812-1815, 1819-1820, 1823-1827, (speaker three years); a Democratic representative in congress, 1829-1835; senator, 1835-1841; governor, 1841-1843.

Finance, in which he reviewed the parts of that document which are designed to make false issues before the Country with great severity, demonstrated that this administration has expended seven millions of dollars annually over and above the income of Government, has drawn in to the payment of these expenditures certain monies appropriated to be invested in stocks for the benefit of Indian tribes, and kept their books in such a way as to conceal that fact. He insisted that the present national debt was larger than was reported by the Secretary, and declared that so far as he could have any control he would insist that a new set of Books should be opened on the 4th of March next—that the old ones should be balanced and the true amount of indebtedness or excess which existed by the providence of this administration, should be made manifest. Mr. Wright asked until tomorrow to reply.

This letter will require no answer, and is written without even the knowledge of any other member of the delegation, as a mark of my regard, and to apprize you of the passing events and *on dits* at the seat of Government. It will, however, at all times afford me pleasure to hear from you when your leisure will permit and to receive any counsel or suggestion you may think proper to communicate relative to matters in which my present position may enable me to be useful either to the whole country or to our mother state.

I am with sincere regard,<br>
Your obed. servt.,

*To James W. Bryan.*            U. Bryan Mss.

Washington City,<br>
Decr. 20th, 1840.

I have had the pleasure to receive your kind letter, and hasten a reply. I regret to learn that the health of Mrs. B. and your own are not improved. It will afford me great pleasure to aid you in the matter of going to Italy, provided I find it proper to urge it. The delegation are disposed to bring to the notice of the President elect, in the most delicate manner possible, the fact that N. C. in a period of more than Fifty years has filled but few of the higher offices, & to suggest that some important appointment is due to her. If he shall be disposed to gratify us, and will designate the place, we will name the individual to fill it, provided he will take our counsels. From present indications I presume we shall be disappointed.

Preston has been to see us today & says that he knows that Webster has been written to by Genl Harrison tendering to him any place in the Cabinet that he may desire, and that he has accepted the office of Secretary of State; that Crittenden will certainly be the Atto. Genl.; Ewing of Ohio Post Master Genl.; & probably Sergeant Secretary of the Treasury; Bell of Ten. at War, and F. Granger[85] of the Navy. In this you see the South would not be represented. And if it be changed I doubt from indications whether N. C. will come in.

If no place in the Cabinet be offered us, nor a principal mission, we surely can command the place of a Chargé. If, however, we should be allowed a station of greater weight, you perceive, there will be more doubt, as to the minor. I have mentioned it in a proper way to Mangum and my brother, both of whom will give a hearty cooperation if circumstances shall authorize a movement on the subject. Mangum tells me, however, that the Kentuckians are speaking of the same place for Menifee of that State, formerly of the Ho. Reps. who is in bad health & desirous of going abroad. I will watch the progress of events, and adopt such course as seems most advisable.

In relation to the office of Collector at Ocracoke, we will hear all the applications, and endeavour to recommend the most suitable person. I was spoken to in Raleigh for Jos. G. Stanly Jr. in reference to it, and Edward Stanly has an application for some one in his district which he will urge. The name of Mr. Hellen was also suggested to me at Raleigh.

Is there a necessity for changing your Post Master? Where there are good officers, who have not prostituted their offices, nor outraged the public sense of propriety, I think they should be suffered to continue. Those of the contrary character should be speedily removed.

I shall write to some of our friends in different quarters, as soon as it is certainly known (I regard now as nearly so) that

---

[85] Francis Granger (1792-1868), a native of Connecticut, graduate of Yale, settled in New York, and became a lawyer. He was active, and mainly unsuccessful in politics, as a Republican and anti-Mason, until 1835, when he served a term in congress, as a Whig. He was later a member, 1839-1841, and 1841-1843, and in the interim he was postmaster general in the Harrison cabinet. He was a member of the peace conference, 1861.

Webster is to be Sec. of State, apprizing them of it and asking them to break it to the public as they deem best. To appoint both him and Sargeant will give the administration a heavy weight to carry at the South, and if Grainger be added, I shall fear the result. If Mr. Webster would decline, then Davis of Mass. could be appointed (by general consent) Sec. of Treasury, and I have no doubt but Mr. Gaston could be Sec. of State; but he, is said to be, resolved on [not] accepting.

There have been two spirited debates in the Senate which you will see, in relation to a repeal of the Subtreasury, & the state of the Finances, but they have been conducted with remarkable courtesy and decency.

I called a few days since on the President. He bears himself with considerable erection, all things considered, tho' Mr. Clay says "his eyes appear as if he had not slept well, or had been crying one or t'other."

I have taken private quarters with Mangum my only messmate as yet; my brother and Rayner will perhaps join us. I have been out but little, and not extended my acquaintance very far.

I hear from Raleigh that W. B. S.[86] has broken loose quite from the Whigs, and is raving most malignantly at everybody & every thing. From what I learn he has made false representations of me among others, which I may notice in the public prints. But his course seems to have been so generally disgusting that he can do little I presume to the prejudice of any one.

I left so suddenly that I could effect nothing for our friend Manly; untill the Bill to locate the Judges was disposed of, it was impossible to say even who would be candidates. But I was at that time satisfied, that no candidate spoken of, could start in the race with much more than the vote of his own Circuit, and therefore advised that Manly should be put in nomination.

I see from the Raleigh papers that the election was to take place last week. If it shall prove as difficult an affair as it was to elect an Atto. Genl., they will be some time about it.

*    *    *    *    *

[86] William B. Shepard.

*To Susan Washington Graham.*                    A.

Washington City,
Decr. 21st, 1840.

My Dearest:

I received your kind letter from New Bern last week announcing your safe arrival, which gave me much pleasure. I regret to learn that Mrs. Bryan still continues unwell.

I have taken private quarters at the House of Mrs. Preuss on Missouri Avenue, one square south of Gadsby's Hotel, & about equidistant from the Capitol. We have fine large rooms and a very neat parlour, & tolerable accomodations in the eating line, and are quite retired from the bustle of Pennsylvania Avenue, which is the Broadway of the City & equals it in noise. Mr. Mangum & myself are sole tenants as yet and will have the controul in admitting others.

We somewhat expect brother James and Mr. Rayner to join us. The former is now on a visit to Phila. to consult Dr. Jackson as to an affection of his throat. I do not believe there is much the matter with him, but he (you know) has his own notions. I suffered considerably last week from a boil, which gave me much pain. After its discharge I sent for a leecher, & had about half a dozen applied, which took away a good deal of blood & I hope will give me permanent relief. He is a more expert hand in applying them than I was in Lincoln on our visit there.

I went the other day to see the President, found him in the company of two or three gentlemen, exceedingly courteous & affable. He is said to be sending off his wines, etc. to Kinderhook, & I presume, will not entertain largely this winter.

If you should prefer it you might come on at once, & return about February, if you did not desire to remain longer. I could meet you at Petersburg, or even at Waynesboro if you find no friend coming the whole way. Such a trip might be of as much service as your visit to Niagara last year. Do however as your feelings indicate or as the interests of our dear children seem to require. I did not intend to write you today as I have written Mr. Bryan, but I supposed you would desire to hear from me during the holidays.

Kiss my Children & be ever mine.

*From William Gaston* A.

Raleigh, Dec. 27, 1840.

I received your letter of the 16th. inst. a day or two before my departure from home to attend the court at this place, and beg you to be assured that as a mark of your regard I value it highly.

You are good enough to say that no answer is required, and I have felt some difficulty in determining whether an answer ought to be returned, to the communication. As it was made without the knowledge of the other members of the delegation I must conclude that the intent of the Body was that I should be ignorant of their purpose, in a certain event, to lay my name before the President elect of the United States, and of course that they should be ignorant of my wishes in regard to what was contemplated. But as the subject has been mentioned to me, and my silence might lead to a mistaken inference, I have deemed it expedient and most consistent with frankness to say to you (leaving you at liberty to make such use of this information as you think proper) that I hope no such nomination will be made. My reason simply is that on the one hand I am reluctant to appear churlish, or to give offense to the People of North Carolina, by rejecting public appointments, and on the other have a sincere desire to keep aloof from political life for the residue of my days.

I avail myself of the occasion to offer you my congratulations on the high proof of the confidence of your country which has recently been bestowed upon you, and to add with perfect truth that had I been a member of the General Assembly I should have most *cordially* concurred in the act.

> With the highest esteem and affection,
> Your friend and obedient servant.

## 1841

*To Susan Washington Graham.* A.

Washington City,

Jany. 1st, 1841.

\* \* \* \* \*

This is new years day, and although it has been snowing and hailing rapidly, I went as is customary with every body, to the levee of the President. Foreign ministers & their suites clad in full Court dress, officers of the Army & Navy in complete uniform, Heads of departments, members of Congress, ladies in gayest attire, private gentlemen, & persons with very doubtful claims to gentility, all crowded together the splendid East room of the White House. I rode up a little after one o'clock, by which time the assembly was beginning to disperse, & remained about an hour. The President exhibited his habitual politeness, but I thought was evidently under constraint and embarrassment. His new allies, Messrs. Calhoun, Pickens, etc., from S. C. were present, I suppose by way of seeing the last of him.

I dined on yesterday with Mr. Merrick,[1] Senator from Maryland, a most worthy and hospitable gentleman, who is keeping house in this City. And on Tuesday evening attended a soiree at Mr. Gadsby's, who has retired from the Hotel a gentleman of fortune, and entertains most sumptuously. So that you may imagine me to have turned out quite a votary of fashion. I am however, rather a looker on, than a participant, and have not sought to extend my acquaintance further than mere civility or accidental circumstances have carried it.

We have at our boarding house, an old Colonel of the British Army from Canada, who served under the Duke of Wellington in Spain and Portugal in 1812 & 13, and the Portuguese Minister to our Government M. Figoniere, both pleasant gentlemen, the former of whom has given us many interesting details of the War in the Peninsula.

Bro. James returned last night from Phila. in good health, and will join us at our boarding house tomorrow.

You may remember that a person of my own name, was formerly in N. C. & imprisoned at Raleigh. A friend of his in Missouri having seen in the papers an account of my election, & mistaking me for him, has written me a letter congratulating on my elevation, and requesting that I will repay him $60. borrowed a few years ago, and that if there be any office to be had, which will probably suit him, to procure it for him.

---

[1] William Duhurst Merrick (1793-1857), of Maryland, a graduate of Georgetown College, soldier of the War of 1812, lawyer, member of the house of delegates, 1832-1838, 1856-1857; Whig United States senator, 1838-1845; delegate to convention of 1850.

It is of course a subject of much merriment with those to whom I have shown the letter.

* * * * *

Mr. Heartt who brought on the electoral vote of N. C. has gone to New Jersey and has not yet returned. Mrs. Stanly is here. I offered my service to wait on her to the Presidents to day but she declined in consequence of the state of the weather. Miss Harriet Jones is to be with her soon.

You do not say what you think of visiting Washington in this month, & returning before March, as I proposed in one of my letters. I am sorry to learn that Joseph gives you trouble. Tell him that Father says he must do what Mother tells him, and that if he will be a good boy Father will bring him some pretty things when he returns. Can William stand alone? Tell John that Father wishes him to be a good boy, and will bring him some candy when he comes home.

Would that I could see you all this evening & give you the blessing of the season. I wish now that I had brought you all with me, as my quarters would make us quite comfortable.

Farewell, my dearest,—May each returning new year find us devoted to each other, and the great duties incumbent on us.


REMARKS OF MR. GRAHAM,[2]

in the Senate of the United States,
on the bill to establish a permanent
pre-emption system in favor of settlers
on the Public Lands.

January 7, 1841.

A motion was pending to exclude foreigners not naturalized, from the benefits of the bill. During the discussion of this point some observations were made by some administration members, which drew from Mr. Graham the following remarks:

Mr. GRAHAM, from North Carolina, rose and said that he had originally entertained no design to participate in this discussion. Those whom he represented (so far as he had ascertained their wishes) were generally oposed to the policy of pre-

---

[2] From *Hillsborough Recorder*, January 28th, 1841.

emptions, and he, himself, concurring in that opinion, had intended to content himself with a silent vote, but for certain doctrines which had been advanced, and facts stated, in the progress of the debate. The bill would have been far less objectionable to him had the amendment prevailed which was offered by the Senator from Kentucky, (Mr. Crittenden) limiting the bounties which it proposed to confer, to American citizens, and excluding unnaturalized foreigners. But, in resisting this amendment, the distinguished Senator from New York, (Mr. Wright) had contended that any one of the states had the right to confer the elective franchise on foreigners without naturalization, according to the laws of the United States, and thus enable them to vote in elections under this government; and the honorable senator from Illinois, (Mr. Young) who has just taken his seat, had stated that this doctrine was actually carried out in practice in his state, for that there, aliens had voted after a residence of six months. He could not but regard such a doctrine as directly in the teeth of the constitution of the United States. The honorable senator from New York, (Mr. Wright) understands this power to belong in a state by reason of the general provision in the constitution that members of the House of Representatives and the President are directed to be chosen by the people of the several states, and that "the electors in each state shall have the qualifications requisite for electors of the most numerous branch of the state legislature." It was unnecessary for Mr. G. to remind one who showed himself so familiar with such subjects of the ordinary rule of interpretation, that all parts of the instrument must be looked to in giving it a construction, and the general words were oftentimes controlled by particular provisions. The section of the Constitution immediately preceding that referred to by the senator from New York, was equally general in its terms—"All legislative powers herein granted shall be vested in a Congress of the U. States, which shall consist of a Senate and House of Representatives." If we look no further than this clause, the Senate and House of Representatives can make laws without hindrance or concurrence from any other department of the government. The words are as comprehensive as any that our language can afford. But in the subsequent part of the Constitution, we learn that no act of Congress shall become a law, unless it receive the approbation of the President, except in cases which need not now be mentioned. Finding this first and broadest declaration of the Constitution qualified and restrained by subsequent provisions our surprise will be the less if we discover that that relied on for the support of the power in question is subject to a like qualification. Let us, in passing, inquire, who are "the people of the several states" by whom representatives, etc., are to be chosen? Who are the people of Kentucky, among whom you, sir, reside? Who are the people of New York? Does any one understand them to include unnaturalized aliens, owing allegiance to foreign governments, and bound to cleave to them in the event of a controversy with our own? But suppose that by the generality of these words they were embraced. The Constitution elsewhere, in express terms, gives to Congress the power "to establish a uniform rule of naturalization," and Congress has exercised that power by prescribing the rule. From its very nature it cannot be concurrently exercised by the general Government, and the states. There cannot, in the nature of things, be a uniform rule throughout the United States, and yet different rules in different states. But it is asked by the senator from New York, (Mr. Wright) shall Congress prescribe the qualifications of voters in the states? By no means. Congress cannot prescribe any qualifications for electors in the states who are native born or naturalized citizens; and even in the case of a foreigner they cannot prescribe to him qualifications *as an elector,* properly so called, but they prescribe the means by which a disqualification under which he labors may be removed; and such disqualification can be removed by no other authority. This construction of the Constitution conflicts with no just rights of the states; on the contrary, the rights of all the others are grossly violated by any one of them undertaking to naturalize aliens in any other mode than that agreed upon in the Constitution of the United States. The states, by the Constitution, have entered into certain stipulations with each other, which none of them can, in good faith, violate. Some of these are of a positive character, such as that they will deliver up fugitives from justice, and fugitive slaves and servants. Others are negative, such as that they will abstain from the exercise of powers themselves which they have delegated exclusively to the General Government. To refuse to execute the former is a crime of omission; to attempt the exercise of the latter is a crime of commission; both alike injurious to the other states. When, therefore, a state admits foreigners to political rights, affecting the action of this government, without naturalization, she violates the covenants of the Constitution, and does injury to her sister states.

Such, (said Mr. G.) is my reading of the Constitution. How stands the question upon authority? I believe that all interpreters of the Constitution agree that the states have alienated exclusive powers of legislation to this government in three cases only: 1st. Where the Constitution, in express terms, granted an exclusive authority to the Union. 2nd. Where it granted, in one instance, an authority to the Union, and in another, prohibited the states from exercising the like authority. And 3rd. Where it granted an authority to the Union, to which similar authority in the state would be absolutely repugnant and contradictory. And it is a little remarkable that all the commentators on the Constitution, from Mr. Madison down—at least as far as I am informed— have selected this very power of naturalization as an illustration of the third class of these cases. In the Constitution of the state which I have the honor in part to represent,—and but for this fact Mr. G. would not now have obtruded himself on the notice of the Senate,—as adopted in 1776, there is this clause,—"Sec. 40. That every foreigner, who comes to settle in this state, having first taken an oath of allegiance to the same, may purchase, or by other just means hold, acquire, and transfer land or other real estate, *and after one year's residence, shall be deemed a free citizen.* "Under this section, foreigners, by taking an oath of allegiance to the state, may yet acquire, hold and transfer lands, but, in the fulfilment of her duties to the Union—and Mr. G. trusted she had fulfilled them all—North Carolina, by her constituted authorities, both legislative and judicial, had uniformly admitted that, by her adoption of the Federal Constitution, and the passage of naturalization laws by Congress, the latter clause of the section just quoted was abrogated, and that foreigners could become citizens only according to the uniform rule established by Congress. And Mr. G. appealed to the honorable senators if it was just towards her, and the other states of the Union, who put a like construction on the Constitution, that other members of the confederacy should adopt a different rule of naturalization. When the Constitution was adopted, it was declared to be intended to secure "the blessings of liberty to the people of the U. States, and their posterity." Aliens were no parties to it. But a provision was inserted by which Congress might admit them to become parties, and to share in its blessings. The Constitution was brought into existence mainly to regulate our foreign relations. To Congress had been given the power to make peace and war with other nations, and there appeared to be a propriety in giving it also the power of determining upon what conditions the people of those nations should be admitted to share with us in the privilege of deciding on the question of peace or war with their native countries.

But, (said Mr. G.) the states have agreed by the Constitution to distribute their relative power in the other branch of Congress, and in the election of a Chief Magistrate, according to the representative numbers of their people, and, so long as these numbers depend on the natural course of increase, or on the inducements which might be held out for emigration from one state of the union to the other, the struggle for power among themselves was one of fair and honorable competition. But, sir, I deny that in such a contest any state has a right to invoke as allies unnaturalized foreigners. This is a subject of vast magnitude, to which I desire to call the special attention of Congress and the country. There is shortly to be a new distribution of power, according to the census recently taken of the people of the United States. Sir, I protest against aliens being enumerated in that census, or, if so enumerated, against any state acquiring members of the House of Representatives, or votes in the Presidential election, by considering aliens, not naturalized, as a part of "the people," of such state. This is an unconstitutional mode of acquiring power, which, if tolerated, would subvert one of the first principles of our confederacy. And, with proper deference to the opinions of others, I cannot conceive a more gross violation of the constitution, a more clear usurpation of power, than for a state to annul or dispense with the laws of naturalization, and swell its own importance and weight in the Union by the aid of aliens owing no allegiance to this country, but bound by the highest obligations to take up arms against it in the event of war with their own sovereign. Such an injury is the more grievous because it operates not so much against this government as against the constitutional rights of the co-states of the confederacy, who had not expressly provided sanctions to prevent such infractions.

Mr. G. would take occasion to remind the Senate that not only personal bravery and adventurous spirit, the qualities so much lauded by honorable senators from the west as characterizing those for whose benefit this bill was intended, that not only these, but the highest degree of virtue and honor might co-exist with a deadly hostility to republican institutions, and he would exhort them to beware how bounties were bestowed on those who owed no allegiance to the government.

Mr. G. said he had not noticed in its proper connection the precedent alluded to by the honorable senator from New York, (Mr. Wright) of the admission of Michigan into the Union with a clause in her constitution allowing foreigners to exercise the elective franchise. If he, (Mr. G.) had been correctly informed in relation to the facts of that case, he did not conceive that it sustained the doctrine contended for by the senator from New York. As Mr. G. had understood, the constitution of Michigan gave the right of voting to the inhabitants of that state at the time of its formation, and the act of Congress admitting her into the Union was by implication a special act of naturalization for the then inhabitants. He supposed such a law was within the power of Congress, and, if so, the case of Michigan was not a precedent for this, to him, new and alarming doctrine; if, however, it were otherwise, he could not admit that a single precedent of Congress could overturn what was, in his opinion, the true construction of the constitution—one of its most important provisions. Mr. G. said that he had no feeling of hostility to foreigners, who were disposed to become citizens according to the constitutional mode. He believed our present regulations on the subject were hospitable and liberal. If they were not enough so, he was ever willing to hear propositions to make them more liberal. He, however, was opposed to annihilating the uniform rule on the subject of naturalization, and bestowing bounties on those who owe no allegiance to our government.

*To Susan Washington Graham.*          A.

Washington City,

Jany 9th, 1841.

My Dear Wife

Your brother George has been here a day and goes this evening towards Raleigh to apply for a license to practice the Law in N. C. He is desirous to settle himself in the middle or Western section of the State, But does not seem determined as to what he will ultimately do. I would be exceedingly glad to have their society with us at Hillsboro', but am still averse to recommend his going there, lest they should not be satisfied. Contentment is often matter of fancy, & is most apt to be obtained when one's own wishes alone are consulted, or at least when no one but ourselves are responsible for what we do. Besides, George has now reached that period of life when he should judge and act for himself. Any information that I can communicate, or aid that I can render, after he has determined where to settle will be cheerfully given. But it is certainly most agreeable, and generally most advantageous to act upon our own opinions about our own affairs.

I went a few evenings ago to a party at Mr. Seaton's,[3] where I met among others, Mrs. Farley, formerly Miss Pearson, who claims to hail from N. C. and was very kind. Mrs. Seaton (you know) is the daughter of old Mr. Gales[4] & also claims kindred with the North State. Mrs. Stanly was there *in good order.* Miss Harriet Jones has not yet arrived. Moustaches, whiskers, epaulettes, stars & ribbons are badges of a Washington party—that is to say among gentlemen. The ladies sport a chain or braid around the head, with a jewel on the forehead. And all waltz like children's tops. Upon the whole, there is rather more freedom of manner than I have seen any where else. But it is a congregation in a great measure of strangers who never met before, and don't care (most of them) if they never meet again.

I was invited last night to the house of Geo. C. Washington,[5] Esq., at Georgetown but declined going. He is said to be more nearly related to the General than any of the family living. I desired George to go over with us, but he declined and we afterwards gave it out ourselves.

Having entered the Senate a new and unexperienced member, I find my time more than occupied by proper attention to my duties there. Super added to which is a correspondence with every body who wants, or wants to know any thing, either private or public.

For the first time since my arrival the ground is freed from snow, the winter thus far having been very severe. I have escaped

---

[3] William Winston Seaton (1765-1866), a native of Virginia, who moved to Raleigh, and married Sarah Weston Gales, the daughter of Joseph and Winifred Gales. He went to Washington to join the staff of the *National Intelligencer,* and became the reporter of debates in congress. He was an anti-slavery, anti-abolition Whig, and was deeply interested in the aims and work of the American Colonization Society.

[4] Joseph Gales (1761-1842), a native of Devonshire, England, editor of the *Sheffield Register,* who came as a political refugee to America in 1795, and to North Carolina in 1799. He founded the *Raleigh Register,* and was a famous editor.

[5] George Corbin Washington (1789-1854), son of William Augustine Washington, and brother of Bushrod Washington, associate Justice of the supreme court.

taking any serious cold, but have not been able to take sufficient exercise.

I regret that our Legislature is about to adjourn without doing any thing for the Western turnpike.

The new President is expected here next week. A painting now being exhibited represents him as an older & inferior looking man than I had supposed him to be.


*From George E. Badger.*                                        A.

Raleigh, Jany. 19, 1841.

\*    \*    \*    \*    \*

I was glad to see you had broken the ice in the Senate,[6] and particularly that you had advocated the only sound doctrine, as to the necessity of citizenship to the possession of the elective franchise. I was the more pleased because a day before I saw your remarks in the N. Intelligencer I had given a written opinion, in clear & decided terms, to the same effect, in answer to a letter of some of our friends in Salem who thought themselves entitled to vote after being domiciled here from ten to twenty years without naturalization. The doctrine you advanced is beyond doubt the true one. It has always been held in North Carolina. At Newbern where the question arose many years ago, the Shff. under the advice of the whole profession there, always rejected the votes of aliens however long resident. Some years ago in the life of the late Ch. Justice Henderson a Mr. Wilson an english Gentleman of learning & high character had charge of the Academy at Williamsburgh and at an election for members of the House of Commons decided to vote. His right was questioned and it was agreed to submit the question to Ch. J. Henderson. Mr. Wilson had all the qualifications required by our Constitution. The C. Justice declared his opinion to be that because of his aliency he could not exercise the elective franchise, and his vote was rejected.

I should have been astonished at the ground taken by Mr. Preston knowing as I do his high mental quality, but that I have had occasion to remark the perplexing effect upon the understanding of the Nullification theory. Once adopted it con-

---

[6] The reference is to Graham's first speech in the senate, on the Pre-emption Bill, delivered January 7th, 1841.

fuses the intellectual operations, and a man can only reestablish a just exercise of the thinking powers by a thorough and total renunciation of that grand political heresy. I can not better express the necessity of a *total* reformation on this subject in order to the possession of a well founded confidence of accuracy in reasoning on any other political subject even remotely connected with it, than in the words of a friend when writing to me lately on a widely different matter. "It requires," says he, "time and reiterated instruction to reform the notions of a people even upon a single point, for our opinions so run into one another, that many collateral matters must be reformed with the principal one." How important then to reform the principal notion in order to a just direction of thought in reference to matters collateral and subordinate.

I wish Preston could *wake up* in regard to Mr. Calhoun's great and dangerous Nullification humbug, use the eyes of his mind, and shake off forever his sluggish submission to that darkening and bumbling error. Until he does he will scarce do his own powers justice on any subject.

We are going on here in our Court very much in the old way. For two days past Winston, Saunders, & Haywood have been fighting over the old bone in Plummer v. Baskervill—& will continue the wrangle tomorrow. But two facts are entitled to special notice for their novelty and importance.

The first is that a Bill passed the Assembly discharging the Shff. of Wake from attendance on the Court & enabling the Judges to appoint a "Marshal of the Supreme Court," under which Col. Weatt has been duly installed. The second is, that for several days past Judge Daniel has appeared and occupied his seat in Court *with his hat on*. Whether he has any thought of joining friend Mendenhall's Society of Friends or whether the change in his Judicial costume has any connection with the defeat of his friend Van Buren I am unable to say.

Leaving you to account for it as you may, the *fact* cannot be denied.

When you have a leisure half hour, I shall be pleased to hear from you. What thought you of Mr. Wm. B. Shepard's flourish?

Respectfully & affectionately
Yours,

*To Susan Washington Graham.*                    A.

Washington City,

Jany. 25th, 1841.

My Dear Wife

I recd your last kind letter on Friday evening & feel some solicitude in regard to your contiguity to the small pox, untill I shall hear of your safe arrival at Kinston. By the exercise of your usual care over the children, I trust you all will escape.

The winter here has been exceedingly wet and disagreeably cold. For the last two or three days however, there has been fine weather.

\*     \*     \*     \*     \*

I dined last week with Mr. Webster. Mrs. W. is with him, a tall majestic figure, without much beauty, but quite ladylike. Mr. & Mrs. Curtis & Miss Leroy of New York, make up their party. He is quite captivated with English style since his return from that country, occasionally sports a white cravat which is said to be now in fashion there, and (Preston says) proposed to him to come out in white silk stockings and pumps.

On Saturday evening the Whig Senators dined together at a restorateur, and settled a good many questions pertaining to the new administration. Among other things it seemed to be inevitable that there must be a called session of Congress about May or June. I mention this to you, though you will please not speak of it untill I come home.

Genl. Harrison will not be here untill next week, the account now is that he will leave Cincinnati tomorrow. Office seekers are coming or sending in from all quarters & I fear the old gentleman will be greatly annoyed.

There is here at present a Chinese missionary Dr. Parker,[7] both a clergyman & Oculist, just from China, who has with him a young man of that nation in the dress of his country. Dr. P. lectured yesterday evening in one of the Churches here, on his visit to that distant region—I went to hear him, but found such a crowd, that I could scarcely get in, & heard with some difficulty.

---

[7] Peter Parker (1804-1888), a native of Massachusetts, graduate of Yale in medicine, who became a Presbyterian minister, and went to China in 1834 as the first Protestant missionary there, giving most of his time to medical work. He went to Japan on the expedition to repatriate wrecked Japanese sailors. He was American commissioner and minister, 1855-1857, and spent the rest of his life in Washington.

I received a letter from Dr. J. A. W.[8] last week in closing one from Mr. James Donaldson recommending Mr. Callender for an office in the City. Mr. T. P. Burgwyn passed here a day or two ago on his way to New York. I did not see him. Mr. B. has been there for some time.

The extra session of the Senate will probably detain me here, untill the 10th or 12th of March. I hope the time will soon arrive, as I long to see you & my dear children once more.

\* \* \* \* \*

*Speech in the Senate on Roanoke Inlet.*[9]

## January 29, 1841

MR. GRAHAM said that, with the indulgence of the Senate, he begged leave to make a very brief statement of facts connected with this bill. Casting your eye on the map of North Carolina, you perceive a peninsula, commencing near its northeastern extremity, and extending southwardly a full degree and a half on the map, and, by the meanders of the coast, at least 150 miles to Ocracoke inlet. On the eastern side of this peninsula is the Atlantic ocean, and on the western a tract of waters navigable for sea vessels, and called, as you proceed from north to south, by the names, successively, of Currituck, Albermarle, Croatan, and Pamlico sounds. These waters are all disembogued at Ocracoke, and although the tongue of land separating them from the ocean is at some points reduced to no more than half a mile in width, there is no access to them for vessels except through that inlet. About one hundred miles north of that was formerly Currituck inlet, through which coasting vessels of light burden passed into Currituck sound. But this gradually filled up, and became closed about ten years ago; and it will be remembered by the Senate that, a few weeks since, I introduced a bill to abolish the port of delivery and the office of surveyor of customs at that place, (which had been a sinecure for many years,) and the bill has passed this body. At a period still earlier, there was another entrance to these inland waters, called Roanoke inlet, about sixty miles north of Ocracoke, at the eastern extremity of Albermarle sound, through which it communicated directly with the Atlantic, and

---

[8] Dr. James A. Washington.
[9] From *Hillsborough Recorder*, February 25th, 1841.

did not then, as now, mingle its waters with those of Pamlico sound on their way to the ocean. Here the vessels of Sir Walter Raleigh's adventure entered, when they planted the first colony on that part of the American continent; and long afterwards it continued to afford an easy and direct passage into the Albermarle and its tributaries.

In process of time, however, a channel has been opened southwardly, through Croatan, from Albermarle to Pamlico sound, there being a considerable declivity in that direction. The whole waters of the sound now flow through that channel, and Roanoke inlet is closed by a sand beach, half a mile in breadth. Thus an unbroken peninsula is formed for the whole distance already indicated, and the entire trade from the Albermarle and its tributaries is forced to seek the markets of the North, whither most of it is carried, by first taking a southern course, to Ocracoke, and thence a contrary direction on the ocean; so that two vessels, the one in the sound, and the other at sea, in the same latitude, may be separated but by a few leagues, and yet each would perform a voyage of from 120 to 150 miles to gain the position of the other. Meanwhile, a wind which is favorable to the prosecution of the first half of the voyage is adverse to the remainder. Each vessel is obliged to double Cape Hatteras, the most dangerous promontory on the American coast, to pass through a difficult and often changing channel at Ocracoke, and to encounter the delay and expense of lighterage. This bill proposes to ascertain if it be not practicable to avoid these impediments to the navigation and commerce of that region by re-opening Roanoke inlet, and affording a direct passage into the Albermarle from the sea. To form an adequate conception of the extent of that commerce, and the shipping which it employs, it is necessary to glance at the adjacent territory. Albermarle sound stretches westwardly, from the site of the proposed inlet, for 60 miles, is generally from 15 to 20 miles wide, and from 20 to 25 feet in depth. Besides several navigable rivers or estuaries flowing into it on the northern and southern sides, it receives at the western end the Chowan and Roanoke, the latter of which waters a greater extent of fertile, arable soil than any river between the Mississippi and the St. Lawrence—a soil whose productions would find their natural and direct route to the markets of the world through Roanoke inlet. True it is, that communications by railroad have been established from the upper Roanoke to Petersburg and

Norfolk, in Virginia; but it is a well known fact that transportation for bulky articles is far cheaper by water than on railroad, and that many of the productions of agriculture cannot be sent to market at all by the latter mode, which would go by the former. No section of the Atlantic states, of the same dimension, furnishes annually greater supplies of agricultural products for market, than the "northern counties" on Albermarle sound. Those on its southern margin and tributaries are, perhaps, equally fruitful, and are likely to have a great increase in their production, by the reclamation of near 100,000 acres of swamp land, now in the course of drainage—a work prosecuted by the state of North Carolina, which has appropriated $200,000 to objects of this kind. In addition to which, and cotton, the common product of the southern states, immense quantities of Indian corn are sent from this section to New York, Providence, and Boston, at the North, to Charleston and Savannah, at the South, and to the West Indies. The exports from agriculture, however, are greatly augmented from the fisheries and forests of the Albermarle country. Besides thousands of barrels of fish, the quantities of staves, heading, shingles, pine lumber, and the products of the pine tree, ship timber and naval stores, exported yearly, are incredible to those who have not had their attention turned particularly to the subject. There are no means of learning the exact value of the aggregate, but it is estimated by those most familiar with that trade, to exceed $3,000,000. per annum, and to furnish employment to more than 100,000 tons of shipping. If such be the value and importance of that trade under its multiplied present disadvantages, what might it not be expected to be, if relieved from its embarrassments by the improvements proposed? As a school and nursery for seamen, it eminently deserves the fostering care and friendly consideration of Congress. It is from the commercial that recruits are furnished to the military Navy; and at a time when there seems to be a general disposition to enlarge and strengthen this arm of the national defence, policy as well as humanity requires that they shall be shielded as far as possible from the perils of shipwreck, and encouraged to embark in the merchant service.

Mr G. said he could not better illustrate the necessity for opening this inlet, and its advantages to trade and navigation, than by reading a few paragraphs from the report of a distinguished engineer, (Major Gwynn,) to which, and to the report by his respected colleague in the other branch of Congress, (Mr. Rayner,) at the last session, he was mainly indebted for the facts already narrated; premising, merely, that *"Roanoke Marshes Light-house,"* mentioned in the report, is situated on the passage between Albermarle and Pamlico sounds. Major Gwynn states that—

"The register of Captain Pew, keeper of the Roanoke Marshes Light house, numbers 1,450 vessels passing and repassing during the year ending December 31, 1839, making the shipping about 100,000 tons; the amount assumed by the committee, which, although remaining the same, shows for that season a considerable increase, when we consider the great tonnage withdrawn from this trade by the facilities afforded by the Petersburg and Portsmouth Rail-roads—the former of which went into operation in 1833, and the latter in 1836.

"The amount of property and lives lost on the coast immediately adjoining the inlet, for a distance of 15 miles on each side of it, presents a frightful list, and a strong appeal to the protection and humanity of the government.

"Between the year 1824 and the present period, there have been (as nearly as I could ascertain) 112 vessels wrecked; which, averaging 50 tons each, would make, together with the cargoes, a loss not much short of $350,000.; and with these vessels 224 souls have found a watery grave.

"The list, fearful as it is, would be greatly swelled if we had the means of adding to it the number of vessels wrecked on the remainder of the adjacent coast, and off Cape Hatteras, in consequence of being compelled, by the closing of Roanoke inlet, to encounter the hazard of passing this dangerous promontory.

"Throwing out of view the advantages to the commerce of the country, as a harbor of refuge from storms in time of peace, the opening of this inlet is an object every way worthy of the nation. And, in time of war, there is no point on the whole coast where a harbor would be more useful, and where one is so much needed, not only for the refuge of coasters from the enemy, but, in bad weather, for privateers and the smaller sized armed vessels, acting offensively."

Sir, (said Mr. G.) this subject has acquired new importance and interest in North Carolina from a survey, under the authority of the state, made during the last year, by the engineer before referred to, of which this report is the result; and since I gave notice of my intention to present this bill, I have received from the Governor of the state a copy of the report, and a series of resolutions adopted by the Legislature at its recent session, urging the work upon the attention of Congress, which I ask leave also now to introduce. It will be seen, by a perusal of that report, that no doubt is entertained by the engineer, of its practicability, and that the Legislature has concurred in that opinion. But as this Government is requested to undertake it, I have presumed that a survey by its own officers would be more satisfactory to Congress, and more likely to ensure their favorable action on the subject, and therefore have brought forward at present, only a proposition of survey. If by that, it shall be again ascertained— as I doubt not that it will—that the work may be accomplished at a reasonable expense, there can be no hesitation, I apprehend, in commencing it at once.

Mr. G. said, before he sat down he would remark that this proposition had no connexion with that system of internal improvement which, under too loose a construction of the Constitution, had been formerly undertaken by Congress, but was since happily abandoned. The contemplated work was strictly within the power over commerce which had been delegated to the General Government, and which made it a corresponding duty of that Government to give to it all proper facilities, and relieve it from embarrassments such as he had shown to exist in that of the Albermarle, and which had been estimated to be equal to a levy of from 15 to 20 per cent on all exports. Had North Carolina not become a member of the Union, the opening of this inlet would have been forced upon her by the just demands of her people. Had she now the power to "lay duties" of tonnage, or "imposts" on merchandise, a moderate rate of levies for twelve months after its completion would defray the entire expense of effecting it.

On motion of Mr. G. the resolutions of the General Assembly of North Carolina, and the report of Major Gwynn, were ordered to be printed, and referred, with the bill, to the Committee on Commerce.

*From Cadwallader Jones.*                    U.

Hillsboro',

Feb. 1st, 1841.

\* \* \* \* \*

Your maiden speech has given us very great satisfaction here, and I heartily congratulate you on your brilliant success, it's force, style and temper were admirable and worthy of imitation in Congress, where slang whanging has been the order of the day so long. Altho' we differ on some points of policy, and even on one in your speech, that difference can never prevent me from being fully sensible of the mind and proud of the success of my neighbour and friend.

I thank you for the documents you were so obliging as to send me; I don't know but that I ought to have acknowledged your kindness before now, but as I intended to write you about my little matter of business in the land office I defered it untill I should do so.

There is nothing new here. The health of our town is good as usual in Winter, tho' we have had so far, the most disagreeable season I have experienced since my residence here. The amount of wet weather is unparaleled, raining almost all the time, and the roads next to impassable. We get a mail through about once in two days and that is brought in a box by four horses. I do suppose the roads were never worse, and I am sure agricultural preparations were never more backward. Altho' the water courses are occasionally very high, I hear of no damage being done; we have had no ice to come down upon us as at the North, indeed we have not been able to get enough to fill our ice houses and the ladies are in great truble at the prospect of not getting our usual supply.

I hear of nothing amiss at your place in town, or country, and believe all are well.

*To Susan Washington Graham.*                    A.

Senate Chamber,

Feby. 1st, 1841.

I was happy to be relieved by your kind letter recd on Saturday evening from the apprehension of the small pox in your vicinity at New Bern. The weather here as with you has been exceedingly wet and unpleasant, & this one of the gloomiest days out of doors that I have ever seen. As you are still at New Bern I fear you did not receive my letter of last week directed to you at Kinston.

*   *   *   *   *

In my next I shall be able to give you some account of the new President, who will be here on Saturday. There are already a good many strangers in Washington, & I suppose the crowd will increase untill the 4th. March.

I have been out but little the past week, attended for half an hour, on one evening, a party at Mr. Pleasontons, one of the auditors of the Treasury. The crowds at such entertainments here are too great to render them very pleasant. I would have been exceedingly pleased to see you here, according to our former conversations on the subject, but your reasons for declining are altogether proper and insuperable. The time however is now comparatively short untill we shall meet again as I trust.

Genl. Edney,[10] an original character from the mountains of N. C., is here, and affords a deal of pleasantry.

As the Senate is in Session I must bring my letter to a close.

Bless my children and Continue your affection.


*From Isaac Dockery.*[11]                                    U.

Dockery's Store, N. C.,

February 8th, 1841.

I suppose as a necessary consequence to the honour and success of Gen Harrisons Administration (independant of general proscriptions) a revolution to some extent in the official service of the Country must be effected.

It is not probable that in the approaching distribution of office that N. C. will share very largely, neither is it characteristick of her Citizens to seek office with much avidity. Circumstances however conspire to induce me to present myself as an exception to the general rule, I will not say a rule reluctantly departed from lest it should be construed as affectation. But to come to the point permit me to say that should you in the exercise of your official

---

[10] Bayles M. Edney of Buncombe.

[11] Isaac Dockery, of Richmond County, who served in the commons, 1832, 1834, 1842.

functions as constitutional adviser of the President feel disposed to present some of your constituents as honest and capable, my name is before you.

I hope that our former acquaintance will be a satisfactory apology for this act of freedom with you, I know not in what light you may view office seekers and more especially this application of mine, but grant that you are disposed to exercise your influence to the utmost, and suffer me to dictate the course I would have you pursue and I would say violate no repugnance that you may entertain towards applications of this sort, let no partiality for a Citizen of your own State influence you, but divest yourself of all feelings of an obligators nature and act strictly in accordance with your own inclinations.

If however you should conclude to interest yourself in my behalf, I should wish my pretentions presented in a modest but respectable light, if an office at all one in which real services may be rendered with a corresponding compensation.

This letter is addressed to you in confidence; if however you should feel disposed I respectfully refer you to Mr. Deberry our immediate representative, other testimonials if required I apprehend may be supplied.

*From Jesse Carter.*                                            U.

Mobile,

February 8th., 1841.

It is with sincere pleasure that I have seen you elevated to your present distinguished post, though differing from you on most political subjects, yet my strong recollection of the days of our collegiate life, (the strongest attachments in life) united to my great admiration of your talents and acquirements, has made your success very gratifying to me. Yes, I can now carry my mind back almost twenty years, when I first saw you, your dress and appearance is still present to me & I have followed your successful and rapid advancement in political influence & power, with the liveliest pleasure, and truly hope you may long be permitted to hold your situation, which I look upon as the most honorable in the gift of our Government, as I know you will do honor to yourself, and reflect back credit upon my old Alma Mater. To which, amidst all my wanderings, my heart turns as the needle to the pole, and am cheered by the hope of being permitted to lay my bones beneath her time honored Sod. Do not think these are

"Vox preterit nihil," they are the sincere feelings of my heart. And a strong source to me of consolation, in the reverses which have attended my political opinions, is that it brings some friends like you on the theatre of public life, which they will adorn by their talents and services.

I have been intending to write you for some time, to congratulate you, but have delayed it until now. I take up my pen, in addition, to recommend strongly to your consideration a friend, though strong political opponent, Daniel E. Hale, Esq., of this City, for the place of District Attorney for the Southern division of this State, if there should be any change, which from all I can understand, ought to take place, though the present occupant belongs to the same party as myself. Yet I think a change would be of service to the Government. This is between us, as the gentleman who holds the office married a near relative of Col. King, of the Senate. Mr. Hale has strong claims for the Office, he is a young lawyer of great promise, and industry, and no doubt is amply qualified to perform all the duties to the entire satisfaction of the Government, & he is certainly one [of] the strongest oponents of the present administration that I have ever seen. He is a brother of Willis Hale, Attorney General of the State of New York, during the whole of the exciting campaign, he was untiring in his exertions for the advancement of the Whig cause. He acted throughout, as Chairman of the young men's Whig Committee, the efficiency of whose organization, with their active and ceaseless exertions, was the cause of the success of the Whig party in this City. I know of no one whose claims are superior to his, upon the new administration. Knowing from your talents and prospective influence, for I know of no one of your age who stands your superior, you will have great weight. So I have taken up my pen, to write to an old friend whom I have known from boyhood, who will believe, and place confidence in, my statements. Do exert yourself for my friend. I assure you, you will be promoting the best interest of the Country, & it will be an appointment exceedingly gratifying to General Harrison's friends in this section. I will take it as a great favour, which will be ever gratefully remembered.

If you should find time, I should be glad to receive a few lines for "Auld Lang Syne," and any documents of interest will be gratefully acknowledged.

Remember me to my old friend, Judge Mangum.

Your friend Truly,

*From Thomas Ruffin.*                                          U.

Raleigh,

Feb'y. 9th, 1841.

Although so new in the station, you, doubtless, begin to experience what demands the constituents of an American member
of Congress think, or pretend to think, they have a right to make
on his time and services. I am sorry to be under the necessity of
adding myself to the list of those who thus obtrude themselves
on you, to the hindrance, perhaps, of your appropriate duties,
or, at least, to the disquiet of the little leisure you might have in
the intervals of those duties. But as the consideration that moves
me to trouble you, is more of a *professional* than a personal nature, I persuade myself you will the more readily excuse the
trouble to which my application may put you.

It seems as if new questions in the law, that is to say, questions
upon which direct authority or precedent can not be found, are
never to have an end. One of that kind is before our Court now;
and the object of this note is to ascertain whether there has, or
has not, been an adjudication on it; &, if there be, to get the
favour of you to take such steps as may furnish us with the information in an authentic manner. The point is, whether the death
of a slave pending an action of *detinue* & after issue joined upon
*non detinet* affects the plaintiff's right of recovery, either upon
evidence on the General issue as going to the *value* to be assessed
by the jury, or plea of the fact *puis darriere continuance;* and,
if in either, in which of those two ways. We can find no English
case to aid us; which, indeed, is not surprising, as this species of
action is not much in use there even now, & until *wager of law*
was abolished it was almost entirely superseded by *trover.* But
we are quite astonished that, as the case must have often happened, especially in the Slave-holding States, it is not a settled
point in American law. Yet, the fact is, that there is scarcely anything on it,—at least, in the books that are accessible to us. In our
own State, there have been cases on the circuits; but no decisions
there on argument, and this is the first case in the Court of the
last resort. In the Reports of *Tennessee* & of *South Carolina*, there
is no case on the point. In *Virginia* there is one, & but one; and
that presents a divided Court & very unsatisfactory reasoning. In
a common place book a case is mentioned in the Court of *Ken-*

*tucky,* that of *Carrol* & *Early* 4 Bibb's Report 271, in which we suppose the point came directly into judgment. If that be so, my brethren & I are quite desirous of seeing the case, the arguments at the Bar & on the Bench, & the judgment. Now, my good Sir, the liberty I am taking is to ask, that you will examine the book— which, we take for granted, is in the Library of Congress—&, if such a case be in it, that you will get one of the numerous clerks of your Committees, *to copy it* for you, so that you can enclose it to me, at as early a day as it can be copied. Perhaps there may be other cases, in accordance therewith, in the same series of Reports, or in those of *Harden,* of the same State, or perhaps in the Courts of Maryland. If so, and you can learn what they are, I shall esteem it a singular favour to have a reference to them furnished to us.

By reason of the absence of some Counsel & the legislative fatigues of others, the arguments occupied less time than usual at this term; & we once thought the term would, therefore, be short. But we find the number of *submitted* cases uncommonly great, & that many of them *ought* to have been argued by Councel & are to be *studied* by us. So, that at present there is no ground to augur an adjournment before the common period.

The health of my brothers, as well as my own, is quite good— tho' Mr. Gaston has been a good deal overcome by the afflicting bereavement of his eldest grand-child, the daughter of the late Mrs. Manly.

Oblige me by offering to your colleague my respects & good wishes; and accept, my dear Sir, the assured esteem and friendly regard of

Your most obed't Serv't


*From Joel R. Poinsett and N. C. Paulding.*          U.

Washington,

Feby. 9th, 1841.

The National Institution for the promotion of Science and the useful Arts, established at the Seat of Government is desirous of procuring specimens of the Natural productions of every portion of the United States and for that purpose respectfully asks your aid and co-operation. The district you represent doubtless possesses many important minerals and vegetable productions which might prove of great value to the arts if they were generally made known.—Specimens of such productions being brought to Washington will not only advance the objects of the Institution, but will prove advantageous to the country whence they come. They will be described by the Scientific members of the Institution and their uses and advantages pointed out and the specimens exhibited to the public in its museum.

You are respectfully requested to bring with you on your return such specimens as you may collect during the ensuing recess. Even a single specimen from each member will be of great advantage to the Institution, and be thankfully received as a tribute to Science.

We have the honor to be
> Sir
>> Your most obt. Servts.


*To Susan Washington Graham.*                               **A.**

Washington City, Feby. 9th, 1841.

I received your letter of the 5th. last night, and as I am a day behindhand in writing you I seize a moment to write from my seat. Genl. Harrison has just arrived in the Cars from Baltimore. His arrival has been greeted by the firing of cannon, ringing of bells, a speech from the Mayor of Washington & the shouts of an immense multitude, who notwithstanding a violent snow storm, still falling, thronged the Avenue above and below the depot for a great distance. I witnessed the arrival of the train, & heard the huzzas of the crowd from the Colonade at the East front of the Capitol. I shall call to pay my respects tomorrow. The new President will be greatly importuned & wearied, I fear, between this and the 4th. of March.

Our mess gave a large dinner on Saturday where we had a goodly number of friends and much wit and good cheer, and on last night I attended a large party at Mr. Hill's in this vicinity, where I saw Mrs. Walsh & Mrs. Farly (formerly Misses Pearson) acquaintances of yours. You maybe perhaps conclude from these indications that I am becoming quite a votary of fashion. This however would be a great mistake. While I am honored by the hospitality which is offered, I confess that I have taken but little pleasure in going into the beau monde since my stay here—I declined therefore an invitation from Mrs. Secretary Woodbury a few evenings ago.

*   *   *   *   *

Except the three appointments of Messrs. Webster, Crittenden, & Ewing, I do not think any Cabinet appointment has been determined on. The Senate is in Session. I write in haste & under interruptions.

*To James W. Bryan.*         U. Bryan Mss.

Washington City,

Feb. 13th, 1841.

The Cabinet has been announced this morning, Towit, Webster, Sec. of State; Ewing, of Treasury; Bell, of War; Badger, of N. C., of Navy; Granger, Post Master Genl.; & Crittenden, Atto. Genl., so you see it all. It is said here to be the ablest Cabinet which has been formed since the days of Mr. Monroe.

We have had a pretty severe struggle with our Southern neighbors for the appointment in that quarter. Our delegation first nominated Gov. Owen for the Navy department, (excepting Stanly). But he was assailed by members from other States as an inferior man; and the President elect signified his intention to form the ablest Cabinet he could procure, and intimated through his advisers that he would prefer Badger. We therefore joined in a recommendation of him. Meanwhile Va., S. C., & Georgia united & pressed Preston for the appointment. So highly however is the devotion of N. C. to true Whig principles valued, that we succeeded against them all.

There is a little murmuring in Ga. on account of the neglect of Nullification, but it will subside. I hope Badger may accept, but I doubt it. The appointment will not add any thing to our strength at home, but it will give the State some character abroad if he shall devote himself to the duties of the department as he should do. It is regarded here as the department promising most reputation to a man of real talent & industry, among them all except the Treasury. If Badger shall decline we will hardly present any other name. You see that Stanly was mentioned for the Navy in the papers, and it gave us a little embarrassment, but the course the thing has taken will set matters right again. I hope our friends in the State will at once give in their approbation. If they knew the struggle which has been made against it, I verily believe, mainly from an habitual indifference (to use no harsher phrase) towards N. C. on the part of her immediate neighbors I doubt not but that they would with one accord say Amen.

You will please not mention the fact of Owens presentment, as he is a gentleman entirely, and has been grossly depreciated by our adversaries. If Badger accepts had you not better continue in the practise in the State. The Supreme Court will be an open field. Write me at once on this point. Webster who is to be Secretary of State is very much the friend of N. C. and on quite a familiar footing with me. I will take occasion to mention to him the mission to Naples, and ascertain who desire it. I learn that Monroe[12] of N. Y. would be pleased to go there. And I shall not present your name unless I learn there is a strong probability of success.

The General has been greatly importuned about the Cabinet, but I have heard but little of the missions abroad. I have however merely called to pay my respects to him formally, the day after his arrival. He seemed to be much fatigued and has dispensed with the ceremony of shaking hands. Webster and Ewing are, I think, his chief advisers.

It may be proper for the New Bern paper to give a short sketch of Badger's history and character, as a native of the place, not omitting his military service under Genl Calvin Jones[13] during the War. For although he fought no battles, his readiness at that time to embark in the Country's service may disarm his political adversaries in their charges of Federalism, aristocracy, etc.

---

[12] James Monroe (1799-1870), of New York, a native of Virginia, a graduate of West Point, who served under Decatur against Algiers, and was aide to Scott, 1817-1822. He resigned from the army in 1832, became active in local politics in New York City, and was a Whig member of congress, 1839-1841. He was later a state senator. He was a nephew and namesake of President Monroe.

[13] Calvin Jones (1775-1846), a native of Massachusetts, a physician, settled in Smithfield in 1795, where he became an active practitioner, medical writer, and botanist. He was also one of the founders, and corresponding secretary of the State Medical Society. He seems to have been the first in the state to employ vaccination in his practice. He represented Johnston County in the commons in 1799 and 1802. He moved to Raleigh in 1803, and was again in the commons in 1807, and was also intendant of the town. He was one of the editors and proprietors of the *Raleigh Star,* an active member of the American Colonization Society, an extensive planter, and militia officer, a trustee of the university, and grand master of Masons. He served as adjutant general in 1807-1808, and was in command of the state troops in eastern North Carolina, and Virginia, in the War of 1812. About 1832 he moved to Tennessee, where he owned some thirty thousand acres of land.

There is every prospect of an extra Session of Congress. Wise and a few other busy Whigs oppose it & may go off, but the general sentiment is in favor of it, to consider a National Bank, the distribution of the public lands, and a Tariff on luxuries to supply the wants of the Government.

Present my regard to all & Believe me

Very truly & affectionately Yours

*To Susan Washington Graham.*        A.

Washington City, Feby. 15th, 1841.

\* \* \* \* \*

The last three days have been bitterly cold but clear. The Potomac is closed with ice & the winds are full of nipping frost. The day after I last wrote you, I called to pay my respects to Genl. Harrison, who has taken rooms at Gadsby's. His appearance is indifferent (so I may whisper to you). His room was crowded with company. I was introduced by Mr. Mangum and remained but a few moments without conversing at all. He seemed worn down with fatigue and had dispensed with the ceremony of shaking hands, owing to the hearty jars he had encountered on his journey hither.

He was visited the day following by the ladies and has also visited and dined with Mr. Van Buren, who returned his call. He will go this week to visit his relatives in Virginia. The City is full of office seekers, and the crowd may be expected to increase untill the 4th. of March. Besides which, I, and I suppose each member of Congress receive about two letter daily requesting, that if there be any thing agoing, in the way of office, that would suit the writer, to put in his claims.

The Cabinet is at length decided on, that is, Mr. Webster, Secretary of State; Ewing of the Treasury; Bell, of Ten., of War; Badger, of N. C., of Navy; Crittenden, of Ky., Attorney Genl.; and Granger, of New York, Post Master Genl. Whether Badger will accept I do not know. There was no serious expectation of the appointment of Mr. Stanly, though the Madam had set her heart upon it. During the past week I have dined with Genl. Van Ness[14] of this vicinity, & attended a pleasant little evening

[14] John Peter Van Ness (1770-1846), a native of New York, and graduate of Columbia, M. C. 1801-1803, was unseated for accepting a militia commission, a lawyer and banker in Washington, who was major general of militia.

party at the house of Mr. L. Hardin whom you know. He has a fine wife, and gave us quite an agreeable entertainment.

I have not heard what the President elect will determine respecting an extra Session of Congress, but I presume it will be called. I will not however permit myself to be absent from you in July. . . . I have escaped colds here most fortunately, but find exposure in the open air for a few days past disagreeably cold. I have not been out of the City, not even over to Georgetown since my arrival.

*   *   *   *   *

I think at present that I will leave here the 5th. or 6th. of March and reach home during Orange Court, that is, provided I find that I can be spared in passing on the nominations of the new President.

How are my dear Boys? Does Will walk yet? Has John learned to talk?

In three weeks from the receipt of this I hope we shall all be together again—In the mean time, kiss my sons. Continue to me your love & believe me

Ever Your

I have written the Overseer to attend to our affairs at home which require immediate care, and some time since to Dr. Strudwick.

A letter from Judge Nash last week informs me that all the negroes and other property of F. Waddell & Miss Sally Moore are to be sold at the County Court at Hillsboro' next week to satisfy debts at Bank. Dr. Strudwick, he adds, will suffer considerable loss as their surety. Mr. Cain will be also a loser but not to so great an amount. This is a terrible calamity upon that family.

From George E. Badger.      U.

Raleigh, Febr. 16th, 1841.

By a letter which reached me from Mr. Stanly the day before your arrival I first learned that such a thing as my nomination to a department was thought of. The tidings took me completely by surprise, for I had not the remotest possible notice of such a thing. Had I anticipated it I should have taken care by a timely letter to you or Mr. Stanly to have prevented such an event. It has placed me in a position of great embarrassment. I am urged by letters from friends in Congress to accept—the claims on me of the State—regard for feeling friends—the duty of aiding in carrying out a true reform—the glory of reconstructing our gallant Navy—all these and other reasons are placed before me, & I am urged by the further thought that if I refuse now N. C. will not have any place in the Cabinet. I have consulted some friends here amongst others Mr. Gaston; he says "if you can possibly bear the pecuniary sacrifice & domestic discomfort, I do not see how you *can* refuse to accept." Now as to personal sacrifices, great as they would be & deeply felt by me, I would not hesitate on that score, if I thought I could discharge the duties of the station with credit to myself and with advantage to the Country. I hold it the duty of those who can, to aid the President elect in his sincere and honorable purposes for the good of the Nation. I do in truth look on this as the great crisis of our affairs & believe if the government be not *now* restored, its restoration can only be hoped by a future revolution.

But then, my dear Sir, how can I hope to fill the duties of the office? I have never been in public life. I have no capacities peculiarly appropriate to it & little of any kind. I could, indeed, honestly and well I trust, advise the President for the good of the Country but how to superintend a department. I love and honor the Navy & have since I knew the meaning of the word. I could willingly lay myself out to advance its honor, but something is requisite to accomplish this better than honest motives & ill assured exertions. I should consider myself happy to add any glory to my native State but I could scarce bear the mortification of having disappointed her expectations and cast a blot on her fair fame.

I honor the President and wish the most brilliant success to his admn. but for that *very* reason I feel (besides others) reluctant, greatly reluctant, to place myself in a position under him in which I might disappoint his expectations and sully the course of his admn.

There are great difficulties with me, & I cannot but feel great though now vain regret that you had not prevented the nomination. You know me to be above any affectation in the matter— Will you let me hear from you? Give me some help on the subject. Let me know what I shall have to do & what I ought to know. Speak to me with *perfect frankness* and say that I ought not to accept, that there is hazard, danger of failure, etc. *say what you think without any reserve whatever* and believe me I shall value the favour of such frankness.

As to the Atty. Genl-ship, I should have felt rather more at home, should have hoped the diligence would have enabled me to succeed. But it would have been an outrage upon the Whig party & upon the nation had Mr. Crittenden been left out & I placed in that office.

I wish I were as well out of the present office.

In my opinion Mr. Stanly's nomination would have been a very good one, and would have been recd. by the Whigs of the old North with glad welcome. The notion about *age* you know I do not regard a matter of attention. He who has passed thirty is fit for most things for which he is likely to be.

But that is, I suppose, out of the question.

I had a letter last night from Mr. Mangum; he says in the case of my acceptance I need not come on untill April. How is this? I have not yet recd. any official notification as to the appointment. Ought I to answer it at once when I receive it, or may I take time to think after receiving it & how long would be proper?

I beg you to express my thanks to Mr. Mangum for his letter. As I am much pressed for time to save the mail I cannot even answer it, using Miller's rule, as to him & yourself. Have the goodness to read this letter to him and ask him to consider it equally addressed to himself.

Mr. Stanly suggests to me in a letter recd. last evening that I should not decline *without first coming to Washington.* Do you concur in this & would it be proper this late? I want to do precisely what propriety may require at least.

Excuse this hasty & ill-written letter which I have no time even to read over & write me on its receipt.

Very truly your friend & obed. Servt.


*From Daniel Moreau Barringer.*                           A.

Charlotte, N. C.,

Feby. 21, 1841.

I write you this note with the hope of obtaining information on a subject that is giving our party *here,* & I suppose, *elsewhere,* a good deal of anxiety. Is it possible that Wise, Mallory[15] & other Southern Whigs are likely to oppose Harrison's administration?

Can it be, that in the moment of victory, and even in advance, that they are intending to join an opposition that will be formidable without their aid? For the the sake of the Country & the success of the great principles for which we have contended, let there be *union*.

Do write me on this subject—& write me fully, in confidence, if you choose.

We learn that Mr. Badger is offered the place of Secretary of the Navy. The Register, (unadvisedly I suppose) intimates that he will not accept. Write to him to accept it, by all means. At this peculiar juncture, there should be a gentleman of distinguished ability at the head of that Department. The reasons must be obvious to you, And although he may not at once be familiar with its details, you know that he will do honour to any station. Besides, I think his appointment will be of service to our party, & will reflect honour on the State.

Will there be an extra Session or not? I fear there is much opposition to it in the Whig ranks of the House. I fear that matters are not going on as favourably to our cause as could be desired. And divisions, if there be any, will be fomented and stimulated by every device of the enemy.

The Candidates for Congress are not in the field here yet. G. W. Caldwell has been nominated by the Democrats, but has not yet accepted; I suppose he will however.

The Whigs are determined to run opposition, & I suppose it probable that I may be nominated as their Candidate. I shall be placed by such a nomination in an unpleasant dilemma. I am not desirous to go to Congress at this time, besides you know that it will be an uphill business to contend against a majority of 1100 votes at the start. On the other hand, I am sensible of the obligations we all owe to the party and the importance of keeping it united. What I may do, is yet uncertain. The Whigs of the district, however, are calculating, without any consent of mine, that

---

[15] Francis Mallory (1807-1860), of Virginia, who had served as a midshipman, 1822-1828, then studied law, only to abandon its practice and study medicine. He secured his M. D. degree from the University of Pennsylvania, and then became a planter. He was a Whig member of congress, 1837-1839, 1840-1843. He was navy agent at Norfolk, 1850-1853, and as such was tremendously helpful to Graham, while he was secretary of the navy. He was in the house of delegates, 1853, 1855, 1857-1858, and was, for a time, president of the Norfolk and Petersburg Railroad.

I must be the Candidate, & I may be compelled to take the field. The chances of success are against us here, but if I do become a Candidate, every exertion will be used.

I wish you, in anticipation of such a contingency, to send me, or get some friend of yours to send me, all the documents, etc., that may be useful to our cause on the subject of a Bank, Distribution of the proceeds of public lands, etc.

If removals are to be made in this State, as I suppose will be, I think there should be, *great caution* should be observed in the selection of proper officers. As to this, however, you are as well advised & better than I can be.

Please answer me on the subject of this hasty letter as soon as you can. *Direct to Concord, N. C.*

With great esteem<br>Your friend, etc.

*P.S.* I am here at Court. Manly does well as Judge, so far. His appointment will give general satisfaction—

*D. M. B.*

*To Susan Washington Graham.*     A.

Senate Chamber,

Feby. 23rd, 1841.

I was very happy in reading your letter of the 19th. which came to me last night, and on this day fortnight I hope we shall be all again at our own home. It is not entirely certain but highly probable.

The newly elected Senators are coming in and there promises to be a majority of our political friends in the Senate on the 4th. March without my presence—

* * * * *

Mr. Badger has been appointed Secretary of the Navy, and has accepted the office. He will be here probably the last of this week. You are mistaken however in supposing that the Navy is a subordinate department. At this time that Head of department has it in his power to place it high in the Cabinet Counsels and in the estimation of the American people.

Washington is becoming crowded with strangers. Several persons are here from North Carolina, and the Governor & several others are to be here by the last of this week. The railroad Company from Baltimore has made arrangements for conveying 5,000 persons at one time to this city. The applicants for office are very numerous, and hundreds of letters daily arrive on the same subject. But the great multitude, I believe, merely come to see the show, and take a jaunt.

\* \* \* \* \*

## ARRANGEMENTS[16]
### FOR THE
### INAUGURATION OF THE PRESIDENT ELECT,

on the
4th. of March, 1841.

———————

The doors of the Senate chamber will be opened at 10 o'clock, for the admission of Senators and others, who, by the rules of the Senate and the arrangement of the Committee, are entitled to admission, as follows:

The President elect;

The ex-Vice President;

The Chief Justice and Associate Justices of the Supreme Court;

The Diplomatic corps;

The Judges of the United States;

Officers who, by name, have received, or shall hereafter receive, the thanks of Congress for their gallantry and good conduct in the service of their country, or who have received medals by a vote of Congress;

The Governor, for the time being, of any State or Territory of the Union;

The ex-Governors of the several States;

Such gentlemen as have been Heads of Departments, or Members of either branch of Congress;

Persons who, for the time being, belong to the respective State and Territorial Legislatures;

———————

[16] Printed document.

Persons belonging to such Legislatures of foreign Governments as are in amity with the United States;

The Mayors of Washington, Georgetown, and Alexandria;

All of whom will be admitted at the north door of the Capitol.

Seats will be placed in front of the Secretary's table for the President elect and ex-Vice President.

For the Chief Justice and Associate Justices of the Supreme Court, in front and on the right of the Chair;

For the Committee of Arrangements, on the floor on the right of the Chair;

For the Diplomatic corps, in front and on the left of the Chair;

Such gentlemen as have been Members of either branch of Congress, together with the Mayors of Washington, Georgetown, and Alexandria, will occupy the eastern lobby.

The circular lobby is assigned to the other persons entitled to admission on the floor.

The eastern gallery of the Senate will be occupied by gentlemen, who will be admitted by the outside northeastern door only.

The circular gallery will be reserved entirely for ladies, who, unattended by gentlemen, will enter the Capitol from the terrace by the principal western door, and be conducted to the rotundo and gallery.

Officers of the Army, Navy, and Marine corps, not entitled to admission on the floor of the Senate under the rule, but who appear in uniform, will be admitted by the same entrance; and all other doors and entrances to the Capitol will be kept closed.

The Senate will convene at 11 o'clock.

The Diplomatic corps, with the Judges of the Supreme Court, will enter a few minutes before the Vice President.

The Vice President will enter the chamber at half-past 11 o'clock with the Committee of Arrangements, and be conducted to the Chair.

The oath will then be administered to the Vice President by the President pro tempore.

The oath of office will be administered to the new members of the Senate by its President.

The President elect will arrive at quarter before twelve o'clock, will be met by the Committee at the entrance, and conducted to the seat prepared for him in the Senate chamber.

At twelve o'clock, those assembled on the floor of the Senate, will proceed to the eastern portico of the Capitol, in the following order:

The Marshal of the District of Columbia;

The Supreme Court of the United States;

The Sergeant-at-arms of the Senate;

The Committee of Arrangements;

The President elect, the Vice President, and Secretary of the Senate;

The Members of the Senate;

The Diplomatic corps;

The Mayors of Washington, Georgetown, and Alexandria, and the other persons admitted to the floor of the Senate, in the order in which they are mentioned.

On reaching the front of the portico, the President elect and Chief Justice will take the seats provided for them.

The ex-Vice President, the Committee of Arrangements, and Associate Justices of the Supreme Court, will occupy a position several feet in the rear of the President elect.

The Vice President, Secretary, and Members of the Senate, will occupy parallel lines next in rear.

The Diplomatic corps will occupy the next position; and the space immediately in their rear is assigned to the late Speaker, Clerk, and Members of the Senate and House of Representatives.

The ladies, and such persons as by the rules of the Senate and arrangements of the Committee are enumerated in the preceding programme, will occupy the steps and the residue of the portico.

On the conclusion of the address, the oath of office will be administered to the President of the United States by the Chief Justice; after which, the Members of the Senate, preceded by the Vice President, Secretary, and Sergeant-at-arms, will return to the Senate chamber.

The Sergeant-at-arms of the Senate is charged with the execution of these arrangements; and, with the Marshal of the District of Columbia, aided by the police of the Capitol, is charged with the preservation of order.

All carriages and horses will be excluded from the Capitol square, whether in the use of the military, or otherwise.

These arrangements have been made with the desire that the greatest possible accommodation be given to the people to witness the ceremonies. The arrangements within the Capitol were, from necessity, formed with reference to the limited capacity of the Senate chamber; and those for the exterior were deemed most appropriate, with a view of affording the assembled multitude an opportunity of witnessing the inauguration.

Should the weather, however, prove unfavorable, the ceremony of the inauguration will take place in the Hall of the House of Representatives.

WILLIAM C. PRESTON,
RICHARD H. BAYARD,[17]
A. S. WHITE.[18]

Washington,
*March 3, 1841.     Committee of Arrangements of the Senate.*

*To Susan Washington Graham.*                          A.

Washington City,

March 4th, 1841.

I have just returned from the great ceremony of the Inauguration of the President of the United States. I have not leisure to give you any adequate idea of the grandeur of the occasion. The crowd in attendance is estimated at from 15 to 30 thousand.

An immense procession of the military of the district of Columbia, of Baltimore & Philadelphia, of the Marine Corps, etc., and thousands of citizens attended Genl. Harrison from his lodgings to the Capitol. He was received in the Senate where we had assembled and where the diplomatic Corps of Foreign Governments had been previously received, (each member of it being clad in full Court dress resembling a military uniform but much richer.) thence we marched in procession to the East Portico of the Capitol, to which a large platform had been added. A stand was prepared for the President & Chief Justice of the United States. From this he delivered an Inaugural address to the great multitude below, in a clear, bold, & strong voice, interrupted ever & anon with shouts of applause & waving of hats from the forest of human heads congregated there. And then took the solemn oath of office which he repeated in still louder tones.

The crowd now responded in defening shouts, and a discharge of Cannon almost shook the Capitol. I occupied a station not far

---

[17] Richard Henry Bayard (1796-1868), of Delaware, graduate of Princeton, Whig senator, 1836-1839, 1841-1845, *Charge d'Affaires* in Belgium, 1850-1853.

[18] Albert Smith White (1803-1864), of Indiana, a native of New York, graduate of Union College, lawyer, who moved to Indiana, and became a railroad president. He was a Whig member of congress, 1837-1839, and senator, 1839-1845. He was a Republican member of congress, 1861-1863, and was appointed a federal judge in 1864.

from him & distinctly heard the Inaugural address, & have no hesitation in believing that it will be acceptable to the whole nation.

I recognized in the assembly many individuals from North Carolina who had come on to witness the occasion, Gov. Morehead, Maj. Hinton, Ex. Gov. Owen, Genl. Owen,[19] Col. Long,[20] etc., etc.

The Senate returned to their Chamber & adjourned. The procession attended the President to the White House, which had been by this time vacated for his reception—I could wish that you had been able to look on the scene, but when I was almost fighting my way, with the new Secretary of the Treasury on my arm through the rotundo, amid a crowd of ladies with whom I was thrown in contact, I thought you would not have had the boldness had you been present to make your progress to the scene of the Inauguration. A goodly number of them succeeded in getting on the platform, although it was specially set apart in the arrangements for the Senate, Corps diplomatique, members of the House, etc.

I never before realized the sight of a great assembly of people. But I must be brief.

I hope to leave here on Saturday morning, and if so will be with you at home by Monday or Tuesday. But this is quite doubtful, and you must not expect me till I come. Should I not be there by Tuesday, you will please look into the round trunk in the office, and take out two bundles of papers tied up with strings & marked "Orange Superior Court" & "Person papers" & send Mr. Waddell.

\*     \*     \*     \*     \*

*From Charles L. Hinton.*                                              A.

Raleigh, March 25th, 1841.

Yours of the 22nd. was received last evening. You will perceive by the Governor's proclamation that he has fixed the very day suggested by you for the election.

We had a meeting last evening to appoint delegates to attend at Hillsborough on Saturday to select a Candidate for the district,

---

[19] James Owen (1784-1865), of Bladen, a planter, who served in the commons, 1808-1811, as a member of congress, 1817-1819, and was president of the Wilmington and Raleigh (later Weldon) Railroad.
[20] Probably William Lunsford Long, of Halifax.

some of them will certainly attend. Many of our citizens think it due to Haywood's feelings to urge his claims but will readily yield to the wish of a majority of the convention. I expect he has calculated on running and might feel disappointed if not selected but we should by all means fix on the strongest man. I am sure such would be Mr. Haywood's wish.

In this County the result would vary very little from a strict party vote with any respectable candidate; many think that Dr. Smith would be the strongest candidate or rather that he would get the larger number of those votes that are to contended for.

\*    \*    \*    \*    \*

*From James Phillips.*                                         U.

Chapel Hill

25th. March 1841.

Governor Swain has just put into my hands a communication to you from the Engineer Department, respecting an application you have been so polite as to make in my behalf. Allow me, Sir, to express to you my sense of the obligation you have conferred on me, & to assure you, that whether your kind efforts terminate successfully or not, I shall regard them as an expression of friendly feelings and shall number them with those which we may treasure up in our memories and reflect on with pride and pleasure in the subsequent periods of life. I have long entertained a desire to see the national establishment at West Point, not merely to get a peep at the outposts and be satisfied with a bird's eye view of the place, & its officers, & cadets, & Libraries, & philosophical apparatus, & *hear* an examination, but to take a closer view, & get, if possible, behind the scenes to see how matters were managed there, & bring away all that I might find useful & suitable to our University. I have attended examinations at several of the Northern institutions and confess I was never satisfied with what I saw and heard, and as West Point has a character for successfully cultivating the mathematics, I have long cherished a hope that I should one day be permitted not only to *see* & *hear,* but to *ask questions,* to satisfy myself of the soundness of their modes of teaching, & if good and practicable, introduce them, or suitable modifications of them, here. Govr. Iredell promised me some 10 or 12 years ago that I should have an opportunity of gratifying my wishes, but it has either not been in his power to perform his promises, or he has forgotten it, & I did not like to take the part of even *appearing* to desire office.

The success, however, of the friends of good order & sound sense in the recent political contest led Governor Swain to think that the time had arrived when I might safely be gratified, and to your personal kindness I am indebted for the prospect of success.

In the communication from the Engineer Department the name of the "Revd. Jones Phillips" is used instead of James. So near the *apex of honor,* the consummation of long cherished hopes, it would be a pity to fail through inadvertance. Will it not be *necessary* to correct this oversight in the officer at Washington & set him right? If so, permit me to ask, as a last favor, that you will do what you consider right in this business.

*To James W. Bryan.*          U. Bryan Mss.

Hillsboro', March 29th, 1841.

I hurried off from Washington about a week before the adjournment of the Senate in order to reach Orange Superior Court. Took cold by the way, the weather & roads being intolerable, and did not get into Court, although I arrived at home on Thursday after a days detention at Chapel Hill by high water, untill Saturday. . . . I have since been at home, will go off tomorrow, on the circuit, and shall have but three weeks to be with my family untill I return to the extra Session of Congress. The call is very inconvenient to me as regards my professional business. I had adjourned over several causes in the Supreme Court from last Winter untill the Summer term with the hope of arguing them myself, but I must, I fear now, abandon them altogether.

My little boy Jo. has been quite sick with Influenza so much so that he was bled, & took Calomel besides large quantities of Croup Syrup, he is now better, but quite feeble. We have all had violent colds, the season has been the wettest within the memory of the inhabitants here, and the cold red earth being saturated with water gives us a humid atmosphere.

Judge Pearson had a laborious week here. A negro was convicted of a most brutal murder of his Master. Another was convicted of manslaughter, a case I removed from Person.

Iredell, Saunders, Haughton[21] of Pittsboro' & Gorrell [22] of Guilford came to attend the Court in addition to the former bar.

Dr. Smith has been nominated as the Whig candidate for Congress here. It is doubtful whether Montgomery or Saunders (Monsieur Tonson) will be his opponent. I regard the result as doubtful. Aug. Shepperd or John Kerr will be the Whig Candidate in Hills. district who declines, & Reed [23] of Rockingham probably the L[oco] F[oco]. Fisher is off, and Rencher or Worth [24] is mentioned as the Whig there. I presume the Loco will run no candidate.

Barringer and Green Caldwell [25] are out in Conners district, and Clingman opposes my brother in the mountains. What are you doing in the New Berne district? With proper management we ought to carry ten districts in N. C. now.

By the bye, is the "New Berne Spectator" no more? I made a formal recommendation of it to the Secy. of State on leaving Washington, for one of the publishers of the Laws. Its quietus was taken so quietly, that I was not aware of its demise. But I now find that it does not come here.

Mangum[26] remained untill he took off the heads of Blair and Rives. By a letter from him yesterday I learn that there is much dissatisfaction among our friends at the appointment of Collector for New York. The competition when I left was violent between

---

[21] John H. Haughton, of Chatham, member of the commons, 1844; of state senate, 1850, 1854.

[22] Ralph Gorrell (1803-1875), of Greensboro, a lawyer and planter, who was graduated from the university a year after Graham. He served in the commons, 1834-1835, 1854, in the state senate, 1856-1858, and in the convention of 1861.

[23] David Settle Reid.

[24] Jonathan Worth (1802-1869), of Randolph, a native of Guilford, lawyer, planter, and promoter of internal improvements. He studied law under Judge Murphey, and became a successful practitioner. He became active in Whig politics, and served in the commons, 1830-1831, and in the senate, 1858-1862. He was twice defeated for congress. He strongly opposed Nullification, and was the author of the resolutions by which the legislature condemned it. He was equally hostile to secession, and twice voted against the call of a convention. He was state treasurer, 1862-1865, provisional treasurer, 1865, and governor, 1865-1868, when he was removed by General Canby. He and Graham were devoted friends, and mutual admirers.

[25] Greene Washington Caldwell (1806-1864), of Charlotte, a native of Lincoln (now Gaston) County, M. D. of the University of Pennsylvania, who served as an assistant surgeon in the army for a short time in 1832. He then studied law and practiced in Charlotte. He was a Democratic member of congress, 1841-1843, superintendent of the United States mint at Charlotte, and a captain in the Mexican War. He was a member of the commons, 1836-1841, and of the state senate, 1850-1853.

[26] Mangum, in the closing days of the 26th Congress, introduced into the Senate a resolution dismissing Blair and Rives as public printers, and took a leading part in the attack on them by the Whigs, which followed.

Curtis[27] & Wetmore,[28] it being regarded as a contest between the Webster and Clay factions. And the success of the former is regarded as a proof of the superior influence of Mr. W. That I think a mistake, although I have not a high opinion of the appointee.

Gov. Owen and others who attended the Inauguration made a written statement as to the propriety of the removal of the collector at Wilmington, shewing his intermeddling in elections etc. If it is desired to remove the Collector at Ocracoke a similar statement should be forwarded to the Secr. Treas.

Badger seems pleased with his new station and made a fair impression at Washington. A letter from Barringer informs me that our friend Manly gets on well, and is popular as a Judge in his riding.

*    *    *    *    *

Professor Phillips is on tiptoe at the expectation of being appointed a visitor to West Point this summer. He wrote me yesterday saying his name was *James* and not *Jones* as it had been incorrectly written in a communication from the War Department, and beging that it might be put right, lest the appointment should fail for misnomer.

*    *    *    *    *

*From James W. Bryan.*                                    A.

Newbern, April 3, 1841.

Your letter dated Hillsboro' reached me by the last mail & I was sorry to learn thereby that you were all suffering so severely from colds & the effects of the late bad weather.

I fear you will find the Climate of Washington very trying to your Constitution, Connected with the unnatural habits incident to a member's life. Many Northern Gentlemen have told me that it is the worst Climate in the known world.

I have had much difficulty about being a Candidate, but I believe the matter is now arranged to the entire Satisfaction of the district. I had Mr. Wm. H. Washington[29] nominated in Car-

[27] Edward Curtis (1801-1856), who had been a Whig member of congress, 1837-1841.
[28] R. C. Wetmore.
[29] William Henry Washington (1813-1860), of New Bern, Graham's brother-in-law. He was elected and served one term. He was a member of the commons, 1843, 1846, and state senator, 1848-1852.

teret & I believe the balance of the district has agreed thereto with great Cordiality; he will be Easily Elected, as he has much popularity of his own & the Locos decline bringing out a Candidate. Shepard positively declines, and has betaken himself with great assiduity to the practice of the law, forming his Circuit in the upper part of the district principally. James Whitfield [30] their next choice I learn will not Consent to run & Dr. Watson[31] their "ultimatum," cannot run & so they have made a virtue of necessity & surrendered the track. I have determined to pursue my profession with as much energy as my health & the Climate will permit & shall be at the Supreme Court this Summer if we send up cases enough to make the trip a matter of interest, etc. I really am sick and sore of politics particularly after the late laborious presidential campaign in which I did my share. I was pleased with the result & am satisfied with the victory, and trust (as I verily believe it will) that it will redound to the honor of our Common Country.

Mrs. Washington is making ready for New York & will leave in a few days. Mary has written on for her permission to join the Episcopal Church & Mrs. W. deems her presence essential to Mary's comfort & advantage.

Whilst I think of it, I would beg to mention that the Spectator makes its appearance for the first time on today on a footing which I trust will be of a permanent character; it would however be particularly grateful, to have the publication of the laws of the U. S. & I hope you will jog Mr. Webster's memory if necessary on the subject. We shall be certain to carry this district for Genl. Harrison. I think that is as certain as any event that can happen.

We have suffered down here most severely from colds also. My children have been much afflicted with them & many of our old inhabitants in the surrounding country have been carried off with pleurisy, etc. Dr. Elias Hawes[32] died of the Effects of Severe Cold. We have also the small pox again in town; it was brought here in a vessel, but as the subject was a common sailor the Measures of the police were so prompt & efficient that there is no danger of its spreading.

\* \* \* \* \*

---

[30] Probably James Bryan Whitfield (1809-1841), of Lenoir County, a merchant, who had served in the state senate in 1840, and was a major general of militia.
[31] Dr. Josiah Watson.
[32] Elias Hawes, a well-known physician of New Bern.

We are getting along very pleasantly on the Circuit & are all much pleased with Judge Baily,[33] he is kind, courteous and gentlemanly in his demeanour to the Bar & as it is a point of honour with us not to be excelled in these matters we endeavour to repay him with interest.

Say to Dr. Smith that he has my best wishes for his success in the approaching Canvass & that I would it were in my power to lend him a helping hand. I wish to go on to Washington & see you all during "Old Tip's" administration, but I fear I shall not be able to make it out. It is so much the fashion in these times to go after office, that if I were to make a start I presume it would soon be bruited about that that was my object. I believe that there is but one office in the Gift of the administration that I want & as that is filled by Judge Potter[34] in our State, it is hardly worth while to think about it, although as my brother Attmore says I am a standing Candidate for the vacancy whenever it happens. We have nothing new here or of interest.

*     *     *     *     *

P. S. I have just left our mutual friend Robert G. Moore the Ed. of the Spectator. He has a son Robert S. Moore[35] a young gentleman of fine talents & acquirements who was at West Point for several years & after leaving that Institution has acquired for himself the reputation of a first rate Civil Engineer having been engaged on some of the principal Rail Roads of the Country; he is also a gentleman of spotless character & of great integrity. Mr. Moore (Robt. S.) wishes the situation of purser in the Navy & if you can aid him in the matter you will confer a lasting favour upon one every way deserving of it, oblige his father very much who is a fast & devoted friend of your & I shall esteem it also as a great favour.

*The Death of President Harrison.*[36]                    A.

City of Washington,

April 4, 1841.

An all-wise Providence having suddenly removed from this life, William Henry Harrison, late President of the United

---

[33] Bailey.

[34] Henry Potter (1765-1857), of Fayetteville, a native of Granville, who had been a Federal judge since 1801. He died the following December.

[35] Robert S. Moore was appointed a purser, 1841. He died in 1845.

[36] Printed circular.

States, we have thought it our duty, in the recess of Congress, and in the absence of the Vice President from the Seat of Government, to make this afflicting bereavement known to the country, by this declaration, under our hands.

He died at the President's House, in this city, this fourth day of April, Anno Domini, 1841, at thirty minutes before one o'clock in the morning.

The People of the United States, overwhelmed, like ourselves, by an event so unexpected and so melancholy, will derive consolation from knowing that his death was calm and resigned, as his life has been patriotic, useful and distinguished; and that the last utterance of his lips expressed a fervent desire for the perpetuity of the Constitution, and the preservation of its true principles. In death, as in life, the happiness of his country was uppermost in his thoughts.

> Daniel Webster,
>     *Secretary of State.*
> Thomas Ewing,
>     *Secretary of the Treasury.*
> John Bell,
>     *Secretary of War.*
> J. J. Crittenden,
>     *Attorney General.*
> Francis Granger,
>     *Postmaster General.*

Washington, April 4, 1841.

The circumstances in which we are placed by the death of the President, render it indispensable for us, in the recess of Congress, and in the absence of the Vice President, to make arrangements for the Funeral Solemnities. Having consulted with the family and personal friends of the deceased, we have concluded that the funeral be solemnized on Wednesday the 7th. instant, at 12 o'clock. The religious services to be performed according to the usage of the Episcopal Church, in which Church the deceased most usually worshipped. The body to be taken from the President's House to the Congress burying ground, accompanied by a military and a civic procession, and deposited in the Receiving Tomb.

The military arrangements to be under the direction of Major General Macomb,[37] the General Commanding in Chief the Army of the United States; and Major General Walter Jones,[38] of the militia of the District of Columbia.

Commodore Morris,[39] the senior Captain in the Navy now in the city, to have direction of the naval arrangements.

The Marshal of the District to have the direction of the civic procession, assisted by the Mayors of Washington, Georgetown, and Alexandria, the Clerk of the Supreme Court of the United States, and such other citizens as they may see fit to call to their aid.

JOHN QUINCY ADAMS, ex-President of the United States, members of Congress now in the city or its neighborhood, all the members of the Diplomatic body resident in Washington, and all officers of Government, and citizens generally, are invited to attend.

And it is respectfully recommended to the Officers of Government that they wear the usual badge of mourning.

DANIEL WEBSTER,
*Secretary of State.*
THOMAS EWING,
*Secretary of the Treasury.*
JOHN BELL,
*Secretary of War.*
J. J. CRITTENDEN,
*Attorney General.*
FRANCIS GRANGER,
*Postmaster General.*

---

[37] Alexander Macomb (1792-1841), a native of Detroit, entered the army in 1799, after training at West Point, and was now the senior major general.

[38] Walter Jones (1776-1861), a native of Virginia, read law under Bushrod Washington, was a soldier in the War of 1812, and was United States attorney for the District of Columbia, 1804-1821. He had a large private practice, and was of counsel in McCulloch *v.* Maryland, and Gibbons *v.* Ogden.

[39] Charles Morris (1784-1856), a native of Connecticut, entered the Navy in 1799. He was with Preble and Decatur at Tripoli, was on the "Constitution" in the War of 1812, and at one time or another commanded the "John Adams." the "Congress," and the Brandywine," when it returned Lafayette to France. Admiral Farragut called him the "ablest sea officer of his day," "the statesman of the American Navy."

*From Bartholomew F. Moore.*                              U.

Halifax, Apl. 5, 1841.

I have rec'd your letter—the contents came safely to hand. For your kindness and trouble be pleased to accept my thanks; tender them also to Mr. Mangum.

I was pleased to observe Mangum's course towards Calhoun; I have no doubt that it relieved many of his warm friends from anxiety. I did not myself doubt Mangum, but I could not be insensible to the existence of apprehensions entertained by others. The truth is we must yield a hearty support to the present administration, if with any degree of consistency we can do so. A breach of any consequence in our ranks will restore the spoils party on the first opportunity. I have a very unlimited confidence in the integrity of Harrison and I am assured that he entertains correct notions on the subject of our finances. I look with much anxiety to the development of his views at the ensuing Session in May. Can we furnish revenue without a revision of the tariff? I think we cannot. All that can be gathered from a prudent revision of the tariff, from land Sales & from all other sources will be needed for years by the Government although it shall practice the severest economy. I am therefore opposed to a present division of the proceeds of the public lands.

One of the chief virtues of this administration, one which is expected of it by the Whig party, is the payment of the public debt brought on us by the profligacy of the past administration. This will require the employment of every resource which we can bring into use without exciting odium. Moreover, our defenses are in a deplorable condition, and money must be had to place them by sea and land on a respectable footing. Can we neglect this? It seems to me that we cannot.

In raising money for these necessary objects can we avoid complaint? I fear we cannot, but we must meet it. Patriotism demands it at our hands that we prepare the Nation for war, although in so doing we arouse the elements of popular clamor. Any measures of this kind must be ably backed by speeches and reports & these must be properly scattered throughout the country. I have observed that the Whigs are too apt to be content with doing their duty without taking the needful pains to convince the people of the necessity of the measures.

Before we parted at Raleigh I brought this to your notice & now let me remind you again of attending to this dissemination of the grounds on which the party act. The enemy is always ready to fabricate and misrepresent and you must provide the means of being seen by the public eye, as *victus in curia.*

If you shall resolve on a National bank, I incline to the opinion that it ought to be either with a small capital or a very large one. A small capital will answer to manage the revenue and regulate the principal exchanges, but in the present state of our wretchedly deranged currency, nothing but a very large capital can accomplish the aforesaid purposes & at the same time provide a circulating medium.

It strikes one therefore, that at present the purpose of the institution should be confined to supplying the place of the subtreasury, and the incidental regulation of exchanges. In proof of time the capital may be increased if deemed advisable so as to regulate the circulation.

Pardon these hasty hints and believe as ever

Yr. obt. servt.<br>& friend.

*From  Nicholas  Carroll.*[40]                          A.

New York & Market St.,

April 7th, 1841.

Since we parted so many matters of deep and startling interest have occured that I believe some account of their effect here will not be entirely without interest to you.

You will remember that the general impression in Washington when you left was that Mr. Curtis would be shelved. By a series of movements, I believe unparalelled in the history of appointments, this position rapidly changed. Senator Tallmadge was nominated by the President, but subsequently at his own request withdrawn. Mr. Crittenden left Washington for the North in the full persuasion that the appointment would not be made. Mr. Clay received the promise of the President that it should not be made. Content with this, he left Washington & reached Balt. on the evening of the 18th. The next day came the news of his

---

[40] Nicholas Carroll was an active "Henry Clay Whig," of New York City.

severe illness. The following day it was known that he was considered in a most dangerous and critical state. At this period, with every reason to anticipate a different decision, R. C. Wetmore, M. M. Noah,[41] & M. L. Davis[42] were thrown overboard, Curtis, Taggard & Lord (all Eastern men) appointed.

The Clay men of our City with almost unexampled unanimity had selected and nominated J. Phillips Phoenix[43] as the Candidate for the Mayoralty. You may judge of their surprize on learning the fact of *the* important oppointments for our City being made in direct violation of the acknowledged majority of our citizens.

One week before this we had every prospect of carrying the City by a large majority. The apathy and despondency of the Tammany Party and the acknowledged bad character of their Candidate almost ensured a triumph. This news fell like a dead weight on our friends, and all spirit and activity ceased. The ground we had taken in the contest at Washington was high and unapproachable. Our objections were not personal to Mr. Curtis, but regarding his public and political infidelity. We asked that he should not be appointed, but did not presume to dictate at all who should receive the appointment. It was but another and most painful instance of the want of faith towards the Republican portion of the party at the North. The opposition to Mr. C's appointment was not local but general, extending even to inland, as well as other than our own sea-board states.

The friends of Mr. Phoenix, among which number I am proud to rank myself one, are determined to back him to the uttermost. We enter the field with no hopes of success, but with a determination to effect all we can by unremitting exertion. Mr. Curtis feels that his position is not a safe one, and I believe at this moment, if we could know the truth, he and their friends deplore their momentary triumph effected as it has been by breach of honor, on the part of the Administration, by an alienation on the part

[41] Mordecai Manuel Noah (1785-1851), a native of Philadelphia, lawyer, playwright, and journalist, divided his childhood between his birthplace and Charleston, South Carolina, in both of which he was a reporter. He was consul to Tunis, with a mission to Algiers. After his return, he was sheriff of New York, founder of the *Enquirer,* surveyor of the Port of New York, by appointment of Jackson. He resigned, and founded the *Evening Star,* to support the Whig party. He was later, for a brief period, a state judge.

[42] Matthew Livingston Davis (1773-1850), of New York, politician, journalist, and the adoring friend and biographer of Aaron Burr, was editor of the *Evening Post.* He was one of Burr's seconds in the duel with Hamilton, was grand sachem of Tammany, and was accused of fraud, and convicted, and later acquitted.

[43] Jonas Phillips Phoenix (1788-1859), of New York, a native of New Jersey, who had been an alderman, and presidential elector. He was later a member of congress, 1843-1845, of the assembly, 1848, and again of congress, 1849-1851.

of Mr. Webster's and Mr. Clay's friends if not a coolness between those gentlemen & expediting an excitement under the effect of which a calamity was induced whose results a nation is now deploring.

I left Washington the Saturday the President was taken sick. From the nature of his malady, his feebleness at the time of the attack, and the excitement mentally and physically to which he had been subjected I feared from the first a fatal termination. That anticipation has been mournfully realized. The hearts of all here are too full and too much grieved to moralize over the scarcely cold remains of this good old man. The respect and sympathy of all classes and all parties here is apparent. A deep and settled gloom appears to rest over our City & upon all its inmates. Today every vestige of business ceased at noon; the bells were tolled, minute guns fired, the shipping and public buildings wore their flags draped with black or half mast & all our places of amusement were closed. To morrow guns are to be fired from sunrise to sunset, and from all our military head quarters the flags are to be displayed shrouded in crape. On Saturday the funeral obsequies are to be celebrated and the representatives of both parties have met to settle the arrangements.

The Republican portion of our party have the highest confidence in Mr. Tyler & singular to relate our opponents are disposed to extend much faith towards him. We all believe that *He* will be President, & allow no behind-the-throne influence to operate upon himself.

You can imagine only partially the amount and extent of absolute suffering in our community. Our business matters are at a perfect stand. Our monetary affairs in a state of perfect confusion. No buildings in progress of erection, and our Manufactories & artizans have either ceased altogether or greatly reduced the extent of their operations. I have witnessed many heart-rending scenes and situations in my native City within the past ten years but I assure you sir there are features of absolute destitution now which we have never before witnessed.

Our foreign relations also are in a most deplorable situation. We now see the folly of putting such men as Pickens at the head of the Comt. on Foreign Relations. His ridiculous report, the small men's popularity-seeking speeches, in the popular branch with the equally reprehensible remarks of certain Senators have had their effect.

A very sound and intelligent friend of mine, a Scotchman by birth, has just returned from a visit to England. He tells me that a strange idea pervades every circle there that we *want* to annex the Canadas. He tells me too that the feeling out of Parlament both with the gentry & commonalty is decidedly and emphatical- ly warlike and that it will require all the Conserveatism of both Countries to avert the danger. I have likewise seen letters from high authority, from the Continent by the last Steamer. They state that we do not appreciate the *real* tone of the English people on this subject. That they who have learned to watch them for half a century think *now* they want to fight. That on the part of the whole French people the most intense devotion to ourselves is manifested and in the event most to be deplored the Tri-color would be as the Lilies of old, side by side with our own banner. This they say would be inevitable for however much Louis Phillipe might desire peace his people would in that event force him out of neutrality.

Altogether, dear sir, this is a fearful crisis in our history; brief as it has been, hitherto its stories are all brilliant. I trust and believe in the patriotism, firmness and integrity of all parties & the disposition partially reached to bury the tomahawk to meet the whole emergencies of our Situation.

On Tuesday the 13th we go into our contest, and if we have not success we shall at all events deserve it.

That evening I shall leave for Washington where, should you have leisure, I shall be happy to hear from you.

Believe me, sir, very faithfully

Yr. friend & servt.


*From Daniel Webster.*                          A.

[April 12, 1841.]

The enclosed will show you, that if Va. & N. C. consumes clocks, nails, furniture &c made in Massachusetts, Massachusetts con- sumes no small quantity of the corn of Va. & N.

Now it seems to me this a great deal better than to compel us to raise our own corn, & to oblige you to buy clocks, etc., of Eng- land, who will not take a bushel of yours.

But I will not make a tariff speech.

We have gone through great events and great agitations. Thus far Mr. Tyler conducts in the best manner possible.

Our intercourse with him is of the pleasantest kind.

I have hopes that he will supply our great loss.

Yrs, with most true regard.

[Enclosure.]

*To Daniel Webster from Sam F. Bridge.*

Boston

April 10th. 1841.

Since I had the honor of handing you Mr. Colman's Agricultural reports, I have ascertained the amount of Indian Corn rec'd at this port coastwise for the years ending Dec. 31, 1835, 1836, 1837, 1838, 1839 & 1840 by which you will perceive the amount for 1840 is nearly double that of 1835.

The consumption of the article has been rapidly increasing for the last five years in consequence of the facility of transportation by our railroads.

You will perceive the quantity was larger by 140,000 bushels in 1838 than in 1840. This was owing to the large quantity received from New Orleans in 1838, but which on arrival was found to be heated & mouldy, altho' bro't on the cob, or unshelled.

In addition to the quantity of Indian Corn, which is almost "two millions bushels," there is a very large quantity of *Indian Meal,* annually rec'd in Boston for the consumption of the State and for exportation. I did not push my researches to this article, but can, if you think it desirable.

I also annex the quantity of Oats, Rye, and Shorts for the same years, which may be interesting or useful.

The principal quantity, in fact nearly the whole amt. of Corn is rec'd from Maryland, Virginia and the Carolinas, and consumed by our manufacturing population, our farmers cannot grow it under 70 cts. a bushel, & therefore they sell their Hay, Potatoes etc. & buy Corn.

Waiting your further commands, I remain

Your frd. & obt. Svt.

Statements of the quantity of Indina Corn, Oats, Rye & Shorts imported into Boston coastwise for the years ending Dec'r 31. 1835. 1836. 1837. 1838. 1839 & 1840.

| Indian Corn | | | Oats | | |
|---|---|---|---|---|---|
| Dec 31 1835 | 948,115 | bushels | Dec 31 1836 | 354,113 | bushels |
| " 1836 | 1,672,251 | " | " 1836 | 351,197 | " |
| " 1837 | 1,725,436 | " | " 1837 | 405,173 | " |
| " 1838 | 1,974,038 | " | " 1838 | 443,657 | " |
| " 1839 | 1,607,492 | " | " 1839 | 439,140 | " |
| " 1840 | 1,834,861 | " | " 1840 | 472,296 | " |

| Rye | | | Shorts | | |
|---|---|---|---|---|---|
| Dec 31 1835 | 23,649 | bushels | Dec 31 1835 | 53,904 | bushels |
| " 1836 | 45,054 | " | " 1836 | 30,742 | " |
| " 1837 | 86,391 | " | " 1837 | 48,634 | " |
| " 1838 | 102,473 | " | " 1838 | 49,082 | " |
| " 1839 | 48,624 | " | " 1839 | 52,755 | " |

N. B. The above is for Boston alone, the quantity rec'd at the other ports in Massachusetts viz Salem, New Bedford, Nantucket, &c &c is not known, but the amount must be large, I should think equal to that of Boston, making *four millions bushels* of Indian Corn annually consumed in the State of Massachusetts.

*From Nathaniel P. Tallmadge.*                                    U.

Washington City, 18th April, 1841.

I have made arrangements at Mrs. Ballards for a Senatorial Mess, at the Extra Session.

Her home fronts the North end of the Capital & nearly opposite the great Northern Gate. It is delightfully located for a Summer residence.

Mrs. B. can accomodate 8 or 10 persons at 8. 9. 10. 11 & 12 dollars pr week. The price will depend upon the size and location of the rooms. *All* the rooms are very neat and comfortable.

I boarded with Mrs. B. during one Session & therefore, can say with confidence, that her table will be well & plentifully supplied, and her house clean and neatly kept.

As I believe that a Mess composed of Senators may be both convenient and agreeable during the Extra Session I shall be pleased to have you join me in the arrangement.

Please direct a letter to me at Poughkipsee N. Y. at your earliest convenience.

*From George E. Badger*                                  U.

Washington, 28 Apl., 1841.

I write a line to make a remark & to prefer a request—First the
remark: I am decidedly of opinion that as far as depends on the
new President the cause of the Country is safe. He behaves with
much dignity and courtesy, is intelligent and appears to realize
what the Country expects from his administration & to be resolved not to disappoint their expectation. Everything here increases my hope of a favorable issue of the administration so far
as the good interests of the Country are concerned. I hope though
that our friends will be as active zealous & confident as if our late
Chief had not been taken from us. Now for the request: I shall
be anxious to have the very *final* news of our elections.

Will you yourself give me returns so far as you can & ask personally or by letter some of our friends to do likewise? It will
gratify me much.

> In great haste affectionately
> Yours.

*From Robert B. Gilliam.*                                U.

University of N. C.,

May 31st, 1841.

\*    \*    \*    \*    \*

Whilst I am in my seat, I will call your attention as a Senator
to a subject which I think may turn out to be one of some importance. I have seen it stated in the publick journals, that Mr.
*Joel Eastman* of N. H. has been appointed District Attorney for
the State of New Hampshire. I have read a letter ascribed to him,
and written as recently as 1838, in which he avows deliberately
Abolition opinions, of the genuine Tappan and Garrison schools.
If the letter be genuine, I have no hesitation in expressing my
opinion, that he ought to receive the countenance of no Southern Whig. You can doubtless procure a copy of the letter at Washington, but for fear of your being unable to get one, I will
forward to you, a paper containing it, if I have not mislaid it.

You will excuse the liberty I take in mentioning this subject
to you. I do so, because I thought it possible you might not re-

ceive any information in the matter, if I did not in this way
bring it to your notice.

I am with high regard
Your friend.

*From John Bell.*                                              U.

June 1st, 1841.

Do me the favor to take your dinner with me tomorrow at
5 o'clock and eat a piec of fresh salmon.

Oblige me by an answer, as the salmon will not keep, and I
hope to be able to find friends enough to consume the entire
fish.

respectfully & very truly
Yours.

P. S. Webster told me he had engaged Mr. Mangum.

*To Susan Washington Graham.*                           A.

Washington City,

June 4th, 1841.

I wrote you a hasty, slovenly note from Gadsby's Hotel on
Monday, merely to let you know, that I had arrived here in
safety. I have since taken lodgings at Mrs. Bowen's near the City
Hall in company with Messrs. Bayard of Del. Clay of Ky. &
Henderson[44] of Miss. all Senators. The last has his wife and grown
daughter here at present, but they will leave for New York in
a few days. We find it more convenient to form a mess, composed
entirely of the members of our own body, as we can then regulate
our meals without reference to any thing but our own adjourn-
ments.

\*    \*    \*    \*    \*

Br. James has, I believe, taken rooms by himself where he is
furnished with breakfast and Tea, & will dine at one of the Hotels.

---

[44] John Henderson (1795-1866), of Mississippi, who, after service in the state
legislature, was United States senator, 1839-1845. He moved to Louisiana, and in
1851 was tried and acquitted of complicity in the Lopez expedition against Cuba.

I called on Mrs. Badger a few days ago but did not see her. I dined in company with Mr. B. at the House of Mr. Bell, Sec. War, on day before yesterday where I met a large party of gentlemen.

Yesterday I called to see the President, whose anteroom was thronged by a goodly company. After waiting a short time Mr. Bayard and myself having sent in our cards, were admitted & spent a few moments with him. He seems much worn down with fatigue, but is quite cheerful and courteous. He politely invited us to come up after candlelight in the evenings if we wished to see him *en negligeé.* It is altogether doubtful how long the Session of Congress may last. The Senate, I think, will go on with dispatch, but there has been much disorder in the House of Reps. and I fear some discord there among our own friends as to measures. I still hope however to leave in course of the next month.

*　*　*　*　*

U.

## *From Thomas J. Holton.*[45]

Charlotte, June 4, 1841.

Having been advised by my friends to write to Mr. Webster and Mr. Granger requesting them to bestow upon my establishment such encouragement as they could consistently with the principles of the Whig Party, I have to request of you the favor of recommending my paper to their notice, especially to Mr. Webster, as he has the bestowing of the publishing of the laws of Congress.

In our District the Lincoln Republican a rabid Loco Foco print, publishes the laws, and I think friends ought to be favored in preference of opponents where the chances are the same. Under other circumstances I should not have brought myself to the notice of these gentlemen, but the Loco Focos having established a Press in this Town by a Joint Stock Company (one of its objects being to prostrate my establishment if possible) I have to rely altogether on my political friends for support.

By conferring this favor you will much oblige me.

Please inform me of your success so that I may know what to calculate on.

---

[45] Thomas J. Holton, proprietor and editor of the *Charlotte Journal.*

*From Duncan Cameron.*                    **M.**

Raleigh,

June 7th., 1841.

I see from the Nat: Intelligencer the Secretary of the Treas'y has prepared, and submitted to the consideration of Congress, a plan for the establishment of a "central fiscal agent," etc.,— this plan, I presume, has been prepared with reference to the views of the President on the constitutional powers of the Government over that *particular* subject, if so, the friends of the administration will favor the establishment of a National Bank, & will be expected to support the Secretary's plan, indeed, they ought to do so, unless there be found—on consideration of it *seriously,* that there is some insurmountable objection to it.

The necessity for establishing a National Bank being *absolute,* the friends of the measure should hazard nothing of it's success, *either* in its progress through Congress, or its adoption by the approval of the President, by a difference of opinion, either as to the structure of the plan, or its details. Some plan *must* be adopted, and it is most likely that the plan proposed and recommended by the Sec'y of the Treas'y will be most acceptable to a majority of the friends of the Administration, & to the President himself. Under this impression, I trust [that] you will hold me excused from a compliance with the promise I made, to furnish you with a sketch of a plan for a Bank,— instead of aiding you in digesting a suitable plan, my views might serve only to create doubts and difficulties in regard to the plan proposed by the Treas'y Depart't, and now under the consideration of the committee.

I have read the President's Message with much satisfaction, it is pretty sane, & what I expected and asked for on the subject of a "fiscal agent," he has gone as far in favour of the conversion as his *former* position in regard to that subject will reasonably allow. Care must be taken by its friends, in issuing the Charter, not to force immediate opposition to it by introducing into its composition any provision unaccaptable to him. His own good sense, and conviction of what is required by the deranged and suffering interests of the Country, must be relied on for approving such a plan as will correct the evils complained of.

I fear you will have difficulty in deciphering this letter—my shattered nerves do not allow me to write legibly at any time,—

and the sudden and intense heat of this section has much increased my inability to write fairly.

Present my kind regards to our friends in Washington, & to your Brother.

*To Susan Washington Graham.*                                    A.

Washington City,

June 8th, 1841.

My Dearest

I cannot deny myself the pleasure of communing with you on this, the anniversary of our happy union. It brings with it recollections, which I delight to cherish and which I hope never to forget.

Five years have now passed over us, since we pledged to each other our perpetual fidelity & love. Years in which we have been made to undergo privations & trials, yet in which we have been blessed, most signally. Though in that period we have to lament the loss of parents and other friends, we may still rejoice, that we are spared to each other, and that our attachment is strengthened by stronger & stronger ties, by the remembrance of mutual good offices and kindness, and by the pledges of affection with which we have been favored in our children. It is pleasant therefore, now in the maturity of our joys & hopes to recur to the Spring time of our love. It may serve also to refresh our sense of mutual obligations & to keep bright the chains which bind us together.

I am every day more and more solicitous to hear how you are, & must beseech you to be careful of your health. It would perhaps not be prudent to venture again on so long a ride as to the plantation.

\*    \*    \*    \*    \*

I believe we have nothing new but political excitement in the last few days. I will send you by the first opportunity some likenesses of distinguished men which are printed here. Washington has a large crowd of strangers of both sexes who throng the Galleries in this hot weather.

I went one day last week to see the races, 4 mile heats. There were many ladies in attendance, & much of style and parade. I was much amused to see the impression made on some of the

Northern members of Congress who are not accustomed to race-fields.

I have cool pleasant quarters, but rather distant from the Capitol, & quite a pleasant mess.

Kiss my children & be assured that five years have made no change in my affections.

*From Frederick Nash.*                                                    A.

Hillsboro',

June 8th., [1841.]

Mr. Norwood delivered me your message. No apology was called for; I did not expect you, the evening you promised to call, for I knew you would be too busy preparing for your absence from home; for the same reason I did not call the next day.

The business to which I wished to call your attention was the following: In Princeton, New Jersey, resides Mrs. Susan Solomons, the daughter of Dr. Samuel S. Smith,[46] formerly President of the College at that place, & grand-daughter of the Rev. Dr. John Witherspoon[47] of Revolution memory. She is a lady, as you would suppose, & in very needy circumstances—has resided all her life in Princeton, & thinks herself competent to the discharge of the duties of Post-master at that place. She writes me that it is understood the Post-master there is to be removed, in which case it would be to her greatly desirable to receive the appointment. So far as a female may be competent to discharge the duties of such an office, it could not be conferred on one in every particular more deserving or better qualified.

I had a short conversation with Mr. Mangum, while here, on the subject, & he suggested I should write to you or to him.

---

[46] Samuel Stanhope Smith (1750-1819), a native of Pennsylvania, who, after graduation from Princeton, became a missionary in Virginia, and raised the money to found Hampden-Sydney Academy (later College). In 1779 he joined the Princeton faculty, and in 1795 he became acting president, and president in 1802. Stern and bitter in discipline, he was liberal in his thinking.

[47] John Witherspoon (1723-1794), a native of Scotland, educated at Edinburgh, became a Presbyterian minister. Emigrating to America, he became president of Nassau Hall (now Princeton) in 1768. He was active in the preliminaries of the revolution, was a member of the New Jersey provincial congress of 1776, and of the continental congress, 1776-1779, 1780-1782, and was a signer of the Declaration of Independence. He was a member of the legislature in 1783, 1789, and of the state convention, of 1787.

The message of President Tyler has given, I believe, general satisfaction. It has one peculiar merit—shortness.

You have commenced business in your house in a spirit highly gratifying to every reflecting man. The spirit of kind feeling & of forbearance exhibited in the debate upon the publication of the Message—particularly as between Mr. Clay and Mr. King[48] is, I trust, the harbinger of a better state of feeling in the Senate. May it continue throughout your deliberations.

The whole country is indebted to Mr. Webster for his masterly reply to Mr. Fox.[49] So much for having master workmen to carry on business. We are looking forward with anxiety for Badger's report, nothing doubting but it will sustain his high reputation & honour the Old North State. The time, so long desired, has come, when North-Carolina can point to her public servants & proudly say—such are the men we delight to honour.

*     *     *     *     *

*From Henry W. Miller.*                                    U.

Raleigh, June 9, 1841.

I have taken the earliest opportunity to comply with your request. The *Yeas & Nays* were not taken on the *passage* of the Resolutions either in the H. of Coms. or Senate. I do hope we shall have a Bank & that too at once. The politicians have, I think, been experimenting long enough. I speak this in due deference to any *Whig* experiments, but not to those of the Locos. I wish that the Honl J. Q. Adams could be any where else but in the Ho: of Repts; It is shameful! The Presdt has called an Extra Session to relieve the distresses of the Nation & *he* is Cocked & primed, ready, to harrass,—yea, *insult* Southern members by his

[48] On March 9th, William R. King, of Alabama, in the debate on the public printing, said that Frank P. Blair had been the "political friend" of Henry Clay, and "his confidential correspondent." Clay replied, declaring Blair a "common libeller," and the *"Globe"* a libellous sheet, and that for King to put him on an equality with Blair was "false, untrue and cowardly." King declined reply or comment at the time, and, on March 14th, William C. Preston expressed regret at the interruption of the "characteristic harmony" of the Senate, saying that he was sure that King meant nothing of what Clay read into his speech. Clay apologized, and King replied that he had no such intention as Clay imputed to him.

[49] Henry Stephen Fox (1791-1846), the British minister, 1825-1851, to whom Webster, then secretary of state, had written an elaborate argument in the McLeod case, which was finally settled amicably. When he was succeeded by Lord Ashburton, he remained in Washington for the rest of his life.

Abolition petition *Fanaticism*. It can be called nothing less harsh, & I hope the House will have sense & decency enough to treat with *contempt* all attempts to introduce such a discussion *at this time*. If it is to come, let it be at the regular Sessions. I do hope the House will check the discussion on this subject at once.

I hope you will give us a speech on the Bank or the distribution of the Pub: Lands. The former would be (I should suppose) best calculated to do good to our cause in N. C.

Any speech or documents you may think interesting or useful will be thankfully recd.

### To Susan Washington Graham.                    A.

Washington City,

June 12th, 1841.

Your letter of the 8th. reached me last night by which time I hope that mine of that date had been received by you. It is most gratifying to me to know that our thoughts were mutually turned on that day, to the event which we have so much pleasure in remembering. Long may we continue to regard it as the commencement of the happiest period of our lives.

On yesterday I dined with the President at the White house, with a party of about a dozen gentlemen, and the ladies of the household, some four or five in number. The invitations were verbal by his son the Secretary on the preceding day to attend at $4\frac{1}{2}$ o'clock. I arrived a little before 5, and about half the company had assembled. After the rest had come in, the ladies made their appearance, that is Mrs. Tyler, Junr., the daughter of Cooper[50] the player, her sister Miss Cooper, Miss Tyler & Miss Harrison from Virginia, grand niece of the late President.

His Excellency did me the honor to assign me to wait on the last, and to take seats on his left. The dinner was well served in the style customary here, of dressing the table with flowers, and carving the dishes on side tables, and handing around the pieces on plates. The conversation was keen, & social, in small parties, and sometimes general, the wine good, & the company quite agreeable.

---

[50] Thomas Abthorpe Cooper (1776-1849), an English actor who was a failure at home, but was a star in the United States from 1801 until his retirement in 1838. His daughter, Priscilla, married Robert Tyler. He held various government posts during Tyler's administration.

A gentleman near me, occasionally jeered the President in an under tone about the table furniture, which was so conspicuous in some of the Congressional speeches last year—especially the golden spoons, which are merely smoked over.

Among the gentlemen present was Cooper, the player, the Father in Law of young Mr. Tyler, who was a guest in the family. He bears the appearance of extreme dissipation but was quite courteous in his manners.

After dinner I walked in the grounds in the rear of the President's House which are quite handsomely improved, commanding a fine view of the Potomac. On returning & being about to take leave, a lady sitting by the President addressed me as an old acquaintance, whom I recognized to be Mrs. McCauley just from Tripoli, having arrived at New York six or seven days ago. She had called on business relative to her husband's office and I remained only a few moments longer.

Mr. J. Cameron[51] & Syme[52] of Petersburg who are here, called for me, and we went to Mr. Badger's but did not find them at home.

*     *     *     *     *

I am still unable to say how long Congress will be in Session. The House of Representatives is a scene of confusion & manifests no disposition to expedite business.

Old Mr. Adams is agitating the subject of Abolition, and he is encouraged by those who wish to waste time & make the Session abortive.

Bro. James has taken rooms not far from me, and is quite well. Kiss my boys, & tell them Father will come back after a while.

---

[51] Probably John Cameron, of Wilmington.

[52] John William Syme (1811-1865), of Petersburg, whose mother was a sister of Judge Duncan Cameron. He was a graduate of William and Mary College. He studied law in Hillsboro under Judge Frederick Nash, and began practice in Petersburg, soon abandoning it to become editor of the *Petersburg Intelligencer*, a leading Whig paper. He also served in the state legislature. In 1856 he acquired the *Raleigh Register*. After secession he became an intense and somewhat violent supporter of the war. In 1863 he moved his paper to Petersburg.

*To James W. Bryan.*          U. Bryan Mss.

Washington City,

June 13th, 1841.

On yesterday the Sec. of Treasury communicated to the Senate a plan of the "Fiscal Bank of the United States" with a capital of 30 millions of dollars, the principal Bank to be placed here. The Government of U. S. to own 1/6, & the States the amount of the fourth instalment of 1836, with power to establish no branches in the States except by the consent of the States, saving merely offices to collect and disburse the revenues of the U. S. It is understood to be a sort of compromise between the President and Sec. of Treasury, and will require essential modifications to make it efficient. Some doubt is entertained whether the President will approve a Charter materially different. The opposition dislike this, but will fall back on it no doubt if we abandon it. Suspicions are entertained that President Tyler designs to run for the succession and that he may break with the Whigs on this question, hoping to carry off a fraction of the party and unite with the Locos. I give it you however as mere gossip which may do him great injustice.

I think we can easily get all our measures through the Senate, but there is very little improvement in the House. The new Speaker[53] is but little better than Hunter,[54] and the uproar & waste of time there are as great as ever. You will see that the Repeal of the Subtreasury has passed the Senate, while the House was getting organized.

President Tyler labors very assiduously every day and must be bored nearly to death with applications for office. I called last week to pay my respects, and was detained a while in the ante room, and then went in ahead of about a dozen persons I found there. I have since had the honor to dine with him in company with 15 or 20 gentlemen and the ladies of the household. His son, you know, married the daughter of Cooper the actor. She and

[53] John White (1802-1845), of Kentucky, who had been a member of the house since 1835. He became a state judge just after his retirement from Congress.
[54] Robert Mercer Taliaferro Hunter (1809-1887), of Virginia, graduate of the University of Virginia, a lawyer, who, after service in both houses of the legislature, was a member of congress, 1837-1843, 1845-1847, and had been speaker in the previous congress. He was United States senator, 1847-1861, member of the Confederate Provisional congress, secretary of state, 1861-1862, and senator, 1862-1865. He was one of the members of the Hampton Roads conference.

her younger sister were of the company as well as the Father, who wears a fiery red face, but was quite genteel in his deportment. A gentleman near me took occasion to jeer his Excellency about the "gold spoons" which on being produced were merely smoked over. He is quite affable, and does the honors of the mansion in good style. Sec. Badger is quite devoted to his Department, and I think, gives general satisfaction. I have seen but little of him since my arrival.

Mr. Sergeant has been offered the mission to England, and will probably accept.

The President is rather chary about removals from office, & I believe will not act except upon a written statement of the causes of removal. I have heard nothing this Session as to Ocracoke, New Bern.

The Loco's are in bad temper, and will resist every measure as long as possible.

P.S. The weather is very warm & dry here. The dust of Penna. Avenue fills the air in all that part of the City.


*From William R. Albright*[55]                    U.

*to*

*William A. Graham and Willie P. Mangum.*

Sandy Grove, [Chatham Co.,] N. C., 15 June, 1841.

I have been looking over the sayings & doings of Congress So far as they have come to my knowledge, & I thought, it might not be taken a Miss by you to Recev a line from me by way of instruction. You know in as much as you are in part the workmanship of my own, not that I know more than you do. or that I know half or quarter as much as either of you. but you know I am one of the democracy of the Country. I am mixing with the Good People of this Section every day & I know what they wish you to do about some things; they wish you to econimize in time & in Money. If Mr. Clay will only hold on the Course he has taken, & he should live four years longer he is obliged to be the President of these United States, I mean to go for Retrenchment & Reform in every instance where it is possible, & for a United States Bank. Our people will be satisfied with nothing

---

[55] William R. Albright, of Chatham, was state senator, 1836-1848, 1852.

short of this, & you had as well go to work at once. Say to Mr. Clay go a head. I have voted for him every time he has been a Candidate for President & that I wish to pick the flint and try it again. The President's Message is much approved off here abouts; we are with him in all its measures, & Especially in the division of the Land Money. I think it the best Method of Reducing the Expens of the Government; the Land Money belongs to the States & let us have it and do what we think best with it & if the Government Needs more Money to Carry on the affairs of the Nation let Congress increase the duties on imports, or Rather lay duties on such articles of Luxuries as are duty free. I do hope to see it stated that W. A. Graham or W. P. M. one or the other has introduced a Bill or is advocating a Bill to lay duties on Silks & wine. I do Really think it is an imposition on our *people* that the Necessities of life should be taxed & that those luxuries, Silks & Wines should be duty free. The People have just found out that it is so & it must be altered, or they will Rise in their might & Chastise their agents for being delinquent in duty.

I wanted also, say to you lookout all those Custom house officers when the salary amounts to much more than is collected by them, let them be done away with. It wont do to hire a Man to work when he does not make for us what we have to pay him. Cut down the salaries of officers. Generally, they can afford to work for less money now as one Dollar is worth as much as two used to be.

I would say, I think you ort to be very carefull how you make appropriations at present, we are in debt. the whole Country is in debt. let use then Get along with as little as possible. I would be glad Mr. Clay would take this view of the subject as well as your selves.

I am weary and must come to a close. Would be glad to hear from you.

Very respectfully yours,

P. S. If you dont obey you need not resign at present. or untill you hear from me again.

W. A.

*To Susan Washington Graham.*          A.

Washington City,

June 19th, 1841.

I have recd your letter of the 15th. and hasten to reply. I am much vexed at the conduct of Isaac, & will write by this mail to Mr. Turner. The breaking into a negro house situated as that is, is not, I think a capital offence, and if it were, I believe, I should feel better satisfied to let the law take its course. The loose discipline which has prevailed among the negroes in our vicinity for some time past, requires some examples to be made. As it is, the punishment in case of conviction would be only whipping and I shall propose to Mr. Turner to chastise him with proper severity, without a prosecution in Court.

Indeed, I much question whether the case is not triable by a single Justice of the peace. I will also aid in getting back the stolen property or pay for such as cannot be recovered. I will determine when I return whether or not I will send him off. You will please therefore to direct him to go to his work at the plantation, and if any person comes for him to submit implicitly. His conduct in breaking custody is almost as censurable as the original crime. Please also direct Mr. Bishop to endeavour to get back the stolen property. I feel the more provoked that you should have been annoyed with this affair in my absence.

\*      \*      \*      \*      \*

Mr. J. Cameron & Mr. Edmunds have spent a week here and have gone on to Kentucky. I have been much fatigued this week, meeting the Bank Com'tee at 10 o'clock, the Senate at 12, and a meeting for the consultation of our friends at 5, every day, untill yesterday.

Affairs are yet in the utmost degree of uncertainty, as to the great measures for which Congress was convened. It will be with some degree of inconvenience that I shall be able to go home in the early part of July as I had hoped, though I still expect to do so. Write me frequently and let me know how you are.

Memorandum.    U.

[June 24, 1841]

Sir:

To meet Mr. Buchanan & silence him and his party, do you call on the Sec'y of Treas'ry and ask him to issue a circular to the several Auditors & Comp'rs., etc., to answer who were appointed under Gen'l Jackson & under Mr. Van Buren, and if the Secretary's call is full, you will be astonished at the answers.

In the 3d. Auditor's office, a Mr. Hampton was from party grounds promoted over the heads of the Whig clerks, by Mr. Woodbury, and Mr. Ewing, the present Sec'y of Treasury, as soon as he was informed of it, countermanded it, and promoted the gentlemen who were entitled to it. Mr. Hampton was a locofoco & belonged to a locofoco Club, which was made known or represented to Mr. Woodbury—this, Mr. Woodbury can't deny— in an other auditor's office, an Irish bar keeper, at Gadsby's tavern, was brought in over the heads of gentlemen old and experienced, & regularly entitled to promotion; he was put *on copying,* while they were kept on *accounts.* Gen'l Jackson had worked at Gadsby's—another vacancy occurred, and the other person, named Overton, a relation to one Judge Overton,[56] of Tennessee, was brought in over these gentlemen—he too was put *on copying,* while they were on accounts—he was so worthless and such a drunkard, that he could not even copy, and got an other person to do it for him; yet he was retained over the gentlemen till he was transferred to an higher station, when the duty ceased by law & he left—: or Mr. Van Buren appointed a Doct. Martin in this same office over the heads of all; the Doct'r admitted he was unfit, and that he could not be an accountant,— and last Summer *Mr. Van Buren* appointed a Mr. Dunscomb over the heads of the gentlemen in this same office—Here, Sirs, is a matter for Mr. Ewing to look into—A circular addressed to the several Auditors, Comptrollers, &c. &c. &c. if drawn up properly, will shew you, what Mr. Buchanan will be ashamed of, & make Mr. Woodbury blush to see.

Let a call be so framed, that the answers must come, so searching, that you will not hear any thing more about removals, &c. I am no office holder, and want none, but give you facts to

---

[56] John Overton (1766-1833), a native of Virginia, who moved to Kentucky, and then to Tennessee, where he was intimately associated with Andrew Jackson. He was a judge of the state supreme court, 1804-1810, 1811-1816.

move on, to meet Mr. Woodbury's conduct, and his party. I have addressed Mr. Mangum, to whom hand this, to frame his enquiries from

Penn.
24 June 1841.

*From James A. King.*                          U.

Brandon, [Miss.,]

June 24th, 1841.

\*   \*   \*   \*   \*

I have purchased an interest in a plantation in La. and early in the Fall shall remove to Mobile, Ala. having formed a co-partnership with Judge Martin in the practice of the Law at that place—Judge Martin formerly of Salisbury, N. Ca. I had for some time determined to quit this State; every thing here is so utterly deranged, and men generally have so entirely cut themselves loose from all restraint, both moral and legal, that I think it becomes all men having a due regard to their welfare and character to abandon the State. For example, we are gravely discussing the question whether we should pay the State Bonds, and the State is divided into Bond and Anti Bond payers; this question for the present is absorbing all others, and I would not wonder if the Anti B. payers succeed at our Fall elections. Ultimately doubtless the honest men of the Country will prevail, but for the present I fear that utter disgrace awaits our State; the contest will be an angry one.

I am requested by an Uncle of mine, Andrew King, to ask your attention to an application he has made for the appointment of Land Receiver at a new land office to be established in this State on the Missi River at Victoria; he has written Mr. Henderson on the subject, & would regard it as a fav'r if you would confer with him about it. I feel free to state that he is every way well quallified for the appointment; he is a gentleman of great integrity of character & highly respectable intelligence and would not fail to give satisfaction to all parties concerned. He was speaking to me on the subject, and I told him that I thought I could take the liberty of asking your attention to the matter. I do not know that you knew any thing of him in N. Ca. If you should have occasion, see Hon'l L. Williams and your brother, both of whom knew him well. I suppose you must be exceedingly harassed with communications of this kind, and it is therefore with some reluctance that I have ventured to trouble you.

I will take this occasion, the first that I have had, to offer you my sincere congratulations upon your election to the Senate. I should like on many accounts to have had *a hand* in that election. I am not in the habit of exulting over political adversaries, but I should have over Haywood and his followers.

But apart from this I am glad to see you in a position where you may render our Country important services, besides acquiring for yourself such a reputation as your friends are anxious that you should and believe that you can.

\*    \*    \*    \*    \*

*To Susan Washington Graham.*                    A.

Washington City,

June 26th, 1841.

I recd your letter of the 22nd. on yesterday, and read with infinite gratification your account of the little boys. I am delighted to hear that Will is walking, and that they all keep me in remembrance. I have hoped to visit you in the course of the next week but as the Bill for establishment of a National Bank is under discussion in the Senate, I would not be excused for leaving untill it is finished.

Possibly I may come the week following but do not expect me too certainly. Public affairs are in a most troubled sea, and it will require the exertions of every one to bring them to a safe result. Indeed, I think, a fortnight now will determine whether the Whig party are to be broken into fragments; I still however hope for the best.

I am quite indignant that Bishop shd. have circulated the false information you mention, and if he persists in it, I hope you will dismiss him from the plantation at once. I have written to Mr. Turrentine respecting Isaac and also to Mr. Norwood, consenting that he shall be whipped in an exemplary manner without the form of legal trial, if the evidence shows him to be guilty. He should be directed therefore to return forthwith to the plantation.

\*    \*    \*    \*    \*

The remains of Genl. Harrison were taken from here today, by a Committee from Cincinnati. Among them I found an old friend and school fellow, Mr. Vaughan, formerly of Camden, S. C. now a lawyer of Cincinati.

The coffin was encased in Zinc, and then, put in a plank box making a very heavy weight. A procession attended it, from the Congressional burying ground to the railroad depot, where an immense crowd assembled to see it embark. The President and Cabinet rode up just before the departure.

Genl. McComb,[57] Commander in Chief of the Army died here on yesterday of Apoplexy. His Funeral will take place on Monday.

\* \* \* \* \*

The heat here has been more oppressive than I remember to have felt it in N. C. Mr. Clay, who is in my mess, rises by 5 o'clock every morning and rides on horseback untill breakfast. I am not so industrious, but usually take a considerable walk with my friend Bayard in the evening.

Many members of Congress from the South have their families with them, and contemplate going to some of the watering places. I wish we could do likewise.

To the hands of a merciful Creator I commit you.


*From Matthias E. Manly.*                                   U.

New Bern,

June 30th, 1841.

\* \* \* \* \*

Since my election to the bench I have abstained as much as possible from all interference in politicks or political appointments. I do not now wish to be understood as recommending the removal of anybody. Your friendly aid is only solicited in the event of the removals being decided upon and when the matter shall regularly come up before the delegation for debate.

I do not know what the views of the Rep. from this district are but take it for granted they are favourable. I am satisfied at any rate that my friends should abide his judg't.

I am obliged to you for documents; Mr. Washington has also been kind enough to transmit important papers, and I will thank you to tender him my best respects and thanks for the same.

---

[57] Macomb.

I have felt deep mortification at the recent proceedings of the house of Rep. There is hardly a man in the country, however rude his own actions and conduct may be, that does does not turn away from it with loathing.

Mrs. McCauley has been here and I think is rather more excentric & comical than she was formerly From her own account I take it you must have had a queer affair with her at the President's Mansion. She says that she wants me to write to the President! or to you about her affairs; what they are I can't exactly learn but (as the phraze goes) I suppose she is up to any thing.

There is a story in circulation here that Mr. Sec'y Badger treated Mr. Southard very rudely at the dinner table of the Sec'ty-of War. How is this?

Your friends here are well There is a great revival of religion going on in all the churches but chiefly in the Baptist and Mrs. Washington is perfectly happy

\*    \*    \*    \*    \*

*To Susan Washington Graham.*        A.

Washington City,

July 2nd, 1841.

My Dear Susan

I write this morning, not that I have any thing to say, except that I am was disappointed in not hearing from you, yesterday afternoon.

There are several gentlemen here from N. C. viz. Gilliam, Roberts of Granville, W. B. Wright,[58] Fayetteville, Jas. Ruffin & Allen Jones, from Alabama. Almost every body who travels in the hot weather takes Washington in his way.

The Sessions of the Senate are quite laborious, Commencing at 10 o'clock & often continuing untill 4 or 5. The Bank bill is under discussion on the question which divides the Whigs.

Bro. James is well.

---

[58] State senator, 1862-1864.

*From Daniel Webster.*                                         U.

Department of State,

July 2nd, 1841.

In answer to your note of the 1st. instant, I have the honour
to inform you, that the papers appointed to publish the Laws of
the present session, in the State of North Carolina, are the
Raleigh Register, The Newbern Spectator and the Highland
Messenger.

> I have the honour to be,
> Sir,
> Your obedient servant,

*To Susan Washington Graham.*                                  A.

[Washington,]

Sunday Morning, July 4th, 1841.

I am much obliged by your letter of the 29th. June, and
although I believe I wrote you a brief reply a few mornings ago,
I seize this opportunity to do so again.

\*     \*     \*     \*     \*

Mr. Bishop should correct Joe at once for his insubordination,
and Isaac also if he was present & did not interfere.

\*     \*     \*     \*     \*

I had yesterday a letter from Parson Witherspoon[59] suggesting
some ideas on the Navigation of our Coast, in which I was glad
to learn that the Wheat crop is likely to turn out well in Orange.

I had yesterday a visit from old Mrs. Royall,[60] who you know
publishes a defamatory paper here, in which she describes persons, characters, etc. And I presume I am to be Gazetted without
much delay.

Last evening Brother James & myself went and took Tea at
Mr. Badger's sans ceremonie. George Little of Raleigh is there

---

[59] The Rev. John Nash Witherspoon, a graduate of the university, D. D.,
Princeton, 1836, A. M., 1853, moderator of the Presbyterian general assembly, 1853.

[60] Anne Newport Royal (1769-1854), of Washington, "Godless Anne Royal," a
native of Maryland, traveller, author, who for some time edited a newspaper
which was vigorously critical of Government officials, and public men generally.
She was convicted in Washington of being a "common scold." She was shrewd
and poisonous.

& has made a handsome speculation in getting a pension for an old woman of $3,000. of which he is to have one third. Mrs. Badger is quite admired in society here.

For several evenings past there has been a military parade of a company of Flying artillery of U. S. troops in the open grounds near the President's House, who have kept up a canonading which has attracted large numbers of spectators; this is the only company of the kind in our service. You may remember that we saw a similar company of British troops maneuvring with a regiment of Infantry at Niagara.

There has been no gaiety in the City this Session; the weather has been oppressively warm, but for a day or two past, it is pleasant. My time has been passed in delving into questions of Banks, currency, etc., and in attending the Sessions of the Senate. Except our social hours at meals I cannot say that it has been pleasantly spent.

For a few mornings I have ridden before breakfast on horseback, which I have found quite a recreation.

*To Susan Washington Graham.*                              A.

Tuesday, July 6th, 1841.

The Senate adjourned over from Saturday untill Tuesday to observe the ceremonies of the anniversary of Independence on the 5th. There were military parades, dinners, processions, etc. The Sunday Schools of the District of Columbia appeared in procession with all their pupils to the number of 2,000, and were addressed in the Capitol grounds by Mr. Southard President of the Senate. The rooms of the President of U. S. were open for the reception of company from 12 untill 3 P. M. I rode up with Mr. Clay & remained about an hour. The company was small, perhaps owing to the shortness of the notice & the fact that the House of Reps. was in Session.

None of the ladies of the Secretaries were there, and no one of the Foreign Ministers.

In the crowd I met with Frank Stanly[61] whom I had not seen for several years.

---

[61] Frank Stanly (d. 1862), a son of John Stanly, of Craven, was briefly a student at the university, and became a Methodist minister.

Bro. James dined with a large company at the President's in the afternoon.

Your acquaintance, Lieut. Russell is here, and desirous to be restored to the Naval reserve.

\* \* \* \* \*

There is no telling when Congress will adjourn. In the course of this week I presume more can be ascertained on the subject. There are various speculations about the President's course on the Bank question, but it is not known what he will do.

I fear I may not be able to be with you for a few weeks. Write me frequently, however, & if you desire I will come.

My blessing on my children.

*From Priestley H. Mangum.*[62]                                           U.

Hillsboro',

July 7th, 1841.

I drop you these lines for information. Appearances in Congress have caused me much uneasiness, and I am apprized that a correct estimate of them can be made only by those whose position at Washington affords an insight into the *under current* of the great stream of events. Why is it that, even in the Senate, there is so much diversity of sentiment upon *Whig measures,* which we all thought in this Country commanded the undivided support of the friends of Gen'l Harrison? Do I correctly perceive, as I think I do, a Cabinet attempt (I mean the Webster portion of the Cabinet) to thwart and postpone Mr. Clay upon the subject of the Bank, under the sinister pretence of going for the only plan of a Bank which Tyler will sanction, & thereby keep together and impart strength to the Whig party, whose success would otherwise be destroyed by the President's veto? When in fact and in truth, the postponement of Mr. Clay is a sweeter morsel than the triumph of our principles to some Gentlemen?

Or is it, that Ewing's plan of a Bank with its Democratic feature of establishing Branches whereby the Constitutional power is virtually surrendered, really is the best? If I were a Whig Congress, I fear I should act the despot. For I am much inclined to think,

---

[62] Priestley Hinton Mangum, of Orange, a graduate of the university, lawyer, teacher, member of the commons, 1832. He was an elder brother of Willie P. Mangum.

that if President Tyler is—in common with Wise, Gilmour,[63] etc these Virginia Whigs in power,—an *impracticable* & under the influence of that clique of politicians; the sooner he stood upon his own bottom, the better. He should take *the responsibility*. And if he proved craven, and shewed the white feather, upon his own head rest the fault—*for my President is dead and I couldn't help it*. But this would not do in practice. If we can't get the best, we will the next best—& if not that, the best we can. Yet it is vexing to see some of your Bank Whigs in the Senate and some of your land-distribution Whigs in the House! What does all this portend?

You can't well imagine how *the party* are chuckling over your divisions. I begin to apprehend that many of our political brotherhood possess but little more merit than our opponents.

Will you write me about these things—all about the political movements among you. For I take it for granted that there are such, & that they are likely to prove ultimately an impediment to the success of those vital principles for which we have been struggling.

We are generally well here—nothing local of any moment. The absorbing subject throughout the land is the critical position apparently of—I can't say with certainty—of the Whig administration, for it is with us growing very doubtful, whether since the death of Gen'l Harrison the Country is to be considered under a Whig Administration, or not. This is the subject upon which the whole thinking Country is seriously, gravely, painfully but silently engaged in the most fearful contemplation.

Say to my Brother that all are well.

Your friend

*From Edmund Strudwick.*     U.

9th July 1841, Friday,

Hillsboro, N. C.

On Wednesday about 2 o'clock P. M. the 7th inst. the little stranger[64] for whom you felt much anxiety arrived safely—in the midst of a smart thunder storm. Mrs. Graham is very well—had a

---

[63] Gilmer.
[64] James Augustus Graham (1841-1909), later a graduate of the university, Confederate captain, lawyer, and state senator, 1870-1872.

"good time"—& is now—for I've just seen her—as well as I ever saw a lady under similar circumstances. I congratulate you, Sir, on being the proprietor of a team of boys—I might say babies— for I believe Joe the eldest is only 4 years of age.

I wrote yesterday to Jas. Ruffin & begged him to make a representation to Mr. Badger in behalf of Dr. Ashe.[65]

If there is anything that I could do to promote his success that I have omitted, if you will be kind enough to suggest it—I'll attend to it promptly.

I take no Washington paper, & will be obliged to you to send me the Madisonian—tri weekly—begin the paper with the 1st of this month.

*From Edward B. Dudley.*                                    U.

Wilmington

July 10th. 1841.

My old friend Major J. D. Ward having been indulged with your frank to convey to me a packet, I trust you will pardon my replying through the same medium, and to ask the favour of you to have the enclosed delivered at your convenience to him. I will take the opportunity to thank you for the friendly disposition which he says you have evinced in his favour. I believed him patriotic and capable to discharge the duties of any office to which he might aspire, & I know he needs something of the kind for support or else I should never have asked your friendship to him. He was a light hearted, thoughless youth & spent without much advantage to himself the property he inherited from his Father, & now in more advanced age, and threatened with sickness I fear will feel the want of it. Endeavouring to be frank and independent he lost the confidence of his political party, and the Clerk of the H. of R. discharged him & I fear without gaining any hold on the Whig ranks "between two stools" he is likely to come to the ground.

My humble opinions having been dragged before the Senate on the subject of Banks, I will take the opportunity to say to you that I verily believe Mr. Clay's bill is the very best expedient which can be devised to releave the Country from its present distress & prostration.

---

[65] William Cincinatus Ashe.

My preference for *remodelling* a system of State Banks under the auspices of the *Federal Government* proceeded somewhat from the station I occupied, and mainly from the difficulty of re-chartering a National Bank, and to avoid if possible the opportunity to demagogues to convulse and revolutionize the pecuniary affairs of the Country to the great injury of all. (And who have we to thank for it). In other things I would give a National Bank the preference.

My plan was not responded to, it is true. Nor was any other reported on, or advocated. If I had recommended a National Bank it would have been avoided with equal if not greater dread. The last Legislatures were afraid, or ignorant, of the subject, and would not touch. The fact is, I believe at least, that if our State was polled, a very great number of our population would be found to be very indifferent on the subject—that they are distrustful of Corporations of any kind & are ready to oppose masses of wealth in corporations or individuals at the polls or elsewhere. None but business men think or care for such matters, & they are not a majority in our State. If both sides of them, I believe, desire a National Bank under the full conviction of its necessity to releave the Country; the Democrats won't say so without you fail to make a Bank which would bring both sides on Congress. If you make a Bank the Democrats will denounce you for the deed, at the same time will be extremely glad to partake of the benefit—even Mr. Calhoun could not prevent So. Ca. from asking a branch, if it was so conditioned, as No. Carolina did in her palmy days of democracy, & that through Mr. Macon[66] for a branch of the old Bank, & so would So. Ca. through Mr. Calhoun of the new, if it could not be otherwise obtained.

Congress is looked to anxiously for relief, & if something is not done, the execrations of the people will be deep & wide.

I regret to see so many frivalous amendments offered to the bill; it seems to be forgotten that there are two sides to a Bank by the friends of the measure, the enemies of course will do all they can to defeat openly & insidiously, but the friends should recollect that *some* inducement should [be] offered capitalists to venture. The odour of such institutions both with Progress

---

[66] Nathaniel Macon (1757-1837), of North Carolina, a Revolutionary soldier, lawyer, and planter, was educated at Princeton, was state senator, 1780-1782, 1784-1785, a Democratic member of congress, 1791-1815, (speaker, 1801-1807), United States senator, 1815-1828, (president *pro tem*, 1826-1828); president of the convention of 1835.

and the People may scare them off. They may refuse to enter an institution where they might be considered as rascals in the face of the Charter and in that way defeat the wishes of your patriotic Statesmen & others. Excuse my scribling I have done, while I have the honor to be,

Very respectfully

Yr. obed't. Serv't.

*From James Graham.*                    U.

H. R., Thursday,

July 15th, 1841.

Mangum has made an agreement with Rives of Va. who is absent that, he will pare off with you, if any vote on the Bank should be pressed *on,* or *before* next Wednesday.

I think there will be no question taken on the Bank in the Senate before Wednesday. Rives will probably not return before Saturday week.

Still you of course will return as soon as you can with propriety. I think the Bank cant pass the Senate.

*To Charles Plummer Green.*[67]             U.

T. J. Green Mss.

Washington City,

July 18th., 1841.

I hasten to acknowledge the receipt of your favor of 14th. inst. I perceive by the R. Register that Mr. Henry will go out no more during the Canvass. So that our Candidates for the Legislature will have a fair field in their respective Counties. I have the most cheering accounts from Orange, Stokes, & Surry, and our Northampton friends, I learn by a letter from one of the Candidates, are in good spirits. Craven, I presume, we shall lose, as there were no Whig candidates at the latest dates, though we had the members in the Commons of the last Assembly. We can afford to lose

---

[67] Charles Plummer Green, of Ridgeway, Warren County, an active Whig, and a friend of Graham. He was a brother of General Thomas Jefferson Green. (*q. v.*)

18 from the last Legislature, and still retain our majority. We calculate on gaining one in Orange, the Senator from Greene and Lenoir, and one perhaps in Stokes, and the prospects are fair for a gain in Columbus.

As to the $6,000 for furniture of President's House, it was contained in the Civil and Diplomatic appropriation Bill, 3rd. March, 1841. You know that V. B. was then President, and had a majority in both Houses. Gen'l Harrison was installed the day after this Bill was approved, and the next Congress did not meet, untill the called session, 31st. May. Our N. C. members were not elected untill May, and so of some other States.

The Yeas and Nays on Bankrupt Law, which have been recently published in most of our papers, shew that it could not have passed but by the aid of Demo. votes. Even the appropriation to Mrs. Harrison was voted for by Buchanan and Walker, two of the most conspicuous men of the party.

I have sent some documents to our friends in Northampton, and will add such others as may seem to be useful.

My impression is that we will carry the State by a handsome majority, though much will depend on the counties you mention as doubtful.

The great subject of agitation now, is the Tariff. The true ground for our friends on that subject is that it is not now, as formerly, a question of laying duties for protection, and raising more money than is wanted for revenue. But the simple state of the case is, that the Gov't costs 20 odd millions of dollars per year. The reduced duties now existing (if by Law we have any existing) yields about 13 millions. Now, the question is, whether the balance is to be raised by a Tariff, in which men only pay as they consume foreign goods, or by direct taxes on lands and slaves, as was done during the war. He who is not for the latter (and no man with us will acknowledge that he is) must agree to raise the amount needed, by a Tariff. Or he is in favor of what is worse than either, and that is withholding supplies, and disgracing the Gov't.

I write you in great haste.

Very truly yours,

P. S. I am afraid we can't adjourn in time to get home to the elections, tho' we hope to do so by the 1st. Aug. I can't therefore say when I will pass Ridgeway.

*From* _____                                              U.

Fayetteville, N. C.,

July 20, 1841.

Dear friend of liberty

I am sorry for my misfortune of not being personally acquainted with your kind honour, as my circumstance at this time is such that I should be acquainted, & certainly I would feel easier in my mind.

I have written a letter on the 30th. of last month to the high honourable Senator from Ky.—Henry Clay—who I think is the most honourable, honest Patriot of this, or any other Country, & I also think he is the most useful man, & the greatest Solomon we have seen since the days of Solomon, King of Israel.

I have written another letter the same day, to the very fine, high honourable Secretary of War, John Bell, who answered it amediately, through his department, with his commanding officer telling me my letter would be attended to as soon as Congress could make an action on the case, & also asking the officer all about, & its use to us running Congress.

The Commanding officer says to me, he recommended the use of it to them in the highest consideration, & that he thought you shorely must have it [in] Congress.

My object is to introduce the sale of one of the finest Spring in this or any other country, it emits some like Three hundred Gals. of the pure, cool, clear, fine tasted, hard, healthy, light water in the twenty four hours, it emits out of the base of a high hill, on which the Arsenal Buildings are agoing on, it lyes with in fifty yards of the Officer's Quarters, now built and a building, & about equidistance from them both, its use can be brought to any of the houses by an incline pump in the Arsenal yard.

Dear good man, I now stand before a stranger, under the necessity of living unacquainted with your kind honour; some of my Whig friends have told me of your good kindness & purfection. I know your are one of our own statesmen, & our chosen & by that means you will be desirus at any rate to doe all the good you can & no harm.

I have got in debt here very lately owing to a friends death, who left a large estate of land amoung which there is a certain plantation is worth Twelve thousand, if it was mine and paid for I would not take any money for it that could be got for it, & there is a debt of Three thousand five Dollars over it, & If I cannot rase the money I cannot go into the purchase.

There was a move made last Congress to buy the said Spring at 5000$, sixteen of the Senators went into the buying it & sixteen others against it & the speaker after some pause went against buying it & by that means lost the sale at that large price, though it is fully worth it, & if your Congress was to see it, you would most shorely say so, indeed, and now for the sake of my necessity I am willing to take the $3500. for it.

There is another Spring close on to this, of the same quality & size, that was sold as follows, one half at $2760, & the other $1950, equal to 4710$ to this Town water company, & now my distress rules me very hard, & shows me to any thing like the usual necessity.

If it should be the will of the Lord that I could get your honour to take my case in to consideration & go to the excelent fine Secretary of ware, John Bell, and also Messrs. Clay and Mangum, and put your head together I am very shore the poor Whig's cause would come out safe, victorius, it will be a shame at any rate if they do not buy it now after geting water out of it so long, all hands of them, or shall the grate honour of the nation subject themselves to beg such small favours of a poore beger like I, or any poor man else. Now as I have always left it to their honour I will do so yet. I should be more than glad if the If I could regulate the friends to go in to the purchase of the Spring, I would gladly come subject to any fare compensation that would satisfy a Gentleman & would think my self favoured from Heaven if your Honour could assist in the very desired business, that would cause such a grate lift to a poor Whig in his distress. I was beged the hardest to change with upposition & they would have my Spring bought & they would give as much credit & help as I wanted. I always loved my country and my God, above all things, I have no more to say but my prayers. May it please the Almighty to rule in your harts & direct your honour in the way of wisdom and peace with all nations now, Amen.

Please to hand this letter to our friend,
Honourable Mangum.

*To Susan Washington Graham.*                                    A.

Washington City,

July 22nd, 1841.

*       *       *       *       *

I believe there is nothing new here of the least interest. Public affairs go on slowly in the Senate. No vote has yet been taken on the Bank Bill, and it is doubtful what will be its fate, though I have more hopes of a settlement of the question, than there has been for some time. I still hope that Congress may adjourn by the middle of next month but that is also doubtful.

I walked yesterday evening to the grounds near the President's House, where a large crowd had gathered to hear the performance of the musical Band from the Navy Yard. But there was such a cloud of dust by the way, that I had but little pleasure in the excursion.

The Misses Gaston are still here but I have not seen them. They appear not to have gone out to any public place in Washington.

*To Susan Washington Graham.*                                    A.

Washington City,

Saturday, July 24th, 1841.

The weather here is oppressively hot, yesterday and today the Thermometer has been at 89 or 90 in the coolest part of the Capitol.

The Senate meeting at 10 and sitting continuously 'till 4 o'clock, the Sessions are exceedingly laborious.

Nothing has occurred since my last of the least interest. The Bankrupt Bill passed yesterday its second reading and will probably become a law. The Bank still hangs in the Senate. It will probably be disposed of, next week, and probably passed with some change from its original form, so as to reconcile all concerned. Having no other news to write you, I am compelled to give you political news.

*       *       *       *       *

I wrote a few days since to Dr. Washington informing him of our recent good fortune, but have not had a reply. Perhaps it may bring like intelligence in relation to his own family.

I still hope that we may adjourn by the middle of Aug.

*To Susan Washington Graham.*                    A.

Washington City,

July 25th, 1841.

I have just read your kind letter of the 22nd which reminds me of the birthday of John. Poor Fellow! amid the cares and anxieties of public affairs here I had suffered it to pass without remembering the fact. I regret to hear of your debility and fear that you will continue feeble during the warm weather; the heat has been intense here for some days. There is something of a thunder shower falling now, and I hope it will become more pleasant.

\*     \*     \*     \*     \*

The weather and lapse of time has somewhat wearied our speechmakers in Congress, and we have hopes of an adjournment by the middle of Aug. but we cannot tell with certainty. Tomorrow will probably determine the fate of the Bank Bill in the Senate, that is, whether it can pass, though it may be some days in getting through.

I am glad to hear from your letter that Wiseman has gotten the portrait, as the members of the family have for a long time desired likenesses of my Father. . . .

*To David L. Swain.*          U. Swain Mss.

Washington City,

July 26th., 1841.

I learn that in the settlement of the debts of the United States, and the several States, in 1793, under an act Congress in relation thereto, there was charged to the State of N. C. $501,000. and to several other States different sums—some more, and some less. In the Bill for the distribution of the proceeds of the public lands, the 4th. Section, (as it passed the House Reps.) requires, that, if any debt be due & payable to the U. S. from any State, the share of such State in the monies to be distributed shall be retained in satisfaction, etc. The section was designed to enable the Government to recover the Smithsonian fund, etc., which have been lent within a few years to some of the States, but it is apprehended that it may extend to these old debts.

I am unable here to obtain the Journals of our Legislature, but my impression is, that this arrangement of the Revolutionary debt (requiring payment according to Federal population, when it was expected to be paid, according to the volume of settled lands) drew forth a violent remonstrance from the General Assembly, and that the State has never, in any manner, admitted the Justice of this balance of debt.

My principal purpose in writing you, is to inquire whether, in the negotiation pertaining to our claim on the General Government for expenditures in the late War, (which I believe was settled under your administration) any offset was claimed, or insisted on, on account of the old claim before referred to, or whether it was waived by the Federal Government.

I do not wish to move an amendment to the Bill, unless it be absolutely necessary, and would be obliged to you for any information in relation to the matter, in your possession. I think it will probably not be taken up for several days, or perhaps a week, (in which time I hope to hear from you.)

You are aware that public affairs are in an uncertain condition here. An attempt is on foot to compromise the Bank question, which I hope may succeed. It will be no doubt determined on, in a day or two.

The session will probably continue untill the middle or last of Aug., and I hope will yet result in harmony & public benefit.

Please present my respects to Mrs. Swain, & Believe me,

Very truly,
Your Friend & Serv't

*To Susan Washington Graham.*                               A.

Washington City,

July 28th. 1841.

On yesterday the Bank Bill passed the Senate by a majority of 3, after having been amended so as to make it more agreeable to a majority of Senators. It will no doubt pass the Ho. Reps. and we hope will be approved by the President.

Other measures are before us which will occupy some time. It is to be hoped not more than two or three weeks, but there is no telling what turn things may take.

I have had your watch repaired, and it is running, but as I found it not to keep the correct time, it is still at the silver smith's.

Mr. and Mrs. Hale[68] of Fay'ville are here, on their way to the North, as I learn, but have not seen them.

Mr. Yarbrough[69] from Raleigh informs me that Judge Cameron and Col. Jones & part of their families have gone to the Fauquier Springs in Va.

I wish very much that I could get home in time to take a jaunt with you to some of the watering places this Summer.

\*    \*    \*    \*    \*

*From William Gaston.*                                                        A.

Raleigh, July 29th, 1841.

I received a letter a few days since from Wm. B. Grove Taylor,[70] the nephew of my late friend Chief Justice Taylor,[71] which has caused me some embarrassment. From my great regard for the writer whom I have known from infancy, as well as from his connection with one whose memory will ever be most dear to me. I have the strongest disposition to render him every service in my power. But I have an invincible repugnance to making application for office in behalf of any one. I may call it invincible *now,* for although it *has been made to yield* under very peculiar circumstances, I think nothing can occur to prevent its having henceforth absolute sway over me. Under these circumstances I have concluded to make known to you the substance of Mr. Taylor's communication, and the facts within my knowledge in relation to his character, and then to submit to your well known

---

[68] Edward Jones Hale (1802-1883), of Fayetteville, a native of Chatham, was trained under Joseph Gales of the *Register,* and then was with Gales and Seaton on the *National Intelligencer.* He bought the *Carolina Observer,* changed its name to *Fayetteville Observer,* and edited it with vigor and distinction. He declined an offer to head the publishing firm of A. S. Barnes & Co., and another to edit the New York *World.* He was a Whig, and in 1860-1861 a Unionist, but, when Lincoln's call for troops came, he became an intense Confederate. He had much to do with the selection of Vance for governor in 1862. After the war, he founded a publishing house in New York.

[69] Edward Yarborough, proprietor of the Guion Hotel, and, later, of the Yarborough House.

[70] William Barry Grove Taylor was appointed a midshipman in 1815, and resigned in 1836. The navy registers contain no other mention of him.

[71] John Louis Taylor (1769-1829), a native of London, came to Virginia in 1781, attended William and Mary College, and settled in Fayetteville. He studied law, represented the borough in the commons, 1792-1794, moved to New Bern, and in 1798 was elected a judge of the superior court. About 1811 he moved to Raleigh. He served as president of the court of conference, and in 1818, when the supreme court was established, he became its first chief justice.

friendship and sense of propriety the decision of the course which shall be pursued in relation to the object of his wishes.

Mr. Taylor (who I believe is at present boarding officer at the Batise, below New Orleans, and commander of the U. S. Revenue Schooner Izard) mentions to me that not long since he had with a boat and six hands captured the Piratical Vessel Independence Captn. De Putren and seven of his crew; that this act had so recommended him to the Citizens of New Orleans that the Municipality, the Chamber of Commerce, and the U. S. Attorney had interested themselves to procure for him the command of an armed Steamer to be stationed on the neighbouring coast, and that he is satisfied that in doing so they act with the general concurrence of the Citizens of New Orleans. He apprehends however that the berth is so good an one that some of the old officers of the Navy may endeavor to have his pretensions superseded. He reminds me however, as is the fact, that he served as a Midshipman in the Navy during the late War, that he is senior in service to all the Cutter Officers, that many years ago upon my application Mr. Crawford [72] promised him the first vacant commission of Captain that should fall in, that he has been rendering for fourteen years the most laborious services as Inspector of the Revenue at the Batise during all which time his home was on a mud-bank, and adds that *I firmly believe* that no individual in the U. States has so intimate an acquaintance as he possesses of every bay port haven & shoal from the Bay of Campeachy to the Capes of Florida.

I feel no hesitation in saying that he is among the most gallant and noble-spirited fellows I ever knew—and I venture to endorse the assurance he gives in his letter that if he gets the command which he asks not a woolly-head is smuggled into Texas or the adjoining country, and every energy which can be required to render such a steamer efficient in protecting lawful trade and putting down fraud and piracy will be fully exerted.

I pray you to believe me my dear Sir
Very truly & with much esteem
Your affectte friend

---

[72] William Harris Crawford (1772-1834), of Georgia, a native of Virginia, whose family removed to Georgia in his childhood. He studied under Moses Waddell, became a lawyer, and rose quickly to prominence. After a brief service in the legislature, he was elected to the United States senate, in 1807, and served to 1813 (president *pro tem.* 1812). He was minister to France, 1813-1815, secretary of war, 1815-1816, secretary of the treasury, 1816-1825. He was a candidate for President in 1824, but suffered an apoplectic stroke, and was not elected. He was a state judge from 1827 until his death.

*To James W. Bryan.*        U. Bryan Mss.

Washington City,

July 30th, 1841.

\*    \*    \*    \*    \*

The Bank Bill has passed the Senate with an amendment as to the Branching power, which was the result of a compromise to procure a majority of the Senate in its favour. It will pass the House without doubt, but there are serious apprehensions as to the course of the President. Mr. Wise, who professes to have the controul of him, sneers at the compromise, and talks confidently of the veto. Others, however, believe that he will approve it. The Cabinet will approve the compromise, and will exert their influence with the President to secure his approval. How it will result, I think, a week more will determine.

The Session of Congress will probably continue for 3 or 4 weeks yet. Our measures are all beset with more or less difficulty. The passage of the Bill for the distribution of the proceeds of the lands through the Senate is uncertain. So many interests are to be conciliated on all these subjects, that it is hard to get a majority for any.

The fate of the Revenue Bill, in the House, will be known today. If it pass there in the present shape, the land Bill can probably pass.

Our greatest difficulties however are likely to arise out of some Executive appointments to high stations, or persons having a strong taint of abolition. If they are rejected we shall identify abolition with the freedom of opinion in all the free States, as it is now identified in many of them, with the right of Petition. On the contrary, if they are confirmed we shall be weakened and perhaps ruined, at the South. Of this, of course you will not speak at present. It is a subject of deep and painful anxiety with us from the South at the present.

\*    \*    \*    \*    \*

*To Susan Washington Graham.*          A.

Washington City,

Aug. 1st, 1841.

My Dear Wife

The date of this letter reminds of the flight of time, and my long absence from home. I hope I may be able to return to you before the end of the month.

George and his family arrived here evening before last, (friday) having lost their baggage on the route. And he was compelled to go back yesterday in search of it. He supposed that it had been put on the train of cars going to the Springs in Va. at the junction of the two railroads on this side of Richmond. If so, he will probably recover it in a day or two. Catherine is here at Brown's Hotel. I went with her yesterday to the Capitol, where the House was sitting, the Senate having adjourned over untill Monday, shewed her the Capitol grounds, Library of Congress, etc. And then visited the Patent office, where I had not been before. Among various other curiosities collected there, is the suit of uniform worn by Genl. Washington when he resigned his Commission as Commander in Chief of the Army. It is in a good state of preservation.

We afterwards rode around the President's square & viewed the grounds and buildings of the different departments, but as C. had a deficient wardrobe she declined going in to be introduced.

I had an engagement to dine with Mr. Kerr,[73] Senator, from Maryland at 5 o'clock, and could not therefore go with her to hear the music at the Capitol, which is customary on Saturday evening, but on calling after dark I found that Wm. Washington had called and gone with her.

If your strength would have allowed it, I would have been much pleased had you come on with George. Or if an opportunity should offer in a week or two, you might perhaps be able to make the Journey. I think you will find it much to your advantage to ride out, and drink a Glass of mineral water at Judge Norwood's[74] before breakfast each morning, or if you would prefer it, to go to the Buffalow Springs[75] for a week or two. You will have a suffi-

[73] John Leeds Kerr (1780-1844), of Maryland, graduate of St. Johns College, lawyer, soldier in the War of 1812, Whig member of congress, 1825-1829, 1831-1833, elector, 1840, United States senator, 1841-1843.

[74] Now known as Occoneechee Spring.

[75] The Buffalo Lithia Springs, Mecklenburg County, Virginia.

ciency of money to bear your expenses if you desire to go, and you should not permit the expense to be of the least consideration.

The Bill to raise revenue by additional duties passed the Ho. Reps. yesterday; they will take up the Bank Bill tomorrow & pass it in the course of this week, probably. Rumors are still afloat, as to the veto of the President, but nothing is certainly known. Mrs. Badger, with whom I dined last week in company with the President & a large number of gentlemen, told me that Miss Polk of Raleigh & several other of her friends, now at the Fauquier Spring in Va. would visit Washington in the course of a week or two. She also stated that Mr. Rayner was an admirer of Miss P.[76] and that she wished him success. Mr. R. has gone home at present in consequence of the death of a brother, to whom he appears to have been much attached.

*To Susan Washington Graham.*                          A.

Washington City,

Aug. 6th, 1841.

\*    \*    \*    \*    \*

Mrs. Stanly will leave here tomorrow for Philadelphia in company with Mr. Battle, formerly of New Bern, who is now here, on his way from Mobile to New York. She is very desirous that her husband shall go on a Foreign Mission, and has had an interview with me this morning on the subject of the Mission to Spain. I, of course, will not decline to give my aid in the matter, as far as it will be available. You will of course not speak of it for the present.

The Bank Bill will probably pass the House today, it is still doubtful what the President will do with it. Rumors are rife that he will not approve it. But two gentlemen who have spoken with him within the last day or two, assure me that he will approve it. I however doubt it. More from the company which habitually surrounds him than from any other circumstance.

The painful state of suspense in which the public, not only here, but throughout the country, has been kept by the mystery which is observed at the White House is most remarkable. Nothing else, scarcely, is talked of, or inquired about, in all circles.

The time of adjournment is like the horizon, which seems to recede as we advance towards it. It becomes doubtful whether we shall not get off before the first of next month.

---

[76] Miss Sarah Polk, later Mrs. Kenneth Rayner.

*From William F. Strudwick.*[77]          U.

Greensboro, [Ala.,] August 6th, 1841.

I saw some time since in one of the Washington papers a notice of an improvement in the construction of *Stoves*. They are made air tight & consume a very inconsiderable quantity of wood, compaired to other stoves.

Will you be so good, as to make some inquiry about it, & let me know, where they can be had? & at what Cost?

I would not have troubled you with this communication, but since *we Whigs* have been *disfranchised*, I have no acquaintance with any of our present delegation, therefore must request in your leisure moments you will obtain the desired information for me.

Your friends here are well.

Respectfully your friend.

P. S. Is there a probability of Dr. *Ashe's* getting the appointment of Surgeon of the Hospital in Mobile?

*To Susan Washington Graham.*          A.

Washington City,

Aug. 8th, 1841.

\* \* \* \* \*

The Bank Bill passed the House of Representatives on Friday and is now before the President; there is still uncertainty as to what he will do. He is allowed by the Constitution ten days to decide. The solicitude on the subject has now become intense, & is the matter of conversation in all circles. Should he refuse to approve the Bill, I fear a universal burst of indignation, and the most direful consequences to the Whig party and the country. If he shall take the counsel of his Cabinet, he will sign the Bill without hesitation, but there is a cabal principally of Virginians, not in political life, who have been about him of late, and will do their utmost to procure a veto. This week will probably determine the fate of the measure.

Judge Cameron's family, Mr. Bennehan & Miss Boylan arrived here yesterday evening from Fauquier Springs, and Col. Jones' party are expected tomorrow. Judge C. is going to Philadelphia in a day or two. And will meet Col. Jones at Baltimore in the course

---

[77] William Frederick Strudwick, a brother of Dr. Edmund Strudwick, of Hillsboro. He was also a physician, and had settled in Alabama some years before.

of a week, whence they are to travel home together. I called of course on them, and will show them such civilities as I can, though my time will be much occupied during the residue of my stay.

I am anxious to be with you in two weeks from the receipt of this, especially as the County Court of Orange comes on then, and hope that I can do so. But am not sure. How I would be pleased to be with you on this Sunday evening! I have spent rather an unprofitable day.

Give my love to Mother & the Children—And be ever mine

*Invitation.*                                                      U.

The President of the U. States having announced his intention of visiting the ship Delaware, off Annapolis on Saturday, 14th. inst. Com: Morris will be happy to see you on board at the same time.

Accomodations will be provided to take the visitors who may accompany the President from Annapolis to the ship.

N. B. Be pleased to shew this card to the Conductor of the cars at Washington; and to the person who may command any of the Boats provided for the occasion at Annapolis.

Monday,
9. Aug. 1841.

*To Susan Washington Graham.*                           A.

Washington City,

Aug. 13th, 1841.

\* \* \* \* \*

Judge Cameron's family have gone to Phila. Col. Jones & his party, including Miss Sarah Simpson, have been here for two or three days, also the Misses Mordecai & Miss Polk. I have called to see them at their boarding house, and met them last night at a party at Mr. Badger's. The young ladies were much admired by the company. Miss Mary Jones was too unwell to go out. I have promised to call and introduce them at the President's when she is better. I do not know whether Mr. Allen Jones has devoted his attentions to Miss Simpson or Miss Polk; he having been an admirer of both. Mr. Rayner, it is understood, is quite devoted to the latter. He has however lost a brother recently, and was not out last night.

The anxiety is every day more intense as to the fate of the Bank Bill. The President has had it under consideration nearly a week, and the rumor is, that he will veto it, but it is not yet certain. Should he do so, it will inevitably lead to a rupture with his friends, and probably a dissolution of the present Cabinet. His return of the Bill is looked for today, and there is of course great curiosity on the subject.

\*   \*   \*   \*   \*

*From James W. Osborne.*     U.

August 15, 1841.

Young Mr. Davidson[78] is on his way to become a member of the law school at Harvard University. It may be important to him to have some testimonials of character and to convey to the officers some evidences of literary attainments in order to secure his admission. Should you write any such in his favour, you may say, (and you would much oblige him & myself by doing so), that he is a graduate of Davidson College, where he sustained a very respectable standing, and since he took his degree about a year ago, he has been reading with diligence a course of history and law preparatory to his entrance into the law school at Cambridge. Of law he has read Blackstone and Kents Commentaries. In private life his character is most unexceptionable. I hope you will interest yourself in his favour as he is himself deeply anxious to avail himself of the advantages of the institution, and his father (Uncle Jacky) sympathizes with him most warmly on the subject.

By this time the state of suspense which in common with other portions of the American people you have felt as to the course of the President on the Bank question will be relieved. Deep anxiety prevails at this moment among our Whig friends in this quarter on that subject. I fear the worst. The indications are certainly unfavourable. It will be a terrible responsibility on the part of the President and his convictions must be inveterate and most

---

[78] Edward Constantine Davidson (b. 1820), an early graduate of Davidson College, after securing his law license, settled in Charlotte. He was a lieutenant of dragoons in the Mexican War, and a member of the commons in 1850.

unquestionable if on such a question at such time he determines to place himself in opposition to the expressed will of the representatives of the people. As far as my information has extended our Senators reflected the feelings of the Whigs on sustaining the propositions of Mr. Clay. The compromise offered by him is certainly the last concession which they think ought to be made on a matter involving so important a principle. It will be fortunate hereafter, when it may be necessary to bring into exercise the power in question, that should the President veto the Bill, there will be but his opinion against the expressed opinion of the representatives of a large majority of our Country.

It will be a matter of deep regret that in the Senate there should be several States in the Union wholy nonrepresented—or partially so—so that its vote is no fair exponent of public opinion.

The dissensions which have occurred at Washington City have had an unfortunate influence on the state of feeling among the Whigs. It has changed the opinions of no one but has depressed the spirits of all. Such dissensions certainly were natural—and to be expected. That they have been in any degree harmonized is the source of greater astonishments. . . .

*To Susan Washington Graham.*                    A.

Washington City,

Aug. 16th, 1841.

I regret very much to say to you that the President has determined to reject the Bank Bill. I had an interview with him yesterday evening in company with several gentlemen, and he announced that his mind was made up, and that a veto message would be sent in the course, probably, of this day. What are to be the consequences it is impossible to foresee. They cannot be otherwise than injurious to the Country, and the Whig party.

Col. Jones' party, who seem to gather numbers every day, left this morning to join Judge Cameron's at Baltimore, whence they are to go down the Bay to Old Point Cft. and expect to reach home by the last of the week. Mr. Rayner is to accompany Miss Polk as far as Baltimore. I do not know what are his prospects of success with her.

Mr. Alfred Jones[79] of Raleigh & Saml. Holt of Orange are also to go with them—& Nat Hill.

A large party went to Annapolis Md. on Saturday to see the U. S. Ship Delaware, which is a 74 ready for sea. They were entertained on board with a sham battle, champaign etc. and returned about dark quite merry.

Mr. Pettigrew is now here, and Mr. J. C. Johnston[80] of Edenton.

I cannot fix with certainty the day of adjournment, but shall look for it with hope and joy.


*To William Gaston.*        U. Gaston Mss.

Washington City,

Aug. 17th, 1841.

My Dear Sir

I forget whether I replied to your letter of recommendation in behalf of Capt. Wm. B. G. Taylor. I have laid the application before the proper department and I will with pleasure afford him any aid, in my power, in attaining the command he desires.

You will have heard before this reaches you, that the President of the United States did on yesterday return the Bank Bill to the Senate with a veto. He assumes the ground that the Constitution gives no power to establish a Bank of *discount* with branches in the States without their assent, but insinuates, and it is said, agrees, that a Bank with agencies to receive deposites and deal in *exchanges* would receive his approbation. The veto message will be considered today, and of course the Bill cannot receive a majority of two thirds in either House of Congress, and will therefore fail. There is much excitement among our friends, but, as yet, every thing has been conducted without any burst of feeling. I very much fear, that we shall not pass any Financial measure, as a substitute, at this Session. Indeed I very much incline to

[79] Alfred Jones, of Wake, who lived on a plantation outside of Raleigh. He was active in the militia, and was regularly mentioned as a "Captain." He fought a duel with a Faucett, of Orange, and was wounded, which so alarmed his adversary, that he disappeared.

[80] James Cathcart Johnston (1782-1865), of "Hayes," Chowan County, a son of Governor Samuel Johnston, and probably, at the outbreak of the Civil War, the wealthiest man in North Carolina. He was a man of great culture, and assembled a large and valuable library, and many portraits, all, with the exception of one of Judge Ruffin, of Federalists and Whigs. Violently opposed to secession, he disinherited his relatives, all of whom favored secession, with one exception, and distributed his property among friends.

the belief, that the President does not desire it. Some of the leaders of the opposition say that, although they will sustain the veto, yet that they cannot coalesce with him. But the great body of them, I think, are disposed to receive him into full communion—or rather to take possession of him. He himself disclaims all idea of going over, but is evidently disposed to fortify himself against his friends as well as foes. Every thing is in uncertainty and there is no such thing as forseeing results. A week more must determine the fate of the Whig party, and of this administration.

I write in great haste and have not time to say more.

> I remain With great regard
> Your Friend & servt.
> Will. A. Graham.

*From William Gaston.*                                           A.

Raleigh, August 19th, 1841.

Occupied as I am with the duties of the Court, more laborious at this term than they ever have been except on one occasion, I can bring no mind to the consideration of the perplexities and dangers which the President's veto brings upon the Whig Party, and of the evils which it menaces to the whole Country. It would argue however an insensibility which I can not admit, if I did not avail myself of your kindness in corresponding with me on the subject to throw out the thoughts crude as they are which have occurred to me.

In the first place it is indispensable to the character of the Party that its proceedings in Congress should be marked by decorum and temper. Violence, and Petulance will lower it in the public estimation, and afford advantages to its Adversary which will certainly be seized. But they are demanded by yet higher considerations. Deeply as the Party must feel the blow from the hands of one, whom it has elevated to the station which enables him to strike, it *must* make allowances for the motives which in his judgment left him no other alternative. It ought not—it cannot be rationally believed—but that he would have infinitely preferred acting with his political friends on this occasion rather than against them, had he thought that this could be done without self-degradation. If no allowance is made for a separation from them, in an isolated though most important case when there is so irresistible a cause for it, the consequence must be a complete disruption of the ties by which he and they are bound together. *All* the objects—great and glorious as they are—for which he and they contended in the late struggle must then be sacrificed. On the contrary a reasonable allowance of justice and toleration from his Whig friends upon this occasion will prevent him from being thrown for support upon men who are unworthy of his confidence, and whose schemes must be ruinous to the Nation. Though the Whig party may not be able to do all the good which it is anxious to accomplish, and to do it as speedily as it may wish, it may do *much,* and in so doing prove itself a blessing to the Country. Time too, the great healer of all diseases not incurable, may effect a co-operation in regard to this very subject, which now seems impracticable. It is my earnest hope therefore that Congress will proceed calmly to act upon the other matters before it precisely as if the Veto (I believe that I shall always hate the term) had not been sent in.

In the next place I would observe that I trust no further attempt will be made at this session to create a Bank. From the desire to get around the constitutional scruples of those who were opposed to an old fashioned Bank, the one lately projected contained many features highly objectionable. Further attempts in this way, should they succeed in procuring a law for the incorporation of such an institution, would give us a ricketty affair that might fail to accomplish the only purposes for which it ought to be established.

I know little of Mr. Tyler personally, but I have always had a high opinion of his honesty of purpose, and in my judgment it is no small blessing to a Community to have a perfectly honest man in the Executive Chair, altho' some of his political notions may be wrong-headed. But if honest men will not aid him, he must seek for aid elsewhere; and with counsellors wanting his honesty and more wrong-headed than himself, the result is the same as if the President himself were dishonest, and unwise.

It is the misfortune of Mr. Tyler and great calamity I regard it, to have imbibed in his youth certain political dogmas, not wanting in plausibility and even partially founded in truth, but as preached and expounded by political zealots, impracticable and absurd, as the revelations of perfect verity. He ought not to be severely blamed for not being able to free his mind entirely from the bondage of his early faith. It requires mighty powers to do this. Such intellects as those of James Madison and of Henry Clay, have been able to effect it—but not until such observation and long experience had demonstrated fallacies too plainly to be over-looked.

I make no apologies for the evident haste with which these remarks are penned. You will regard them I am sure as evidence of the personal esteem and affection with which I am, my dear Sir,

Truly your's

A.

*From Henry K. Burgwyn.*[81]

Boston,

Augst. 22nd, 1841.

If there be any seeming impropriety in addressing you in the manner I am about to do, I hope you will find an excuse for it, in the situation: I am here placed, a Southerner, shut up, as it were, for some two months among Northerners, hear'g every day their feel'gs opinions expressed on all the various affairs of public interest, that are now before your "honorable body"; Among these there is none, that seems to excite so *universal & absorb'g* an enquiry as whether the Southern Senators are about to vote against the nomination of Abolitionists to offices at the *North*—out of the way of the Southern interests—simply on the ground that no Abolitionist must be allowed to hold any office? even here? in other words, that freedom of opinion is not to be allowed among any of the Petty Officers of Govern'mt.

This question has been agitated recently, from the fact that several Northern papers have stated—see the N. Yk. Commercial of the 17th 18th. inst.—that the nomination of Mr. Ed Everett of this State, & Gen'l Wilson[82] Of N. Hampshire, had & would continue to be opposed on *this* ground. I can truly say that the disappoint'nt consequent on the Veto & the loss of the Bankrupt & Land Bills, would not excite one *half* the feeling of indignation among all classes & parties if it were to be the case that these two appoint's were voted down by Southern Senators *on the ground*

---

[81] Henry King Burgwyn (1813-1877), of "Thornbury Plantation," Northampton County, a wealthy planter.

[82] James Wilson, Jr., (1797-1881), of New Hampshire, was educated at Middlebury College, and became a lawyer. He was a member of the lower house of the legislature, 1825-1837, (speaker, 1828), 1840, 1846, and a member of congress, 1847-1850.

that the *peculiar tenets* of these Gent'n were *denominated Aboli-tion principles.* It would unite all parties, both personal foe & friend of Mr. Everett, & create a feeling of animosity against us, that would destroy the feeling of good will now almost universal among the better informed at the North towards us, and would go far—as a personal friend said to me today—"to make us all Abolitionists." These gent'n say that Mr. Everett is no Abolition-ist, that he lost his election because he refused to accede to the principles offered to him by an Abol'st Committee, & lost it solely on that ground; that he is opposed to slavery in the abstract they say has nothing to do with it. In my replies during the course of the various arguments I have held, I state that most assuredly the South will not suffer an Abolitionist to represent us at the Court of a Power that is only wait'g a favorable opportunity to destroy that institution among us by any means they could bring to bear upon the Southern Country, even by the employ'nt of Negro troups to excite our slaves: but that the South would *not* call Mr. Everett an Abolitionist if his principles are those I hear avowed to be his here. (indeed I am sometimes inclined to think Mr. Ed Everett has been confounded with his Brother who is a Locofoco and Abolitionist) and of course would not oppose his nomination on *that ground;* indeed the South would feel inclined to give the representation of our Country at the Court of St. James to a New Englander, both on acc't of the present preponder'ce of Southern and Western men in office, & that a more speedy & satisfactory adjus'nt of the Boundary question would ensue from the fact of their more immediate interest in the settlement of the matter & being more familiar with the premises. That the South would not do what they blame the Abolitionists for attempting—viz—to in-terfere with Northern feelings & relations among themselves & wholly apart from any Southern connexion or influence whatever. If you Northerners with an officer of customs, or any similar one who may be a an Abolitionist in his principles, in God's name have him, we care not, but when the question is whether we shall place the interests of the South in the hands of a man whose creed is that he is doing "God's will"—as they term it—when he is arousing our slaves to cut our throats, that he may destroy an in-stitution among us that his own ancestors chiefly founded, when, I say, our interests are to be thus deposited, and he who ought to be their guardian is to be surrounded by those most desirous of destroy'g them, & who would be glad to see Slavery & the Cotton

Culture destroyed with us, that they might flourish with theirs in the East, then it would be suicidal in us not to prevent it.

Pray if it be not against the usual etiquette, let me hear from you on this matter; it is one of more than a little interest here & I must say I think justly so, & I have heard enemies of Mr. Everett say he would unite in opposing such a mov'nt among the South'n Members. You cannot imagine the joy that the late ac'cts of the passage of the Bankrupt Bill & other mov'nts have created among us. The Loco's fired 100 guns on the veto, the Whigs intend send'g them money to fire 100 more as soon as we have the "Exchange Agent" passed. Bancroft the Great Loco here said Tyler would not go far enough to suit his party, nor the Whigs & would be drop'd by both.

*To Susan Washington Graham.*                    A.

Washington City,

Aug. 22nd, 1841.

I had but little expectation of being here still, when I left you. But such is the uncertainty of political affairs that no definite opinion can be formed of the duration of the Session. The veto was discussed in the Senate on Wednesday by Mr. Rives & Mr. Clay & disposed of. The general opinion here is that Mr. Clay has never made a more eloquent speech since the war, than he did upon this occasion. It was a severe criticism but personally respectful to the President who is said to have taken it with good humor. But I fear he is surrounded by influences which will make it difficult to unite with him on another measure. A Bank Bill has been however introduced into the House, which, it is supposed, will meet with his approbation, but I believe it is far from being certain. The Land Bill drags on in the Senate & its passage is doubtful; and so of other measures.

We have a new batch of North Carolinians here every few days. Mr. Lassiter called on me last week, & I had expected to see him again, as he told me he was going to Orange Court this week. But I presume he has gone.

. . . An old acquaintance from New Orleans who knows Mr. Scott of Hillsboro' told me that he had seen him in Texas; that he had a leg broken by a fall from a Horse a year or two ago, and that the fracture never healed; that this infirmity had prevented the confirmation of his appointment as a Judge, which was conferred on him by the President of that Republic. And that he was but little improved in his fortune. I mention this to you, but suppose it is not proper to communicate it to the family.

\* \* \* \* \*

I regret to hear from Princeton that my nephew, young Witherspoon, & another student had been severely injured in a fight, which seems to have been somewhat general, among the students on the arrival of the veto there. I hope it is not a serious injury.


*To Susan Washington Graham.*          A.

Washington City,

Aug. 27th, 1841.

I write merely to keep you advised of the probability of the time of the adjournment of Congress, because of your anxiety on the subject, rather than because I have any thing to communicate. The Land distribution bill passed the Senate yesterday, and has gone back to the House with some amendments. There is no doubt that it will become a law, unless our Veto President shall reject it. There is however no prospect of that, so far as I can hear.

The Senate is today engaged in the discussion of the Revenue Bill, which will consume several days, after which we shall have the new Bank Bill, which has already passed the House. I fear we shall be found here, two weeks hence, for besides what I have mentioned, the Executive business of the Session (passing on nominations to office) will take some time.

The relations of the President to Congress are not better than they have been. The report now is, that he will veto the new Bank Bill, and I fear it is too true. If so, a breach with him is inevitable. He seems indeed to be too weak, to form or to propagate a scheme of his own, but is changing his ground every day, or at least at every new consultation of his domestic advisers. In short, he seems to have no mind of his own, upon the whole subject of Finance. This of course, I write only to you, as I know with what avidity the declarations of a public man are caught up, & repeated for purposes of mischief.

Mr. Botts of Va. a friend formerly of the President, has put forth a violent publication against him in consequence of an imprudent letter of his, which was written to a friend in Richmond, having been unexpectedly published.

\*     \*     \*     \*     \*

*To Susan Washington Graham.*                                    A.

Washington City,

Aug. 29th, 1841.

I again write you without any thing to communicate, except that the period of adjournment is still uncertain. The Session must continue however, more than a week yet, and I shall not be able to reach Granville Court next week. If I can reach our own Court the week following I will deem myself fortunate.

Yesterday the Senate was engaged on the Revenue Bill which will consume the greater part of next week, after which comes the new Bank Bill. The House of Reps, owing to a strictness in their rules of proceeding have nearly finished every thing before them & are now ready to adjourn, but there is a disposition in the Senate to extend the Session with the hope of defeating measures, and the rules of the body are at present such as to allow an abuse of the priviledge of speaking to an indefinite extent. The prevailing report is that the President will disapprove the new Bank Bill, which has been formed in accordance with his views, (if he has any); If this be true, it must inevitably separate him from the Whigs. Indeed, such a feeling of distrust has already grown up between them, that there can hardly ever be a cordial reconciliation.

I attended last night a party of gentlemen at Mr. Crittenden's. The President came in late, the company being in high glee, and many of them having not seen him since the veto. Mr. Clay with his never failing self possession greeted him very cordially, "Well Mr. President what are you for?" (After a pause of embarrassment on the part of the latter) "Wine, Whiskey, Brandy or Champagne? Come show your hand." The P. replied that he would take a drink of whiskey, and they accordingly drank together with a good deal of merriment.

I went to hear the music at the Capitol yesterday afternoon, where I met Mrs. Badger. In walking with her about the grounds, she said that they expected soon to return to N. C. and I should not be surprized if at the adjournment of Congress, the Cabinet should be dissolved. It is a most singular state of things now, that another set of persons know far more of the intentions of the President than the Cabinet Ministers.

\* \* \* \* \*

*From Thomas S. Hoskins.*[83]                              U.

Edenton, N. C., Aug. 30, 1841.

I have had the honor of receiving from you the most admirable and conclusive speech of Mr. Morehead [84] of Ky. on the Fiscal Bank Bill, also the remarks of Mr. Washington of N. C. in the Ho. of Representatives on the same subject, for which you will please accept my sincere thanks. It is with pleasure that I now address you but a few lines, for the first time since you have occupied the distinguished station of U. S. Senator from the Old North State. I was very much gratified at your election, & hope you may long continue to hold the same office, to assist the great patriots, & distinguished Statesmen of the Country, (the Whigs) in dispensing blessings & posperity upon a now suffering people.

What a calamity it was,—the death of our beloved Harrison! Nothing *could* have happened to compare with it. It has placed a man in the Presidential Chair, who was not even *thought* of by one in a thousand, when we cast our votes for the lamented Harrison for that elevated station. A man too who does not "understand the true principles of the Government," & does not "carry them out," particularly as regards the late Bank Bill. I have just read Mr. Clay's speech on the Veto, & I think he completely uses it up—tears it all to atoms—leaves not a spot upon which Tyler can stand. Clay is our man. He *must* be & *shall be* our next President by the help of God. I recd. a short communication from him the other day, for which please tender him my thanks, & also for his admirable & inimitable speech on the Veto. That Veto makes Clay President, beyond a doubt, on the 4th. March 1845. I suppose Tyler will also veto Sergant's Bill from the House, unless

[83] Thomas S. Hoskins was an ardent Whig. He represented Chowan in the commons, 1835-1836.

[84] James Turner Morehead (1797-1854), of Kentucky, was educated at Transylvania, and became a lawyer. He was a number of times a member of the legislature, was lieutenant governor, 1831-1832, and governor, 1832-1836.

the term *"Corporation"* will cause him to forget that it savours of a *Bank*.

Notwithstanding the loss of the Bank however, I am pleased to see that you have done much that will no doubt redound to the good of the country. I see that Humbug Benton raves and rants occasionally about the bank ruffians, bank bullies, etc. He must cut a contemptible figure when he acts so.

The Va. Cabal I suppose, stands no chance. One of them, Mallory, has been completely used up by his Norfolk constituents. It was with great reluctance that I gave up my seat in the commons. But I had got married, gone in the country to farming, & could not well leave home at the time of the meeting of the Assembly.

I should be pleased to hear from you, & also to receive other able speeches in pamphlet form, should others be at any time conveniently at your command.

*To Susan Washington Graham.*                    A.

Washington City,

Sept. 5th, 1841.

This, is the anniversary of my birthday, and brings with it the ten thousand recollections, that are incident to such an occasion. I had most fervently hoped to spend it with you, but have been doomed to disappointment. It induces me, however to look back upon my life, as it has been, & is, and presents vividly before me, those, to whom I am attached by the tenderest ties.

I hope Congress will adjourn in time to allow me to reach home by this day week, or the day following. I was very much tempted to break off with George and Mary, who left here yesterday, and will have reached Hillsboro' by tomorrow or the next day. George did not apprize me that they were here untill a few moments before they left. You will therefore excuse me for not writing by them.

The President has signed the Land Bill, and has now before him the new Bank Bill which it is believed he will reject as he did the former one. If so, he will necessarily separate from his friends. The Senate has now before it, the Revenue Bill, after disposing of which there is but little business of importance except to pass upon the nominations to office, some of which will be much contested. My hope is that the business will be so far advanced that I can leave here on friday next, though I may be detained longer.

I attended last evening a party at Mr. Badger's, and on Thursday evening preceding, one at Mr. Bell's. The Cabinet seem disposed to make merry, as if they were in no trouble. But I very much apprehend a dissolution. The President was not out last night, but was at Mr. Bell's. He is evidently laboring under great anxiety, and if he could divest himself of the small squad, who have had charge of him during the Session, I have no doubt he would gladly sign the present Bill. His approval of the land Bill, will effectually separate him, I presume, from the other party, and he is destined to have an irregular & hobbling administration, from which I apprehend the country will experience but little benefit.

\* \* \* \* \*

*To Susan Washington Graham.* A.

Washington City,
Sunday morning,
Sept. 12th, 1841.

I had packed my trunk on friday & was ready to set out then for home, so as to have been with you this morning, but have been prevailed on to stay by reason of the importance of the business before the Senate. The President has rejected the second Bank Bill, and Messrs. Ewing, Bell, Badger & Crittenden have resigned their offices. Mr. Webster & Mr. Granger, the other two members of the Cabinet, had not resigned today, though I hear that the latter will probably do so. The President has nominated to the Senate, to fill the vacancies made:

Walter Forward [85] of Penna. Secy. of Treasury.

John McLean[86] of Ohio, now a Judge, Secy. of War.

A. P. Upshur[87] of Va. Secy. of Navy.

H. S. Legare of S. C. Atto. General.

---

[85] Walter Forward (1783-1852), of Pennsylvania, lawyer and Democratic editor, who had been a member of congress, 1822-1825, delegate to the state convention of 1837, and a treasury official. He was secretary of the treasury until 1843.

[86] John McLean (1785-1861), of Ohio, a native of New Jersey, who moved to Ohio by way of Kentucky. He was an editor, a war Democrat, 1813-1816, a judge of the state supreme court. He was postmaster general, 1823-1829, and, declining the war and navy portfolios, was appointed to the supreme court, and served until 1861, apparently always hoping to be President.

[87] Abel Parker Upshur (1791-1844), of Virginia, educated at Princeton and Yale, became a lawyer. He served in the house of delegates, 1812-1813, 1825-1827, in the convention of 1829, and on the court of appeals, 1827-1841. He was a champion of state rights, and of slavery. He was killed by the explosion on the "Princeton," later in the year.

These gentlemen are all Whigs, and I do not know that they can agree together, better than the late Cabinet. We are destined to have a stormy & troublesome time during the whole reign of Mr. Tyler who is a weak indecisive man, having no mind of his own, but is driven about according to the suggestions of others.

Messrs. Wise and Stanly had a personal rencountre on the floor of the House of Reps. day before yesterday which was well nigh leading to a general fracas. It was however suppressed and has been reconciled. Mr. Wise received a mark or two on the face which he carries yet.

Great indignation and disgust at the course of the President is felt throughout the country. And it is probable that publications will be made by some of his Cabinet to shew his indecision if not perfidy. Nothing else is talked or thought of here.

I regret exceedingly that I shall not be able to get home in time for my business in Court this week. Congress will adjourn on Monday, tomorrow, and I shall probably be able to leave here on Tuesday so as to reach home on Thursday or Friday.

I am much tantalized by the detention here, and will break off, at the first moment when I can be spared.

I have been looking out for a boarding house for us next winter, but do not know that I shall make any engagement, untill you come on, & examine, so as to make an agreeable selection.

*To James W. Bryan.*                     U. Bryan Mss.

Washington City,

Sept. 13th, 1841.

Congress will adjourn today. You have heard no doubt of the veto upon the second Bank Bill. Messrs. Ewing, Bell, Badger & Crittenden resigned their offices on yesterday, and there has been nominated to the Senate Walter Forword of Pittsburg, Penn, now Comptroller of the Treas. to be Sec. of Treas. Judge McLean of Ohio, Sec. of War. Judge Upshur of Va. Sec. of Navy, Mr. Legare of S. C. Atto. Genl.

Mr. Granger was waited on by the N. Y. delegation and requested to resign, & I hear, did so on Saturday evening.

Mr. Webster continues, it is said, at the special request of the President, who desires him to stay untill he weathers through the pending difficulties with England.

You can well conceive of the excitement which prevails. The President has lost the respect of almost every body, and if revelations are made of the facts attending the passage of the last Bank Bill, he will stand convicted not only of imbecility & folly but of treachery also. I learn that before the Bill was introduced, (he being waited on by some members of Congress who were sent to consult him) he called a Cabinet Council where it was discussed some time, and he yielded his assent to it in the very words in which it was introduced and passed. And then drew the title of the Bill in his own handwriting. Yet you see the veto comments on the title with reprehension, as well as on the act itself. The Cabinet have therefore not left him for mere disagreement on a measure, but for trifling and treachery towards them. For weeks past the correspondent of the New York Herald has been a constant and favored guest at the White House & is seen escorting the President's daughter at public places, though he has been daily writing libels on every member of his Cabinet. They were not consulted about the last veto and never saw it untill published. Indeed, for some time past no persons here have been more ignorant of the designs of the Executive. Poor silly man! he seems to have surrendered himself to the keeping of a small clique, and I should not be surprized if he lost his understanding altogether long before the end of his term. Disapproving all systems of Finance which have ever been tried, he begs Congress to adjourn and allow him a few months to see if he can discover one which *"per se"* he can approve. The Locos will not take him up, though they use him. The new Cabinet has strong Nullification tendencies, and there is reason to believe that he expects to build on it a third party with the aid of the "Corporal's guard" now about him.

There is great regret in the social circles here at the dissolution of the Cabinet. The Secretaries and their ladies have added a charm to society in Washington which it had not derived from the officials for many years before.

Mr. Badger procured the nomination of your friend Moore to a Pursership in the Navy, and I hope it will be confirmed today. It is said that the Cabinet will put forth an address, and there is a proposition to do so by the Whigs in Congress, but I fear that the matter may be overdone. The weakness and folly of the President may be exposed by the Cabinet, but if Congress also assail him, he may persuade the Country that he is persecuted.

The nomination of Everett to England will probably be confirmed today. With much difficulty I have brought my mind to sustain it, though he wrote a most foolish letter to the abolitionists when last a Candidate for Governor. But the Legislature has previously passed resolutions of the same purport. And it seems more proper to withhold from Massachusetts, appropriations for defence, or to retaliate in any other way on her than to deny confirmation in office to one of her citizens for saying he approved the resolutions.

I hope to leave here tomorrow and reach home on Thursday or Friday. This is the week of Orange Supr. Court, which I am compelled to lose as well as that of Granville last week—

\* \* \* \* \*

*From James W. Osborne.* A.

Charlotte,

Oct. 16th., 1841.

The character of an office seeker is at all times odious, and any one of right sensibility reluctantly troubles his friends with solicitations for such an object. But I am peculiarly situated, and under existing circumstances, I have banished the objections which arise from my own feelings, and venture to ask your aid, if there exist no objections with yourself in obtaining an appointment under the general government. I am convinced that it is required by my welfare that I should leave this state; at all events, it is sincerely my wish to do so. Yet I am bound to it by obligations to which no well disposed mind can be insensible. And my wish is to keep up an intercourse with North Carolina, and at a future day return to it, an office, therefore, which I could properly fill, & the emoluments of which would leave me something beyond the expenditures incident to it, seems to me the only practicable mode of effecting my object. My friends have suggested to me to become an applicant for the appointment of chargé des affaires in Texas. I am interested in a planting interest in Louisiana, not very distant from the Texan Capitol, and which it is most inconvenient to me at this time to superintend. This consideration would make the office at that quarter acceptable. And tho' I know it is the duty of such officers to reside at the foreign Capitol, yet the relations of the United States to that Government are so well settled, and the points of diplomacy are so few, that that requisition will not be rigidly enforced. If the appointment can be obtained, I should be gratified to have it. Its salary, I suppose, would be more than the expenditures incident to the situation, and its duties would, I presume, imply no great difficulty. Success in the application will, I am aware, depend wholly on the influence which may be exerted by ones friends. But, as I understand it, such offices fall within the control of the department of State, and depend chiefly on the officer who occupies that department. With the delegation from this State, my acquaintance is not very intimate, nor very general. I knew Mr. Mangum when a boy, but since I came into life, I have known little of him. Of his disposition in this matter, I can therefore form no opinion. With Mr. Rayner I am better acquainted than with almost any other Whig of our delegation in the House of Representatives, and I might hope for his assistance should no other person interfere. I have submitted this matter to you—have communicated with no one else—and would be guided by your advice in relation to the matter.

Respectfully,

*From B. Baker, H. W. Miller, C. L. Hinton.*          U.

Raleigh, N. C.,

Nov. 9th, 1841.

The Whigs of Wake County have tendered the Hon'l George E. Badger a public Dinner as a token of their respect for his private character, and in approbation of his public Course, which he has accepted, and he has signified that on Saturday next it will be convenient for him to meet his friends.

We have been appointed a Committee to say to you that it will afford much pleasure to those of your personal and political friends who may be present, to have your Company on that occasion & we do hope you can find it convenient to attend.

We are with sentiments of
     high respect and esteem,

Your Ob't. S'vts,

*From David L. Swain.*                                    U.

29 Nov., 1841.

Your predecessor Judge Strange franked at my instance some hundreds of the annexed circular,[88] and Gov. Davis[89] when Senator, was the medium of a protracted correspondence between Mr. Bancroft and myself on the subject of Am. History.

I am preparing for publication in the Am. Quarterly Register at Boston, a catalogue of the graduates and of those who have recd. literary distinctions at this institution, from its foundation to the present time.

Fortified by the precedents loco-foco and Whig, above referred to, I venture to beg of you as *a Trustee,* either to send me half a doz. franks to be used for the purpose stated and that only, or to let me transmit the papers to you at Washington, that you may send them from there under your frank. Doct. Montgomery (much to my surprize, I confess) tendered his services to us, in the latter mode. I did not avail myself of his kindness, but Dr. Mitchell did in various instances.

My dispatches will be ready in two or three days.

*To David L. Swain.*                                    A.

Washington City,

Dec'r. 5th, 1841.

Your letter was handed me after I set out from home, for this City. I send herewith several franks for disseminating the documents of which [you] make mention, and I will with pleasure aid in sending abroad any other papers pertaining to the University which you may forward to me here.

\*   \*   \*   \*   \*

You wrote me last session for a copy of the census, etc. I was unable to procure one then, even for my own use. I will, if I can obtain it, send you one in a short time.

The members of Congress are coming in. I believe there is nothing new in the political circles beyond what you see in the

---

[88] The letter was written on a printed letter of the executive committee of the Board of Trustees, dated April 15th., 1837, containing the curriculum, the entrance conditions, and the laws and regulations relating to the university.

[89] John Davis, of Massachusetts.

papers. There seems to be no prospect of a reunion between the Whigs & the President.

I will be pleased to hear from you occasionally during the session.

*To James W. Bryan.*          U. Bryan Mss.

Washington City,

Decr. 22nd, 1841.

I had intended to have written you before this, but have been so much engaged that it has been omitted.

In public affairs there is a great dearth of news. The Fiscal Project of the Sec. of the Treas. is in today. The report accompanying it bears Webster's mark strongly, and is an ingenious appeal to the public. There has been no expression of opinion in relation to it, except Benton's attack when the President's message came in. It meets but little favor as yet, among the members of either party, but no prediction can be made, as to its ultimate fate.

Decr. 27th. The foregoing was written several days ago, when I was interrupted. I now resume, the Senate being in Session. Nothing new has occurred as yet, things are still in a state of quietude. The President has given thus far a dinner on each Friday. I had the honor to be present on the second occasion—thirty or Forty were there, taken about equally from each party. Wright of N. Y. being on the right hand, and Evans,[90] M[aine], on the left. He is playing, I think, for the Loco Focos, though he professes to stand indifferent between parties.

We have taken lodgings on Penna. Av. not far from the Railroad depot, in a small mess consisting of ourselves, Miss E. Washington, and Gov. Morehead's family from Kentucky. There are more ladies connected with the members of Congress at this Session in the City than have ever been here before. The Winter however does not promise to be very gay, as the new Secretaries, with the exception of Webster, are boarders only in the City. Nevertheless, with so many families present, we can have abundant society, in a more quiet way.

---

[90] George Evans (1767-1867), of Maine, a graduate of Bowdoin, a lawyer, who had been speaker of the lower house of the legislature, Whig member of congress, 1829-1841, and was senator, 1841-1847.

Mr. Clay is here, and has been sick with a cold since the commencement of the Session untill today, when he is present in his seat. He will continue here not more than two months when Crittenden will come in to his place. His health is not permanently bad, but the result merely of cold contracted on his journey.

The Locos profess to be in high spirits and so long as they do not nominate a Candidate for the Presidency, they will cohere, but when that takes place, there will danger of a severance.

The events of this Session will try very much the strength of party connexions. The Tariff will be an apple of discord among the Whigs, and may produce a new explosion in the Cabinet. The Secretary of the Treasury being as you see, a Tariff man, and even higher toned, I learn, than his report indicates.

The Fiscal project, you perceive, has gone into the hands of a Com'tee in the House, of whom a majority are friends of the President, or as they are called here, the Corporal's guard. The Madisonian complains of this; I don't know what they will produce. The Senate has not yet determined what Com'tee to consign it to.

Preston moved last week to print a number of extra copies of the Secretary's plan. Buchanan[91] asked delay, saying, that he designed to make some remarks and was then unwell. And on his motion it was postponed 'till today.

I see that the Locos are calling meetings every where to send delegates to a Convention in Raleigh. Montgomery's faction in Orange, propose Brown for Gov. and condemn the relief of the Railroad Cos., etc., in the two last Legislatures, thereby giving a blow to some of the most prominent of their own party. Brown would be a stronger Candidate than Henry,[92] though Morehead can beat either, very easily. I think our friends should turn out in full force at their Convention in the Spring, or it will have a depressing effect upon the spirits of the party.

[91] James Buchanan, of Pennsylvania, then a senator.
[92] Louis D. Henry.

1842

*From William Gaston.*                                    U.

Raleigh,

Jany. 5th, 1842.

Since my arrival at this place I received a letter from Mr. Isaac Guion of Newbern stating that he was an applicant for the appointment of purser in the Navy, and requesting from me any little aid I could afford him in effecting his object. This I trust will be received by you as an excuse for troubling you with this communication.

Mr. Guion is a young man, I suppose about 24 years of age, and now holds the office of Teller in the Merchant's Bank of Newbern, the duties of which I understand that he performs to the entire satisfaction of his employers. Altho' the salary attached to the office affords him a decent support, it does not furnish the means of improving his condition in life, and he is naturally solicitous to engage in some business which may prove more profitable. He is a good accountant, has an unimpeached character, and is of business habits. It would afford me much gratification if he could obtain the situation which he desires, and I entertain the confident belief that, if he should, the duties of it would be discharged with fidelity.

You must, I think, have been acquainted with his father, John W. Guion. He was the Cashier of the Bank for many years, and no Institution ever had a more upright or faithful officer. At the time of his death, which occurred about two years since, he was among the oldest friends I had on earth, and a better man it has seldom happened to me to meet with. He left a family of many children, who had been carefully trained up in the paths of virtue, but left very slender portions wherewith to commence their career in life.

I will thank you to exhibit this letter to Mr. Mangum and to Gen'l Saunders, both of whom, I believe, were well acquainted with the late Mr. Guion, and who I hope will feel an interest in the success of his son.

Believe me, with great regard
Your friend & obed't Serv't

*To David L. Swain.*          A. Swain Mss.

Washington City,

Jany. 6th, 1842.

I desire to know what were the terms on which the Proc. money of our State was issued, and what were the causes which kept its credit up, or at least that of some of it, untill a particular period, I believe about 1808. Was it not a legal tender between individuals or receivable in payment of taxes, under the Laws which created it, notwithstanding the prohibition in the Constitution forbidding future "issues of Bills of credit"? And did not our Banks for some time receive & use them as specie? I feel confident that there was some peculiarity in our Legislation, which kept a part of it equal to specie. But I have not the means here to make the investigation.

My reason for desiring this, is that Mr. Calhoun in 1837 referred to our paper money as an illustration of the success of Government paper, which he then considered as the best of all currencies.

Will you do me the favor to give me your views of this subject, which I know you investigated thoroughly, during your Legislative & Executive career.

I desire also to know whether the Merchant's Bank at New Bern has suspended specie payments with the other Banks. My impression is that they have not suspended, but that exchange is no better between New Bern and New York, than between Raleigh and that City, thus contradicting certain theories now in vogue in the Country.

Please inform me if you have this information, though I will write to New Bern for the same matter.

There is but little new here. Woodbury is making a speech against "the Fiscality" as it is called, in which he is endeavouring to justify his policy in the Treasury department. He inveighs with vehemence against the plan of the Secretary, as all his party have done. Our friends are equally opposed to it, except the Webster section and the conservatives. All however say they won't take it as it is. But think that something may be made of it, "and the people expect something." It will be referred of course, but I do not now suppose that any thing effectual can be made of it.

Mangum and Barrow[1] have made pretty spicy attacks on Tyler, as you see, and the great body of our friends have no confidence in him. His entertainments embrace both parties, and about equal numbers at the same time. And he refuses to remove any more officers, & when vacancies occur, he nominates some personal favorites. In one or two instances persons removed by Harrison.

*From David L. Swain.*                                    U.

Chapel Hill,

Jan. 11th, 1841. [1842]

Your favour of the 6th. was rec'd by this morning's mail.

I recollect very distinctly Mr. Calhoun's reference to the history of our paper currency. I intended at the time it met my eye, to furnish a newspaper paragraph for some of our editors, but ultimately concluded to abide by the determination not to enter into political speculations, while in my present position. In 1828 and 1829, when a member of the Ho. of Com. and again in 1834, at the instance of Mr. Wilder of Ga., I was induced to examine with some minuteness every source of information within my reach, in relation to our revolutionary Bills of credit. I have preserved many things, in various shapes, but they make parts of bound vols. that cannot be conveniently transmitted. I will give you some abstracts however, and if you need more particular information, will endeavour to supply it in answer to such inquiries as you may propound.

The first emission of Bills of credit was in 1713, the last in 1785. The total amount emitted during this period of 42 years, was £29.133.350 or $72.833.375. The total value of real estate in N. C. in 1798, was $28,000,000, and the whole wealth of the State real and personal, was doubtless of less value than the amount of this debt. In Jan. 1778 the scale of depreciation was $3\frac{1}{2}$ to 1—Jan. 1779—6 to 1—Jan. 1780—32 to 1—Jan. 1781—210 to 1—Jan. 1782—800 to 1.—At the latter rate—(800 for one) it was rec'd and absorbed at the Treasury in payment for entries of land.

Of the various emissions made during the Revolution, or previous to the adoption of the Federal Constitution, the two last

---

[1] Alexander Barrow (1801-1846), of Louisiana, a native of Tennessee, educated at West Point, lawyer and planter, served in the state legislature, and was United States senator, 1841-1846.

(in 1783 and 1785) of £100.000 each, were made a lawful tender in the payment of debts. The Bills were of two denominations only, 40 S. or Five Dollar Bills and 20 s. or $2.50 Bills. These emissions were of course unaffected by the provision in the Federal Constitution that no State "*shall*" emit Bills of credit. They continued a lawful tender, until they were absorbed in the payment of subscriptions for Stock in the old State Bank in 1811, and burnt. Notwithstanding the immunity afforded by the tender laws at the period of the adoption of the Federal Constitution, they had depreciated at the rate of 2 for one, and the utmost extent which they *appreciated* at any time was 5 to 4.

You doubtless are old enough to recollect when the old Forty Shilling Bills were current at $4, although it was an indictable offence, and various Scotch merchants were indicted and punished at Hillsboro, for refusing to receive these at the rate of 8 Shillings to the Dollar.

The amount of Proclamation money (as it was called) in existence when our first Bank was introduced by stealth in 1804, under the name of "the Marine and Fire *insurance* company of Newbern," is supposed to have been between 2 & $300.000. The Banks of Newbern and Cape Fear divided 10 per-cent annually until the establishment of this State Bank in 1810 by issuing notes *ad libitum,* and thrusting these brown, ragged, hideous, lawful tender at all applicants for gold and silver.

The great object sought by the creation of the State Bank, was to deprive the Banks of New Bern and Cape Fear of this *shield,* and it was, as you doubtless recollect, one of the conditions of the charter that it should be redeemed by 1815.

In 1811 Mr. Stanly[2] published his famous pamphlet entitled "Common Sense," in defence of "old Proc," and the old Bank, and against the Bank of the State. I regret that I cannot send the pamphlet. The following extract in the peculiar manner of that remarkable man, will give you some idea of the spirit and argument of the whole.

"It is alleged this paper money will not pass out of the State. This is true, and in my opinion this confinement of a certain portion of our Cash to our own market is a most valuable quality; the more so certainly that this fleeting commodity called money can have imparted to it, the quality of *sticking by us.*"

[2] John Stanly.

"The man who has saved money enough to speculate, and goes to Virginia or Maryland to buy Negroes, the trader who is indebted for goods to the Northern merchant, the foreign creditor or his attorney having pursued to judgment and Execution his delinquent creditor; the man who is about to leave the State, and who having sold his property here and removed, calls once a year for his payments; these are the men who want *Dollars* for their purposes abroad, and these, if not the whole, are certainly nearly the whole whose occasions require specie."

"The first certain, inevitable consequence (of the withdrawal of this currency) will be to convert every existing debt due from the citizens of this State, not only judgments and executions, but bonds, notes and book accounts into a *"hard money debt"* and to expose the property of every unfortunate debtor to sale by execution for *Gold and Silver only."*

Prof. Roberts[3] who returned from Newbern on Monday last, thinks that the Merchants, is not a specie paying Bank, except so far as relates to a supply of change, but is not certain.

So much in relation to what you; none with respect to information that I desire.

And first will Mr. Spencer[4] send Prof. Phillips to West Point.

Secondly, are we not entitled to some books among those published by Congress, that have not been sent us, and if we are not, cannot you obtain them for us? The executive and legislative documents of each Session, are transmitted regularly and we have received a copy of Gales and Seatons edition of State Papers and the two Vols. of Clarke & Ferns Doc. History. We need particularly a late edition of Gordon's Digest, and more especially a copy of the Diplomatic Correspondence of the Revolution, and would be thankful for other favours. Are we not entitled to copies of these and of Gales and Seatons Register of Debates?

If you revive your Bill in relation to monuments to Gen'l Nash and Gen'l Davidson, is not the Campus of our University, the most appropriate location?

---

[3] John Jones Roberts (1819-1908), a native of New Bern, graduate of the university, and professor, 1841-1842. He later became an Episcopal minister, and spent the rest of his life teaching, in Massachusetts, and New York.

[4] John Canfield Spencer (1788-1855), of New York, a graduate of Union College, lawyer, soldier in the War of 1812, Democratic member of congress, 1817-1819, member of, and speaker of, the state assembly; secretary of state of New York, secretary of war, 1841-1843, secretary of the treasury, 1843-1844. In 1844 Tyler nominated him to the supreme court, but the Whig majority in the Senate, enraged by his support of Tyler, refused to confirm him.

I fear that my caligraphy gives little evidence of the favourable effects of time, upon my physical constitution.

*From William W. Holden.*[5]                    U.

Raleigh, 18th January, 1842.

Application has been made to me by several Whigs here to engage with Mr. Lemay[6] in the Editorship of the Star.

Mr. Miller has kindly proffered his services and influence in the premises, and has written to our Whig delegation in Congress upon the subject. Mr. Lemay is perfectly well qualified to conduct the Star, but his other engagements are so numerous that he has little time to bestow upon it. The object of this communication is, to request you to use your influence with the Whig delegation, and to impress upon the party in this State the necessity of a plan similar to the one I propose.

If the Whigs will give me $200 and Lemay $100 I will engage to do all I can through the ensuing campaign; and this sum, I am persuaded, can easily be obtained. If the Whig delegation should take the matter up, and write to Mr. Lemay urging the plan, I make no doubt he will assent to it.

Be pleased to inform me as soon as possible with regard to it.

Very truly your friend

*Speech on Roanoke Inlet.*[7]

In Senate,

January 28th., 1842.

MR. GRAHAM, on leave, introduced a bill making an appropriation to reopen Roanoke Inlet.

---

[5] William Woods Holden (1818-1892), a native of Orange, a Whig editor, and then the editor of the influential *North Carolina Standard,* of Raleigh, the father of secession" in the State, who boasted, not without reason, that politically, he had "the power to kill and make alive." Defeated for the Democratic nomination for governor and senator in 1858, he became a Unionist, and opponent of secession. He was a delegate to the convention of 1861, and voted for secession. Always opposed to the war, and hostile to the Confederate government, he was a peace candidate for governor in 1864, but was defeated. Johnson appointed him provisional governor, and he was defeated at the first election. Having become a radical Republican, he was elected in 1868. In 1871 he was impeached, and removed from office.

[6] Thomas J. Lemay edited several papers in North Carolina. He later moved to Alabama.

[7] From *Congressional Globe,* January 28th, 1842.

Mr. G. said that, although he had given notice of his bill several weeks since, he had delayed asking leave to introduce it, until he could obtain certain information which he desired, from a distinguished Civil Engineer, who had made a survey and report under the Legislature of North Carolina, on the subject of re-opening Roanoke Inlet. The work was one of deep concern to the people of that State, whose General Assembly, at each of its last two sessions, had adopted resolutions urging it upon the attention of Congress as, in the highest degree, important to the commerce and navigation of the Union. He held in his hand a copy of these resolutions, and of the report of the Engineer, (Major Gwynn) to which he had already alluded, and wished to lay these on the table for the information of the Senate, and of the Committee to whom they might be referred. He would, therefore, enter into no discussion of the object of the bill at present, except to remark that Roanoke Inlet was once the direct channel of communication from Albermarle Sound to the Atlantic Ocean; that, in process of time, it had been filled up, and the waters of the Sound were compelled to seek an outlet by forcing their way southwardly to Pamlico Sound, and thence through Ocracoke Inlet to the sea. By the change which had taken place, vessels from the Albermarle, or any of its tributaries, bound to New York, or any northern ports, were obliged to take this southern direction out to sea at Ocracoke, and to perform a voyage of more than one hundred and twenty miles to return to the latitude of Roanoke Inlet or Nags Head, encountering in its progress the expense of lighterage over shallows, the risks of a narrow, difficult, and often changing channel, before reaching the ocean, and then the peril of doubling Cape Hatteras, which mariners more dread than almost any part of the American Coast. This bill contemplates reopening the ancient entrance to Albermarle Sound, near sixty miles north of Cape Hatteras, by proposing a passage through a sand beach, about one-half or three-quarters of a mile in extent, and thus avoid all the difficulties and dangers of the present course of navigation. It will be seen, in the report of the engineer, that the commerce, now laboring under these impediments, amounted annually to at least $3,000,000., that it furnished employment to more than 100,000 tons shipping, is one of the best nurseries of American seamen in all of our coasting trade, yet that the burdens under which it is carried on, and the frightful loss of human life which attends it, for want of the old Inlet, are almost incredible.

Whether, therefore, the work proposed be regarded as opening a new harbor of refuge for our commerce from an enemy in time of War, or from the frequent and violent storms of that Coast, as relieving our seamen and vessels from the dangers of shipwreck, or as freeing the commerce of one of the most productive sections of the Country,—a section more extensive in territory, and more populous than several of the States of the Union,—from burdens of of the most oppressive character, it equally demanded a favorable and immediate attention of the Government.

*Newspaper Comment.*[8]

"Hon. Wm. A. Graham, of N. C.—This Senator is the brother of James Graham, who has long represented the "Buncombe" district in the popular branch of Congress, and has a number of years been an active politician. Previous to his elevation to the high position he now occupies, he was elected to the State Legislature, and was chosen Speaker of the lower house. He is in the prime of life, of medium size, light hair and complexion, blue eyes, very expressive—handsome forehead, high and arched. His features are of the Grecian cast, and the expression of his face is strikingly agreeable and intelligent. According to all physiological rules, he must be a man possessing a good deal more than common intellectual qualifications. He is exceedingly modest in his demeanor, pleasant in his private intercourse, happy in his disposition, and enticing in his manners. He is very studious, and enjoys a very high legal reputation; is conversant with constitutional law, and has a clear, sound and philosophical mind. There is nothing about him of a doubtful character,—rather avoids than seeks applause,—and every movement he makes is founded upon a substantial basis. As a Senator he will, I imagine, be found more useful in the committee rooms than in debate, though there is no reason why he should not take an active part in discussion; for he has a good voice and a pleasing delivery; and what is better than all, a logical mind, highly cultivated. Let him be where he may, he will be always sure to command profound respect, both for the beauty of this intellect, and the excellency of his heart."

---

[8] From the *Hillsborough Recorder,* February 3rd, 1842. Quoted from the *New York Mercury.*

To *James W. Bryan.*          U. Bryan Mss.

Washington City,

Feby 10th, 1842.

My engagements have prevented me from writing you as often I had wished. The events transpiring here have not been of much general interest, but there has been the customary amount of gossip, scandal, etc.

My children have not been well for a week or two past. John now has the measles, and I presume of course the two younger children are to take it. Jo. has had an attack of fever which yielded to a dose of calomel, and some lighter medicines.

Susan and Cousin Eliza are quite well, and are somewhat pleased with the society of Washington. The latter has been to numerous parties, and amuses us much with a fac simile of the dancing of Lord Morpeth,[9] who is now here, and who is said to be so proficient in the saltative art. He seems to be an unassuming gentleman, and takes great interest in the observation of our affairs.

There has been no public entertainment for him, but he has received hospitalities from many gentlemen in private. Dickens (Boz) has been feted magnificently at Boston, and is to be again at New York.

Moffitt the Methodist preacher (Chaplain of the House) is a great lion here just now—and is a real stage player in the pulpit. The crowds which gather to hear him are greater than attend at any of the discussions of Congress. And he is as much a subject of Tea Table chat as any other gentleman who has separated from his wife, and is under suspicions of bad *morals.* He has a musical voice, sings like a Nightingale, and recites poetry in the true theatrical manner & elocution, and strings together all the Heroes, demigods, Poets, philosophers, & sages of antiquity, touches on gravitation, steam, electricity, etc., and thus fills out an hour and a half. There have been some criticisms on him in the New York express, which are Capital caricatures.

There is no prospect of an agreement between Congress and the President on the Currency and Finances. He is so poor an imbe-

---

[9] George William Frederick Howard (1802-1864), 7th Earl of Carlisle, who, until he succeeded to the title, had the courtesy title of Lord Morpeth. He had been fifteen years in Parliament, had been chief secretary for Ireland, and was later lord lieutenant. He spent a year in America.

cile that there is no such thing as keeping terms with him. His nominations are made, with reference to his own popularity solely. We shall be able to disappoint him on some of them, and but for Webster's control in a part of New England he would not have the semblance of support, in the Senate. Some of his favorites we shall blow up—others will pass with reluctance. He seems disposed now to make some removals, but appoints loose Whigs instead from whom he exacts fealty to him.

Waddy Thompson has been nominated as Minister to Mexico, Washington Irving to Spain, and will be both confirmed. A Mr. Blackford [10] (one of the numberless tribe of Virginians who absorb all the offices of Government) is nominated to Guatamala.

Bradford [11] of Phila is nominated for district Judge, in place of Binney, who declines. Botts has placed Upshur in deep difficulty by his last publication, proving that he has been an unqualified and boasted advocate of a dissolution of the Union.

The Secretaries are all Boarders in the City, except Webster, and I believe, entertain no company. It is rumored that the Secy. Treas. will go out upon an office. He is certainly unfit for his place, and I have it from unquestionable authority that Webster wrote every word of his Report on the Fiscal agent.

You have seen the proceedings of the House in the case of Adams' Petition to dissolve the Union. He is a great nuisance, and the prosecution has been a great force. On yesterday Gilmer[12] Proffitt,[13] etc., asked to be excused from serving on the Com'tee of Foreign affairs with him, and were taken at their word. I do not know who succeeds them.

Mr. Clay will resign about the last of March and be succeeded by Crittenden. He will not go to N. C. this Spring, as some of our friends desire, but tells me *in private* that he wishes next winter to go to New Orleans and Cuba and will probably return by way of Charleston, and visit Raleigh during the Session of the Legislature.

---

[10] William Matthews Blackford (d. 1864), of Lynchburg, Virginia, lawyer and editor, appointed charge d'affaires to New Grenada, and served from 1841 to 1844. After his return, he edited the Lynchburg *Virginian*.

[11] Thomas Bradford.

[12] Thomas Walker Gilmer (1802-1844), of Virginia, who was a Whig member of the house of delegates, 1829-1836, 1839-1840, (speaker, 1839-40), governor, 1840-1841, member of congress, 1841-1844, secretary of the navy, 1844. He was killed a few days later, by the explosion on the "Princeton."

[13] George H. Proffit (1807-1847), of Indiana, a native of Louisiana, merchant, lawyer, member of the lower house of the legislature, 1831-1832, 1836-1838, was a Whig member of congress, 1839-1843. He was nominated minister to Brazil, but was not confirmed.

Our delegation here feel much anxiety that there should be a respectable turn out of our friends to the Convention at Raleigh in April. We have also suggested the propriety of at once nominating Clay for the Presidency. Tyler has not only disappointed us on the currency, but withdrawn from us his confidence, set himself up for reelection contrary to his repeated and vehement declarations before his election. Nor has he, in twelve months from the beginning of his administration proposed a single measure of reform or economy. Will you think of the propriety of an immediate nomination, and if you do not go to Raleigh, suggest your views of it to our friends there. If it will not aid us, it should not be done, but would it not be an advantage to have a distinct flag up in the summer elections?

I have not seen Mr. Henrys acceptance of the nomination for Governor, but am told that it goes beyond Allison and Wheelers report at Raleigh. A great effort will be made upon Craven, Northampton, Halifax, Orange, Stokes, Surry, and Rowan, but with united action we shall be able to carry the State.

Old Poindexter[14] of Miss. has been introduced at my boarding House within a day and is in a bad humor. He came here last March for an office—was soured with Harrison for not giving it to him. When Tyler succeeded he had much influence over him, and was appointed one of a Commission to investigate the N. York Custom House. He says now that he has discovered the most astounding frauds in the Custom House, but that as he implicates Curtis as deeply as Hoyt, Webster (a devoted friend of C's) has prevailed on the President not to receive the Report. He has called twice, and didn't see Tyler; has written and received an answer, but that is not satisfactory, and he swears that he will not call again untill he is sent for. If he is not appeased he will make an explosion. You have perhaps seen in the papers that he quarrelled with one of the other Com'ers and challenged him; and accuses him of bribery, etc.

This is but a part of the running gossip. I must defer more for the present.

---

[14] George Poindexter (1779-1855), a native of Virginia, who, after settling in Mississippi, was attorney general, member of the assembly, and delegate in congress, 1807-1813. He was a soldier in the War of 1812, Federal judge, 1813-1817, member of congress, 1817-1819, governor, 1819-1821, United States senator, 1830-1835.

*From George McClellan.*          A.

Philadelphia,

Feby. 14, 1842.

Although my attachment to our good Whig cause has been so often discouraged by untoward circumstances it has never been thoroughly disheartened. I still feel impelled to go onwards & try once more for success: and I have promised my friends to take to the stump for that noble old fellow Henry Clay in the next campaign. You must excuse me therefore, for troubling you with this hasty expression of my sentiments upon a matter which is likely to affect our prospects seriously in this district, if not in the whole State. Many of our best friends have thought it very impolitic to quarrel with Mr. Tyler upon the now odious Bank question, and prefer to let him go quietly with a decent appearance of party support through his term of office. They disapprove of any such opposition as may tend to break up the integrity of our party, and heartily desire to preserve an unbroken phalanx for a sally at the next Presidential election. Among the chief of these has been my old friend and neighbor Thos. Bradford, Esq. who I know has always been the unwavering friend & admirer of Mr. Clay, and upon whose influence in our cause I calculate as fully as upon the coming seasons. Now to allow him to be put down by the influence of any of Mr. Clay's avowed friends in the Senate will destroy every prospect I have indulged of a final triumph of my hopes. The whole of our large band of Judicious and temperate Whigs who have preferred to keep John Tyler as long as possible in the ranks of their party will become disgusted, and I fear will leave us to our fate.

But I need say nothing to you on this point. What I desire particularly to state to you is my knowledge of Mr. Bradford as a man, and his claims for your support of his nomination before the Senate as a Judge of the District Court of the U. S. Notwithstanding all the representations which may have been made to you I beg you to believe that the testimony of all the worthy of the Bench and Bar here is absolutely & unqualifiedly in favour of his thorough qualifications for the appointment. There can be no doubt of his learning, abilities, or (what is of most consequence in this case) of his John Locke's strong, round-about common sense. The excellence of his character as a gentleman and a Christian cannot be questioned. I know no one of greater purity and honour in this City. He is descended from one of the most distinguished families in our Country. You must be familiar with the brilliant reputation of his former Uncle, Wm. Bradford,[15] the Attorney General of the U. States under the elder Adams. But his own virtue will prove his best commendation. Since 25 years ago his brother, the late Samuel Bradford failed, involving him to a very large amount by endorsements in two of our principal Banks. Since that period Thomas Bradford, although poor, has devoted one half of his entire professional earnings to the discharge of these debts, for which he never received any advantage whatever. I know that he has paid more than 60,000 dollars in this way for the pay't of his endorsements in principal & interest.

In the mean time he has raised and educated a large and accomplished family of children by unremitting toil, without grumbling to his friends, or asking the Banks to abate a shilling of their claims. The public will respect such a man; and his numerous friends will indulge feelings of resentment against any body of men who shall appear to lay the heavy hand [of] opposition upon him.

I lay this disinterested statement before your impartial mind, and beg you to present my warmest regards to Mr. Clay, & mention the facts to him.

My excellent old friend Mr. Chauncey has written upon this subject to Mr. Huntington;[16] and I beg you to read that letter for a corroboration of my testimony.

*From Elisha Mitchell.*                                         U.

University of N. Ca., Feby. 16th, 1842

I have been engaged during a considerable part of a week in unpacking and arranging a collection of minerals purchased for us in Vienna by J. Randolph Clay,[17] lately Charge'd' Affairs of

---

[15] William Bradford (1755-1795), of Philadelphia, a graduate of Princeton, Revolutionary soldier, state attorney general, 1780-1791, judge of the state supreme court, 1791-1794, United States attorney general, 1794-1795.

[16] Jabez Williams Huntington (1788-1847), of Connecticut, a graduate of Yale, Whig member of congress, 1829-1834, judge of State supreme court, 1834-1840, United States senator, 1840-1847.

[17] John Randolph Clay (1808-1885), a native of Philadelphia, lived with John Randolph of Roanoke, his godfather, while he was educated in Virginia, and went with him to Russia as secretary of legation. He was charge there, 1836-1837, secretary of legation at Vienna, 1838-1845, and acting charge, 1839-1842, again secretary of legation at St. Petersburg, 1845-1847, charge at Peru, 1847-1853, and minister, 1853-1860.

the United States in that City. They have come to us in good order and the whole business appears to have been well executed for us.

I wish to advise him of their safe arrival and perhaps engage him to make other purchases. When the appointment of Mr. Jenifer[18] was announced in the papers it was stated particularly that Mr. Clay was retained as Secretary of Legation, but when Mr. Jenifer sailed for Europe no great while since, he was said to be accompanied by some person (I forget whom) as Secretary of Legation.

You can I presume easily ascertain whether Mr. Clay has been or is to be removed and whether therefore a letter from me is likely to find him in Vienna as also whether it will be of any use to correspond with him about further purchases. Will you do me this favour and inform me at an early date?

Furthermore, I procured from Russia to be exhibited to the classes three Platinum coins—12. 6. and 3. Rubles. I should be very glad to inform them at the same time what the inscription and legend are; and with a view to that have copied them as they appear on the larger coin. The word Rubles I can make out, and I suppose a part of the legend to state that the platinum constituting the coin is from the Oural mountains. The only Russian book we have is the N. Testament in Ancient and Modern Russ.

You will not wonder therefore that I should be at a stand.

I have formed the opinion of M. Bodisco,[19] the Russian Ambassador that he is a worthy man and well liked in and about Washington with the exception that his having married so young and pretty a lady displeases the younger portion of the hangers-on about the public offices, who would have preferred that she should be the wife of some one of their own numbers.

Could you get this inscription interpreted for me, the pronunciation in English letters and the meaning either from M. Bodisco or from some one of the attachés of the Legation, or is such proceeding altogether improper and preposterous? you will judge.

I had even thought of going farther, and getting you to ask M. Bodisco, if he had an old Russian spelling book to give it to me, or if he were going to send to Russia for one for his boys to send

---

[18] Daniel Jennifer (1791-1855), of Maryland. After service in the legislature, he was a Whig member of congress, 1831-1833, 1835-1841. He was minister to Austria, 1841-1845. He fought a duel with Jesse A. Bynum of North Carolina.

[19] M. A. de Bodisco.

for me too. But suppose that such begging of a spelling-book from a foreign Ambassador, by a professor in an University through the medium of a venerable Senator might be a thing unheard of in the Annals of Diplomacy. I abandoned the idea altogether.

*From James C. Turrentine.*[20]          U.

Hillsborough,

February 16th, 1842.

I have made out a list of voters as well as I could remember as to their polaticks and marked the letters W. for Whig, & V. for VanBuren, opposite their names. I have tried to select the young men and those who did not take political news papers. I have tried to class them as to the proper post office as you will see. I have no doubt failed in some instances, in remembering their Polaticks & the proper office, Yet I think it will be correct in the main. I should have liked that you could have had the list earlyer but my business prevented. Nothing new here. Your people are well as far as I know.

*[Enclosure.]*

Voters at Hillsborough election Aug't. 1841.

W. John N. Clark
W. Alexr. M. Kirkland
W. And. Mickel
W. John Bain
W. James Webb jr.
W. John Douglass
W. Alvis Bishop
W. A. F. Long
W. George McCawley
W. Henry Webb
W. Allen Petty
W. Benjamin Kinion
W. James Collins
W. Thos. D. Cate

V. Robert Hastings
W. Tyrie B. Ray
W. Lawrence Kinion
W. Anderson Armstrong
W. Charles L. Freeland
W. Thomas Griffin jr.
W. Arch'd McCawley
W. John Brown
V. Alvis Durham
W. Harrison Scott
W. Eaton Walker
W. Henry Witherspoon
W. Duncan Nichols
V. Allen Collins

---

[20] Sheriff of Orange County.

V. Stephen Clark
W. Tho. W. Holden
W. John Wilkerson
V. William James
V. Joseph McCullock
V. Williamson Burton
W. Wilson Jackson
W. William H. Thompson
V. James W. Clark
V. James Thompson (of Josh
W. James Jackson (Stiller
W. Paul Kinion
W. Andrew Borland
W. James H. Pratt
V. John Duly
W. Cameron Craig
V. Porter Thompson
W. David Hayes
W. Adam Douglass
V. General Baker
V. Willie Andrews
W. Nath'l D. Bain
V. Nathaniel Bain
W. Thomas C. Hayes
W. James Long
W. Charles Long
V. Richard Williams
W. John I. Freeland
W. William Duskin
V. David D. Paul
V. William Gatler
V. Frederick Williams
W. William Dixon
W. Wm. H. Holden
V. Lemuel Pickett
W. Jno. U. Smith
V. Hugh C. Reeves
V. Sidney Tapp
W. Andrew Shanklin
W. William Wolf
W. Thomas Long

W. Thomas Pratt
W. John Walker
W. William R. Walker
W. James Sykes (of Tho.
W. Hugh Faucett
W. John C. Latta
W. Silas M. Sink
W. Alex'r Dixon
V. David McKee
W. Stephen Jackson
W. David Tinnen
W. John Sykes
V. Samuel Thompson
V. Charles Jordan

### Hillsboro'

V. Calvin Hill
V. Wm. Ward
V. Rich'd Cheek

*Voters at Chapel Hill election* )
                                    )
                                    )

V. Dr. Henry Lloyd
V. Green Andrews
W. Irai Ellis
W. Wilson Watson
V. Chas. L. Cooley
W. Catlett C. Tinner
W. Thomas Hogan, jr.
W. Pinkney Sykes
V. Duncan Anderson
V. Wm. F. Smith
V. Wm. H. Brown
W. Julius Watson
W. Alex'r Borland
W. Jno. Hobbs (David
V. Abisha Faucette
V. Henry Cheek
V. Wm. F. Jones jr.
V. Thompson Maris
V. Alex'r Findley

*Morrow's*

W. Thomas Faucett
W. Jno. Cate (of Milly
W. David Roach
W. Rich'd A. Standford
W. Elijah Pickard
V. Sidney Lindsey
V. David Anderson
W. Henry Whitted
V. James N. Strayhorn
V. William Woodard
W. David W. Craig
W. Jno. Faucette (Sam'l
W. David Lockhart
W. Daniel Thompson
W. Arch'd Borland
W. James N. Craig
W. Joseph L. Turner
W. Samuel Smith
W. Robert Faucette
W. James P. Clark
W. Calvin Smith
W. Samuel Holman
W. and C. Murdock
V. Ralph Thompson

*Morrow's*
*Lindley's Store—*
*Jno. Newlands P. O.*

W. Jonathan Zachary
W. Dr. Abner Holton
W. Merritt Roberson, Sen.
V. John Bingham
W. Oliver Newland
W. Brice Carter
V. Miles Davis
W. Samuel Kirkland
V. Benjamin McCawley
V. Stephen Lloyd
W. C. W. Snipes
W. Wm. I. Hogan

V. Abel Madray
V. Josiah Madray
V. Camel Lloyd
V. Jehiel Atwater
V. Thomas D. Faucette
V. Henry Andrews jr.
W. William Strain
V. William Brewer
W. Alex'r Cheek
W. John Morrow
V. Jno. Andrews
W. Thomas Weaver
W. Thomas Burrhus
V. Alfred Boothe
W. Matthew McCawley
W. James Crabtree
W. Wm. O. McCawley
V. George Nevills
V. Charles Nevills
W. Wm. S. Bradshaw
V. Wm. Perry
W. Hosea C. Smith
W. Jno. Crawford, jr.
W. Wm. P. Morrow
W. Dr. Alex'r Morrow
V. Sam'l Thompson (of W'm)
W. Thomas Brewer, jr.
W. Jno. Moore
V. Geo. B. Morrow
W. Alfred Pickard
W. Wm. Smith
W. James S. Morrow
W. Richd. Howard
V. Jno. J. Roberson
W. And. M. Steel
W. Saurin Standford
W. Sidney Whitted
V. Berry Andrews
V. John Pickard
V. Thomas Thompson (of Josiah)

V. Hawkin Strowd
W. Thos. E. Oldham
V. Samuel Bradshaw
W. John Lloyd
W. James Newland
W. Daniel Foust
V. Robert Cheek
W. William Bradshaw
W. Hiram Johnston
V. James Stewart
V. Robert Grahams
W. Isaac Holt
W. Peter Foust
V. Jno. Cable
W. William Johnston
W. Thomas Woody
V. Samuel Stockard
W. James Roberson
W. Nathaniel Woody
W. John Foust

Cummings election )
John Stafford's    )
Snow Camp **P. O.** )

W. John Kirkpatrick
W. William Wells, jr.
W. Fred Stafford
W. William Thompson
W. Sam'l Kirkpatrick, jr.
W. Jeremiah Piggott
V. Thomas Lloyd
W. Jno. W. Pritchard
W. William Weaver

Voters at Morrow's   )
   election          )
Clover Garden Post   )
   Office            )

W. Jesse Durham
W. John Morris
W. James Morris

W. Wm. M. Crutchfield

*Fogleman's Election*
*Hunt's House P. Office*

V. Jno. S. Fogleman
V. Louis Wilson
V. Rich'd Leavins
V. Michael Roberson
V. Henry Fogleman
W. Michael Shoffner
W. James F. Shelton
V. David Bennett
W. Peter Shaffner
W. John Webster
W. William Webster

*Michael Holt's P. O.*
W. Daniel Albright F. R.)
V. David Graves
W. W. A. Carigan
W. David Andrews
V. David Roberson
W. Jno. A. Crutchfield
W. Henry Edwards, jr.
V. Alfred Thompson
V. Patterson Thompson
V. Jno. J. Durham
V. Wm. P. Thompson
V. Henry Crutchfield

*Albright's P. O.*
W. Fisher Clendinen
V. Thomas Truitt

*Haw River P. O.*
W. Wm. M. Rogers
W. Jeremiah Harden
W. Rob't F. White
W. Daniel Harden
W. Geo. W. White
W. Jno. Harden
V. Jeremiah Bason
W. Jno. G. Albright

W. Samuel White, jr.
V. James Jones
V. Jno. Cheek, majr
W. Rich'd Glass
W. Stephen Glass
V. Joseph B. McMurray
W. Robert Moore
V. Jno. Thomas
W. Maddison Phillips
W. Martin Ghaskill
W. Peter Foust
W. George Ghaskill

*Patterson's Store*
*P. Office*
V. David Patterson
W. Calvin Johnston
V. William Mosier
V. Standford Steel
V. Thomas Steel
V. Isaac Patterson
W. Samuel Coble
V. George Patterson

*C. F. Faucett's P. O.*
W. William Jones
W. Abel Faucette
V. John Raney
W. Thomas Grayham
V. Lewis Dishong
W. Uriah V. Bacon
V. Jacob O. Hurdle
V. Phillip Crawford
V. Jesse Gant
W. James Faucette, jr
V. Benjamin Raney
W. Thomas White
V. Josiah Hurdle
V. John Crawford
V. William Crawford
W. Martin Coble
V. Jacob Huffman
W. James Ferrell

W. Daniel Shaffner
W. Emanuel Clapp
V. Jacob Neese
W. William Smith
W. Julius Coley
W. William Coble
V. Martin Neese
W. David Clapp

*Albright's P. Office*
V. George Albright
V. Jacob Rich
V. Jno. Holt
W. George Lay
W. Samuel Curtis
W. Joseph Holt
W. Peter Boon
W. Lewis Boon
V. William Tarpley
W. Jeremiah Holt
W. John S. Turrentine
W. David L. Ray
W. Willis Sellars, jr
W. William Foust
V. Wm. Holmes
W. Milton Holt

*Mason Hall P. O.*
W. Thomas McCracken  (Tho.)
V. Willie Mebane
V. John Nelson
V. Paisley Nelson
V. Anderson Thompson
W. Joseph W. Steel
V. John Hamilton
W. James McCadams
W. Rowan Tate
W. Joseph Tate, jr
W. Thomas Tate
V. Wm. H. Goodloe
W. Green D. Jordan
W. John A. Mebane
W. Wm. S. Moore

V. Jno. M. Paul
V. Paisley Kirkpatrick
W. James Johnston
V. John Stevens
V. Jno. Corden, jr
V. Henderson Fowler
V. Hugh Kirkpatrick
V. William Kirkpatrick
W. Rutherford Love
W. John Adams, jr
V. Nevils Courton
V. Grandison Garrison
W. Bedford McCray
V. Henry Garrison
V. Dickey Hurdle
W. Johnston McCawley
W. Wagstaff Maynard
V. Anderson Watson
V. Obediah Hurdle
V. Harrison Muden
V. Jno. Griffis
V. Geo. Outlaw
W. Jonathan Harvey
V. Jacob Hurdle, jr
V. George Jordan
V. Jno. Faucette (of Wm.
W. George Walace
V. Jesse Tate
V. Jacob Dickey
V. John W. Shaw

*Post Office at
Trollinger's Bridge P. O.*
W. Henderson Crawford
W. George McCray
V. Samuel Crawford
W. Willis Sellars sr
W. Jacob Holt
W. Abel Griffis
W. Henry Bason
W. Stephen White

*P. Office at Col.
James Moore's.*
W. William Brannock
V. Thomas Palmer, jr
V. Tho. Palmer, Sen'r
W. Thomas Moore
V. James Ross
V. Andrew Ross
V. David Barber
V. Thomas Ross
W. Edw. Brannock
V. Caleb Busick
V. John Ireland
V. Thomas Danilly
V. Sam'l P. Foster

*Lee's P. Office*
W. Wm. Anderson
W. Sam'l Hargraves
V. Empson Walker
W. Wm. Ward
V. Lambert Murray
V. John Benson
V. Thomas Bird
W. Juniah Hale
V. John Enocks
W. William Eccles

*P. Office Cedar Grove*
W. Tho. W. Hughes
V. William Roberts
V. Asahel Moore
V. Henry Malone
V. Spency Henslee
V. Sam'l P. Moore
V. Thomas Pope
V. David A. Taylor
W. James Crawatt
V. Samuel Dunn
V. Joseph R. Hester

*P. Office Sam'l R. Wood's.*
V. William Jordan

V. Robert Faucette
V. Sam'l McBroom
V. Sam'l Madden
W. Rich'd Breeze
W. David W. Jordan
V. Hugh Woods
V. John M. Ray
V. Charles Ray
V. James Ray
W. Nelson P. Hale
V. Joseph Brown
W. Ezekiel Laws
W. Cyrus Laws
V. Elza Harris
W. Thos. Carrington
V. Hugh Montgomery
W. Jonathan Nichols
V. James Montgomery
V. John Woods
V. Joseph Medding
V. Alex'r Robinson
W. Jno. B. Leathers
W. William McKee
V. James Woods
W. Felix G. Wilson
V. Mark Parish
W. Robert Hale, jr
W. Person R. Nichols
V. Charles Wilson

*Red Mountain P. Office*
V. Squire D. Umstead
W. Hinton Mangum
W. Wm. D. Parker
W. Jno. Barnwell
W. Rob't Morrow
V. Noah Mitchell
W. Rob't Tate
V. James McCadams
V. David McCadams Sen'r.
V. Shadrack Ward
V. Robert Whitted

W. Albert G. Bird
W. Beaufort Benson
W. James Ward
V. Allen Compton
V. Jno. Squires
V. Wm. Benson
V. Hugh McCadams

Horner's election
W. Thomas Garrard
W. John Peed
W. Augustin Riggs
V. Ellis Roberts

*Pratts. Burgh P. O.*
W. Duke Glenn
V. Andrew Turner (Israel)
V. Joseph Procktor
V. Jno. P. Cole
V. Fred. Horner
V. David R. Allison
V. Edward Riley
V. Wm. McCullock
V. Bogan Ray
W. Wm. Barlow
W. Joseph Barlow

*Turner's Mill Post Office.*
V. Washington King
W. John Collins
V. Harvey Roundtree
W. Washington Laws
W. John Wilson
W. James Ray, jr
W. Eli Carrol
W. Baldy Nichols
W. Wesley Carden
W. Jesse B. Geer
V. Anderson Malone
W. Harris Woods
V. Gray Barber
V. Hiram Vickers
W. Reaves Mangam
V. Lewis Hutchins

W. Rich'd Peed (Round
 Hill P. O.)
W. Wm. Piper (Stagville P. O.)
W. Fendal Southerland " "
W. John Duke (Red Mount.
   P. O.)
W. Stephen Tilley " "
W. Thomas Hale " "
W. Joseph Lunsford " "
W. Wm. Beasley (R. Hill
   P. O.)
W. Yancy Boling (Red Mo't
   P. O.)
W. Wm. Duke, jr " "
W. William Mangum " "
W. Benton Ray R. Hill
W. Moses Leathers   "
W. Jno. Garrand Red Mtn.
W. Green Mangum  " "
W. Sam'l Forsythe   "
V. Willis B. Dillard
V. James M. Gilbert
W. Thomas I. Leigh
W. Robert Jeffers
V. Stephen Horn
V. Mark Rigsbee
V. Arch'd Rigsbee
W. James N. Patterson
W. John Burroughs
V. Elisha Glenn
V. Hargis Glenn
V. Ben Johnston
V. James Ferrel, jr
W. Jno. C. Lewis
V. George W. Rhoades
V. John Vickers
V. Thos. W. Gooch
V. Henderson May
V. John Hancock
W. Hargis Farthing
V. William Procktor

V. Reuben Cardon
W. Thomas Farthing
V. Thomas Christian, jr
V. Ezekiel Hailey
V. Allen Hutchens
V. Allen Ferrill
W. William Cain (of Allen
V. James A. Pratt
V. William J. Duke
V. James Stagg
V. Jesse Clinton
W. William W. Guess
W. Anderson Cheek
W. John Cheek
V. Anderson Ferrell
V. Jacob Bledsoe
V. Samuel Merritt
V. John Barbee
W. Pleasant Scoggins
W. M. C. Herndon
V. James Vickers
W. Caslett Herndon
V. Rowland Cook
V. Henry S. Marconi
V. John Marconi
V. Willis Roberts
V. David George
V. Gabriel Barbee
V. Hugh C. Lyon
V. Hiram B. Dalohite
W. Henry M. Scoggin
W. Joseph L. Moring

*Wm. Trice's Store P. O.*

V. David Vickers, jr
V. Chesley Herndon
W. John Neal
V. Alsa Carrol
V. Marck Pickett
V. Moses H. Turner
V. Willis I. Vacun

W. John Leathers
W. Presley Cardon
W. Arthur Bobbitt
V. and Turner (Jno.
V. John Cole (Sam.
V. Henry D. Trice

V. Charles Carrol
V. Harden Couch
W. Anderson Rhodes
V. Chesley P. Trice
V. Zachariah Rhodes


*From G. Robertson.*[21]          U.

## Moon's Creek,

### Feb'y. 17th, 1842.

I send this to let you hear that the Whigs of Caswell are alive, and intend holding a Whig meeting on the 7th. of March.

There is no division among the great Whig Party of Caswell. I was a Tyler Whig at the close of the extra Session. I thought Capt. Tyler honest in vetoing the Bank bills, and was disposed to stick to him, but when his man, John Jones, announced continual appointments of Democrats, I then thought Botts right, but the Madisonian's attack on the Whig party is enough to convince any Whig that Tyler is not one of them.

I have been a subscriber to the Madisonian for 4 or 5 years. I always thought a great deal of Mr. Rives and I became a subscriber because I thought it was a Rives paper. I want you to pay off my a/ct to the editor & send the bill & I will send you the Cash; I would send it at this time but don't no the amount. I have only pd. $5. some 3 or 4 years ago. I owe some $15. or 20. I can't stand it's abuse of Judge Mangum, he ought to have a small drubbing. *Send him this way & he shall be Lick'd.*

I see you and Judge Mangum Split on the repeal of the Bankrupt Law. We say here, give it a trial before the repeal. there is not a Tyler man in my acquaintance, and I have not heard a man speak in favor of the Tylercasity or Fisicality of the Finance project among the Whigs. the Democrats say you all will be forced to take it, they chuckle at our Situation, they think to beat Our Worthy Gov'r. on the Tyler Split. Where they will get their aid from—I don't know.

At our Meeting I will see what can be done for our Whig friends at Washington, the Independant and True Whigs.

---

[21] G. Robertson of Caswell County.

Times are so hard and our friends a little cool, I fear but little can be done.

My address you no is at Yancyville. I have set $5. to pay for the Independent One year, And the Madison I want stop'd.

Mr. Kerr Sends his respects to you & says all things will be right in the old North State. Accept of my best wishes for your Helth & god fortun, and believe me yours,

Very Respectfully.

P. S. My Respects to Judge Mangum

*From J. A. Norcom.*     U.

Plymouth, N. C.,

Feb'y. 20th., 1842.

I saw, a few days past, that you had introduced a bill for the purpose of re-opening *Nag's Head,* or Old Roanoke Inlet, in N. C.

I observed that it had passed its second reading, and had been referred, etc. Will you be so good as to inform me what your opinion is as to its ultimate fate in the House of Representatives, for I expect nothing less than its passage in the Senate, that body being heretofore noted for its gravity, intelligence, & Independence, etc.

Though I saw incidentally a few days past, that the Senate came near a disturbance caused, as I suppose, by Mr. T. Benton. I was sorry to see it, for I have great hopes in the Senate of the U. S. in maintaining the dignity of our Country, and it is my opinion (If intitled to one) that the thing should be nipped in its bud, by expelling positively the first man that attempted to break in upon its dignity and character; for God's sake don't let the Senate of the U. S. degenerate in its dignity of character, like the House of Representatives, the veriest undignified body that can be conceived of, pretending to decency and Intelligence. Though why should I say any thing of the House of Representatives, for I am not, nor have I been for some years, represented there, prefering to stay at home and not vote, untill the people shall have some regard for themselves, and for the character of our common Country.

*To John M. Morehead.*                                    A.

Washington City,

February 23rd., 1842.

It is my painful duty to announce to you the death of the Hon.
Lewis Williams, which took place today, between 1 & 2 o'clock.

He was attacked suddenly on night before last, with plurisy,
and sank rapidly, notwithstanding all the efforts of Physicians.
I have not time to write more, but feel it my duty to give you
early information of this calamitous event.

*Speech On Lewis Williams*[22]

United States Senate

February 24th., 1842.

Mr. President: I was a spectator of the melancholy event which
is announced in the message from the House. It was the result of
a sudden and violent attack of disease, which, defying all remedy,
proved fatal in less than thirty-six hours from its commencement.
On Monday Mr. Williams was in his seat until the close of session
of the House. On Wednesday, within little more than an hour
after the meeting of the House, he lay a lifeless corpse. Of the
dreadful lesson which is taught by this most unexpected calamity,
it is fitting that others should speak with more propriety than
myself. But the occasion gives rise to a few reflections in which
I hope to be indulged. A public servant has been struck down by
the hand of death almost in the harness of his public labors—a
man whose long life of near sixty years has been devoted to useful, honorable and patriotic service. The occurrence is well calculated to arrest the ordinary course of thought and action here,
and to turn our minds to the contemplation of that awful change
to which we are all ultimately destined. It reminds us, too, that
the older men are passing away from the public councils, and
naturally excites some inquiry as to the life and character of him
who has so long shared in the deliberations of Congress, and in
the gratitude and confidence of his countrymen.

Mr. Williams was a native of the county of Surry, North Carolina, in which he always continued his residence. His education

---

[22] From the *Hillsborough Recorder*, March 10th, 1842.

was liberal, having been graduated at the University of his native State, and having remained some time subsequently as a tutor in the same institution. Not very long afterwards, he was chosen by the Legislature a member of the Board of Trustees of the University, of which he was ever one of the most vigilant, active and faithful guardians. Anxious to be useful in the employment of the country, he seems early to have contemplated a public career. In the year 1814 he was returned from the county of Surry one of the members of the House of Commons in the General Assembly of the State; and, although a young man, he took a prominent part in the proceedings of the ensuing session. In 1815 he was elected the Representative in the Congress of the United States, of the 13th. Congressional District, which embraces the county of his residence; and at every election since that time he has been returned by the same constituency to the same station. Of his talents and services as a member of Congress, it would be superfluous to speak here, in the scene of his labors, and among his early and later associates. His legislative history is incorporated with the history of the country for more than a quarter of a century, in one continued series, and is found in the journals and documents of the House, the reports of its committees, and the register of its debates during that period. Few members of the House ever performed more useful and laborious service than did Mr. Williams for many years, while he acted as the chairman of the committee of claims, in adjusting the numerous demands on the Government which grew out of transactions connected with the late war with Great Britain. And none, it is believed, ever possessed the confidence of his associates in legislation in a greater degree. With a mind patient, laborious, and strictly impartial, he applied himself diligently to this branch of the business of Congress, and was found so generally accurate that his opinions acquired the greatest weight. His continuous service for so many years not only made him the Father of the House, by seniority of membership, but his intimate acquaintance with public affairs, his enlightened views of the structure and policy of our Government, and his inflexible honesty and manliness of character, rendered him one of the most valuable of the public counsellors. But, sir, it is not so much his public action in the high places of the country, and his capacities to be serviceable there, that I wish particularly to mark. His character will bear closer examination and a severer scrutiny. I wish to bear my humble testimony to the eminent purity of his private life and moral integrity, and to speak what I believe is the common sentiment in his wide circle of acquaintance, that during his long public career, neither the angry contests of parties, the tempting of ambition, of avarice, or vice, have sullied his name with a single action which should cause one moments regret to his friends. In his public conduct he was manly, frank, ingenuous, and devoted to his duties. It happened to me in my boyhood to have been sent to school in one of the counties of his district; and I well remember to have witnessed the feelings of gratitude, of kindness, and affection, with which he was cherished by those who so early, and constantly honored him with their confidence, and whom he repaid with such fidelity and disinterested service. Always moral, he became later in life a religious man, and uniformly regulated his conduct by the principles of virtue and a conscientious conviction of duty.

But it was in the charities and kind offices of private and domestic life that Mr. Williams was most favorably known and appreciated. Although he never contracted the relation of marriage, there are those by whom his demise will be as deeply deplored as would be that of their immediate parents. He was a member of a numerous family, the head of which acquired an honorable fame by his patriotism and service in the war of the Revolution, and by his public spirit and elevation of character, in after life. A twin brother of my lamented colleague now presides as Judge in the courts of Tennessee. His elder brother, Colonel John Williams, was distinguished for his gallantry as an officer during the late war, and for his talents and character at a subsequent period, as a Senator in this body from the State of Tennessee, and in our diplomatic service abroad. A third brother was for a long period the Adjutant General of the State of North Carolina. The two latter, though deceased, have left children. Others of his brothers, and near relatives yet survive, and are among the most enlightened, hospitable and liberal gentlemen, both in North Carolina and Tennessee. On the families of these, the intelligence of their bereavement will fall as the thunder from a cloudless sky. To these, however, wherever situated, it will be consoling to know that, though the pangs of his dissolution were severe, they were of short duration, and that he met his fate with the calmness and resignation which arises from the consciousness of a well spent life, and the hope of an immortality beyond the grave.

In reference to the message of the House, I beg leave to present certain resolutions.

*Resolved,* That the Senate has received with deep sensibility the communication from the House of Representatives, announcing the death of the Hon. Lewis Williams, a representative from the State of North Carolina.

*Resolved,* That in token of sincere and high respect for the memory of the deceased, the Senate will attend the funeral at 12 o'clock tomorrow, the hour appointed by the House of Representatives, and will wear crape on the left arm for thirty days; and as a further mark of respect—

*Resolved,* That the Senate do now adjourn.

*From George C. Mendenhall.*[23]        U.

Carthage, Moore, N. C.

Feb. 26, 1842.

We are to have a prodigiously hard fought Battle out & out the Summer of 1842, hopes run high on the part of the Vans— I cannot call them Democrats because they are not so. We have had a Whig meeting here this week, & appointed Delegates to Raleigh 4th. of April next.

Last night a Van meeting was had & Resolutions adopted and among others inviting Gov. Henry to visit Moore, which I had before heard he was to do in May. It is a little likeing the Vans are willing to kick off Strange if they could; not having added much weight to their cause heretofore. And further it is a little thought that Strange & Haywood & especially the latter wish Henry to be, or run for, Gov. to have him out of the way, not only that one of them might be Senator by the Lo. Co. Legislature which is to be elected this year, but also in case of a Van President next after Tyler. N. C. must & will have a Cabinet appointment, & then if Henry could sooner be supplied with, or in the way for office, such appointment would fall on others & not him.

Mr. Henrys letter will be one considerable, if not the principal Subject of discussion the Summer Campaign. I may or may not be in the field, but whether or not, I should like well to be furnished with the facts, & at good length too, which will prove

---

[23] George C. Mendenhall, of Guilford, an able and successful lawyer, an active Whig, who served in the commons, 1828-1829, and in the state senate, 1840-1842. He was a devoted supporter and friend of Graham.

much, if not most, of that Super-Extra, magnificent production to be unfounded.

Judge Nash & all the Bar are well.

I had intended writing you sooner, & will likely again. I wish to write to Mr. Shepperd shortly.

I fear we shall have but a small majority of Whigs in next Assembly N. C.


*From Priestley H. Mangum.*                                    U.

Hillsboro',

March 2nd, 1842.

We occasionally hear from you and Willie, thro' the papers & with that have been compelled to make a virtue of necessity in not complaining. But hereafter that quiescent course will cease to be a virtue. Difficulties begin to thicken around us, & every man will be called on to do his duty. And first of all in point of time, as well as in point of importance, & efficiency, our Senators must at least *seem* not to have forgotten their fitful and jealous constituency.

Last week I was in Raleigh where I heard complaints from our friends of the silence and inattention of our Senators to that portion of the State. They say that as this District is represented in Congress by a L. F. they think they have a right to expect some notice from our Whig Senators. Major C. Hinton & others. You must bestir yourself and drop leters to our *chief friends,* if they don't contain anything of importance. The mere fact of receiving notices of that sort *imparts strength.* Men are men, & like the ladies, are not insensible to suitable attentions.

Louis D. Henry is here. On yesterday he addressed the people from the C. H. steps in a tirade of three or four hours length. Brother Waddell's politeness got the better of his discretion, and prevailed upon a reluctant Court to give way and tender the C. H. to Mr. Henry. I don't relish this thing. The speaker is the most reckless demagogue I have yet heard. His fluency is great, & has at his finger's ends the whole of the slang, misrepresentation, unfairness, & sophistry of the most thorough Loco foco newspapers. But upon the whole, his Circus-like mimicry and buffoonery nutralizes the many good things he says, & by reason thereof, I think his effort proves powerless, if not decidedly injurious, except in *the sole* particular of stirring up the venom of the bitterest portion of the Democrats.

You know the Whig State Convention is to take place on 4th. April; before then, Morehead will not, I suppose, present himself before us. But I think Mr. Henry should be met by Whig speakers wherever he goes. Others think differently, and I have been overruled upon this point here this week.

I read with pleasure your remarks on the occasion of the death of Hon. L. Williams. We feel apprehensive on the score of health in your City. The Season has in an eminent degree favoured the disease of which Mr. Williams is said to have died.

I can't say how matters are going; I can hear nothing definitely that seems to indicate any loss of strength to the Whig cause in the State. Yet I fear. I think the Whigs will rally. The Democrats will make a great rush, and it is remarkable what feeling of hate and poison seems to influence many of the party.

Write to your friends often, & but little, for you won't have time to write long letters to as many as you ought to notice.

*To James W. Bryan.*        U. Bryan Mss.

Washington City,

March 8th, 1842.

I recd your letter a few days ago, on the subject of Mr. Gibbs appointment as Collector of the Port of Beaufort. And will with pleasure concur in his nomination.

*    *    *    *    *

We are very anxious that there shall be a respectable assemblage of our Whig friends in the Convention of the 4th. of April.

Mr. Clay has been invited by a Com'tee at Raleigh to attend on that occasion. He has consulted us as to the propriety of his going. And believing that it is politic to nominate him at once for the Presidency, and that on that account it would be indelicate for him to be present, we have dissuaded him from attending. Some of the delegation thought a nomination premature, and that it might be against us in the Summer elections, but a majority of us think differently. It should be well considered by our friends in the Convention, and a nomination made or not, as may be deemed advantageous by the Convention.

By the bye, I promised Mr. C. some time since to procure for him some of the seed of the longleaved pine. Will you be so good as to send me a few of them? I suppose half a dozen would not exceed 2 ozs. the extent of my frank.

The Report of Tallmadge has been postponed 2 weeks; they desire, I doubt not, to put it off untill Mr. Clay leaves the Senate, and hope to enlist many friends after that event. From certain billing and cooing, there is some prospect of a Union between the Loco focos and conservatives. Webster's section of the Whigs is ready to agree to any thing agreeable to the administration. Boz[24] has not yet arrived. It is feared that Lord Ashburton[25] is lost on the Caledonia.

\* \* \* \* \*

I hear that Henry has opened the Canvass for Gov. by a speech at Hillsboro' last week. Our friends think he made no impression.

*From Citzens of Florida.* U.

St. Augustine, Flo:

10th March. 1842

The undersigned inhabitants & planters of Florida beg leave respectfully to call your attention to the memorial addressed by them to Congress at its present Session, on the subject of their losses and sufferings by the Seminole War.

We are induced to address you on this occasion by the confidence we feel in the justice and reasonableness of our claims, and our conviction, that if such be their character they will not fail to engage your attention and enlist your support.

The undersigned trust that in examining into the grounds of these claims, and the merits of their demands, it will be steadily borne in mind, that the War, by which they have suffered so much & which still continues to devastate the Territory, was neither brought on by any act of the people of Florida, or commenced at their instance, but was the result of the unadvised attempt of the Government to remove the Indians without the

[24] Charles Dickens.
[25] Alexander Baring (1774-1848), 1st. Baron Ashburton, British Minister to the United States. Famed as a business man, he came to the United States and married in Philadelphia. He had represented various constituencies in Parliament, between 1806 and 1835. He supported economic reform, but opposed Parliamentary reform, and was a leader in the final compromise.

presence of a Military force, sufficient to command respect and
prevent the outbreak which the known opposition of a majority
of the nation to the measure, and their repeatedly expressed
determination to resist it, gave warning & reason to expect.

Through this fatal neglect on the part of the Government, the
inhabitants of the Territory were left without protection on the
breaking out of the war, and exposed to those disasters and
losses which form the subject of their claims. They hence look
with the fullest confidence, for indemnification & relief from the
same hand, to which the injury (however undesignedly inflicted)
is properly chargeable: the more especially in this case, where
the dictates of justice will be found to coincide with those of good
policy—as with the renewal of their means, the industry & enterprize of the inhabitants will be also renewed and once more set
in action, a general settlement of the country promoted, and thus
an important auxiliary be provided towards a speedy and efficient expulsion of the Indians.

> We are,
> Very Respectfully,
> Your most obed. Servts.
> David R. Dunham.
> G Humphreys.[26]
> W. H. Simmons.[27]

*From David W. Stone.*[28]                                    U.

Raleigh, N. C.

March 11th, 1842.

I received a few days since the very excellent and able Report
of Mr. Tallmadge on the Exchequer Plan for a fiscal Agent and
am very much obliged to you for your kindness in remitting it
to me. There are but one but two amendments that I would make
to it;—I would have no commission charged for issuing certificates
of Deposite lest it should drive away Depositors, and I would al-

---

[26] Colonel Gad Humphreys, rose from lieutenant to lieutenant colonel, and
brevet colonel in the army, between 1808 and 1821. He was Indian agent, 1822-1830,
and actively engaged in territorial politics.

[27] Dr. William Hayne Simmons, of St. Augustine, a man of high character and
standing, served on the commission to locate the capital, and was on the territorial
council in 1823.

[28] David W. Stone, cashier of the Edenton branch of the State Bank, and, at this
time, cashier of the Raleigh branch of the Cape Fear Bank,

low no Banks to be made agents or used as Depositories; they as a body have never acted with good faith to the Government & I don't believe ever will; there are to be sure some few and honorable exceptions, but they are so few that I would not voluntarily trust the system again. With these amendments I would adopt it with all my heart as it seems to me it cannot work otherwise than well, if the agents to put it in operation are at all competent to the task. I think too that it would be an improvement to prohibit their taking the Notes of any Bank that issued & continued to issue for 12 months notes of a less denomination than 5 Dollars; by so doing it would have a strong tendency to suppress the small note circulation and infuse silver and gold in the currency of the Country, which is the only healthy state for it; the wanting exchange and not buying it, is most excellent, and the selling exchange will have a happy tendency to equalize and *purify* the currency, as it will make plain to the people that this great difference of exchange (as it is falsely called) of 10—15 & 20 per cent, is not exchange in fact, but the depreciated Bk notes in which it is paid, and that very proof will have a mighty influence in making them correct the evil, and if Banks can't or won't pay, but suspend to make larger profits (as most of them do) if forcing them to go into liquidation and cease to palm their notes on the Community as money, when they are daily and hourly refusing to redeem their promises and are taking advantage of the discredit caused thereby to purchase them in *by way of Exchange* at a discount of from 3 to 20 per cent. We want some such correction & Demonstration, & believing that Mr. Tallmadge's plan would so operate, I for one would be rejoiced to see it adopted.

There is no local news of interest, except that from indications so far this Summer's political campaign in the old North State promises to partake a good deal of the excitement of 1840.

*From Daniel S. Crenshaw.*               **U.**

Forestville, [Wake Co.,] N. Ca.

March 16th, 1842.

by your attention I have received several Speeches, reports, and procedeings of the present Congress, for which please accept my warmest acknowledgements and allow me to beg your kindness still farther by procureing the Army Regulation and subscribe for the Army and Navy Chronicle for me. I would not trouble you so far but the first Book cannot be had here and I am unacquainted with the names and address of the Editors of the last. I will refund whatever you may advance on sight. Our Governor's Election is waxing pretty warm and the Standard is growing very inquisitive about Icehouses, from a number of such *seeming* extravagances the Locos are determined to excite the populace as much as possible, but I do not believe that they (with all their self confidence) are sanguine and I have recently had a fair opportunity of ascertaining this fact from the warmest partisans of Warren, Nash, Edgecomb & Martin. I believe with all their bright prospects elsewhere they are not Egotists enough to claim the *Old North State* we are looking up to the 4 Apl with anxiety and hope to see our Favourite of the West Mr. Clay, at our Convention at Raleigh. no definite arrangements are yet entered into by the Whig party for running Candidates for the Legislature from Wake. we are exerting ourselves to make the Locos split and at present they have two Candidates allready in the field for the Senate. Messrs Whitaker and Shepard both are making public speeches and vowing that neither will resign

our only hope in the Senate is to lie in ambush until the eve of the Election then raise a Scouting party and fire a still shot into the enemy's ranks. make my respects to Mr. Stanly tell him there is one other Whig than himself has beaten Gen'l Wilson and given him Edgecomb with his *feesimple right* to all its *interests* which right he publicly proclaimed in a public speech at Tarboro on the day of our Election there. I do not however claim my promotion as a party triumph for I am indebted to the more liberal and Patriotic Democrats for my success, and political influence would have excited stronger prejudices against me but for the fact that Gen'l Wilson & his friends were so sanguine they thought it unnecessary until it was too late, and the possibility of my beating never occurred to him until Northampton voted. we should be most happy to see you in Raleigh at our Convention on the 4 Apl

I am verry Respectfully & Truly
Your H'ble Serv't

*From James W. Bryan.*                           U.

Newbern,

March 19th, 1842.

I am unable at present to procure the Seed of the Pine for Mr. Clay, as it is too late in the Season for them, but will forward them to you, whenever the proper season arrives for gathering them.

\*     \*     \*     \*     \*

Our town is very dull and but for an excitement against Mr. McRae for preaching against the Temperance Society there would be a sort of atrophy in the place. Politics are dead here also. I think the Locos will carry this section of the Country very easily; they are very active. The Whigs are the reverse and seem to be dispirited and dead. . . .

Mrs. W. has had the fences of the old Castle repaired and it begins to look up somewhat, although it requires even now a considerable expenditure of money to put it in order.

I am desirous of going Northward this Summer after my Circuit is over but the times have come down upon us so hard that I do not know how I shall make it out; it would be a convenient matter in that way for me to mingle the multum in parvo by being a visitor at West Point, if the post is not in too great request, and if you can conveniently procure the appointment do so, but if not I pray you not to mention it, for I have such a horror for office seeking & so much contempt for such applicants that I think the whole matter does dishonor to all concerned. I have done the powers that be a little service but I ask them no pay for it and will not place myself in the attitude of a beggar, however convenient the matter may be to me, or severe the pressure of the times. I therefore leave it to your sound discretion.

We have Judge Battle with us and are all much pleased indeed with him; he is patient, good tempered, and a very good lawyer. The next term of the Supreme Court will present a fearful array (in numbers) of cases. Judge Gaston told me that the appeals were very numerous in all the Circuits he had heard from.

\*     \*     \*     \*     \*

*From Ralph Gorrell.*                                    U.

Greensboro

March 22nd. 1842.

\* \* \* \* \*

Mr. Waddell handed me a letter from you to him last week in which you express a desire to be informed what are the opinions about Mr. Clay's coming to Raleigh at the approaching Whig Convention and also as to the policy of his being nominated in that Convention as a Candidate for the presidency. As to the first point I think very clearly that he ought not to be there, and that his presence at that time would be attended with no beneficial results to the Whig party, and in this opinion, hereabouts, our friends generally concur. We would all be proud that our old State should receive a visit from Mr. Clay at a time when that visit would be productive of advantage to him, our cause, and our Country, but I believe that time is not now. That he *ought* to be nominated by the Convention I have no doubt and that he *will* be nominated by it I have as little doubt. Our Whig meetings throughout the State are nominating him. You will have perceived before this reaches you that at a Whig Meeting in Bertie, Outlaw and Cherry have both declared strongly in his favour, and the latter has said that he will be at the Convention and intends to have his name put in nomination. The Whig meetings are also denouncing Tyler and the party want some name to rally around, and Sir whenever Mr. Clay's name is put in nomination in my opinion our disspirited & dispersed forces will gather around his banner and under his name we will acheive another glorious victory not a fruitless victory as our last was made by the treachery of (Captain Tyler) but a victory which will fill our Country again with contentment, prosperity and happiness. There is no Whig in my knowledge that thinks or talks of any body else for the next Presidency but Mr. Clay, and this being the case why not put his name in nomination at once. If he is nominated and the Whigs rally around him to a man which I am confident they would do this strong expression of public favour will prevent the names of others from being brought before the Country, and by a temporising course difficulties of this kind may be reasonably expected.

Please present my best respects to Mrs. Graham and tell her that in walking by your residence, which I did several times last

week I observed that the trees shrubs and flowers in her yard and garden were blooming as sweetly as if she were there altho——
                "born to blush unseen,
        And waste their sweetness on the desert air."
                        Sincerely your friend


*From Samuel L. Southard.*[29]                                 U.

                                        Washington,

                                March 25th, 1842.

I am still too unwell to attend to my duties in the Senate, & desire that you will occupy the chair for the day.
I am respectfully.


*From Charles L. Hinton.*                                      U.

                                        Raleigh,

                                Apl. 4th, 1842.

Yours of the 2nd. was recd. by last nights mail.
I write a line to say that our Convention is numerously attended, and I have never seen the Whigs more determined on a hard fight than at present. They number about Two hundred and fifty, forty Counties represented.

After the lethargy and indifference which I had supposed was felt in our ranks I had no expectation of seeing them so suddenly aroused, the best feeling prevails, there was yesterday some difference of opinion as to the policy of nominating Mr. Clay at *present,* but they have yielded and I don't know that there will be a dissenting voice. The Committee will report this morning; they will hand in an able address, accompanied with diverse resolutions setting forth the principals of the Whigs, denouncing Mr. Tyler, and expressing their entire confidence in Mr. Clay.

The question of Vice President will be left for future arrangements.

I refer you to the Register of this morning for a more detailed and interesting account of the proceedings. This meeting will do much good to the Whig cause in this State, every man will return home inspired with increased confidence.

---

[29] This letter is an example of a large number received from Mr. Southard during this period.

*From John M. Morehead.*                          A.

Raleigh,

April 7th, 1842.

The measure of any Whig's desires would have been amply filled had he been present at our Convention.

Supposing that you will see it in the papers I shall not attempt to give you a detailed account; I can only say that it was every thing it should have [been] in numbers, talents, deportment, dignity, etc., every one left us yesterday & today (except a few) delighted that they came.

I am extremely glad that Mr. Clay did not come; that was my opinion from the first—that he should not do so.

Now it is the movement of the people themselves. You will perceive there is no resolution authorising his nomination to be communicated to him. We did not wish to call upon him to accept the nomination; it will be time enough for him to do so when many States have spoken in his favor.

You will perceive I am directly recommended to take the field this campaign, if I do I only regret that the Presidential Canvass is not now before the people. I should like much to lead Clay triumphantly through the State, as we did Harrison; & with the same exertion it can be done. I will do half the work this Campaign & leave the balance to my successor.

Your suggestions and documents are recd. and duly noted, & you will confer a favor to give me any suggestions you may deem important, and forward me any thing that you may think important.

I saw a letter written by Mr. Stanly to Miller giving a statement of Mr. Henry's time of service and his pay as Commissioner, etc. Can you procure for me an *authenticated* statement of that Commission, and whether he had his draft in the U. S. protested, & all the little matters attending it? It is said that he made some speculation in the matter some way—have it certified Stanly can put you on the track.

He is demagoging very much indeed it is said he suppasses any candidate we have had.

Say to your Brother, that the suggestions in his letter were duly attended to.

I go up in the morning to Greensboro to bring my little girls home.

We shall have a merry Canvass this summer, & I think you had as well come home as soon as convenient.

*To James W. Bryan.*        U. Bryan Mss.

Washington City,

April 11th. 1842.

\*   \*   \*   \*   \*

I have also addressed a note to the Secretary of War on the matter of Visiter at tho Military Academy. Ever since I have been in Congress, Swain has urged the appointment of Professor Phillips as one of the Visiters, and last year Bell declined to appoint him, under circumstances which were not pleasant to me. I accordingly renewed his application the past winter, before your letter was received. As we had no visitor last year, I proposed your name to Spencer also, (and sometimes they have had two or three from one State). Since the Raleigh Convention, however, I have but little hope that the wishes of the N. C. delegation here will have much weight in any future appointments to office. I desire however, for the present at least, that they shall not be able to say that they did not know that any appointments were desired by us.

The proceedings of the Raleigh Convention have been received by our friends here with great joy. Winthrop[30] of Boston told me he admired the spirit, but thought it premature. I reminded him that N. C. had heard that before. It was the reply made to the people of Mecklenburg by their friends in Congress when the declaration of Independence was announced to them.

Lord Ashburton arrived last week, and has entered on the negotiations of his mission. He is a good looking man, and appears to have good address. Webster piloted him into the Senate last week for half an hour. He has three or four distinguished young Englishmen with him. As yet there are not developments as to what he and Webster are doing. The latter is weekly assailed in

---

[30] Robert Charles Winthrop (1809-1894), of Massachusetts, a graduate of Harvard, who studied law under Daniel Webster, served in the lower house of the legislature, 1835-1840, (speaker, 1838-1840), Whig member of congress, 1840-1842, 1842-1850, (speaker, 1847-1849), United States senator, 1850-1851. He was defeated for senator, and for governor, in 1851. He had wide reputation as an orator. He and Graham were later closely associated, as trustees of the Peabody Fund.

the Globe, and many things are charged to him in the highest degree discreditable. Some at least of which are no doubt true. His moral character is so shocked that I doubt whether he could now pass the Senate for a Judicial station, for which his eminent abilities so admirably fit him. Tyler is more controlled by him than by any member of his Cabinet, and will use all his official power to prevent the election of Clay.

The Clay dinner came off yesterday; the Ball will take place next week. After which he will set off for the West.

I fear that the land Bill is in danger, with the Executive and many members of our own party flying the track.

I hope you will return to New Bern by the time of the election. With the spirit gotten up at the Raleigh Convention, I think we shall be able to carry the State.

## Speech on the Loan Bill.[31]

### In the Senate of the United States.

### April 13, 1842.

Mr. President: In the division of the labors of this body it has not fallen to my lot to have any especial charge of the finances and expenditures of the Government. But, being called upon to vote for an additional loan for the public service, I have felt myself constrained to examine whether it was demanded by necessity; and being now satisfied that such necessity exists, I must bespeak the patience of the Senate while I endeavor to show its existence, and the causes by which it has been produced.

For more than five years past, the expenditures of this Government have exceeded, very far exceeded its revenues. By an official document from the Treasury Department, now before me, it is plainly demonstrated that in four years, from the 1st. of January, 1837, to the 1st. of January, 1841, the expenditures were above one hundred and twelve millions of dollars, whilst, in the same time, the aggregate income from revenue was but eighty-four millions of dollars in round numbers, being an average annual expenditure of twenty-eight millions, with an annual revenue of but twenty-one millions of dollars. I omit the fractions of millions to

[31] *Speech of Hon. William A. Graham of North Carolina, on the Loan Bill, Delivered in the Senate of the United States, April 13, 1842.* Washington: Printed at the National Intelligencer Office, 1842. The North Carolina Collection, University of North Carolina. Brackets and parentheses are found in the original.

simplify the statement. It thus appears that, during that space of time, expenditure exceeded revenue by twenty-eight millions of dollars. [See appendix.]

In the four years from the 4th. of March, 1837, to the 4th. of March, 1841, the precise period of Mr. Van Buren's Administration, the excess of expenditures over revenue is still more surprising. It amounted to more than thirty-one millions of dollars, being an average annual excess of expense over income of near eight millions per year—an expenditure greater in four years than would have been yielded from the average revenues in five years and a half.

Such having been the condition of our monetary affairs during the past Administration, the wonder is, not that we are compelled to borrow now, but how they have avoided a greater debt heretofore. Having expended thirty-one millions of dollars beyond their income from revenue, that would naturally be expected to be the amount of debt which they left to their successors on the 4th. of March, 1841, instead of five and a half millions, which they admit. Such would have been the amount of debt left by them upon the country, had they, like other Administrations, had no other means to expend but such as they themselves raised. But, sir, it was their good fortune to inherit a full Treasury, in ready money, and to have falling into it, at convenient periods during their term, millions upon millions of capital stock, (not current revenues), which had been laid up by the Government from the contributions of the people in previous years. The surplus in the Treasury was seventeen millions of dollars, nine of which had been directed to be transferred to the States, as the fourth instalment under the deposite act of 1836. Nine millions more were received by them from debts due to the United States, principally, almost wholly, for the sales of its stock in the late Bank of the United States, at $115. per share. Adding these together, you have twenty-six millions of dollars of extraordinary means, over and above the revenue, expended by the late Administration. Yet, in addition to this, they borrowed five and a half millions of dollars by the issue of Treasury notes, which were outstanding at the end of their term, making in all more than thirty-one millions of extraordinary means. Recollect, too, that this was during a period when they had a tariff of duties on all the principal articles yielding revenue, averaging forty per cent. Yet, sir, we who feel bound to vote for this loan, are taunted by the adherents of the late Administration, by being told that we are running the nation in debt. This reproof, if deserved at all, would come with better grace from those who could show a better administration of the finances while in their charge. The distinguished and able Senator from Pennsylvania (Mr. Buchanan), proclaimed in this discussion the other day, that a Whig administration, in the short space of thirteen months, was, by this bill, about to consummate a public debt of seventeen millions of dollars, in addition to that of five and a half millions of dollars, which he admits was contracted by their predecessors. Sir, this may be very criminal; but, take it without any of the palliation or apology to be found in the deficiency of the revenue, and the wants of the public service, did the Senator and his friends do better when they had possession of the Government? The very first act of Congress, at the called session under Mr. Van Buren, was an act to borrow nine millions of dollars which had been given to the States by the bounty of Congress; (I say given, because, although in legal form it was but a deposite for custody, in substance and intention, at least on the part of many, it was a gift) ; and in the act of Congress to which I refer, the transfer is merely postponed until the 1st. of January, 1839, but a repeal of the gift is avoided. This was the first movement of Congress under that Administration, and the second is like unto it; that is, an act to borrow ten millions of dollars by the issue of Treasury notes. By deductions equally fair with those of the honorable Senator, it is shown that, not in thirteen months, but in seven months after coming into power, the Administration of Mr. Van Buren borrowed nineteen millions of dollars. This was alleged at the time to be indispensably necessary, because of the indulgence given to merchants on duty bonds by an act of that session, and the failure of the deposite banks to pay the amounts due from them to Government; and that these measures were to be merely temporary until those means could be realized. But, although the merchants and the banks paid up what they owed, yet the fourth instalment was never paid to the States, of whom it was borrowed, and Treasury notes were kept afloat by issuing and redeeming again and again, leaving five and a half millions outstanding when that Administration closed.

[Mr. Woodbury would remark to the Senator that there was yet due $100,000., or $200,000. from the banks of Mississippi, and he believed $80,000. from the Bank of the United States.

Mr. Evans: No, the last has been paid. The Mississippi banks are all who have not paid.]

MR. GRAHAM resumed. That is too trifling an amount to constitute the slightest apology for failing to pay the fourth instalment, and redeem all the Treasury notes issued. It bears no proportion to the nine millions of the former, and the five and a half millions of the latter. It now distinctly appears that the States lost the fourth instalment which had been promised them, and a permanent debt of five and a half millions was fixed on the country, not by reason of the defalcations of "the merchants and the banks," which, for some time, were represented as the sources of all the ills which befell the Government, but because the expenditures during the last Administration were raised to an annual average amount of twenty-eight millions of dollars per year. With a revenue admitted to be deficient by their very first acts of legislation, and which, by regulation of the compromise act of 1833, was to decline materially during their continuance in authority, a system of expense was pursued, which not only overran the yearly incomes and exhausted all the earnings of previous years, but superadded a national debt besides. A guardian who should thus manage the estate of his ward, would find no just cause for wonder in his removal from office.

We are now told however, that, although the average rate of expenditure was large, the graduation was downward; and it has been repeatedly a matter of boast, that, in the last year of Mr. Van Buren, the whole amount expended was but twenty-two and a half millions of dollars. And it is vehemently contended, that the experience of that year shows that sum to be the amplest amount for annual expense; and, indeed, that it should fall below it. Sir, I hope it will be found to be enough for the yearly support of the Government. If we can avoid war, I hope to see the annual expenses reduced to twenty millions. But a very casual examination of the legislation of 1839-'40 will show that the reason why no more than twenty-two and a half millions was expended in the latter year was, that the Administration had no more to expend. The seventeen millions which they found in the Treasury were gone; the nine millions of debts which they had collected were gone, in addition to their current revenues; and a Presidential election being on hand, it was not deemed prudent at that moment to resort to the taxing power to raise new supplies. The perennial fountain of Treasury notes, it is true, was still kept open, but for sufficient reasons it was not expedient to swell the amount of those in the monthly published statement. What, then, was the wise measure of economy and retrenchment which was adopted to bring down expenses to income? Was an useless branch of service cut off? Were all the objects which yearly cost the Government money examined, and those struck off and discontinued which were not supposed to be worth what they would cost in taxes upon the people? No, sir. A new expedient was devised. Appropriations were made as usual in all branches of expenditure; Congress thereby declaring that the objects of appropriation were proper, and were still to receive the patronage of Government. But a proviso was inserted in the appropriation bills, authorizing the President of the United States *"to postpone* the expenditures" in case of a deficiency of revenue; "such postponements, in each case, to be *merely temporary,* or until the close of the next session of Congress," manifestly implying that these subjects of appropriation, though suspended momentarily for the want of money, are all, thereafter, to be resumed and finished.

If, by such resorts as these, the public expenditures were reduced in 1840 to twenty-two and a half millions of dollars, it furnishes surely no occasion for the authors of that reduction to boast of their economy, nor to accuse their successors of extravagance in completing the works which they had begun. In the military establishment, the expenditure was nearly a million less in 1840 than in 1839. Why? Because, under the authority of these provisions in the acts of Congress, the President could arrest the operations of the mechanic and laborer on the public works with his hammer or trowel in hand at midday, and whilst his contract was yet unexpired, though the walls of the barracks or quarters in which they labored were but half finished, with an assurance, however, that the works were not abandoned, but only suspended until Congress should provide additional means for carrying them on; meanwhile the Presidential election will be over. In like manner, seven or eight hundred thousands dollars are saved by suspending the works on fortifications, and leaving the half finished walls of your fortresses to wind and weather, until the Treasury should be replenished. Mr. President, this course of temporary reduction, to make a fair showing in the arithmetic of expenditure, so far from being economy, was neglect of duty. Either the military establishment and the system of fortifications—the number of men in the army, and their barracks and quarters; the armories, arsenals, forts, etc.,—should have been permanently lessened, or adequate revenues should have been provided to support and carry them on efficiently. The policy which was adopted necessarily exposed the public property to dilapidation, expressly intended no permanent reduction in expense, and threw over upon the year 1841 many of the pecuniary burdens which properly belonged to 1840.

Mr. President, in tracing the causes of the enormous average expenditure of twenty-eight millions per year during the last Administration, I believe it will be found to have been chiefly owing to their having had a redundant Treasury, which they had not been obliged to provide for themselves—as the heir of fortune is generally a prodigal, while the son of industrious poverty, who must needs accumulate for himself, is economical from habit and necessity. In my humble opinion, the first and prolific source of that system of expenditure, as well as of many of the other evils under which the country now labors, was in withholding the fourth instalment from the States. It deprived the States of a boon which they had a just right to expect, under the provisions of the act of 1836—a boon which was held out to them as a sure resource for more than twelve months; upon the reasonable expectation of which, they had commenced public enterprises, and incurred debts, and which, though taken from their grasp almost at the very moment when they were about to clutch it, was still suspended over their heads, like the bow of promise in the heavens, until the turbid and overflowing waters of public expenditure were raised high enough to absorb it. That many of the States would have become deeply embarrassed, independently of the action of this Government in this particular, I do not doubt; but that the embarrassments of many of them have been hastened and increased by the loss of the fourth instalment, I believe, is equally certain. To them, in their peculiar condition, it was everything; to us, I fear, it has been worse than nothing. With it, the last Administration expended in their four years, one hundred and eleven, or one hundred and twelve millions of dollars. Without it, they would still have had one hundred and two, or one hundred and three millions, giving for average annual expenses near twenty-six millions per year—enough for all reasonable purposes —enough, the country will say, nay, has determined, for all the good that was accomplished.

By yielding this to the States, one of two results must have happened, either of which would have had a happy effect, in mitigating the severity of our present embarrassments—either a material reduction of expenditures, to correspond in some degree with the rate of income, or a timely provision of means for support, by reason of which the suddenness of our present difficulties would have been avoided. I listened on yesterday with much pleasure to many of the remarks of the Senator from South Carolina (Mr. Calhoun), on the dangers of allowing expenditures to exceed income, and the tendency of an overflowing Treasury to produce extravagance. And I could but regret, that those maxims, so true in themselves, had not been applied in 1837, and the 4th. instalment allowed to go to the States, instead of being retaken into the Treasury of this Government, thereby affording the means for extravagance.

[Mr. Calhoun, said the Senator, was not here, and of course [we] could not know the reasons which had induced him to vote for withholding the 4th. instalment from the States. He was opposed to collecting moneys for distribution, and went for distributing in the first instance only because there was a surplus on hand. When it was needed, he voted to restore it to the Treasury. But he had uniformly voted against extravagant appropriations.]

Mr. Graham said he had not been examining the votes of the Senator for purposes of censure, but was calling his attention, and that of the Senate, to what I conceive to have been an unfortunate mistake, in giving to the Government temporary means so far to exceed its regular income in its expenditures, and to carry them to a height from which the present state of our finances would demand so abrupt and hasty a descent. As it is, a service now costing you twenty odd millions of dollars per year is suddenly let down upon means not exceeding thirteen and a half millions; and its weight is accumulated by a public debt of five and a half millions, left by the last Administration, bearing an annual interest of 330,000. dollars. To meet this deficiency what have we? Instead of surplus, we have debt; instead of extraordinary means falling in, we have a daily increasing charge of interest; instead of a tariff of 40 per cent, we have one nearly approaching 20 per cent, and that upon little more than half the imports. What then is to be done? If we propose to borrow money to defray the present expenses of Government, we are told that we are running the nation in debt. If we propose to levy duties to furnish a permanent revenue, we are taxing the people. If we suggest retrenchment, and cutting off such parts of the public service as are not most needed, we are told there is imminent danger of war, and that the most vigorous preparations for it should not be omitted. Mr. President, our whole duty in this emergency seems to me to be comprehended in three propositions:

1st. Borrow such sum, upon the best terms you can obtain, as will relieve your present necessities, and save the public honor from disgrace.

2nd. Reduce your expenditures to the lowest point which is consistent with an efficient public service.

3rd. Levy such duties upon imports as are necessary for an economical administration of the Government, and no more.

But, sir, our opponents have one panacea for all the difficulties of the times. Take back the proceeds of the lands, say they. A direct proposition to that effect was early introduced by the Senator from Missouri, (Mr. Linn). And no matter what may be the particular subject under consideration, it is perpetually moved by way of amendment. Now, let me ask in all candor, if they are resumed into the Treasury, of what avail are they? Last year the nett proceeds but little exceeded a million of dollars, and it is exceedingly doubtful what they may be in years to come. To say nothing of the immense quantities in the hands of speculating companies, the very fact that large grants were made to the several new States, by the distribution act, embracing in the whole, I think, near two millions of acres, with the liberty of selecting choice qualities—grants already perfect because made by the statute itself, and incapable of repeal, whatever modern democracy may urge to the contrary—will make those States our competitors in the market, and, apart from the depression of moneyed affairs, must diminish the receipts from that source. But, suppose the annual proceeds to be three millions of dollars, the maximum that has been estimated here, what is this, compared with fourteen millions, the amount by which the Secretary of the Treasury informs us the current revenue of the year will be deficient? With or without the lands, therefore, the necessity for a loan is exigent and unavoidable.

But, Mr. President, were it otherwise, I would ponder long before I could consent to disappoint the just expectations of the States and the people, in regard to these lands. No subject has been more discussed or better understood in this country for the last ten years, than that of the distribution of their proceeds among the States. None ocupied a more prominent place in the Presidential canvass of 1840. None was more distinctly or boldly put forth as a leading article of his creed of policy, in his letters, speeches, and addresses to his fellow-citizens, by the illustrious man who was then called on to preside over us. And, whether we look to the results of elections, the proceedings of popular assemblies, or State Legislatures, no measure on which parties in our country have divided has, so far as I recollect, so many and such unequivocal evidences of public opinion in its favor.

Sir, to my mind it is clear that the Constitution of the United States does not contemplate the public lands as among the means for the ordinary support of the Government. When the venerable men who framed that Constitution breathed into the nostrils of this Government the breath of life, and prescribed the laws by which it should live, and move, and have its being, they declared upon what element it should subsist. Aware of the vital importance of the money power, which not only affords the supplies of peace, but the sinews of war, they proclaimed, as the very first of the authorities of Congress, the power "to lay and collect taxes, duties, imposts, and excises" for the purpose of paying the debts and providing for the common defence and general welfare of the United States; not such "taxes duties, imposts, and excises" as shall be necessary for the purposes expressed, in addition to, or after applying the proceeds of the public domain, but an absolute power is conferred, limited only by the application to constitutional objects. As to the public lands, nothing is said of them as a means of supply; they are not mentioned at all in the first three articles of the Constitution, which emphatically create the Government, by constituting a Legislature, Executive and Judiciary, and are brought forward in the latter part of the fourth article, not as a source of contribution to the Treasury, but a public property, the disposal of which is committed to Congress. "Congress shall have power to dispose of, and make all needful rules and regulations respecting the territory, or other property of the United States." How Congress shall dispose of it, whether by sale or gift, whether on one object or another, is not defined. The trust is without limitation, in the words of the Constitution. And for instruction as to our duty in administering it, we are thrown back upon the directions of the donors in the deeds of the ceding States. These declare them a "common fund for the use and benefit of *such* of the States as have become, or shall become, members of the confederation, or federal alliance," etc. And here let me remark, that I recognize no distinction between the disposition of the lands ceded by the States, and those acquired by treaty. The great man, (Mr. Jefferson), by whose negotiation our first great purchase of public land was made, entertained strong doubts as to the power to do so, and it was surely a doubtful question. But that difficulty being overcome, and the question settled by practice, the lands thus acquired became "territory of the United States," to be "disposed of by Congress" in like manner with other territory. That that other territory was not looked to, in the Constitution, as a resource to pay current expenses; and that it was intended for the benefit of the States severally, I have endeavored to show. To enter no farther into the argument, to me it does appear that the cessions of North Carolina and Georgia, made after this present Government was established, and in full operation, granting their territory to the United States, not for revenue, not for the benefit and enjoyment of the United States as a political corporation, but for the use and benefit of "the United States of America, *North Carolina* and *Georgia inclusive,* according to their respective and usual proportion in the general charge and expenditure," etc., (the same in substance with the grants of Virginia and other States, which ceded under the old confederation), afford an early exposition, not only of the designs of those States themselves on this subject, but of the general understanding of the deeds of the other States at that time.

But, sir, the whole legislation of Congress in regard to these lands shows that they have never been considered as standing on the basis of the revenues of the nation. The immense grants which have been made, from time to time, to States, State corporations, benevolent institutions, and as charities to meritorious foreigners in distress, who have come among us, would never have been attempted, or allowed, out of a fund which had been raised by taxation, direct or indirect. And for a series of years past, the leading statesmen of all parties seem to have concurred in the opinion that, within a short period at least, the proceeds of the public lands ought no longer to be relied upon as a source of revenue; the difference between them being that those with whom it is my pride to be associated, adopting the policy of the eminent Senator from Kentucky, (MR. CLAY), who has recently retired from this body, were for an equitable distribution of the land proceeds among all the States, while our honorable opponents, approving the suggestion of General Jackson on this subject, were for ceding the lands themselves to the States in which they are situated. In his message of December, 1832, the then President says: "It is desirable, however, that in convenient time this machinery (the land offices) be withdrawn from the States, *and that the right of soil and the future disposition of it be surrendered to the States respectively in which it lies.*" I need not refer you to the report of the experienced Senator from Alabama, (Mr. King), at the head of the land committee of that session, and the speeches of other distinguished gentlemen of that political school, to show that in both parties there has been a general concurrence in the propriety of "looking to the custom-house for revenue," and that the real contest upon the subject of the lands has been between a general and equitable, and a local and partial distribution. The evidences upon this point have been abundantly furnished by the Senator from Indiana, (Mr. Smith), upon a recent occasion. I must therefore be pardoned, Mr. President, if I cannot yield to the eloquent appeals which are almost daily addressed to us against withdrawing the land fund from the exchequer of this Government, and giving it to the States. But yesterday we were told that the lands should be considered *worthless* for revenue; now we are assured from the same quarter, that they are as the purse of Fortunatus. You have only to retain them in hand, and wish, to obtain whatever treasure you want. While without them, you can neither get money, nor credit. These appeals, sir, are but the afterthoughts of the advocate, after a decision against him upon the points made at the hearing. And when the people are persuaded, as they are constantly, that every dollar of land proceeds distributed creates a necessity for new taxation, they will not fail to remember that those who oppose distribution when the Treasury is empty, did it with equal earnestness when it was full; they will reflect that this taxation will be the same whether the land proceeds are taken from the Treasury by the plan of distribution, in which the people of each State get their due share, or those other plans of surrender, cession, or graduation, by which the whole is given to a few States. And, in this connexion, let me remind you that, if there were objections to the passage of the distribution bill, there are objections to the repeal likewise. As I have shown already, two millions of acres of land have been granted to certain States by that bill, which are incapable of being recalled. With what propriety can these grants be allowed to remain, as they must remain, in full force, whilst those States to whom the grant was of money only, are to be deprived of its benefits?

I have said, Mr. President, that the authors of the Constitution did not rely upon the public lands as a means for the ordinary maintenance of Government, and in my humble opinion, to effectuate their design of making this a Government of limited powers, confined to comparatively few objects, it ought to be restricted to those modes of supply pointed out in the Constitution. All history will verify the fact, that those nations have been most remarkable for purity and correctness of administration, for the strictest accountability of public agents, and have longest preserved their liberties, who have kept their ruling powers constantly dependant upon the contributions, direct or indirect, annually levied upon the people. As a certain writer has remarked, "they who would trample on their rights are restrained by the want of their money." This general truth applies with tenfold force to a Government, like that of the United States, far distant from the great mass of the people whom it affects, and so complicated in its structure and diversified in its operations, that, to keep up a minute knowledge of its details of administration, federal politics must be made, to a great extent, an exclusive profession. That period of our history, when peculation and embezzlement were most rife, when the responsibility of public officers was least rigid, when salaries were unregulated, and the gains in many offices were almost what their holders desired, and when appropriations were most extravagant, was the period which I have reviewed in the first part of these remarks, when revenue was not redundant, but grossly deficient, but when there were surpluses and extraordinary means in your coffers, which the Administration had nothing to do with but to expend. Think you, sir, that, in any other state of the Treasury, a district attorney would have been allowed to receive emoluments greater, by more than one-half, than the salary of the President of the United States—greater, according to his own declaration, when about to leave office, than "any citizen of a free republic ought to receive:" that marshals, collectors of customs, and postmasters, would have been permitted, like Roman pro-consuls, to enrich themselves to immense fortunes out of the offices created for the public benefit alone, and oftentimes by like instances of official abuses—abuses to which no corrective was applied until the 3rd. of March, 1841, the very last day of the late Administration, when a clause was inserted in the appropriation bill, a kind of bequest to pious uses upon the death bed repentance spoken of by the Senator from South Carolina, (MR. PRESTON), restraining the compensation of these functionaries to six thousand dollars per annum for the future.

Sir, adversity is not without its uses. Lamentable as is the present condition of the public fisc, it will compel us to at least an earnest endeavor at economy and retrenchment. When the question comes to be determined, as it must now be determined, whether any particular office, institution, or department of service, is worth to the public what will be required in taxes for its support, I have an assured hope, that sinecures will be abolished, a more rigid accountability established, and our system reduced. Without any desire on my part, you, sir, have done me the honor to place my name on a committee on retrenchment, raised during the present session on the motion of my friend from Kentucky, (Mr. Morehead) , and I have felt it my duty, in the intervals allowed by other and prior engagements of my time, to look somewhat into the public expenditures, both past and proposed. The estimates of the Secretary of the Treasury for the present year, amount to twenty-four and a half millions; that is, for the civil list, four millions, less, by nearly one million, than have been its expenditures for the last six or seven years. By rigorous examination I doubt not but that hundreds, thousands, perhaps hundreds of thousands more may be saved in this branch of the service; but if you wish to save millions, you must go into the War and Navy Departments. Wars, it has been long known, cost money; and we are learning by experience that rumors of wars are also expensive. For many years past, we have been threatened with hostilities, and I rejoice that there is now a prospect that these difficulties with foreign Powers approach a termination— I hope a peaceful termination. In the event of actual war, I shall be willing freely to contribute every thing to the national defence. But if we are to have peace, I am not for maintaining such a system of armament as would only befit a great militray empire. The estimates of the War Department, including Indian Affairs, etc., for this year, amount to about eleven and three-fourths millions of dollars—a sum equal to the whole cost of the Government twenty years ago, though less than has been expended in that Department for the last few years. Those for the Navy Department are near eight and three-fourths millions, being two and three-fourths or three millions more than has been applied to that service annually for several years past. Bating this excess, the estimates for this year are less than were the expenditures of the boasted fourth year of Mr. Van Buren's Administration. And, Sir, with the most sincere desire to see an efficient system of defences, and without any pretension to professional knowledge in such matters, I am unable to approve that rapidity and extent of increase contemplated by the Heads of Departments in the reports at the commencement of this session, unless in open prospect of immediate war. We have seen from the repeated declarations of the Senator from New Hampshire, (MR. WOODBURY), as to the appropriations of Congress exceeding his estimates, when Secretary of the Treasury, that Mars and Neptune prevailed over Mammon when the Treasury was full; and we are obliged to avoid yielding too much to their influences now that it is reduced.

But, sir, I weary your patience. I rose but to explain the real unhappy condition of our finances and expenditures, the causes which led to it, and my conception of the mode of relief; to show that the question of the passage or rejection of this bill, is a question of affording or withholding the necessary supplies to the Government of our country. Such being our condition, I voted for it as I did for the issue of Treasury notes under the last Administration. I will not stop the action of the Government by denying it the means of going on, no matter who may be in power.

### From Tod R. Caldwell.[32]                         U.

#### Morganton.

#### April 22nd, 1842.

I take my pen for the purpose of asking the favour of you to send me, if you can conveniently do so, some Congressional documents. I have, contrary to my own inclinations, consented to be one of the Candidates for the next Legislature, and as I have heretofore had very little to do with politics and feel that in order to give sufficient support to our, the Whig, party it will be necessary to devote some of my time to political matters before the Campaign commences. You will therefore confer a favour by sending me from time to time such documents or speeches delivered in Congress, as you may think will be of advantage to me and assist me in defending the Whig policy, since the election of our lamented Harrison of course by Whig policy, I do not mean Tyler measures. And if it will not be asking too much of you I would thank you to mark with your pen or pencil such parts as should most particularly require my attention, I am this

---

[32] Tod Robin Caldwell (1818-1874), of Burke, a graduate of the university, who, up to this time, had taken no active part in politics. An intense Whig, he served in the commons, 1842-1844, 1848, 1858, in the state senate, 1850, and in the convention of 1865. He became a Republican, and was elected the state's first lieutenant governor in 1868. After Holden's impeachment, he was acting governor, 1870-1871, succeeding him as governor after his conviction, and serving until 1874.

particular for the reason that I never have paid much attention to politics and because I perceive from signs which I think indubitable, that there will be a desperate effort made by the locos to carry Burke. I do not however apprehend the slightest danger, but think that it will not be amiss to be well armed and ready for the fight.

We have had the honour of the Hon'l L. D. Henry's company in our district for the last month, he has been to several of our Courts, Buncombe, Yancey, Burke & will be at Rutherford week after next, he had an appointment to address the people at this place on last Wednesday, but failed to do so, altho' he was present; his excuse was that he did not feel well enough tho' he rode into town 5 miles in the morning and back again in the evening. I think that the true cause was that he was advised by his friends that his best policy was to keep dark, lest he should arouse the people and determine them to go to the polls, and if they did they would be sure to vote against him; he left this place today for Charlotte, but says that he will again be among us. Gov. Morehead is also to be here in June and will sweep every thing as he goes.

I will be pleased to hear from you as soon as your convenience will permit.

### *From William R. Walker.*[33]                            U.

#### Wentworth,

#### April 22nd., 1842.

Your letter acknowledging the recipt of the money which I had collected and forwarded to you, came to hand in due time. The invitation therein contained, to correspond with you, is most cheerfully accepted. Yet I confess that, in commencing a correspondence of this kind, being one exclusively of friendship, I experience a difficulty in finding matter with which to interest you, that, it is to be hoped, will be removed by our subsequent correspondence, if I am to be honored by its continuance.

As to the complexion of politics in North Carolina, I deem it unnecessary to write, since, from your numerous correspondents in the State, and your association with our delegation, you are

---

[33] Probably William Richmond Walker of Rockingham County.

doubtless much better acquainted with it than I possibly can be, exiled as I am from every other part of the world.

I have read with very great pleasure the letters of Mr. Clay to the respective Committees in answer to theirs, inviting him to the Convention recently held in Raleigh. But his valedictory to the Senate, although remarkable for eloquence, for benevolence to the entire Senate, and pathetic in the extreme, was read with sincere regret. Since it announced the separation from that body of one who had long reflected honour upon the same. And I fear likewise, from the signs of the times, his separation from the service of his Country. This withdrawal, however, appears to have endeared him more closely to his friends, and to have produced with his opponents that feeling which is the natural consequence of injuries inflicted when reparation cannot be made.

I think it probable nevertheless, that his resignation at this time (whilst the entire Harrison party (or at least the intelligent portion of it, who are seething with rage at the base defection of John Tyler) have the utmost confidence in him, and whilst the current of popular opinion, which for some time has been turned against him, and which now begins to run favourable) may afford some hope that he will yet be elevated to the Presidency. Especially since the loco focos appear to have lost the charm of Jackson popularity, have lost the influence of the patronage of the Government, and have no prominent man in their own ranks who has any considerable popularity.

Last week I attended the Superior Court of Stokes, and for the first time since I have been at the bar, saw his honour, John M. Dick, upon the bench. And "inter nos" I found him a much meeker man than I had even anticipated. In his courtesy to the bar, and his independence and fairness in meeting cases far surpassed some of the other gentlemen of the bench.

The practice of the law, or rather, the practice of going to Court, has for me as yet few charms, neither does it give me many fees. If ever a poor fellow was tired of his apprenticeship, or afflicted, *deeply* afflicted, with melancholy for want of professional success, I am he. For the sake of a location at which I expected practice I exiled myself from society, and until recently had no prospect of that success which, for pecuniary as well as professional reputation, I much covet. My prospects in this County begin to assume a more promising appearance, and I think ultimately, my practice will be entirely respectable.

There is a habit here amongst the young men of the bar, of acting the demagogue for practice, but, much as I desire success, I have as yet been too miserly to pay the price of honour for the little pittance which might be picked up in this manner. And amongst those who have recently come to the bar, there is not one whose intellect should discourage any one who has any respect for his own capacity. Had I not commenced my profession late in life, or had I an estate which would justify my waiting for the moving of the Waters, my want of success would not be a source of any uneasiness. But I have now arrived at that period of life at which it is proper, if ever, to settle myself. Should I fix my affections upon a lady of no property, I have not an income sufficient for supporting us, if upon one of wealth, I could not bear the idea of depending upon the portion which I might receive from her to support myself. So that the melancholly of which I complain, arises not from any apprehension that I shall not eventually succeed, neither from any actual or apparent want of means to support myself individually, but from the reflection that for a time, at least, I am doomed to single blessedness, and to a separation from intelligent society. We have, however, in the County, as you know, some quite intelligent and hospitable citizens, and of their hospitality I frequently partake.

Accept my acknowledgements for the public speeches, etc., which you forwarded to me. I do not expect to see you at our Superior Court, but hope I shall have the pleasure of meeting you in Hillsboro' after the adjournment of Congress.


*To Messrs. Gales and Seaton.*[34]                    U.


Washington,

May 2nd., 1842.

In the Southern Literary Messenger for April, 1842, is "An Essay on the Civil Law, by a Lawyer of North Carolina," which is creditable to the taste and learning of the author. But on page 251 of the work, I observe the following note on a certain passage in the essay by the editor:

*"Peine forte et dure.*—Unless recently amended, this dreadful judgment is to this day required by the laws of North Carolina.

---

[34] Editors of the *National Intelligencer,* of Washington. The letter was reprinted, in the *Hillsborough Recorder,* May 19th, 1842.

For, if we mistake not, the terrible sentence of *peine forte et dure* was inflicted by one of her Courts only a few years ago. When the prisoner was arraigned for trial he stood mute, and refused to plead either guilty or not guilty. Whereupon he was laid on his back upon the bare floor of the court house, great weights, as great, and greater than he could bear,—were placed upon his body, and in this condition he was fed with ditch water from a spoon *till he died.* We challenge the universal jurisprudence of modern Christendom to out-Herod this. We call upon our correspondent, and every other friend to humanity, to use their influence in erasing from the statute book of the good old North State this disgraceful and barbarous penance."

Editor Southern Literary Messenger.

That an editor at the Capital of Virginia, distant not more than ten or twelve hours' travel from that of North Carolina, and with a copy of the Statutes of the latter State at least as near to him as the Executive office in Richmond, should have ventured upon a statement so uncalled for, and so unfounded, in a publication aspiring to a higher character for candor than the ordinary news-paper press—a statement than which Hall, Trollope, Marryat, *et id omne genus,* have put forth no calumny on our country so ridiculously extravagant, is certainly a matter to be regretted by all the lovers of that literature to which the Messenger professes to be devoted. Had the editor deigned to consult the first volume of the Revised Statutes of North Carolina, which reduces into but little more than 600 pages the whole body of her public statute law which is now in force, from *Magna Charta* of Great Britain until the year 1837, he might at least have spared his appeal to the "friends of humanity" to use their influence in erasing a barbarous provision from her statute-book. He will there neither find the *peine forte et dure* of three centuries ago, nor any thing which even a barbarian could mistake for it. But, on the contrary, an express provision, that, "if any person arraigned shall stand mute, of malice, or will not answer directly to the indictment, in every such case it shall and may be lawful for the Court to order the proper officer to enter a plea of *not guilty,* on behalf of such person; and the plea so entered shall have the same force and effect as if such person had actually pleaded the same."

The readers of the Messenger who may chance to read this, will judge whether the code of North Carolina is wanting in humanity, or the editor of the Messenger in accuracy of information on a subject which he volunteers to illustrate. This provision, it is true, was inserted in the Revisal of 1836 for the first time. But it was not then inserted because the old doctrine of *peine forte et dure* had ever prevailed in the state. All such statutes and parts of the common law of Great Britain as had been theretofore in force and use in the colony, and as were not inconsistent with the new form of government, were adopted by act of the General Assembly in 1777. But there is no history or tradition of the existence of this barbarism, "in force or use," at any time in the colony, and it is manifestly inconsistent with certain declarations in the Bill of Rights, which forms a part of the Constitution, adopted in 1776. It therefore never had a foothold in her criminal law. And with an acquaintance somewhat familiar with the Reports of cases decided in her Courts, which reach back nearly to the period of the Revolution, and with a personal acquaintance with, I believe, every professional man in the State now living, who has been at the bar for as much as five years, I have never read, or heard of any incident in the proceedings of those Courts which could furnish even a suggestion for the tale of atrocity which is told with so much minuteness, and dwelt on with such holy horror by the editor of the Messenger, as having been realized "in one of the Courts of North Carolina only a few years ago;" a tale which, if true, would degrade a North Carolina Judge below the level of a Scroggs,[35] or a Jeffries,[36] exhibit her unsurpassed system of enlightened jurisprudence as no better than that of our English ancestors in the worst times of feudal despotism, and her free and gallant people as not only patient spectators, but the ready and willing instruments of a most cruel and savage murder.

So sheer and baseless fabrication is hardly to be found in the adventures of Munchausen. Yet the story is told with a precision of description which might almost indicate a personal attestation, and more in sorrow than in anger. The unlucky culprit having been "arraigned, stood mute; whereupon he was laid upon his back upon the bare floor, great weights—as great, and greater,

---

[35] Sir William Scroggs (1623-1683), lord chief justice of England, educated at Oxford, noted for his violence and partisanship, particularly in the trial of Catholics, that he was known as "Mouth," "undoubtedly one of the worst judges that ever disgraced the English bench."

[36] George Jeffreys (1648-1689), judge and lord chancellor of England. He was utterly corrupt, and is best remembered for his conduct of the "bloody assizes." He died in prison.

than he could bear—were placed upon his body, and in this condition he was fed with ditch-water from a spoon till he died." This last idea of the ditch-water is, I think, a refinement upon the old mode of torture, and I apprehend has no precedent in the year books. It was probably suggested to the writer by some of the incidents which history records as attending the death of the second Edward; and, as he was wholly unrestrained by any facts in drawing his picture, it would have been more graphic had he adopted the mode of killing by which that ill-fated monarch came to an end. As it is, it is altogether doubtful whether the modern victim made his exit by the pressure of superincumbent weights, or, like Socrates, perished from drink; whereas there could have been no mistake in heated iron.

I am aware, Messrs. Editors, of a habitual disposition in certain quarters to disparage the character and institutions of North Carolina, and to affect those patronising and ridiculous airs of superiority which many upstart foreigners have assumed towards our country in general. Whether the editor of the Southern Literary Messenger is to be included in this category I know not. If he be, there is some consolation in being able to perceive from this, his first effort, (so far as I have known,) that, like those aforesaid foreigners, his attempt at disparagement is too destitute of truth to do much harm among persons of tolerable information. I will not "challenge the universal jurisprudence of modern Christendom" to a comparison with that of my native state, lest, like the editor of the Messenger, I should be found arrogating an omniscience which indicated that I knew nothing of either. But I will venture to say to the intelligent reader of the Messenger, who may disport himself in "the gladsome light of jurisprudence," that in no State of this Union will he find a Constitution more redolent of genuine, rational, American freedom—a more liberal, well defined, just, and humane code of laws, and more benevolence, firmness, and general intellectual ability in their administration, than in the State of North Carolina.

I am, with high respect, your obedient servant,

### From Thomas S. Hoskins. U.

Edenton, N. C. May 9, 1842.

I have just had the pleasure of receiving & reading your most *excellent* speech on the "Loan bill," delivered in the Senate on the 13th ult., a copy of which you honored me with. I am greatly indebted to you for thus thinking of me occasionally. I have also previously, during the present Session of Congress, had the honor of receiving from you, other speeches & documents, for which you will please accept my grateful thanks.

Judge Berrien's[37] able Speech on the "Repeal of the Bankrupt Bill," which you or Rayner one sent me some time back, has accidentally been mutilated, & as it is such an admirable speech, I should be pleased to receive another copy, if any are afloat now. For I take great pride in preserving these speeches in pamphlet form. By the bye, this man, Berrien, is one of our ablest men, in my opinion, from his speeches.

I have intended writing you before now, but I know you must be a good deal bothered with so general a correspondence, as all public men are apt to be.

When I read that great man's farewell speech in the Senate, from "Henry Clay of the U. S." (as Mr. Badger says,), I felt as if we had lost him forever. But I hope not. I hope we shall have the benefit of his councils in a higher sphere yet. The Old North State has, you see, taken the lead. I hope we may be successful. But prospects appear gloomy. The elections all go against us. And the Old Dominion still continues to disgrace herself. She is the meanest State in the Union, except perhaps Mississippi. 'Tis true however that the Whigs are too much disheartened by the conduct of *their* Capting Tyler, are almost prepared to give up in dispair, thinking after a long 12 years struggle they fortunately obtained the ascendancy, that providentially they lost it in one short month, & have to struggle for another four years, with a somewhat dark prospect ahead. It is too bad;—almost past endurance.

And our old friend Lewis Williams, "the father of the House," has gone !! I was very much grieved at the event. But we all have to go, sooner or later,—the high & the low.

I was very much pleased at your's and Rayner's notice of the sad occurrance. I have understood that Rayner was going to get married & abandon his seat in Congress. I hope it is not so. Tell him it *must not* be. I see by the papers that the apportionment Bill will probably give N. C. the same representation, (13). If

---

[37] John Macpherson Berrien (1781-1856), of Georgia, a native of New Jersey. Educated at Princeton, he settled in Savannah. He was solicitor, judge, captain in the War of 1812, state senator, and United States senator, 1825-1829, resigning to enter Jackson's cabinet as attorney general. He resigned in 1831. He returned to the senate as a Whig, in 1841, and served to 1852.

so his District will remain the same; & we have no other man to depend on. He is our main-stay. If it should so turn up that we could add Bertie to our District, & Rayner *quits,* then we should rally under the flag of Cherry, a host within himself. I see Stanly & Wise are continually quarreling. They will have to shoot each other yet, I expect.

My respects to Judge Mangum & Rayner. I should be pleased to hear from you again.

*To David L. Swain.*          U. Swain Mss.

Washington City,

May 10th, 1842.

You will perceive by the published list in the papers, that we have not succeeded in procuring the appointment of visiter to the Military Academy for our friend Professor Phillips. I know not on whose recommendation the appointment of Gen'l McRae (as published) has been made. No one of the Whigs of our delegation, I have satisfied myself, made any recommendation of him, or knew that he was an applicant. Mr. Washington, who has just returned from New Bern, says that it is not Gen'l McRae, but Gen'l A. F. Gaston who has been appointed, there was a letter of recommendation in his behalf, sent in I believe by the representative from his district. But I do not know that any other person joined in it. Or that he did more than send to the department the letter he had received.

I have so little confidence in the Secretary of War, however, that I can conjecture nothing of his motives of action. I have never been introduced to him, & know him only as "Secretary War," the inscription on his card, according to the style of the present Cabinet Ministers. Under such a set, there can be little hope of regular or rational action.

Your Friend Mr. Baring[38] has been here recently on a visit to his kinsman Lord Ashburton. I had the honor to dine a few days since, with his Lordship, who is entertaining in a magnificent style of hospitality. He is exceedingly plain in manners and mind, And is certainly very far from being the man to argue questions of international Law with Mr. Webster.

---

[38] Charles Baring (1773-1865), of Charleston, a native of England, a member of the famous family of bankers. He had a home at Flat Rock, there in Buncombe County where Swain probably met him.

There has been a very violent quarrel between Messrs. Stanly and Wise, and I doubt whether serious results may not ensue. Of this, however, say nothing as coming from me.

*From Priestley H. Mangum.*     **A.**

Hillsboro'

May 12th, 1842.

You have to look to your friends to be informed of small matters at home, which altho' unimportant are sometimes well enough to be known. In the first place, I tender you my acknowledgements for your several favours, including your valuable speech on the Loan Bill; and especially for your spirited and timely defence of the Old North State against the ignorant & wanton assault of Virginian insolence. *This thing will tell!*

You have long since heard all about our State Whig Convention. One remark in reference to it. I never saw a finer spirit among our friends than that occasion evinced, and what under other crises would clearly indicate that victory was to crown our efforts in the approaching Summer Elections. I could not ascertain, after the most anxious inquiries of delegates from all quarters, that there was any known defection from the Whig ranks in the State. And yet I confess I have my misgivings as to the complexion of our next Legislature; this you may put down as the result of those timid apprehensions common to advanced years. But I would fain have it believed that I am not yet an old man. I fear the result, because the "floating Capital" of the Country & perhaps no State has more of that curse than this—may likely be carried by the force of the senseless cry of our opponents on the score of *the promise of better times* not being redeemed; notwithstanding the least intelligence would see that the fault was not with the Whigs; and as little honesty on the part of the adversary, would compel an admission of this truth. The pecuniary pressure of the day will hurt us more than any thing else, and it seems to me, that that argument might be most triumphantly and successfully met provided we should bring into the field proper speakers, and there was a proper material to be acted upon. The more I think of it, the better I am satisfied that Jno. Tyler deserves to atone for his unmanly vile treachery, in the merciless hands of the hangman.

Last week at Granville Court, there was rather an embarrass-ing "position;" the more to be regretted as one of your friends was the prominent actor. Previously to Court week, some spirited young men from the "Back side of Tar River." who had been delegates to the State Convention & had doubtless gone home strongly tinctured with a loathing for every thing like "Tylerism," prevailed upon some of their most respectable Whig neighbours to join them in a letter to their Senator Johnston,[39] & Com-moner R. B. Gilliam, calling upon each for his views upon cer-tain Whig measures. Mr. Gilliam is now between wind & water upon a U. S. Bank. Mr. Johnston gave a written answer, not exactly as *we* would have had it, but upon the whole pretty good & safe. Mr. Gilliam was much perplexed, not exactly certain whether this thing, or that thing, was the right thing, but how-ever defered giving an answer untill Court Week, on account of the pressure of other business. Well, we from Hillsboro' & Raleigh, upon reaching Court & hearing of the matter, & learning that Mr. Gilliam had made it known to some of his friends that he had declined being a Candidate for the Assembly because of his pecuniary interests, etc., set ourselves to work to accommodate difficulties by suppressing the written correspondence, which was designed by the young men to be published; and by inducing the young men to believe Mr. Gilliam was a proper good Whig, & by trying to prevail upon Gilliam to consent to run.

On Tuesday was their Whig meeting, got up to nominate Candidates. Mr. Gilliam was there to answer the letter in his speech, & did so in a manner, I suppose, to suit that Whig atmos-phere, but he could not take Mr. Clay's Bank Bill (Jno. Eaton, etc., clapping!!) he was not prepared however to say that he was against a Bank, prefered Ewing's—*that* perhaps contained objec-tionable features—Went for Mr. Clay, if he should be the nominee of the Whig party, was opposed to the President's Land distribu-tion repeal message, & to Jno. Tyler in every thing, & hoped and begged the people would let him off from being a Candidate, etc.

A committee was raised, including some of the young men afores'd, who reported a ticket of Candidates, Mr. Gilliam & others, & so the thing went off. Mr. Gilliam talks of backing out after awhile.

In Orange there is some stir. At our Feb. Court, from the vote of the Magistrates upon the question of a new Court House, a

---

[39] William A. Johnson, state senator from Granville.

suspicion occurred that Dr. Montgomery was secretly manoeuvering to unite his "peculiar friends" with persons in the East of the County. By help of this view, I prevailed upon Sam Holt at the State Convention to agree to harmonize with us in regard to the *Division Question.*" You must know that we are anxious and determined if possible, to seperate the local question of dividing the County from National politicks in our August Election; & that our plan is, for the Court at May by an order to direct the Shrff. to poll the votes of the people at every Election precinct, for & against Division, & for the Whig Ticket to pledge to carry out the will of the Majority. Lately, as you will see from the Recorder, Montgomery and son-in-law had a meeting at High Falls, & avowed their determination to go for *a Central division,* & nothing short of it, & carried it in their Meeting over a respectable minority. The proceedings of that Meeting have lighted the torch in all that Country. Those people believe that an attempt at a Central division would defeat every thing on the subject, hence they are holding meetings among themselves, contra; & our Whig friends over the River are writing us that every thing is going on well there. The prospect now is favourable. It is obvious that Dr. Mont. & Gen'l Allison are mutually jealous of each other. Mont. may attempt to bring out Candidates from the extreme West and East, including himself, & the Allison faction, which is the stronger, will probably make a ticket independantly of Doct. Mont. One certain good, it may be assumed, is gained, viz: The way is opened for seperating the local question from the politicks of the County. I doubt not that Doct: Mont is *soured* with his party for their having passed over him so silently in getting up a Democratic Candidate for Congress last Spring; & that his purpose now is, to advance himself upon the question of a "Central division," if possible. This may, or may not, benefit us. I want you to send documents, etc., to the following persons, viz: Tom Holden,[40] Wm. Lipscom, Henderson Parrish (Red Mountain) & Doctor C. Parrish. I suspect the old Doct is cooing in that quarter.

As to our Candidates, I expect we shall have Giles Mebane, H. K. Nash,[41] Doct. Holt,[42] Oldham, & a Stony Creek man or H. Parker.[43] Waddell lately is almost in the notion—or keeps dark

[40] Thomas Holden was a man of considerable influence in Orange County.

[41] Henry Kollock Nash (1817-1897), of Hillsboro, graduate of the university, a lawyer, who was a member of the commons in 1842.

[42] Dr. Samuel Holt.

[43] Commonly known as Hay. Parker.

on the subject that he may enjoy the flourish of declining a nomination. But the Cty. Convention will not nominate him, unless he previously indicates a willingness to accept in the event of his being nominated. For I myself should be unwilling to throw upon Mebane[44] the unpleasant reflection of his being run after Waddell shall have declined. I think that much is due the zealous, self sacrificing devotion of Mebane to the cause heretofore.

I have thus gone into details at the hazard of incurring the charge of violating good taste. But some of those details may possess interest, as you are removed from the scene of action. Yet I ought to have remembered that you are unfitted for their enjoyment by reason of the high matters constantly pressing upon your attention.

What are you likely to do in furtherance of the great Whig principles for which we fought, & bled, & perhaps died, in the memorable campaign of '40? Has the mock dignity of President Tyler collected around him a formidible show of friends? or awed into submissive obedience any stout Whig heart in the Senate? or in the House? or is it likely to sway villages or States? or to suppress the Suffrage faction in little Rhode Island? Will you be able to hold a wholesome rein in the Senate upon his nominations? Will the Whigs be able to keep the ascendancy in both Houses of Congress? And when will you adjourn? These are subjects of some moment, & particularly the last, inasmuch as we hold that every dollar saved is two made.

*To James W. Bryan.*        U. Bryan Mss.

Washington City,

May 14th, 1842.

So far as I can hear from N. C. I think our friends are getting ready for the contest in August, and are generally well organized. But in the New Bern district, we fear, that the Counties may be lost by the failure of suitable candidates to offer themselves. Could you not, at the Carteret and Jones Courts, do something in inspiriting our friends with proper hope, and bring out influential men? In Craven also, Washington is fearful that there will be difficulty in getting out Candidates. My impression is, that we shall lose nothing of consequence in the other districts.

---

[44] Giles Mebane.

There is great excitement here, in consequence of the affair between Stanly and Wise. Process has been sued out on the affidavit of F. S. Key.[45] Stanly eluded the officers, and is now in Maryland. Wise has been arrested, and carried before the Judge of the district, and yesterday and today, he and his Va. Colleagues are enlightening the Judge on the subject of Parliamentry priviledge. Wise refuses to enter into recognizance to keep the peace out of this district. On the ground that the Judge has not Jurisdiction beyond the district. The Judge has taken no notice of the Assault and battery committed by Wise on Stanly last Saturday, which would give a clear right to bind him for his appearance at the next district Court. In the mean time, should he kill or injure Stanly, he may be punished with the utmost extent of severity for the assault and battery. You need not be surprized to hear that they have fought in the course of the next week. I can't see any possibility of escape.

Dr. Jas. Washington and sister were here last night, and went on today to Phila. He had a fall into Roanoke River (which was likely to cool off his love) but only gave him a shake of the ague which kept a day in Richmond.

I dined a few days since with Lord Ashburton, who is entertaining in a magnificent style of hospitality. He is however, a plain, mercantile looking person, and certainly not the man to discuss questions of International Law, with Webster.

\*    \*    \*    \*    \*

*To Paul C. Cameron.*    U. Cameron Mss.

Washington City

May 20th, 1842.

My Dear Sir

I received your kind letter in due time, and regret that I have so long delayed a reply. In relation to our friend Waddells becoming a candidate, I think with you that our success in Orange will much depend on it. I had written him some time before the receipt of your letter to that effect, and may drop him a line

---

[45] Francis Scott Key (1779-1843), a native of Maryland, a graduate of St. Johns College, who had been a law partner of Roger B. Taney, and United States attorney for the District of Columbia. He is best known, of course, as the author of "The Star Spangled Banner."

again, in a day or two. If however in full view of all his duties private as well as public, he cannot give his consent to offer, I doubt not it will be for reasons which cannot be complained of by our friends, and much as I desire it on every account, I feel therefore restrained from urginig him with too much importunity.

You have no doubt heard of the quarrel between Stanly & Wise, the former is still in Maryland, and the impression is, that a fight cannot be avoided, but how soon a matter of some doubt. Wise is under recognizance in $3,000 to keep the peace, and not to leave the district for the purpose of a duel with Stanly, this however it is understood will not have effect as to the latter provision.

We are all agog about the rebellion in Rhode Island. Every mail is looked to for news of bloodshed, and outbreak. Dorr the pretended Governor, has organized a force and is guarded constantly. By the last account he has seized some pieces of Artillery, and threatened an attack on the Arsenal. The President at first manifested proper firmness, but I very much apprehend as is his nature, he is vacillating, as usual. Had he acted with the energy of General Washington, in the case of the Wiskey insurrection, by sending a sufficient force at once to put down all insurrection, it would have ended without loss of life. But in present circumstances there is imminent danger of collision, and with a large portion of the Locofoco party here, encouraging the insurgents, the excitement may be greatly extended, especially, as the insurgents profess to be contending for the popular doctrine of the right of universal suffrage. Dorr is president of an abolition society, and of course goes for the largest liberty. And upon his doctrine a majority without regard to color, or condition, have at any time a right to overturn the existing Government, and set up their will in its stead.

I fear the session of Congress is to be unusually long, there is no mode of preventing it, as there is much business yet necessary to be done.

I hope our friends in Orange will make the best selection they can of candidates. I have taken some pains in endeavouring to spread correct information among them, and think there is no cause for despondency in a fair contest. Indeed I have the most sanguine belief that we shall carry the state by a decisive majority.

&#42;　&#42;　&#42;　&#42;　&#42;

*From Denison Olmsted.*                                    U.

Yale College, May 17th, 1842.

I thank you for your able Speech on the "Loan Bill," which I have read with equal interest and instruction.

You are aware, perhaps, that teachers as they grow old, are always prone to appropriate to themselves a large share of the honors acquired by their pupils.

Whether it be this common frailty or not I do not know, but certain I am that nothing affords me more pleasure than to witness the advancement of those in whose early education I bore even a humble part.

I beg you to present me very respectfully to such members of the North Carolina delegation as may remember me, and believe me.

Very Respectfully & Truly Yrs,

*From James W. Bryan.*                                    U.

Newbern,

May 24th, 1842.

I wrote an Editorial for the Spectator the last week and nominated three Candidates for Craven, all of which seems to take very well. At Carteret last week I caused them to call a Whig meeting to nominate their Candidates there, and matters seem to be getting along very well in the way of politics.

\*     \*     \*     \*     \*

We are all on the tiptoe of expectation to hear from Stanly & Wise. Newbern feels great interest of course, in Stanly, and all wish him to come off conqueror in the contest. It is an affair to be much regretted by the whole Country.

\*     \*     \*     \*     \*

*From Nicholas Lanier Williams.*[46]          U.

Panther Creek, 25th. May, 1842.

By last nights mail I rec'd a letter from Joseph L. Williams[47] dated the 18th inst. at Raleigh, saying that in a conversation with you, a few days before he left Washington, that you expressed much solicitude as to the probable fate of the Whig ticket in Surry

The Whigs of this County nominated their candidates at our last Court, Col. R. C. Puryear[48] for the Senate; H. P. Poindexter N. Boyden, and Jesse Franklin[49] Esqr. for the Commons. This ticket cannot be beaten by any other, which may be brought out in oposition to it. I think you may be well assured that Surry is safe.

We had considerable difficulty in getting Puryear, and Boyden, before the people again; they both positively refused at one time, and Puryear went off to the South on business and to avoid a nomination just before Court. I was prevented by a sick child, from going to Court myself, but I wrote to several of my friends to have Puryear nominated for the Senate in his absence, that I thought it was the only way we could hold him on. Puryear has since returned and has consented to run.

If the other Counties will bring out as strong a ticket, as we have done, the Whigs will have a very large majority in the Legislature.

---

[46] Nicholas Lanier Williams (1799-1886), of Panther Creek, Surry County, a member of the distinguished Williams family, was an able man of high character and wide popularity and influence. He was, briefly, a student at the university, and long one of its most devoted Trustees. He became a somewhat extensive planter, and, while keenly interested as a Whig, in politics, he never sought office, his short service on the council of state in 1864 being his only acceptance of any appointment. He was a brother of Lewis, Robert, John, and Thomas L., and uncle of Joseph Lanier Williams, who made history, not only in North Carolina, but in Tennessee, Mississippi, and Louisiana. He is, perhaps, most widely remembered today through the fame enjoyed by the products of his distillery.

[47] Joseph L. Williams (1807-1865), of Tennessee, above referred to, was educated at the university, and at West Point. He was a prominent lawyer, and a Whig member of congress, 1837-1843.

[48] Richard Clauselle Puryear (1801-1867), of Surry County, a native of Virginia, a lawyer, who served in the commons, 1838, 1844-1846, 1852, and in the state senate, 1840. He was a member of congress, 1853-1857, and of the Confederate provisional congress.

[49] Jesse Franklin (1760-1823), a native of Virginia, who came to North Carolina during the Revolution, in which he served, being at King's Mountain and Guilford Court House, among other battles. He served in the commons, 1793-1794, 1797-1798, in the state senate, 1805-1806, was a member of congress, 1795-1797, of the senate, 1799-1805, (president *pro tem.*, 1804-1805), 1807-1813, and was governor, 1820-1821. He was commissioner to treat with the Chickasaw and Cherokee Indians.

I am really sorry that I had not the pleasure of seeing you at Washington in my late visit to that place. I called at the Senate twice to see you; once you were occupying the Chair, and the other time, you were not in the Senate. I requested Mr. James Graham to inform you of my disappointment.

I should be glad to hear from you at all times.

*From Priestley H. Mangum.*                    U.

Hillsboro',

May 30th., 1842.

Don't be alarmed, for I promise you that I am not intent again upon inflicting a long letter upon you.

Our doings of last week being over, I will give you a sketch of the results, & the whys and wherefores. Previously to Court, I was satisfactorily informed that in the eastern part of the County, and particularly within the range of the Round Hill Election, there was cause to fear a loss of some twenty-five votes, unless a controlling influence from the neighborhod was brought to bear upon the Election. That fact led to the proposing Hav. Parker to the consideration of our friends early in the week. Cain Creek desired a candidate, but was divided between Oldham & Wm. Thompson. Again Stoney Creek had its aspirations, Faucett & Col. Grahams. Waddell's coming in rendered it indispensable to take but one Candidate from those three sections. Hillsboro' was against Parker, as he never could go for any thing that was not *of self;* but over the River, part of Cain Creek, and some scatteringly all over the County, pointed to Parker as preferable for the 4th. Commoner. We had informal meetings on Tuesday and Thursday Evenings, to pave the way to a harmonious action. On Thursday Evening, to avoid heartburnings on this point, I stated our belief of a probable loss from the character of the River population, but left it entirely with our friends abroad to decide, professing a willingness to take H. Nash as the Eastern Candidate, if others should decide not to take Parker. That, I thought, ought to satisfy friends with me and mine. Whether it has done it, I don't know. The difficulty being over thus far, Waddell was cause of a much greater one. Not untill Monday did he say to his friends that he would accept of a nomination. Between March Ct. and May; our friends over the County, having lost sight of

Waddell, had been looking to Mebane for the Senate, which led to neighbourhoods cherishing with more fondness the expectation of more candidates in the Commons than our number would admit of selecting with Waddell, viz: Flat River, Cain Creek, over the River and Nash, all could have been served. As to Grahams, public opinion was well settled against him, & pretty well that no candidate from Stoney Creek would impart strength to the Ticket. But Waddell consents. Mr. Cameron's letter, the Chairman of the Central Committee's letter at Raleigh—all of which I suspect you & Willie had a hand in—were to Mr. Waddell irresistable! He consents, and we thought that altho' he is eternally injuring the cause when not a candidate, he was most available & efficient in the heat of a Canvass, & most terrible to the Enemy. But great opposition appeared against him from our political friends, over the River principally, but a good deal over the County. He was much alarmed, & would have burst forth, as usual, but for Judge Nash & a few of us. It was apparent that it could be settled only in the Committee that might be raised, two from each Captain's Company, selected by the delegates of each Company; to report a Ticket of Candidates. John Norwood had zealous friends in opposition to Waddell, as had Giles Mebane. Well, we go into Convention, the Committee is raised, its members having been selected in the early part of the day by the delegates of each Company, with strict reference to the Senate principally, and to the fourth Commoner, and after the absence of an hour or so, they reported Waddell in the Senate, G. Mebane, H. Nash, Doct. Holt, & Hav. Parker in the Com's., & unanimously adopted by the Convention. The candidates accepted. (In the Committee the vote stood 32 for Waddell, 16 I believe for Mebane, 6 for Nor'd—all this is secret.) But unanimity prevailed as far as the public knows. Gov: Morehead, soon after the Convention closed its business, addressed the public from the Porch of the Lodge, and gave us one of the very best of popular speeches, which told. All things look well in the County. By order of Ct. the vote upon *Central* division is to be taken, & that question will be separated, I think, from politicks this summer.

*From  Giles  Mebane.*                                    U.

## White Oak,

May 30th, 1842.

More than a month ago I wrote a letter to the Editors of the Inteligencer requesting them to change the address of my paper so as to direct it to Mason Hall *via Raleigh and Hillsborough.* They have paid no attention to my request and the grievance I then laboured under continues unredressed—Which is the tardy and irregular receipt of the Inteligencer. It comes to me from Greensborough and often two Nos. together. The P. M. in Greensborough told me the same paper for subscribers in the eastern part of the State came to his office. I have heard complaints of the same kind about Yanceyville, & I believe Mr. Thorn stoped his paper because it came so irregularly. I wrote to the Editors because I disliked to trouble a friend with such a matter. But I must request you to write a note to the Editor directing them to write on the envelope of my paper: Via Hillsborough. I believe the paper is regularly Rec'd in Hillsborough & I wish mine to come in the same mail.

At May Court Gov. Morehead came to Hillsborough & spoke to a large assembly of people. The Whigs in the County are generally stirred up for the Summer *campaign.* The Governor is very sanguine as to the ascendancy of Whig principles in the State & the next Legislature. Our County ticket of candidates I suppose you have seen in the Recorder. I think with proper and usual elections we shall be able to carry it through in triumph. A supply of such reports as have been made by and to Congress exposing the Van Buren administration would be very acceptable to me. I have seen a number in the papers but would be pleased to have them in pamphlet for convenience. I would be glad to receive any speech or document containing the best views on the bank or tariff question so far as Mr. Clay is to be vindicated. The State convention having nominated him his name will mingle more or less with our election.

I see the True Whig requests from members of Congress the names of their constituents who would like to take that paper. I have not seen but one or two Nos. and do not know it's character if you think it an efficient auxiliary you may hand in my name as a subscriber.

*From J. Kerner.*                                      U.

Scotts Creek, [Haywood Co.,] May 31st, 1842.

I see from the public prints and the action of the Senate, that a Treaty is now pending, or proposed, with the Cherokees East the Mississippi. You will pardon me for suggesting the propriety of such a treaty.

Under the provisions of the Treaties of 1817 & 19, many of the Cherokees held reservations within the limits of Haywood & Macon Counties, that Treaty provided that the Reservee possessed only a life Estate in the Reservations—the State has questioned that title, by that Treaty the children are to possess the fee simple title at the death of the Reservee. Many of the Reservees are dead and the heirs are in the act of commencing suits in ejectment against the purchasers under the State, and But for the timely interference of Mr W. H. Thomas, the Cherokee agent, Suits would have been going on at this time. On enquiry you will ascertain that numerous suits have already found their way into the Courts of Tennessee.

I have recently spent some 6 or 7 days in the neighborhood of the Cherokees in this County; the best understanding exists Between them & the whites. Much anxiety is felt by the Citizens in relation to the Legal Estate of the heirs in the various Reservations in this vicinity; the value of property Jeopardized Can not be less than $20 000. A Treaty of that kind to rest and provide for the removal of the Cherokees West in a friendly way at some future day as they may desire to go, after the old & infirm are no more, would give Satisfaction Generally.

At a Council held some 8 weeks ago—I was present—and from Rumors circulating I was surprised to find that not so many as one was found willing to go West; by the next mail I will give you such information as can be selected in Relation to the proposed Treaty.

## Speech On The Districting Clause

*of*

The Apportionment Bill [50]

*delivered*

## In The Senate Of The United States,

## June 3rd., 1842.

MR. PRESIDENT: I am aware of the impatience of the Senate to vote on this bill, and of the urgency with which the State Legislatures, either now in session, or shortly to convene, demand speedy action upon it. But, as the provision contained in the second section of the bill, requiring members of the House of Representatives to be chosen in every State by single districts, is about to be established by a law of Congress for the first time, and as it has been inveighed against in this debate as an innovation, not solicited or desired in any quarter, contrary to the faith and spirit of the Constitution, and forbidden by its terms, I, who give to it my cordial approbation, must claim your indulgence to offer my views in its defence.

I have listened attentively to the new, bold, and ingenious theory of the honorable Senator from Alabama, (MR. BAGBY) [51] who has just taken his seat, affirming that the election of members of the House by general ticket, as it is called, where each and every elector votes for as many members as are to be chosen from the State, is the only constitutional mode of election; and, by consequence, that the practice which has prevailed for fifty years in four-fifths of the States of the Union is utterly at variance with the true meaning of the Constitution. Those who adopt this theory, which implies that the contemporaries, and many of the framers of the Constitution did not comprehend its true import on this important subject of representation, and that the action of the Federal Government, as well as that of almost every State, for more than half a century, has been erroneous in regard to it, will look with some charity upon whatever of novelty

---

[50] From a reprint from the *National Intelligencer,* 1842.

[51] Arthur Pendleton Bagby (1794-1858), of Alabama, a native of Virginia, a lawyer, who served in the lower house of the state legislature, 1821-1822, 1824, 1834-1836, and was speaker, 1822, and 1836. He was state senator in 1825, governor, 1837-1841, and Democratic United States senator, 1841-1848, resigning to become minister to Russia.

there may be in the uniform system of election by districts, as now proposed. Their own idea, that the general ticket system is the only constitutional mode of choosing Representatives, is not only novel, but fraught, as I conceive, with danger to the Union itself; inasmuch as, practically, it would enable four, or at most five, of the twenty-six States of the Confederacy (should they be so disposed) to control the most important branch of the National Legislature. The construction of the Constitution, as I understand the argument of the Senator, is derived solely from the direction that members of the House of Representatives shall be chosen "by the People of the several States;" and he insists that it is an abridgement of the right of suffrage not to allow every elector to vote for as many members as are to be elected from the State of which he is a citizen. The error of this construction I apprehend to consist in allowing too much force to mere general words, without reference to circumstances which restrain and control their generality. The very same sentence of the Constitution proceeds to negative the supposition that the whole "People are to vote, by requiring the electors to "have the qualifications requisite for electors of the most numerous branch of the State Legislature, thus excluding a large portion (perhaps the majority) of those who are properly denominated "People" of the State from the right of suffrage altogether. The bills of rights in many of the State constitutions declare that "all political power is vested in, and derived from, the *People only;*" and that "the legislative authority shall be vested in two distinct branches, both dependent on *the People.*" But no one has ever inferred from these general expressions, that members of the State Legislatures are, each, to be elected by the entire body of the People of the State.

Having reference to public convenience, as well as to the true theory of representative government, every State has directed its Legislature to be constituted by divisions of the People choosing representatives, each for itself, and these, together, forming its General Assembly. The impropriety as well as the danger of attaching too much importance to mere general terms, without reference to anything else, is most strikingly manifested by adverting to the very first words of the Constitution. If the expression, "we the People of the United States," is to be allowed the same liberal interpretation which is sought, for the purposes of this argument, to be given to the terms "People of the several States," then the confederated character of the Government is gone, and it becomes the Government of the aggregate mass of the People of the Union.

Sir, I will not venture to assert that either of the modes of election now in question is unconstitutional. So far as I can perceive, in the discretion of Congress, or, if Congress deem it inexpedient to make regulations, in the discretion of the State Legislature, either mode may be adopted without running counter to any of the literal inhibitions of the Constitution. But, from some examination of the history of this subject, made during the progress of this discussion, I will undertake to demonstrate that the district system of representation was the one contemplated and expected by the framers of the Constitution. Although the question is no where decided, or distinctly made, between those two systems, in the general convention which proposed, or in the State conventions which adopted, the Constitution, so as to indicate the one or the other as the only allowable mode, yet it is manifest that the district system was in the mind of every man who thought upon the matter of representation, as it was upon the tongue of every one who spoke or wrote in relation to it, during that anxious period when the question of adoption was pending before the American People. In the 56th. number of the Federalist, Mr. Madison, in treating of the House of Representatives, and in combating the objection of the opponents of the Constitution, that the members of the House would not have sufficient local information to be fit Representatives of the People, employs this language:

"Divide the largest State into ten or twelve districts, and it will be found that there will be no peculiar local interests in either, which will not be within the knowledge of the Representative of the district."

In the succeeding number (57) of that great commentary on the Constitution, pursuing the same subject, he asserts, in substance, that, were the objections of its opponents read by a person who had not seen its provisions relative to representation, he could suppose nothing less than that the mode prescribed by the State constitutions was, in some respect or other, very grossly departed from. He then adds:

"The only difference discoverable between the two cases is, that *each Representative of the United States will be elected by five or six thousand citizens,* whilst in the individual States the election of a Representative is left to about as many hundreds."

Again: In discussing the objection that there could not be adequate representation in the House, after drawing some arguments and illustrations from the British House of Commons, he adds:

"But we need not resort to foreign experience on this subject, our own is explicit and decisive. *The districts* in New Hampshire, in which the Senators are chosen immediately by the People, are nearly as large as will be necessary for Representatives in Congress, those of Massachusetts are larger than will be necessary for that purpose, and those of New York still more so. In the last State the members of Assembly for the cities and counties of New York and Albany are elected by nearly as many voters as will be entitled to a Representative in Congress, calculating on the number of sixty-five Representatives only. It makes no difference that, in these senatorial districts and counties, a number of Representatives are voted for by each elector at the same time. If the same electors at the same time are capable of choosing four or five Representatives, they cannot be incapable of choosing one. Pennsylvania is an additional example. Some of her counties which elect her State Representatives, are almost as large as her districts will be by which her Federal Representatives will be elected. The city of Philadelphia is supposed to contain between fifty and sixty thousand souls, it will therefore form nearly two districts for the choice of Federal Representatives."

Such was the view of the mode of representation in the House held by the father of the Constitution, when, almost with the wisdom of inspiration, he was urging its adoption upon his jealous and doubtful countrymen, as necessary to their tranquility, liberty and happiness. Not only does he, in express terms, assume that the district system of choosing Representatives is to be everywhere established as the natural one under the Constitution, and that cities (Philadelphia being the example) are to be divided for that purpose, but he also unequivocally negatives the idea of elections by general ticket, by declaring that, unlike the senatorial elections in the State of New York, where four or five members were voted for at the same time by each elector, the choice of Federal Representatives would be limited to one in each district.

Such, also, was the opinion which seems almost universally to have prevailed in the State conventions which deliberated on the reception of the Federal Constitution. I will detain you by referring to the only notice of the subject which I find in the debates of the convention of 1788, in North Carolina, which rejected the Constitution. Mr. Galloway,[52] a strenuous opponent of the Constitution, stated, by way of objection to it, that all the members of Congress would probably be taken from the seaboard; to which Mr. Steele[53] immediately replied, that this objection was groundless, as the State would probably be laid off into districts. There was no response to this latter allegation, and it would seem to have met with general acquiescence.

But, sir, we have more substantial evidence of the expectation, not to say intention, of the founders of the Constitution, than that embodied in their contemporaneous speeches and writings. Their "faith" was shown also by their "works." In Virginia, where lived Washington, the President of that illustrious assembly which produced the Constitution, and Madison, its chief author, advocate, and expounder, in New York, Massachusetts, the Carolinas, every where except Georgia and Connecticut, the district mode of elections was established with the very beginning of the Government; and in nearly all of the original States it remains to this day. To question its constitutionality now, is to question the validity of the whole body of laws enacted since the first elections to Congress in 1789.

It is said, however, by the Senators from New York and Pennsylvania, (Messrs. WRIGHT [54] and BUCHANAN,) that the bill proposes an innovation not desired or solicited from any source. I trust that I have already shown, if historical evidence can prove anything, that the district system of elections is not, of itself, an innovation of which the framers of the Government (were they living) would complain, and its toleration for fifty years, almost with unanimity in the old States, and its adoption in nearly three-fifths of the new, affords somewhat decisive proof that it coincides with the general wish of the American People. I have, moreover,

---

[52] The two Galloways, James and Charles, were delegates from Rockingham County to the convention of 1788. The one referred to was undoubtedly James, who had been a member of the commons from Guilford, 1783-1784, and from Rockingham, 1786-1789. He was prominent in the convention.

[53] John Steele (1764-1815), of Rowan, whose only previous public service was as a member of the commons in 1787. He was an active and ardent Federalist. He served also in the convention of 1789. He was later commissioner to treat with the Cherokees, and Chickasaws, boundary commissioner with South Carolina and Georgia, member of congress 1790-1793, and comptroller of the treasury, 1796-1802. The rising tide of democratic ideas defeated him twice for the United States senate. He was a member of the commons, 1811-1813.

[54] Silas Wright (1795-1847), a native of Massachusetts, a graduate of Middlebury College, who became a lawyer, and settled in New York. He was Democratic state senator, 1824-1827, brigadier general of militia, and was elected to congress, 1829, but accepted an appointment as state comptroller, instead of serving. He was United States senator, 1833-1844, and governor, 1844-1846.

some evidence to show that their approval of it has gone beyond mere toleration—that, such a favorite has it been in their affections, they have repeatedly demanded that it should be established and secured to them by the Constitution itself. The State whose servant I am, has been so devotedly attached to the district mode of representation, that when her Legislature repealed that system of choosing electors of President and Vice President, and established the general ticket, though a decisive majority of the People, in the parties of that day, were with the Legislature in general politics, yet this change produced no little excitement; and it could only be excused and the repeal prevented, upon the ground that similar changes in other States had rendered it a necessary act of self-defense—an argument which our subsequent history has shown to have been but too true; since now, in every State, the electors are chosen by general ticket, except in one, where they are elected, not by the People, but by the Legislature. Foreseeing that a like alteration might be generally made in the manner of electing members of the House of Representatives, and deprecating such an innovation, her servants here, as well as her General Assembly, raised their voices at once in favor of the district system; and, to render it *permanent* as well as uniform, throughout the Union, both in the choice of Representatives in Congress and presidential electors, they demanded an amendment of the Constitution. As early as the session of 1813, Mr. Pickens, a highly intelligent and respectable member of our delegation in the House, an old associate and friend of the Senator from Alabama, MR. KING, [Mr. King nodded assent,] offered resolutions of amendment to the Constitution to that effect. At the succeeding session of the Legislature, resolutions on the same subject appear to have been passed by both Houses, and transmitted to the other States of the Union. Here let me remark to the honorable Senator from Virginia, (Mr. RIVES) —from whom I regretted to hear that he would vote against this section of the bill, although he concurred with us in believing that the district mode of representation was wisest and best, lest its establishment by law now might, in the contest of parties, lead to what he greatly dreaded, the enactment of the general ticket system hereafter—that, in his State, as well as my own, the manifestations of public opinion have been strong in the preference of the district system. On the 18th. of April, 1816, in the House of Representatives, Mr. Pleasants,[55] of Virginia, laid before the House a communication from the Legislature of that State, reciting that—

"The Legislature of North Carolina, having proposed the following as an amendment to the Constitution of the United States: That, for the purpose of choosing Representatives in the Congress of the United States, each State shall, by its Legislature, be divided into a number of districts equal to the number of Representatives to which each State may be entitled.

These districts shall be formed of contiguous territory, and contain as near as may be, an equal number of inhabitants, entitled by the Constitution to be represented. In each district the qualified voters shall elect one Representative, and no more."

Then providing for the choice of electors of President by districts, in like manner, and concluding with a resolution declaring that it is expedient to adopt the said amendment.

The Legislature of Massachusetts adopted like resolutions about the same time.

On the 21st. of January, 1817, Mr. Pickens, of North Carolina, presented to the House the proceedings of the Legislature of that State, referring to the "resolution of the Commonwealth of Massachusetts as being the same in principle with that adopted by the General Assembly of North Carolina at the last session;" then repeating the specific amendments of the Constitution desired, I believe, in the very words which I have before read in the communication from the Legislature of Virginia, and ending with resolutions in favor of their adoption—the whole being embodied in a report signed "R. M. Saunders, Chairman," and certified to have passed both the Senate and House of Commons *unanimously*, by John Branch, speaker, and Robert Williams, clerk, of the former; and of the latter, James Iredell, speaker, and Pleasant Henderson,[56] clerk.

At the session of 1820, the Hon. J. S. Smith, of North Carolina, representing the district in which I reside, offered similar resolutions of amendment to the Constitution, in favor of the district system of choosing representatives and electors; and, on the 25th.

[55] James Pleasants (1769-1836), of Virginia, a graduate of William and Mary, lawyer, who was frequently a member of the legislature, was a representative in congress, 1811-1819, and senator, 1819-1822, governor, 1822-1825, and a delegate to the convention of 1829.

[56] Pleasant Henderson (1756-1842), of Granville, a Revolutionary soldier, who studied law under his brother, Richard Henderson, was for many years a legislative clerk of one sort or another. He was also for some time, steward of the university. As a young man, he pioneered in Tennessee and Kentucky, and a few years before his death he moved to Tennessee.

of January, 1821, the vote of the Representatives of the People on the resolutions was, yeas 92, nays 54; so the proposition to amend the Constitution failed, for want of a majority of two-thirds in its favor; but the recorded vote is a strong indication of popular opinion in favor of the districts.

The subject, however, was not permitted to sleep. At the session of 1823, Mr. McDuffie, of South Carolina, presented resolutions, I believe, in the very words of those of Mr. Smith, and during that session submitted an elaborate report, in which the expediency of the district system of electing both Representatives and electors is argued with great ability. I do not perceive that the resolutions were pressed to a vote at that session, but the argument of this report vindicates the propriety and necessity of this mode of election in a masterly manner.

[Mr. BUCHANAN said he did not know that he would speak on this subject; but, as the Senator appeared in some of his remarks to refer to him, he wished to say that the precedents cited, all proposed to amend the Constitution so as to establish the district system. This bill proposed to do it by a law of Congress, prescribing that districts should be laid off by the State Legislatures. He desired to hear how Congress obtained that power.]

MR. GRAHAM resumed. The Senator has done me the honor to attend to my remarks, and hence I may have, in some degree, addressed myself to him. I am sensible of the constitutional difficulty suggested by that Senator, though it does not appear to me insurmountable, and design, before I conclude, to meet it fairly. I have referred to these matters in our history thus far, with no view to the question of constitutional power, but to show what has been public sentiment in and out of Congress, in regard to district representation, and to quiet the apprehensions of those who seem to dread popular tumults and collisions between sovereign States and the Federal Government, from the establishment of that mode of representation which the People from the first expected, have so generally exercised, and with such an approach to unanimity, have adopted in their own States, and called for throughout the Union—a mode of representation which almost every Senator who has participated in this discussion admits, in his individual opinion, to be the best, but which, from doubt as to the power to ordain it in this manner, on the part of some, from an apprehension that its adoption now, may be understood to spring from motives of party advantage, and that, in a revolution of parties, it may be succeeded by the general ticket system, on the part of others, fails to receive that powerful support to which the admitted merits of the district system would seem to entitle it. Whatever force there may be in these objections, I flatter myself that the direful consequences which gentlemen anticipate from the passage of this law, will never be realized. If it be unconstitutional, it yet proposes an object so near to the hearts of the People in general, that its constitutionality will be tested and decided, in that calm, deliberate and unimpassioned manner which is so necessary to the preservation of all our institutions. If it be constitutional, then the superiority so generally conceded to it will prevent its repeal in any mutations of mere party, much less its being superseded by the general ticket system, which finds so little favor for its own sake.

Mr. President, we are told by Mr. Madison, in the Federalist, what is indeed sufficiently evident without the authority of his great name, that the peculiarity which distinguishes the two Houses of Congress is, "that one branch is a representation of *citizens,* the other of States." Here, the People of the States are represented as aggregated communities, or political corporations; in the House, they are represented as individual members of society—in that capacity in which they are required to contribute to the Treasury of the Government, and to furnish blood and bone and muscle for its defence in war—in which they enjoy the great fundamental rights of life, liberty and property, prosecute for violations of their rights in courts of justice, and suffer judgment for offences against the laws enacted by Congress, as well as by their immediate State Legislatures. And the prohibition of the Constitution against originating revenue bills in this body was designed to secure the individual man against exactions even proposed by the Representatives of the State of which he is a member, and to give the initiation of the laws on this most vital subject to those direct Representatives of the People with whom they share a common local interest, the atmosphere of a common neighborhood, and whom they must meet face to face at the ballot-box; nor does it seem quite to consist with the spirit of this regulation, although I have admitted that the letter will allow it, that those Representatives should be chosen by all the electors of of State, instead of subdivisions or sections of the people. Thus chosen, they would seem to be more appropriate Representatives of the States, as communities, having derived their authority from a vote of the majority of the whole People, than even members of the Senate, who are elected by the State Legislatures. No one has ever thought of applying the general ticket system in the choice of members of the State Legislatures, and yet popular representation was not intended to be more complete in any of them than it was in the House of Representatives, on the subjects committed to the jurisdiction of Congress. The very idea of it implies, at least, if we can form any opinion from the usage of mankind, not that the people are to determine the choice of Representatives by the majority of the State or nation in the aggregate, but by elections in divisions of greater or less magnitude; and, accordingly, we find in every free nation, with any great extension of country— I of course exclude the minor Grecian republics, with territories no larger than the county in which I reside—that the representative assemblies of the People have been chosen by counties, parishes, departments, districts, by whatever name called. It ensures that personal and intimate acquaintance between the representative and constituent which is of the very essence of true representation, and makes political promotion depend as much upon the personal and virtuous character of the candidate, as upon his talents and abilities; whereas, in the great contests of entire States, the responsibility of the individual elector being less, there is but too much danger that tickets may be made out of those having address, or adroitness in party management, without reference to private character. Sir, we learn from contemporaneous history, that a principal and powerful objection to the adoption of the Constitution was, that in the representation under it, from the largeness of the electoral bodies, the choice would too often fall on those favored by fortune, or, in the language of the objectors, (as preserved by those sages who replied to them) on the "wealthy and well-born." However erroneous this objection of jealous freemen was then shown to be, while districts, as we have seen, were alone contemplated, it applies with decisive force to elections by general ticket, for a considerable number of members; not that wealth has the influence which was then apprehended, for it is comparatively seldom in this country that very opulent men have been elected to places in the public councils; but combinations may be formed, by the management of party leaders, and party allegiance appealed to for their support, by which the People, who pursue their daily avocations at home, deprived of all choice, are left no alternative but acquiescence, or not to vote at all. Thus, he who aspires to a political career, without enjoying the favor, perhaps the acquaintance, of the few who control in such matters, (and obscure have been the beginnings of many who have attained the highest eminence,) has before him the hopeless task of traversing the entire State, to make known his qualifications and his principles, and to encounter at every step of his progress the combined opposition perhaps of two sets of party candidates, and the denunciation of the entire party press. Sir, in my opinion, no more effectual mode of preventing the free choice of the People, and of excluding from the House of Representatives many of its most shining ornaments at all times—young men who, without adventitious aids, but by the mere force of mind and character, under the fostering genius of our institutions, have worked their way thither—could be devised than the establishment of the general ticket system in the larger States of the Union. I have already adverted to its disastrous effect on the Government itself, by throwing the absolute control of the popular branch of Congress into the hands of five or six States who already possess the power, by the general ticket system which they have adopted, of choosing a President of the United States.

But, Mr. President, much as the district system is recommended to us by the considerations of expediency, of its conformity to the true theory of representative government, and to expectations of the immortal patriots who formed our Government, we cannot adopt it by law here, unless we possess the constitutional power. The Senator from Pennsylvania (Mr. Buchanan) has already intimated that the repeated propositions to amend the Constitution in relation to it, indicates that the power to do it by law was doubted or denied. Sir, that suggestion is not sustained by anything which I have observed in the history of these propositions. On the contrary, Mr. McDuffie, in his report, to which I have alluded already, does not urge the amendment to the Constitution upon the ground of a want of authority in Congress to make laws for its regulation, but to put it beyond the control of fluctuating and temporary legislation—to make the system "*permanent*," and not subject to change, as well as "uniform." [Here Mr. G. read several passages of the report, in support of this statement.] So far as an opinion is expressed on the question in dispute, it is in favor of the power now claimed.

"It has been seen" (says he) that "the times, places, and manner" of electing members to this House are now liable to be prescribed by the Legislatures of the several States, "*subject to the controlling and superseding power of Congress.*" These latter words are in italics, and need no strained interpretation to show that the author conceded quite as much power to Congress over this subject, as is asserted by the present bill.

Here, sir, let me also notice certain proceedings in several of the State conventions which deliberated on the adoption of the Federal Constitution, referred to, and much relied upon in the argument of the Senator from New York, (MR. WRIGHT.) It seems that, in seven or eight of the States, North Carolina being one, the conventions declared "that Congress shall not alter, modify, or interfere in the times, places, or manner of holding elections for Senators and Representatives, or either of them, except when the Legislature of any State shall neglect, refuse, or be disabled by invasion or rebellion, to prescribe the same." And I first supposed the Senator to insist that this was a construction of the clause in the Constitution regarding elections, and an exposition of the sense in which it was understood at the time of ratification. But it appears this was an amendment proposed by these conventions, predicated on the opinion that the Constitution, as it stood then and stands now, did authorize Congress to interfere and make regulations at pleasure; and the Senator, as he subsequently explained, only referred to these proposed amendments as manifestations of the wishes of those States; and he thence argued that it would be disrespectful and a breach of faith towards them, to pass this bill. If we are to be restrained in the enactment of laws under the Constitution as it is, by what was proposed by way of amendment in the various State conventions, we shall soon be stripped of our most important and beneficent powers. Take as illustrations these, which I select at random from twenty six amendments, besides a bill of rights of twenty articles offered by the Convention of North Carolina, "that no navigation law, or law regulating commerce, shall be passed without the consent of two-thirds of the members present in both Houses;" that no standing army or regular troops shall be kept up in time of peace without "two-thirds" in like manner. These crude suggestions of the jealous spirit of freedom, if the Senator's argument be correct, would require a repeal of perhaps half our laws pertaining to commerce and navigation, and more than half of those respecting the army. Many objections and propositions of amendment were no doubt made to the Constitution on its first presentation, which were soon afterwards abandoned, even by the authors. At the very first session of the first Congress, ten amendments were proposed and adopted, which were speedily ratified, and appended to the Constitution; and at that very session this identical project of an amendment to limit the power of Congress over elections, which the Senator from New York tells us had received the approbation of so many States, was proposed in the House of Representatives and rejected—not only failing in a majority of two-thirds, but not receiving a numerical majority—ayes 23, noes 28; among the latter being James Madison, Jr., and other distinguished members of the Convention of 1787. (House Journal, 21st. August, 1789). North Carolina, by her second Convention, acceded to the Union the November succeeding, well knowing what amendments had been approved by Congress and what rejected, (her assent to the Constitution being given on one day, and to the ten amendments on the next,) without any proposals for additional amendments. And, from that day to this, there has been no renewal of the proposed restraint on the power of Congress over the regulation of elections, from any State whatever. So far as these proceedings, therefore, have any force as authority, they show an admission of the power of Congress; a solicitation of some States, before the Government was tried by experience, to take it away; a refusal by the Representatives of the People in the first Congress, by a decisive majority, even to submit the question to the amending tribunals for consideration; and an acquiescence in that determination ever since.

If we examine the words of the Constitution, there really seems to me to be little room for cavil on the question of power. They are these: "the times, places, and manner of holding elections for Senators and Representatives shall be prescribed in each State by the Legislature thereof; but Congress may, at any time, by law, make or alter such regulations, except as to the places of choosing Senators." I understand it to be admitted that, by virtue of these words, Congress does possess the power to lay off the districts itself, but that it has not power to direct them to be laid off by the State Legislatures.

[Several Senators in opposition declared that they did not make this admission.] [57]

Mr. Graham said he had so understood the concession, and it was, at all events, he conceived, too plain to be controverted. He recollected the declarations of some that Congress could not, in good faith, interfere, until a State was in default, by failure or negligence, in respect to its elections. But the language of the Constitution is, that Congress may *"make or alter."* Now, omit the

---

[57] Brackets throughout appear in the original.

disjunctive power to "alter," and the reading is, "Congress may, at any time, make such regulations"—create anew such "regulations." What regulations? Obviously those of time, place, and manner of the elections. I proceed, therefore, to the position assumed by the Senator from New York, (MR. WRIGHT,) that, although Congress may possess the power to lay off districts throughout the United States, by law, you cannot prescribe a system of districts by your law, and call on the State Legislatures to carry it into effect. His assertion is, if you touch the subject, you take all into your own hands, and must go through with it. Is this so? Are time, place, and manner *tria juncta in uno,* and indivisible? Can you not regulate time without interfering with place, and prescribe manner without meddling with either time or place?

[MR. WRIGHT assented.]

Well, then, how is it that manner is a unit incapable of division, and must be completed, in all its details, by the hand which prescribes its general outlines? Does not the major include the minor? If I have a right to go twain, can I not go one mile? If, when you designate time or place, without more saying, the State Legislatures are still bound to regulate the manner of elections, by what discrimination is it that, when you declare the manner only, they are not bound to carry that manner into effect as fully as they are obliged to appoint time and place? The manner and places of choosing presidential electors belong, under the Constitution, exclusively to the State Legislatures. The time of choosing them "Congress may determine." Congress has declared that they shall be elected within thirty five days before the first Wednesday in December, in every fourth year; and the Legislature of each State, without offence to its sovereignty, has fixed for itself the day of election. Yet, according to the reasoning of the Senator, Congress, having interfered with the time, was bound to appoint the precise day in every State. Why may not Congress declare that Representatives shall be chosen from such equal districts as the State Legislatures shall prescribe, as well as that electors shall be chosen on such day, within a month, as those Legislatures shall set apart? In the execution of the power contained in the before-recited clause of the Constitution, the State Legislatures are unquestionably the trustees of the People, in the absence of action by Congress; but they are liable to be controlled, or entirely superseded, whenever Congress does act. And, if I may be allowed a still further professional illustration, whatever particle of authority Congress does not assume over the subject, inheres in them as absolutely as the use and possession of an estate cohere in our law, except so far as they may be separated by the intervention of a power of appointment. And they are bound, as a part of their constitutional duty, to supply any defect which may be left in the regulations prescribed by Congress in this behalf, as fully, to all intents and purposes, as they are required to make regulations, out and out, if Congress shall leave the entire subject untouched. If there were nothing to confer this power on Congress but the word "alter," it signifies a change only in part; and what more literally corresponds with an alteration of the regulations of a State than declaring that, instead of one or five districts, it shall arrange as many districts as it has Representatives?

But we are told that we have no power to pass this law, because we cannot enforce its execution by penal sanctions; and an urgent appeal is made to us by the Senator from New Hampshire, (MR. WOODBURY) to know whether an armed force, or a writ of mandamus is to be sent to the State Legislatures to compel them to lay off the districts. No, sir, neither. No one ever conceived the idea of compelling a free Legislative Assembly to do, or not to do, any thing by physical force, or the precept of a court of justice. The crime of omission or commission in their constitutional duty, like that of parenticide among the Athenians, is provided with no legal sanction, but left to the oaths and consciences of men, to an accountability to make public opinion, and to that constituency whose rights have been outraged or neglected. The preservation of this Government greatly depends on the faithful fulfilment of the duties imposed by the Constitution on the State Legislatures. If a majority of them shall fail to elect Senators, (as one has done,) —if five or six of those in the largest States shall fail to make regulations for choosing electors of President and Vice President, in conformity to the laws of Congress, the Union would be as effectually dissolved as if we who are sent to the legislative halls of this Capitol should obstinately refuse to attend in our places, and pass the laws annually necessary for the support of the Government. It is faith, honor, conscience, and not the "hangman's whip," on which, at last, rest the blessings of this noblest human institution which has ever been devised for the security, the welfare and happiness of man. The duties of the States, under our Constitution, are not to be determined by their liability to punishment, but by the covenants into which they entered by that instrument. If, by the Constitution fairly construed, they covenanted to yield and conform their legislation to that of Congress in the regulation of elections, as I have endeavored to demonstrate, they are as sacredly bound to keep that agreement as if the world in arms stood ready to enforce it. And, in reply to the asseveration so often repeated, that we cannot issue a mandate to the State Legislatures, let me say, once for all, the Constitution issued the mandate fifty years ago that the legislation of the States in this particular might at any time be superseded by that of Congress, either wholly or in part only. Instead of issuing an unwarranted mandate to them, we do but pass a law, to which our common constituents, the People, speaking through the Constitution, require that their legislation should conform. But, although there is no method of compelling a State to action in the performance of her duty, yet if, when she has acted, her conduct be not conformable to the Constitution, or a law made in pursuance thereof, the act is simply void, and every tribunal before which it comes for adjudication is obliged so to declare it. If, therefore, notwithstanding the law, a State should return members according to general ticket, the House of Representatives, as judge of the election of its members, would be under the necessity of pronouncing the election a nullity. I speak of what would be the decision of the House, not only from its obligation to support the Constitution and laws, but because it has already decided. This bill comes to us with all the weight of authority which can be given to it by the approbation of the august assembly which is hereafter to expound and enforce it. In view of this, I have regretted to hear the intimations of Senators that certain States would not conform to it, but would elect by general ticket, and raise the question before the House. Much as I should regret to see the members of any State bringing up such a controversy in the House, so strong are my convictions of the importance of district representation to the country in all coming time, that I cannot withhold from it my approbation, from apprehensions of any such result. But, sir, when I look to the expectation, the desire, and the practice of the fathers of the Constitution in favor of the district system—the hold it already has in the minds of a great majority of the people; when I contemplate its beneficent effects in protecting the smaller States from possible combinations of the great, and the individuals from the oppressions of the mass, and remember the patriotism, forbearance, and devotion to the Union which characterize our State Legislatures, I cannot anticipate controversy in relation to the execution of this law; or, if it shall arise, I doubt not that it will be conducted and determined with the quietness, dignity, and mutual toleration so necessary to ascertain truth, and so salutary in preserving in their true essence, both the Federal and State authorities. In that spirit Congress now acts, in merely providing the mode of representation, but leaving all the details of interior arrangement to the Legislatures of the States, whose local knowledge and personal acquaintance will enable them to consult the popular convenience and the popular wish in the formation of districts in a far greater degree than can possibly be done here. All must at once perceive that this mode of interposition is the least exertion of the authority of this Government, and leaves the amplest field of power and discretion to the State Legislatures which is at all consistent with the great end proposed.

### *From W. R. Albright.*                                U.

Sandy Grove, N. C., 3d June, 1842.

I wish you to send me a copy of Mr. Poindexter's Report on the expenditures of the Publick Money, and also please state to me when it was, that the Appropriation of $6000 was made to furnish the President's House, was it at the Extra Session, or was it not at the latter part of the last Session under Mr. Van Burens Administration I have lost the time and wish to know it, it will be brought against us, as extravagant.

I also wish to know how much of it has been used, whether all or part only, I also wish to know how much was used in the purchase of Furniture for President Jackson in his 8 years, & how much in Mr. Van Burens 4 years, and any other information that you may think adviseable.

I must here be permitted to return you my thanks for the documents you have already sent me. Could you not send me another of Mr. Simmons[58] Speaches. You sent me one & I loaned it to some one & do not know who.

We will soon commence the Campaign with a greater zeal than I had expected. I was at Hillsboro Court last week, when & where each party made out Tickets as you have heard, I Expect, & I never saw the Whigs more sanguine in Orange. Governor More-

---

[58] James Fowler Simmons (1795-1864), of Rhode Island, manufacturer, United States senator, 1841-1847, 1857-1862.

head was there & he Addressed the people Effectually I thought; he is in fine health & spirits, no doubt of his election. Mr. Henry mistook our People he over Shot himself, it is no go. Mr. Henry has quit the Field for the moment on accnt. of bad health.

Mr. Mangum & yourself should use great industry in giving your friends in Orange information. Give them such Speakers as will furnish them with weapons to fight with, and Orange is safe, a desperate effort will be made by the Loco focos to Get a Majority in the next Legislature to turn you out of the Senate & put Mr. Brown back again; he is a Candidate for the Senate from Caswell, without opposition.

It is reported here that our fine Col Rencher has left us is it so, or do you know about it, how is his Health, Ort you not Adjourn and come home, these long Sessions of the Whigs & nothing done will ruin the Whig Cause. You ort to come home, I know it.

*From Henry K. Nash.* U.

Hillsboro', June 7th, 1842

I dislike very much troubling you as often as I have done lately, about matters in which you take little or no interest. I hope however that as the matter now on hand is not entirely uninteresting to you, you will pardon me for troubling you again. You have seen I suppose that I have been nominated as a Candidate for the next Assembly. It is my desire to prepare myself somewhat better than I am at present on those points that are likely to be brought before the People this Summer. We are resolved, I believe, to come out openly and boldly on the subject of a Bank, and to advocate it strenuously. That together with the Distribution Act, will be vigorously assailed by the Locos. They also intend to denounce Mr. Clay, and expect to do it with effect before the people. Proscription is also another one of their hobbies. I should be glad if you would send me any papers that you may think would be of service. I think we shall be able to beat them again this Summer.

*From Hugh Waddell.* U.

Hillsboro', June 8, 1842.

You have no doubt been much surprised at my obdurate silence & I am myself ashamed of it, but the truth is that I could not reply to either of yr. very kind letters without saying what I knew would be disagreeable to you & which on that account it gave me pain to say, viz. that my situation was such as to prevent me from again taking the field politically, & this I *must* have written if I wrote at all, up to our County Court, which is just over & during which a change of my resolution on this subject was brought about by several concurring circumstances, not the least of which was the wish you expressed & my confident belief that should I be successful it would be of ultimate benefit to you. Earnest wishes expressed at home, many letters from abroad, & on the very day on which your last arrived I recd. from the Chairman of the Central Committee of the State at Raleigh, a mandatory epistle which would take no refusal, all combined to overthrow my previous determination & when I found on Friday morning our friends would take no refusal I yielded, but even then, there was a trivial circumstance which had nearly determined me to refuse, but I will not trust it to the possibility of publicity by mentioning it here, as this may be opened or never reach you, but will tell you when we meet. There seems now much enthusiasm & several changes for us, viz, in the Hawfields Paisley Kilpatrick,[59] who will I hear go for me for the first time, Abel Griffis who is loud mouthed for the whole ticket, old Jas McRae, father of Geo. (who was so true before) & others. But the contest *must* be a very severe one & one of the purposes of this hasty line is to beg that you will furnish me with all the armour *defensive* & all arms *offensive* which can be had.

We shall be liable to assault on many points I fear, not so fatally however on the general or national questions, as on those of State policy. Many of our friends in the Legislature were induced I fear to go too far on sundry works of Improvement which cannot justify the expenditure in our day. Yet such is the enthusiasm of our people in the great National commotion, that these local matters will be soon forgotten & if we can rouse then as you did 2 years since we may carry all before us. My own notion is that the Whig Party has now no alternative, but to avow that Clay & a U. S. Bank, are both *indispensible* to the salvation of the Country; if I am right in this, give me the best argt. & most sucsinct view on the Bank question & I will prepare to maintain this "agst. all comers."

---

[59] Paisley Kirkpatrick.

Write me *at length* at yr. earliest convenience on all matters
which you deem important in this campaign for to speak truth
I have so thrown myself, *on purpose,* out of the way of these
things for 3 or 4 years past that I know nothing about them.

We are all gratified at the complimentary manner in which
both Mangum and yourself are spoken of in the papers & I really
thought the other day that we were going to be too big for our
breeches when I saw yr. name with a western gentleman as spoken
of for the Presidency of the Senate & then saw Mangum actually
receive it.

The last Register alluding to our Ticket called "Orange" a
glorious old County & so she is, to furnish 2 Senators in the U. S.
& have even a decent modicum of talent left for domestic use.

\* \* \* \* \*

*From John W. Norwood.* **U.**

Hillsborough,

June 13th, 1842.

Inclosed I send you the names of our Committees of Vigilance,
arranged not according to the appointment, that is by Captain's districts, but according to their Post Offices. We had a full
& encouraging meeting on Saturday of the Central Committee for
the County, by whom these Committees have been appointed.
And an Executive Committee, consisting of Dr. Strudwick, Dr.
Long,[60] & I, have been charged with preparing and addressing to
each Committeeman a printed Circular, encouraging them to the
contest, & briefly stating the principles & measures for which we
contend. This paper will immediately be issued. It would have
been well to have consulted you & Judge Mangum on the subject,
but with Waddell's assistance we must do what we can.

If we succeed in properly arousing the Whig party, we will
carry the whole ticket. And the movement, with regard to these
Committee of Vigilences, is mainly with the view of aiding in this
purpose. The recent defeats of our party all over the Country
have greatly elated the Democrats, & discouraged the Whigs, and
we have hard work to do; but it can be done. We will need, however, all the aid which you can give us, and I have by the direction of the executive Committee forwarded the names of the

---

[60] Dr. Osmond Long (1808-1864) was a well-known Orange County physician,

Committee men, hoping that our friends in Congress may have it in their power to help us by sending then to their proper post offices useful papers and information. My own impression is decidedly that the question of a National Bank can be made the most popular subject which has been used in Elections for years past. The Country is ripe for it—for the last six months I have put it to every Democratic client who has been in my office, & I sincerely believe they will not follow their party against that measure any longer, *if the subject is properly managed.*

The ticket which has been nominated does not give entire satisfaction, but the objections to the several individuals composing it (& especially Waddell) will be lost sight of long before the election. The ticket of the Democrats has given great dissatisfaction to the party.

It would be well for our friend Mangum to remember that if he is not particularly attentive to us, we will say he is getting above us.

We think it not presumptuous in us to expect the assistance of all our Whig friends in Congress from the State, for the fate of the Whigs in Orange is in every event important to us. And it is made the principal seat of attack by the other party.

This letter of course is intended for Judge Mangum as well as yourself, but I thought it would be rather formal to give it a joint direction.

We hear the most encouraging tidings from several parts of the County, & I think a fine spirit is getting up. . . . off this in great haste, but hope it will answer the purpose.

## [Enclosure]

Cannon Bowers, Thos. Brewer jr, Jas Bishop, (White Cross) Newman Cates, Goodman Neeils, Shiffy T. Lindsay, Chas. Nevill
   (Chapel Hill) Isaac Holt, Jno. Newlin, Jas: Robinson, Merritt
   Robinson, Oliver Newlin, Brian Carter, Peter Ferist (of Mary)
   (Lindley's Store)
   Jno. Stafford, Solomon Allen, Calvin Johnston, & Joshua Dixon
      (Snow Camp)
   Alex^r. Albright, Jerrimiah Piggott, Samuel Coble, W^m Eulis,
Eli. Eulis (Rock Creek)
   Dan: Albright Jno. S. Turrentine, Jno. C. Long, David L. Ray,
Joseph Holt, D^r Ben. A. Sellers, Jas Whitsett, W^m Rogers (Albright P. O.)

Jno. Freeland. Jno. Hardy, Nicholas Albright W^m N Ruffin, W^m Faust, W^m Rogers, (Haw River P. O)

Abel Griffis, Jas: Johnston, Willis Sellers, Henry Bason, Henderson Crawford, Stephen White (Trolinger's Bridge)

Handy Wood, Joseph Albright, Anderson Newson, (McDaniel's P O)

Absalom Harvey, Jas: Moore, Admund Brannock, Jno. W. Wilson, Thos: S. Swift (Moores Ville)

Jas: McCaddins, Stephen Glass, D^r. I. A. Craig, Richard Glass, Robert Thauson (of Jno) Robt. F. White, Saml. Cain (Haw River)

Alex^r. KirkPatrick (Haw Fields) Capt. W^m Bradsher (Mt Willing)

Alex^r. Dixon, Geo Ray, Iv. Barlow, Saml. R. Wood Richard Breeze, Felix Wilson, W^m Barlow, Person Nichols (Walnut Grove)

Andrew Murdock, Adam Duglass, Allen Brown, Jno: Walker, Jas: Roberts (Hillsborough)

Elis: Holden, Arch^d Cain, Jesse Lewis (Eno Mills)

Green D. Jordon, Lemuel Mebane, Jno. A. Mebane, Jo. Tate, Wilson Watson Thos: McCracken (Major Hale) Hugh Wilson (Haw Fields P O).

Gabriel B. Lea, Jno Barnwell, Eli Murray, W^m Vincent, Saml. Hargrave, W^m Murray, (Pleasant Grove)

Chesley F. Faucett, Geo. Hurdle, Jas: Grahams, Thos: Grahams, Bennett Hazell, Geo Wallace (Faucett's Store)

Revd Enoch Crutchfield John        Mud Lick.


*From William A. Johnson.*                          U.

Granville, June 15th, 1842.

As the time of our State elections is drawing near our democratic friends are crowing somewhat loudly and taunting us with haveing made charges of extravagance and corruption against the State administration, which we either could not, or dare not attempt to sustain by authentick proof; and haveing seen in the newspapers the report of the committee on publick expenditures in House of Representatives, and some notices of the report of the commissioners appointed to investigate the affairs of the custom house in New York, which go very far towards fastening upon them all the charges made by the Whigs, I have to request that you will do me the favour, to procure and send on to me as speedily as possible a copy of each of those reports, as well as the report of the retrenchment committee appointed by the house if it can be obtained.

On Saturday last at a Battalion Muster in this County Genl. McClanahan, backed and supported by his co-labourers, made a regular, and I conceive a most reckless onslaught upon the Whigs, charging that, instead of the retrenchment and reform which they had promised, they had run the government in debt $14,000,000; and that $15,000 had been appropriated to defray the expenses incured by the Whig committee for electioneering purposes, and said he had the proof; this was news to me, and I hope you will be so good as to furnish me with some information upon the subject in a private communication.

If it will not be taxing your goodness too much I would be exceedingly obliged to you in the same communication to give me the names of all the democratic senators who supported the appropiation to Mrs. Harrison and the bankrupt law.

Be pleased to ask Mr. Mangum if one certain William Russell [61] did not solicit his aid in obtaining an office under Harrison's administration, and to state if he pleases the grounds upon which the said William based his claims; I should not have troubled you or the Judge with this last request but for the fact that the said William is a candidate and making much noise in these parts.

*From Jesse Turner.*                                                   U.

Van Buren, Ark.,

June 15th, 1842.

I thank you for the copy of your able and interesting speech on the Loan Bill, delivered in the Senate during the present Session of Congress, which came to hand a few days ago. The measure was doubtless called for by the emergencies of the Country and should have rec'd the support of all parties. You seem to have an extremely anomalous state of things at Washington, or to use the appropriate language of Mr. Clay, "President without a party, and a party without a President."

---

[61] William Russell was elected to the commons at the election which followed.

This deplorable state of things, the disappointment of our fondest hopes, and the bitter reflection that our great triumph of 1840 has utterly failed thus far in yielding us the fruits which we anticipated, through the defection and treachery of our chosen Vice President, seems to have had a most paralyzing and unpropitious effect upon the spirits and energy of our party. A succession of disasterous defeats in the State elections has been the consequence. Whether we can recover from this tremendous paralysis by 1844 is questionable. With that great and gallant leader, Henry Clay, for our Candidate, I hope we shall be able once more to reinstate our party and cause upon the elevated ground which we occupied on the 4th. March 1841. I am pleased to see that my native State takes the lead in presenting the name of Mr. Clay to the nation. The old North State is now appreciated. Several of her first men are in the Councils of the Country, and it is understood that she thinks and acts for herself, uninfluenced by her imperious neighbors. But I fear Mr. Stanly, who is a favorite with the Whigs through the Country, is not acquitting himself well in his affair with Wise. It strikes me that, under the circumstances, he should neither have apologized, nor accepted an apology. *His distinguished Sire could not have acted thus.*

I should be most happy to hear from you often and should you see any of my friends when you return to "old Orange" please give them my respects. Remember me to my early friend Mr. Mangum, and believe me

Your friend truly

Jesse Turner

of Hawfields.

*From Jesse H. Lindsay.*[62]                                    U.

Greensboro, N. C.,

June 22nd, 1842.

The Citizens of Greensboro, having met in the Court House, on motion of Gen. Jno. M. Logan,[63] Jesse H. Lindsay was called to the Chair, who explained the object of the meeting, to take

[62] Jesse Harper Lindsay (1808-1886), a graduate of the university, cashier of the Greensboro branch of the Bank of Cape Fear, a member of the commons, 1835-1838, of the state senate, 1844. He was a leading citizen of the town, with many business interests.

[63] John McClintock Logan (1797-1853), a native of Ireland, merchant, town officer, and major general of militia.

into consideration the sudden and unexpected cutting down of
the mail from Raleigh to Greensboro. On motion of Jno. A.
Gilmer,[64] Dr. D. P. Weir[65] was appointed Secretary of the meeting.

Jno. A. Gilmer submitted the following preamble & resolutions, to wit:

Whereas the convenience and necessities of the community
satisfactorily shewn to the Post office department in the year
1838 induced the head of that department to increase our mail
facilities by giving us a daily mail from Raleigh to Greensboro,
with which we were well pleased and much benefited.

Whereas the route was bid off by gentlemen, then strangers to
us but who we had well hoped would have conveyed the mail
thereon with the ordinary regard to the public convenience and
their own credit and profit.

Whereas we believe there were other men, had it not been for
the interference of the present contractory, who would have
taken the contract on terms essentially as favorable to the department and in the discharge of the duties thereof have met the
wishes of the community and the government.

Whereas in pain and disappointment we have witnessed the
gradual diminution of our mail facilities—but the alterations heretofore being to a small extent, altho' not consulted by the contractors in relation thereto, we had not complained, but having
with great astonishment learned for the first time that the contractors have succeeded by their individual representations or
otherwise, in getting the route cut down to a tri-weekly mail.

And whereas we learn that the new arrangement will destroy
all connection with the other mails heretofore in connection at
our town, and in truth owing to the arrivals at Raleigh give us
but two Northern mails per week.

Therefore, it is unanimously resolved by the citizens of Greensboro' that the public convenience requires a daily instead of a
tri-weekly mail from Raleigh to Greensboro'.

Resolved further, that the causes and circumstances that induced the alteration from a tri-weekly to a daily mail remain
the same.

Resolved further, that it is the opinion of this meeting that

[64] John Adams Gilmer (1805-1868), lawyer, state senator, 1846-1856, Whig candidate for governor, 1856, member of congress, 1857-1861, where he quickly rose to
prominence. He declined a seat in Lincoln's cabinet, and was a member of the
Confederate congress, 1864-1865. He was a delegate to the National Union convention, 1866.

[65] D. P. Weir was treasurer of the Greensboro Mutual Life Insurance Company.

the Hon. Post Master General in giving his sanction to this alteration was either misled by interested individuals for an individual purpose, or misinformed as to the wishes and convenience
of the Community.

Resolved farther, that in executing mail contracts public convenience should rather be consulted than private interest, and
that good faith requires the original contract to be fulfilled.

Resolved further, that a copy of these proceedings, signed by
the Chairman and Sec'ty be forwarded to the Post Master General
thro' our Honorable Senators Messrs. Mangum and Graham,
and our immediate representative the Hon. A. H. Shepperd with
a request to them to call the attention of the department to
the importance of our office, not only to us, and the surrounding country, but being a distributing office to all the Western
and South Western part of the State, and use their influence to
re-instate this contract—which, on motion, was unanimously
adopted.

D. P. Weir, Sec'ry.

### *From James T. Littlejohn.*[66]          U.

Oxford, June 23rd, 1842.

Mr. Johnson (our late Senator & now the Whig Candidate) has
just left me and at his request I trouble you with this communication.

Mr. J. I hope will not be hard run. I hope & think he will be
easily elected. A better Whig never was & it would be much to
be regretted were he not elected. He has our old friend Elijah
Hester[67] to contend with, who bye the bye, is not easily to be
beaten. Johnson says he is in want of some public documents,
such as the Report of the Committee on Public Expenditures,"
Report of Commissioners (Poindexter's) investig. Custom Ho,"
Report Committee on Retrenchment"—and indeed any documents or speeches that you think will be of service to him. Something on the 'Restriction of the Veto' would not be amiss.

I have paid so little attention myself to what has been spoken
in Congress this session, that I am unable to select matter best
calculated to aid us in our Canvass. I should however like a

---

[66] James T. Littlejohn, of Oxford, who was a member of the commons in 1844.

[67] Elijah Hester was a member of the commons, 1835, 1838, and of the state senate,
in 1842.

Copy of Meriwether's[68] speech, as well as one for Johnson, if to be had.

We have a full ticket on both sides. I think with industry & proper management, the whole Whig Ticket can be elected. Gilliams quitting I dont think has injured us as much as our friends were afraid of. My own opinion is, that we can elect the whole ticket as easily without him as with him, if proper exertions are made, though G's place as a Speaker cannot be supplied & his own election was certain, but what we have lost in him individually is supplied by the locality of the present ticket.

Since commencing I have concluded to make this a joint letter to you and Mr. Rayner, and will beg the favour of you both to send to Mr. Johnson, at Dutchville P. O. Granville Cty the desired papers, and such others as you may think he will need. I think Mr. J. said he had written to one of you, but desired I would write to you both.

I think Morehead will beat Henry about 7,500.


*From Weston R. Gales.*                                                A.

Raleigh,

July 1, 1842.

I have just received your last favor, and merely drop this line to say, that you are doing more than all our Members of Congress together, to enlighten the public mind, and I so stated to the Central Committee yesterday, without committing you to any particular act.

Waddell, who was present, confirmed the statement. By the bye, he seems sanguine of success, not only for himself, but the whole Ticket.

It is a singular fact, that with the exception of your brother James, and yourself, I have not received a line from any Whig Member, the present Session. The facts you have disclosed to me, particularly the items in regard to the Bankrupt Laws and Fisher's Bank Bill, have produced a very favorable effect. The latter I shall continue to harp on. I have an article in today's Register, with an extract from the Report, which I find in print, but it is

[68] David Meriwether (1800-1893), of Kentucky, a native of Virginia, trader, farmer, lawyer. Democratic member of the lower house of the legislature, 1832-1845, 1858-1885, (speaker 1859), delegate to convention of 1849, state secretary of state, 1851, United States senator, 1852, governor of New Mexico, 1853-1855.

a little singular that neither the Bill or Report can be found in the Archives of State, nor, indeed, can any other document of importance, bearing Fisher's impress.

As Mark Britain would say, it looks *ominous*. My inability to find these papers, delayed a notice of the matter. Waddell has been furnished with the Report, Journal, etc., and thinks Santee—Ann a case.

The gentlemen of the Bar from various parts of the State, in attendance upon the Supreme Court, give the most encouraging accounts of the prospect. The only County from which we really hear bad news is *Craven,* which seems disposed fairly to entitle herself to the name. No Whig Candidate is yet out, though John H. Bryan says the County is certainly Whig.

The Central Committee have written to Atmore, but had not Mr. Washington better interest himself in the matter.

We hear that Wadsworth[69] will run, if a full Ticket is started, not otherwise. It will be a burning shame to let the Loco Focos take a *snap judgment* against us there.

Morehead is carrying every thing before him in the West. He says, Henry will never meet him again.

*From John F. Poindexter.*                                          U.

Germanton, July the 1st, 1842.

I have for some time been thinking of writing to you, but have put it off from time to time hoping to find something that would interest and please you; nothing of the kind has yet transpired. Our people here are becoming a good deal excited upon the subject of the pending elections. Gov. Morehead delivered a speech on last Monday in this County, I was not present but am told that his speech was a good one and was well received. The Gov. has gone West and is to address the people every day or nearly every day between this and the election.

In this County the Whig ticket for the Legislature is not yet filled. Dr. Wm. Withers[70] is a candidate for the Senate and Dr. William Walker for the Commons—please furnish them with such papers as they may use with advantage.

---

[69] William B. Wadsworth, of New Bern, had been a member of the commons, 1838-1839, and was again a member, 1848. He was state senator, 1862.

[70] Dr. William Withers, of Stokes, had been a member of the commons in 1840.

I think in a few days we shall complete our ticket, but by whom I am not yet advised. I have been trying to bring out friend Shober,[71] and I think he is somewhat in the notion. Matthews[72] & Covington[73] were nominated by the Whigs, but decline being Candidates, I think Matthews would have yielded to the wishes of his friends, but that he had the misfortune two weeks ago to lose a brother, who died of fever. Covington, I believe will not run.

I do not think that we have lost any thing in this County, but believe that if we can manage to get our people excited as heretofore, we will be able to do as well as we have done for the last four years. Some of the moderate Whigs have become somewhat dissatisfied on account of Captain Tyler's treachery, but they will still vote with us if they are properly attended to, and we will endeavour to have that done.

It is possible you will hear from me again when we shall have completed our ticket.

Please present my respects to Mr. Shepperd and say to him that I will write to him in a few days.

*To Samuel F. Patterson.*[74]        U. Lindsay Patterson Mss.

Washington City,

July 7th, 1842.

I owe you an apology for not earlier replying to your letter. Mr. Forward requested that I would wait untill the 1st. of July, when I first applied to him, and when that time arrived he had gone to Philadelphia. I now enclose you his letter; the terms are not inviting, and I have concluded not to go into a loan. With the wretched, vacillating man at the head of our affairs, there is no certainty that any duty bill will pass at this Session, which will escape a veto. And if Congress shall adjourn without providing means to meet our liabilities, the stock must depreciate much. In the state of uncertainty, therefore, which exists, I do not think

---

[71] Probably Emmanuel Shober, state senator, 1819-1820, 1822, 1824, 1827-1828.
[72] Caleb H. Matthews had been a member of the commons, 1835-1838.
[73] James M. Covington had been a member of the commons, 1836-1840.
[74] Samuel Finley Patterson (1799-1874), of Wilkes, (now Caldwell), a native of Virginia, who came to North Carolina in 1814. Long a legislative clerk, he was state treasurer, 1835-1837, president of the Bank of the State, president of the Raleigh and Gaston Railroad, state senator, 1846-1848, 1864-1865, member of the commons, 1854-1855, delegate to the convention of 1865. He was grand master of Masons, 1833-1834. He was also a most successful farmer.

U. S. loans a desirable investment, and would not go into it at par.

I would be glad to obtain 20 shares of stock in the Bank of the State N. C. if it can be had at par. If you can without inconvenience effect such a purchase for me, I will be obliged.

Congress will sit untill the first of August—possibly longer. The vacillating papers which have heretofore supported Mr. Tyler, are now denouncing him, and I think it impossible to avoid a rupture in his Cabinet.

[*Enclosure.*]

*From W. Forward.*

Treasury Department,

July 7th, 1842.

I have the honor to acknowledge the receipt of your favor of the 6th inst.

All the negotiations made by this Department, for Stock under the loan act of the 15th of April 1842, have been made at par, where the offers were for sums under one million. I am not prepared to depart from such terms.

Upon a receipt of a certificate of deposite in the Bank of Virginia, at Norfolk, or the Bank of the Metropolis, at Washington certificates of stock for a corresponding amount, will be issued to the order of your friend.

I regret that the arrangements of, and requisitions upon this Department, will not allow of such deposit in any of the Banks of North Carolina, but I trust that in selecting the nearest depositories of the government, such facilities will be afforded, as will enable your friend to make the desired investment.

I am with great respect
Your obd't serv't

*From J. H. Long*                                                        U.

July 7, 1842.

I have only time (while the mail waits) to observe. That of all Measures ever adopted by Congress since the Alien & Sedition

Law, I firmly believe the Bank-rupt Law is at this time the most Odious in the estimation of all classes of Men having any pretensions to honesty.

Its not only so hereabouts but as far as my travels or acquaintance has extended. It is doing more to allay the zeal of Whigs than every thing else. Tho I believe there is as many Whigs in this State as ever and it will be so found if they can be got to the polls.

Can't the Bank-rupt Law be repealed forth-with?

You have no Idea of its abuse. If suffered to opperate 'till another session it will do Incalculable injury to the honest and indulgent Creditors throughout the Country.

### From John A. Barnett.                    A.

#### Roxboro,

#### July 8th, 1842.

I have taken the field against Mr. Williams & I think with a tolerable prospect of success If I can obtain a little assistance from You; the assistance I need is a few documents relative to what has been the course heretofore persued by the Government towards Publice officers who have died in the service of the Government as the principle charge here against The Whigs is the donation to Mrs. Harrison & particularly against You as You voted for it; another Charge against You is that You refused to refund to Gen'l Jackson by Your vote the thousand dollar fine by a New Orleans Judge.

I tell the people I am perfectly willing for Gen'l Jackson to have the money refunded to him & that I believe You are also providing the bill refunding it does not censure the Court that imposed the fine. Mr. Williams stated that You so cloged the bill with amendments that the democrats themselves could not vote for it.

I think Mr. Choate in a Speech he delivered in Congress refered to several Cases where Congress had made handsome donations to officers who had died in the Service of the Government & as I Cannot now lay my hand upon it please send it to me. If I mistake not there were some democrats who voted for the donation to Mrs. Harrison; please give me their names & the States they reside in.

I wish You to write to me informing me what Course You are willing to persue relative to the $1000. fine; I would prefer Your writing a letter I could publically use; If you think proper to send any document or make any Communications to me please direct them (under cover) to George A. Smith, Milton N. C.

Your Compliance with the foregoing request will much Oblige

Your friend.

*From Giles Mebane.*                                            **U.**

White Oak, July 10th, 1842.

We have come over the County as far as Turrentine; the gathering is there tomorrow. So far there is an increased Whig strength & a manifest want of harmony & confidence among *locos*. When *rogues* fall out, etc. I have no time for the amusing incidents. One specimen must suffice. We have drenched them with *Henry's bitters* until confession is had from them that Henry is only taken as *a choice of evils*. The *File Leader* leads in evil & that evil is tied to a dog's tail, as the *gallant Henry* said he was in Hillsborough.

We are under great obligation to you for doc's. No one complains of your sending them but the old file Leader he thinks it mighty hard that Mr. Graham should furnish the people information when his election comes on next Winter. He is the only one that has said He would vote against you & he only to get such a good democrat as *Bedford*.[75]

I think now we shall carry the whole ticket triumphant. I send you enclosed one dollar for the True Whig.

Eli McDaniel, P. M., near your friend Michael Albright, who has named his son after you, says Eli will not let him have the papers you send him until they have lain in the office weeks. The office is of little use I understand & might be abolished. Eli intends moving this Fall if his creditors will let him. Such a Miscreant ought not to be P. M.

Can you not pass bank bill after bank bill & revenue bill after revenue bill until his accidency shall pile up a mountain of *Vetoes* that will make his throne shake under him? The people will surely sustain Congress against a *petty tyrant*.

---

[75] Bedford Brown.

*From  Charles  L.  Hinton.*                    A.

Raleigh,

July 12th, 1842.

Yours of the 9th. was recd. last evening. I shall write to Gov. Morehead by tomorrows mail inclosing your letter to me togeather with a letter from the Sec. of the Treasury which has been recd. since he left for the mountains. I think it probable he will authorise me to go on; if so I shall have the pleasure of seeing you in Washington.

I send you a letter from the Gov. to his Secretary which will give you an idea of his feelings on the election. I dont believe any Loco calculates on Henry's success. We have thought the Legislature somewhat doubtful but are more sanguine at this time, indeed we feel pretty safe. The Whigs are more roused than I expected to have seen them. During the present term of the Supreme Court, men from every quarter have been here, and general determination among the Whigs to do their best, but they say some of our Congressmen dont aid them as much as they might, particularly Mangum who they suppose has more leisure since his late elevation, a letter from a distance has a great tendency to spur up, and a document among the Country people is read through a neighborhood circle. Your Brother's circular is a *most excellent* document, like all his circulars it is peculiarly adapted to the rank and file.

It is now 5 o'clk, I have just left Rayner—poor fellow he is as badly scared as tho' he were to be led to the gallows at 8 o'clk which is the appointed hour for him, tho' he says he will *try* and get there.[76]

We shall have a large party; all the old Lady's children have *convened.*

13th.

Rayner is *certainly* married, a very large party. Had you not better ascertain whether the Treasurer pays off the amt. due the States and write me, as it would be unnecessary to go on without a probability of getting the money.

--------
[76] This was his wedding day.

*From Frederick J. Hill.* U.

Pittsboro,

July 13th, 1842.

Your esteemed favor of the 22nd. ulto. directed to Wilmington reached me at this place and I thank you for it as well as for the accompanying Doc't.

I do not know that I can add anything to the intelligence which I doubt not you receive from your numerous corrispondents in the State; but as I had the pleasure of hearing the Orange candidates a few days since; I cannot forego the pleasure of stating to you the *decided advantage* they obtain at every point where they meet their competitors. Old St'a Ann carrys a consciousness of defeat in his cadaverous visage, and sanguine expectations are entertained of the success of the whole Whig Ticket. Mebane is a most efficient campaigner, quite equal I think to our friend Waddell. Squire Stafford and Mr. Isaac Holt heard the candidates on four seperate days, and concur in the opinion above stated.

As to the Gov's Election no fears are expressed, no doubt seems to exist, but I am not as confident of carrying the Assembly ticket, much the most important one in my estimation. Northhampton, Craven, Bertie, Stokes and Granville and in the order in which they are enumerated are the doubtful counties. I know nothing however calculated to excite alarm which is unknown to you except perhaps that we have a very weak Ticket in North Hampton and the Dem'ts a strong one; of my own prospects I can say nothing only that I have been absent since the 10th. June and do not expect to be present again before the 1st. August. You will perceive too that Mr. Tyler has thrown the weight of his name (or rather that which hangs around the office he accidentally fills) into the canvass to my prejudice; his letter, however, contains a spurious evasion of the statement made by me to my constituents, and altho' from an attentive Perusal of the same he does not deny my statement yet to a cursory reader it is such; and so I must construe and answer it. I stated to the People of Brunswick that he, Mr. Tyler, while at the Harrisburg Convention (not in Convention but in conversation) stated to Gov'r Owen and myself that his views on the Bank question had undergone a change and that his constitutional objections he thought ought to yield to the various Executive Legislations and Individual discussions of the question. I further stated that he was a zealous advocate of the claims of Mr. Clay to the nomination of the Convention.

The death of Gov'r Owen deprives me of the strongest Testimony in the case, altho' I think I have sufficient to establish the fact. Among your Congressional acquaintances can you furnish any thing bearing upon the matter. 'Tis probable, I think, that Mr. Archer[77] was acquainted with the views of Mr. Tyler; please make enquiry of him or Mr. Boardman[78] of Connecticut, or any other member of Congress who was at the Convention; where I am known I doubt not my statement will be fully vindicated, but as it is a question of veracity I desire it settled beyond the reach of cavil. I have already replied to the letter but as the controversy may be continued I wish to be fully prepared.


*From Daniel S. Hill.*                                          U.

Louisburg No. C.,

July 14th, 1842.

It is very important that we should be prepared to meet the Loco-focos in Franklin on the Tariff Question & on the enomous expenditures of the Present Whig Congress. If you could forward me the reports of Committees of Retrenchment made by Summers[79] of Va., Stanly, & others, your Speech on the Loan Bill (I think it is I thot I had it in the Intelligencer but cant find it) two or three copies of yr Bro' Circular on the subject of the appropriation to Mrs. Harrison. On the Tariff will you do me the favor to give me some of yr. views on the subject. The L Focos charge the Whigs with Voting to Tax the consumers of the south for necessaries & blankets, etc. Please refer me to some speech or Document by which we can turn the tables upon them by showing the similarity between the Tariff the Whigs propose &

---

[77] William S. Archer of Virginia.

[78] William Whiting Boardman (1794-1871), of Connecticut, a graduate of Yale, studied law at Harvard and Litchfield. He was a member and speaker of the lower house of the legislature, 1836-1839, 1845, 1849, 1851. He was a Whig member of congress, 1840-1843.

[79] George W. Summers (1804-1868), of Virginia, educated at Washington College, (now Washington and Lee University) and Ohio University, began the practice of law in Charleston. He was a member of the house of delegates, 1830-1832, 1834-1836, a Whig member of congress, 1841-1845, a delegate to the convention of 1850, and to the peace conference, 1861.

Woodbury's recommendation While Sec. of Treasury, & the fact that V. B. Expended $7,000,000 annually more than his recpts while the Tariff was double what is now under the compromise bill.

Excuse the liberty I have taken in troubling you as well as the hurried manner of adressing you; we are trying to run a Whig through from Franklin & have no doubt if matters continue as they are but that we shall succeed. The Excitement of 1840 will be nothing to compare with the enthusiasm that the Mill Boy lights up in the hearts of the Whigs of the *old North*. The Whigs are every where in high spirits & determining to do their duty on the 4th. Augst.; they are certain of a Whig Legislature Whig Governor & Whig Senator.

I am in hopes you all will come home before August. for I believe that the success of Mr. Clay in '44 depends upon the vote No. C. gives in Augst.

*From Edwin G. Reade.*[80]                    U.

Roxboro, July 16th, 1842.

I am so much pleased myself at the fair prospects we have of electing two Whigs from Person that I supposed the news would not be altogether uninteresting to you.

Little John Barnett—as he is generally called—opposes Williams[81] in the Senate & although I do not think his election *certain* yet I think it *very probable.*

There is not much difference between the Whig & dem. vote in the Senate & Williams cannot unite his party. When Williams speaks of the apropriation to the widow Harrison Barnett tells him of his $10,000 vote to the Wake Forest Institute & this ruins him with the Hardshell Baptists.

Barnett manages the canvass remarkably well. He has hardly a personal enemy in the county & some who will not vote for him will not vote vs him. Two years ago Williams solicited

[80] Edwin Godwin Reade (1812-1894), of Person County, farmer, lawyer, American (Know-Nothing) M. C., 1855-1857, was elected a delegate in 1861 to the convention which the people refused to call. He was appointed to the Confederate senate in 1864 to fill a vacancy. He was a judge of the superior court, 1864-1865, delegate and president of the convention of 1865, and associate justice of the state supreme court, 1865-1878.

[81] Probably John W. Williams, the incumbent, who served, 1838-1842. He was a delegate to the convention of 1835.

Hester[82] to oppose our sherriff. Hester did so & Williams did not vote for him. I understand he thereby loses the Hester influence which is considerable.

There are four democratic candidates in the Commons. Jones,[83] Chambers,[84] Hiram Saterfield,[85] & John A. Holloway,[86] One Whig, James Holman[87] who is decidedly the best informed man on politicks in the county. He makes a strong farmer-like speech about an hour long which tells remarkably. He knows every thing that has been done for a number of years & who did it. If all the dem. candidates hold on there is *no doubt* of his election. They have tried very hard to call off two but they have hitherto failed. They cannot unite on any two, & if they could I should then think Holman's chances very fair.

If we can elect two Whigs I shall greatly rejoice for more reasons than one but chiefly for one.

James Graham's address is very satisfactory & is of service to us. Every body says Morehead will be elected.

The contest in Granville is doubtful I fear we shall lose our ticket.

Mr. Norwood informed me that they were doing well in Orange; probably the whole Whig ticket would succeed Henry Nash's election thought to be certain. He seems to take *very well.*

If you have any thing that would help on our candidates please forward it to them.

*From Samuel F. Patterson.*                    U.

Raleigh, July 20th, 1842.

\*     \*     \*     \*     \*

Our political contest is waxing pretty warm. In this County we have a most beautiful Dog fight between old Sam Whitaker[88] and J. B. Shepard. They have been quarreling ever since the

---

[82] Robert H. Hester, who was state senator, 1844-1850, and a member of the commons, 1856-1858.

[83] Robert Jones was a member of the commons, 1832-1835, 1838-1840.

[84] Moses Chambers, member of the commons, 1836-1840.

[85] Hiram Satterfield of Person, member of the commons, 1842.

[86] John A. Holloway, member of the commons, 1842.

[87] James Holeman, member of the commons, 1846-1848, 1852-1854, state senator, 1862-1864, 1865.

[88] Samuel Whitaker, had served in the commons, 1822-1830, and in the state senate, 1834-1840. He was not elected in 1842.

campaign opened and every day I understand it gets worse and worse. On Monday one of Whitaker's sons struck Shepard whilst he was speaking publicly in consequence of some epithet which he applied to his father.

To day I learn that Mr. W. H. Haywood has gone to Busbee's (the place of the tax gathering) with the avowed purpose of taking the hide off Shepard, from neck to heel, for some remarks which Shepard is said to have made in his public speeches about Haywood and also about his father-in law Mr. Graham.[89]

It is understood that Haywood is decidedly opposed to Shepard and as decidedly in favour of Whitaker. Hence the cause of Shepard's attack upon him.

Our Candidate in the Senate old Natty Warren[90] as they call him, glides along very smoothly and avoids as much as possible being drawn into a controversy with either of the others, which I think is decidedly the best plan. Should both the democrats hold on, of which there seems now to be no doubt, Mr Warren will certainly be elected, and our Candidate for the Commons (Dr. Hicks) [91] is very sanguine of his election also.

The last accounts from Orange were very favorable. The Whigs are in high spirits and seem confident of success.

I understand that a few days ago at a public gathering while Mr. C. Jones was addressing the people and pretending to read from some document (one of Gov Morehead's speeches I believe) evidence to sustain his position, Mr. G. Mebane detected and convicted him of reading it falsely and perverting entirely the meaning of the evidence relied on. Mebane exposed the trick to the people which I understand had a most powerful effect.

In some of the Western Counties we hear our friends are managing badly. In Wilkes particularly they have out too many Whig candidates and consequently two Locos have come out, who unless some arrangement can be made to induce a part of the Whigs to withdraw, I fear will be elected. I have to day written several letters to my friends there to endeavor to produce some better understanding among the Whigs, and Mr. Badger has also written with the same view. I hope sincerely some accommodation will be effected before the election comes on.

---

[89] Edward Graham (1765-1833), a native of New York, a graduate of Princeton, who studied law under John Jay, and settled at New Bern. He became a distinguished lawyer. He was a borough member of the commons, in 1797.

[90] Warren failed of election.

[91] Dr. Hicks was also defeated.

The Governor was at Lincolnton on Saturday the 16th, was to be at Morganton yesterday, and is to be at Statesville tomorrow. All accounts from him are of the most cheering character, and we have now no doubt of his election by a large majority.

Henry's letter has dispirited and dissatisfied his party very much, and they are now abusing each other for having brought out opposition at all. Your brother's circular I think will do great good to our Cause. It is indeed a most excellent document just at this time, and is the very thing our people wanted. I wish it had come out a little earlier; I fear it will not get into circulation as extensively as it ought to do.

I am glad to find that the House has passed the Tariff bill, and hope you will be equally successful in the Senate. I believe that nothing but reasonable protection to our own manufactorys & an old fashioned U S Bank well restricted in its provisions will ever bring our matters straight again.

I did not however sit down to write a letter on politics and will therefore conclude.

by subscribing myself,<br>
Very respectfully,<br>
Your obt. Servt.

*From John M. Morehead.*          U.

Salisbury,

July 24th, 1842.

I am this far on my way Eastward, canvassing as I go, according to my appointments advertised in the Whig papers.

I was West as far as Franklin (Macon) but could not visit Cherokee & have time to return to Rutherford Court, nor could I visit Yancey.

The politics of the whole West is sound, I think, decidedly improved from Publicity beyond the mountains.

I understand that Mr. Calhoun reported at Washington that Henry was seen to be elected, & as Mr. Fisher is there now, I suppose there will be confirmation.

I profess to be no prophet, but I will hazard this prediction: If the vote of the State is as large as in 1840, say 80,000, I will beat my opponent *at least* 10,000; if 60,000 I will beat him 8,-000.

I think we shall secure the Legislature, but our friends do badly in some parts of the State. I have done every thing I could in my part of the State to try to secure the Legislature, but in some Counties I could not get things arranged as I wished.

But we shall secure the Legislature.

I cannot get ten minutes to write a letter day or night; we are as enthusiastic as in 1840.

I write to thank you in the name of the Whigs of N. C. & of the U. S. for your very opportune circular; it is reprinted and largely circulated.

It is just what it should be.

Shew this to your brother, with my respects. I have not time to write him—almost broke down—but feel like I shall hold out until the election.


*From William H. Owen.*[92]                                    U.

Chapel Hill,

July 25th., 1842.

My Dear Friend;

For, if you will allow me honour, I shall never feel disposed to apply a colder epithet to you. The generous recommendation which you gave of me to the Trustees of William and Mary has impressed me with lasting gratitude.

The kind exertions of several friends of yourself, in particular, had placed success almost beyond doubt, as I inferred from two communications from President Dew, and other intelligence which I received from William and Mary. My sanguine expectations of success were shared by my friends at this place; but when the golden prize was almost within my grasp, I felt constrained, both by duty and inclination to withdraw my application, in consequence of the irreconcilable opposition of my Mother and Sisters, particularly of the former, who was firmly impressed with the belief that the climate of Williamsburg would be fatal to the family. Several of my friends, (among them Mr. H. Waddell, & Pro. Green) expressed similar apprehensions, and the latter, as well as Mr. Hooper, advised me to withdraw my application. On consideration of the foregoing motives, I indulge the hope that

---

[92] William Hayes Owen, a graduate of the university, who served as a tutor, 1835-1843. He was a professor thereafter at Wake Forest College.

you will attribute my course neither to fickleness, nor to any want of a proper appreciation of the kind exertions of my friends.

Before I conclude, I wish to make a remark personal to yourself. I did hope that your public conduct, admirable in all that becomes a Senator, would gain for you the approbation of every member of the Whig party, at least; but such is not the case. I have learned from authentic sources that there is a strong disposition to run Judge B—r against you,—and what do you think is the charge against you, why—prudence!! excessive prudence, degenerating into selfishness, for fear of compromising yourself. I know of but one other instance of Prudence being considered a blemish, viz: Gen'l Lee, when rebuked by Gen'l W. for his retreat at the battle of Monmouth, replied that he had been taught by his Excellency some of that "rascally virtue called Prudence." But, "Nullum numen ab est, si sit Prudentia." You are not at liberty to mention the foregoing information in connection with my name—it might compromise me. You see that I, too, have learned a little prudence.

If the hint I have given you shall occasion uneasiness, rather than impart desirable information, I shall regret having given it, and can only plead friendly concern for your political interests.

There is but little news at this place. The Institution has resumed its operations, under more favorable auspices than were anticipated at the end of the last Session. We have nearly 170 Students.

The President will make a Northern tour in the beginning of the fall,—Prof. Roberts retires in October, and the Rev. Mr. Deems[93] is to come into the Faculty, with the title of Assistant Prof. of Rhetoric. . . .

The foregoing, printed pages will, I hope sufficiently explain themselves.

I am with sentiments of exalted regard, & warm friendship,

Your obliged humble Serv't

---

[93] Charles Force Deems (1820-1893), a native of Baltimore, graduate of Dickinson College, a Methodist minister, who came to North Carolina as an agent of the American Bible Society. He was a professor in the university, 1842-1848, and at Randolph-Macon College, 1850-1851, held pastorates, and taught in several places. In 1865 he went to New York, and established and edited *The Watchman*, a newspaper designed to promote reunion, and was pastor of the Church of the Strangers. He was a prolific writer. He was instrumental, through his intimacy with Mr. Vanderbilt, in the founding of Vanderbilt University.

[*Attached Letter.*] [94]

CHAPEL HILL,                               1842.

DEAR SIR,

I have conceived the plan of opening a Female Boarding School
in the family of my Mother, and have chosen this method of
communicating our views, because it allows us to do so with
greater familiarity than is compatible with a newspaper notice,
although the latter has the advantage of giving more extensive
publicity, and also that of being a better vehicle for the circulation of certificates and references. But in regard to these I will
at present only remark, that, so far as competency can be established by the testimony of others, I can satisfy the most sceptical
by reference to many of the first characters and scholars in this
State, and likewise to some in Virginia.

The Moral and Religious instruction of the girls will, in a
great measure, be under the direction of my Mother. Two of my
sisters, under my superintendance and arrangement, and with my
frequent assistance, will teach to the extent of their ability; where
they fail, I will endeavor to supply the deficiency. I have a sister
who has been resident at Chapel Hill for several years, whom
I have carried through a pretty extensive course of Latin and
French. In teaching her the latter language, I have been kindly
and efficiently assisted by the accomplished Professor of Modern
Languages in the University. The acknowledged abilities of the
able assistant in the department of Mathematics, can, and will be
called into requisition if necessary.

The part of our plan which I like most, and to which I wish to
invite your particular attention, is, that we shall have no vacation
during the two *college* vacations. The object of this arrangement
is, to allow me to give my undivided attention to the girls during
the college vacations, which together amount to *three months,*
or *one fourth* of the *whole year.* Parents can send for their
daughters whenever they think proper, and keep them at home
as long as they deem consistent with propriety and their interests.

As we shall not be under the necessity of employing teachers,
since we have them in our own family, we can afford to instruct
girls on more moderate terms than usual.

Such, sir, is the outline of our plan. To you who know me,
it is, I hope, needless to say that it is almost impossible to bring

---

[94] Printed circular.

more or weightier influences to bear upon an instructor in the discharge of his duty than those which will operate upon me; a sense of honor, regard for reputation, gratitude for confidence conferred, delight in the occupation, and that which would be the all-prevailing consideration with many, self-interest, all constitute so many securities for the faithful performance of my part of the incumbent duties.

My friends who know me best can testify that I have long manifested a deep anxiety on the subject of Female Education, in my humble way, I have both spoken and written in its behalf. I regard it as the most extensive and most unoccupied field of usefullness that can be presented to the philanthropist. Let it be cultivated, let its natural beauties, which have been so long left to flourish in wild luxuriance, be nourished and directed by the plastic hand of cultivation, and soon they will diffuse a refreshing and vivifying fragrance, the incense of enlightened purity, that will pervade the length and breadth of the land, under the influence of which presumptuous ignorance, impudent venality, and heartless selfishness would be rebuked. Of course I have no expectation of being a reformer in this neglected field, yet it may be allowed me to throw out the above views, as a motive, at least. But enough about our own qualifications. I have less hesitation in speaking of the INCIDENTAL advantages of the place. It is needless to speak of its healthfulness, this is well known; its picturesque beauties are equally so. But that which renders Chapel Hill unrivalled as a desirable place for the education of young ladies, is the intellectual character of its social intercourse, and even of its amusements. Long before I had ever dreamed that my Mother's family would come here to reside, I had thought a thousand times that I would rather a sister of mine should be educated here than at any other place in the South. In the first place, there is here enough of society for rational enjoyment, and the accomplishment of manners, but not enough for the introduction of the frivolities of fashionable life, and its consequent distractions; in the second, all our exhibitions are far more frequent, intellectual and improving to the young than those of any other village in the State. The public addresses, speeches, experiments, and exhibitions which take place during the year would, if equally distributed, average, perhaps, one for every fortnight. To all of these admission may be easily obtained for the young ladies. From the facts just stated, it is evident that *here* a young lady's PRACTICAL education woud go hand in hand, and keep equal pace with her *theoretical* instruction. She would not be taught as a nun or novice, but when she had gone through a course here she would be prepared to enter upon the active and efficient duties of her sphere.

The Superintendant regrets that the compass of a letter does not allow him to give so full an exposition of his views as he desires. He differs from many in regard to the manner and kind of instruction proper for young ladies; and whilst he will in all cases make it a point of conscience to attend most respectfully to the particular wishes of parents as to the instruction of their daughters, he begs that he may be restricted as little as possible in this respect; he is willing that his views should stand or fall, by the proficiency or deficiency which may be exhibited in the *education* of a young lady whom he has carried through a FULL course. He subscribes to the observation of Addison, that "good manners are a perpetual letter of recommendation;" he will therefore give as much attention to the POLITE branches of education as he may think they deserve, but his chief aim will be to impart a PRACTICAL, A USEFUL education; one that may be made *available* in after life, for the instruction of families, or the acquisition of a support in a reverse of fortune. He will endeavor to teach principles, as well as facts, to discipline the mind, as well as furnish the memory. Many, competent to form a judgment on the subject, hold the opinion that, in all its *essential branches,* female education is a half century in the rear of male. No justification for this state of things can be found in any necessary or inherent incapability in the female mind to acquire the ABSTRUSE and ABSTRACT, as well as the POLITE and ORNAMENTAL. The Superintendant thinks he has observed, in his limited experience, that under the operation of equal motives and equal external advantages, the female intellect is as apt as the male in the acquisition of those subjects which are sometimes considered as appropriate to males only. He does not deny that the former may have less TASTE for these severe studies; he is only speaking of capability.

Amid the disasters in trade, and failures which for years past have spread gloom and despondency over our land, women have frequently appeared in new and interesting points of character, and exhibited dormant and uncredited energies. Whilst bankrupt husbands have, in too many instances, given themselves up to despair, or what is worse, to the accursed bowl, their wives have, with a hero's fortitude and an angel's meekness, regulated their households in conformity to their altered fortunes, and betaken themselves to the teaching of youth as a means of support. Who, in view of such a contingency, does not wish that the rising female generation may be educated for the *shade* as well as the *sunshine* of life?

I foresee several obstacles to the realization of my wishes, but chiefly these two; first, my being a single man; but I am not a very young one, and in one sense I have been the head of a family for years. Ever since my Mother and her four daughters have been here, I have been the sole male head; besides, it not unfrequently happens that the assistant teacher in a female school is a much younger man than myself. Secondly, the erroneous impression that exists in the minds of some in regard to the manners of our students; this, I know from long experience, does the young gentlemen of the institution great injustice. I am convinced that their association with ladies is as delicate and deferential as that of the young gentlemen of any other village of the State, with the additional recommendation of being more intellectual, as their oportunities are greater, and their number larger. Already can the influence of the limited female society of our Literary Metropolis, be observed in the greater polish and amenity of manners of our students.

### Terms.

For tuition in English, board, and all the necessary expenses of lodging, (washing excepted,) $16.00 per month, one half of the charges for the year payable in advance. If Latin, French, (or Greek) be studied, there will be an extra charge of $1. per month. Music, of course, an extra charge.

Very respectfully,
Wm. H. Owen.


*From James Martin.*                                          A.

Mobile,

July 26th, 1842.

I received with no little gratification your speech in pamphlet on the apportionment Bill. For although I had read it in the Intelligencer I was glad to have it in a less evanescent shape. The speech was read by me with the more pleasure because it reflects so clearly the grounds taken by the late Governor when a Senator from this State, in recommending and being mainly instrumental in introducing here the general Tickett in place of Districts in the Election of Members of Congress. The representation by districts would have been three to two, and the two would have represented a majority the population and the Wealth of the State. North Alabama however having comparatively few slaves has the ascendancy in votes, and hence the voice of the South is not heard in Congress. Mr. Bagby is an agreeable man, and a fluent ingenius speaker, but his powers of discrimination may be fairly judged of by his argument upon the principle involved in the Bill.

The Election for the State Legislature commences here this day week each party have their candidates, who divide as well on the Currency question as upon Politicks. The Whigs are for discontinuing Banking by the State the Democrats for a partial discontinuance only. The Whigs think the system is inherently wrong. That the management under it is corrupt and the plan is corrupting. The others contend that the corruption grows not out of the system and of course can be reformed.

So that it is seen here that Whigs are opposed to State Banking and Democrats are in its favour. The covert reason is, that Loco Focoism is in the ascendancy in Alabama, and this rotten State Bank system tends to continue their misrule. So much for our local politicks.

The Whigs proper interest is on the increase among us and I trust will be in the majority in 1844. Another matter, which concerns myself chiefly I would invite your attention to. I believe I coincide with you entirely in Politicks. Now I should like an appointment to be made by the President. It is the Judgeship for the Western District of Florida. I would not nor would you do any thing derogatory to my principles to obtain it. If with this reservation I could obtain that appointment I should be gratified by it. The office is now vacant, and I mention this to you in confidence. You may use my name or not as you may see fit. The Judge resides at Pensacola the most healthy point upon the Coast.

Our Crops are exceedingly fine, never since I have been in the Country have I had so good a prospect.

Please to present my respects to your Brother. His circular is just the thing for the time and that Section of Country.

*From Frederick J. Hill.*[95]                                    U.

Pittsboro

July 27th. 1842.

Your esteemed favor of the 22nd. Inst. has been received and I beg leave to tender you my thanks for the interest you manifest in the question of veracity between his accidency Mr. Tyler and myself. I had thought of having my reply, with the letters of Messrs. Miller and Cherry Published in the Intelligencer, but really from the coincidence of my statement with the Speech of Mr. Matthiot [96] in the Ho. Reps, the charges of Mr. Botts, and the declaration of Mr. Stanly and all these too, following so immediately the incontrovertible Publication of Mr. Ewing have placed the miserable matter so low in the estimate of all good men that I felt it would not be magnanimous to give further publicity to his ignominy; my only desire has been to be placed in a proper position before the reading Public and if the opposition Papers would have published my reply without garbling it, I should have preferred that the matter should never have gone beyond the limits of the State. I observe however in the Carolinian this morning (the Paper in which Mr. Tyler's letter first appeared) what purports to be my reply and published at my request, but omitting the most reliable Testimony, the letters of Messrs. Miller and Cherry. The Editor of the Standard too altho' he has not positively declined the Publication has thus far failed to do so and I presume when the Election is over he may insert such a mutilated statement as made its appearance in Mr. Henry's organ at Fayetteville Under these circumstances some of my friends here think it ought to be published in the Intelligencer; as to myself I am satisfied that my assertion is fully sustained and would prefer the matter to rest where it is. I am not willing unnecessarily to add to the National disgrace the Country now suffers in its worthless and unprincipled head; if however my friends think that it is due to myself that in

---

[95] Hill was a delegate to the Harrisburg convention, and voted for Tyler. After the break with Tyler, Hill, questioned about it by a Whig committee in Smithville, stated that, sitting in the room occupied by himself and Governor John Owen, Tyler had declared that his views on the Bank question had changed, and that he believed it indispensable, and no further question of its constitutionality should be raised. Tyler replied, June 5, 1842, denying Hill's statement.

[96] Joshua Mathiot (1800-1849), of Ohio, a native of Pennsylvania, lawyer, state legislator, and a Democratic senator, 1807-1811, and now a representative, had just bitterly attacked Tyler.

self-defence I should proceed further, it must be done. Will you then be kind enough to confer with Messrs. Mangum and Rayner on the subject; and do in the premises what in your judgment ought to be done.

Tomorrow morning I set out for Brunswick in order to attend the Election; all the accts I receive from them speak favorably of the result, but you know the disadvantage of two months absence immediately preceeding the day the votes are taken.

I have no additional information to communicate as to the final result only that a gentleman from Halifax with whom I conversed a few days since speaks favorably of our prospect in Bertie and North Hampton. Branch and Fisher may Brag as they Please, but I confidently believe Morehead's maj'ty over Henry will be larger than it was over Saunders.

As to the Legislature, I repeat, I am not as Sanguine as some of our friends, tho' I think we shall survive, but by a diminished majority.

If the result is known in the Southwestern Counties before I leave there I will drop you a line; in the mean time believe me very truly

and Sincerely
Your friend

### From Charles Plummer Green[97]     U.

Ridgeway, N. C.,

July 30th, 1842.

I received by due course of mail your very kind favour of the 18th. Inst. for which you will please to accept my thanks. The suggestions have been of service to our friends in Granville particularly in relation to the Tariff question. I am just from that County where I heard all the Candidates address the people at several different places, & I regret to say that our friends appear not to understand, as they ought to do, the question now aggitating the public mind. I would not be at all surprised if we are defeated, at least a part of the tickett, though they all are sanguine.

---

[97] Charles Plummer Green (1810-1843), a native of Warren County, gold miner in Western North Carolina, founder and editor of the Boydton *Virginia Expositor and Southern Advocate*, which he sold in 1836 and began to study law. He was in Texas for a time thereafter.

I am in hopes of hearing from Governor Morehead to day saying that he will be in Oxford on Tuesday or Wednesday, if he is, we are safe.

Is it not possible for you to get to Orange by Thursday it may be important to count every vote, besides great good would be effected by an address from you giving an account of what Congress has done during this "long session," as our opponents often say. You might "pair off" with some Loco.

I hope you will pardon me for troubling you to get me as many of the Lithographed prints of Mr. Clay from a Daguerreotype plate now for sale in Washington, as the within will purchase. I understand they can be had at eight Dollars per dozen. You will please to leave them at Ridgeway, where I hope to meet you on your way home.

Give my respects to Judge Mangum. Should there be a print of the Judge, I will thank you to get me one.


*From Charles Plummer Green.*                    U.


### Ridgeway, N. C.

### August 2nd, 1842.

I hope you will pardon me for again trespassing upon your time, which I would not now do, did I not think it important to put you upon your guard against an intended coalition between certain men from the *Nag's Head* region, and the Locos in the next Assembly. this was attempted in part a day or two previous to the meeting of the last Legislature but it was no go. Now it is very desirable with a few Whigs in the East to send a Senator from that section & Wm. B. Sheppard [98] is that man, & if not him, Mr. Cherry would like to fill that station. This is not all conjecture on my part. I have several reasons for believing so. I heard through a prominent Loco Foco a few days ago, that the latter gentleman (I think) told him that "you would not be a candidate for reelection & if you were that the Nag's Head people would not vote for you." I am confident of the correctness of the above as the same gentleman on our way to the Whig Convention spoke with confidence that you did not desire to remain longer in the Senate. I thought at the time his

---

[98] Shepard.

*desires* might influence in a great measure his belief. I would not be supprised if some of that clique should try to "soft sawda" as Sam Slick would say, Mr. Rayner, thinking that he might be induced to lend his aid to defeat your election. Now, my dear Sir, let me advise you by no means to suffer a word to drop which could by possibility give them any pretext to force you to decline a reelection, as your election will be beyond doubt if we have a majority of even *one* in the Legislature. I fear not that the great body of our opponents will make such a disgraceful intrigue to elect any other Whig in your stead, as many of them I know would go for you in preference to any Whig in the State, and it would be treason worse than Capt. Tyler, should a portion of our friends go for a Loco to defeat you. There are a thousand good reasons why you should not leave the Senate, a most prominent one is that Sheppard & Judge Mangum could not harmonize together, in fact I had rather have a full blooded Loco Foco than to have Sheppard, his course towards you and the Judge, (you will recall that he did not vote for you) ,[99] ought not to be forgotten, at least it never shall by me.

If you have no objection read this to the Judge, he will readily understand the movement. I would not be surprised if a certain *ex Judge*[100] in Raleigh, of our party would not like to fill your shoes. I know your honesty and your good opinion of mankind, therefore must again say *beware of false friends.*

I should be please to get a line from you.

I hope for the best from Granville but have fears. I will go there to the election, the cars is about to start so I must close, with the best wishes of your friend.

### *From Richard C. Puryear.*                                    U.

Huntsville, August 5, 1842.

We have sustained a complete Waterloo defeat in Surry Yes, the county which *proudly* gained the ship has again fallen under the dominion of *pretended* Democracy.

---

[99] Shepard, after Graham's election, made a furious speech, amounting to a personal attack on Graham, and denouncing the election to the senate of two men from Orange County.

[100] This might refer to George E. Badger, or Romulus M. Saunders. The latter was an active candidate when the Democrats controlled the legislature, but the context would indicate that Badger was meant.

I was taken sick about the middle of the campaign and Dobson[101] passed over half the county without opposition and availed himself of every advantage which my absence afforded him. Boyden and Poindexter fought gallantly every day but all in vain. The people cried loudly for the promised reform and retrenchment and could not be convinced that Congress might not have done much in those matters without the aid of Tyler. They loudly denounced the bankrupt law and though all the Whig candidates except Mr Boyden were opposed to it, they charged it upon us as a Whig measure and compelled us to bear the responsibility.

The burial of Genl. Harrison and the appropriation to his widow were loudly complained of and considerably diminished our vote. In vain did we refer to similar cases from the death of Washington through the administration of Jackson & Van Buren down to the present time. The predudices of the rabble were awakened by the demagogue and your own experience has taught you the difficulty of satisfying and allaying such feelings by argument and reason.

I dread to hear from the general result. God grant that it may be different from that in our County, and that you may again be returned to the Senate.

Nothing but a desire for the accomplishment of that object and the reorganization of Congressional districts could have induced me to become a candidate. As respects myself I do not regret the defeat and if we have a majority in the Legislature I am content.

P. S. All the Loco Candidates in this County came out strongly for a National Bank.

*From Samuel F. Patterson.*                    U.

Raleigh, August 8th, 1842.

I have only time to give you the unwelcome intelligence that we are beaten beyond all doubt for the Legislature. Our returns of course are as yet but partial, but enough is known to make it certain that we are beaten. Stokes & Surry have both gone against us which makes a difference of 14 Votes at once. We have also lost one in Chatham, and rumour says that we have lost Doct Hill in Brunswick—these in addition to other losses of which

---

[101] William P. Dobson, state senator, 1818-1819, 1830-1834, 1836, 1842.

you have no doubt heard. Wilkes is the only Whig County as yet heard from that has maintained her position entire. Morehead's majority there is 1224 Votes and notwithstanding they had two Whigs & one Loco Candidate for the Senate, and five Whigs and one Loco for the Commons they have elected all Whigs by large Majorities. Our party have managed badly; in many of the Counties they had too many candidates and in others they split their tickets. The Rail Road question too operated greatly against us, to say nothing of Captain Tyler's treachery and other questions of general policy. We think there can be no doubt of Morehead's election, though his majority will be much diminished.

### From Henry K. Nash. U.

Hillsboro, August 12th, 1842.

I have to apologize for not having replied to your letter of the 1st. inst. sooner; I was at Wilkerson's hard at work, when your letter arrived; it was taken out of the office by Dr. Strudwick, who forgot to give it to me until I was about to set off for Chatham Court. I should have written then, but supposed that some of our friends had already done so. In fact our defeat was so unexpected and astounding, that everyone I suppose was unwilling to be the first to communicate it to our absent friends; at least such was my case.

Over-confidence and the most disgraceful apathy on the part of our friends, or some of them, was almost the sole cause of this result. The question of "Division" or "no division," also injured us. It was Jones' course on this question which gave him the Whig votes he received at this place, and which beat Holt & Mebane and elected him. He received about 74 Whig votes in this place alone, I mean at this election precinct.

The conduct of the Whigs here, has had another, and worse effect even than that of electing the Democratic ticket. It has exasperated our friends in all parts of the County to such an extent, that they do not hesitate to say, that they will never again support any man who comes from Hillsboro, and also that they will do all in their power to divide the County. Indeed I think they have abundant cause for offence, the conduct of the Whigs here was inexcusable, and bitterly so many of them, now that it is too late, repent it.

The State is still Whig, though there is no doubt but that the Democrats have decided majorities in both branches of the Legislature. Morehead is elected, I think, by a majority of between 3 and 4000.

I see that the Revenue Bill has passed the Senate without amendment, I suppose the President will Veto it.

I suppose we may expect Mr. Mangum and yourself home, at least by September Court.

*From James Graham*[102]                                              U.

*to*

*The President of the United States.*

**H. R.,**

August 24th, 1842.

There are about Twelve Hundred Cherokee Indians remaining in my district in North Carolina. The appropriation for instituting a commission to adjudicate their claims for spoilations, and so on, has just been made by Congress.

I recommend to you as suitable persons for said Commissioners, Nicholas Woodfin[103] of Asheville, N. C., and Haywood Guion of Lincolnton, N. C.; both are gentlemen of integrity, intelligence, and independence of Character, and well qualified to hear, examine, and decide questions according to justice, law, and equity.

I recomend also James Robinson Franklin in Macon County, N. C., as a gentleman of strict honesty, and fine business talents, and well quallified to to be appointed enrolling Agent to enroll and assist in removing the Cherokees now in North Carolina to the Country west of Arkansas. Mr James Robinson is not only capable, but I believe he has, and deserves the confidence of the Indians, and unless they confide in a man, he can do little or nothing towards their removal.

They will not go *voluntarily* with any man they do not know and esteem.

---

[102] Autograph copy.

[103] Nicholas Washington Woodfin (1810-1876), of Asheville, an able Whig lawyer, deeply interested in internal improvements and public education, who was state senator, 1844-1852. He was a delegate to the convention of 1861, and, during the Civil War, agent of the state at the salt works in Virginia.

The Indians in N C reside entirely I believe in Cherokee and Haywood Counties.

Your prompt attention to this subject will greatly oblige my constituents and their Representative.

James Graham.

P S Mr. John Timson, a Cherokee Chief of N. C. is about removing West. He deserves and I hope will receive every facility to enable him to go West. He is an Honest man & a good Citizen.

J. Graham.

*From James Graham*                    U.

*to The President of the United States.*

H. R., August 29th, 1842.

You asked me a few days since if the Commissioners to be appointed under the Cherokee Treaty of 1835 required the sanction of the Senate, or were appointed by the President alone. I believe I answered by the President alone; and in that I was mistaken, as I learn from the Indian Bureau that the former Commissioners were appointed by and with the advice and consent of the Senate. I would also recommend Harvey Miller of Rutherforton, North Carolina as a young gentleman well quaelified to be Secretary to the Board of Commissioners.

Very Respectfully
Your obt. St.

*Letter from Committee.*[104]

Henderson, N. C.

September 17th., 1842.

At a meeting of the Whigs of Granville, Warren, and Franklin, held here today, the undersigned were appointed a committee to tender to you and your colleague, the Hon. WILLIE P. MANGUM, a Barbecue, given by the Whigs of the above named Counties, and to request you, in conjunction with Mr. M., to designate a day for the same. In tendering to you this mark of the high con-

---

[104] From the *Hillsborough Recorder*, October 20th., 1842.

sideration of your fellow-citizens, in this section of the State, we feel that we are incapable of adequately describing the warm feelings of attachment, and the sincere sentiments of admiration, with which you are regarded by those whom we represent. Your career in our National Councils has been short, but it has been marked by an ability, integrity, and faithful adherence to pledges, made out of office, that have at once placed you among the great statesmen of the day, and given you new claims to the high regard and affection of the citizens of your native state.

The late session of our National Legislature has been, perhaps, the most memorable in the annals of our country, and never was the firmness and patriotism of men more thoroughly tried, than were those of the Whig members of that assembly. Opposed in every measure for the relief of a distressed and suffering country, by a party whose only aim was its own ascendancy, and deceived, thwarted and warred upon by a weak and treacherous Chief Executive, the course of the Whig members must have been unusually difficult and embarrassing. Yet, surrounded as they were, by so many, and so apparently insuperable obstacles, they have been unfaltering in their course, untiring in their zeal for their country's weal. A grateful people have watched with deep emotion, each step in their enlightened, liberal and manly policy, and they will, most assuredly mete out to them their proper reward. As for the Whigs of the good Old North State, they are ready to assemble, by thousands, at the festive board, and do "honor, to whom honor is due."

An early answer is respectfully requested.

We are, with considerations of the highest regard, your friends and fellow-citizens,

C. H. Wiley,[105] C. P. Green, H. J. Robards, V. Winfree, A. E. Henderson, D. S. Hill, John Read, J. B. Littlejohn, R. F. Yarborough, R. Bullock, N. R. Tunstall, T. N. F. Alston, J. Person, S. G. Ward, H. J. G. Ruffin.

---

[105] Calvin Henderson Wiley (1819-1887), of Guilford, author, educational leader, Presbyterian minister, a graduate of the University. He became a lawyer, was a Whig member of the commons, 1850-1852, and in the latter year a Democratic legislature created a department of schools, and elected him superintendent. He was a passionate advocate of universal, free education, and from then until the outbreak of the Civil War, the school system made wonderful progress, and was far in advance of the rest of the South, and compared favorably with most of the North and West. War interrupted this progress, and reconstruction practically closed the schools for many years. Wiley's writings included two novels, *Alamance* and *Roanoke,* and he also wrote an interesting *North Carolina Reader.* He founded and edited the *North Carolina Journal of Education.* After the war he was general agent of the American Bible Society.

*From Frankfort Whig Committee.*                          U.

Frankfort, Ky., Sept. 23d, 1842.

Sir:

It is the purpose of the Whigs of Franklin to hold a Whig festival at or near this place on the 26th of October in honor of the
Whig members of Congress in order that the friends of the good
cause may celebrate the noble stand which our party now occupies
before the world.

We know Sir that this position has not been attained without
arduous exertion and much self denial on the part of those who
as the Representative of popular rights in the Congress of the
United States have so gallantly contended not only against a
powerful vigilant and organized political opposition but also
against the usurpations and follies of an Executive who should
have been an ally and not a foe. The Congress has adjourned with
the unbroken confidence of the nation leaving the Executive in
the undisturbed possession of the Nation's contempt. It is gratifying to hear from all sources that the Whig members of Congress
are every where received with open arms by their Constituents
and it is cheering to witness the enthusiasm which attends their
triumphant return.

Kentucky has especial reason to be gratified with those demonstrations, as she has maintained through good and through evil
report all those principles that give to the Whig party their dis-
tinctive character and she observes with pride that her own distinguished Statesman is honored equally at home and abroad by
his admiring countrymen. We expect Sir that most of the distinguished politicians and tried Whigs will be with us on this occasion and we hope it will suit your convenience to be one of the
number.

It will give us pleasure to meet you at the festive Board and
we can promise a welcome in the cordial style of old fashioned
Kentucky hospitality

Very Resply.,

Yr. ob. sts.

| | |
|---|---|
| WM OWSLEY | JAMES DAVIDSON |
| J. SWIGERT | N. C. GOODLOE |
| P. SWIGERT | W. D. REED |
| LYSANDER HOOD | JNO. C. HERNDON |
| THO. B. STEVENSON | G W CRADDOCK |

*To Calvin H. Wiley and others.*[106]

Hillsborough,

September 24, 1842.

GENTLEMEN: I have had the honor to receive yours of the 17th. instant, tendering to me and my distinguished colleague, Mr. Mangum, a Barbecue, proposed to be furnished at Henderson, on such day as we may designate, as a testimonial of the regard and approbation of the Whigs of Granville, Warren and Franklin. I thank you for the too partial and appreciating terms in which the personal feelings of many of your Committee have prompted you to convey to me the invitation of those you represent; and beg you to assure them of my deep regret that my avocations, both private and professional (after a long absence from home) deny me the leisure necessary for such a meeting at any early day, and therefore compel me most unwillingly to decline it. With no portion of my constituents would I have more gladly met, at the festive board, and freely commune on the present state of our public affairs, than with those of Granville, Warren and Franklin. Nowhere are there more firm, true-hearted, intelligent and patriotic Whigs, men whose honest and disinterested approval is most gratifying to a public servant, as it fortifies his own consciousness of adherence to duty in trying circumstances.

You, gentlemen, have not undervalued the embarrassment and difficulties which the majority in the present Congress have been forced to contend. Opposed and assailed on every measure, from the burial honors of the lamented Harrison, to the highest question of national policy, by a powerful and factious party, who, though they left to their successors a public service costing on an average 28 millions of dollars per year, (exclusive of the peculation and embezzlement so frequent under Mr. Van Buren's Administration) and a revenue system yielding less than 14 millions, refuse to raise the means to supply the deficiency—though they left a funded debt of 5½ millions bearing interest, and Government engagements to the amount of 20 millions more, will not provide for their payment. Though they habitually borrowed monies for the Government during a period of four years, clamored most loudly before the people, when loans became necessary to fill up the vacuum they had created. Though thus opposed and

---

[106] From the *Hillsborough Recorder,* October 20th, 1842.

assailed, the Whigs, as a party, have carried through both Houses of Congress every measure which they proposed for the relief of the country. But our opponents have found, in the defection of the acting President an ally, making the minority more powerful than the majority of Congress. Although as yet the fact is attempted to be concealed, he has become theirs to every intent and purpose, of party benefit and advantage—theirs in sympathy, in defamation of the Whig party, in the dispensation of patronage, and the use and abuse of his vast powers of appointment and removal—theirs in every thing, except for his own honor and advancement. He cannot be their candidate for the succession; they spurn the very idea. But he will be used to the utmost extent of appointments, removals and vetoes, to promote the election of their candidate. Had the Republican Whigs of the present Congress been pursuing the desperate game of party policy of which he has accused them, they would have left him in the hands of his new allies, to get through a term to which he has accidentally succeeded, as he might. But they have felt that their duties to the country remained to the extent of their powers, however much he has failed in his. They have proceeded to the enactment of measures deemed necessary for the public interest, regardless of what he might approve or reject. Yet, so freely has his interposition been thrust upon their labors, that the chief benefits which they are permitted to tender to the country are of a negative kind. If during the late long and arduous session, but little has been done, as is untruly asserted by those who intend reproach, it may be truly affirmed, that much of the extravagance and folly of the late administration has been *left undone*. The contingent expenses of Congress have been reduced at least one hundred thousand dollars, and principally in the item of public Printing. A new and more rigid accountability is introduced into the public departments, by what has been heretofore left at discretion as incidental expenses. And after all the land has rung with cries of extravagance, the appropriations of this first regular session of a Whig Congress for the service of the year, chargeable on the Treasury, are less than twenty and a half millions of dollars—seven millions less than the average annual expenditure under Mr. Van Buren, and two millions less than even the last year of his administration, when such extraordinary efforts were used to appear economical. By a discharge which Congress has directed in the course of the ensuing year, of more than five thousand men from the standing army, there is a prospect of a still lower reduction of the amount required from the people, for the support of Government. But as to those measures of positive advantage to the people, by which soundness is to be restored to the currency, our commerce revived, and our prosperity thoroughly re-established, they must be delayed until a change in the Executive opinion. Meanwhile, a numerous and lately dominant party applaud all vetoes and usurpations of the Executive which tend to thwart the Whig majority, and the people are familiarized to the idea that the President is a sovereign, whose opinions, not only of constitutional construction, but of expediency also, are to set at naught all the wisdom of Congress. And that whether this rejection of a bill arise from simple imbecility, from vindictiveness or revenge, it is to be justified because it disappoints political opponents; thus precedents are formed which are to become laws hereafter, and the free constitution of our fathers degenerates into an elective monarchy. It was a remark of a most sagacious man, that where annual elections end, tyranny begins. Yet the course of passing events is to confirm the doctrine that we have in effect but one election in four years, all others being designed to conform the Legislative assemblies to the will of the Executive then chosen.

To correct this downward tendency of the present times, and to restore the Government to its healthful and proper action, the only sure reliance is on the ballot box, at the next Presidential election, accordingly the Whigs of the country from Maine to Louisiana, are already aroused for that contest; and I rejoice to believe that our prospects of success are most cheering. With one only candidate in the field, to whom the proudest in our ranks think it no disparagement to defer and give place, and that candidate a man who has illustrated every important period in our history for the last thirty-five years, by his eloquence and courage, his patriotism and wisdom—a man at the mention of whose name in any part of the world an American heart beats quicker and prouder—when that candidate is Henry Clay, and the issue is for the re-establishment of the just balance of the Constitution, and the true prosperity of the people, we need not dread the result. The more especially in view of that other controversy, now no longer concealable, as to who shall be the candidate of the party opposed to us, or whether amid their divisions, that party can have any one candidate. We have had our troubles and trials, but are at this day as firmly united as ever—theirs are but beginning. And it remains to be seen whether they can present the same united front in the contest for the succession which they have exhibited in opposition to the Whig measures for the relief of the country—or whether more than one aspirant to the Chief Magistracy will not find himself like the fabled Actaeon, victimized by those followers whom he vainly flattered himself that he was leading to victory, that would inure to his benefit.

I am, gentlemen, with the highest respect and esteem, your friend and servant,

*To Charles P. Green.*     U. T. J. Green Mss.

Hillsboro',

Sept. 24th, 1842.

I received this afternoon your letter inclosing the invitation of a Committee to the Barbecue at Henderson.

Your note by the Post rider reached me on Thursday evening, and I remained at home yesterday, in the hope that I should have the pleasure to see you at my house.

With your letter I have one from Judge Mangum, suggesting his views of the propriety of postponing the proposed Barbecue for the present; these, he, no doubt, communicated to you verbally.

My professional engagements as well as my private affairs render it highly inconvenient for me to be present on such an occasion, at any time this fall, but all these I would readily forego to meet our good friends of Granville, Franklin, and Warren, in the manner proposed, did I not believe it better, in every aspect of our affairs, to postpone the meeting at least for the present.

I have not time to go at large into my reasons for this opinion, as I desire to dispatch this by the mornings mail, but these I am confident have been, partially at least, suggested to you in the conversation of Judge Mangum. Should our Whig friends who have so kindly tendered this manifestation of their approval and confidence, think proper at a future time (say next Spring after the adjournment of Congress) to propose such a meeting, I will make any sacrifice to be there. That however is too distant a time for an engagement, and must be left to future arrangement, and the inclination and convenience of the Whigs of that Section.

No portion of my Constituents, I feel well assured, is composed of more high spirited, patriotic & devoted Whigs. And there are none, whose approbation of my public course, could be more gratifying than theirs.

I must beg therefore of you (whose friendly regard has been so often exhibited in acts of kindness towards me) to make all proper apologies for the course we are taking in most respectfully declining the invitation.

I will forward to you by the next mail, my reply to the Com'tee. which will reach Henderson, I trust by Wednesday.

My present purpose is merely to acknowledge the receipt of your letter, and my personal obligations for your zeal & kind offices in this matter.

I am very truly,<br>Your Friend an Serv't.

P.S. I will send the invitation with my letter, according to your request.

I hope you received the likenesses of Mr. Clay.

*From Charles P. Green.*                    U.

Ridgeway, N. C.,

October 5th., 1842.

I received a few days ago yours of the 24th. ult., & also your answer to the Committee of invitation, the last I sent on to the Register for publication. On yesterday I received a private letter from Judge Mangum, informing me that he had been quite unwell ever since I left his home, consequently he had not been able to reply to our letter.

I regret not having the pleasure of visiting you, which I fondly anticipated when I left home, but failing to find the Judge at his home, & not meeting with him at Mr. Cain's, compelled me to give up my trip to Hillsborough.

Notwithstanding I would have been glad to see you both at the proposed Barbecue I am pleased that you declined it this fall, as I am clearly of the opinion that next spring will be a much better time for political effect, & is advocated in the meeting at Henderson. I now give you fair notice to hold yourself in readiness to attend there immediately after the adjournment of Congress, when we hope to have a great gathering of the people, which must be followed up by similar movements in different sections of the

State. Upon this subject the Judge & myself had a most unreserved conversation.

I beg you will pardon me for alluding to what you may consider premature, but I do it from the best motives, and for many good reasons, which I deem unnecessary to mention at present. I already hear the names of several gentlemen from the Eastern part of the State spoken of as candidates on the Whig tickett for next Governor, Rayner, Manly, Collins, & Sheppard, neither of whom, in my opinion, will answer to make "a bruising race."

Soon after the result was known, that the Legislature was Loco Foco, I named to a number of my friends that I thought the Whig party ought, by all means, to run you for that station, since then I am much gratified to find a great number of your friends agree with me. I am aware that, should you consent to be the candidate, it will put you to great personal inconvenience, besides a sacrifice in a pecuniary manner,—though I think I know you too well to count the cost when patriotism calls to duty.

I hope you will take the subject under consideration, but in no wise to throw any impediment in the way of your nomination should it be the wish of our party at a proper time to bring you before the people.

I much prefer Collins to either of the others, one of whom I never will vote for to fill any office.

I fear that the Whigs, in their zeal to elect Mr. Clay, will lose sight of the right kind of man for Vice President. John Davis is too timid, too much under the influence of Webster, too much Tariff to suit the South, not enough anti-abolitionism & besides, has done nothing that he should be so highly honoured. As to Tallmadge, I consider him a poor opponent to Rives, I see that his friends, under his guidance, are making strong efforts in New York to start a Ball, though I do not think it will roll out of his State. North Carolina has a man of the "right stripe," I mean your colleague, who could, in my humble opinion, get the nomination if he was to do as all other men do who succeed to high station.

Mr. Clay is quite an old man, & may not live to the end of his term, and it would be bad to make another failure—if it was not for a few in our State who never fail to underrate the prominent men within her limits, together with some who forever act the part of the Dog in the manger, Mangum might get the nomination in the National Convention, particularly if some State would lead the way. When do you think the Convention ought to take place? I think it ought to be at Baltimore, & the Judge says in May, 1844. Who do you think now stands the best chance for that office? Is it possible for Mangum to get the nomination, etc., etc., etc. Badger has great influence with the Raleigh papers, & he is *very friendly* to Mangum. They could give him a start, and a start is all. Will you attend the Court at Oxford before going to Washington? I saw Batt Moore of Halifax a short time ago, who says that he will "set up" to the Locos upon any important question. It would be well for you to give him, from time to time, such information as you think will be of aid to our cause.

\* \* \* \* \*

*From James W. Bryan.*                                        A.

Newbern

Oct. 25th. 1842.

We were much pleased to learn by Mr. Henry K. Nash that you were all well and also that you had located yourself comfortably and delightfully in Mr. Kirkland's house, which he purchased from the Rev. Mr. Green.

\* \* \* \* \*

We have no news here. Our Bankrupt Court terminated it's Session on yesterday; a large number were emancipated from the Slavery of debt and seem to be in high spirits, etc. This is a law for weal or woe. Messrs. Palmer, Nash & Winslow were in attendance to represent the distant and non resident petitioners.

I suppose you will figure largely at Raleigh this winter before their mighty Locofoco highnesses. North Carolina has disgraced herself in this last election, and it will take a series of years and of triumphant Whig victories to atone for this shameful and disgraceful abandonment on the part of the Whigs of correct and manly principles. I shall, I think, eschew politics as being productive of nothing but chagrin and bitter disappointment and leave them to more ambitious aspirants.

I had made up my mind to decline a Candidacy for the Solicitorship of this District, but the Whigs and *some* of the Locos urge me to run & I suppose I must do so and thus add another to the many victims that are to be sacrificed by Loco foco misrule, to Whig supineness.

\* \* \* \* \*

*From Charles L. Hinton.*                                **A.**

Raleigh,

Nov. 20th, 1842.

I write on a scrap of paper, the best in reach, to say I think you
should spend a day or two in our town on your way to Washington. You owe it to your old friends from a distance.

As usual on the Sabbath preceeding the meeting of the Legislature, all is bustle and confusion. I have seen but few members
myself but learn there is much caucaussing in squads, a general
feeling for a general turn out of all Whigs. Genl Marstella[107] has
been here for two days I presume he will take Manly's[108] place,
& Busbee,[109] Freeman's;[110] it is uncertain who will take Miller's.[111]
It is understood Dr. Montgomery is a candidate for Sec. of State,
about a dozen for Comptroller, Dr. Watson[112] and Gov. Branch
for Treasurer. These are the rumors of the morning and I presume correct, about fifty candidates for door keeper.

Col. Brown[113] and Genl. Sanders[114] are very busy, it is said
neither will yield.

The Whigs as far as I have learnt intend having their regular
Candidate for every appointment, and vote for no other.

*From George C. Mendenhall.*                              **A.**

Monday night,

Nov. 28th, 1842.

Yours of the 25th. Inst. was recd to-day & I am sorry I had not
written you sooner, for I frequently thought of it, but supposed

---

[107] Lewis H. Marsteller, of Wilmington, a native of Virginia, who served in the
commons, 1832-1834, in the state senate, 1835-1838, and was chief clerk of the
commons, 1842. He had also been clerk of the court, collector of the port, a major
general of militia. He was an amateur actor, and was a prominent figure on public
occasions.

[108] Charles Manly had been clerk of the commons, 1830-1840. Defeated in 1842, he
again served, 1844-1846.

[109] Perrin Busbee, of Wake, who was clerk of the commons, 1848, 1852.

[110] Edmund B. Freeman (b. 1796), who was clerk of the supreme court for thirty-
seven years.

[111] Henry W. Miller of Wake.

[112] Josiah O. Watson of Craven.

[113] Bedford Brown.

[114] Saunders.

you were likely crowded with letters from this City. The Whigs of the Commons had a meeting on Monday the first day of the Session at 10 A.M. some 40 odd present where I presided. We there left all at will to vote for DoorKeepers & Engrossing Clks but resolved upon opposition as to the Speaker & Clks of the House as you saw by the papers, and in that meeting informally agreed to put you in nomination which will Surely be done, when ever the Locos bring on the Election. They were twice in Caucus & could not agree on Senator, & they are now a third time this night in Caucus. Brown out runs Saunders, and Saunders 'tis said is violent & cuning, but holds on, much to our special satisfaction, he has said if *Caucused out* he can *go out,* and if his Party can do without him, he can do without them. I now think from what I have heard that Brown will prevail tonight. So Busbee their Clk. told me, who is a Haywood man. We shortly hear nearly all they do, & tomorrow I shall hear the Caucus decision tonight.

The Whig*s all—all* stand firm, and I think will; & let them elect their own Senator, for they, the Locos say one *must* be elected, & they cannot go home without it. I have since the 9 o'clk bell returned from Judge Mangum's Room, he thinks in the end, after many Ballotings, it would be perhaps best for the Whigs to elect Saunders rather than Brown. Only for the reason that more political Capital could be made of it hereafter in 1844. But this I think will not be done. Wm. Hill is elected 150 to 13—Strange 149—no opposition, Poindexter's[115] Election not reached yet; he is here and tolerably certain, if not caucused out tonight. Collins[116] is no doubt gone—and Hinton may hold his post, for they can't do without both, and have all new hands. Jno. H. Wheeler is here for Treasurer—Craige[117] for Solicitor, & Nat. Palmer[118] for Comptroller, all tramping and trampoosing about. Jno. Branch looks clean and grey, & makes low Florida Bows, but whether a Seeker of health, Office or Religion, is not distinctly set forth of Record; he is merely about where loaves are plenty, perhaps in case of a Snarl among the dogs.

I cannot close this till I hear tomorrow from the "Monarch of all it surveys" the Caucus of this dark, & cold, *to all*—and fatal night *to some.* I will try & report the dead and wounded, so far

---

[115] John F. Poindexter.
[116] William F. Collins, of Nash County, state comptroller, 1836-1861.
[117] Burton Craige.
[118] Nathaniel J. Palmer was a Whig lawyer, of Orange County. He moved to Raleigh, and was a candidate for various offices, and edited several newspapers including one at Hillsboro.

as the morning news shall have ascertained. We have done but little in the Assembly. Our Table is being piled high, with the most indigestible relief laws, ever known this side our great Western waters. Our safety is in having a tolerably fair Committee on the Judiciary. If Batt Moore comes & is added thereto, we shall be nearly secure from such unwise, unmeaning, & wreckless infractions.

It is growing late. But notwithstanding this democratic rule, in these democratic days, please give my warm Respects to our friend Hugh Waddell, Esq., for this is not a justifiable cause of Proscription.

[P.S.] Mangum is as warm a friend of yours as ever made a track. Tuesday—House of Commons.

R. P. Cardwell[119] moved to bring on the Election for Senator this day 2 weeks & nominated one Bedford Brown; agreed to by our House—no other nomination as yet. I hear Saunders is increasing and has improved from 22 to to 27 votes in Caucus. Clarke[120] is Caucused out in favor of Rodman[121] for Solicitor, the Whigs will vote for Clarke

I asked Cad Jones if Saunders would be nominated he very hesitatingly answered that he did not know.

Jo. Caldwell[122] introduced a Resolution denouncing repudiation; a Resolution by Byrd[123] of Yancey to divide out our funds and make Loan offices in each County—this is most melodious.

Tuesday night—*I* by authority shall nominate the Hon. Wm. A. Graham for the Senate; call at my Room as you pass, and *you* shall know all Whig proceedings. We have 70 or more of the best Whigs that ever lived; Dr. Shade P. Allen[124] No. 1. I hate—I abhor!

---

[119] Richard P. Cardwell, of Rockingham County, member of the commons, 1838-1842.

[120] Henry Selby Clark, (1809-1869), of Beaufort County, an unsuccessful candidate for solicitor, member of the commons, 1834-1836, of congress, 1845-1847.

[121] William Blount Rodman (1817-1893), of Beaufort County, a graduate of the university, studied law under William Gaston, and became an able lawyer. He served on the code commission in 1854. He was also a planter. A secessionist Democrat, he rose from captain to major in Confederate service, and later, from a military judge to colonel. He was a Republican delegate to the convention of 1868, where he rendered valuable service as a restraining influence. He was one of the commission to prepare a code of civil procedure, and served as a justice of the supreme court, from 1868 to 1879.

[122] Joseph Pearson Caldwell (1808-1853), of Iredell, studied law under his brother, David F. Caldwell. He was state senator, 1833-1834, member of the commons, 1838-1842, and member of congress, 1849-1853.

[123] Samuel Byrd, of Yancey County, was a member of the commons, 1842.

[124] Dr. Shadrack P. Allen, of Beaufort County, member of the commons, 1840-1842.

in my soul—my very soul—to give you up—I will not! till I think the Nation Commands.
12 at night on Tuesday.

*From William C. Preston.*                                    U.

Columbia,
S. Carolina,
Dec. 4th, 1842.

\*   \*   \*   \*   \*

It is understood that Mr. Calhoun has designated Barnwell Rhett as his successor, and that if it be ascertained, as it probably will be, that the State is not prepared for such a degradation, they may decline to accept Mr. C's resignation. There are ten candidates of whom Judge Huger is the strongest. It is doubtful whether McDuffie will be able to go on. A bullet in his back keeps him sick.[125]

With the highest respect
I am, Dear Sir
Yr obt. Servt.

*From George C. Mendenhall.*                                 U.

Late Sunday-night Decr. 4. 1842.

My dear friend:—

There is much in your personal appearance, your manner, and *may be* in your presence. Affairs on our part must not go by *default.* You know I slightly insisted upon your staying tomorrow; I have doubted since whether I should not have pressed the matter more strongly. Your appearance at our Bar of the House would fire the already anxious feelings of our friends & make the strong, stronger & rouse their Resolutions almost to the tenacity of Death.

We cannot otherwise than expect to sacrifice you at last. And would to God it could be upon the Holy Altar of Principle.

I cannot, I will not insist that you should stay—and then for our almost heavenly & certainly Spartan Band, as it were, in your face by the uncontrollable force of Circumstances to Vote not

---

[125] In 1822 George McDuffie fought a duel with William Cumming, of Georgia, and was so seriously wounded that he was never again a well man.

against (for this would be Treason) but not for you, in the bitter hour of trial; but I merely suggest whether you had not better spend one last, ill-fated political day with us, for expiring lights often beam the brightest.

*From Edmund Strudwick.*                                          U.

Hillsboro',

December 5th, 1842.

Mrs. Graham begs me to announce to you the birth of another son,[126]—this event occurred this morning between the hours of 2 and 3 o'clock. I am happy to add that under the circumstances she is as well, as the phrase goes, as could be expected. Mrs. Graham leaves to you the selection of a name for this fifth leader.

You have carried with you the latest news from our Legislature. I can therefore furnish nothing on that subject. The probability of your election is becoming stronger every day with your friends here; indeed we shall be disappointed if you do not retain your seat as our Senator; if you are ousted we have but little choice about your successor.

*From James P. Espy.*[127]                                        U.

To The Friends of Science.

———————

Last summer I announced to my correspondents, and the public generally, that a "form for keeping Meteorological journals would be prepared and sent to all those in the United States, Bermuda, West Indies, Azores, and the Canadas, who should signify a willingness to co-operate with me in my endeavors to find out all the *phases* of storms which occur within the range of the wide-spread simultaneous observations about to be established."

———————

126 Robert Davidson Graham (1842-1904). He was in later life a graduate of the university, Confederate captain, farmer, lawyer, secretary of the U. S. civil service commission, and chairman of federal board of pension appeals.

127 James Pollard Espy (1785-1860), "Storm King," a native of Pennsylvania, a graduate of Transylvania, a lawyer and teacher, who won wide reputation by his theories on weather, and his lectures thereon. He was at different times connected with the war and navy departments, and the Smithsonian. He was a member of the American Philosophical Society. Arago said, "England had its Newton, France its Cuvier, and America its Espy."

I have to announce now that the "form" is completed, and arrangements are made to strike off a sufficient number to supply all who shall express a wish to aid in this most important undertaking. It is my intention to lay down, on skeleton maps of the United States, by appropriate symbols, all the most important phases of the great storms which come within the range of our simultaneous observations; and thus it is hoped that we will be able to determine the *shape* and *size* of all storms, whether they are *round* or *oblong;* and if oblong, whether they move *side-foremost,* or *end-foremost,* or *obliquely;* and their *velocity* of motion and the direction which they take in all the different seasons of the year; the *course* that the wind blows, in, and beyond the borders of the storm; the *fluctuation* of the barometer, and *change* of temperature, which generally accompany storms, and the *extent* to which their influence is felt beyond their borders.

Now, as many of these particulars can be observed as well without meteorological instruments as with them, it is manifest that all who will send me a faithful account of the winds and weather will essentially contribute to the great end in view. Editors of papers, too, who notice great storms, may be of much service by mentioning the time of greatest violence, and the direction of the wind, and time of change, and sending a paper containing the account to the *Surgeon General's Office, Washington City,* with the word "Meteorology" marked on the corner of the envelope. All papers and journals thus directed will come to my hands, as I am now attached to that bureau; and, after being carefully collated with each other, will be deposited in the archives of that office, to aid the future meteorologist in developing laws, which the present state of the science may not enable us to detect. Let none think their *mite* too insignificant to be thrown into this common treasury.

I am authorized by the Secretary of State to request all our Ministers, Consuls, and other Diplomatic and Commercial Agents of the United States in foreign countries, to whom the "form" is sent, to transmit to the *Department of State* the journals which they may keep, or procure from others, that they may be immediately placed in my hands.

All masters of vessels sailing in the Atlantic, or Gulf of Mexico, are requested to send a copy of their "logs" to the *Surgeon General's Office* immediately on their landing at any port in the United States.

If the chain of simultaneous observations could thus be kept unbroken entirely across the Atlantic, the value of the whole system would be much increased.

Journals, according to the adopted plan, will be kept at all the military stations of the United States; and the Secretary of the Navy has given orders for the same to be done at the naval stations, and in ships of war on our coast. Forms also will be sent to all the light-houses and floating-lights, and many of them will at least keep journals of the wind and weather. Governor Reid, of Bermuda, has promised to send me journals from that island, and I have the promise of various journals from Canada, Newfoundland, and Nova Scotia.

There are many of the colleges of the United States from whom I have not yet had such promise; but I now appeal to them *all,* with confidence, to unite in their efforts to perfect this most interesting science.

There are one hundred and three colleges in these United States, and very many high schools; and, as it is known that barometric fluctuations accompany storms, it is manifest that the direction in which storms move, and their velocity, may be ascertained by observations made on the barometer alone, at these various institutions.

The number of observations cannot be too great.

James P. Espy.

Surgeon General's Office,
  Washington,
    December 6th., 1842.

*From George C. Mendenhall.*                         U.

Raleigh,

Wednesday night,

Decr. 7th, 1842.

No doubt you have letters from many friends here every mail, tho' Sometimes this is Supposed by too many of us & our friends thereby neglected.

To-day Gen'l Hawkins[128] moved for another voting for Senator, which with many noes however carried & is laid on the Table

[128] John Henry Hawkins, of Warren, a graduate of the university, a physician, member of the state senate, 1830-1832, of the commons, 1835-1836, 1840-1846.

in the Senate and we agreed to the Senate's proposition to vote tomorrow at 12. The voting after you left was nearly as before. There has been much talk with us here & the Saunders men have been so informed, that if they will aid in making fair Senatorial Districts in the State, the Whigs will elect Sanders—I have talked so several times, but I have taken a second & further view of the matter & have recalled my sayings so far as I could, & so informed J. T. Morehead & other Whigs, that we could not give such a pledge, for the Districts might be made so that we should not Complain much, and if we did not *then* elect Saunders, we should be charged and reproached with a breach of plighted faith, and it might be that about that time party fury might rage high, & the Brown men or some 15 of them rush over uncontrolled to Graham, & pray where should we be? The Dems have tried to fix on a third man, and cannot agree upon any, but Strange and Ruffin,[129] & neither will likely accept, & they can agree upon no other. A leading Saunders man has been to J. T. Morehead & threatened positively to go over to Brown, but I know a platoon or 2 of them who will not, & it is fraud. Some doz. Whigs may vote for Saunders tomorrow.

Jim Sheppard[130] is going for Collins for Comptroller if Rand[131] does not run, & says there is more honesty among the Whigs than Democrats.

Sheperd's Locoism got him 16 votes for Atto. Gen'l., and Tho. Bragg[132] going against Poindexter elected Whitaker[133] over him.

There is no telling where we shall get to, yet.

Brown cannot be elected in 1000 years, if the Saunders men don't desert *him*, and I think nothing short of some governing, rigid leader of these 2 factions will or can ever bring them together—I mean some great ring leader of the Party coming to Raleigh and operating in Caucus, if Caucus can be assembled,

---

[129] Chief Justice Thomas Ruffin.

[130] James B. Shepard.

[131] Nathaniel G. Rand.

[132] Thomas Bragg, Jr. (1810-1872), of Warrenton, educated at the Partridge Academy, at Middletown, Connecticut, and at the university, became a lawyer, and did not enter public life until his election to this session of the legislature, when he was already distinguished in his profession. He was a Democratic elector in 1844, 1848, and 1852. He was elected governor in 1854, and served two terms, defeating Alfred Dockery and John A. Gilmer. He was United States senator, 1859-1861. He was Confederate attorney general, 1861-1862.

[133] Spier Whitaker (1798-1869), of Halifax County, attended the university briefly and became a lawyer. He was a member of the commons, 1838, and attorney general, 1842-1846. He then moved to Iowa.

which is very doubtful now, for some swear they will never go into another.

A letter from H. Waddell Esqr. today reprobates our going over to Saunders in any event. I answered him.

We have nothing interesting, except a printed card from Mr. Badger was publicly handed round by the Door keeper to day to every Whig member, inviting us tomorrow at 7, to his house, and not one to a Loco here. I fully expect this will produce excitement on the other side, and in fact I cannot understand it. I talked with Judge Battle today, & he could not either; it seems about to be a Whig Levee.

Palmer, Y. Patterson & Gen'l Cowan[134] hold on for Comptroller yet, and J. H. Wheeler[135] for Treasurer, and we have a Resolution before us to abolish the Comptroller office. Perhaps to erect an Auditor's upon its ruins, and avoid proscription. Avery[136] introduced it.

### From George C. Mendenhall.                                          U.

#### Raleigh, Thursday night,

#### Decr. 8, 1842.

Today 2 more votings come off for Senator. Some Whigs voted for Saunders, & his vote was 45, yours 55, & Brown 63 twice over. The Whigs have no idea of giving over yet, if at all.

There is a full Loco Caucus tonight to try & reconcile, and every Whig member invited to Mr. Badger's & we now go. So it seems like a double Caucus—for not a Loco is invited to Badgers.

---

[134] William James Cowan, of Wilmington, a graduate of the university, member of the commons, 1816-1817, 1821.

[135] John Hill Wheeler (1806-1882), a native of Murfreesboro, graduate of Columbian University, studied law under Chief Justice Taylor, and served in the commons, 1827-1830. He was secretary of the commission on the French claims, 1831-1834, superintendant of the mint at Charlotte, 1837-1841. He moved to Lincoln County, and was state treasurer, 1842-1844. He was again in the commons in 1852, and Minister to Nicaragua, 1854-1857. He was the author of *Historical Sketches of North Carolina,* and *Reminiscences of North Carolina.* Both were highly inaccurate, but nevertheless valuable. The former, which played up Democrats and minimized or ignored Whigs, won a popular title of "The Democratic Stud-Book."

[136] William Waightstill Avery (1816-1864), of Burke, a graduate of the university, studied law under Judge Gaston. He was a member of the commons, 1842, 1850-1852, and state senator, 1856 (speaker), 1860. He was chairman of the state delegation in the Democratic national conventions of 1856 and 1860. He was a strong secessionist, and was a member of the Confederate provisional congress. He was killed by Kirk's raiders in 1864.

We shall hear tomorrow most likely & I will write again.

Doake[137] & McLean[138] Went off to Saunders—not to remain—all well. Cad Jones said both B. & S. would be rolled off the track. I dont believe it.

[P.S.] The Jackson $1000. resolution was on to day by Satterfield from Person.


*From John A. Young.*[139]                                   U.

Raleigh,
North Carolina.

December 9th., 1842.

Gen'l Patterson informed me that you wanted a Directory, and I herewith forward you one.

Our proceedings of yesterday you have in today's Register, we did not vote today for U. S. Senator, but agreed to vote tomorrow at 12 o'clock. The postponement was not by Party concert, nor is it believed was intended by its movers to affect any Party purpose. Your Competitors are both still in the field, and so far as the Whigs know, will continue to press their claims.

If it is in my power at any time to inform you of any important *move* concerning your election, or communicate any thing of moment in relation to it, I will do so with much pleasure.

Mr. James Graham has not yet arrived.

It would afford me much pleasure to hear from you, or Recieve Communications from you at any time.


*From George C. Mendenhall.*                              U.

Raleigh, Saturday night, 11 P.M.,

Decr. 10, 1842.

Yours was today recvd. Nothing further has been done on the subject of Senator. We heard distinctly the Dems. could not agree in their Caucus. I think some Brown voters will go over to L. D. Henry next time, tho I do not think Henry will yet be put in

---

[137] William Doak, of Guilford, member of the commons, 1838-1844.
[138] Joel McLinn, of Guilford, member of the commons, 1842.
[139] John A. Young, of Iredell, a member of the commons, 1840-1842.

nomination. There seems rather a flagging of the Brown party; he himself took sick under the operation & could not be present at the Convention Comparing the votes for Gov. but was in his seat today & looks badly—I mean badly for *him*. Things are just in the condition about Senator that *nobody knows nothing*. I glory to hear Saunders intends holding on to the bitter end; no Whig has gone off from you only temporarily—every one to a man can be called back at a word—and the only matter of difficulty now is, whether it be possible to get enough actually to go over to Saunders to elect him—even if it was thought best, and we all tried to get them to do so. There is not a Brown Whig here, tis true as I wrote you, but how many Saunders Whigs there are upon a full & close vote is very doubtful. I think likely upon *one more* voting, we may give Saunders an addition of a few over 45, and then call off the dogs and leave the Locos to a true Locofoco fate. I feel almost irresistably induced to write you every mail at the present crisis of affairs. There seems rather fear & alarm & almost consternation among both factions. I shall not withdraw your name.

We had a meeting of the Trustees of the University tonight, 13 present, & if 20 could be had our late Atto Genl. would go overboard.

McDowell County passed the House 3rd time today.

We have nothing interesting.

*From George C. Mendenhall.*                              U.

Raleigh, Sunday night 11,

Decr. 11, 1842.

Tonight we had Gov. Morehead, Pope,[140] Moore,[141] Barringer, Long, Foreman,[142] & McLean, all together. We had letters from Washington, assuring that Saunders would be withdrawn on tomorrow unless the Whigs went over. We don't believe it, but all prefer Saunders to Brown, nor do we believe a further voting will be moved for a few days. We know not what to do, but some

---

[140] Benjamin A. Pope, of Halifax, attended the university briefly, and was a member of the commons, 1840-1842.

[141] Bartholomew F. Moore.

[142] John L. Foreman (1808-1844), of Pitt, after two years at the university, became a planter. He was a member of the commons, 1833-1835, 1838-1842, state senator, 1844.

10 more Whigs will vote for Saunders next time, and then we will consult again.

I have now burnt your letter. It is thought by some that to elect Saunders that both Brown & Henry are done with Public life & Saunders out of the way in past. As to his resigning in a year none of us believe that; if we did, he would be elected at once. We are, I might say, altogether dispairing of electing you, but whether enough of Whigs will go over to Saunders to elect him I know not; if required there were enough awhile & may be yet, but several will never go for either. We are anxious to district the State right first.

On the Senators election write cautiously & confidentially & to a few only. I cannot tell how we shall act in the end; I much fear not satisfactory to ourselves, tho' we are a United Band. The present Whig belief here is, for the benefit of the Whig cause, to run Saunders up to Brown's vote and there stop for awhile, and our Whigs unwillingly do this, but most are ready to do what they are directed to do for the cause.

I have never seen everybody so much at a loss exactly what to do, and those of us—yes, all of us—who give directions for others to vote for Saunders—all, every man himself, strongly holds on & votes for you himself; letters come thick and strong to us to elect Saunders at once. We think we can judge best of this who are here, so far as N. C. is concerned.

There may be an agreement among the 2 factions & all gone at once, but we do not think so. We have not yet come to the period for final action, nor do we have much idea when or how we can.

All I fear is that of making a blunder at a wrong time.

Every sort of game is endeavored to be played off upon us by both factions, but we are not yet to be frightened or deceived.

We are in absolute uncertainty.

Farewell.


*From George C. Mendenhall.*                                    U.

Raleigh, Tuesday night, Decr. 13, 1842

Another day has passed off & nothing more done about Senator & it is said will not be till Thursday & I think then no election, for Saunders will get over 50 votes & Brown, I think, cannot gain many votes. Nelson[143] of Stokes said Brown would be elected in the end. McRae[144] of Cumberland says he will not vote next time for Brown but for Henry.

There seems a strong disposition here among the leading Whigs to go over to Saunders after awhile, in fact all is uncertainty yet. Shultz[145] of Stokes went over from S. to Brown & is mad with his Saunders friends & they at him it is said.

Caldwell's Resolutions[146] on Repudiation were postponed till Monday next, Catawba is a County, and McDowell & Union passed the Commons. There is very little here interesting in any way. Nelson said Brown would be elected next time, but I have no idea of an election for some votings yet myself. We are generally well.

*From George C. Mendenhall.*                               U.

Raleigh, Decr. 14th, night, 1842.

There is great exertions going on here—and an evident giving way of the Saunders party. Tonight is another Caucus tis said by adjournment. Therefore I now suppose this was the reason that no Election was to come on till Thursday.

The Standard is out to day strong for Brown as you will see. The Carolinian out against both & for Henry, but abusing the Locos for having no election.

The Brown men today seem rather flushed with Success, or the prospect of it. I still think the Saunders men will stand one more fire, and unless Saunders is well nigh or quite even with Brown their Phalanx will give way—not all—but enough to elect Brown.

Letters come here from different parts of the State saying, go for Saunders if - - - Graham cannot be elected. We are in rather a staggering condition, for if Brown is to be elected, we wish all that voting to vote for you; but again if all drove back now from Saunders, he will be withdrawn—or rather they will go over & vote for Brown & not withdraw him.

---

[143] Albert F. Nelson, of Stokes, a member of the commons.
[144] Duncan Kirkland McRae (1819-1888), of Cumberland, a member of the commons, journalist, consul to Paris, Confederate colonel.
[145] Jacob Schultz, of Stokes, a member of the commons.
[146] Joseph P. Caldwell, on November 29th introduced resolutions expressing abhorrence of repudiation, by certain states, of their debts.

Russell anxiously enquired if any of Browns friends had said they had rather see Graham elected than Saunders. Barringer & myself assured him such was the Report. Wilder told me to day he did not know what to do for he had charge of Saunders name & he was blamed very much, & he should be compelled against his will to give way, Unless he percieved a fair prospect of Saunders increasing his vote.

We are not to be deceived by all these statements & intimations tho there seems now a stronger prospect of a Union than ever in the course of this week.

We did but little in the House to day. The Committee on Finance & Biggs[147] at their head have had a correspondence with the Gov., & have adopted a Resolution tho not yet offered, declaring that the Literary Board have or had not power by law to invest the $22 000. in Rail Road Bonds endorsed by the State. Brown at the head of Banks moves slow, no doubt waiting the final & hoping happy result of the Senators election.

We have not heard for a few days from Washington except a letter from Stanly pressing for Saunders election, if you are hopeless. I heard of, but did not see the letter. Biggs and Bowers[148] work like dray-horses to find some flaw, error, or mistake somewhere to add to their capital in 1844.

*From George C. Mendenhall.*                    U.

Raleigh, Decr. 14th, 11 at night, 1842.

Since writing the enclosed, yours of the 12th was recvd, and I soon found there was on hand, before I had recvd. it, a general stew.

Barringer, Batt Moore, & others all conclude tomorrow a number of us must vote for Saunders, and nothing else will do. We intend thereby, whether Saunders is withdrawn or not, to prevent an election, and then postpone all further action and tomorrow night go into Caucus and try our strength, for Gee & many others are *ditch-men,* & some are pledged, and I believe Saunders will

[147] Asa Biggs (1811-1878), of Martin County, lawyer, delegate to the convention of 1835, member of the commons, 1840-1844, of the state senate, 1844, 1854, Democratic member of congress, 1845-1847, United States senator, 1855-1858, Federal judge, 1858-1861, delegate to convention of 1861, Confederate judge, 1861-1865.

[148] George Bowers, of Ashe, state senator, 1812-1817, 1848-1854, member of the commons, 1842.

be almost or quite elected shortly, for every Whig is hopeless as to your election.

Moore came here a ditchman & hands off, but he is now strong & fully going for Saunders to strengthen the Calhoun party for the time being. Next to put down Brown forever also to avoid Saunders running for Gov. again, & furthermore to create an unreconciliable difference between Saunders party & the Loco focos proper, etc.

Albright will lead off for Saunders and J. T. Morehead will go, & Col. Joyner will on a 2nd voting go over, and even Shad P. Allen will likely strike off first in our house.

So you see the thing is up.

Your friend
farewell

I hate to write this letter, but the truth is always required of me.

*From Joseph B. Hinton.*[149]                    A.

Raleigh, N. C.,

Decr. 14th, 1842.

Mr. Benton's bill for repealing the Bankrupt law is so invidious and unjust to those whose cases are still pending in the Courts under the law, that I should think it will stand no chance of passing either branch of Congress in the form he has presented it, at least I hope so. The law has done much good & harm; much good to thousands of families hopelessly undone without it, and much harm to a just and magnanimous party which enacted and sustained it, but when the strifes of the present day have past, I cannot doubt but the mede of praise will be awarded to its friends, and it will be deemed as wise as beneficent and humane—maugre all the clamor and slang of the present times. Mr. Badger thinks that it is a mistaken idea that it will be good policy in a Whig Congress to repeal it. However that may be, of one thing there can be no doubt, and that is this: that so invidious and unjust a method of repealing it, as Mr. Benton's, ought to find no favor any where. If the law is to be repealed now, at least let it die in its *present form,* and the cases now pending in the Courts to be

---

[149] Joseph B. Hinton, of Beaufort County, who represented his county in the state senate, 1829-1830, 1832.

placed on the same footing as those already decided under it. If the law had been enacted as Mr. Benton proposes now to make it, in its last moments, it would have been an utter abortion as to all useful purposes. Not one in a thousand who has sought relief under the present law, would have gone into Court under Mr. Benton's modification of it—not one in No. Ca most certainly would have attempted it. One in the million might possibly get 2/3ds of his creditors to *sign consent* for the discharge of their debter, upon a surrender of all, but in this State, hardly the first case would have been found to do it. We go for the stuff, and when the stuff is got, then we reluctantly let go our grip of the hide and tallow. There are thousands of cases now depending under the act in the United States, and in N. C. several hundred; and the Judges are hastening proceedings by special Courts, in this and the next month, to dispose of all they can, before the repeal of the Law, and thereby to relieve as many as they can. But if the law be *now* changed as Mr. Benton proposes, these cases are to be decided upon wholly different principles than those upon which they commenced—and wholly different from those cases already decided under the act. This would be monstrously unjust to all concerned. I am one of those concerned, and as such, and in the name of some hundreds of other unfortunates in this State, I pray you, and our whole delegation in Congress, whether in favor or against the Law itself, to leave us upon the same footing as those whose cases have been decided; by leaving the law unchanged up to its repeal, at least so as not to affect cases now depending and commenced under the law as it now exists.

I was left a portionless orphan at 3 years of age, & had to be the architect of my own fortunes, but my industry and enterprize made me master of all of $25,000 worth of property at 40 years of age, but then having had to pay the debts of others for whom I was unfortunately security to amt. of not far from $20,000 and other losses, my affairs became embarrassed & after struggling with various success until last Spring, in the hope that Congress would pay my claim of $20,000 for French Spoilations & thereby again enable me to be independent and comfortable—a Case upon the only unjust claim against me for about $200—the object of which was to force my wife to sell her separate property & pay it, or my friends to do it—drove into a Bankrupt Court upon the advice of my friends, & in so doing I surrendered to the Assignee not far short of $30,000 worth of property, or what ought to be worth it, including my Government claim. But if the law had been as Mr. Benton would have it, I certainly would have made no such surrender, but struggled on as I could, without any resort to a Bankrupt Court. I am very sure I express in this, the sentiments of every other applicant in N. C. & probably 99 out of every 100 elsewhere.

The plot thickens here. The last three days have been busy ones in whipping the faithful into the ranks, and it is confidently said to day, among the Brownites, that they have accomplished their purpose, & on friday they intend to withdraw Genl. Saunders & elect Mr. Brown, & the fact that the Standard has to day pulled down the Generals flag and run up Mr. Brown's, & its attempt to frighten the impracticables into the ranks, and the fact that Mr. Brown has to day for the first time in a week, looked cheerful & at ease, induces me to think there is truth in the statement. But I know there are some of the Saunders men who still swear they will not be driven from his support. If 30 of them, or even 25 of them are *pluck,* on the next trial, Genl. Saunders will be the Senator—as in that event the Whigs I am sure would give him a majority over Mr. Brown. The zeal of the Standard and others to day, is intended to prevent such a result, and secure Brown's election at the expense of the sacrifies of the Genl—for some of their leaders don't hesitate to say openly, he has ruined himself with his party by suffering his name to be run & pushing his pretensions, when vetoed by the Caucus. I am a Saunders man & if you cannot be reelected, as it is clear the Whigs cannot do that at present, I do wish our friends to aid the Genl. in triumphing over a selfish clan who have used his influence & now kick aside the ladder.

Day before yesterday, Mr. Shepard introduced into the Senate a bold measure to be the order of the day on friday next. It is to authorize the issue of one million of Treasury notes to be divided among the Counties of the State, & by means of loan offices to be lent out to the people at $3\frac{1}{2}$ percent, reimbursable in 3 years; on pledges of real or personal security. Weldon N. Edwards[150] denounced it at the threshhold as a violation of the Constitution

---

[150] Weldon Nathaniel Edwards (1788-1873), of Warren, a native of Northampton, was educated at the Warrenton Academy under Marcus George. He was a member of the commons, 1814-1815, member of congress, 1815-1827, state senator, 1833-1846, 1850-1854, (speaker 1850-1854), delegate to the convention of 1835, president of the convention of 1861. He was able, balanced, and effective. A devoted Democrat, he had the confidence of the Whigs as well.

& monstrous! To day this same Mr. Shepard introduced another Bill, "Concerning Banks." It forbids our Banks to pay out any other bills than those authorized by our own Legislature—under fine and imprisonment—& forbids the Banks to suspend specie payment at any time hereafter; if for 30 days they forfeit to the State Treasury 3 per cent on all their circulation, if for 3 months, they forfeit their Charters & go forthwith into a close of all their matters. Mr. Brown seemed startled at so bold a measure & moved its reference to the Judiciary Committee! Unless I am mistaken, many of the party won't come up to the scratch when the time comes, and will curse Mr. Shepard for his temerity.

To day the Senatorial Districting Com. reported, and as far as I could hear or judge from the reading I am of opinion very few political changes are made by it, as very few of the Dists are changed. I learn that the probable report on the Congress'l Dist's will be 5 to 4. Mr. Rayner's can't be altered to his disadvantage, but Mr. Stanly's will. And yet, with Nash & Martin hitched on to it, if the Whigs are wise when all the Richmonds of the *party* take the field, they will have the game in their own hands.

*From George C. Mendenhall.*                     U.

Raleigh, friday night, Decr. 16, 1842.

To write now is rather to write a blank letter. We had no voting to-day & no talk of it. The Lo-co party met in Caucus tonight. I wrote you or Mr Rayner the result of our last vote—that the time had come as we believed here for action & a number more of us voted for Saunders, running him up to 56. The Brown party are alarmed above measure.

To-day after Mr. Sheperd on his million Bank or Treasury notes, Mr. Bedford Brown held forth some 2 hours most luminous in real *Brown Style*—a Crowded Senate—the house adjourned for want of a Quorum—and such real rearing and charging & Bank abuse was never heard. Mr. Cooper is next entitled to the floor. Brown is *agin* Sheperds moneyed affair. The Committee on Finance and on the Literary fund are thro their Chmn., Biggs, trying to get into a difficulty with the Gov., but he has many cool admirers around him and is willing to be advised.

We now have a certificate issued by the State in 1783 for 19.2—3 before the Assembly, barred of course by our act of 1799, and perhaps the Genl. Government ought to pay it. We are against repudiation, and yet we understand some 20 or 100 thousand dollars are still out.

The original Certificate is produced here & is genuine.

I should like to have some information on this subject—if convenient but not otherwise. Since the death of Lewis Williams I do not know who to enquire of.

To pass repudiating Resolutions and refuse to pay a just and unsatisfied Debt, because old, is incongruous.

A most deadly effort will be made to drive the Saunders men from their strongholds. Shultz now votes for Brown & Rea, and Dr. Bracken[151] voted for Tho. Ruffin last time.

The Whigs have no meeting appointed and it is yet uncertain whether enough of Whigs will go over to elect Saunders unless some Brown men come back.

I thought there would full enough of Whigs go where necessary for S., but it is not now so certain.

If Saunders is withdrawn, every Whig goes back and votes for you unless a false march is suspected by us on their part & then we vote in part for Saunders to prevent an election.

We are on doubtful ground, but hold the balance of power.


*From George C. Mendenhall.* U.

Raleigh, Decr. 18, Sunday morning, 1842.

Last night we the Whigs sat in Convention till ½ after 11 at night—or later—Badger made a long & able speech. Manly & Bryan & Clingman also spoke, and we had speech after speech, and I never have heard men abused so, as both Brown & Saunders, & *both* by all were placed on equal footing, & each worse than the other if possible.

It was in Convention agreed for me to withdraw your name Monday or at the coming on of the next voting. If a Committee of 5, two of the Senate & 3 of the Commons reported to me that enough of Whigs would go for Saunders to insure his election; poor

---

[151] Julius C. S. Bracken, of Orange, a native of Caswell, member of the commons, 1842.

Col Joyner, and Howard [152] & Jones[153] of Wilkes, & Jefferson,[154] & Baxter[155] & many others yielded with apparent heartfelt sorrow, as did every Whig there, but the time has now come and we were compelled to act at once.

No man upon Earth need desire more warm feelings of friendship, nor to be spoken of in terms of higher regard for talent, ability, dignifying, manly, & high minded honorable course of conduct in public & private life than yourself. Sir, it was a meeting of Whigs most solemn! it was like cutting the ligaments of regard and Friendship and plighted troth between man and wife; for us to conclude to leave our favorite, gallant, and beloved leader, and march over to the succor of an enemy, a common enemy.

We may have done wrong.

May the Great God of Heaven forgive us.

No doubt before you could answer this there will be a Senator.

> Your friend
> farewell

It is said Dobson & some others are giving or given way from Saunders. We had about 60 Whigs together or near it, & the object of the Commitee was to ascertain whether enough of Saunders men still remained firm to him, who aided by the Whigs could elect him; if not, all Whigs would then vote for Graham, but I understand this morning there are 32 Saunders men who hold on—it was reported all were gone but 18. I shall know tonight before I sleep because the Committee are to report to me.

---

[152] James W. Howard, of Jones, member of the commons, 1831, 1834-1836, state senator, 1842, 1846.

[153] Edmund Walter Jones (1811-1876), of Wilkes, (now Caldwell) County, graduate of the university, state senator, 1842, from Caldwell, 1868, (did not attend), delegate to conventions of 1861 and 1875, member Council of State, 1866.

[154] Thomas Jefferson, of Rutherford, a native of Virginia, member of the commons, 1836, 1840-1842, of the senate, 1844. He was a Whig leader in his county. He later moved to Arkansas.

[155] John Baxter (1819-1886), of Rutherford County, member of the commons, 1842. He moved to Henderson County, and was again in the commons, 1846, 1852-1865, (speaker, 1852). He moved to Knoxville, where he was a strong and active Unionist in 1861, sat in the convention of 1870, and was a judge of the United States Circuit Court from 1877 to his death.

*From Hamilton C. Jones.*                                    A.

Wilmington,

Decemr. 18th, 1842.

Several of our profession assembled here to attend the Dist. Court of the U. S. have seen with much concern the propositions sprung most suddenly upon Congress to repeal the Bankrupt Law, and they have requested me to address you on the subject. The proposition of Mr. Benton to repeal the law with a saving that imposes duties and restrictions not held out by the law, would be most hard & unjust. We fully appreciate the motive that induced you to propose a continuation of the law as it stood, to the 5th. of December but to cut off all from its protection who have filed petitions since that day. Now my dear Sir you have no idea of the pain and dissatisfaction such a *saving* would give to a large class of unfortunate individuals and their friends. Why not let the repeal take effect from its passage with a saving of all those who had filed their petitions before that time? Or at least why not save all who had filed petitions before they had notice that such a measure was contemplated? Many had sworn to their petitions and let them lie in the hands of their attornies till they could come down to this Court where the necessary orders could be obtained: these persons have with great difficulty raised some money for the cost and secured from $25 to 50 dollars for fees relying on the benefit which was promised them by an existing law of their Country: all this they will have to loose if they are not brought within the scope of the saving: they clerk and attorney will say that it is not their fault that the duty is not performed which they engaged to do. So they must pay their fees and lose what they have paid if this is not done. Besides this, they have laid open their affairs and exposed themselves to be harrassed and oppressed for having done what the law invited them to do. Fictions of law usually are adopted to forward the purposes of justice, but your proposition by relating back to 5th. of December will work hardship and injustice to such as have come on without any intimation of any such thing. If any are to be saved why not all. All are upon the same footing as to merit and any law that does not save all would be partial and unreasonable. And we do not see why it would not be as easy to get through a saving for all as for some.

We do not say that the law ought not to be repealed. But if Congress has done wrong in passing the law it is no reason they should do wrong again in repealing it. We humbly concur that it would be more manly and that they would stand better even with the opponents of the law to take care of that unfortunate class of individuals whom their own act had made more helpless and wretched. No clamor of the crowds or bitterness of political enemies ought to make a party do wrong to save themselves and a little wrong ought just as much to be avoided as a great one in such a case. We feel persuaded that you can not far differ with us in these sentiments and as a part of your constituents and from our positions well knowing the cruel disappointment it will work we ask you so to enlarge your proposition as to put all petitioners on the same footing.

*From S. O. Butler.*                                                U.

Cincinati,

(Confidential)                                December 18th., 1842.

The known hostility of the Senators from Ohio to the Bankrupt Act, prevents my writing them on the subject of the repeal of that law, which from present indications, will take place this session. I do not suppose that any suggestions from a Whig would find favor, either with Mr. Tappan or Mr. Allen.[156] From those reasons I have taken the liberty to address you upon the subject, thinking (from your notice in the Senate of your intention to offer an amendment, so that the repeal shall not effect those who petitioned before the commencement of the present session) that you might take into consideration the propriety, and indeed the obvious justice, of the suggestions I now trouble you with. All men of proper feeling and sentiment feel a great repugnance to availing themselves of this mode of cancelling their debts, and evidently the odium which attaches to those who are obliged to publish their dishonor to the world in the shape of a petition for the benefit of that act! And I would most respectfully suggest to you, if gross injustice would not be done to those whose applications have thus been made public, if the law should be repealed,

---

[156] William Allen (1803-1879), of Ohio, a native of Edenton, N. C., a lawyer, Democratic member of congress, 1833-1835, United States senator, 1837-1849, governor, 1874-1876,

and leave them with all the *odium,* without extending to them the benefit of that act. The law was passed to induce the honest and unfortunate debtor to surrender all his property, for the benefit of his creditors equally, and those who have made their petition since the Session of this Congress, as well as before, could not possibly believe that the law was to operate as a snare to him, to induce him to suffer the *extremest* mortification a high minded and honorable man is capable, and then to leave him with his debts uncancelled and his character *stigmatized* as an *unsuccessfull* applicant for the benefit of a law which was intended for the good of all. I am one of those who, had the Bankrupt act never been passed, would never have been obliged to resort to the act myself, and my case is only one of thousands. My endorsements for friends have compelled me to this course also, as, after the passage of the act *preferences* could not be given, and therefore I had to stand my chance with the other creditors, whereas, had the act never been passed, my confidential endorsements would have been secured, and I should have been safe and solvent, and could have met *all* my own obligations! And now, within the last ten days, I have been compelled to make public my own inability to meet my engagements promptly, and in addition to the mortification, I am also called upon to endure the agony of an anticipated repeal of the law, which will cut me off from its benefits, because I did not make my application a few days earlier. I beg you not to think, my dear Sir, that I have explained my individual case, supposing that it would influence you, but mainly to shew you the situation, that repeal of the law would place thousands in, who did not petition before the commencement of this Session. If the people demand the repeal of that law, would not they be just as well satisfied to have the appeal take effect on the 4th. of March next, when this Congress expires, and thereby give *all* an opportunity to avail themselves of it. This course, it does strike me, is the one dictated by a spirit of philanthropy and justice, and I would most earnestly, but humbly, ask you to give the suggestion some thought, and if your views are in accordance therewith, and your sense of duty to your own immediate constituents, will permit you to so modify your amendments as to permit all who *have* petitioned, to reap the benefit of that act, you will receive the heartfelt gratitude of thousands of unfortunate debtors, who are now trembling with fear and anxiety, expecting its repeal. Not having the honor of a personal acquaintance with you, an anonymous signature would no doubt be as satisfactory as my real one, but I venture to solicit your kind indulgence for the liberty I have taken, and subscribe my real name, and remain,

Your Obed't Serv't.

*From George C. Mendenhall.*    U.

City of Raleigh, Monday night,

Decr. 18, 1842.

The Whig Committee consisting of H. G. Spruill,[157] Jones of Wilkes, Barringer, Leach,[158] & Halsey [159] at the Meeting of the House this morning reported to me that there were Whigs enough with the Saunders men who would vote for Saunders to elect him, and directed me to withdraw your name.

Accordingly when the Senate agreed to our message to Vote, I rose and with pain to myself and I know to every Whig who heard it, withdrew your name. Forthwith Bragg nominated Haywood, & he got 5 votes, Brown 61, and Saunders 78 votes; another message was sent to the Senate to vote immediately, and G. B. Jones [160] nominated Michael Hoke who is now here, and the Senate laid it on their Table. An attempt was made to bring on the election of Treasurer to day & the Locos opposed it, and it produced much warm debate, but the Senate adjourned & then we did, & so the matter stands. Only the Loco party have a meeting tonight and they will cause a political Earthquake or rally their forces altogether.

There is nothing else new or changed in our City. I think Badger's Party went off without complaint, for that night the Locofocos were all in Caucus.

We are generally well, and get on very slow with Business You see the Locos now have 3 of their Party—yes 4— all on the track. I never saw such confusion and consternation, and such pale faces as when your name was withdrawn. Cad Jones & C. Graves seemed wholly out of sorts.

It is thought Brown will be withdrawn tomorrow. I think Saunders will be elected. There is much bitterness among our

---

[157] Hezekiah G. Spruill, of Tyrrell County, member of the commons, 1831, delegate to the convention of 1835, state senator, 1836-1842.

[158] Julian E. Leach, of Randolph, member of the commons, 1842.

[159] Joseph Halsey, of Tyrrell, member of the commons, 1842, state senator, 1844-1848.

[160] John B. Jones of Currituck, member of the commons, 1831-1833, 1840-1844, 1854-1856, delegate to the convention of 1835.

foes. Cardwell charged an unholy alliance today in the house, and then withdrew it as to the Saunders men, etc.

It is most horrid to be placed in our condition.

*From Charles L. Hinton.*                                    U.

### Raleigh

#### Dec. 19th, 1844. [1842].

My apology for not answering your letter sooner is the great electioneering excitement in which my feelings have been enlisted.

\*     \*     \*     \*     \*

We had another balloting for U. S. Senator to day, Sanders[161] came within two votes of being elected, his own men flying the tract, your name being withdrawn, the Register, I suppose, will give you the particulars. There will be a Caucus to night to try and fix on a third man—Hoke is here and spoken of.

It is believed if a second balloting could have been had to day, that Sanders would have been elected. I now doubt very much whether Sanders can rally his forces.

20th. in the morning.

I have reason to believe that they fixed on Haywood last night in Caucus—Brown and Sanders will both be withdrawn.

My own election is very doubtful.

*From Henry K. Nash.*                                    U.

#### Raleigh, December 19th, 1842.

I have been waiting until some dicisive action should be taken by our friends on the subject of the Senatorial election to write to you.

Against the advice and consent of several of our friends (myself among the number) it has been determined by our friends—a majority of them—that it is the duty of the Whig Party to withdraw your name from that contest and unite upon Genl. Saunders. I will not unite with them in any such course, and there are several others who occupy the same ground.

---

[161] Saunders.

I think our friends will find they have committed an egregious error; I hope however it may be for the best.

I will write to you as soon as the election takes place.

*To James W. Bryan.*                              U. Bryan Mss.

Washington City,

Dec. 21st, 1842.

\* \* \* \* \*

There has been quite a sensation here for a day or two past, in consequence of the hanging at the yard arm of the Brig Somers, at Sea, of Midshipman Spencer,[162] a son of the Secretary of War, for mutiny. By order of Commander Sledell McKenzie,[163] author of "A year in Spain." You will see a detailed account of it in your papers. As yet public sentiment justifies the Execution as an act of necessity. A Court of Inquiry, however, will investigate the whole matter.

The proceedings of Congress have had little interest thus far, and promise not much during the Session. The Bankrupt Law will probably be repealed. Benton is making war on the late British Treaty in every mode that he can devise, to affect Webster and Tyler, and through them Calhoun. The latter is in rather low spirits, I think. The election of Judge Huger, a Union man, as his successor, over Pickens and Rhett,[164] has been discouraging to him. And the party here after their successes in so many State elections, look generally to Van Buren as their Candidate for the Presidency. Calhoun however is disposed to hold off, and advises Saunders to take the appointment of Senator from the Whigs, if he can get it. I expect to hear tonight that he is elected.

Cass arrived here yesterday from Paris, and is ready to come out upon a little solicitation. Old Col. Johnson is quite willing, and Buchanan nothing loth. Benton however will bully them into a

---

[162] Philip Spencer.

[163] Alexander Slidell MacKenzie. The Navy Register gives the date of his death, 1848. The case caused much excitement and loud demands for MacKenzie's punishment. A court martial was ordered which exonerated him completely.

[164] Robert Barnwell Rhett, (born Smith) (1800-1876), of South Carolina, a lawyer, served in the lower house of the legislature in 1826, was elected attorney general, 1826, was a Democratic member of congress, 1837-1849, United States senator, 1850-1852, delegate to the convention of 1860, and a delegate to the Confederate provisional congress, 1861. He controlled the policies of the influential *Charleston Mercury* for many years, and edited it for some years.

nomination of Van Buren. And then it is to be seen whether Calhoun and Johnson will submit.

The Whigs have to consent to a National Convention to bring out a Candidate, but I think Clay can easily obtain the nomination. He is now on a visit to New Orleans and is to be received with wonderful demonstrations.

I have just recd. mail from Raleigh and find that Saunders wanted three votes of election, and there was an adjournment, and probably Haywood was agreed on in Caucus.

*From Charles L. Hinton.* U.

Raleigh,

Decr. 31st, 1842.

Yours of the 24th. was rec'd last night, I am sorry your proxy was not directed to some other person as I am not a stockholder and can't act. Monday will be an important day with them, as there will be a proposition to surrender the Charter[165] to the Legislature, it will be supported by the principal stockholders and I expect a resolution will be introduced in the House to day directing the individual representing the State stock to vote for a surrender, if it passes the house it will certainly pass the Board, so you see we are likely to be placed in an awkward position with regard to the Banks. The Locos say, and I have no doubt will, if the Charter is tendered, accept it, and establish a bank on the faith of the State with a Capital of several millions such at least is the general feeling at this time.

The reason assigned on part of the stockholders for surrendering is, the great abuse by the opposite party, for you will discover from the resolutions and speeches that the managers of the Bank are treated as a parcel of swindlers, it will disarm them, of at least this one strong weapon that has been most effectually used against the Whig party.

Were I a stockholder, I should vote against it as ruinous to the Public, we shall not be able again to get Capitalists to invest in any Bank in the State, it will force them to seek a foreign investment.

---

[165] The Bank of the State was about to surrender its charter.

*From Susan Washington Graham.*                    **U.**

Hillsboro',

Decr. 31st, 1842.

My Dear Husband,

I received by this morning's mail your letter of the 26th. and also one of a later date, containing a check for Dr. Webb. I gave the envelope of the New World to Will and told him there was a letter from Father, the little fellow kept it all the morning and was as much pleased as he would have been with the handsomest toy in Washington. He has an affectionate disposition and is very fond of little "buddy Wobert" as he calls him, frequently comes and asks me to let him see his pretty little blue eyes and says "I do lub him I do." He resembles Will more than the others and is *much* the largest of all my infants. The other boys try to play with him sometimes but they are most amused in listening to Will's speeches to him. He bids fair to be a good deal of a Wag.

I wish you could have the little creatures around your knees for a while. They are very fond of you and whenever they object to getting their book I merely have to ask them if "I must tell Father that they didn't say a lesson today." They have missed saying a lesson only three or four days since you left us. Joseph learns slowly but remembers pretty well.

Dear little James has just come to me and I asked him what must I tell Father? his little face brightened up and he looked around in every direction as if he expected to see you. Whenever asked where you are, he points to the door and shakes his head and says "gone—gone."

One page to your boys, which I hope will not be entirely devoid of interest for you.

Mr. Turrentine hired out Barbara and Charity on Thursday last, Barbara to Mr. Kerr of Chapel Hill for $25 and Charity to Miss or Mrs. Martha Kirkland (Sister of Mr. Hogan) for about $19—so Charity said—Isaac is well or nearly so; he went out to the plantation Monday Morning. Abram went out there to spend his Christmas holiday and I sent Henry and his medicine with the directions, by him to Sally. Henry is much better, and in a fortnight will probably be entirely well.

Dick brought in the waggon Thursday morning to haul wood, and said that Joe cut his foot so badly on Tuesday that he couldn't walk. Dr. Smith has not yet sent the timber here.

I have had the chimney from the other lot hauled over.

Old Mrs. Bryan came to see me in great tribulation about Mr. Laws threatening to "throw them out doors." She said Dr. Parks had given them a lot of ground and they had sufficient timber excepting a few logs to build their house and would be very glad to get the logs of the old kitchen that had fallen down. I told her you had left directions with Mr. Laws about the house and lot and I could not interfere but that she might tell Mr. Laws I said she could have the logs if he would let her take them away. She afterwards came and got permission in writing for them to be hauled away. Upon reflection I thought perhaps I had transcended my authority in allowing her to take them, but it is not at any rate a matter of much consequence.

The supply of shocks was finished a fortnight since. I sent to Mr. Bishop to know if there were any in the neighborhood for sale. He sent in a load by Dick from the plantation and said he knew of no one that had any to spare.

I intend getting some oil cakes for the cows next week. Old Suke is so poor that I shall dislike to take the milk from the calf. I inquire frequently of Lizzy about feeding them but I know they are not as well attended to as if I could see them occasionally.

I intended writing a *long* letter, but Robert continues to fret so much that I must bid you adieu for the present but will try to close my letter in the morning in time for the Mail.

Sunday Morning—A happy "New Year" to you [page torn] May you be spared to enjoy many more.

*  *  *  *  *

I shall spend a lonely New Years but I hope not an unprofitable one. Adieu my Beloved one

May the blessing of God be with you.

Ever Yours

1843

*From George C. Mendenhall.*       U.

City of Raleigh,

Jany. 12th, 1843.

We have had much difficulty about Col. Wheeler giving his Bond as Treasurer. We have by a joint Resolution extended the time from the 22nd. ult. to the 23rd. Inst. and he has obtained the names of 16 members of Assembly, it is said, and has gone to Bertie, etc., this morning with Judge Saunders son for a witness. We have been in awkward fix without a Treasurer thus far. The 2 Speakers approved, & the Gov. disapproved his Bonds, and a controversy arose & facts etc., but the Gov. will be sustained.

The business of legislation goes on slowly. The Congressional Districts as reported from Committee have passed the Senate & most likely will the House. We still have much before us, & not much time. We sit nearly all the time day & night— no time, & no room, for Caucus now. You no doubt saw our actions on the Bank Resolutions.[1] The Locos are sick of them & I think the Banks will in the end rather be sustained, than injured by any of our proceedings. The Political Resolutions[2] are a long ways behind everything. We don't intend to stir them, but if the Locos do, as a Mr. Barnes said here once—there shall be "Speaken upon them." The Locos are afraid of the Whigs on all party measures where "Speaken" can likely arise, and we have & will give notice that no Democratic Resolutions pass without full debate.[3] We shall give no relief to the People by Bill or Resolution, unless it be by adjournment *sine die*.

We are generally well. We cannot adjourn before the 23rd. Inst.

### *From George C. Mendenhall.*     U.

Raleigh, Jany. 12, 1843.

(Confidential)

You are no doubt fully aware that it was intended on the part of the Whigs to hold a Caucus here not to nominate but to fix

---

[1] During the session many resolutions were introduced by Democrats into each house, providing for investigation of the Bank of the State, and the Bank of Cape Fear. Some of them passed one house or the other, but none obtained the concurrence of both. In the midst of extended discussions of the subject, the Bank of the State offered to surrender its charter.

[2] The political resolutions referred to were introduced in the commons by Cadwallader Jones, Jr., and were finally, after much discussion, and Whig opposition, passed by both houses. After asserting the right of the legislature to instruct the senators, and their duty to obey, they went on to declare opposition to taxation designed to promote the interests of particular occupations at general expense, condemning the tariff act just passed, as unwise, dangerous, and unconstitutional, and also a violation of the Compromise of 1833. They included also, sharp condemnation of the bankrupt law, and a demand for its repeal, a demand for the refund of General Jackson's New Orleans fine, and an endorsement of the veto power of the President, and closed with instructions to the senators and a request to the representatives to carry them into effect.

[3] This statement is mild, for the Whig minority waged a quite successful war of opposition and delay, day after day being spent on proposed amendments, and motions to adjourn. Cloture was then undreamed of in North Carolina.

on some person to be hereafter nominated by a Convention hereafter to be held, to be run for the Governor of this State. At the
last Whig meeting in Decr. last, a Resolution was adopted to
assemble the 2nd of Jany. and it seemed to have been wholly
forgotten. I attended alone. We still think of having a Meeting
for that purpose, & to appoint a Committee to invite Mr. Clay
to this State when it may suit him to come. I have several, yes a
number of times been determined on writing a private letter to
you, on the subject of your running for Governor, and asking
a private answer, but I have from time to time felt a backward-
ness in approaching you on that subject.

Col. Barringer has requested & insisted that I should write to
you and request an early answer, as we expect to adjourn the
23rd Inst. I think I can say with certainty that it is the general
belief you are the strongest man who could be placed upon the
Whig ticket in N. C. for Gov., and there is no prospect of any
other being fixed upon unless you refuse, & then Charles Manly
would most likely to be the next man. Our friend K. Rayner, I
think will not now be taken up by the Whigs for Gov.

I am very unwilling to make any request of you that I ought
not, but it does seem as if there should be some little conference
upon this subject, before anything like formal action.

Should you feel yourself at liberty to give any intimations or
to decide upon this important matter, please drop us a confidential line, and no Eye shall see it but those allowed & specially
mentioned by yourself, and the letter shall be forthwith burnt.

*From George C. Mendenhall.*                              U.

City of Raleigh,

Jan'y. 13th, 1843.

By the mail last night I wrote you a line—with one enclosed—
upon the very subject mentioned in yours received this morning.
I shewed yours to Moore, Barringer & Badger & no others.

I cannot tell when we can or shall have a Whig meeting here.
I was pleased with all your suggestions, except that of declining
a nomination for Gov. We have nobody else but Manly whom
we can successfully run, & the Locos have none but M. Hoke, &
I do not think he has folly enough to try it.

You know the Gov. disapproved and the 2 Speakers approved
Wheeler's Bonds.

The Committee of investigation have taken the Evidence in writing of D. W. Stone that the name of Perry Carter had no seal, on friday morning the 30th ultimo & he so informed Wheeler. Then the evidence of Dr. G. C. Moore that J. H. & Sam J. Wheeler came from Murfreesboro to his House at 10 at night & shewed the Bonds & then *they* told G. C. Moore that Carter signed at dark at Murfreesboro & they told him he had omitted the seal, and that Carter then told those 2 to tell Dr. Moore to add the seal & he would be bound by the act, and that friday evening the 30th J. H. Wheeler in Raleigh reminded Moore, and he then in pursuance of this verbal authority thus sent added the seal.

This Evidence will go to the Commons Tomorrow with a Report by Bragg favorable to Wheeler & with leave to withdraw his Bonds; he is now gone to Bertie for others. It is said 14 Loco Members have signed for him, & Stallings, B. Brown & W. N. Edwards among them. Wheeler has lost ground here, by being detected in incorrect statements; he will be Treasurer however in the end.

The Bank Resolutions which passed the Commons are amended by the Senate & will not pass the Commons as amended, for many Democrats are sick of them.

We get on very slowly indeed.

We have 50 thousand Dollars of Wilmington Rail Road Bonds to pay & to pay now; this is bad for the Whigs.

We shall have the Interest for the Gaston Road to pay to add to our list of Burdens. The Whigs have however a general advantage throughout this Session.

*To James Webb.*    U. James Webb Mss.

Washington City,

January 14th., 1843.

I have rec'd your letter informing that 40 pieces of the Gold I left for Mr. Albright were sovereigns, instead of half Eagles. I never opened the packages after receiving them at this place, except when I delivered them to you, and supposed that it was all American Gold. You will, of course, let Mr. A. have the sovereigns at 4.85, and charge me with the difference between that and $5.

There is nothing new here, I believe, the weather of late, mild for the season. The business of Congress does not afford much of general interest. The Committee of ways and means has reported in the House unanimously, against the Exchequer scheme of the President, and nothing can be done on the subject of the currency at this session.

The jealousy between the friends of Messrs. Calhoun & Van Buren as to the next Presidency, is becoming more and more apparent. Gen'l Jackson has lately taken distinct ground in favor of the latter, in a letter to a public meeting in Philadelphia, and he will doubtless get the nomination of their National Convention.

The Bankrupt Law will probably be repealed, but it is more doubtful than it was, at the beginning of the session. The Locos have made political capital by abusing it thus far, and now they want its benefits in their private affairs.

F. S. Tay, an eminent lawyer of this district, died suddenly a day or two since, on a visit to Baltimore.


*From John Umstead Kirkland.*               U.

Hillsboro', N. C.,

Jany. 16th, 1843.

\*     \*     \*     \*     \*

. . . We are getting along here much after the old sort, Whigs & Democrats are much disappointed at the doings of the Legislature. I have myself never known as much nonsense to emanate from a Legislative body within my short experience. I hope their constituents will hold them to a rigid account.

Your Family are all well and indeed so far have enjoyed an unusual exemption from the Scarlet Fever which has prevailed to great extent & in families with much fatality throughout the County.

*From Charles L. Hinton.*                    U.

Raleigh,

Jany. 20th, 1843.

\* \* \* \* \*

The resolutions of instruction are still under discussion in the house.[4] B. Moore has had the floor for a part of two days and occupy it again this morning; he is making an excellent speech for Buncombe.

Col. Wheeler returned last night and I suppose will present his bond today. Report says some of his Loco friends will have their names taken off, if so another difficulty will probably be presented. I think the party are heartily sick of him, indeed they are sick of the most of their doings, and would retrace if they could, for every act has had the tendency to bring them into disrepute. They have disappointed themselves, their friends in the Country are disappointed and dissatisfied, every act has had a tendency to elevate the Whig cause.

Tonight the Whigs will have a meeting to make arrangements for future operations.

Yourself and Manly are spoken of for Governor


*From Charles L. Hinton.*                    U.

Raleigh,

Feb. 1st, 1843.

\* \* \* \* \*

The members have left except some two or three attending the Supreme Court, and our town is quiet. The citizens nothing do but talk over the incident of the late session and lay schemes for the postponement of debts when pressed by creditors which by the bye is no small matter, for really I have never seen the embarrassments of Wake anything like as great before. Our Banks I presume will be much more liberal in their discounts which will afford some relief. The course pursued by the Democrats in the Legislature on the Bank resolutions is generally condemned by all intelligent members of the party in this and the adjacent counties,

---

[4] The introduction of resolutions declaring the right of instruction of United States senators, brought about a prolonged debate in each house.

we think they are completely check mated on that subject, and given us sufficient capital on all others for the next two years.

I attended a Whig Caucus, no nomination was made for Governor or any preference expressed in the meeting for any individual. Manly, Bryan, Rayner and yourself were spoken of during the session, the general impression was that you were much the strongest of the party, and I expect you will be strongly urged to accept the nomination.

Our representative, Col. Massey,[5] has run away (it is thought for Texas) leaving his neighbours between five and six thousand dollars, minus.


*To Charles P. Green.*                                    U.

T. J. Green Mss.

Washington City

Feby. 17th. 1843.

I have read with great concern your letter to Mr. Mangum respecting the unfortunate Texas prisoners lately captured at Mier, and immediately afterwards met with Mr. Van Zandt,[6] the Texan charge here, from whom I was happy to learn that your brother[7] was not among them. He informs me that he has been written to, by you, and has today replied in such way as I hope will relieve your anxiety. The gentleman by the name of Green, who has been captured (he tells me) is Thomas Green, a son of Judge Green, of Tennessee. He has no middle name as your brother has, both being personally known by Mr. Van Z.

---

[5] Dempsey B. Massey.

[6] Isaac Van Zandt, of Texas, charge d'affaires, and later, minister of Texas to the United States, who was active in Texas politics and diplomacy. He was a candidate for governor in 1847, but died before the election.

[7] Thomas Jefferson Green (1801-1863), a native of Warren County, who attended, for a time, the university and West Point, but did not graduate. He served in the legislatures of North Carolina, Florida, Texas, and California, and also in the Texas congress. He reached Texas just after the outbreak of the revolution against Mexico, and, commissioned a brigadier general, raised a brigade in the United States. He led the expedition against Mier, was captured, and later escaped. He set the Rio Grande as the boundary of Texas, was the first public advocate of a railroad to the Pacific, and before he left the state became a famous breeder of racing stock. In California, he was a major general of militia, and, in the legislature, drafted and introduced the bill establishing the University of California. He returned to North Carolina just before the Civil War, and lived at "Esmeralda," his plantation, until his death.

Having received this information, I did not call on Almonte,[8] with whom I have no personal acquaintance, although we have exchanged cards.

I beg you to be assured, that had the fact been as you supposed, I would have omitted nothing, within my power, to aid your brother in obtaining liberation. A son of Mr. Crittenden[9] was taken at Mier, and his friends have procured, without difficulty, a letter to Santa Anna, from Gen'l Almonte, asking the interposition of his clemency. Letters were also written to Gen'l Thompson, who, I doubt not, will do every thing in his power in behalf of the unfortunate persons, now prisoners in Mexico.

I will make further inquiry, from Mr. Van Zandt, as he receives intelligence from his country, and will apprize you of it, should it affect your brother.

I am happy to be able to make you this communication, and hurried as it is, I hope you will read it to your venerable Mother, as an assurance that her son is not in the custody of the Mexicans.

I received from you a letter before I left home, which I failed to answer, because I hoped to meet you in passing Raleigh on my way here.

We have no news in Washington of any interest.

Judge Mangum desires me to present his respects, and that you shall consider this a joint letter.

*     *     *     *     *

*From Robert Hall Morrison.*                                    A.

Cottage Home,

March 6th., 1843.

A few weeks since, I received the portrait of Father Graham, which you were kind enough to have drawn and forwarded. I

---

[8] Juan Nepomuceno Almonte (1804-1869), of Mexico, was educated in the United States. He was aide to Santa Anna in 1836, was later secretary of state of Mexico, and was minister to the United States, 1841-1845, when, upon the annexation of Texas he demanded his passport. He was a candidate for President, but after defeat, was minister of war, and ambassador to France. He fought with distinction in the war with the United States, and was minister to Washington in 1853. He supported the establishment of the empire, and in 1864 was appointed by Maximilian marshal of the empire. He fled to France at the downfall, and died there.

[9] George B. Crittenden (1812-1880), a native of Kentucky, graduate of West Point, began the study of law, tired of it, and went to Texas. Captured at Mier, he was freed through the efforts of Webster and Waddy Thompson. Re-entering the army, he rose to major in the Mexican War, and to lieutenant colonel afterwards. He resigned in 1861, and, entering the Confederate army, became a brigadier general. He was state librarian of Kentucky, 1867-1874.

have for some time been looking for an opportunity of sending you the money for it; but meeting with no private conveyance and feeling that it ought to be paid, I have concluded to enclose it by mail. Enclosed you will find $45., which I understood, through Bro. John Graham, was the price. If in this I am mistaken, please to let me know it, and I will forward the balance, if there should be any.

\*    \*    \*    \*    \*

The pressure of the times is felt as sensibly as it has been. Those who are free from debt are very independent; but a large am't of property, even in this region so long noted for stability, has changed hands, and much more doubtless will do so before better prospects are realized.

Much of the Cotton from this Section of the State has already been sold from 4 to 6 cents. Dispair of any relief from measures of the Government, during the present administration, seems to be general among both parties.

I have much regretted that among other evils flowing from the temporary success of a reckless party, you were called to lost y'r Station in the Senate. But there is much consolation in the assurance, that faithful Services and unbending integrity cannot be obscured, much less prostrated, by the rage of proscription. Every uncompromising adherent to principle, who retires before the waves of party violence, carries with him all that is worth having.

The measures of the last Legislature, if I am mistaken, will do more to cure the State of the *chills and fevers* of democracy than any thing that has taken place for the last ten years.

The Whigs of this District are about to hold a Convention to nominate a Candidate for Congress. There is, I understand, some excitement, if not division, in th'r ranks. Gen'l Edney rather claims the field. Mr. Osborne and Mr. Barringer each have their friends, who wish th'r nomination.

\*    \*    \*    \*    \*

Dr. Alexander's family are tolerably well now, after a good deal of sickness in the fall. Sister Violet has another (Daughter) I think it is.

Uncle Sam'l Wilson died recently.

\*    \*    \*    \*    \*

*From E. Dyer.*                                    U.

Washington City

March 16th, 1843.

\*   \*   \*   \*   \*

Judge Mangum is still here. He has been confined to his room for a few days, by cold & fever. He expects to be off, for the good old North State, in a day or two.

Mr. Tallmadge is also confined to his room, and has been quite sick.

It is rumored here now, that the Secretary of State[10] will not go to England; but that he will retire to Massachusetts, and become a Candidate for the Presidency—upon Mr. Cort Johnson's[11] hobby.

Whether he will have the countenance and support of the Government, the Lord only knows.

Wishing you good health, with every other blessing.

*From James Graham.*                              U.

Raleigh, March 26th, 1843.

\*   \*   \*   \*   \*

I have ordered 100 of my Circulars to be sent to you at Hillsboro to be disposed of as you may think proper.

I left Mangum, Rencher & Stanly at Washington. The two last are preparing Circular letters to the people.

[P.S.] I have a strong suspicion that Tyler will offer Rencher some appointment. I seriously fear G. W. Caldwell is to supercede Gaither in the Mint.

J. G.

*From Joshua Tayloe.*[12]                          U.

Washington, N. C.,

March 30th, 1843.

It is in contemplation by the Whigs of this County to give a public Barbacue some time in the month of May in honor of our

---

[10] Daniel Webster.

[11] William Cost Johnson (1806-1860), of Maryland, lawyer, state legislator, 1831-1832, Whig member of congress, 1833-1835, 1837-1843, delegate to convention of 1836.

[12] Joshua Tayloe, of Beaufort County, for many years collector at Ocracoke, state senator, 1844. He was the progenitor of a line of distinguished physicians in Washington, N. C.

late Representative, Edward Stanly, to which entertainment *all* Whigs of this Congressional district are to be invited.

It is important that we should make the affair as improving as possible, to give us a good start in the comeing Canvass, which will probably be between Stanly and Arrington.[13] It will therefore be of consequence to have as many of our prominent friends with us as can be prevailed on to attend, and more particularly the company of yourself and Mr. Mangum is desired.

The more likely to effect our object it has been suggested that I should write you informally and enquire at what time in May it would be most convenient for you and Mr. Mangum to attend, that we might make our arrangements accordingly.

Will you be so kind as to consult Mr. Mangum and let me have an answer at some early day. I need hardly add that you will be received most cordially by your Whig friends in this district.

With much respect,

Your obt. Servt.

*From Bartholomew F. Moore.*                           A.

Halifax,

April 20th, 1843

Your esteemed letter of the 12th. Inst. came to hand on yesterday. The subjects on which it treats have commanded my very serious deliberation for several weeks. Within the last ten days I recd. a letter from an active Whig friend of Warren, urging the same views expressed by you in relation to the movement in Franklin. They are my own. I am decidedly of opinion that the locos take the lead in nominating a Candidate. You very truly say we can gain nothing by heading them in the selection of a Candidate, nor by running with them *pari passu*. We ought to avail ourselves of the local position of our Candidate, and this can be done only by regarding the local position of the loco Candidate. Perhaps by refraining from taking the field now, our opponents may become divided amongst themselves, if so let the division become fixed before we stir. These views were recently expressed

---

[13] Archibald Hunter Arrington (1809-1872), of Nash County, a lawyer, and planter on a large scale. He was a Democratic member of congress, 1841-1845, and a member of the Confederate congress, 1862-1864.

through our village newspaper, and the Whigs here respond to them.

In regard to the question who shall be our Candidate (and I think we ought to have one) I am decidedly of opinion that he ought not to come from the same County in which the Candidate of the opposition resides.

It is now, I think, almost settled that Daniel [14] will be the nominee of the democrats, and all that a Whig Candidate from this County could do would be to prevent inroads on the party here. Party divisions have so long existed here that in the event of both Candidates coming from this Country the battle must be fought in the other Counties of the district, and both being strangers, without any personal influence, party would be the sole consideration of support. A Candidate from any other County of fair pretensions would do better than one from Halifax. Such is the opinion of intelligent and candid friends with whom I have conversed, and to whom I have taken the liberty of mentioning your views. These considerations ought to be decisive with me as a good Whig, against permitting my name to be put in nomination, and, fairly canvassed, ought to decide every Whig in the district. My personal ambition does not interfere with my idea of duty, and these and other objections of a private kind are absolutely conclusive with me. I feel flattered by the partiality in which my name is held by the Whigs of Orange, and nothing but a deep sense of duty to the common cause and to myself could induce me to take so immoveable a stand. Allow me to say to you, that there is a very strong & warm current of feel in your favor in my County. Most of us look to you as a Candidate for the Executive chair, and we do not apprehend any diminution of the respect we entertain for you, If you would do us the favor to permit your name to be placed before the people in the approaching Congressional Canvass. All the reflecting Whigs, now that Daniels nomination wears the aspect of great probability, look elsewhere than to the County for a champion, and your name most readily occurs to them. Whatever resolution you may come to in regard to a district nomination, the nominee for the Gubernatorial office whoever he may be, will be obliged to yield himself to his party. And you, my dear Sir, will come before the Convention with strong demands for your services. In the event that you

---

[14] John Rives Jones Daniel (1802-1868), of Halifax, a graduate of the university, member of the commons, 1831-1834, Democratic member of congress, 1841-1853. Later, he was a lawyer, and planter in Caddo Parish, Louisiana.

may be chosen, refusal will be out of the question, and now let me ask you, if a canvass for Congress in this district would not materially promote Whig success in that most important struggle. I address myself as a *Whig* to you as a *Whig,* desiring more, by far. the success of our cause than any personal triumph.

If, however, you will not, as you say, be consenting thereto, then the question arises, and it is really a difficult one, whom shall we put in harness for the cause? It is certain that policy demands a Candidate, and it is equally certain that that Candidate should be able to uphold the Whig cause with ability, and it were better that he should already be known with advantage to the public. And moreover he should, in my opinion, come either from Granville or Orange. I confess I am at a perfect loss, unless we take either Waddell or Gilliam. As to the latter, I understand that he will not run, and on some Whig principles of great importance, as the Bank question, does not agree with us. I speak doubtingly as to his opinions, and therefore desire my surmise may not be repeated; I esteem him greatly and would not wrong him for the world. Waddell would do well; he would command the advantage of local position and is already favorably known to the people. His address is popular, is an overmatch for Daniel in speaking, appearance, and the art of *getting along.* If neither he nor Gilliam will take the field, and you persist in holding back, I declare myself aground.

In respect of the time when it may be most prudent for us to make demonstration, I think about the first of June will be the favorable time. The opposition, by that period, will have developed its true character, and its legitimate traits, and the canvass after that period will be less inconvenient to the Candidate, if he should be a practising lawyer, than if it were to commence earlier. Your suggestion of that time suits my views.

In the mean time, can you not take the liberty of addressing to some one of the gentlemen who composed the Franklin meeting, a letter giving the views of Whigs of different parts of the district on this subject. They may without something of this kind feel a mortification that may may beget indifference. I would be gratified if you would.

By accident in part, neglect of others to perform their duty, the Whig address has fallen to my lot. I have written it and sent Barringer a copy for his perusal & criticism. I shall send it to Raleigh early next week for publication. I greatly fear it will fall vastly short of expectation and of what it ought to be. In its composition I have been without aid, and almost without documents, depending on memory of the transactions as they transpired. I have postponed committing it to the press till I can have an opportunity of reading it to some of our Whig friends at my Supr. Court next week. I should feel myself particularly fortunate if I could have the benefit of your counsel on its pages before it went out. You know how dangerous it is to write a book. I hope, although it has been delayed, it will serve us some good turn in the Congressional canvass.

When you did me the kindness to visit me at my sick chamber in Raleigh, just on the eve of your departure for Washington, you had little cause, from my conversation, to suspect that, in any event, I would go for Saunders in his controversy with Brown. Yet it so happened that my opinions became changed and I think now, that if we had succeeded in electing Saunders, we should have accomplished a signal good to the Whig cause and inflicted a lasting injury on the democrats; the event has made me still more anxious to have succeeded. I dislike Haywood as a politician exceedingly, and I lament that he was finally selected to fill *your* place.

But enough of this.

> With much & true regard,
> I am truly your friend.


*To James W. Bryan.*          U.  Bryan Mss.

Hillsboro,

April 30th, 1843.

I seize a moment before setting out for Rockingham Court to reply to your letter of last week. I heard at Guilford of the heavy calamity which had befallen your town,[15] but did not know that Mrs. W. and myself had suffered so largely untill my return, the day before yesterday. At this distance and without accurate knowledge of the state of the walls of the house (whether they fell in or are still standing) I am unable to determine what is best to be done with the ruins—My impression is, however, that it will be best to sell the whole of the rubbish and the ground also for the

---

[15] On April 18th, 1843, a destructive fire occurred in New Bern which, according to the newspapers, destroyed one hundred and twenty houses. The Grahams were among the heavy losers.

best price that can be obtained. I have no purpose ever to rebuild, and I presume also that Mrs. W. has not. If therefore she will consent, I will be under additional obligations to you to dispose of it as you deem best. Whatever course may be adopted will be satisfactory to me.

\* \* \* \* \*

The Monied pressure continues unabated in this section. No Whig Candidate for Congress here as yet—Daniel will be the Loco, no doubt.

*From Bartholomew F. Moore.*          U.

Tarboro,

May 23rd, 1843.

There seems to be great difficulty in getting a candidate for the district. From the papers I do not discover that the Whigs in your section have made any movement towards that object. We must not permit the election to pass by default. We must have a rallying point, we must keep the spirit stiring striving and struggling. You can command more votes than any man in the district, yes by several hundred; But if you have *absolutely* declined the candidacy, we must concentrate on some one.

Mr. Gee[16] of my county is not only willing but anxious to enter the lists against Daniel and will do so unless restrained. He will not discuss on the hustings, although a man of excellent good sense and could make, with a little preparation, a good practical speech. He can command more votes in Halifax than any one from the county. His family connexions in Franklin & Warren are extensive and influential and he is well known in both counties. He is a jovial fellow; in a crowd King of joke and laughter—liberal with his purse and a decided Whig—Dislikes Daniel, and I believe would traverse the district. Now what say you to him; I have thought that our true policy was to select some one who would discuss actively and boldly and if none such could be found willing to encounter a canvass, then we ought to run some one well known to the people, yourself, Joyner, or Waddell. In this I may be mistaken at least so far respects the concentration on the still candi-

---

[16] Sterling H. Gee, of Halifax, who was a member of the commons, 1835-1836, 1840-1844.

date, and perhaps it may be better to have Gee with his mode of electioneering than a candidate who lies at home.

Speedy action now must be taken, and unless some other will come out and discuss, I am for putting Gee before the people. Decide quickly; and if you think proper, give Gee a small notice (*non committal*) in your paper.

Last week at Halifax we had a Whig meeting at which we adopted a resolution appointing a Committee with power to take such measures as may be deemed expedient in relation to selecting a candidate for Congress.

Do you deem it proper to appoint such Committee?

If you run Gee, he ought to have a quasi nomination in the district. The hour of event has arrived.

Farewell.


*From James Graham.*                                      U.

Rutherfordton,

May 25th, 1843.

*    *    *    *    *

I am busy travelling through my extensive district and find my opposition proceeding mainly from the *Democrats,* the *ultra* Whigs and that class of people who always desire a change, or something new. I think I shall be elected, but *all the aspirants* in the District are making opposition to me.

I shall leave here tomorrow for Cherokee County Court and continue on that side of the mountain in attendance on the County Courts untill July. I have not yet been in the most Western part of my district.

My votes are all approved, but my vote on the Distribution Bill, and so soon as the people learn we had *to borrow* 12 millions on the day after we distributed three millions, they generally become satisfied with my vote.

The Bankrupt Law is the most odious law among all classes of people I have ever known, and Mr. Clay's popularity is very seriously injured by it in this part of the State.

*To Willie P. Mangum.*[17]                                     U.

Raleigh, June 22, 1843.

At the request of Mr. Nathl. Green, who is here, I inclose you a letter addressed by Genl. T. J. Green, from his prison in Mexico. to the President of U. S. The General sent the original to his mother, and expressed a wish that a copy might be sent to each of the senators from N. C.

I need not say to you that if any mode of interference in behalf of Genl. Green shall suggest itself to you that it will be highly gratifying to his family & friends, that you should embrace it without delay.

*To Weston R. Gales.*[18]                                     U.

Hillsborough,

July 22nd., 1843.

A friend has called my attention to an article in the N. C. Standard, which I had not before seen, in which I am charged, in substance; 1st., with receiving mileage as a member of Congress, beyond the amount allowed by law; 2dly, with receiving compensation as a member while I came home to attend a Court.

The most material part of the article is as follows:

"Wm. A. Graham, Hillsborough, am't rec'd     $1,132.00
R. M. Saunders, Raleigh,                           1,086.40
                                                   ———————
                                                         45
Distance from Raleigh to Hillsborough,
40 miles, doubled 80, pay                               32
                                                   ———————
                                                       $13.

Days charged by both from 31st. May to 13th. September, 1841, inclusive, and yet Mr. Graham came home to attend a Superior Court."

To show that my mileage is excessive, it is assumed in this article that that of Gen. Saunders was correctly charged; that he wrote to the Post Master General for the distance from Washing-

[17] From *Publications of the Southern History Association,* Vol. III, pp. 115-121. The enclosure referred to is also there printed.
[18] From the *Raleigh Register,* July 25th, 1843.

ton to Raleigh, and received for answer that it was 288 miles, etc. I have been told today, that Gen. Saunders, at a recent public meeting in Chatham, reiterated both the above allegations in regard to myself. He has, therefore, if this information is correct, made himself the endorser, if he be not the original author of them. It certainly would have been more *manly,* if such imputations were intended to be made, to have spoken of them where I had an opportunity of hearing. I was present at the discussion in Raleigh, where such charges were freely preferred against *others,* by Gen. Saunders, but no allusion even was made to *me,* in connexion with them. Are they true in respect to me? I deny the correctness of that standard, by which it is proposed that I shall be judged. I deny that General Saunders, according to the document to which he makes reference, received pay for only 288 miles as his distance from the city of Washington, though he insists that that is the true distance for which he was entitled to compensation.

| | |
|---|---:|
| His whole compensation for the session referred to, was, as we have seen, | $1,086.40 |
| The session consisted of 106 days, at $8 | 848. |
| | ———— |
| | 238.40 |
| Leaving for mileage, 576 miles, double of 288, at 40 cents per mile is, | 230.40 |
| | ———— |
| Excess above the distance he claims, | $8. |

So that he has received pay for 298 miles, as his true distance, notwithstanding the letter of the Post Master General. If I have committed any error on this subject, which I utterly deny, it was with no such lights before me as that letter afforded. The law allows compensation at a given rate, "For every 20 miles of estimated distance, by the *most usual road"* from the place of residence to the Seat of Government. When called on by the Secretary of the Senate for my distance, I told him I was unable to give it with entire accuracy, that the road travelled was by Raleigh, and my distance beyond that was 40 miles. I stated to him the distance from place to place as far as Richmond, Va., and asked his aid in estimating it from there. By the result thus obtained, my account was settled, and I have no reason to doubt that it was done with correctness. The Post Office book referred to, in the Standard's article, represents Hillsborough as nearer to Washington than Raleigh. It could, therefore, furnish no true guide in my case. For the writer of that article does me no more than justice, in admitting that I am entitled to the additional mileage from that place to this, as a part of the usual road. Indeed, it is manifest that the nearest Post route is not, but that the most usual road travelled over, of course paid for, is the standard for estimating mileage. I am aware that there has been complaint for years, that in this portion of the compensations of Members of Congress, there were abuses which require correction, and I uniformly contributed my aid where any real effort has been made to reform tham. But I deny that I have at all participated in any such abuse.

As to the other charge, that I came home to attend a Court, and received compensation during my absence on that business, it is without the least foundation in truth. At the extra Session referred to, I was present at the adjournment, and did not reach home until the latter part of the Court week, in September. The only occasion when I ever left, by reason of professional business, was at the Executive Session, called at the inauguration of Gen Harrison—then I remained until after all the important nominations had been acted on, and left a few days before the adjournment. *But my pay stopped with my departure.*

Will you do me the justice to publish this in the Register?

Very respectfully yours,

*To Weston R. Gales.*[19]

Hillsboro',

August 5th, 1843.

A communication of the Hon. R. M. Saunders, in the Standard, referring to my letter to you on the 22d. July, requires some notice from me.

In the Speech of that gentleman at Raleigh, he affirmed "the table of Post Office distances" to be the rule by which the mileage of members of Congress should be estimated, and having produced that document, he declared that Messrs. Rayner, Stanly, and many other members of Congress had received excessive allowances for mileage, and that any one would discover this who should compare the table of distances with the accounts of these members.

[19] From *Hillsborough Recorder,* August 24th, 1843. Quoted from Raleigh Register.

That the Post Office table furnishes no rule on the subject of the mileage of members, I said in my letter to you; and the correctness of my position will be apparent from several considerations. First, from the language of the Act of Congress giving the mileage. It provides that each Senator and Representative shall receive "eight dollars for every twenty miles of estimated distance by the *most usual road*," etc. Most usual for what? for transporting the mail?—surely not—but most usual for travelling by public conveyances. This is evident from a subsequent provision in the same law, in these words "and each member of the Senate shall be entitled to the same, etc., allowance for, etc., travelling to and from any meeting of the Senate," etc. It is an allowance for *travelling*, to be compared, not by the distance *actually* travelled, but by that usually travelled by public conveyances.

Secondly—from the Retrenchment Bill, of Mr. Arnold, for supporting which Gen. Saunders seems to think himself entitled to special commendation; for one of the amendments proposed by that Bill was to *make* the Post Office estimate the rule for computing mileage in future—a provision useless, and indeed absurd, if it had been the rule already.

Thirdly, from the uniform action of the members and officers of the two Houses for more than twenty years, by none of whom (except General Saunders) is it believed that the Post Office Table was deemed to furnish the rule; but on the contrary, by all of them the usual route of travel was considered the only proper guide. But now we learn from Gen. Saunders that the table, *per se,* is not the rule, but the table corrected by ascertaining the true distance of travel. The General, it seems, wrote to the Postmaster General and learned that in his own case, the table and the fact did not agree, and he, in consequence of this information, charged not according to the table, but according to the supposed fact. Now, when the General wrote to the Post Master as to his own case, did he consult him as to the proper distance of Messrs. Rayner, Stanly, and the other members referred to? If so, why did he not give the result of those inquiries? If, as I suppose, he did not do this, then in the only case in which he consulted the Postmaster General, he found that the table was erroneous, and he himself disregarded it. Why, then, did he propose *that* as the rule for others, by which he had not governed himself—and why did he assume the estimates of a table to be right as against others, which by the only instance in which their correctness had been tested, he himself had found to be erroneous. This was bringing forward evidence to accuse others, which he knew was not worthy of trust; it was requiring them to submit to a rule by which he was not willing to govern himself—and it was more than this. As Gen. S. affirmed the Post Office table to be the true rule of calculation, and condemned others for exceeding its estimate, while he gave no intimation that he had rejected it in his own case, was it not the natural inference of all who heard him, that his *own* account had been settled by that rule, which he had just declared to be the true one? Whether Gen. S. designed to produce this inference, which he knew was contrary to the truth, he only can determine. This much, however, is certain, he alleged the rule, condemned others for not adhering to it, and was at the same time perfectly silent as to the fact that he had disregarded it.

The table of Post Office distances being thus set aside as a governing rule, in the calculation of mileage, both by the confession and practice of Gen. Saunders himself, it is difficult to understand why a committee, consisting of the General and the Postmaster, should be a more appropriate medium of adjusting the mileage, than was furnished by the consultation of the Secretary of the Senate and myself. The Postmaster was not an Officer of Congress—neither the law nor the practice of that body gave him any power of interference; he had nothing to do with it; and the General might just as well have called to his assistance any Clerk in the General Post Office, as the head of that Department. The difference then between the General and myself is merely this—I resorted to the usual and proper mode of estimating the distance, and he to one which, though not improper, was certainly unusual. I see no reason to admit that the result in his case was accurate, rather than in mine; but, if it were so, my effort was as sincere as his, and a mistaken calculation, I presume even the General himself will admit, constitutes no offense.

The other charge made against me in the Standard, and endorsed by Gen. Saunders, he alleges that I have evaded, but this allegation, like most others that he has introduced into his gratuitous and unprovoked attack upon me, is without foundation. That charge, as I understood it, was, that while paid for the whole extra Session, I came home to attend a Superior Court. Knowing that I did not come home to attend any Court during the extra Session, and that I had left Washington before the close of the Executive Session of the Senate in the Spring of 1841, and did attend a Court, I naturally supposed this absence was the subject of reference. I answered the charge supposed to have been made, by stating that I was present at the close of the extra Session, and though I left the Senate while in Executive Session, in the Spring, yet my pay stopped with my departure. This the General considers but a small affair, and supposes I might have lost a day's pay. If he had been as careful to ascertain and to recollect facts, as he seems to have been intent on making charges, he might have learned that the Executive Session referred to continued from the 5th. to the 15th. of March, and that I left Washington a full week before its termination.

The charge, I now learn is, that I was absent on some other occasion, and without deduction of pay. I was absent once during the extra Session. I came home on an occasion of indisposition in my family of the deepest interest to me as a father, and a husband. Finding, on reaching home, that the crisis was over, I took the very next Stage on my return to Washington. My absence lasted six days, of which period four days and nights were spent on the road. I consulted with a friend as to the propriety of deducting pay for these days of fatigue, expense, and anxiety, but was told that, under the circumstances, my absence was not voluntary, but compelled by a necessity which fell under the equity of that provision of law which allows pay to an absent member detained by sickness. This view struck me as correct, and I acted accordingly, and I very much doubt whether, either for the absence or the pay, any honorable man in the United States will deem an excuse required.

As Gen. Saunders seems to have made an investigation somewhat particular into my absence from Congress, it is not uncharitable to suppose that when he alluded to my hurried journey home, he was informed of the necessity which caused it. Why did he withhold that information from those to whom he made the charge of absence? Why, but because he knew that to have communicated that information, would have been to fasten attention upon the difference between a short absence, under the influence of considerations having the force of physical coercion, and a long and voluntary absence in the prosecution of a lucrative profession, and would thus have made his charge against me recoil upon himself.

As to Mr. Arnold's Bill, of which the General seems a great admirer and advocate, and which he has drawn, rather unnecessarily, as appears to me, into this discussion, I have but a few words to say. I was opposed to that Bill as a whole, because it proposed a very large deduction from the pay of all officers, Civil and Military, which is within the control of Congress, and because it proposed *no* reduction of the pay of the Congress who were to pass it, but a large reduction of the pay of their successors. The first would have been a cruel injury to a large class of meritorious public servants, and the second provision made us to be generous to the country, not at our own expense, but at the expense of those who should come after us. I thought besides, that the compensation of members was not excessive, and ought not to be reduced, but I was very decidedly in favor of fixing a common criterion by which to determine mileage. Whether my views were correct or not they were certainly adopted without the bias of interest, for it was then ascertained that I was not to be a member of the ensuing Congress, and the passage of the Bill would not have affected my own interests a penny.

But surely the self complacency of Gen. Saunders in the support he gave to this Bill rests on a slender foundation, for if the present rate of compensation be not excessive, why should it be reduced at all? And if it be, why should not the reduction be applied to those who judged it excessive?

One other remark, Sir, and I will encroach no further on your columns. When Gen. Saunders in his Raleigh Speech, at which I was present, produced the Post Office table—announced it to be *the* rate by which mileage should be estimated—accused several members of Congress by name, who were absent, with overcharging, and referred his auditory to the book and accounts for proof— the inference was inevitable, that he had been engaged in the laudable business of making the examination, to which he invited others. When afterwards, in another Address, at which I was no' present, he added my name to those which he had before singled out for accusation, it was certainly not an overstrained inference that I was in the first instance omitted because I was present, and in the second, named because I was absent. That such conduct deserved to be called *unmanly*, none surely could doubt, and to some, might seem to merit a harsher epithet. But it seems the inference I so naturally drew was mistaken, and that the discovery as to myself was made after the Raleigh Speech was delivered. I am glad to learn that it is so, and desire to express my felicitations to the General that the continual success of his electioneering appointments yet left him leisure to pore over the table of Post Office distances—that each day of diligent inquiry added somewhat to his store of matter for vilification; and, though I cannot praise the spirit which prompted his efforts, his industry is undeniably entitled to commendation.

And I think, Sir, I may congratulate myself, that after all his energy of inquisition, he has been able to produce but two charges—one supported by proof which he himself has discredited, and the other which, if he deems an offence, he is the only man in America who would.

Of the flourish about facing with which the General very appropriately and characteristically concludes his note, I shall say nothing, because it deserves no reply which it would become me to make.

I am, Sir, very respectfully,

Your b't serv't,<br>Will. A. Graham.

*From Charles P. Green.*    A.

Rockbridge County, Virginia,

August 5th, 1843.

Your kind letter in answer to mine I received several months since, which found me quite indisposed with a long attack of Branchitis, together with a cough strongly indicating that my Lungs are or may be effected, which has caused me, under the advice of Phicicians to travel on horse-back, consequently I set off two weeks ago in company with my niece in a Barouche & an out horse to ride, whenever I feel able. I am still feeble, though suffer none from travelling. I fear the Mineral waters, therefore do not think I will go much West, but take a trip rather North-East, so as to get home on or before the last of this month & if sufficiently recovered go South to spend the Winter.

I regretted that I was prevented from taking part in the political contest just ended in our State. I have not heard a word from the elections yet, but take it for granted that in our District Saunders is elected. I hope you yet will be prevailed upon to run for Governor. I do say in all candour that I think it important to the success of our cause in the State. I rejoice to hear that "old Hal" is going to visit us.

My Mother, who is now quite an aged person, is desirous of giving several negroes to a widowed daughter who labours under the misfortune of owing debts which will more than cover the property, consequently got the advice of a Lawyer, to write that clause in the will so as to prevent the creditors from selling said negroes which clause here follows, though the same has been submited to others whom give it as their opinion that it cannot be done, either to a Trustee for her benefit during life & then go to some specified person named by my Mother, nor in the way as you will see. I wish you to give me your opinion whether it is practical or not. The creditors will no doubt make every effort to invalidate.

"I give and bequeath unto A. B. my negroes in trust that he shall receive the hires and profits of said negroes and apply the same to the support and maintenance of my daughter Sally M. Ward during her life in such manner as said trustee shall in his discretion deem most admirable and at the death of my said daughter I give the said negroes & increase to such person or persons as my said daughter may by her last will and testament or by any other suitable instrument of writing, bequeath or give the said property to; and in case my said daughter shall omit to exercise the power or right of disposing of said slaves hereby confided to her, in that event I bequeath the same to be divided among my heirs at Law."

Please write to me at Ridgeway, N. C. where I shall probably be *soon*.

With the highest regard<br>I am your friend truly

*From George E. Badger.*                                    A.

Raleigh,

August 12, 1843.

I fear you will have blamed me for the delay in the appearance of your letter and still more I fear that you may disapprove what I am now to offer in explanation of that delay.

When I took your letter from the post office, I went immediately to Gales and read it to him. It was at once apparent to me that you had done what a wise man should never do, you had written for the public in a great hurry and in great irritation—an irritation justly provoked it is true by the coarseness and illtemper of Saunders' note and a hurry natural to one who, reacting to resent such littleness and illiberality. Still from the circumstances in which you wrote, you were inexcusably led from the calm and dignified tone of your first letter to copying something of the spirit of Saunders so far as your character would admit such a result. There was a vein of *petulance* running through the whole tissue of your letter, very unlike, permit me to say, the whole bearing of William A. Graham and quite unbecoming the retired Senator. Besides this your haste had rendered your statements obscure and your argument involved. Some things you had omitted which ought to have been injected and one or two matters were introduced which seemed to me, not to forward if they did not impair the force of your reply.

After taking a day or two to think what I should do, convinced that I could not execute the trust you had confided to me of *correction* without rewriting the whole, I at last, but with much fear and trembling, concluded to *"take the responsibility."* Yesterday I handed Gales what I had produced and had a conference with him as to the part I was assuming; he fortified me in my doubtful and wavering action, Said you had certainly written too much temper and hurry and advised me strongly to let what I had prepared be printed.

Now, my dear Sir, I pray you to acquit me of impertinent interference, and if I must stand answerable for exceeding my powers, do not accuse me of presumption and self conceit. Of one thing you are sure, I have acted from the most sincere affection for yourself and an anxious desire both as your friend and as a North Carolina Whig that you should always retain unimpaired that high character for dignity of manner, elevation of sentiment, and coolness of description which you have in so eminent a degree attained and in which both my friendship and patriotism so sincerely rejoice.

I have stricken out all such expressions as "ferreter"—"recklessness" pharisaical," "self righteousness," etc., which I thought were undignified. I have included a short reference to these considerations to shew the rule of mileage accounted for by Saunders to be incorrect: 1st. the phraseology of the law. 2. [illegible] & 3 the uniform practise of the two houses. I have put a concluding sentence refering to Saunders' gasconade about facing, which without giving him any insult will make him feel and at the same time by treating it rather jocosely preserves your attitude of superiority. In short that I have left out every *expression* or *epithet* which was objectionable on the score of taste, etc. You will find on the whole I think that he fares worse on the rewriting than in the original, while no insult or cause of offense is offered him.

Now, my dear Sir, can you pardon me? If you do I shall be gratified indeed. If not—I say "Strike—but (first) hear me."

Most affectionately,<br>Your friend and obed. Sevt.

P. S. I have altered the date of your letter, so as to bring it down a few days later for a reason you will understand by the last paragraph of the letter.

2 P. S. I have altered the conclusion & restored the date.

[Enclosure.]

The Honable William A. Graham, Senator U. S.

By mileage . . . . . . .          $284.—
By per diem pay from 8th.
December 1842, to 3d. March,
1843, making 86 days @ 8.

688.—<br>$972.—

Contra

January 9, 1843 to cash $500.
      "   "    Ditto    50.
     24  "    Ditto    50.
February 20  "    Ditto   100.

700.—

Due 3 March, 1843 - - - - -          $272.—
   March 1, 1843 To Cash  -          272.—

The Hon'ble William A. Graham—

By 710 miles travel @ 40c

$ 284.—

by per diem pay from
6th. December, 1841,
to 31 August, 1842,
making 269 days @ $8.
per day

2152.<br>$2436.—

## *Contra.*

$ 2,436.

| December | 31st. | 1841 | To Cash . . . . | $200.— | |
|---|---|---|---|---|---|
| January | 7th. | 1842 | Ditto . . . . . . | 100.— | |
| " | 19th. | " | Ditto . . . . . . | 200.— | |
| February | 4th. | " | Ditto . . . . . . | 100.— | |
| " | 19th. | " | Ditto . . . . . . | 250.— | |
| March | 5th. | " | Ditto . . . . . . | 100.— | |
| " | 16th. | " | Ditto . . . . . . | 120.— | |
| " | 26th. | " | Ditto . . . . . . | 50.— | |
| April | 1st. | " | Ditto . . . . . . | 80.— | |
| " | 14th. | " | Ditto . . . . . . | 100.— | |
| May | 9th. | " | Ditto . . . . . . | 150.— | |
| " | 25th. | " | Ditto . . . . . . | 75.— | |
| June | 4th. | " | Ditto . . . . . . | 100.— | |
| " | 10th. | " | Ditto . . . . . . | 45.— | |
| " | 18th. | " | Ditto . . . . . . | 33.35 | |
| " | 29th. | " | Ditto . . . . . . | 60.— | |
| July | 5th. | " | Ditto . . . . . . | 150.— | |
| " | 22nd. | " | Ditto . . . . . . | 125.— | |
| August | 3rd. | " | Ditto . . . . . . | 150.— | |
| " | 10th. | " | Ditto . . . . . . | 50.— | |
| " | 20th. | " | Ditto . . . . . . | 50.— | 2,288.35 |
| | | | | | $  147.65 |
| August | 29th. | " | | | 147.65 |

## The Hon. Mr. Graham, Senator U. S.

| | | |
|---|---|---|
| Mileage 710 miles travel | @ 40¢ | $284.- - |
| By perdiem pay from 10 Dec'r 1840 to 3d. March, 1841, making 84 days | | 672.- - |
| | | $956.- - |
| By detention on January to seat of Government by storm for 3 day @ $8 | | 24.- - |
| | | $980.- - |

## Contra.

| | | | | | |
|---|---|---|---|---|---|
| Feb. 1 | 1841 | Cash | $50.- - | |
| 9 | " | Ditto | 100.- - | |
| 25 | " | Ditto | 250.- - | |
| March 3d. | " | Ditto | 250.- - | |
| 3 | " | Ditto | 480.- - | $980.- - |

By per diem at special Session
from 4 to 7 March 1841 inclusive
making 4 days @ $8. _____ 32.

### Contra.

March 6. Check _____ 32.

## The Hon'ble William A. Graham.

To mileage _____$ 284.- -
To per diem pay from 31 May to
11 September 1841, making 104
days at $8. per day _____
$1116.- -

### Contra.

| | | | | |
|---|---|---|---|---|
| June | 28th. | 1841 | —By Cash | $ 50. |
| July | 8th. | " | —Ditto | 108.09 |
| " | 26th. | " | —Ditto | 50. |
| " | 31st. | " | —Ditto | 50. |
| August | 21st. | " | —Ditto | 50. |
| Sep. | 6th. | " | —Ditto | 80. |
| " | 9th. | " | —Ditto | 727.91 |

$1116.

*To J. H. Hedges.*                                                    U.

Hillsboro', N. C.,

August 31st, 1843.

In reply to your letter of this day's mail, I have the honor to state that the professional gentlemen of this County who have been longest at the bar, are

Hugh Waddell
John W. Norwood
P. H. Mangum
Wm. A. Graham

Hillsboro',
N. C.

Raleigh, the seat of Government, is 36 miles distant, where reside,

The Hon. Geo. E. Badger
Geo. W. Mordecai
John H. Bryan

Raleigh,
N. C.

also of the profession.

Very Respectfully,
Your Obed't Serv't,

P. S. Any of these are worthy of confidence.

*To James Graham.*                                                    U.

Hillsboro',

Sept. 1st, 1843.

Dear Brother

I rec'd your letter the day after the elections from the Rutherfordton, & regretted to learn that you had lost your election. The combination against you was such as has been rarely seen in a contest of the kind, and I doubt not, will resolve itself again into its original discordant elements, long before the parties to it shall have received the rewards which they promised themselves in forming it. I am glad to find that you look on the result with the equanimity which becomes a man conscious of having done his duty faithfully and fully.

W. P. Mangum is now here, and expresses deep regret at the decision. Indeed with the body of the people in this part of the State I find your publications have had more effect in forming public opinion than those of any other individual, and intelligent Whigs in this quarter have looked to your reelection with great interest on that account.

You may have seen in the Raleigh papers that I have been drawn into a controversy with Saunders as to some personal matters. The fellow has been completely disgraced, in being detected in getting fees for obtaining pensions, while receiving his per diem as a member of Congress, (as much as Five Hundred dollars in a single case—$200 in another, etc.) and when charged by Miller with this, and other matters, he sought to divert public attention by false allegations against others. I contented myself in the first instance by a simple explanation. But in replying to his vulgar and impertinent publication I designed to make him feel his degredation and shameless prostitution. I inclosed the letter to Badger, however, with a request to look over and correct, and he modified it so much as to impair its force, and make it merely defensive. The matter has thus ended.

. . . I made a good crop of wheat, and have fine corn, both here, and at the plantation. My Courts are now beginning again with the Co. Court here this week. I find that I can readily command a share of important business in the Courts, and have nearly determined to quit the County Courts except in Orange, but there is not much of important litigation. There are however now several cases of contested wills on hand, and two capital felonies, in which I appear, to be tried at the Superior Court, week after next.

I go day after tomorrow to Paul Cameron's on way to Granville Superior Court. Judges Nash and Bailey have left here for their circuits below. Manly is to hold our Courts.

Suppose you come down and spend a few weeks with us the latter part of this month. I will have then, an interval of a week or two of leisure, and we will be very glad to see you. . . .

I believe we have nothing new in Hillsboro'. I hear that Judge Settle was baptized in his neighborhood a short time since, became a member of that Church.

* * * * *

The Tennessee elections will fix the Whig majority in the Senate U. S. for the next Congress. The Locos here are mortified at the late elections in this State, and are despairing of Calhoun as their Presidential Candidate. They are now disposed to attempt a sort of Military assault with old Dick Johnson.

---

*From John Howard.*                                    A.

Randolph-Macon College, Virginia,

Sept. 18th, 1843.

As corresponding Secretary of the Franklin Literary Society, it is my pleasant duty to communicate to you information of your unanimous election by that body, to address it and the Washington Lit. Society, on the second Tuesday of June '44—the day preceding the next Commencement of R. M. College.

In selecting an individual to speak on that occasion, it became us, in consideration of the honor both of the Institution and its Societies, to choose one whose literary attainments qualify him to discharge ably to duty imposed, and whose reputation as an orator would call together a large assemblage of the people. Such men were, President Tyler, Judge N. B. Tucker[20] of Wm. and Mary College, Gov. Gilmer, etc., who have hitherto addressed the two Societies. Be assured, Sir, that we use not the flattery which youth often pays to exalted merit, in saying that we know of no one better qualified than yourself to speak on such an occasion and to succeed the distinguished gentlemen who have honored us by their efforts.

It is, therefore, the unanimous wish of the Society of which you have long been an honorary member, that you will come and stand where *they* stood to "delight and enlighten;" and thus give to Virginia and to the world, another evidence of the talent which dignifies and adorns the *"Old North State."* ___ ___ ___

I am, dear Sir,
With the highest regard,
Your obt. Servant
Cor: Sec: F. L. Society,
R. M. College, Va.

---

[20] Nathaniel Beverley Tucker (1784-1851), of Virginia, graduate of William and Mary, lawyer, and soldier of the War of 1812. Appointed a judge in Missouri Territory, he lived there, 1815-1831, during which time he was a violent opponent of the Missouri Compromise. When he returned, he was professor of law at his *alma mater*. He was a defender of state sovereignty, and intensely pro-Southern in his politics, all of which was reflected in his writings. His best known work was "The Partisan Leader."

*From Thomas P. Devereux.*          A.

Raleigh,

Oct. 10th, 1843.

I performed the promise I made you, Morehead & Hines last Friday, & had a very full conversation with Mr. B,[21] in which I stated to him my firm conviction that it would not do to nominate Mr. Stanly; in this I was warmly seconded by Mr. Singletary,[22] who spoke as well for the interest of that gentleman, as for the good of the great cause. Mr. B. seemed to think that Mr. S. had beed badly treated, as the various paragraphs in the papers were not upon the authority of the editors alone. He however expressed his wish that the cause should triumph rather than *the* man, or any *one* man, & his entire willingness to go into convention with an eye single to that purpose, and to sacrifice every personal prediliction to the desired result.

Having read this much, you must permit me to add that however valuable these declarations may be— (I do not confine them to Mr. B.) —there will be a greater or less influence exerted from the fact that the candidate is one who is acceptable to every body— one above all kind of political and personal exception, & who will firmly and cordially unite all parties, or sections of parties. I never have taken any deep interest in a canvass, not that I have not felt as much as any other person, be he who he may, but a due regard for the success of my party has kept me from taking an active hand in the melee. I am therefore almost a "looker on in Vienna," & it is proverbial that a stander bye sees more of the game than a player. I am deeply impressed with the truth that we are on the point, not of a division, but of a joint contest, owing to the fact that *all* are not heartily united on the man. I see as plainly as if written with a sun beam that you are the only person who will be acceptable to the *whole* Whig party, against whom no one will object, but in whose nomination *all* will concur, as being the very best that could be made, & the candidate who will heal all personal or national feelings; in fine, who is certain of being elected. I do not say any other, or all others will be beaten, I think otherwise, but you will most certainly be elected. I may

---

[21] George E. Badger, who was a connection of Stanly.

[22] George E. Badger Singletary, of Beaufort County, later a captain in the Mexican War, and colonel in the Confederate Army, who was killed in a skirmish at Tranter's Creek, North Carolina, in 1862.

speak strongly, but I think I speak truly. Now permit to ask if you cannot make the sacrifice for one term? I know it is a grievous sacrifice, but I take the liberty of saying to you with more force than I did to Badger in the year 1841 when appointed Secretary, "I do not see how, you can avoid making it. I think it a deep misfortune, but your public professions require it." The Whig party with one voice, settled upon you for the highest and most honorable office they had it in their power to bestow—for good (not for evil) they united you to their cause. You consented to the union. They now say to you "we want your name—nay, your services—for two years; we wish you to aid us in effecting the grand object of our struggles—with you for our candidate we are certain of success—with another name we may succeed in the gubernatorial election—but that is only a part of our plan—the greater object is to carry the Legislature—to elect a President— without your aid we shall endanger the two latter," they might add, but as it is no inducement to you it would be useless "that your reward would be all the political distinction they could bestow." Now my dear Sir permit to argue the point a little. I premise that I think & admit it to be a sacrifice, it has no charms for me, but with your standing & character, you can at once re- sume your station at the bar;—if you wish to give up all political aspirations, it is a most respectable and graceful point from which to retire; if on the contrary further political advancement would be agreeable to you, your own observation must convince you that it is the vantage ground for the contest.

In conclusion permit me to say that my objections to political life is mainly involved in the habits which it generates; with the settled solidity of your character there is no danger on this head— the sacrifice is the personal and pecuniary one of the Canvass, & two years abstention from your business. You are young; two years I hope will not form any large portion of your life. I should dislike to argue you to any state which would be essentially in- jurious to you, but I pray you to reflect seriously on the subject: What is a great move for me.

I will with great pleasure attend the convention if I can have the honor of nominating you.

> Believe me
> Very Respectfully &
> Sincerely
> Yours.

*From James W. Bryan.* **A.**

Beaufort,

**Oct. 13, 1843.**

Your favour of the 10th. inst. was forwarded to me at this place. Perhaps I may have rather singular notions on the subject of slavery, but I have always had a reluctance to sell them against their will. As Clara has never been guilty of any unpardonable offence I am rather unwilling to separate her from her "kith and kin" without being somewhat provoked to it. I have been how-ever greatly "be-deviled" on the subject of servants & have had so many unhealthy & fashionable maid servants that I am getting rather sore on such matters. It seems that Clara cannot enjoy her health here; she is complaining at times, & I am reluctant to have her services when unwell & this of itself upsets my domestic affairs. I was willing to gratify her in going to your town, & tho't as she preferred going there, that she would be very willing to reside there. I must beg of you to say to her that I do not wish to sell her unless she desires it, & also to request you to hire her out & perhaps before the next year expires she may have regained her health; as she is in the upper country she must at least make an experiment of it. We have supplied her place with another servant & of course have no use for her here. This too is Ann's wishes on the subject & I am content with it also. I feel assured that Mrs. Cameron will be pleased with her as she is (if she chooses) a first rate servant & knows both the duties and pro-prieties of a servant very well indeed. If she desires it I will send her boy Lemuel up & perhaps ultimately she may be willing to take up her abode in Orange. I have some scruples in casting them off *nolens volens.*

I am sorry to trouble you so much in this matter, & trust that you will have no reserve in calling on me for any services I can render you.

I have just heard from Newbern by tonight's Stage. Another attempt has been made to fire the town. I believe in advising you of the late fire I informed you that an attempt was made to burn up Mr. James Stevenson's residence and store; that failed as the first was extinguished. Since then a Mr. Green who occupies Mr. Lamotte's Store on the County Wharf has made an effort to burn up his store & effects it is rumored to get his insurance. The "Counter tables" were all prepared & put into a "good's box"

& set fire to, but the fire was discovered bursting out of the roof & put out. The Intendant was to have had him arrested on today for examination, as all the circumstances point alone to him as the "author & finisher" of the whole matter. The character of Newbern is going down rapidly; it seems now to be conceded that Williams set fire to his store to get the insurance money. I trust for the credit of the town that these rumors may be without foundation on investigation.

Newbern is becoming very sickly. Genl. Pasteur[23] who came down on today from that place says that Dr. Hughes said he had thirty new cases on Friday & Chapman had as many. Mrs. Dr. Masters is dead, also a child of Tho. J. Emery's, a Captain Davis, etc.

I think you are right in wishing to decline the nomination for Governor although if you should alter your mind we should give you a hearty and manly support in this quarter. I have become disgusted and worn out with the party politics of the present day and have determined to "make my bow" to all active interference in them. I think the office of Gov'r has become somewhat degraded by the miserable system of demagogueism which by a sort of common consent is now attached to it in seeking popular favour on the stump at every grog-Shop and carttail in the Country. It is asking too much in my humble estimation of a gentleman to "stump it" throughout the State. We would give any gentleman the same vote down here without these appeals to popular prejudice. I think you would run better with us than Stanly. Badger has written to Stanly that he must be the man by all means; it is bad counsel for Stanly and I am sorry he has given it to him. We have nothing new among us—the young people seem to be getting up some hymeneal festivities which may not be uninteresting to the female part of your family. Alex'r Blount is to be married on the 26th. inst., Dr. Justice & Miss Guion on the 17th. inst., & others are in embryo. It is rumored that Judge Manly having failed with Miss Owen at Pittsboro will lead Miss S. Simpson to the altar this winter. I give you this as *rumour* as I know nothing more about it.

*   *   *   *   *

23 Thomas J. Pasteur.

*From Richard Hines* [24] *to Willie P. Mangum* [25]          U.

Raleigh,

Oct'r. 18th, 1843.

Private

Taking it for granted that you feel a very deep interest in the coming Gubernatorial election is the cause of my troubling you with this letter. It is not doubted that every true Whig in the State is, like myself, willing to sacerafice all personal preferences in the selection of a Candidate, and to go heart and hand in the support of the nominee of the Convention to be held in December.

It will however be admitted by all to be of the first importance that the Convention should select for our candidate the man most capable and best calculated to sustain and advance our cause, and most likely to obtain the greatest number of votes. In short every thing for principles but nothing for men.

From all that I have heard and seen here, I take it for granted that either Stanly, Manly, or Graham will be the nominee of the Convention. I shall therefore confine myself to their claims, not because I think the other gentlemen named are less worthy but because I think the public feeling at present is not in their favour. If however the State was not to be Canvassed, I think Col: Joiner[26] would be the decided favourite.

All admit Mr. Stanly has many and strong claims upon the Whig party, but it is urged against him that he is too young, rash and indiscreet, and not a successful electioneer, as is proved by the falling off of his vote in his old district at the last election, having beat Arrington only about fifty votes in the Counties composing his old district.

That the Quakers with many moderate Whigs would not vote for him on account of his violence, and his nomination would bring out every Loco vote in the State, and cause one of the most bitter contests ever witnessed at any election. It is also believed

---

[24] Richard Hines, of Edgecombe, and later of Raleigh, an influential Whig, who had been a member of the commons in 1824, and of Congress, 1825-1827.

[25] This letter, as will be seen from Graham's letter to his brother James, of Nov. 26th, 1843, was addressed to Willie P. Mangum. A penciled note on the envelope follows: "Mr. Mangum begs leave to present his respects to Mrs. Graham & the Ladies—He had hoped to make them in person & hand the enclosed letter, which Mr. M. desires Mr. Graham to see—It is marked "private,"—but Mr. M. deems it not improper to exhibit it to Mr. Graham—It is one with four others that he received by the last mail all of the same tenor—Nov. 3rd, 1843."

[26] Andrew Joyner.

by many that he would loose many votes in the Western part of the State on account of the old Federal politicks of his father, his own partiality for J. Q. Adams and his father's uniform opposition to the West and the many personal enemies he made whilst in the Legislature. For these and other objections it is feared his nomination might endanger that triumphant success important at all times, but particularly so at present, as all eyes will be turned to us being the first to speak in the great presidential campaign.

To Mr. Manly who is a gentleman in the best and most extensive sense of the word and would make an excellent Governor, it is objected that he has never made any sacrifice for the Whig cause that he has been the recipient of many favours and some patronage at their hands that he is by marriage connected with a clique here that has been raised and supported at the public expense, that one of his brothers in law has been governor[27] that the other is now one of the Senators in Congress from this State[28] and one of the most odious men in the State to the Whigs. That never having been in the Legislative councils of the Country, he is of course not very well informed in its political history, and his physical ability to canvass the State is much questioned by many who know him best.

The opinion is universal as far as I am informed that Mr. Graham is the most popular man of the three, and can command the largest vote probably by thousands, that he is looked up to as one of the leading politicians of the Country, well informed in its political history, and well qualified in every respect to increase the popularity of our cause and to defend our principles successfully whenever and by whoever assailed, and that the Whigs would unite in his support with more cordiality & zeal than either of the others, and that the Locos would opose him with much less warmth and bitterness than either of the others. It has been also stated here that Mr. James Graham is at present very luke warm and considers himself badly treated by the Whigs, and in case of Mr. Stanly's nomination it is by no means certain he would sustain him, whilst if his brother is nominated it will bring out all his strength and probably be the means of once more uniting our party in that very important district.

I have prefered stating the objections and views of others to the different persons named, rather than my own. I might say

[27] Edward B. Dudley.
[28] William H. Haywood.

much more, but hope I have said enough to satisfy you how things are getting on here at present. I am decidedly of the opinion that Mr. Stanly or Mr. Graham will be the nominee of the Convention. I therefore consider it of the first importance to our party that we should know at once whether Mr. Graham will serve if nominated for two years if no longer as the report is very industriously circulated that he will under no circumstances consent to be a Candidate. A decision that every leading Whig here, as far as I know does not believe Mr. G. can make in justice to his political friends in this, their hour of greatest need. Unless he has resolved to retire altogether from political life, having received from our hands at once one of the highest offices in its gift, and had we had the power would beyond all doubt have received it again.

I wish it distinctly understood that I entertain personally the most friendly feelings towards all the gentlemen named, and that were I to consult my own feelings I should hardly prefer Mr. Graham as my acquaintance and intercourse with the other gentlemen are of much older date and more intimate terms.

From letters recently received from Mr. Clay we expect him here in March. He expects to come from New Orleans by way of Charleston. What will be the most suitable mode of accomodating him here.

I consider myself authorized to say that a very large majority of the leading Whigs here concur in the views I have taken in this letter. Will you have the goodness to assertain from Mr. Graham his views about the matter and let me know his determination and what you think had best be done as soon as your convenience will admit, and oblige one who has the

> Honor to be very sincerely
> and truly your friend
> and obt: serv't

[P.S.] Since writing the within our friend Maj'r Hinton called in and authorizes me to say he fully concurs in the views I have taken. We concur in the opinion that it is very important *that something should be done at once to preserve the union and harmony of the Whig party, which he now believes to be in great danger.*

*From James W. Bryan.*                                    U.

Newbern,

Oct. 19th, 1843.

The last Newbern paper will exhibit probably rather an extraordinary publication of a Whig meeting here at which you will perceive I presided. During the whole week I was most laboriously engaged in Court & did not see the proceedings on paper before they were published in the paper. The original draft of the resolutions which I saw and drew before I was called to the chair evinced no preference by name for any Candidate for Gov'r but acquiesced in the choice of the Convention. A short time after the meeting was organized the town was again set on fire and the alarm caused us to adjourn until the next day, when the committee reported the resolutions which you will see published. *No* resolutions whatever were passed upon the subject of inserting the proceedings in the newspapers and the resolution to publish them in papers in favour of Stanly, Clay, etc., are the creation of the fancy of the Secretary which I am made to sanction by his own insertion of my name with his own at the bottom of the same. The whole affair is so ridiculous and at the same time the relations growing out of it of so delicate a character as to make a public allusion to them, rather disagreeable.

I felt this as due to you, as being my first and decided choice of all the Candidates, or rather, persons named as Candidates, for the office of Governor.

Charles Shepard died on Wednesday night last—he had an attack of the bilious fever, and sunk under his last chill.

*To Hugh Waddell from Weston R. Gales.*           U.

Raleigh,

Nov. 2nd, 1843.

*     *     *     *     *

Mr. Manly has peremptorily declined the use of his name for Governor. His determination is inflexible. Graham would have got the nomination any how; and now, I presume, there will scarcely be a dissenting voice. It is hard to "buckle fortune" on a man's back "whether he will or no," but as little disposed as I know Mr. Graham to be towards an acceptance of the nomination, there is no other choice. He will be forced into it, *nolens volens,* and his friends might as well prepare him for it. I have always known he was our strongest candidate. He will unite *all* our friends, and neutralize many of our opponents.

*From James Graham.*                                           U.

### Rutherfordton,

### Nov. 5th, 1843

I received your letter written at Raleigh. There is a total indifference in this Section to politicks. *Three* efforts were made here this week during Court to get up a Whig meeting to appoint Delegates to the Convention at Raleigh *before* it succeeded. Many of our substantial and influential Whigs have seen so much selfishness and personal advancement in the conduct of those who claim to be leaders in the party that they are disgusted and discouraged, and manifest an unwillingness to do any thing to Sustain the party.

The Meeting which authorised the appointment of Delegates this week did not exceed 20 or 30 persons; Although it was held in the Court house about one o'clock in the day of Court.

I regard the Whig cause in N. C. as in imminent danger from the general apathy and personal jelousies in this District among those who aspire to fill high stations. Among the few who will speak at all on the nomination for Governor, Mr. Stanly appears to have but few friends. His vote for the Bankrupt Bill and the Tariff Bill would injure him very much, beside his indiscretion. Manly will make a good run, if he can sustain himself on the stump.

If this district *gives way,* of which there is great danger, the Whig candidate, no matter who he may be, will be hard run, if not beaten. I have not expressed this opinion, because I do not wish to discourage any Whig any where, but the elements of discord are abroad in the Mountains. I shall be but little in the district during the coming winter, as I expect to go to Tennessee where I will probably remain some months.

I think you will act wisely to hold fast to your determination not to suffer your name to be run before the convention to nominate a Candidate for Governor, Some of my friends have been kind enough to ask leave to nominate me for that office, and I have promptly and positively refused, & requested that no more should be said on that subject. It is a poor office; and the Whig who gains it next Summer will labor hard for it.

If the Convention will adopt some plan of organization and system of just policy to unite and strengthen the Whig party we may be saved; but without some such effort we will be defeated.

*From Thomas P. Devereux.*                          A.

Conaconara,

Nov. 6th, 1843.

I am in receipt of your letter of the 29th. ult. by which I am more flattered than interested—for I confess that I do not view the subject in the light you do. In the unreasonable number of candidates spoken of by the Whigs & in the character of the men I see much cause for alarm.

The most prominent one[29] (who caused my conversation with our mutual friend) will be beaten I verily believe. Your opinion is well founded as to the probable success of an indifferent Whig candidate, but there are a vast body of staid men who will not vote for him—many men of probity intelligence and virtue in all its phases who will not vote for a professed duelist—a noisy quarrelsome bragadocio who is easily bucked out by one more noisy and more quarrelsome.

My notion is that we must nominate you & leave the responsibility on you.

Very sincerely
Yours

*From Charles L. Hinton.*                          U.

Neuse River,

Nov. 15th, 1843.

The subject of the Governor's election is one in which we all feel deeply interested, not so much on account of the individual to be selected as the impulse it is to give to public feeling during the next summer.

---

[29] The reference is, of course, to Edward Stanly.

I have recently met with intelligent individuals from the lower Roanoke, the seaboard and the mountains, all of whom concur in the decided opinion that public sentiment is settled on you as the Candidate.

Now, my dear Sir, I have no doubt you consider the acceptance of the nomination as repugnant to your interest and inclination, but your situation towards the party must compel you to yield both, and accede to the wishes of the convention, or you must cease to occupy that high stand in the Whig ranks you at present hold. This is the opinion expressed by many intelligent Whigs who speak not for the individual but for the cause. It is your service next summer rather than in the executive office we are looking to, the crisis will then have passed and the Whig party triumphant or disbanded.

You have probably heard that Manly has preremptory declined having his name before the convention; should you do so I fear it will produce much confusion in our ranks.

I am induced to write these few lines in consequence of a conversation we had when I last saw you, in which you were not only disposed to decline but to publish a card to that effect.

### *To James Graham.*                                     U.

#### Hillsboro',

#### Nov. 26th, 1843.

When I last wrote you from Raleigh in relation to the election of Governor, I did so at the request of Hinton, Morehead, & others who were in constant intercourse with Manly, & were in possession of his intentions and wishes. I presented the same views to our friends on the Circuit with whom I conversed untill I reached Rockingham. There to my surprize a letter from the Govr. to Jas. Morehead was shewn me, written for my perusal, in which it was stated, that Manly had positively declined, and would under no circumstances consent to be considered among those, from whom a selection was to be made, and urging that I must yield to what he stated was the general wish. It struck me with surprize, and even excited a stronger feeling, as the reason assigned for abandoning a position before the party, which he had held for nearly twelve months, viz ruin to his fortune, cannot be the real one. I gave but little heed to the matter however untill

I came to Caswell, where my mail was sent me from home. In which I found letters from R. Hines to Mangum, & from Gales to Waddell urging that I was the choice of the State and must consent—also the Hillsboro' paper of that week, the leading article of which, prompted, I presume, by Mangum, insists that I am generally preferred, and although "it is known to be far from my inclinations yet if nominated that I could not refuse," etc. On coming home I find a letter from Hinton in the same strain, saying that he had seen persons from all sections of the State, & that I would be nominated unquestionably. In mean time public meetings in several Counties (some of them by advices I have no doubt from Raleigh) have made nominations of me. A large meeting is expected here this week with a similar design. But I will endeavor to prevent a nomination in it.

I am placed however in a situation of painful embarrassment. The office is the last in the State that I would wish to fill, to say nothing of the sacrifice of business & fortune. Yet, I apprehend, the nomination is about to be thrust upon me, and I do not see how it can be declined. I now regret that I did not publish a card in the Summer, as I proposed to do but was dissuaded by Morehead and Hinton, saying it might injure the prospects of Manly, by encouraging others.

I have not given my assent to any one, but on the contrary discouraged the idea. When however the delegates go from here, they must be in possession of my views, and I have thought under the circumstances that I could not do less than to say that though decidedly averse to it, if it were the unanimous wish of a Convention representing all parts of the State, I could not decline. But if a respectable minority did not desire it my friends should withhold my name. I wish very much, that I could have an interview with you in relation to it, and although it is late, I would be glad you would write me on the receipt of this, what I should do under the circumstances.

\*    \*    \*    \*    \*

[P.S.] We have four criminals confined in Jail for Capital felonies. We hope to see you as you go North in Jany. The wedding of Mr. Ruffin[30] was a large party.

Hubard[31] M. C. from Va. was here with a party from Halifax.

---

[30] Peter Browne Ruffin, son of Judge Thomas Ruffin, married Mary Rebecca Jones, daughter of Cadwallader Jones, of "West Hill."

[31] Edward Wilcox Hubard (1806-1878), of Virginia, graduate of the University of Virginia, planter, Democratic member of congress, 1841-1847, Confederate treasury official, colonel of militia, 1864,

I was absent on the Circuit, but my family & all the world beside was there.

### From Daniel M. Barringer.                                U.

Washington City,

Dec. 3rd, 1843.

I was anxious to see you on my way through Hillsboro' to say a few things to you in relation to our State politics. Your letter to me was duly rec'd., and I concurred entirely in its contents, with the exception of one thing, and that was, that you thought you could not accept the nomination as our Candidate for Governor. I write you now, merely to say, that if you are nominated, as I hope you will be, that you *must* reconsider your former purpose & *run on the ticket.* I know it will be disagreeable to you, & you will have to make sacrifices. But I think your acceptance due to your friends, to the party, and yourself. I have considered this matter in all its bearings, & this is my *deliberate conviction.* You are the strongest man with us in the West, where our opponents count much on the popularity of Hoke. He will play the demagogue a good deal, but you will find him quite manageable after you hear him once or twice.

I write you this letter in haste, as the mail is about to close.

Our friends here are in good spirits. J. W. Jones[32] will probably be Speaker.

Write me whenever you can conveniently.

### From George E. Spruill.[33]                                U.

Raleigh,

December 11th., 1843.

Hon. W. A. Graham:
Sir:

In compliance with the request contained in the resolutions herewith enclosed, I have the honor to inform you that, at the Whig Convention held in this place the 7th. inst., you were unan-

---

[32] John Winston Jones (1791-1848), of Virginia, graduate of William and Mary, lawyer, delegate to the convention of 1829, Democratic member of congress, 1835-1845, (speaker, 1843-1845), speaker of the state house of delegates, 1846.

[33] From the *Raleigh Register*, Dec. 29th, 1843. The writer, George E. Spruill, was a planter in Warren County. He was educated as a physician, but never practiced.

imously nominated as the Whig Candidate for governor, at the election to be held in 1844. I have the pleasure of adding, that your nomination was received by the Convention, not only with unanimity, but with the most hearty and enthusiastic approbation.

It will afford me, as I am sure it will the Whig party of the State, great satisfaction to learn from you, your willingness to accept the nomination.

With sentiments of the highest regard, I am very truly,

> your ob't serv't,
> George E. Spruill.
> President of the Whig Convention.

### [Enclosure]

### Resolutions of the Whig Convention.[34]

### December 8, 1843.

*Resolved,* That William A. Graham be, and he is hereby nominated as the Whig Candidate for Governor, at the election to be held in 1844.

And this Convention, taking into consideration the great importance to this State, and to the Union, in the contest of 1844—and the efforts which have been made, are now making, and doubtless will continue to be made, to misrepresent the principles of the Whig party, and to advance the destructive doctrines of what is miscalled the Democratic party; and having entire confidence in the soundness of the Whig cause, and the honest and patriotic feelings of the great body of the people, do hereby express their wish and expectation that Mr. Graham will, as far as possible, canvass the whole State, and place before his fellow-citizens, the true grounds on which the Whig party rest their cause, and vindicate its claim to general support.

*Resolved,* That the President of the Convention communicate to Mr. Graham their resolutions, and desire him on the part of the Convention, to accept the nomination.

---

[34] The enclosure is missing from the letter. The resolutions of the convention are taken from the *Raleigh Register,* of December 12, 1843.

These resolutions, constituting a party platform, are typical of North Carolina party platforms throughout the ante-bellum period, in their reference to national issues only. The absurd absorption of both parties in national politics led to practically complete inattention to the needs of the state, with disastrous effects upon the state and its people.

*Resolved,* That the nomination of HENRY CLAY, for President of the United States, made by the Whig Convention of April, 1842, still meets the unanimous and cordial approbation of the whole Whig party of North Carolina; and therefore,

*Resolved,* That this Convention do adhere to the said nomination, and declare Henry Clay to be the first and only choice of the Whigs of North Carolina for the Chief Magistrate of the nation.

And this convention, having entire confidence in the wisdom and integrity of the National Whig Convention, to be held in Baltimore in the month of May next, and nothing doubting that they will be careful to select as a candidate for the Vice Presidency, an intelligent, consistent, and trust-worthy Whig: Therefore,

*Resolved,* That the Whigs of North Carolina will support for the Vice Presidency, the person who may be nominated by that Convention.

*Resolved,* That Edward B. Dudley of New Hanover, and George E. Badger of Wake, be appointed delegates to the Whig Convention which is to assemble in Baltimore in the month of May next.

*Resolved,* That for collecting and disbursing the public revenues—for facilitating and equalizing exchanges, and for furnishing a currency of uniform value, a National Bank is and has been (to the Government and to the people of the Union) a convenient, proper, and necessary instrument; and therefore,

*Resolved,* That such an institution, with the safeguards and improvements in its organization which experience has suggested, ought to be established by Congress.

*Resolved,* That no more revenue should be collected by the General Government, than is or may be necessary to an economical administration thereof; that the revenue necessary for this purpose should be collected by duties upon imports, and not by direct taxation; and that in adjusting these duties, such a discrimination ought to be made as will countervalue the oppressive restrictions imposed by foreign nations, upon our commercial intercourse with them, and incidentally afford just protection to American industry.

*Resolved,* That this Convention is deeply impressed with the importance of immediate and thorough organization of the Whigs of North Carolina, and doth therefore earnestly recommend that Clay Clubs be established forthwith, in every County, and that subordinate Clubs or branches be extended to every precinct or local subdivision of the County, according to the general plan as recommended by the Convention of April, 1842; and the Convention has the firmest conviction that if this plan of organization be adopted and actively pursued, the elections in 1844, for Governor and Electors, of President and Vice President, will show a greatly increased Whig majority, and the next legislature will represent truly the Whig State of North Carolina.

*Resolved,* That the public Lands of right belong to the several States of the Union, and the purposes for which the same were originally ceded to the United States having been accomplished, the General Government holds the same merely as a trustee for the parties so entitled thereto; and therefore,

*Resolved,* That the distribution of the proceeds of the said Lands, amongst the States of the Union, ought to be no longer denied or delayed.


## To George E. Spruill.[35]

### Hillsboro',

#### December 18th., 1843.

Sir:

I have had the honor to receive your letter, enclosing the resolutions of the Whig Convention, which assembled at Raleigh on the 7th. inst., and conveying the intelligence that I had been unanimously nominated by that body, for the office of governor of North Carolina, at the election to be held during the next year. To have been thus distinguished by a body so respectable for its numbers, intelligence and patriotism; and the exponents of such a constituency as it represented, is a mark of approbation which can only be surpassed in my esteem, by a sanction of the nomination by the people of the State.

That I was deemed worthy, by such an assemblage, to occupy a place which has been adorned by a Caswell, a Johnston, a Davie, and so many other eminent citizens—men who have illustrated our name in war and in peace—is an honor, to which I cannot be insensible, and which I shall ever regard among the choicest recollections of my life. But, however gratifying to an honorable pride, your communication awakens feelings also of a different character. It breaks in upon my plans of life, my professional and

---

[35] From the *Raleigh Register*, Dec. 29, 1843.

agricultural pursuits, and demands a sacrifice of interests which cannot well be spared from my family. I had, therefore, most earnestly and anxiously hoped that the choice of the convention would have fallen on some one of those able and virtuous citizens whose names have been connected with this subject, and whose disinterestedness and zeal in the Whig cause, is only equalled by their devotion to its principles. Nevertheless, with my conceptions of duty (however much I had wished it otherwise,) I have no alternative but to accept the nomination. Without stronger reasons than any which I have to urge, I could not hold any other person justified in refusing a call from such a source, to lend his name and his efforts to the support of principles, which, I verily believe, lie at the foundation of the enduring prosperity and happiness of the country.

Though your letter requires no further reply, I deem it due to the occasion to express my entire concurrence in the opinions of public measures, embodied in the resolutions of the Convention. For forty years, of the fifty-four that our Government has existed, we have had a National Bank. That it was useful to the Government, as a depository of the public moneys, and a fiscal agent in their transmission and disbursement, is proved by the unquestioned fact, that the Nation suffered not one cent of loss, nor any delay or expense in the transfer and payment of its funds, to the amount of hundreds of millions in all parts of the Union, by any of the operations of the Bank. That it also facilitated and lowered the rate of exchange, and furnished a currency, equal or nearly so, to the precious metals, good alike in all parts of the Union—in Main and Louisiana—in North Carolina, Michigan, Illinois, and Missouri, are likewise facts which have passed into history. Whether like advantages have been shared either by the Government or the people in their pecuniary affairs, whilst we have had no such institution, our recent experience, and the reports of Mr. Dallas and Mr. Crawford as to a former period, will enable us to answer.

The Charter of the first Bank, having been passed with the approval of President Washington in 1791, for a term of twenty years, and having been found in practice to answer the ends for which it was designed, no other mode of administering the finances, or of equalizing exchanges, or giving soundness to the currency, was agitated or discussed, until about the time of the expiration of that Charter in 1811. It was then supposed that all the benefits derived from it could be obtained through the agency of Banks chartered by the States. Accordingly, the old Bank expired, and the experiment of State Banks was made.—President Madison, who had been the ablest and most zealous of the opponents of the first Charter in Congress, and who had concurred in the propriety of suffering it to expire, after a trial of the State Bank system for four years, and finding it to fail his expectations, magnanimously surrendered his long cherished theoretical opinions, and called on Congress to readopt the system which had been found useful in practice. A Congress, a majority of whom had partaken of those opinions, convinced by the same process of experiment, responded to the call, and established the Bank of 1816. Thus no other system became necessary to be devised for another period of twenty years. During this time the public moneys were safe, and our entire currency and exchanges attained a more perfect state than was enjoyed in any other country. As the end of that term approached, those who opposed the Bank sought for a substitute, which would effect all its beneficial objects, and be free from the objections which they entertained to it. To make sure of a wise provision of a substitute, and to enable the country to undergo the transmission without derangement to its affairs, they commenced their work early. It as proclaimed that the agency of State Banks would be again resorted to. The States were exhorted to establish Banks, with a view to carry out the new system, and the people were told that under it, not only would the finances of the Government be as well, or better, administered than they had been by the Bank of the United States, but that the exchanges would be at least as low, and the currency as sound. Accordingly, the State Banks were trebeled in number and capital, the deposits of the public moneys were taken from the Bank of the United States before the end of its Charter, and placed in them. They were encouraged to lend freely, and especially to furnish a bountiful supply of exchange; and for three years, the country was assured by the most triumphant assertions of the public functionaries, that the experiment had succeeded in every particular. While yet the notes of exaltation at this great achievement in finance and currency was still sounding in our ears, in May, 1837, the bubble burst, the system failed, the Banks suspended payment, their paper depreciated—and with twenty millions of its money on deposit in the vaults, the Government was obliged to resort to an issue of Treasury notes to satisfy its daily expenses. By arrangements and indulgencies, they have since all paid up the amounts then held in deposit, except it may be, a comparatively small sum. But the event showed, and their former advocates now admitted, that they did not answer the expectation of the country. What was next to be done? A like magnanimous sacrifice of the pride of opinion, with that which characterized Mr. Madison, and the Congress of 1816, would have counselled a return to the safe and tried paths of experience. But Mr. Van Buren, then the President, had proclaimed "uncompromising hostility to the Bank of the United States," and must needs propose some new scheme. He therefore brought to the consideration of Congress the sub-treasury system; by which, abandoning all care, over currency and exchange, as not within the powers of the Federal Government, (except so far as the former is embraced in the power to coin money, and regulate the value of foreign coins,) it is proposed that all the dues of Government shall be collected in gold and silver, and be kept by individual depositories. I have not space to discuss that project here. Let it suffice to say, that it proposes to abandon a safe, practical method of administering the finances, and regulating the currency and exchange, for the speculative opinions of those, who signally failed in the State Bank system, on which they professed equal confidence. Or, rather, that we shall prefer to our own American, successful experience of half a century, the experience of continental Europe and of Asia. But it has been condemned by the judgment of the American people, and most unequivocally by those of our own State.

Whilst, however, I advocate the establishment of a Bank of the United States, it is not for the sake of the Bank, or to favor the stockholders, as is sometimes unfairly charged by those holding opposite opinions, but for the public benefits that are expected to flow from it. Whatever abuses have existed in former institutions, (and I doubt not there have been many,) they should be guarded against, and prevented for the future. To say that this cannot be effected, is to deny ordinary wisdom to the Legislature, which has the power to fashion the Charter at their will, or to suppose unfaithfulness or corruption in those, who are to expound or to execute the laws. To forsake every scheme, into the administration of which abuses may creep, instead of lopping off and suppressing the abuses as they are discovered, would be to make government itself a constant series of new experiments. That a Bank affords the cheapest mode of keeping and disbursing the public moneys is manifest, since no compensation is paid for this service, however great may be the amount, or distant the place of payment from the place of receipt. That it is *safest*, is equally evident, for whatever embezzlements, frauds or accidents may happen to the Bank, its whole capital stock, as well as other means, are liable to make good the deposits in its vaults. There are advantages which recommend it as a fiscal agent of the Government. It was found in practice to possess another quality—that of lowering exchanges, and forcing the local Banks to keep their circulation in a sound state; which renders it particularly desirable to North Carolina, and those other States which do not find a market for the largest part of their productions within their own limits, but carry them to other States, and from the necessities of trade, receive in payment the currencies of Banks over which their authorities have no control.

I was one of the earliest of those who advocated in the Legislature of the State, the policy and justice of distributing the proceeds of the public lands among the States of the Union. I do not consider this funds as having been contemplated by the framers of the constitution, among the means for the ordinary support of the government, and it has not been considered so by others. If we have reference to the immense grants which have been made of it, from time to time, to States, State corporations, benevolent institutions for education and other purposes, as well as to individuals—grants which would never have been supposed within the powers of Congress, if it had been required that they should be satisfied by equivalent sums of money out of the public treasury. I will only add on this topic, that my conviction of the propriety of distribution has only been confirmed by the nearer view of the subject, which I was enabled to take from a position in the public service which I recently occupied. And I cannot but regard it, as most unfortunate for the country, that the acting President thought proper to arrest these two great and beneficient measures by the exercise of the Veto power.

The collections of revenue, and the objects and amount of its expenditure, are always matters of just and deep solicitude to the people. The public judgment has long since determined that in times of peace the Federal government should raise its revenues by duties on imports, rather than a resort to direct taxation. And I most cordially subscribe to the opinion of the Convention, that no greater amount should be collected than is necessary for an economical administration of the Government. From the year 1816 to 1837, a period of twenty-one years, the revenues not only paid all the current expenses of Government, but yielded an average excess annually of 11½ millions of dollars. This surplus was absorbed in the payment of the national debt, arising out of the Revolution and the late war, until its extinguishment. We are now happily under no necessity to provide any continuing excess for such purpose, our debt being comparatively inconsiderable. All that is needed at present, is an amount which shall defray the annual cost of a proper peace establishment, with a moderate, temporary, excess, until the present debt shall be discharged. The question has arisen, whether, in levying such an amount, discriminations should be made in the duties on particular articles, for the encouragement of American industry, and to countervail the restrictions of other nations, or whether a light rate shall be collected on all articles without distinction. I have no hesitation in saying, that whilst I think the Government should collect the least amount of money which may be necessary for an efficient public service, in laying duties to raise such sum, I would incidentally afford protection to American interests, when they were deemed of sufficient importance to deserve it, as well as counteract the effects of restrictive regulations on our trade, by foreign nations wherever it should appear expedient to do so. To act otherwise, in the present condition of the commercial world, would be for the Nation to surrender the great principle of self defense and self protection. I did not vote for the tariff now existing. Some of its duties were higher than I approved, but in the vacant condition of the Treasury, I would not have withheld from it my support, had an amendment, which I offered, proposing a distribution of the proceeds of the public lands among the States, been incorporated in the Bill. If it shall be found to yield a greater revenue than is needed for the Government, (which it has not yet done) or if its provisions are found, on trial, burthensome to the citizens by increasing greatly the price of commodities, it should be modified so as to meet either contingency. We have seen that in the period already referred to, ending in 1837, the revenue largely exceeded the public expenditure. It has been far otherwise since. Under the operation of the Compromise Act of March, 1833, the income of the Government from customs, gradually declined until 1842; and although it has considerably revived since the passage of the act of that year, it seems not yet equal to the public necessities. But what amount per annum ought to be considered economical for expenditure in time of peace? During the four years of Mr. Van Buren's administration, the appropriations for current expenses averaged per year more than 28 millions of dollars. The appropriations for the year 1842, by the last Congress, were but a small fraction above 20 millions of dollars. And this, in the face of estimates from the Executive Departments, coined for 24½ millions. Yet, I have not understood that the public service has in any way suffered by the curtailment. The appropriations for 1843, and the first half of 1844, made at the last session of Congress, for like objects, were less than 25 millions for the whole 18 months, being at the rate of less than 17 millions per year. I point your attention, Sir, to these facts in passing, to show that the great revolution of 1840 has not been without its fruits, in the promotion of economy and reform, however the defection of the acting President has enabled him to thwart Congress, and disappoint the hopes of the people in other respects.

The benefits of the Federal Government depend so much on the conduct of the Executive Chief Magistrate, that I rejoice to find the Republican Whigs throughout America disposed, with one voice, to call to that high station, a man who has never disappointed friends, nor deceived even foes, who has rendered most important and approved public services to the Union for a period of 35 years, and who is admitted by the judgment even of his opponents in political sentiment, to be one of the best specimens of American character that our institutions have produced. If our efforts in the next contest shall be crowned with success, as we have every reason to hope and HENRY CLAY shall be called to the head of the Republic, the country may look forward to a restoration of its prosperity, and a new career of happiness, under dignified, enlightened and thoroughly patriotic counsels.

I will endeavour to comply with the request of the Convention that I shall visit the different sections of the State, so far as I shall be able to do so, consistently with other engagements.

With my thanks for the cordial and kind manner in which you have been pleased to execute your office,

I am, with profound respect,

Your obedient servant,<br>Will. A. Graham.

George E. Spruill, Esq.,
    President of the Whig Convention,
        Warrenton, N. C.

*From Daniel M. Barringer.*          A.

## House of Rep.,
## Decr. 27th, 1843.

Nothing new. It is now certain that Van Buren will be the nominee of the Dem. Tyler's party will be against him. Our Whig friends are very sanguine & in fine spirits. N. C. must do her best Summer. I have reason to think that it will be important for you to spend some time in the mountain Country as early as possible. I have no fears of your election,[36] but I should regret any decrease in the Whig vote. In my own District you will get the whole & perhaps more than the Whig vote.

I shall be glad to hear from you often. I write you now in haste.

* * * * *

*To James W. Bryan.*          U. Bryan Mss.

## Hillsboro',
## Decr. 28th, 1843.

* * * * *

I find myself exceedingly perplexed by the nomination for Governor, which has been forced on me, and especially the resolution of the Convention calling for a Canvass of the State. My professional business never promised better reward, and I have sundry improvements both of this place and my plantation on hand, which I desired to superintend in person. Withal, the office is one for which I have never entertained the least partiality.

We have no news in Hillsboro' Christmas has been a dull affair to all but the negroes. The weather has been mild and genial as early Spring.

---

[36] Shortly after this, on January 8, 1844, Samuel F. Patterson wrote to Edmund W. Jones: "You have no doubt read with attention the proceedings of the late political Convention held in this City. . . . The greatest unanimity of views and opinions, & the greatest harmony and good feeling prevailed throughout the whole sitting. You have no doubt also read the admirable letter of Mr. Graham, accepting the nomination. With such a leader, and such a cause, the Whigs can hardly fail of success, unless they are most shamelessly negligent in the performance of their duty."

*From John Steele Macnamara.*                                          U.

Salisbury,

Dec'r. 29th, 1843.

The acquaintance which some years ago I had the honor of forming with the late Senator from North Carolina, will, I trust, excuse me for taking this occasion to express to him the high gratification with which I learned the result of the deliberation of the late Whig Convention at Raleigh, and in particular the nomination which it had the good fortune to make of a candidate for the gubernatorial Chair.

Fully persuaded that the elevation of the person thus indicated to the highest dignity within the gift of the people of his native State, would not only subserve the best interest of the people and party of which he has long been a distinguished leader, but also promote the welfare and prosperity of the commonwealth; the humble efforts which in my limited sphere it may be in my power to make will be most cheerfully contributed to effectuate an object so desirable. In anticipation of this event, and counting with perfect confidence upon its occurrence, I trust it will be considered no breach of modesty in me to make a suggestion which being prompted by considerations of a nature personal to himself would perhaps have come with a more scrupulous propriety and a better grace from some third person.

The Legislature of the State has thought fit to support the dignity of the Chief Magistrate by assigning to [him] four Aides. Should the successor of the present worthy incumbent see proper to avail himself of this provision and in considering the claims of this Section of the State, should he deem the undersigned a suitable person for that appointment, an obligation would be conferred of no small magnitude, and one which would ever merit the warmest thanks of the favoured recipient.

I have the honor to be,
With sentiments of the highest regard
Your Obt. Servant.

1844

*From Reuben Clarke Shorter.*[1]                    U.

Chapel Hill

Jan. 21st. 1844.

Having had the honor to be chosen one of the Managers of a
Party to be given in June to the graduating class, if you will
honor me by being my assistant Manager,[2] you will confer a
very great favor on

Your humble servant

If convenient to Mr. Graham, an answer is very desirable immediately

With much esteem

*From William Blanding*[3]                    U.

Charleston,

Jany. 22nd, 1844.

As one of the Corresponding Committee of the Whig Club of
Charleston, I have the honor of informing you, at a late meeting of our Club, your name was unanimously directed to be en-
rolled among the Honorary Members of the association.
    I am with the highest Respect

Your obt. Servt.

*To James W. Bryan.*            U. Bryan Mss.

Raleigh,

Jany. 26th, 1844.

You have no doubt heard of the death of Judge Gaston on
Tuesday evening last at 8 o'clock. He had been in Court untill
after two. Complained on leaving the Bench and was supported
by Jas. Morehead into the Gov's office, where he was very ill—

---

[1] Reuben Clark Shorter, of Barbour County, Alabama, attended the University
of North Carolina, and became a lawyer and legislator in his native state.
[2] This is an example of an interesting practice at the university. A few years
later, the persons thus selected were, more fittingly, entitled honorary managers.
[3] William Blanding, a well-known Charleston lawyer. The preliminary organization of the famous Palmetto Regiment took place at his residence, and he
became a captain in it, and served throughout the Mexican War.

Dr. Haywood [4] was called in, and by the use of stimulants he was revived. He taken in a carriage to his lodgings, and after wards seemed much better, talked cheerfully, etc., but about 8 o'clock he complained loudly of coldness in the breast or stomach, and soon expired, the Dr. says of Apoplexy. His funeral was to have taken place today, but is postponed till Sunday.

You will see in the papers the proceedings of the Bar and Court on the melancholy occasion.

\* \* \* \*

*From James Graham.*                                            U.

### V. Furnace,

### Jan'y 30th, 1844.

I received your last Letter, but not until about *six weeks* after it was written; and of consequence not in time to answer you before the Whig Convention met to nominate a Candidate for Governor. It is not necessary to say anything now about the propriety of your acceptance.

Your Letter of acceptance is a good paper, the sentiments and stile are sound and plain. In the present want of organization among the Whigs of this State; and the want of energy and industry and tact among the present delegation of Whigs from N. C. in Congress, I presume you must have very onerous duties to perform: and the more so, as the Whig Press of our State are conducted with very little ability and an obvious want of tact and popular address among the people.

It would lighten your labors very much, as well as advance the Whig Cause, if a public Meeting were held in every County of the State at next Spring Superior Court to nominate popular and able candidates for the next Legislature. That being done, then if our Whig Delegation in Congress would send suitable documents, speeches, and Letters that were short, plain, just in principle and full of patriotism, then the people would see and understand the true and naked questions at issue between the opposing parties. The Whig Papers should call forthwith on all Democratic Candidates to declare unequivocally who is their *first choice*

---

[4] Dr. Fabius J. Haywood (1803-1880), a graduate of the university, M.D. of the University of Pennsylvania, at this time the most prominent physician of Raleigh.

among the Candidates for the Presidency. Gov. Morehead, being much at leisure, might write excellent Newspaper Articles.

\*  \*  \*  \*  \*

I have been very busy on my plantations. I have sent to Market (Columbia) 8 Waggon Loads of Cotton. I hope in the Spring to send 12 or 14 more. I think in the coming Spring you had better sell your Lands in this County at what you can get—I am preparing to do so with mine that lye in detached parcels.

P. S. The death of Judge Gaston makes the complexion of the next Legislature a new subject of interest. Badger ought to be the man to succeed him.

*From Robert B. Gilliam.*                                                    U.

Oxford,

Jan. 31st, [1844.]

\*  \*  \*  \*  \*

It will be no news to you, to be informed that your nomination is universally acceptable amongst our Whigs, as it indeed seems to be everywhere. I have all along been satisfied, that the Whig cause in the State at this juncture required your nomination, but knowing the severe personal and pecuniary sacrifices it would cost you, I forebore to press the subject upon your consideration.

The sudden death of Judge Gaston has caused a very great sensation amongst all classes in this place. Every one seems to regard it as a National loss. It will be difficult to supply his place on the bench and I fear the political complexion of the Council will increase the difficulty already existing. Will the Governor nominate to the Council, as is contemplated by the constitution, or will he submit the election to that body, as was done by Gov. Burton, and I believe, by some of his successors? If the nomination is made by the Governor, who will be his nominee? I should be glad to hear from you, if you have the leisure.

*From Robert B. Gilliam.*                                                    U.

Oxford,

February 2nd, 1844.

\*  \*  \*  \*  \*

I think it likely that you will be called on for a political speech at Court, in such a way that it will be difficult to resist it. There is much anxiety to hear you, of which you will no doubt be very distinctly apprised upon your arrival. I take it for granted, as you make no reference to it, that Mr. Hoke will not be here at March Court, and if he should come at another time, I am satisfied it is of the highest importance that you should meet him. This County, as you know, is debateable ground, but with proper care, the prospects are decidedly in favour of the Whigs. I should not like for Mr. Hoke to have the *last say* on you. If you are to make but one speech in Granville, I wish it to be when the adversary is here; not that I consider Mr. Hoke formidable in argument, but he has a good address, and I suppose is pretty well skilled in party Slang. At any rate, when he comes, I wish you to be here too.

If your engagements will permit, I would be glad you could get to Oxford a day or two before Court, and spend the intermediate time at my house. By the way, if you think it best to speak at March Court, I should be glad to know pretty soon, that I may take some pains to call the attention of the people to it.

I have no idea of again embarking in politicks, except as a private soldier. Certainly not for some time to come. I shall not be an indifferent spectator, nor should I be if I felt less interest than I do, in the approaching Presidential election.

Whilst your flag is flying, I can never be indifferent or inactive.

### From New Hanover Committee.[5]    U.

#### Wilmington,

#### February 4th., 1844.

We discharge with pleasure, the duty imposed upon us by the "New Hanover Clay Club," to inform you of your election to its honorary membership, and to ask that you will meet the Hon. Henry Clay in Wilmington, and unite with us in receiving and welcoming him to North Carolina, upon his arrival in our beloved State.

It seems particularly meet, that the *favorite son of North Carolina* should welcome by his presence the landing of the *favorite son of the Union,* upon the shores of North Carolina. We therefore confidently hope that you will be with us upon that occasion.

---

[5] From the *Hillsborough Recorder,* March 7th, 1844.

You will be definitely apprised of Mr. Clay's arrival, as soon as it can be done with certainty.

As an additional consideration for visiting us, we would suggest, you would then have an opportunity of seeing a greater number of the people of this District in Wilmington, than upon any other occasion which is likely to present itself.

With high consideration, we are your friends,

> Edward B. Dudley,
> Robert H. Cowan,[6]
> F. C. Hill.[7]

Com. New Hanover Clay Club.

*Invitation to visit Western Counties.*            U.

Franklin, Macon Co., N. C.,

Feb. 5th, 1844.

The position you occupy before the people of N. Carolina is our apology for adressing you at this time.

In your letter of acceptance of the 18th. Dec'r '43, you signify your willingness to "visit the different sections of the State, so far as you shall be able to do so consistently with other engagements."

Now we would respectfully suggest that when you arrange your plans, if possible, you will so arrange it as to visit this place and Murphey. It would be inconsistent with our present purpose to state the reasons in detail which make the course important.

The principal are these: The people of these two counties, particularly of Cherokee, are largely indebted to the State for their lands. An act of the last legislature made it obligatory on them to pay all the interest on their bonds up to Jan'y 1st. '44; and if they neglected or refused to comply against the 20th. of Jan'y it was made the duty of the agent to bring suit against them for the principal. We will just say the time is past and few are saved!

You, Sir, would have to be among us to understand fully the difficulties against which we have to contend. A new Country

---

[6] Robert H. Cowan (1801-1843), of New Hanover, a prominent citizen, who sat in the commons, 1824-1825.

[7] Frederick C. Hill, of Wilmington, editor of the *Advertiser*, a Whig newspaper,

is to be opened—the means of raising money limited,—and worse, where is the money?

The people now expect to be sued; and if they escape being *mashed up and ground up,* it will be by the mercy and forbearance of those who execute the law!

Yet these people express a willingness to pay for their lands, and in a late Memorial from the people of Cherokee to the Governor and Treasurer they say "we will pay so soon as we can do so consistently with the good of our families." Placed in this situation, they look for relief to the next Legislature, and they will expect and demand such treatment from the State as their peculiar and embarrassed situation requires.

You would of course expect that they have become quite sensative on this subject, as all persons will do when the welfare and happiness of themselves and families are involved.

Now, Sir, the impression is trying to be made out here that a Western man has feelings and interests in common with the Western people, and therefore it is a matter of interest for them to place a Western man in the Executive Chair.

These counties will doubtless give a large Whig majority; yet in order to insure success it is important that the people should be attached to their man as well as to their principles. And if they can be satisfied that an Eastern man will feel an interest in their prosperity, then, with our principles, we will triumph.

If you feel desirous to make yourself more fully acquainted with the condition and wants of the people of these counties, we would respectfully recommend you to Jacob Siler,[8] Esq., Agent for the collection of Cherokee Bonds, who is better acquainted with the condition of the people than any other man in Western Carolina—whose devotion to Whig principles is undoubted, and who, we are sure, will take great pleasure in giving you any information he possesses. His address is Franklin, N. C.

Please excuse any seeming impropriety in addressing you on this subject, at such length.

---

[8] Jacob Siler, of Macon County, a tanner, who had been a Whig member of the commons, 1835, 1838-1840. He and his brother, William, married sisters of David L. Swain.

Our only motive is to serve our Country & our cause, and if we can do this we are satisfied

> Believe us, Sir
> With great respect
> Your ob't Serv'ts
>> JNO. Y. HICKS[9]
>> N. H. PALMER
>> J. F. GRANT

*From Henry Clay.*                                          A.

## N. Orleans,

### Feb. 6th, 1844.

I received your friendly letter, an acknowledgement of which has been delayed by my absence from this City. I should be most happy in meeting Mrs. Graham and yourself, and accepting the hospitalities of your house. I am sure that I should be no where more tranquil or happy; but I am afraid that it will not be in my power. We will see when I get to Raleigh. I have announced the 12th. of April for my arrival there, where I purpose remaining a few days.

I anticipate the necessity of stopping a day or two at Wilmington, and a short time at the other places indicated by you on the route from that place to Raleigh. But I must trust to my friends to spare me as much fatigue as possible. I am particularly anxious to avoid public entertainments with their train of excitements. Some recent experience of them admonishes me of the absolute necessity of my avoiding them.

I saw, with very great pleasure, your nomination as Gov'r of the old North State, and I cherish the confident hope of your easy election. Still I should have preferred that you were in another situation, where the whole Union would have been benefited by your Services.

I congratulate you on the bright and cheering prospect of the Whig cause. There is scarcely a speck in the whole political horizon.

Do me the favor to present my warm regards to Mrs. Graham, and believe me ever

> Truly Your friend

---

[9] John Y. Hicks served in the commons, 1846-1848.

## To New Hanover Committee[10]

February 16th., 1844.

Gentlemen:—I have the pleasure to acknowledge the receipt of your letter, informing me of my election as an honorary member of the New Hanover Clay Club, and requesting that I will be present and unite with the citizens of Wilmington, in receiving and welcoming the Hon. Henry Clay, upon his expected arrival in that place.

Be pleased to declare to our associates of the Club, that I duly appreciate this mark of their confidence and respect, and most cordially unite in the objects of their association.

I have long entertained a desire to visit Wilmington, and the region of the lower Cape Fear. The Town from which the royal Government was compelled to take its flight, hurling back a Parthian arrow in the shape of a proclamation; and a region renowned for its early, bold, and decisive stand in favor of the principles of the revolution, as well as for being the scene of some of those spirited events which aided to give it success; events on which general history has as yet but dimly shed her light, but which are calculated to flatter the pride and elevate the feeling of every true-hearted son of North Carolina.

It will afford me particular pleasure to make this visit, at a time when your citizens purpose to do honor to the great American Statesman, whose enlightened labors, and disinterested devotion in the cause of the country, has identified him with all the great events in our history, for the last forty years. Without accident, therefore, I promise myself the gratification of being present on that occasion.

I am under obligations, gentlemen, for the terms in which you are pleased to convey your invitation, and am, very respectfully, your obedient servant,

Will A. Graham.

---

[10] From the *Hillsborough Recorder*, March 7, 1844.

*From Thomas Turner.*[11]                    **U.**

Windsor, N. C.,

Feb. 17th, 1844.

Having occasion to write you the enclosed letter on business, and unwilling to give you by itself so dry a chip as that, I shall accompany it with a dish of politics, merely to show you where I am in such matters, and in the hope of rendering myself agreeable to you for half a minute.

If I were asked how I liked the last election by our Legislature of a Senator in Congress, I should say, I preferred Haywood to either Saunders or Brown. But for all that, that the election did grieve me mightily in my affections, in my politics, and in my desire to see public affairs, especially in our own State, conducted with a decent regard to steadiness, to probity, experience, intelligence and wisdom.

But the world will work so! No one may expect to see it steadily advance in right principles from right motives. It is contantly jostled in it's saddle by its jockey companions, who somehow contrive to manage it to suit their selfish ends and purposes. Yet, every now and then, say once in 50 to 100 years, the disinterested and patriotic are highly gratified to see it get the start of the jockeys and to make large strides in the path of virtue and improvement. This start, our share of it, is trying now to take in the election of Henry Clay; and should it succeed, we may hope, with his aid, and the aid of others of a kindred spirit, to see it take one of those strides, and to continue in that course, by throwing so many and such large obstacles in the way of the selfish, as that they shall impede its progress no more.

Among the obstacles to which I allude, are these; 1st. But one term for the service of the same person as President; 2nd. some measure that shall prevent the party in power, (for the time) from making political capital of the offices of the Country; 3rd. Distribution of the sales of the public lands, for the benefit of the States severally in such and so permanent a manner, as that politicians shall never gamble in them, nor make political capital of them, again.

---

[11] Thomas Turner, of Plymouth, about whom little can be discovered, other than that he was on terms of friendship with Ruffin, Murphey, Graham, and other well-known men in the State.

The history of the world is but biography. Take it for any age, and the memoirs of a few individuals of that age are its history. I am sick, sick at heart of such histories; and it is time that history should be something more than the memoirs of individuals. Who but must be sick of the history of any Country, in any age, when they see it nothing more than a record, wherein the sum of the whole is that the few who go entirely for the public good, utterly regardless of their own, are slandered, thwarted, defeated in every effort, by the jockeys who in that and other ways, seemed to twist public affairs to the promotion of their own wicked and selfish ends, regardless if they impoverish or render miserable and wretched every body else.

Such is the history of the world, excepting, (as I said before) a few bright spots for a short time. Such has been the history of our Country of late years; and such (to bring my letter to a close without farther reference or remark) such, I am persuaded, would be the history of our last Senatorial election could it be fully and faithfully written.

With the greatest regard
I am, dear Sir
Yours truly.

The Senate of the United States at this session have given me the greatest satisfaction in rejecting the nominations of Henshaw,[12] Spencer,[13], Cushing,[14] Porter,[15] Hill[16] and Profit. They

---

[12] David Henshaw (1791-1852), of Massachusetts, a prominent politician and business man, who had served in the state senate in 1826, was an advocate of a free bridge over the Charles, was a banker, and founder of an insurance company. He was prominent in building, railroad and was one of the founders of the anti-Federalist *Boston Statesman.* He organized the Calhoun-Tyler group in the State. Tyler nominated him collector of the Port of Boston, and the senate had just rejected him.

[13] John C. Spencer, who was nominated for secretary of the treasury.

[14] Caleb Cushing (1800-1879), of Massachusetts, a graduate of Harvard, a representative in the General Court, 1825, 1833-1834, 1850, senator, 1827, Whig member of congress, 1835-1843, colonel and brigadier general in the Mexican War. He supported Tyler, and ultimately became a pro-Southern Democrat. Tyler nominated him on the same day as minister, and as commissioner to China. The senate rejected the nominations, but later confirmed him for the lesser post. He was president of the Charleston Democratic convention, actively aiding the Southern wing of the party, but he became a Unionist after the firing on Fort Sumter. He was of counsel in the Alabama claims dispute, and Grant nominated him chief justice of the United States, but the senate rejected him.

[15] James Madison Porter (1793-1862), of Pennsylvania, lawyer, state judge, legislator, delegate to the state convention of 1837-1838, railroad president, who had been nominated for secretary of war, *ad interim,* and rejected. He was the founder of Lafayette College.

[16] Isaac Hill (1789-1851), of New Hampshire, a native of Massachusetts, editor and politician, had served in the state senate, 1820-1823, 1827-1828, in the lower house, 1826. He made his Anti-Federalist paper, the *New Hampshire Patriot,* a

seemed to have said in these rejections, "Down with political gambling", or in other words "no more trading in politics". I regret that they did not also reject Wise. But I concede that they had good and sufficient reasons for it, unknown to me, and beyond my conjectures.

Down, down! I say with this trading in politics.

But hush! Stop my pen! thou art weilded by no body! It matters not who is President, nor who is not, nor who is up, nor who is down; I shall never have any but a fancied interest in public men, public offices and public affairs. But yet the fancy that can give me that fancied interest, can and does fill me with indignation as I see Vice triumphant, or happiness when Virtue prevails. It is, however, all fancy but the feeling.

U.

## Invitation from the Democratic Whigs
## of the City of New York.

New York,

Monday, Feb. 19th, 1844.

The Democratic Whigs of the city of New York, represented in their general and central committees, have jointly resolved to celebrate the fourth day of March next as the great day of National hope, the expected consummation of the labors and triumphs of the friends of Henry Clay. They have made arrangements for such exercises on that occasion as will excite and gratify the true Whig feeling, and awaken among all present a sense of their responsibilities in view of the associations and rememberances of the time. They design to commence on that day the action that shall place the Whigs of New York on high ground, and that shall result in the redemption of this city from Locofoco misrule, and in its honorable enrollment among the great Whig cities of the Union. With this view they have appointed Mr. D. Francis Bacon, to deliver an address before them on the evening of Monday, the fourth of March, in the Broadway Tabernacle in this city.

power in the State, and influential elsewhere, was a Democratic United States senator, 1831-1836, and a member of the "Kitchen Cabinet." He was governor, 1836-1839. He was throughout his career an intense advocate of internal improvements. His appointment as second comptroller of the treasury had just been rejected.

Appreciating your honorable and faithful services to that great Whig cause, which unites our sympathies and purposes, and desirous to share with you on that occasion the enjoyment and inspiration arising from such assemblies of the true friends of liberty and good Government; we most respectfully request the favor of your presence with us at that time, that we may be encouraged by your sanction and animated by the associations suggested by the sight of those who have added honor to public distinctions by the manner in which they have sustained them.

Your presence will add much to our enjoyment; and we hope for the pleasure of meeting you at that time with the voice of welcome from many thousand Whigs, who gratefully remember your varied Services to the Cause, and the man, and who have resolved to be "faithful to those that have been faithful to them."

Yours respectfully

| | |
|---|---|
| Henry E. Davies[17] | Morris Franklin |
| Nathaniel G. Bradford | James Kelly |
| C. S. Woodhull[18] | James S. Thayer |
| | Corresponding Committee. |

*From Hugh Waddell.*                                          A.

Hillsborough,

March 1st, 1844.

My dear Friend!

I have this moment learned that Mrs. Graham is thus far on her way to Greensboro'. I need not say with what a throb I heard this most grateful intelligence. May God speed her, & bless her anxious eyes with the sight of a rapidly convalescent husband!

Immediately on hearing of her arrival, I dispatched a servant with a note to her giving the very latest advices I had of y'r situation & was rejoiced to be able to report you better & improving.

---

[17] Henry Ebenezer Davies, judge of the supreme court of New York, assigned to the court of appeals.

[18] Caleb S. Woodhull was a lawyer of New York City. Later, while Graham was secretary of the navy, Woodhull, who was president of the Congress Hill Cemetery, wrote him of a movement to have the body of John Paul Jones brought back to America for interment in the cemetery. Graham was so far interested that he authorized Admiral Sherburn to bring it back on the U. S. Frigate, "St. Lawrence." *General Letter Book, Secretary of the Navy,* Vol. 45. p. 211, Archives of the United States.

Richard Ashe[19] who was at my House when the fact of Mrs. G's arrival was announced, immediately proposed to me (if I approved it,) that he should go in person & offer to accompany Mrs. G. to Greensboro'. I did approve it & he has now gone to wait on her. I was pleased to see it. But my friend, if anything could compensate for the pangs of disease & more than all for the pangs of anxious hearts which beat only for us, it would be found in the manifestations of sincere affection & respect with which we are greeted by all manner of persons if we have so lived as to deserve it. And this present attack, I fondly hope, will ultimate only in proving to you two things, first that the God whose mercy has carried you thro' two severe & long protracted diseases heretofore, has once again appealed to y'r heart & by shewing you the perilous and unsteady footing with which we traverse the very edge of a precipice every day of our lives, he may perchance fix *y'r mind* upon the only subject on this earth worthy of its high & elevated character.

(This may seem rather strange language from me, but I assure you I am becoming more and more convinced of the great truths of the Christian religion.)

The other end for which it will have pleased God to send this visitation, as I humbly trust & believe is but ancillary to the first, viz, to satisfy you how deeply and immoveably is the "immediate jewel" of your character *set* in the affections of all who know you, & *therefore* of how great benefit to others might the example of such a man be. *We* have no concealments I trust; certain am I, that if any man has ever felt *too proud* to *flatter* another I have been that man: when therefore I say to you that this community & indeed persons from all parts of the State have without exception & without respect to party joined by acclamation in their ardent and affectionate expressions of regret at y'r illness & as warm and enthusiastic prayers openly uttered for y'r recovery I speak the words of truth & yet they are so seldom true when spoken of other persons as scarcely to be credible. My own experience has known nothing like it, for one of y'r age & indeed with two exceptions, of any age. I was here about to close a letter already too long for a sick man to read, but Dick Ashe has just returned, elated with the idea of his accompanying Mrs. G. He is a fine spirited lad. As to y'r business, we have taken the best care of it—all helped to dispose of it in the way you w'd like

---

[19] Richard Ashe of Hillsboro.

to hear it was disposed of. The very common & illiterate men from the woods would come to me in open Court & beg me to lend them Dr. N's letter that they might go out and read it in groupes. Dick will tell you that I have risen from my Sofa to which I have been for 3 hours confined with headache to write this letter & am now in part surrounded by clients.

Dick can tell you all current news.

May God bless and restore you to the arms of y'r friends & prepare you soon to meet the proud anticipations of y'r Country is the prayer

of y'r constant & affect'e
friend & servant.

P. S. Beg Dr. N. to excuse my failure to reply to his Kind and valued favour of today by reason of a dreadful head ache.

H. W.

*From S. Bulow Erwin.*[20]                    U.

Pleasant Gardens,

March 2nd, 1844.

At a meeting of the "McDowell County Clay Club", held on the 22nd. *ult.* On Motion the following Resolutions were unanimously adopted. (i. e.)

"Resolved, That the Hon. William A. Graham be elected an honorary member of this Club, and that the Corresponding Secratary notify him, and request his acceptance of the Same.

further, Resolved, That he be invited to visit and address his fellow citizens of McDowell County, at such time as may suit his convenience."

I take great pleasure in communicating the enthusiasm and unanimity manifested by the meeting on the adoption of the above Resolutions. It shows what may be expected of the Whigs of the *"Western Reserve"* in August and November next.

The Club believes that McDowell County is the strongest Whig County according to population, in the "Mountain Dis-

[20] Sidney Bulow Erwin (1821-1908), of "Pleasant Gardens," McDowell County, who, after a year at the university, became a lawyer, but did not practice. He was a member of the commons, 1848-1850, and was in the navy department in Washington from 1851-1861.

trict." They are determined to use all honorable means to confirm that belief.

Clay and Graham will sweep through the mountains like a tornado.

In conclusion permit me respectfully to request, that the wishes of the Club expressed in the foregoing Resolutions may meet with a favorable response.

An early answer is desired.


### From Thomas Ruffin.          U.

#### Allamance,

##### March 6th, 1844.

Dear Graham.—

After having given your friends so serious a fright I think you are in duty bound to take all needful steps to put their minds at ease again. At Raleigh I heard the most alarming accounts of your situation, which, of course, gave me the utmost anxiety. From that I have been much relieved by learning, since I have returned to Orange, that your attack has been rather a painful than a perilous one. Yet I can not say, that I am not still uneasy about you: at least, I should feel quieter if I could hear occasionally and directly that you are convalescent. The accounts would be the more satisfactory, if, coming from yourself, they gave practical proof that you were getting up again. But should you not be able to write, we should be very much obliged to Mrs. Graham, or, in case her engagements about you forbid, any other friend, for a note by the Stages, to say how you are getting, etc.

Of course Mrs. Ruffin & I shall expect you here for a night & day or more, on your return to Hillsborough.

With much sympathy with Mrs. Graham & much solicitude about yourself, I am, dear Sir, as ever

#### Your affectionate friend

*From Robert Hall Morrison.*                                A.

to

*Susan Washington Graham.*

Cottage Home, N. C.,

March 9th, 1844.

Dear Sister

We have heard with painful emotions of the sore illness of your Dear Husband—not however until today that he was dangerously sick. I would Start by the first Stage to see him if the Situation of our family would admit of my leaving home. Our Children have both the measles and the mumphs, and Some of them are very sick; and new cases are occurring daily in our family.

My hope is still strong that the Lord will hear the prayers that are offered in his behalf, and spare his life to be a blessing to his family and to Society. I trust you have learned where to place all your trust in times of trial and under the darkest events of a mysterious, but wise and merciful Providence.

The Lord reigns over all things; me and all our friends and all our interests are in his hand. He too is a Gracious Sovereign and a Kind Father to all his Children.

Go to him with humble but firm Confidence. Lean upon his Almightly arm & rich promises, for the Support which earthly things cannot give. If he has more days for your Husband to live, as I trust and pray that he has, your prayers will be answered. Do not be dismayed or cast down.

*They that trust in the Lord shall be as Mt. Zion and cannot be removed.*

*Cast all y'r care upon him for he careth for you.*

We should be gratified to hear as soon as convenient how he is. Mary & the family join me in much love and tender sympathy. May the Lord be with you in this affliction.

*Invitation to a Whig Meeting.*                           U.

Sommerville, [Tenn.],

March 16th, 1844.

At a Convention of Whig Delegates assembled in Sommerville on 22nd. February last, among other things it was "Resolved unanimously that a Whig Mass Meeting for the entire Mississippi Valley be held in the City of Memphis on the last Wednesday in May next."

It becomes our duty as a committee for the County of Fayette to invite to this Meeting distinguished Whig advocates from abroad. To no one do we more cordially extend such an invitation than to yourself. Your position as the Whig Candidate for Governor of North Carolina, your devotion to the success of sound Whig principles, your acknowledged talents as a Statesman, all unite to entitle you to our highest respect, and would render your acceptance of this invitation most truly gratifying to the Whigs of the West. We ask you then to come, and by your presence and your eloquence to aid and cheer and animate us on the occasion alluded to. Trusting that it may suit your convenience to comply with our wishes, and that we may number among our guests at this proposed meeting one who has won for himself a proud distinction not only in his native State, but in the Senate of the United States, we tender to you assurances of our great regard and esteem,

Very respectfully

CALVIN JONES, GRAN. D. SEARCY, L. P. WILLIAMSON, B. DOUGLASS, P. T. SCRUGGS.

*From Hugh Waddell.*      U.

Pittsborough,

March 21st, 1844.

My dear Friend!

Constant and laborious engagements for the last fortnight have prevented me from writing you. I heard by Richard Ashe what greatly relieved my anxieties, viz that though *slowly,* you were, in the opinion of your Physicians, surely getting well; from time to time we have continued to receive the same intelligence & I *know* it must gratify you to hear that on each occasion it was received by all who knew you, (apparently "without distinction of parties") with sincere joy.

Had it been *possible,* I would long since have been with you, aiding at least in nursing, if not assisting to relieve in some degree the tedium of your confinement. After the arrival of Mrs,

G. I must acknowledge that I felt less on the subject of your tedium & of course that it was matter of little real importance who else was with you after her arrival. It is true I rely much on the skill of your Physicians, but have never to this hour been made acquainted with the *precise* danger to which you were exposed. I trust in God whatever it may be, the crisis is now past & that we may shortly have the true pleasure of welcoming you once more to your home.

All regrets are vain, & I shall not therefore indulge those which so naturally arise while thinking of you. Much and ardent anxiety has been expressed by your political friends, that you might not, perhaps, be able to canvass the whole State, unless your recovery was more rapid than they anticipated, to this I have always replied that there was no doubt of your doing your whole duty, if not to be done at the peril of your life. But if any danger to your health were threatened or the slowness of the recovery should prevent your canvassing the State, one thing was certain, viz that you could get a better vote & stay at home than any other man in the State & this seems agreed.

Hoke will probably be happy to stay himself at home, as he does not entertain any real hope & it will furnish some excuse (that he was less known than you) for the dreadful drubbing he is doomed to receive.

I see your distinguished successor, Haywood, "has given himself to Fame" by introducing 6 Bills to reduce everybody's pay except his own & "if encouraged" promises to produce 26 more Bills of like tenor & date for the 26 States. How short his *career* has been,—for he has now effectually killed himself.[21]

The veriest Demagogue, except Cotten, that I have seen, says it is contemptible, & Judge Dick cannot help saying "what a pity it is."

I have very much to say when we meet, but it is now 12 at night, & Judge D. starts at sunrise.

Give my most respectful & kindest regards to Mrs. G. & believe me your ancient and constant friend.

---

[21] On March 14th, 1844, William H. Haywood served notice in the senate of his intention to introduce "at an early day," not six, but ten bills, reducing from March 5th, 1845, the salaries of the president and vice president, of the justices of the supreme court, and all other Federal judges thereafter appointed, and regulating and fixing the salaries of all the heads of departments and their subordinates, and all territorial officers, and limiting the tenure of cabinet officers to two years.

*From Hugh Waddell.*      **A.**

Asheboro,

March 29th, 1844.

My Dear Friend!

I have heard with sincere joy of y'r arrival at home, and pray God you may rapidly recover from y'r late attack, in which prayer I know there are many others, not only here, but in every part of the State who sincerely join.

Were it not that the price is rather high for such gratification, one might almost consent to be ill to have the assurance which you now have, how truly & how highly you are esteemed by your countrymen. Hearing that you stood the ride so well has greatly encouraged me in regard to y'r case: the fear I had of the *hazard* of removal is now dispelled. You are under the best advice, yet I may be permitted to suggest two things from experience. viz, that you should abstain as long as possible from *all business,* especially of a political character which must necessarily be exciting & also that you take regular & only *moderate* exercise for some weeks. We all feel a common property in you now & therefore assume the right in some degree to direct what should be done with what belongs to us. There is abundant time to think of the proper course in reference to the Canvass; in no event would I think of moving, "till I felt entirely restored & ready for effective action. As for the contest there can be no ground for solicitude: you can distance y'r competitor & never leave home & although I am anxious you should visit certain parts of the State for the effect it would produce on the County elections for the Legislature, I think the benefit not so great as to justify your running any risques to achieve it. Besides, y'r indisposition will be ample excuse for failure to visit *all* the parts of the State.

The deepest regret I feel, next to that felt for y'r dreadful suffering and protracted recovery, is, that you are prevented from meeting Mr. Clay under such circumstances as would have added to his pleasure in visiting the State, & to y'r own fame in the eyes of the whole Country: Thinking of this matter the other day I said I thought it not improbable that Mr. Clay, if possible, would come to take you by the hand in y'r own house: It would be in character with him, for I *know* from the *best authority* that you have no *personal* friend who deplores more than he, y'r late illness: He may be compelled by promises to Virginia to deny himself the gratification of visiting you. but I yet hope to hear of his giving you this mark of his affection & esteem. Being as you know a dreadful *proser* I have to ask pardon for the infliction of so long a letter as this on a sick friend; it is cruel, & I hope Mrs. G. will be gracious to my informity & forgive it. Should I live to see you once more I have very many things to say, on the subject of "the prospect before us."

If it be not too much to ask may I hope that *by the hand of some friend* you will address me at Salem a short line saying *particularly* how you are; it will be to me a high gratification, but will be also authority for answering the "1001" questions daily asked me on the subject. If I could suspect a Democrat of sincerity, the expressions of regret at y'r illness daily used by many of them w'd go far to induce the belief that y'r votes would not be confined to the Whig party.

As "the Spring returns, the vernal joys y'r better years have known," will return, I trust, bringing health in every breeze & gratitude to God in every pulsation of y'r frame, for his goodness in restoring you to y'r family, y'r friends, & y'r Country: all this is the fervent prayer of one who "in all time of y'r prosperity, in all time of y'r adversity" has been y'r friend.


*From Paul C. Cameron.*                              U.

Fairntosh,

Orange County,

April 6th, 1844.

I had fully intended, before this, to have visited Hillsboro', with the single object of acquiting myself, in what I regard the first of social duties, towards a sick friend; But the state of things in my family have been such, as not to suffer me to go from Home.

I desired to express my anxious sympathy for you in your long and dangerous illness: and to assure you of my deep solicitude for your speedy and *perfect* recovery. Suffer me to say, that in your wide circle of friends, few if any, have looked with a more sincere and anxious solicitude, for a favourable issue.

Gladly do I offer you my cordial congratulations at the prospect now before you. Again in your comfortable Home, nursed as you will be, and surrounded by faithful friends and physicians, I shall be sadly disappointed if I do not hear of your daily improvement.

I can offer you no inducements to visit me, but if, in the progress of your convalescence, you should feel disposed to go abroad, for exercise and change of place, be assured, no friend will "open his gate wider."

I fear I shall be hardly able to get to Raleigh on the 12th. but "I will if I can." I fear the reception of our illustrious guest will not be equal to public expectation. *Your* absence will be universally regretted. Mention me in words of kind respect to Mrs. Graham.

I am too much of a countryman to resort to any of the formal ceremonials of society, and I pray you to regard this as the offering of your

attached friend.

*From John M. Morehead.*                    U.

Raleigh,

April 8th, 1844.

I am extremely happy to see that you are able to ride out, & hope ere long that Richard will be himself again.

My object in writing you this line, is this.

I do not know what effect your affliction may have upon your spirits, after you have become able to think about political matters, and something of a despondency, & dread of encountering a severe campaign may produce in passing upon yr mind, wholly inconpatible with what I believe to [be] the interest of the Whig causes & [I] assure [you] in some parts of the State the character of yr affliction is supposed to be much more serious & permanent than it is—& among the inconsiderate, who may think a powerful canvass indispensible, some intimations may be thrown out that you ought to withdraw & let some one, able to canvass take the place, etc., etc.

Now, Sir, I think I know N. C. as well as any man in it and you must take no step nor give any intimation of the slightest disposition to withdraw. If you [are] so badly afflicted as to induce the belief that you would not survive your term of service it would have a serious effect upon our prospects.

But with an assurance that you would eventually get well, we can carry you through triumphantly, & let you keep your bed through the Summer.

I wish you therefore to write me by Friday at least, a most cheering letter, giving a flattering account of yr rapid recovery, & evince in it a lively spirit & firm resolve to make a vigorous campaign, & carry terror & dismay into the enemy's camp— (or rather, carry conviction to their bosoms) & make Clay triumph in N. C. [by] thousands. I wish this letter to give satisfaction to our friends throughout the State, & write it in such way that it may be published. If we deem it proper, & you may, if you choose, make it in reply to this, & you may consider this as calling you out upon any subject, upon which you wish to say something & yours a reply to my letter.

Let your letter to me have no reference to what I have principally suggested, but answer me as if this letter was written to enquire after yr health & to invite you to come down if you can, which I heartily invite you to do—accompanied by a request that you shall not do so, unless you are fully able to stand the ride. I send this letter by a private conveyance, as I omitted to write you by last mail.

Mr. Clay was detained [page torn] Columbia, so that he is this day, Monday, in Charleston, & consequently can't reach here before Friday evening, which we much regret.

Dr. Knox was kind enough to call & give me an account of yr condition, with which I was much gratified.

Yrs

sincerely


*To Richard Hines.*[22]


Hillsborough,

April 11th., 1844.

I deem it due to the relation in which I stand to the people of the State, to offer an apology to those of our fellow-citizens who may be assembled at Raleigh, on the 12th. inst., for my not being present, to join with them in manifesting proper respect for the distinguished Statesman, who is now the guest of North Carolina.

---

[22] From *Hillsborough Recorder*, May 2nd, 1844.

I have so far recovered from a tedious and painful illness, which I recently suffered, that I am released from the prison of my sick room, and able with some aid, to walk out in the grounds contiguous to my house. But I am too much enfeebled to leave home and participate in the joyous meeting, which I doubt not you will have in Raleigh. I have, however, every reason to hope for a speedy restoration to perfect health, and that, ere long, I may be able to visit the different sections of the State.

Have the goodness to convey to our friends, who, from every indication, are gathering in great numbers, my sincere regret that I am denied the pleasure of being with them, and to assure tham that under other circumstances, no one would go farther, or submit to greater inconvenience or sacrifice, in paying due honors to Henry Clay; with whom a personal acquaintance somewhat intimate, has only served to confirm and increase that sense of his exalted patriotism and high qualifications for administering the Government, which had been inspired by a knowledge of his national reputation. I also tender my congratulations on those demonstrations of public opinion, now so generally exhibited, which render his elevation to the Chief Magistracy of the Union, almost a matter of absolute certainty.

I am, with high respect,
Your ob't serv't,

*From James W. Bryan.*        **U.**

Newbern,

April 13th, 1844.

I was gratified to learn from Ann that you had improved so much as to be able to leave the house, etc., and that you were regaining your strength. We have had great anxiety and concern for your welfare, and have been pained to be advised of your sufferings and illness. You must be prudent or you may looze all you have gained; I fear you will find your political Campaign matters too much for you and I think you and Col. Hoke had better dispense with your popular harangues, etc.; I have always been opposed to it, and have ever regarded it as beneath the dignity of the office, but in this I know I am overruled by a large majority of our friends. The enthusiasm in behalf of Mr. Clay at Goldsboro' was a perfect outburst of popular feeling; many democrats have declared their determination to do him justice in the approaching election by voting for him, but I am sorry to say to you, that the excitement of his coming among us has not reached our decaying town; we are dead here both as to politics and religion and when the few turpentine trees that surround us give out, I think we shall "cave in." We shall give you the full strength of our vote in August, but I hope you will find it convenient in every respect, to visit us, and let us hear from you.

\*    \*    \*    \*

We have no news of interest among us, except that we are to have three weddings (I hear from some of the fashionables) next week. It is rumoured that a Miss Shaw is to be married to a gentleman from Wilmington on the 22 of April, Mr. Sparrow to Miss Blackwell on the 23rd, & Mr. James Shepard to Miss Donnell on the 24th; all this is during our Court week. So you see we are in a fair way to have a busy time of it. The "Old Castle" remains in *statu quo* and every time I see it, I regret that you did not agree to let me sell it. I am satisfied that nothing can occur to add to the value of our real estate, in this section of the State.

\*    \*    \*    \*

. . . Would you like to have any book of Judge Gaston's as a reminiscence?—his library is to be sold.


*From Henry Clay.*                                                    U.

Raleigh,

April 15th, 1844.

I received at this place your favor of the 11th. inst., and I regret extremely to hear of your continued indisposition, not only on account of itself, but because it deprives me of the satisfaction of having the gratification of seeing you in your own State, as I always hoped to do. For that purpose, I should be delighted to visit you at your own residence, but it is one of the privations incident to my journey that the public takes complete possession of me, leaving me no leisure for individual intercourse. Were I a freeman, at liberty to do as I please, I should accept the tender of your hospitality with great avidity, but my engagements to the public deny me that happiness.

Cordially wishing the speedy restoration of your health and tendering to Mrs. Graham my affectionate regards, I am truly,

Your friend
And obed<sup>nt</sup>. serv<sup>nt</sup>,

*From Thomas P. Devereux.*          U.

Raleigh,

April 15th, 1844.

I hoped to have had the pleasure of seeing you here, but am very much pleased to hear of your continued amendment. Do not expose yourself—a canvass is very desirable, but we can beat them even if you stay at home. I had some part in getting you into the scrape, and am of course but merely just when I do all I can to aid you. If you are able to canvass the low country counties the sooner you begin it the pleasanter for you, May and June being our most delightful months. The Almanac will tell you when their courts sit. My children will be coming up the country between the 5th. & 15th. of May & I think most certainly by the 20th. my carriage will have returned. I shall stay down the country until the 20th of June. My carriage & horses shall be at your disposal when you will intimate to me your wishes, but recollect that if it will alarm the democracy to see you riding in my carriage, I will not be mortified if you think best to travel on your own hook—being quite accustomed to such estimates of my insignificance.

We have had a glorious time; everything has passed off well, even in the tour of Loco Foco counties extending from Wilmington to Halifax, excluding the latter, which is most truly Whig. The reception was very warm, it was peculiarly so at Goldsborough Weldon & Henderson. I have seen old men shed tears upon more than one occasion. The upper part of New Hanover is the darkest part of the world; I verily believe that the natives there would prefer hearing a banjo to seeing all the great men of all parties.

God bless you & restore you to perfect health.

*From Robert B. Gilliam.*                              U.

Oxford,

April 27th, 1844.

\*   \*   \*   \*   \*

I am most sincerely rejoiced to hear of your improved health. Your situation has been a subject of universal concern amongst your political friends, and of still deeper anxiety amongst those who are connected with you by the ties of personal friendship. I trust soon to hear of your taking the field in complete armour, partly for political reasons, but much more from the satisfaction I shall receive in hearing of your complete restoration to health.

The prospects in this County are very decidedly favorable to the success of the Whig cause. With respectable management, we can carry the County *easily*.

Should you have occasion to come to Oxford during the campaign, or to travel in this direction, I shall be highly gratified if you will make my house your headquarters.

With the most earnest wishes for your speedy and complete restoration to health,


*From Haywood W. Guion.*                              U.

Lincolnton,

May 4th, 1844.

I have just returned from the Mountain district, & having had a consultation with our Whig Brethren, have concluded to address you a few lines. Throughout that region there is scarcely any defection in our ranks visible, although Hoke was nominated for the express purpose of weakening us in our Stronghold

With the exception of Yancey County, he will have no Whig votes worth speaking of. But to Yancey it is deemed advisable that you make a visit during the Summer & devote some little more time to it than its size & worth really entitles it to. The people in that County are very flexible, & have been known to change several times in a single campaign. Gen'l Gaston resides there now, and is acting a part at once pitiful & despicable. He is a real Loco Foco demagogue, although he will not *fully* acknowledge it. He is denounced & discarded by the Whigs. His popularity and influence are great in Yancey, & some effort should be made to seduce the County.

Into this County & Catawba you need not make any appointments, in fact I think, & so do others, that it will be advisable to travel around them both.

We are in the midst of the highest *local* excitement imaginable. The question of repealing the new County of Catawba, & also of removing the Court house from Lincolnton have drawn out double sets of Candidates, who argue the questions with great warmth and bitterness. Hoke, living in town & being opposed to the division, & having taken an active part to defeat the new County bill at the last Session, has rendered himself extremely unpopular. Many of his old L. F. friends will refuse to vote, & a large number will shew their resentment by voting for you. His loss in the two Counties will be very great. If you come into the Counties, you will be called upon to give your views upon division, repeal and removal, & give it as you may, nothing will be gained but something will be lost. If you have time in a letter to speak against the removal of our Court house, & also against the present division line as approaching too close to Lincolnton (if such are your sentiments) I may use it to advantage with some few of our town Whigs, who intend voting for Hoke. Only do this if you have leisure and inclination, without, we can get on, for matters are really favorable as they stand. Could you not stir up our Central Committee, & the Register, to urge the necessity of having active Whig Candidates out in every County? It strikes me that we are backward this Spring, & that without more energy we shall lose the legislature.

If you have occasion to write West address:

D. F. Ramsour,[23] Murphy, Cherokee, N. C.
M. FRANCIS,[24] Waynesville
JOHN BAXTER, Hendersonville, Henderson County
N. W. WOODFIN or
JOSHUA ROBERTS

Asheville

[23] D. F. Ramsour, a hotel keeper, one of the first residents of Murphy.

[24] Michael Francis, of Buncombe and Haywood, a native of Scotland, educated at Edinburgh, a keen and scholarly lawyer, learned in the law, and "irresistable before a jury," also a forcible and logical platform speaker. He was an immense man, weighing three hundred and thirty pounds, and was jovial and widely popular. He represented Haywood County in the commons, 1842, and in the senate, 1844-1846.

W. E. Mills[25]
Gen. E. Bryan[26] or
Wm. Twitty or
J. G. Bynum

                                        Rutherfordton
For Yancey or Burke address
Tod R. Caldwell, or Col. B. S. Gaither.
For Caldwell Co. address James Harper[27] or A. C. William-
son.

Hoping to hear of your complete recovery and final success, I subscribe myself,

                        Yrs truly.


*From Robert B. Gilliam.*                                 U.


                        Oxford,

                                May 7th, 1844.

I am in the midst of a circle of your friends, who have been
debating for some time as to your plan of operations. We have
unanimously concluded, that there is not time now to give sufficient notice to enable you to commence the campaign in this
County on Monday, or indeed any day early in next week. We
would venture to recommend this course, that you should gratify
your friends in Montgomery and Anson, and join Mr. Hoke at
some of his appointments as soon it can be done consistently
with your convenience.

This will enable you to reach Fayetteville by the 25th. and to
continue your appointments through the Eastern section of the
State, sufficiently early to avoid the dangers that might attend your
visit there, at a later period in the season.

Other considerations have aided in bringing us to this Conclusion. It is to be presumed, that Mr. Hoke will make a tour through
this section of the State, and we think it *very* desirable that you
should be with him. We trust that our views will correspond with
your own. We have debated the matter very earnestly, and we are

---

[25] William E. Mills (d. 1850), of Rutherford, lawyer and planter, who was
a member of the commons, 1838-1844.

[26] Edmund Bryan, a prominent and influential citizen of Rutherford County.

[27] James Clarence Harper (1819-1890), of Caldwell County, a native of Pennsylvania, who grew up in Ohio, and moved to North Carolina in 1840. He laid off
the town of Lenoir, and was a merchant and manufacturer there.

satisfied that it is the best practicable arrangement. The other advantage attending it, will be that you can give general notices through the papers in Raleigh and elsewhere.

Mr. Waddell, Dr. Herndon, Mr. Littlejohn, Mr. Cameron, & Mr. Hill all concur in these views—and direct me to communicate them to you.

Hoping to have the pleasure of seeing you in the Campaign, I am with the warmest
  regard, Your friend.

The Whigs have brought out a *good* ticket to day, one that will be elected.

      R.B.G.


*From Hugh Waddell.*

[On back page of letter]

My dear Sir!

I will only add a line to say after much consultation with friends here that the course proposed by Mr. Gilliam is, I think, the best. Perhaps the fact that you will meet Mr. Hoke at certain points ought to be immediately announced by the Register & Carolina Observer (Mr. Hale's paper is so called I believe) & this will draw full meetings & when you meet, yr. subsequent line may be chalked out to suit yourselves, & will not *necessarily* keep you *together;* I am particularly anxious that yr. visit to the East may not be prolonged beyond the middle of June, or perhaps the 20th.

Every thing here is looking well. How do you like the nomination for Vice President? J. T. Littlejohn says Mr. Clay was understood at Washington to have been *very* much pleased with the nomination of Mr. Frelinghuysen.[28]

There is, he says, strong talk now of running Tyler for Pres't & Dick Johnson for Vice, by the Democrats, but this is surely not so. He says there were 100,000 at Baltimore and the Va. elections are glorious.

---

[28] Theodore Frelinghuysen (1787-1862), of New Jersey, a graduate of Princeton, soldier in the War of 1812, lawyer, attorney general of New Jersey, 1817-1829, United States senator, 1829-1835, Whig candidate for vice president, 1844, president of Rutgers College, 1850-1862. He was a member of many religious and charitable organizations.

*From Robert Hall Morrison.*                               U.

Cottage Home, May 7th, 1844.

Your kind letter was recd. yesterday. We were gratified to hear that you were recovering so fast from yr. long & sore affliction. I trust you will not suffer the strong desires of the public to see and hear you, to make too heavy demands upon your strenth.

We had heard last week (by letter from Bro. James) of the death of Bro. Jo's widow, and the condition of his children. Mary inclines strongly to the opinion that they ought to be brought to this Country if their Grand Mother is not living, wh. seems to be her impression.

I have written to Bro. Jas. that we would take the Daughters if he should think it best to bring them, and no better plan should occur to him. Our family is large, but we feel willing to do any thing we can for their welfare. I am glad you have written to him in reference to your purpose touching the sons.

I know of nothing better for them, as you have a good School in Hillsboro' & are near the University.

We have been expecting Sister Susan to come up & pay us a long visit this Summer, and were gratified to hear that she is resolved to do it.

Our family has recovered from the measles after a long continuance. General health prevails.

The Whigs are in good spirits in the West. Much solicitude has been felt for yr. recovery.

Perhaps it might be well to take some steps at an early period to inspire Confidence in the public mind that your recovery may be hoped for, as I learn that reports of a very different aspect are circulated in Lincolnton and, it may be, in other places. If you begin the Canvass, this knowledge will follow as a necessary result. All it seems to me, that is wanting, is the assurance that your health will be restored, to secure an overwhelming majority. Mr. Hoke begins on the 11th and will be at Fayetteville on the 25th. inst.

Tell Sister Susan that we will look for her & all the children and that we expect her to consider Cottage Home as her home while in the West.

We hope too to have pleasure of seeing you often while going to different places around us in your expected circuit.

Mary joins me in love to all.

Yours very affectionately.

*From John M. Morehead.*                              **U.**

## Raleigh,

### May 11th, 1844.

I am pleased to learn by yours of the 9th. that you feel like campaigning. I got here tonight from the upper country, where I was detained a few days by indisposition. I wish I had come by Hillsboro'. I differ so totally from your Granville friends that I still think you had better return to the East after leaving Chatham.

If I had selected a part of the State for Hoke to waste his time in I should have selected Stanly, Montgomery, Anson & Richmond. He can do no harm there & from the distance you could not meet him from Pittsboro before Anson. I should like very well for you to meet at Moore & Fayetteville but I think you will do much better to return Eastward from Pittsboro.

You will see that from 18th to 25th Hoke covers but little ground, in a thickly populated county, in a good part of which Gen'l Dockery will not allow him to charge a man.

Now if I recollect rightly, Courts sit on 3rd. Monday 20th. in Wake, Halifax, & Waynesboro—all of which you can attend easily by rail-road. Here on Monday, Wednesday Halifax, Thursday Waynesboro, Friday I think you can be at Sampson, & Saturday at Fayetteville with him—here is but one day lost in the week, Well return by Stage to R. Road, come back to Waynesboro, and be at Johnson Court 4th Monday, go back to Waynesboro, take R. Road to nearest point of Duplin Court House (say 15 miles), go there & thence if time allows to Onslow, Carteret, Craven, etc., so as to get to Northampton by 1st Monday of June.

As it is impossible for me to make the appointments for you now, sick & broken down riding today, and Judge Nash starts very early in the morning, I shall throw out these suggestions for you, brothers Manly, Waddell, & Co., get the Almanacs, see the days & Courts & fix them among yourselves, & send the list to Gales for publication, as I expect to leave for Wilmington with my family about Wednesday next, but I think up to Duplin. My suggestions are the thing. Always keep near the R. Road, and then distance is nothing. I spoke in Smithville Friday night, frolicked Saturday, spoke in Wilmington Saturday night, Kicked up heels Sunday spoke in Waynesboro Monday, & Halifax Tuesday, and actually became melancholy for want of employments, as the [illegible] points were only 200 miles apart.

I shall tell the R. Roads to frank you & Hoke to—old Nick if you choose to go & as I go down I will advise our friends to have conveyances ready to take you from the road to the different points, which they can see by reference to your appointments.

I have not seen a man since I returned, except Judge Cameron & Nash, who called in since candle-light, and the last of whom was proudly Knight of the King's Bench and took the robes of office—with the motto in his crest *"fiat justitia ruat coelum."*

As I have taken this week something less than 16 oz. of Quinine, & my ears are roaring, my head spinning, & senses reeling, I hardly know what I have written or said, but command me when you choose, & if sober I'll try to obey.

God bless you, Waddell, Manly, & all the other Whigs good & true.

Don't forget to tell Charlotte that she is our own dear full-blooded Cousin to Guilford, & that she must prove the relationship next August.

*From Bayles M. Edney.*                                    U.

Lincolnton,

May 13th, 1844.

I am just home from my mountain circuit, & allow me to say to You, that it is all important that You should pay those Whigs a visit, before the Election, For a variety of reasons, a few of which I will assign. One is, that the party of Whigs which voted for Clingman, feels some coolness towards Mr. James Graham, and that prejudice will operate to Your injury & many of them do not yet know, but You are the same Graham, & that *impression* is sought to be made by our Adversaries, whenever they think it will avail them.

Secondly, Mike Hoke has recently been round that circuit, useing every effort, to secure a Whig influence & to some extent has succeeded. I know several Whigs of influence, in their neighborhood, who intend going for him, unless changed before the Election. His social swagering manner is well calculated to captivate & please the unlettered men of the mountains. He tells them privately, that he has nothing to say against Mr. Clay, that the

Governor of Nor. Car. has nothing to do with Politics, simply has to sign Captains Commissions, etc., & that the State, as far as the Democrats are concerned, will (between Clay and Vanburen) let the Election go by default, for Mr. Clay.

Thirdly, that the Election is peculiarly local, & has nothing to do with National politics, that a generous Whig might well, without any sort of impropriety, vote for Mr. Clay, & Mike Hoke.

Fourthly, that he lives in the West, and that it is all important that the West of all parties, should unite upon a Western man for Governor, be his politics what they might. He has done many acts of Personal friendships, for leading Whigs of different Settlements, & thereby gained their pledges. These, and many other reasons, which I could mention, make it expedient that You should come. There are very few who know any thing of You Personally, & all are anxious to see You. Just come, and let them see You, & You will thereby secure a large vote, that will otherwise be lost.

I have laboured for you, like a Hero, from the first, & at the beginning, before we had our State Convention, I was the only public Advocate You had in these Western Capes. I got them right at last, & have been stumping for You ever since, & I have promised them all, that they should doubtless see you during the *Summer.* But *little* can be done *in the East,* anyway, & the West is the Field for labour.

Mike is much stronger privately, than Publicly, & he does not wish to come to the West, any more, believing He has done the best for himself, & so he has, & He is therefore, now trying to decoy You off to the East, Keep You from the West, & therefore, Keep down excitement, for his own benefit. But don't be hoodwinked; Come here, I say to you again, Your Election depends upon it, I tell You. Write me to Hendersonville, or to the [illegible] & have some days appointed right away, so People may know You are coming, & come You must, so write me soon & let me know Your course. I feel a deep interest for You, & nothing would afford me more unmixed satisfaction than to see You riding head & neck, with Henry Clay. I know these mountain People, and know the *food* to feed them on, & what I say to You, is the only food that can at this juncture of affairs gratify their apetites.

Very respectfully
Your obedient Servant.

*From Francis Joseph Kron.*[29]                    U.

Attaway-hill, [Stanly Co.,]

May 16th., 1844.

Mon cher Monsieur,

We of Stanly were much in hopes that your precious health had sufficiently strengthened to enable you to gratify your many friends here with a *personal acquaintance,* particularly on the occasion of Mr. Hoke's visite, (which happened yesterday) so that the antidote might have closely followed the poison. There has been no harm done, however, and when Mr. Hoke had concluded his long, very long address, there were but a few of his hearers, nearly all Whigs, (a loco foco is the rara avis) who could not, by the knowledge of the faith that is in them, tell where the speaker's seeming argument was lacking. He took for the theme of his *exordium* the Whig aphorism. Principles, and not men, from which he complained that all parties were straying. He then contended that our *principles* were wrong, and undertook to prove their erroneousness by partial statements of their application when the Whigs came into power in 1840. He commenced with the Bankrupt law, upon which, however, he recorded your negative vote, and dwelled with great pathos and an unreasonable accumulation of details on its various bearings. Next, he took up the distribution bill, charging the Whig Congress with defeating its own law by inserting a damning clause in it; that the same law was conditional for the old States, making its existence depend on the contingency of the duties raising above 20/00, whilst it was unconditional in [illegible] the new State, which by it [torn] of thousands of acres of land. Then he came to the tariff, charging the Whigs with bambouzaling the people by covering the premium to the manufacturers under the deceptive term of *minimum duty.* The bank bill was to complete the demonstration of his proposition. Here he felicitated the Whigs that Cap. Tyler had furnished them with an excuse, for had that bill passed, he

---

[29] Francis Joseph Kron (1798-1883 (or 1888), of Montgomery (now Stanly) County, was born in Germany, but under French rule, studied medicine in Paris, and married there. The date of his emigration is unknown, but he was an instructor in French at the university in 1824. He then took a course at the University of Pennsylvania, and settled on the land of his wife's uncle in Montgomery County, where he spent the rest of his life, engaged in the practice of medicine. He seems to have been an excellent physician, had much learning, and a keen mind. The date of his death, because of injury to his tombstone, is uncertain.

said, most calamitous would have been the consequences. Then he repeated numbers of the ever refuted arguments against all banking institutions; he wound up, however, with a plan of his own, namely, to place bank and individual notes on the same footing. From all this he concluded, with apparent exultation, that our principles were wrong, that they could not stand the test of experiment, and that we had better begin to review them. The Harangue was brought to a close by an appeal to the sympathies of the people for the annexation of Texas. Here he touched none of the objections to the scheme, he did not pretend to give a statement of the case, he read some abolition resolutions in Massachusetts on the subject, and seemed to think he had proved by figures the advantages to the Union from Annexation, by stating that a reverse condition would necessitate an expensive line of Custom-house offices, and be an incentive to smuggling.—

Such is an outline of Mr. Hoke's long, but temperate harangue. His pointless jokes raised no haw! haw! and his pathos could not draw the least exclamation from the few of his creed within his hearing. The Whigs of Stanly were determined not to be run over, and in case of rough usage, Mr. Hoke would have been replyed to, but as he was studiously courteous in form, we paid him back with an attentive hearing, leaving him his doctrines, and sticking to our own. In one instance only, we felt like retorting on him, that was on his endeavouring to excite a prejudice against you for your vote on the policy which gives the election of governor to the people. He said *it was fair to state the records.* Otherwise he was complimentary to your abilities and moral worth.

I am told that your opponent made pretty much such a speech on the previous day in Rowan and Cabarrus. Do not let this however, deter you from coming among us, if you safely can; our people are so enamoured with their glorious principles that they are never tired to hear them told over, and told by you, their enthusiasm will kindle still higher and confirmed affection sink deeper its roots in their hearts.

With my best wishes for your health, I am most sincerely
Votre admirateur depuis long-temps,
Votre ami pour toujours
Francis
Albemarle, Stanly.

P.S. Please remember us with our Hillsboro' friends & benefactors.

*From W. E. Mills, George W. Logan,*[30]
*and Walter Rutherford.*[31]                    U.

Rutherfordton,

May 30th., 1844.

The undersigned have been commissioned by the citizens of the County of Rutherford, to invite you to attend a celebration at this place, on the approaching anniversary of our Independance, and participate in the Festivities of the occasion. The people of this County were among the first in the State to ratify your nomination as the *Whig Candidate* for Governor. They have long admired your political course, and duly appreciate the distinguished services which you have rendered your Country. They long to see you among them, and have an opertunity of tendering you in person, their congratulations.

The undersigned take pleasure in dischargeing the duty which has been assigned them, and do most respectfully and earnestly solicit your acceptance of the invitation given.

You will be pleased to give us an answer at your earliest convenience. We have the honour to be your friends & fellow citizens,

[Attached letter.]

*From  W. E. Mills.*                    U.

My Dear Sir

I have for some time intended addressing you & urging upon you the importance of visiting the West, and particularly this District. Mr. Hoke attended our Spring Courts, and was very busy in electioneering privately, but would not declare his sentaments publicly, he made strong appeals to his personal friends, and may get some Whig votes. I think if you could address the people in these mountain Counties we might be able to give an increased Whig majority that would be glorious after the extravigant caluculation the Democrats have made on Hoke's personal popularity. I am very anxious you should be here on the fourth, as you would then have an opportunity of seeing more people

---

[30] George W. Logan (1815-1899), of Rutherford, lawyer, clerk county court, clerk and master in equity, member Confederate congress, 1864-1865, delegate to convention of 1865, member of commons, 1866, superior court judge, 1868-1874.

[31] Walter Rutherford, justice of the peace, 1836-1850, lawyer, owner of the *Western Carolina Republican.*

than on any other occasion, as our Court dose not come on untill after the Election. I would not have considered it so important for you to visit this County was it not that we are so much split up on local questions that there is dainger of loosing sight of more important matters. The Democratic Candidates have come out in favour of a division of the County, and are thus endeavouring to draw off public attention from National politicks. Our County Courts commence at Cherokee on the first Monday in June, and come regularly round, to Macon, Haywood, Henderson, Buncombe, Yancy, Burke, Caldwell, & McDowell, which last will be the week of the Election, so that our Court & Cleveland come after the Election.

If you could inform me of your appointments I would have them published. I am glad to see that your health has so much improved as to enable you to commence the Canvass. I have no fears of your election, yet I think it advisable for you to visit this section of the State in order to counteract Hoke's personal influence. Write me and let me know what course you will take;— your Brother has not yet returned, he will be back in June.


PLAIN THOUGHTS FOR THE WEST.[32]                    U.

[June (?), 1844]

In 1824 the People of the Western Counties voted for Gen. Jackson as President, and his election was defeated by the corrupt bargain between Clay and Adams.

In 1828 the people of the west again voted for Gen. Jackson, and he was elected President against the opposition of Clay and Adams combined.

In 1832 Henry Clay was the candidate against Gen. Jackson, and the people of the west voted for Jackson, and elected him triumphantly.

---

[32] This printed circular, the only one I have been able to locate, is among the Graham papers. It is important for the light it throws upon the opposition campaign. Hoke, in his speeches, always had good things to say of Graham. The *Hillsborough Recorder* said, Sept. 5th, 1844; "It is a bad cause which requires such means for its support, and we cannot think it will add much to the credit of the political jugglers at Raleigh that they have thus essayed to support their candidate. . . . The redundant tide in November will convince them that they have not gained anything by their mediocre, but disgraceful infamy." But to the Whig press—and to most of the Whigs—all things Democratic, whether men, measures, or arguments, were infamous.

Col. HOKE was a Jackson man then, as he has been all the while, and is now. He is now a candidate for Governor; but the people of the west are called upon by his opponents to put down the western candidate, because he is not for Clay! Will they do it? They ought not; and it is hoped they will not do it.

Has Henry Clay ever done as much for the west as Michael Hoke? Does he love North Carolina, and the West in particular, as Michael Hoke does? It cannot be pretended.

The writer of this does not intend to traduce Mr. Clay; but candor obliges him to say (what all honest men will admit to be true) that, guilty or not guilty, the people of the *West*—the people of *North Carolina*—the people of the *United States,* have been opposing his ambitious efforts to be President just twenty-one years! He has been again and again defeated, censured and condemned. And if it were a crime in Col. Hoke to suspect him, he but erred in common with the West; he has the excuse too, of having derived his suspicions from the identical people who are invoked to proscribe him—to proscribe him for having faith in them and in their opinions! Besides, the most clamorous partizan-deriders of Col. Hoke in 1844, were themselves the most violent accusers of Mr. Clay in 1828. They admit now that they slandered Mr. Clay at that time. Will not the people see that they are just as liable to misrepresent Col. Hoke at present?

But, it is asked, what has Col. HOKE done? He went to the Legislature in 1834, a young man, and served from year to year 'till 1840 inclusive; and men of all parties in the West are challenged to point out the occasion during his whole term, when he was not foremost in defence of western rights, and in the protection of western interests! Is that nothing? He voted for the Convention bill, in 1834, to give equal representation to the people. He voted, too, to give to the people the *election of Governor.* MR. GRAHAM, the competitor of Col. Hoke, voted to strike that out of the Convention bill. So much of the bill as gave the Governor's election to the freemen of the State, Mr. Graham voted to expunge! His vote stands recorded against him in 1834; but in less than ten years after it, Mr. Graham is asking the same people to give him their votes for Governor! He asks western men to do him this honor, to the prejudice of their own able, eloquent, accomplished, Hoke.

In that same year Col. Hoke, though a young member, successfully defended the *debtors in the West for Cherokee Lands,* in a manner that, if fully known, would be gratefully remembered by all those people. The facts were these: The Senate passed a resolution directing suits to be commenced upon every bond which was not paid up in a short period afterwards. But in the House of Commons it was referred to Col. Hoke, J. W. Gwinn, and another. They reported an amendment, permitting the debtors to renew their bonds. And, by the influence and good management of Messrs. Hoke and Gwinn, the amendment was adopted and indulgence granted to the debtors. The writer of this knows the facts to have been as stated; and the laws and journals of 1834 confirm his recollection. Do the people of Haywood, Macon, Yancey, etc., call this nothing? The debtors for Cherokee lands who were not crushed and ruined by suits and execution sales, in 1835, owe it more to Col. Hoke, and J. W. Gwinn's agency, in the Legislature of 1834, than to any other cause! Such recollections speak directly to the hearts of these people; and they will not reward Col. Hoke for his faithfulness by proscribing him in 1844!

When Governor Swain was a candidate for re-election in 1834, before the Legislature, and it was proposed by some of Col. Hoke's party to proscribe him—and he was, in fact, opposed by Moseley—because he did not go for Van Buren as President, Col. Hoke said *no;* and he voted against his party, for the *western candidate,* and Gov. Swain was re-elected.

So when the *west* were without a single Judge residing amongst them, Col. Hoke not only voted for the western candidate in the Legislature of 1835, though of the party opposed to him, but, to the knowledge of the writer of this essay, Col. Hoke refused to let this own name be put up when it was certain he would have been elected! He was faithful to the West, and true to his friends, at the cost of his own election to the Bench! Such men are not to be safely proscribed. The West ought to cherish them.

And again in 1836, when he was a democratic leader of the Legislature, his devotion to the rights of the western counties impelled him to cast aside the trammels of party, and to put up the name of Judge Pearson, because, he said, the West were entitled to share in the honors and priviledges of the Bench. It is not saying too much to affirm, that without Col. Hoke's influence, there would not now be in that section west of the Yadkin, a single Judge of North Carolina!

The friends of Col. Hoke ask no more for him than he has done towards others. The advocates of the western candidate for Governor, should be found amongst all parties in the west. He has been true to the west: the West should be true to him. Michael Hoke, though faithful to democracy, has been true to all parties in the West; all parties in the West should now prove true to Michael Hoke, the western candidate for Governor!

*From James Graham.*                                        U.

New Orleans,

June 4th, 1844.

\*     \*     \*     \*     \*

This City and State afford great facilities to make and spend money. The lands are very rich, but subject to frequent inundations. The boat in which I ascended Red River took several families out of their dwelling Houses which were surrounded by water and their entire Crops were destroyed and the plantations left a dreary waste full of deep holes and sloughs.

The Mississippi River is now so high that the Rain water runs on each side of all the principal streets through the City toward the Lake.

I will leave here this evening on the steamer Missouri for Memphis and try to collect the money that is due Ann Eliza. Her Town Lots at Memphis are fast depreciating in value owing to the business of the City following the boat Landing down the River by the formation of obstructions at the former landing near the mouth of Wolf River.

\*     \*     \*     \*     \*

*Campaign Speech*[33]

Fayetteville, June 1, 1844.

Mr. Graham remarked, that he appeared also before his fellow citizens as a candidate for the office of Governor of the State, and in the remarks he should offer, he would be guilty of nothing in the slightest degree to infringe the liberal feelings of his honorable opponent. Before he proceeded with the discussion, lest he should forget it, he would speak of a subject which had first been

---

[33] From the *Hillsborough Recorder*, June 6th, 1844, quoting *Fayetteville Observer.*

broached in a paper published in the town of Mr. Hoke's residence, and recently spoken of by Mr. Hoke at other places, but
not here to-day. He alluded to a vote he gave in the Legislature
of 1834, relative to a change of the Constitution to give the election of Governor to the people. His opponent charged that he
had voted against that amendment. The circumstances were
these: In 1833 he was one of a Committee who addressed the people on the subject of Convention. In that Address, various amendments, including the election of Governor by the people, were
advocated. In 1834 he was a member of the Legislature. It was
very doubtful whether the bill to call the Convention would pass.
It could not pass without some Eastern votes, and the vote would
be very close. In this condition of things, his friend, Mr. Outlaw,
from Bertie, appealed to him to vote for leaving out the election
of the Governor by the people, stating, that if that were omitted,
he would vote for the bill. With the hope of thus securing the
other great objects of the bill, including the reform of the representative system, by which 3000 men in one county might be
allowed more political power than 300 in another, which might be
lost without Mr. Outlaw's vote, as they had often been lost before,
he did vote for Mr. Outlaw's motion to strike out, though contrary to his own wishes and opinions, as previously expressed.
The motion was rejected, and he then voted *for* the bill, including
the election of Governor by the people. After the Convention met,
Gov. Branch, Mr. Macon, Mr. Weldon Edwards, Judge Daniel,
and other Democrats, who were members of the Convention,
voted against giving the election of Governor to the people, and
Mr. Macon spoke against it, and finally voted against the whole
amended Constitution because of that provision, and biennial,
instead of annual, elections. His friend, Mr. Hoke, he said, had
since that time, in 1838, voted for Mr. Branch for Governor, and
he really thought, therefore, that he could not entertain any very
strong opposition to his (Mr. G's) election on that ground.

Having disposed of this matter, Mr. Graham proceeded to
notice Mr. Hoke's objections to the action of the 27th. Congress.
Having complained of all these measures, we had a right to hear
from him, what he was in favor of? He objected to the Bank, what
else would he have? A National Bank, properly guarded, and the
sub-Treasury, was the real issue. Did Mr. Hoke abandon the Sub-
Treasury, to which he had never once alluded? Mr. G. read from
a Democratic Address to which Mr. Hoke's name was signed in
1838, in which the Sub-Treasury was spoken of as "the great

measure of deliverance and liberty," involving all other questions. What has become of it? We hear nothing of it now. The
Whigs propose an institution, properly guarded, to disburse the
public funds, and regulate the currency. In the forty years of
existence of a Bank, it had collected and disbursed more than
500 millions of dollars of public money, without the loss of a cent
to the government. No individual could do this. He showed its
use in regulating a vitiated currency, than which there is no greater curse. Every State has an interest in the currency of other
States. But all may make Banks at discretion. Shall government
act the Shylock, by adopting a system by which only gold and
silver shall be collected, thus drawing the specie from the interior
to the ports, making State Banking unprofitable, and taking away
the great tools of trade—for money is the agent of trade? The
effect in Europe, wherever tried, has been to reduce wages to 2
or 3 pence a day. A well regulated credit system is as indispensible
to the people as a supply of blood from the heart. It is said by a
distinguished foreign traveller in the United States to be the one
main cause of the rapid advance and great prosperity of this country. The young American operates upon a moral capital which
fire cannot burn. Mr. Hoke had told us that Mr. Tyler had done
without a Bank, but he did not tell us that all the money has been
deposited in State Banks, as it was under the Sub-Treasury itself.
That is the reason it has been managed so well and cheaply. There
was no divorce of Bank and State.

Mr. G. was glad to hear his opponent's liberal remarks about
our State Banks. But astonished at his proposition to discard
every thing that *may* do harm. Shall we abandon every blessing
and every institution because it may be abused? Shall we abandon
the army because it was once disgraced by the treachery of Arnold,
or the surrender of Hull? Shall we abandon government itself
because it *may* be made an engine of oppression? Surely not!
Guard, correct, amend, but do not destroy. Look at the aggregate
of good or evil. If good preponderates, retain it.

The arguments that capitalists would have to call in the aid
of the constable to get the money for investment, was an argument against all Banks and public improvements. But there was
plenty of capital, which would have come out from its hiding
places if the Bank bill had gone into operation. Capitalists had
hoarded, because they did not know what was to be the action of
government, which, for 7 or 8 years, had tended to make the rich
richer, and the poor poorer.

In reply to Mr. Hoke's remark about office hunters in Washington on the accession of Gen. Harrison, Mr. Graham said it might well have been expected that there would be a good many vacancies. All the defaulters who had been retained in office for fear that their removal would injure the party, would necessarily go out, and of course there would be many offices to fill.

He did not consider the land fund as forming any part of the revenues of government. After the payment of the public debt, it was expected and intended to be enjoyed by the States severally. Congress has not treated it as a public fund, they have made grants of more than 5,000,000 of acres to the States, for Internal Improvements, Colleges, etc., besides every 36th. section for Schools, to say nothing of grants to corporations for benevolent purposes, and to foreign exiles who have come among us. From 1828 to 1841, alone, 2,600,000 acres have been granted for Internal Improvements. Mr. Calhoun proposed to cede the lands to the States in which they lie for 50 per cent of what they might bring, and afterwards for 65 per cent, and take the bonds of the States. That, however, was before the days of Repudiation. Mr. Graham defended the allowance of the 10 per cent to the States in which the lands lie, as a matter of justice to them, and the grant of 500,000 acres as a matter of benefit to the United States in the increased value of the rest, and because of similar allowance to other States. And besides, the grants of 500,000 acres having been made by statute, could no more have been repealed than the grant by this State to a private individual could be repealed or divested. He showed that it was not the fault of the Whigs that the Distribution was repealed. They passed the law, and the President vetoed it. Cited Gen. Jackson's well known and emphatic recommendation in his message of '32, of cession to the States in which they lie, and Mr. King of Alabama's report, that we should look to the Custom Houses and not to the lands for revenue. Thus showing that the true contest on this subject of the Public Lands between leading men of the two great parties of the country, was between local and partial cessions on the one hand, and a general and equitable distribution among all the States on the other, neither regarding it as a fund on which we are to rely for revenue for the support of government.

In reply to Mr. Hoke's remark that the Whigs of this State had condemned the pre-emption principle in the resolutions which caused the resignation of Messrs. Brown and Strange, and yet that the Whigs of Congress had embodied the pre-emption in their land bill, Mr. Graham showed the entirely opposite character of the two systems of pre-emption. They were as unlike as a monkey was unlike a man. Under the old system, a wealthy man hired a score of men to settle on as many separate tracts of the best public lands, and in a short time he would thus acquire a right to buy them all at the lowest price, and send off his men to settle other tracts in the same way; and thus all the best lands fell into the hands of wealthy speculators, who then sold them to the poor emigrant at high prices. Such were the pre-emption laws of the Democratic administrations. But the pre-emption law that the Whigs passed, provided, under the surest guards, against any but the actual settler getting its benefit, and he cannot have it more than once, nor if he owns 320 acres elsewhere, nor with a view to sale, but for himself alone to settle. It is a pre-emption law for the benefit of the poor man who moves off to the new lands, and to defeat the schemes of the speculator.

There was nothing Tyler had done that he more regretted than the veto of the Distribution. He had looked forward with deep interest to the vast benefits that would flow to North Carolina from the devotion of this fund to purposes of Education and Internal Improvements.

He contended that the people of North Carolina had made up their minds in favor of distribution, in favor of a National Bank, and against the Sub-Treasury. In 1817 the whole Legislature, except four members in the Senate, had voted to ask the establishment of a Branch of the Bank in this State. Brown, Saunders, Wilson, and other leading Democrats had voted for it. In re-chartering our State Banks, and in creating the Bank of New-bern, (which Mr. Hoke himself voted for,) there was provision made, by universal consent, that they might deal in the stocks of the then U. S. Bank, or any future U. S. Bank. In 1838, North Carolina denounced the Sub-Treasury. And at the last session, the resolutions of the Democratic party did not object to either of these Whig measures, or advocate the Sub-Treasury. Why? Because the party must have felt that to do so would be unpopular, and contrary to public sentiment.

But he thought his opponent could not object to a Bank with 20 millions capital for the whole country, when he himself had voted for the Charleston, Louisville, and Cincinnati Bank, with a capital of 12 millions for the four States of North and South Carolina, Tennessee and Kentucky.

He adverted to the great change of ground of the party on the subject of our local Banks. Two years ago they were denounced as manufactures of rogues and swindlers, and guilty of every species of evil. And yet, when the party got into power in the Legislature, what did they do besides keeping up the same clamor, to put down these evils? Nothing. This was a confession that the evils they had charged did not exist. He was glad to hear this concession to the great conservative principles of the Whig party, that our Banks have been well managed, and have furnished a sound currency. He regarded it as leading to the establishment of other Whig principles.

As to the Bankrupt Law, he did not vote for it; but he thought it had been no disadvantage to the country. So far as his observation had extended, no one had been discharged under it who could, or would, have paid his debts without it. But it was now repealed.

Neither did he vote for the Tariff, because he disapproved of some of the duties, but chiefly because the distribution clause was not in it. He offered an amendment to insert the distribution clause, and if that had been adopted, he would have voted for the bill. But he was for sustaining because its action was beneficial to the country, and until it shall yield an amount sufficient to support Government, and pay off the public debt, and then, if it shall yield an excess, that it should be reduced to the revenue point. But perhaps he might save himself and his opponent some trouble by pointing to the present Democratic Congress, where one of the party had moved to lay McKay's bill on the table, and they did lay it there. They found they could not better the Whig Tariff, and they had therefore best say nothing against it, until they could agree among themselves on something better. Until then, they should come and help us. Under which candidate will they get a change of the tariff? Buchanan, Johnson, Van Buren, and Cass were all in favor of protection. [Here Mr. Hoke interposed as to Mr. Cass. But Mr. Hoke was wrong. Cass's letter of Feb'y 8, 1843, avows his advocacy of Protection, as both constitutional and expedient.] [34]

He felt sure that the people were about to settle this, as all other great questions, right, on a basis of protection to the Industry of the Country. Why does government protect the shipping interest without complaint from any one? Why cannot I ship one

_____
[34] Brackets appear in original.

hundred bales of cotton from Wilmington to New York in a foreign vessel, or take passage in one from one American port to another? I could probably get either much cheaper in a foreign vessel; and our opponents say we ought to be allowed to buy where we can buy cheapest. But it is true policy to nurse our sailors, who are to bear our flag in triumph over the ocean in times of war. And the fishing bounties are paid for the same purpose. But all this is Protection—Protection to American Industry, promoting our Nation's prosperity and Independence, in peace and war; just as the Protective Tariff promotes them. We have the right to discriminate. Under the acts of 1816 to 1836 government collected money enough to pay expenses, and 11½ millions a year besides. But the compromise act so reduced the revenue that it was absolutely necessary to pass a new law to raise money enough to support government. Van Buren expended 31 millions more than his revenue in 4 years. His average expenditures were 28 millions a year. The average appropriations since, are less than 20 millions. When he left office, the revenue was only 14 or 15 millions, and a debt on hand. What was to be done? The Whigs were obliged to pass a Tariff to obtain means to support government. They had curtailed the expenses, so that for the last year and a half the appropriations had only amounted to about 17 millions a year. And since Van Buren went out, there had been no fraud, defalcation, or loss of revenue. These were fulfilling Whig promises.

As to the minimum principle which Mr. Hoke complained of so much, it was introduced in Mr. Calhoun's Tariff of 1816, and continued in every one since. Public men of all parties had advocated it, and it did not seem possible to dispense with it. Mr. Hoke had asserted that the protective principle of the tariff is altogether for the benefit of the Manufacturers, and yet he complained of the protection of Wool, Hemp, Sugar, etc., which were not manufacturing but agricultural interests. Laces, Jewelry, and other articles of small bulk and high value, are taxed low, because they would be smuggled so easily if a high duty were laid on them. Mr. Calhoun himself advocated this principle in regard to gold watches, in the bill of 1841.

Duties do not necessarily increase prices; and we have found that under this Tariff, prices of Manufacturers have not risen, except when the raw material has risen. Foreign ministers at Washington understand this matter. When a duty is to be laid on articles from their country, they present their memorials against it to members, knowing that their countrymen are as able to pay the duties as the United States, thus admitting the principle for which we contend, that duties are often paid by the foreign producer, and not by the consumer. In every country the protective system exists, and we cannot, without great disadvantage, dispense with it.

Mr. Graham next spoke on the veto power, and then paid deserved respect to the character and services of Mr. Clay.

As to Texas, Mr. G. said, if all other subjects were of no importance compared with that, his opponent ought to go for Tyler. That was *his* measure, and they ought not to deprive him of it. Mr. G. is against the Treaty; not that he is against Texas coming into the Union when she can do so without entailing a war upon us, and requiring a violation of our solemn Treaty with Mexico, and a sacrifice of our honor as a nation. He denounced in the strongest terms the act of Mr. Tyler in sending the Army and Navy to the Texas and Mexican frontiers, as an unauthorized levy of war by the President alone. Equally did he condemn the President's doctrine that Texas was ours till the Senate rejected the Treaty. He scouted the idea of re-annexing Texas, when the Treaty conveyed an immense Territory, including Santa Fe, Chihuahua, etc., that neither the United States nor Texas ever had a shadow of claim to; Territory embracing several Mexican cities, which have always been in the quiet and undisputed possession of Mexico. She still claims Texas, and our government and Texas have repeatedly acknowledged that Mexico is waging war for its recovery. It is true we might take Texas by force, and it might be very convenient and desirable to have it. And so it might be, convenient and desirable to me to have the lands of my neighbor, who is poorer than myself. Yet I have no right to take them, and should dishonor myself by doing so.

He showed the difference between the condition of Mexico when we attempted to negotiate with her for Texas in 1825, and that of Texas now. And above all, insisted upon it, that all parties have officially admitted the existence of the war Mexico is waging for the recovery of Texas, which she claims as her own Territory. The English Minister has expressly declared that England has no idea of interfering with Texas. If this is true, it is perfectly satisfactory. If not true, it will be the proper time for us to interfere when we find it untrue. And, suppose we possessed

Texas, we should have still a frontier beyond it, more remote, more difficult to defend. It is much more extensive, and more likely that we should then be annoyed through Mexico, and the next step would be to take Mexico also. Let us first set our own house in order, improve our own great nation, and in due time we shall have Texas, without war, and without a violation of honor. He rejoiced that this was not altogether a party question, and that one of the most able and influential of the Democratic party, Mr. Benton, had taken strong and conclusive ground against the Treaty in a speech lately delivered in the Senate.

In conclusion, he said, that if his fellow-citizens should elect him Governor, he would devote his time, and whatever he possessed of ability, energy, and loyalty, to the interests of the State.

*From William E. Mills.*                                    U.

Rutherfordton,

June 17th, 1844.

I have received your Letter & this day had your appointments published as follows:

Monday, the 1st. July at Morganton, the 2nd. Glass Store (near Brindletown) 4 Rutherfordton, 6 Ashville, 8 Waynsville, 11 Burnsville, 15 Logan Carson's in McDowell, 17 High Shoals (Lower end of this county) 18 Shelby, 20 Lincolnton, 22 Catawba, 24th. Statesville, 26 Charlotte—I had great difficulty in making the appointments, but after consultation with Col. Bynum, & other friends, I made the above, we thought it important that you should address a large assembly in this county & feared that we could not get the people out again so soon after the 4th. & determined to have you here on that day. We are split up on local questions & think that you can be of great service in arousing and [page torn] the Whigs; you will be at Asheville on [page torn] Court where you will have a large crowd. You will see that we have been compelled to leave Henderson out, they are all Whigs & no dainger there, they will attend at Ashville; we thus get you to Burnsville on Thursday of Court. I think there will be no dainger beyond the Mountains.

A decision of the County is now splitting us here, the Democratic Candidates came out for it, but refuse to discuss National politics; I am in the field & closely engaged, so that I will not be able to meet you untill you reach this place.

Col. Bynum will meet you at Morganton & accompany you to this place, we will have the whole County here; I see that Hoke is on your track, but I hope you will make an impression that can not be effaced.

I trust the appointments I have made for you will not press you too hard; I no fears of your Election, but I fear they may elect a Democrat from Burke & perhaps two from this County unless we can unite the Whigs. The Democrats here have not yet taken up Polk, they are waiting instructions from Hoke.

I will send you several papers containing your appointments so that some of them will be certain to reach you.

Col. Gaither will probably meet you at Wilkesborough. Pore it on the [page torn] where ever you go.

Your friend

*To Susan Washington Graham.*                         A.

Lexington,

Thursday, June 20th, 1844.

I arrived here yesterday afternoon, and still continue in good health. I reached Mr. Turrentine's in good time on the evening I left home, and Greensboro' by the next day at 10 o'clock. You may imagine my feelings in going back to my old room, in which I had recently suffered so much—Mrs. Strozzi was waiting in great anxiety the return of her husband from Fayetteville, and wept freely when she was informed that I had not seen him for about three weeks. She had expected him for about a week before I arrived, and hoped that he would journey by Hillsboro' & come on with me. In the course of the day, however, he arrived and relieved her fears.

I addressed the people in the afternoon, and went next day to Salem, where I met many kind & cordial friends among the Moravians of that place. I had passed through it long ago, when a boy, in the stage, but had not remained long enough to gratify curiosity—I went to the Church where they have the largest organ I ever saw, the burial ground, etc. There was a vacation in the school, and I was therefore not carried there. The number of pupils is about 160.

On Monday morning I went up to Germanton the Court House of Stokes, made my address on Tuesday, and came from there by way of Salem on yesterday to this place. I wish to finish today in time to reach Salisbury this afternoon. A Superior Court was in session at Germanton held by Judge Settle, and Messrs. Morehead, Gilmer, Kerr, etc., were in attendance. My friend Mr. Walker was also there. He is a candidate for the Legislature in Rockingham.

You should give directions that the horses should be fed on oats after they are harvested, and not with corn.

The weeds should be cut off from about the old shuck house and the oats stacked there after filling the stable lofts. The hay may be stacked in the meadow, if there be not time to haul it up.

If Dr. Strudwick buys the horse we spoke of, you should let Abram drive him with Jerry in the waggon hauling wood etc. before you set off Westwardly.

I am anxious that the 1st. of August should arrive as I am heartily tired of the tour I am making. I think I can meet you in Lincoln by the middle of July. You had better take three days from Hillsboro to Salisbury—say 1st to Smith's—2nd Brummell's 3rd Salisbury, or stay all night at Greenesboro, & come from there to this place, & reach Salisbury to dinner. You could send Ed. Scott (if bring him) home from Salisbury.

The Locos are to have a festival in honor of Mr. Polk at Charlotte on the 23rd. of July, to which they have invited guests from abroad.

### From Charles Cotesworth Henderson.[35]      U.

Lincolnton, N. C.,

July 22nd, 1844.

On yesterday our Friend H. W. Guion, Esqr., informed me that Burton Craige, Esqr., had asked you a question as to some statement you had made to me at this place, but Guion said he got so mad at Craige interrupting you, that he could not remember the Question; and this morning Gen'l Daniel Seagle[36] a Democrat of this place, told me he heard the Question, and said it was so:

---

[35] Charles Cotesworth Henderson, of Lincoln County, a leather manufacturer, who made a substantial fortune in Texas lands, and was a contractor in the building of the Charlotte and Columbia Railroad.

[36] Daniel Seagle (b. 1796) of Lincoln, merchant, farmer, and general of militia.

"did you not tell Cotesworth Henderson that if you was elected Governor, that you would use your influence to prevent the Court House from being moved from Lincolnton," which you promptly answered in the negative, and very correctly too; and I told Seagle that instead of your telling me you would use your influence in that way if elected, you expressly told me, that if you was elected Governor you would not become the Patisan of either Party; and I then told Seagle what you had said to me in our conversation, you observed that you understood H. Cansler intended to call you out on that Question, I told you it was a mistake, Cansler did not intend to do so, and after some further conversation you said you did not think the Legislature would repeal the Law, but thought they would move the Line up, so as to leave the Court House at Lincolnton, I observed that I thought myself that the Law would not be repealed; but that in as much as Wray had concealed our Petitions, etc., that it would not be more than right to Repeal the Law, to which you gave no opinion.

Now when I stated this conversation to Canseler & Isaac Lowe, I did it to them as Friends, considering together for the best interest of our Repeal Candidates, and without the least suspicion that they would betray me, and have it used in the Governor's Election; We Whigs and Democrats had been consulting together as to the most prudent course to be taken in our conduct towards you in this place while addressing the people, that would not give our Whig Friends, (in certain Sections of the County where they had no interest at stake here, but intended to support our Repeal Democratic Candidates) no cause to complain of us.

I have traced the matter up, and find that Robert Williamson,[37] Jun., informed Hoke of it, and he had got it from the fourth or fifth hand, and did not hear a correct statement of what I said you had told me; and I have no doubt but Michael Hoke got Craige to ask you the Question, as Guion says they took a long walk together at Newton, before you spoke there that day. I observed to Guion on yesterday, that if he had have thought of it, and got some one in Catawba (after you got through your speech) to have asked Hoke, if he had not told some persons in Lincolnton, that he had traveled all over the Eastern part of this State, and conversed with all the Candidates for the Legislature, and had the whole matter fixed so that they would not move the Court House from Lincolnton, that he could have put Hoke in a bad

[37] Robert J. Williamson (1813-1858), of Lincoln County, a lawyer who was clerk of the county court, 1845-1853, clerk of the superior court, 1855-1858.

Box; he said he did not think of having the Question asked him, but said he told several influential Whigs in Catawba of the circumstance, and that they would use it well against him; and he has gone up through Catawba to day, and told me he would call to see several influential Whigs, who are Division men, and get the circumstance well circulated before the Election.

I have thus given you a full statement of matters; but I do not do it, fearing that you might suspect that I told the conversation which passed between us, with a view of injuring your Election; as I am satisfied you will not think so; but will attribute it to some degree of imprudence in me, in my great zeal to promote the Election of our Repeal Candidates, without ever suspecting for a moment that it would be used in the Governor's Election; and I do not think it will injure you any, as I know the people in Catawba will not believe in the professions he made there on last Saturday, and particularly after they hear what he told some persons in this place, what he had done on his Trip in the East.

I am with sentiments of high respect,

*From James W. Bryan.*                                    U.

Newbern,

Aug. 3, 1844.

Official Returns for the County of Craven 1844

| Precincts | Govern: | | Senate | | | | Commons | |
| --- | --- | --- | --- | --- | --- | --- | --- | --- |
| | Graham | Hoke | Partin | Berry | Street | Dewey | Washington | Prentiss |
| Newbern | 285 | 114 | 27 | 87 | 112 | 105 | 289 | 292 |
| Russells | 25 | 24 | 13 | 14 | 24 | 24 | 25 | 25 |
| Whites | 54 | 77 | 36 | 20 | 82 | 71 | 63 | 53 |
| Big Swift Creek | 40 | 127 | 78 | 14 | 122 | 123 | 40 | 41 |
| Little Swift Creek | 15 | 45 | 30 | 9 | 46 | 44 | 16 | 13 |
| Lathams | 8 | 71 | 43 | 4 | 70 | 71 | 8 | 9 |
| Beards Creek | 79 | 27 | 16 | 41 | 27 | 30 | 76 | 77 |
| Bay River | 81 | 73 | 44 | 55 | 72 | 79 | 78 | 75* |
| Adams Creek | 74 | 31 | 12 | 43 | 34 | 37 | 71 | 69# |
| Ives | 19 | 33 | 17 | 13 | 32 | 31 | 19 | 19 |
| | 680 | 622 | 316 | 300 | 621 | 615 | 685 | 673 |
| | 622 | | | | | | | |
| | 58 | | | | | | | |
| | maj. | Dem. | Whig | Dem. | Dem. | | Whig | Whig |

\* Not official but believed to be correct.
\# This is correct.

I had intended to keep you advised of our political operations throughout the Canvass, but I have been for some time deprived of the use of my right hand, having put out of joint one of my fingers on my right hand, and have therefore been disabled from writing. I now use my pen with great difficulty.

Newbern, you will perceive, gave you a large vote, & your majority in Craven is 58. We succeeded, as you will also see by the above returns, which I send you of the vote in electing the two Whig Commoners, Washington & Prentiss.

We have lost the Senator by 16 votes. I was at Carteret this week & set them a going there. I took good care that the precincts should be supplied with your votes (printed).

Jones gave you a majority of 40 or more votes. I shall hear from Carteret to night. Lenoir has given you a good vote also. I have not rec'd the returns from there but have seen several of our friends who represent it to be an *extraordinary* vote. The Loco Candidate for the Commons is defeated in Lenoir & I think we may calculate on receiving the support in the Legislature of the one who is elected. Your vote in the East will exceed Morehead's.

I left my family all well at Beaufort on Thursday morning last, having left there at that time to attend an Election in this County on the South side of Neuse.

\*     \*     \*     \*     \*

I write with such extreme difficulty that I am compelled to omit much I wished to say. I will send you the full returns.
P. S. The Beaufort Stage is in, but brings no returns of a definite character.

### From John W. Cameron.[38]                                U.

Rockingham,

Aug. 5th, 1844.

To redeem my promise I write to you, though I have but little information to communicate. Our village is badly situated for the early reception of election news.

In this County the vote for Governor was Whig 678, Democrat 113. In 1842 it was Whig 655, Dem. 92. The Democrats have increased their vote, but the Whigs have increased their majority two votes. Never did men make a more desperate effort than the Democrats in this County did on the day of the election—every artifice that an unscrupulous ingenuity could devise was resorted to. But, considering the extraordinary exertion made, the Texas Humbug, and that Hoke made two long, windy speeches in Richmond, we have done nobly.

The evening we parted with you at Wadesboro' I came home. The other delegates all remained about Wadesboro', or started and turned in by the way side; but for my part I was determined

---

[38] John Worthy Cameron, of Richmond County, a graduate of the university, lawyer, and journalist, a member of the lower house of the legislature, 1865.

to give neither sleep to my eyes nor slumber to my eyelids until I reached Rockingham.

At the River I was met by the gentlemen and escorted into the village about midnight. Next day Mr. Deberry *entertained* the crowd for an hour, and a half, in a very agreeable manner. Your humble servant then *detained* them for a like period, after which they went off as well satisfied as could be expected, considering how anxious they were to see their favorite Whig candidate— the "Goliath of the Whig Party." By the way, I made a tolerably neat, oily excuse for you.

Big Wat,[39] I am told, is exceedingly vain-glorious of the manner in which he bore up the standard of his party at Wadesboro', says both sides claim the victory, etc. Never was Jackass prouder of the mark of a lion's claw than he is of the scars you left upon him. And so stoutly does he strut through the streets of Rockingham, that all who see him are in pain lest he will tread himself under foot. How proud it does make a little man to get his posteriors kicked by a great man!

In Anson the Whigs have lost ground since 1842—their majority being some fifty six less than it was then. In Robinson the Democrats have carried the day by a small majority—forty, it is reported—but the information as to the amount of the majority is not much to be relied on. In Moore, Street,[40] Whig, is elected. In this County and in Montgomery I am informed the Whigs have held their own for Governor, but cannot hear the precise vote from sources to be relied on. Dr. Worth,[41] Whig, is elected in Senate from Moore, and Montgomery. In Anson all Whigs elected.

In great haste,
respectfully yours.

---

[39] "Big Wat," presumably, was Walter Francis Leak (1799-1879), of Rockingham, who, after several years at the university, became a lawyer, and a large planter. He was active in Democratic politics, was a member of the commons, 1821, 1931, state senator, 1832, delegate to the convention of 1835. A strong secessionist, he was a delegate to the Charleston convention of 1860, and the convention of 1861.

[40] Donald Street, who served only this one term.

[41] John Milton Worth (1811-1890), of Randolph County, abandoned the study of medicine to become a gold miner, farmer and merchant. Through his natural ability, sound common sense, and high character, he became one of the most influential men in the state. He was, as state senator, 1842-1844, 1848, active in support of public schools, and internal improvements. A Union Whig, he opposed secession, but supported the Confederacy, was colonel in the senior reserves. He bitterly opposed radical reconstruction, was again state senator, 1870-1872, and state treasurer, 1876-1885. He played a large part in the adjustment of the state debt, and reforms in taxation. Through all these years, he was an active business man.

*From Nicholas Carroll.*                                      **A.**

New York,

180 Prince St.,

Augt. 27th, 1844.

If such proffer be no intrusion in the chamber of the invalid, most earnestly & heartily do I congratulate your State, *more* than I do you, for your election. *They* have gained a great deal, and to enable them to do this, you had to make a correspondent sacrifice. It is very natural for young men to feel peculiar gratification in the success of a young man, & you must permit one of that number, in humble & modest friendship, to offer my song of praise for a consummation devoutly prayed for, and to hope that for *you*, in your public & private life, the proverb "extrema gandii luctus occupat" will drop its negative preposition, and hereafter read "that is joy without annoy."

I felt all along that your majority would be trebled at least if your health would have permitted you to have taken the stump— but notheless that, you have the honor & pleasure of coming to the Executive Chair supported by a Legislature Whig to the core. God grant that so Mr. Clay shall come into the Executive Chair of the Nation. And if the unselfish cordon that are linked in brotherhood & the truest fraternity, the Union through, can effect this great result it will be done. But it is not wise to close our eyes to things about us & to rest secure upon a partial victory.

I did never much affection for Seward & certainly *he* is taking in this State *very strange* means to help Mr. Clay's friends to secure permanent power. But we have sounded the tocsin and the venom of the cowardly 'copper heads,' who couched in our path, is as harmless as the worm, and we can crush or torture at our pleasure or will. I feared such treason as that of 1839 *could not, would not,* 'die & make no sign.' It *is* alive, in more shapes than one, but against the "devoted & dauntless guard" that will hem the way betwixt them & president Clay, their ambushes and wiles will be as harmless then as their poison is now. There *is* & there *is to be* a go easy league between Webster & Seward & Evans & Choate[42] and others. I dare not speak of it plainly, but its hydra

---

[42] Rufus Choate (1799-1859), of Massachusetts, a graduate of Harvard, Whig member of congress, 1831-1834, senator, 1841-1845, attorney general of Massachusetts, delegate to the convention of 1853.

head will be upraised and Mr. Clay's Inauguration will be scarcely done, when they would dictate *their* terms or prepare to 'bake his funeral meats.'————But enough of this. We, the young men of New York, as watchful as the eagles of our Adirondack mountains, will win this field, and our trophies will be lasting & permanent. Our alarm has been good for us; We can & we will carry New York & count her majorities in thousands. We can & will have an U. S. Senator, who will not be a Tallmadge. We will beat here—every where—but we must fight for it. There is no retreating foe before us, but ever delving and always mining, we must labor by daylight that they do not suddenly blow up some fastness & watch by night that they steal no march upon us. If we win we rescue our Country from her greatest peril; if we lose, then vanishes forever the heritage of our children.

\* \* \* \* \*

*From George E. Badger.* A.

Raleigh,

Sept. 21st, 1844.

\* \* \* \* \*

I shall *certainly* go to the Alamance meeting unless prevented by some event which will make it physically or morally *impossible*. I wish you would write me a line to say what is my best route to that place, and where Mr. C. whose invitation you gave me lives. Should you see him, offer my thanks for his kindness.

While writing allow me to mention another thing. I learn that several Whig Senators are prepared to vote for *Stone*,[43] the present Loco Clerk of the Senate, Among others Mr. Lindsay of Guilford on account of some relationship. Now if this is done, great offense and even deep disgust to the Whigs fairly generally and to our devoted Whig friends in Franklin;—they look on him as one of the most bitter and furious, and malignant Locos in the State, and they declare they will look on the Whig triumph as no triumph if he is retained by the Whig Senate. Now cannot you do something to prevent this result?

---

[43] Thomas G. Stone, of Franklin County, clerk of the senate, 1836, 1842-1844.

*From Christopher C. Battle.*                           U.

Raleigh,

Nov. 9th, 1844.

The high office to which the people of your native State have elevated you, requires four Aids de Camp, and if you have not already made a selection I trust that it will not be considered an intrusion for me to present my name as one I think qualified for the station.

For six years I have been attached to a Volunteer Company at this place, and have refused high appointments, & the burthen of too much muster is becoming oppressive, and having served a reasonable time in that service it would give me some relief and great pleasure to be promoted as brevet Colonel & Aid to the Governor of North Carolina.

I present my name now, that I may be among the early applicants for that post of honor, and hope that you will regard it as an application in which I desire not to interfere with any wishes or partialities of yours.

Very respectfully

*From William D. Cooke.*[44]                          U.

Staunton, Va.,

Nov. 18th, 1844.

During the past Summer I have received several letters from gentlemen in N. Carolina on the subject of establishing an Institution for the Deaf & Dumb. In a letter I received from the Rev. Mr. Burwell [45] of your town, he suggested the propriety of writing to you on the subject. I am the more inclined to do this, as from the short interview I had with you last Spring, as well as from

[44] William D. Cooke came to North Carolina from Staunton, Virginia, where he had been the head of the Deaf and Blind Asylum. In 1845 he was elected principal of the newly established state School for the Blind in Raleigh, and filled the place until 1860.

[45] The Rev. Robert Burwell, a Presbyterian minister, and his wife, born Anna Robertson, both natives of Virginia. He was called to a church in Hillsboro in 1835, and in 1837 they established a school for girls which won considerable reputation. They moved then to Charlotte. After the close of the Civil War, they established a school in Raleigh, which became a forerunner of Peace Institute.

your known reputation for extended benevolence, I am led to believe, that the subject of making some provision for the education of this unfortunate class of our fellow beings, will meet with that consideration from you, which it deserves.

When I left N. Carolina last Spring it was suggested by Gov. Morehead, that if possible, I should commence a school, before the meeting of the Legislature, but I have been unable to accomplish this, owing to the want of the necessary funds.

From what I saw of the people during my trip, I am inclined to believe that an appropriation by the Legislature for the purpose of establishing such an Institution, would meet with general approbation, from all parties. If the Legislature should not be inclined, at once, to go to the expense of erecting buildings for the school, they might commence on a small scale, without much expense, and gradually expand. It was the understanding when I left last Spring, that during the Session of the Legislature, I should visit Raleigh with Young Albright and give the members an opportunity of witnessing the advantage of education to the deaf and dumb, as well the manner of teaching them.

My object in writing to you is to ascertain your views on this subject, that I may be governed accordingly in my future actions. May I trespass so much on your time, as to request you to give me your views, and any suggestions that may occur to you on this subject? If you should think it best for me to visit Raleigh, what time would you suggest as the best for the purpose?

The plan I proposed of establishing an Institution for the deaf and dumb in N. Carolina, has excited the greatest animosity in the minds of those connected with the Institution in this place, against me. They are anxious that N. Carolina should send all her pupils to Virginia, instead of having a school of her own, and in order to accomplish this, the board have determined to send the teacher of the deaf and dumb and the teacher of the Blind, to the Legislature of N. C. to induce them to send to Virginia instead of having their own Institution, and this too, when they are unable, for want of funds and buildings to receive near all that apply for admission in their own State.

It will be for the people of North Carolina to decide whether they will appropriate money to be sent out of the State or whether they will prefer to keep it within their own bounds, and have their children educated under their own eye.

It may be well to state, that if necessary, I can command the assistance of the best deaf mute teacher in the country and that if

I succeed in my plans, I am determined to make the school second to none in the United States.

Will you do me the favor to let me hear from you as early as possible?

With respect<br>Your Ob't Serv't.

To James W. Bryan.        U. Bryan Mss.

Hillsboro',

Nov. 25th, 1844.

I would that my recommendation could have any effect in procuring the appointments for your friends desired in your last letter. Their disappointment and regret, however, at the result of the Presidential election, cannot exceed mine. I can scarce even yet persuade myself that it is so. I can perceive nothing in the result affording promise of advantage to any interest of the Country, as a compensation for the degradation of the national character in the person of the successful candidate, and the means of his elevation. We are to have, I fear, four years of faction and cabal, in our public affairs, and hard times in every private interest. Nevertheless, I cannot bear the thought the Whig party is to disband or relax its efforts. Although I shall probably never see a candidate for the Chief Magistracy for whom I shall have as great a personal admiration as I entertain for Mr. Clay, yet I deem the conservative character of the Whig party so essential to the preservation of our institutions, that I should deeply regret its dissolution. Even though unsuccessful, the sense of its vigilance and the rectitude of its principles are a powerful check to the downward course of Locofoco-ism.

Our friends in the Senate at Raleigh have done well in forcing the Locos to elect a Whig speaker,[46] though in a majority of those present.

But our press is miserably deficient, in not holding up to public censure the conduct of the Locos in attempting to force upon the Senate a presiding officer of that party, and thus to get the chances of the succession to the office of Governor against the decree of the people. The policy of the Locos will be to make the session

---

[46] Burgess S. Gaither.

abortive, and when the public interest makes action indispensable, to raise a clamor against it before the Country.

This is the week of our County Court, the last of my operations at the bar for the present. The sacrifice I am about to make has been in every stage an unpleasant one to me, and as events have turned out, I fear will be of but little worth to the Country.

\* \* \* \* \*

I will go to Raleigh a few days before the 1st. Jany. but not remove untill the Spring. I hope to be able to come back so frequently as to keep my affairs at my plantation in tolerable train. My receipts at the bar, with every disadvantage of sickness and canvassing, have this year been very good. Of course my parting with the profession is not an agreeable one. Pearson has been on our Circuit, and done a great deal of business. I do not think he will be before the Legislature for the place of Judge Nash, though he is looking in that direction. At all events, from what I hear, I presume the Legislature will confirm the Executive appointment. I think by a united effort in your section you might get something done for the Navigation of the Neuse by steamers. I am trying to get our people to move on the subject of a Turnpike road from Raleigh West,—if no further than Greensboro'. I have not seen so many emigrants from the State passing through this section for the last ten years. The current had for a measure ceased for some time past.

\* \* \* \* \*

*From James Cornick to John M. Morehead.*        U.

Dismal Swamp Canal Co.,

Norfolk,

November 27th., 1844.

By order of the Board of Directors of this Company, I take great pleasure to transmit to the Executive department of the State of North Carolina a statement, showing the quantity of produce, etc., passing through this Canal.

Your Excellency will perceive the immense amount of articles which, when valued, would amount to an enormous sum; that is passed through the Canal to Market, with so little risk, that Insurance is seldom made, thereby saving a large amount to the planter and consumer, this produce would have to find a market, and it must be very evident that the cheaper it is transported to a market, whether by *Sea, River, Canal, Railroad,* or Waggon, the planter must be benefitted in proportion.

These matters we do not undertake to judge, knowing as all experience has proven, that trade will find its way in the cheapest and best mode offered, and that the State is too much alive to the interests of its Citizens, not to give facilities to that mode best adapted for that purpose.

At this time there are some very fine Steamers of the most approved construction of *Iron,* built expressly for the upper Roanoke navigation, and if the trade from above the Falls can be brought to that point, great facilities will be given to a Market, which, in its broadest sense, opens all the principal Commercial Towns to this inland Navigation, between Roanoke and New York, and we think with great economy to the producer.

> I have the Honour to remain,
> Your most Ob't Hum. Serv't,
> President.
> Dismal S. C. Company.

### [*Enclosure.*]

Produce passed through the Dismal Swamp Canal during the Year ending on the 30th. September, 1844.

*Inward i.e. North*

- 2,768 Bales Cotton
- 38,708 bbls. Fish
- 24,511 bbls. Naval Stores
- 358 bbls. Spirits
- 724 bbls. Spirits Turpentine
- 569 cwt. Bacon
- 459 Kegs Lard
- 543,082 bushels Corn
- 6,219 do Flaxseed
- 91,216 " Wheat
- 25,842 " Peas
- 12,650 " Potatoes

- 4,395 Cooper's Bolts
- 207,070 Cooper's Staves
- 29,160 fence Rails
- 8,469 Cords fire wood
- Sundries, or non enumerated articles, paying Ad-valorum Toll of ¼ of 1 p. ct. on *Value.*
- Value $127,600.

•Outward (to the South.)
- 39 Qr. Casks of Wine
- 2,042 bbls. Spirits

2,310 Cubic Feet Mast Timber
110,743 " " other Timber
181,142 " " plank and
scantling
394,040 pipe Staves
4,831,570 hogshead ditto
362,700 barrel staves
2,903,064 long Shingles
2,344,210 two ft. Shingles
24,588,110 building Shingles
79,800 Garden Poles

2,935 bbls. Pork
4,061 bbls. Flour
646 bbls. Fish
355 bbls. Bread
109 bbls. Beer
574 bbls. Sugar
134 Hhds. Sugar
645 " Molasses
258 " Spirits
1,510 Bags Coffee
1,265 boxes dry Goods
851 boxes Hats
1,254 Boxes Soap and
Candles
992 Kegs Nails
182 Kegs Gun powder
187 Crates (earthern)
Ware
291 Casks Cheese
2,198 Casks Lime
73,258 bushels Salt
94 Tons Iron
675 Kegs Tobacco
Sundries, or non enumer-
ated articles, paying Adva-
lorem Toll of ¼ of 1 p. ct.
on their Value.
*Value* $372,000 Dollars.

True copy from the books.

James Cornick,
President.
Dismal Swamp Canal Company.

November 27th., 1844.

*From Hugh Waddell.*                                      **U**

Raleigh,

Decr. 5th, 1844.

Your friends here have frequently expressed the desire to see
you, but they have been told that you would not be here until
about Christmas. Nevertheless I am sorry you are not with us;
it may be somewhat selfish to be sure, as there are sundry matters
on which I should have been pleased to have your opinion.

There is now before the Senate a Bill prepared by our friend
B — r[47] called "a Bill concerning Jury Trials," in which the act
of 1796 is at least *made plain.* Some of our fearful men are scared,
but generally the Bar stands up. It forbids the Judge in trial of
cases before Juries to do more than *recite* the evidence & uses
the words "he shall make no comment on the said evidence,
either by way of repeating the arguments of the Counsel or *otherwise.*" It furthermore authorizes Counsel to argue the whole case,
as well Law as fact, *to the Jury,* but with the express authority to
the Judge (except in State cases) to lay down authoritatively the
Law to the Jury.

When properly understood it is no more than a Declaratory
Statute of what the profession has always considered the settled
Law of this State.

I suspect, as it has been reported by the Judiciary Committee,
of which I am Chairman, that their Honors will *give it to me*
hereafter on the Circuit, though *I* did not introduce the Bill.
Elliott [48] of Randolph did it at my request.

Yesterday we had the solemn ceremony of the Electoral College
and I felt as though I were at the obsequies of a departed friend.
Kerr and Osborne have done themselves immortal honor, as I
learn at this great meeting of Whigs, & Poor Cherry, who seems
to be under some malignant star, croaked so much & talked so of
*judging Polk by his acts* as very much *dissatisfied* his friends, and
I have heard him cruelly censured. The truth is, he has never

---

[47] Presumably George E. Badger. The bill passed and became law. It gave
parties, or their counsel, the right to argue to the jury not only the facts in the
case, but the law as well. *North Carolina Laws, 1844-1845,* Chapter VIII.

[48] Henry Branson Elliott, of Randolph, a graduate of the university, two years
later than Graham, member state senate, 1842-1844.

been himself since Moore[49] was beaten by Caldwell. He seemed exceedingly vexed, though he was told with much truth that his District had less right to complain than any other, as Bailey was elected especially to please it, and had left.

Some friends say that he (Cherry) is determined to prevent the West from talking him up for Gov'r, as he says he will not run and is acting thus to effect his object. If so, God knows he will soon succeed from what I hear from the West in the last few days. He has fallen much with them.

You are no doubt pleased with the Judicial appointments of Nash and Caldwell. We talk of an 8th. Circuit, but I doubt. Pearson we learn was very keen. A leading Democrat told me that the friends of P. among Democrats had *required the party* to unite on him & then kicked at [page torn] & got worse & worse.

I wish you could be here, as Dr. Hill, Dudley & others will be here now for some days; the Town will give Gov'r M: an *entertainment* of some sort.

Mrs. G. ought to be down were it only (like all other *new female* sovereigns) to shew her subjects "how *gracious* she be."

*Notification of election.*        **A.**

Raleigh,

Decm. 10th, 1844.

By joint resolution of the Senate and House of Commons, the undersigned have been appointed a Committee to inform you, that you have been elected and declared Governor of North Carolina for the Constitutional term commencing on the 1st. day of January next, And also to ask at what time it will suit your convenience to take the oaths of Office.

In discharging the pleasing duty thus assigned us, we beg leave to tender to you our hearty gratulations on this event, so auspicious to the State & so honorable to yourself

HUGH WADDELL        On part of the Senate
W. E. MILLS
J. B. JONES        On part of the H. C.

---

[49] Augustus Moore (1803-1851), of Edenton, a graduate of the university of Graham's class, and a prominent and successful lawyer. He was elected a superior court judge in 1848, and resigned almost immediately after taking his seat on the bench.

*To James Graham.*        U.

Hillsboro',

Decr. 15th, 1844.

The school at this place having terminated its session, & a change taking place in the instructor, I sent George on day before yesterday to Greensboro, to enter the Caldwell institute. He has been so badly taught that he has not yet learned how to study, and is by no means sufficiently versed in English to commence the Latin. He is therefore not prepared to derive much advantage from the ordinary course of Academic instruction. At Greensboro' one of the professors, Mr. Lindsley,[50] devotes himself entirely to teaching English, and I have directed him to continue in that department untill he becomes a good English scholar. He was two or three months in the Academy here, but did not make satisfactory progress, owing to the time of his teacher being engrossed with the Latin and Greek scholars. I did think of carrying him to Raleigh, & entering him in a Military school there, but supposed it was not adapted so well, to advance him in other learning. I have sent him to board with his teacher, Mr. Lindsley, who takes but four boarders and promises to overlook his morals and deportment. He is a graduate of Princeton & brother of Dr. Lindsley[51] of the Nashville University. They prepare young men at the institute for the Junior class at the University, and the instruction is said to be more thorough than in the lower classes at Chapel Hill. I think it should depend on the capacity George exhibits in his present studies whether he takes a regular classical course. He seems free from any vice, & kind & affectionate in disposition with understanding enough to make a scholar, but idle-minded, and rather wanting in energy; the former from want of proper teach-

---

[50] The Rev. Silas Condit Lindsley, a native of New Jersey, a Presbyterian minister, who came to North Carolina in 1830 to teach in Oxford. He taught in Greensboro, 1831-1836, and then became a teacher in Caldwell Institute.

[51] Philip Lindsley (1786-1865), a native of New Jersey, graduate of Princeton. He became a Presbyterian minister, was, successively, professor, vice president, and acting president of Princeton. During that time he declined the presidency of three colleges, and, later, of six more. He declined the presidency of East Tennessee, (later University of Nashville), but later accepted, and served from 1826 to 1850. He was bent on making the institution a great force in the life and thought of the South, but never secured the necessary means. He was succeeded by his son, J. Berrien Lindsley. He was an editor, missionary, moderator of the Presbyterian general assembly. He became a professor in New Albany Theological Seminary.

ing heretofore, and the latter from the debility & lassitude of the climate in which he has been brought up. . . .

I propose to go to Raleigh on the day after Christmas, so as to spend a few days in learning the routine of business in the Executive office before I am installed. I must, this week, prepare something of an inaugural address, which I would be glad of an opportunity to exhibit to you. Susan will go down with me to remain a week or two, but we will not remove untill, probably, March. What with settling of accounts, and professional and plantation affairs, I shall be very busy, untill I leave home. I fear our Legislature is so occupied with the idea of a short session, & the apprehension of doing something that may destroy party ascendancy, that the session will prove abortive. Our financial affairs present a subject of serious embarrassment, and it is much to be doubted what course is best to be taken with them.

The result of the Presidential election has unsettled everything in the business operation of the Country, and I think we can calculate on no improvement in any thing for the next four years. I greatly regret to hear that there is doubt of the election of Maj. Hinton to the office of Treasurer, Stedman[52] of Chatham being a candidate, & the Locos and a part of the Whigs disposed to support him.

Paul Cameron has taken 100 hands to Alabama a few weeks since and purchased a plantation in Greene Co. at $30,000.

I think my health more robust than it has been for some time.

Very affectionately Yours

*From Hugh Waddell.*                                                    U.

Raleigh,

Dec'r 15th, 1844.

My engagements on the Judiciary and other Committees occupy so much of my time that I really have scarcely had a moment to devote to a friend & hence I have written you but once since my arrival. Our friend Judge Nash, who urged me to write him, has been treated like yourself very scurvily, having been written to only once.

---

[52] Probably Nathan A. Stedman of Chatham.

This being Sunday, I thought I would claim some of the fore-
noon, tho' generally I might say with Mr. Pope, "Sunday is no
Sabbath day to me."

In looking at the two houses, one is struck with their general
appearance of respectability, but they by no means deserve the
character given them by the Press, of being bodies of more than
usual ability. One or two members of each house are certainly
gentlemen of respectable talent and information, but they are too
few in number either to give character to the bodies or even to
influence their action. This latter fact you will admit to be true
when I say that Moore & Cherry of the House & Boyden and
Francis of the Senate so far from influencing the action of their
respective Houses, have proved fatal to all the projects they advocate, by pressing with more zeal than prudence their views &
sometimes with a certain contemptuousness of manner, not the
most *winning*.

A certain Bill concerning Judy Trials has been read a *second*
time in the Senate & amended by striking out the whole of it
except the first section which allows the Counsel to argue their
whole case as well of Law as of fact to the Jury. The Bill I think
you would approve of if you could see it, although I know like
myself you are no friend of *alteration* which may even *seem* to
diminish the power of the Judiciary

Shepperd [53] moved the amendment, & curs'd him I believe only
then because he thought it would vex me. It is now lying on the
table, & we may get it through yet in the primary spirit of it by
a small amendment in the Commons.

This letter you will see, was commenced on Sunday & not being
able to finish it that day (by reason of a visit of half dozen
friends) in time for the mail, I now shall try to conclude the miserable scrawl. It is wretchedly uninteresting, but I cannot give
you anything very private or of party character, by so hazardous
a channel as a private hand. When you shall be here I'll tell you
much most villainous trickery which will surprize you not a little,
on account of the persons *concerned*. You will find your *new place*
most troublesome in every particular, as I learn from Morehead,
and if I could do it I would gladly relieve you of the horrors of
keeping a Loan office of $300,000. as laborious as any other Loan
office, & the 2 Boards, (Int. Imp't & Literary Fund) are of themselves fruitful fields for constant labour all the year round, but

---

[53] James B. Shepard.

never producing a harvest. But desiring this so much I fear there will be no hope of restoring the Gov'r of N. C. to his rights by this Assembly; the very Documents and accompanying Messages from the Gov'r are voluminous beyond belief.

Hearing that your intended residence (the *Palace!* God save the mark) was almost without necessary furniture, I got my friend Col. Tayloe[54] to present a resolution raising a Committee on the subject of furnishing *your House* properly; the resolution was carried without objection & Tayloe (of Beaufort & Hyde) knows what genteel furniture is, & will do his best to make the Lady Governess Graham as comfortable *nearly* as *she is at home,* though I believe it is not *nearly* after all.

Having just received your last favour *directing* engagements to be made for the "Royal Cortege" at Yarbrough's, I shall obey with fidelity and alacrity & will apprize you forthwith of the result of my application, perhaps before Mr. Laws leaves town, in which event I will add a P. S. to this and will leave room therefor.

My profound and most Loyal duty to the better part of the Sovereign Executive Power of N. C.

As ever faithfully your friend

Have called on Yarbro' & he says you *shall have rooms* if he turns every body else out of doors. I'll try to fix every thing for you.

*From John M. Morehead.*                    U.

Raleigh,

Dec. 20th, 1844.

I shall be pleased to know when you will be here—I think it will be no time lost for you to spend a week here before I leave; there are a great many little details of facts that I could suggest to you, which I cannot think of at the moment, that will be of service to you; I felt the want of them when I first went into office.

There are other matters & suggestions of a private and domestic nature that you might find of service.

I expect to give my last executive blow-out on next Tuesday evening, and the young ladies were about sending you & Madam & Miss Washington tickets, but I told them I was going to drop you a line, and would mention it.

---

[54] Joshua Tayloe.

Mrs. M. & myself will be pleased to have the company of your-self and Lady, & Miss Washington, & other friends whom you may bring with you.

Let me hear from you.

Yrs respectfully.

# INDEX

## A

Abolitionism, discussed, 222, 232-234.

Adams, John Quincy, agitates for abolition, 196-197; mentioned, 181, 195.

Alabama, political situation in, 364-365.

Albright, William R., advises Graham and Mangum, 199-200; identified, 199n; letters from, 199-200, 336-337; requests information on expenditure of public money, 336-337.

Allen, Shadrack P., identified, 285n; mentioned, 397.

Allen, William, identified, 404n.

Almonte Juan Nepomuceno, sketch of 418n.

American Whig Society, elects Graham honorary member, 4.

Anderson, Albert, mentioned, 63.

Anderson, Alexander Outlaw, identified, 132n.

Apportionment Bill, speech on, 320-336, 364-365.

Archer, William S., mentioned, 354.

Arrington Archibald Hunter, identified, 421n.

Ashburton, Lord [Alexander Baring], arrives in Washington, 285; entertains, 307, 312; feared lost, 277.

Ashe, Richard, identified, 497n; mentioned, 483.

Ashe, William Cincinatus, mentioned, 211.

Avery, Clarke Moulton, identified, 50n; issues invitation, 50-51; letter from, 50-51.

Avery, Waightstill, identified, 391n.

## B

Bacon, D. Francis, invited to address Democratic Whigs of City of New York, 477.

Badger, George E., appears for State in suit for western lands, 37-38; appointed delegate to national Whig Convention, 457; appointed secretary of navy, 161, 163, 167, 168; congratulates Graham on speech, 146-147; disturbed over Democratic victories, 524; entertains in Washington, 207-208; honored by Wake County Whigs, 243; invites Whigs to his home, 391; letters from, 146-147, 164-166, 189, 435-439, 523; mentioned, 4, 37, 111, 119, 121-122, 131, 161, 163, 167, 168, 195, 199, 206, 207-208, 211, 239, 240, 357, 369n, 382, 440, 443, 530n; mentioned as successor to Judge Gaston, 469; offers advice, 435-437, 441; opposes repeal of Bankrupt Law, 397; relates events in legislature, 147; resigns from cabinet, 239, 240; responds to appointment, 164-166.

Bagby, Arthur Pendleton, identified, 320n.

Bailey, John Lancaster, identified, 65n.

Baker, B., invitation from, 243.

Bank, National, discussed, 132, 183, 192, 196, 198, 209-210, 211-213, 217, 218, 219, 222, 224, 225, 227, 228, 229-230, 234, 236, 237, 238, 239, 241, 340, 370, 457, 461-462.

Bank of the State, surrenders charter, 409, 412n.

Bankrupt Law, deplored, 349-350, 370, 397-398, 412n, 426, 511; repeal debated, 403-404, 404-406, 408, 415.

Banks, discussion of, 14, 44-48, 77, 88-89, 121-122, 211-213, 248, 250-252, 399-400, 409, 412, 416, 459-462, 508-511.

Barbour, Philip Pendleton, identified, 120n.

Baring, Alexander [Lord Ashburton], identified, 277n.

Baring, Charles, identified, 307n.

Barnard, Daniel Dewey, identified, 82n.

Barnett, John A., letter from, 350-351; mentioned, 355; requests information for local Whig campaign, 350-351.

Barringer, Daniel Moreau, insists that Graham accept gubernatorial nomination, 455; letters from, 166-168, 455, 465; mentioned, 94, 176, 394, 396, 406, 413, 419.

Barrow, Alexander, identified, 249n.

Battle, Christopher Columbus, applies for position, 524; identified, 29n; letter from, 524.

Battle, William Horn, identified, 87n; letter from, 87; mentioned, 281, 391.

Baxter, John, mentioned, 493; sketch of, 402n.